# The Politics of West German Trade Unions

First published in 1986, this book assesses the politics of the West German trade unions in the context of their larger role as major actors in the polity. By focusing on the historical realities of the labour movement both before and after 1945, the study explains the extent to which organized labour solidified and challenged the dominant structures of politics and authority. It examines the metalworkers' union, the construction workers' union, the printers' union and the chemical workers' union and shows how the industrial reality of each organisation helped shape its political outlook and strategic thinking.

This book will be of particular interest to students of trade unions, industrial relations and political economy in West Germany.

# The Politics of West German Trade Unions

Strategies of Class and Interest Representation in Growth and Crisis

Andrei S. Markovits

Routledge
Taylor & Francis Group

First published in 1986
by Cambridge University Press

This edition first published in 2016 by Routledge
2 Park Square, Milton Park, Abingdon, Oxon, OX14 4RN
and by Routledge
711 Third Avenue, New York, NY 10017

*Routledge is an imprint of the Taylor & Francis Group, an informa business*

**Publisher's Note**
The publisher has gone to great lengths to ensure the quality of this reprint but points
out that some imperfections in the original copies may be apparent.

**Disclaimer**
The publisher has made every effort to trace copyright holders and welcomes
correspondence from those they have been unable to contact.

A Library of Congress record exists under LC control number: 85030002


ISBN 13: 978-1-138-65098-5 (hbk)
ISBN 13: 978-1-315-62502-7 (ebk)
ISBN 13: 978-1-138-65099-2 (pbk)
ISBN 13: 978-1-138-65101-2 (set hbk)
ISBN 13: 978-1-315-62498-3 (set ebk)

# THE POLITICS OF THE WEST GERMAN
# TRADE UNIONS

To my Father, Ludwig Markovits;
and the Memory of my Mother, Ida Ritter

# THE POLITICS OF THE WEST GERMAN TRADE UNIONS

Strategies of class and interest
representation in growth and crisis

## ANDREI S. MARKOVITS

*Associate Professor, Department of Political Science, Boston University*

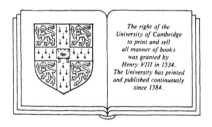

The right of the
University of Cambridge
to print and sell
all manner of books
was granted by
Henry VIII in 1534.
The University has printed
and published continuously
since 1584.

CAMBRIDGE UNIVERSITY PRESS

Cambridge
London   New York   New Rochelle
Melbourne   Sydney

Published by the Press Syndicate of the University of Cambridge
The Pitt Building, Trumpington Street, Cambridge CB2 1RP
32 East 57th Street, New York, NY 10022, USA
10 Stamford Road, Oakleigh, Melbourne 3166, Australia

First published 1986

Printed in Great Britain at the University Press Cambridge

*British Library cataloguing in publication data*

Markovits, Andrei S.
The politics of the West German trade unions:
strategies of class and interest representation
in growth and crisis.
1. Trade-unions – Germany (West) – History
I. Title
331.88'0943    HD6694

*Library of Congress cataloguing in publication data*

Markovits, Andrei S.
The politics of the West German trade unions.
Strategies of class and interest representation in growth and crisis
Bibliography: p.
Includes index.
1. Trade-unions – Germany (West) – History.
I. Title. II. Series.
HD6694.M373 1986    331.88'0943    85-30002

ISBN 0 521 30513 6

CE

# Contents

# Foreword

It has become commonplace for many political scientists – as well as for quite a few makers of public policy – to look upon the fates of national political economies as determined not just by the three "factors of production" (human labor power, capital and natural resources) described in economics textbooks, but by one further ingredient. According to this view, the growth and stability of capitalist economies, as well as their capacity to absorb the shock waves caused by crises and discontinuities in the global economy, are also conditioned by the way in which class conflict is cast into certain institutional arrangements. Consequently, these institutional arrangements must be considered a "factor of production" in their own right.

Institutional arrangements peculiar to certain countries (e.g. the Japanese, the Swedish, the French, and the British systems of institutionalized class conflict), by which these societies manage or fail to cope with endemic cleavages of interest, show a remarkable degree of persistence over historical time. They also show a degree of specificity and non-transferability that must frustrate those who believe in the possibility to transplant or imitate "successful" institutional designs elsewhere. But also – and this is the point the social scientist must address with the highest priority – such continuity does not obtain by virtue of some historical inertia, nor is it guaranteed by the sheer weight of some national tradition or institutional heritage. Rather, continuity must be seen as a *process* of identical reproduction, which may or may not occur. It is only in the historian's retrospective analysis that continuity appears to be governed by some iron law of institutional tradition. As we look closer and examine the point of view of conflicting actors, their projects, interests and the environments in which they find themselves, we come to perceive the dilemmas, uncertainties and potential disruptions implicit in the web of routine practices. If continuity must therefore always be considered precarious and uncertain, how do we account for the cases in which it does persist, and how do we explain those instances in which it does not?

It is, in my view, the exemplary achievement of Andrei Markovits' study of the German Trade Union Federation (DGB) and four of its member unions to provide us with a detailed picture of the dilemmas, conflicts, antagonisms and imbalances that make the continuity of the post-World War II institutional arrangement of class and industrial relations in West Germany so fragile while at the same time also delineating the political, intellectual and economic factors that have up to now contributed to maintaining institutional stability in this country's industrial relations. Continuity, as long as it prevails, is nothing but the outcome of a continuous conflict over the continuation of an institutional pattern of which no component is guaranteed or sanctified by history, power or reason.

While this underlying theme of Markovits' research is of substantial intellectual interest even to scholars and students who specialize neither in trade unions nor in the post-war history of West Germany, both of these categories of specialists will find the book a highly valuable contribution to their particular field of interest. As far as its contribution to a general theory of labor movements and trade unionism in advanced capitalist societies is concerned, Markovits uses the West German case to explore the entire range of organizational and political problems that any form of collective action on behalf of employees' interests must confront. The dilemmas which Markovits examines include whether to organize along (party) political and ideological lines or to represent employees in a "unitary" and non-partisan way; whether to centralize bargaining power or to decentralize it in accordance with more syndicalist models; and how to find a viable demarcation between industry level and company (or plant) level negotiations and industrial action. Markovits also addresses broader issues confronting the labor movement, among them: how to relate to the state, the government and political parties; whether to treat the interests of employees as "class" or "group" interests; how to relate the three substantive interests that employees share (namely increasing real wages and welfare state transfers, improving working conditions [including a satisfactory work time regime], and achieving full employment), and how to deal with the painful trade-offs that exist among these interests. Markovits explores the heterogeneous factors that led to the settlement of most of these questions after the "hour zero" of the military and political breakdown of Nazi Germany in 1945, which followed twelve years after the real "hour zero" began for the German labor movement immediately following the fascist takeover in 1933. The author does so in a rich and well-documented narrative of the development of the labor federation's and the four unions' post-war history, while keeping a keen eye on the ambiguities, conflicts, counter-intuitive consequences and frustrated expectations that were associated with every key decision involving the West German unions' structure and strategy.

As is well known, the West German trade unions gravitate around the four principles of unitarianism (*Einheitsgewerkschaft*), industrial unionism (*Industriegewerkschaft*; "one plant, one union"), a federal structure granting considerable autonomy to individual unions, and a strong reliance on legal guarantees to protect the interests of employees via reform legislation, labor courts and other agencies of state power. In addition, there is the common interest of unions *and* employers' associations to make collective negotiations on wages and working conditions the exclusive domain of the "social partners," i.e. to keep the state out of direct incomes determination. What Markovits is able to show in the course of his extensive analysis of economic, political and historical data, however, is the fact that these principles do by no means constitute a solidly built institutional structure. Rather, he argues, they are just the framework of ongoing strategic debates, challenges and conflicting interpretations. As far as the unions themselves are concerned, the two opposing tendencies within this intra-labor field of tension are accurately labelled "activism" vs. "accommo-dationism" advocating, respectively, militant self-reliance and an "expan-sive wage policy" vs. legally guaranteed status rights. The same cleavage describes the opposition of a more inclusive model of class politics to a model of special interest group politics. More specifically, what becomes clear in the course of the author's many detailed accounts of the junctures and turning points of West Germany's post-war labor history is the peculiar logic of *Verrechtlichung*, a mode of regulating industrial conflict that relies heavily on reform legislation and its juridical implementation. The unions have been partly attracted and partly repelled by this model of *Verrechtlichung*. On the one hand, the attraction of obtaining legal status and protection lies in the fact that it allows unions to utilize state power for the promotion of employees' interests – and thereby to "save" their own power resources. On the other hand, labor's status rights come with a price tag, as the holders of state power tend to demand and enforce, according to their own logic of exchange, a "responsible" union strategy in return. The resulting entanglement of unions in corporatist arrangements may well undermine, as the activists have always worried, the unions' capacity to organize, mobilize and utilize their own resources in the interest of employees. This poses the additional danger that, in future configurations of conflict, the unions would be rendered defenseless if a government should repeal legal guarantees and status rights of labor. Both the famous works council legislation and the co-determination legislation of the early fifties, which together are often seen as the industrial constitution of the Federal Republic, and both of which were the outcome of a peculiar alliance between social democracy and Catholic socialism, are at once the outgrowth of class conflict and an obstacle to its further development. It is in the context of these strategic debates that the old question of contract vs. status poses itself again and again: is civil society the level of social reality at which a stable and desirable form of societal order can emerge, or must the state impose such order upon society? The activist unions, often inspired by Old Left as well as New Left theories of the capitalist economy and society, argue for the former position, while the accommodationist unions (who typically see the state not just as law-maker and law-enforcer, but also as their more or less direct source of employment) tend to adhere to what is often called a "state fixation."

Markovits draws a comprehensive and detailed picture of how the partly overlapping conflicts and dilemmas of state vs. civil society, labor vs. capital, and activist vs. accommodationist labor strategies were conditioned and accentuated by changing political and economic "opportunity structures." To the best of my knowledge – and in spite of such major research works on German trade unions as those authored by Joachim Bergmann, Otto Jacobi and Walther Müller-Jentsch on the one hand and Wolfgang Streeck on the other – the interaction of institutional structures and environmental conditions which emerges in the political economy has not yet been analyzed in the German social scientific literature with similar degrees of historical comprehensiveness and specificity as it has by Markovits in his impressive study.

The major rupture, at least in recent history, is marked by the year 1974 when, after a brief period of social-democratic-led reformism (1969–74), the successor to Willy Brandt, Chancellor Helmut Schmidt, was confronted with a rapidly worsening situation of mass unemployment (which has since reached post-war records of close to 10%). Simultaneously, the Free Democratic junior partners of Schmidt's coalition government became increasingly assertive of a neo-liberal economic doctrine, while on the left side of the political universe new social movements and – as the seventies drew to a close – the Green Party appeared on the political scene. It was under these rapidly changing economic and political conditions that the unions of the DGB had to come to terms with – and respond to – the unpleasant truth that the organizational resources of unions were dwindling under the impact of the employment crisis, and that effective means of ameliorating this crisis were in fact beyond the reach of union strategies. This became clear after the struggle for the introduction of the 35-hour week – led by the labor federation's two most activist unions, the metalworkers (IG Metall) and the printers (IG Druck und Papier) – failed to achieve any substantial success along the lines of "work-sharing" in the protracted and bitter strikes of spring 1984.

This defeat resulted from, among other things, the fact that, while general employees' interests exist in *three* dimensions (wages, working conditions, employment levels), only *two* of these are admitted as "negotiable" items and thus as objects of potential collective agreements. The level of employment is considered either as a mere by-product of autonomous investors' decisions or as something that must be indirectly determined through the economic and fiscal policies of the federal government. Markovits emphasizes cogently the highly divisive potential of the employment crisis for a unified and "unitary" union strategy. The crisis – and the absence of promising strategies by which organized labor could respond to it – amounts to a structural temptation for unions either to exclude the unemployed and the marginally employed from their effective representational domain, or to resort to special deals and political exchange arrangements with the incumbent government's economic policy makers. Labor could also choose to allow a shift of the arena of industrial conflict to take place, i.e. from industry-level negotiations to company-level bargaining. All three options would compromise major tenets and basic strategic principles of the DGB and the more activist unions. These consequences for the West German trade unions – some of them analyzed in this study, some additional ones emerging only since this research has been concluded – are bleak indeed and may well put into question the much-praised stability of the West German industrial relations system.

Whenever we try to understand and explain political actors and action, the hard methodological choice is whether and to what extent we want to rely on the categories, perceptions and interpretations the actors themselves employ, or to what extent we want to stay within the boundaries of a supposedly neutral, objectivist (and objectifying) conceptual language of the social sciences. It appears to me that Markovits' study resolves this dilemma, as well as the related ones of values vs. facts and of historical narrative vs. systematic analysis, in quite a fortunate way. The tight interweaving of the points of view of political actors and their political motivations on the one hand, and certain consistently employed key theoretical categories (such as stability and change, union and party politics, activist and accommodationist tendencies within organized labor) on the other, make the book an excellent representative of the case-study approach. Its findings and results testify to the potentially advantageous position that an observer from abroad can exploit when studying a field as complex and sensitive as German union politics. The fact that Markovits is extremely knowledgeable about and evidently sympathetic to the causes of labor politics, combined with the "detachment" from organizational routines and shared experiences afforded by his status as a foreigner, may have facilitated his access to the field and its actors beyond what a "native" German scholar could have easily achieved. In any event, this book is much more than just another introduction to German post-war domestic politics and industrial relations, although it certainly performs this function well. It is foremost a profound and critical inquiry into the foundations, the fates and the acute ambiguities of what some German politicians have celebrated as the "Modell Deutschland," which this book helps substantially to demystify.

Bielefeld, December 1985                                         Claus Offe

# Preface and Acknowledgements

As this book reaches its final stages of production in early 1986, the West German trade unions find themselves confronted by two challenges. The first concerns an integral part of labor's routine, namely the beginning of yet another bargaining round with the employers. The second centers on labor's effort to find a solution to an acute crisis, which in this case involves the concerted efforts by the three governmental coalition parties and the employers to revise parts of an existing law so as to make calling and implementing a strike much more difficult and costly for the unions. Responses to routine and crisis have continuously informed the development of the unions as major participants in West German public life. One of the major purposes of this study is to demonstrate how the West German organized labor movement's handling of routine and crisis in the Bonn Republic has helped create and defend democracy in the Federal Republic, the most successful political construct on German soil to date.

This book argues – perhaps provocatively – that without a strong, organized labor movement the Federal Republic would not only be a much less prosperous country with a far less successful economy, but – more significantly – it would not boast one of the most stable democratic polities in the world. Given Germany's tragic recent history, which entailed the breakdown of democratic institutions – and, not by chance, the destruction of independent trade unions – the book's claim should have a universal urgency.

As an American political scientist with Central European Jewish origins, my scholarly and political interest in the German labor movement forms a key part of a larger commitment to a better understanding of Germany and Germans in the twentieth century. I have been involved in analyzing post-Nazi Germany, particularly the Federal Republic, by finding answers to the following two questions: (1) What makes West Germany sub-stantially different from previous political formations in twentieth-century German history? And (2) How deeply rooted are these differences in the German past and are they firmly enough institutionalized in the present to guarantee a future free from the horrors of the past?

This study of the West German trade unions forms the first part of a scholarly trilogy which seeks to find some satisfactory empirical answers to these two questions. I wanted to devote a substantial amount of my intellectual energies to an understanding of one of the few institutional arrangements in modern German history which from their very beginning upheld the ideals of democracy, even if they failed on occasion to devise appropriate strategies in democracy's defense. Concomitant to concluding the first part of the triology with this volume, I have broken ground on the next two installments, an effort which has thus far yielded only a number of journal articles. But both projects – on the West German Left and on German–Jewish relations in the Federal Republic – will eventually result in book-length studies. This task will be greatly simplified if I am fortunate enough to be able to count on the continued emotional support, intellectual stimulation and deep friendship of a large group of people in both the United States and Europe. Without them and their unique institutional environments the present volume would have never been conceived, let alone completed.

I would like to proceed chronologically in expressing my gratitude for the generous support which I received in the course of this project. It all started in the fall of 1975 when, having just defended my doctoral dissertation at Columbia University, I arrived at the Center for European Studies at Harvard University for what was going to be a one-year post-doctoral intellectual binge. I already knew the Center to be the most exciting environment in the United States for young scholars working on Europe. The fact that eleven years later I have yet to leave the Center bespeaks of its formidable influence on me. Indeed, like family, I am convinced that the Center cannot be abandoned. As the celebration of the Center's fifteenth birthday in the fall of 1985 amply demonstrated, Center "graduates" readily internalize wonderful experiences they enjoy during their sojourn on Bryant Street. In addition, such memories inform their activities as scholars and teachers wherever they may be in the world. For having created and continued to foster such a unique intellectual and humane environment – and one in which I have been fortunate to learn a great deal – special thanks are due to Stanley Hoffmann, the Center's chairman, and Guido Goldman, its director.

But as anybody who has ever been associated with the Center knows, Abby Collins, the assistant director, is this institution's be-all and end-all.

Her contagious dynamism, intellectual vision, organizational savvy and deep personal caring have made the Center a special institution for all Europeanists. Abby's friendship and support since the first day I set foot in the Center remain without any doubt my most cherished gains.

It was with Abby's encouragement that Peter Gourevitch, Peter Lange, Andrew Martin and George Ross embarked on a project in 1976–77 which analyzed trade union responses to the economic crisis in Western Europe. By the fall of 1978 they had submitted a research proposal to the Ford Foundation, which received funding in 1979. At this point, these prominent Center associates asked me to join them for the purpose of researching the West German case. I am very grateful for their trust and confidence at a relatively early stage of my academic career. Before embarking on our respective field trips, the original "gang of four" was augmented by Stephen Bornstein, Maurizio Vannicelli and Christopher Allen. These eight researchers eventually produced two volumes on trade union politics and economic crisis in five West European countries. This project formed the basis for the present book. I would like to extend my special thanks to Stephen Bornstein, George Ross and Christopher Allen who offered many a helping hand over the years, well beyond the normal duties of good colleagueship. Christopher Allen in particular, my co-author on a number of journal articles and conference papers on the West German union movement, and also on the West German section of the Center-sponsored project, proved to be a trusted friend, and I continue to respect his knowledge and opinions.

While I was very well prepared for my trip to the Federal Republic at the end of 1978 due in good part to the excellent inventory of literature on German unions in Harvard University's Manpower and Industrial Relations Collection, I relied on only three contacts in the Federal Republic to help me during the initial stages of my research: Wolf-Dieter Narr, Volker Bahl and Angelika Bahl-Benker. Their friendship, counsel and concern provided invaluable help at the time and they continue to be among my dearest friends and most respected colleagues anywhere in the world. Their extensive contacts within the unions and trust in my project enabled me to affiliate with the Wirtschafts-und Sozialwissenschaftliches Institut (WSI) of the German Trade Union Federation (DGB), which in turn initiated a lasting relationship of mutual confidence and respect between the Federal Republic's union officials and myself. While at this point I truly would like to name over one hundred West German unionists and academic colleagues whom I had the pleasure of consulting in the course of this project, I refer the reader to the list of interviewees which constitutes Section D of the bibliography. At this juncture, I can only express my deeply felt gratitude to a select few in each of the cities where my research led me over the years. First and foremost I owe special thanks to the director of the WSI in Düsseldorf, Heinz Markmann, whose confidence in me opened crucial doors and whose kind hospitality welcomed me at the institute in a manner which has made me all but a permanent member of this organization.

Other colleagues in Düsseldorf whose assistance proved invaluable for my project were Ulrich Borsdorf, Hans-Otto Hemmer, Reinhard Jordan, Hartmut Küchle, Gernot Müller, Detlef Perner, Hartmut Seifert and Ulrich Zachert. Also in Düsseldorf I am greatly indebted to Gerhard Leminsky whose encyclopedic knowledge about unions in the Federal Republic and special readiness to share this knowledge in the most unselfish manner are well known among scholars of German labor relations.

In Frankfurt I would like to extend my heart-felt gratitude to Iris Bergmiller, Rainer Erd, Otto Jacobi, Karl-Heinz Janzen, Jürgen Jöns, Jutta Kneissel, Rudolf Kuda and Klaus Lang. Rüdiger Bouillon, Karl Hauenschild, Hermann Rappe and Gunter Rose have earned my special thanks for their help in Hanover. Werner Vitt deserves much of the credit for the insights which I gained into his union, IG Chemie-Papier-Keramik. His devotion and dedication to the German labor movement were among many of the nuances which could not appear in the pages of this study but which made the research such a rewarding and often moving experience for me. In Stuttgart the help and hospitality accorded to me by Detlef Hensche, Willi Hoss, Rolf Seitenzahl, Franz Steinkühler and Hajo Vitzthum will never be forgotten.

Friends and colleagues in West Berlin who gave generously of their time and readily shared their experiences with me were Elmar Altvater, Knuth Dohse, Hajo Funke, Eckart Hildebrandt, Jürgen Hoffmann, Ulrich Jürgens, Frieder Naschold and Wolfgang Streeck. I am also grateful to Werner Sengenberger in Munich and Martin Osterland in Bremen for their continued expert advice and deep personal friendship over the years.

True to the international nature of this project, I am not only deeply indebted to people in the United States and the Federal Republic for their encouragement and support, but also to four Englishmen whose assistance and concern proved indispensable for the completion of this volume. David Childs' insightful comments and helpful criticisms on earlier versions of the manuscript, offered in the most constructive form of collegiality, provided a major incentive to conclude this study. Gordon Smith's kind hospitality in allowing me the use of his spacious office during the summer of 1984, when the London School of Economics and Political Science invited me as an Academic Visitor, permitted me to conclude three chapters in what has been one of my most productive summers to date. Last but certainly not least I would like to express my deep appreciation to my editors Michael

Holdsworth and Richard Fisher at Cambridge University Press whose expertise and professionalism coupled with their understanding and humor have succeeded in making the whole publication process a truly rewarding and fun-filled experience for me.

In addition to the initial eight months spent in the Federal Republic in 1979, for which I owe special thanks to the Ford Foundation, I would like to acknowledge with gratitude a three-month summer grant extended to me in 1980 by the International Institute for Comparative Social Research of the Science Center Berlin, and a six-month research fellowship given to me by the Hans Böckler Foundation in 1982. Two Wesleyan University faculty research grants between 1980 and 1983 also provided welcome financial help for the completion of this project.

I would also like to take this opportunity to thank a number of students who at one stage or another helped me in various ways to cope with the usual chores accompanying the writing of a book of this kind. What has given me additional joy in this context was that most of these students not only benefitted directly by their association with the project, whether in the form of writing a senior thesis on the metalworkers' strike in the steel industry or simply by getting sufficiently interested in things German to spend one summer at a university in the Federal Republic, but that they also became close personal friends with whom I continue to stay in touch. Here I would like to mention Karen Donfried, Kenneth Gibbs, Gary Herrigel and Richard Kreindler.

Stephen Hubbell, formerly one of my star students at Wesleyan University, served as an excellent editor in the final stages of the manuscript's production. He also proved to be a meticulous and thoughtful proofreader of the pageproofs, which had to be returned to the publisher in a relatively short period of time. In spite of considerable pressure, Steve never lost his wonderful sense of humor, while at the same time retaining the high standards which he always pursues in his work. I would like to thank him for his loyal friendship which, I hope, will continue to manifest itself in our amicable disagreements about various aspects of German politics.

My most profound thanks and deepest gratitude belong to Thomas Ertman who more than any other individual has helped me complete this book. From the first moment I met Tom in June of 1980, at which point he was still an undergraduate at Harvard College, I was convinced that I had made the acquaintance of an unusually gifted young man, and one who was destined to make his mark in a later career as a social scientist. In the subsequent six years, I can barely recall having written a professional paper without consulting Tom in the process. This close intellectual trust also dominated the production of the present volume, where Tom's influence and counsel became indispensable to me. As is readily visible to the reader, Tom's labor on Chapter 6 and 7 was sufficiently extensive to make him a co-author of these two chapters. Most important of all, my six-year association with Tom has been an enjoyable and rewarding learning experience for me. Be it Argentinian history, Czech literature, Italian opera, Australian cricket or West German trade unions, Tom not only knows them all in great detail and with the proper historical perspective, but he also has the rare gift of being able to fascinate his listeners with his intellectual preoccupations and knowledge. Tom has in the meantime become a successful doctoral candidate in the Sociology Department at Harvard University. Despite the usual pressures of graduate school and the particular ones associated with the high expectations in Tom's exceptional abilities, he continues to enjoy the catholicity of his interests while he delights his friends with his impressive "Allgemeinbildung." I only hope that the future will continue to see our collegiality and friendship bloom as they have in the past.

I would like to take this opportunity to thank Connie Procaccini and her able staff at Mulberry Studio for the impeccable typing of this book's manuscript. Their reliability, expertise, empathy and humor always provided me with the necessary assurance that everything would be finished on time bearing the mark of high-quality work produced in an atmosphere of cameraderie and congeniality.

No sustained intellectual effort could ever be successfully concluded without the unconditional emotional support of friends, colleagues and family. The list of those individuals who fall into the all-important category of simply being loyal supporters would be far too extensive to be enumerated here in its completeness. Still, I would like to mention a few very special friends who stood by me in good times and bad and continue to do so. They are Paul DiMaggio, Michael Freund, Oliver Holmes, Jerome Karabel, David Karen, Jerrold Katz, Dennis Klein, Jeremiah Riemer, Rosalie Siegel and Jeff Weintraub. Ellen Zucker's constant encouragement and deep afffection meant more to me than she will ever know. She, like all others mentioned in these acknowledgements, deserves much of the credit for this book's merits. Its shortcomings, however, remain my sole responsibility.

Cambridge, Massachusetts; January 1986          Andrei S. Markovits

# INTRODUCTION

Although the West German economy has experienced some problems in recent years – hardly unusual given the global economic crisis – it has distinguished itself by its remarkable resilience and prosperity. Concomitant with this economic stability, the Federal Republic has enjoyed a political order dominated by a liberal democracy. The two have thus far reinforced each other so that the worries of many political analysts in the early years of the Federal Republic who feared a repeat of Weimar have remained largely unfounded. On the other hand, however, their suspicions have not been seriously tested precisely because the Federal Republic has never experienced conditions similar to those that plagued its Weimar predecessor. While the "Bonn is not Weimar" syndrome can be attributed to several objective international and domestic factors, there are also many subjective or voluntaristic dimensions which have contributed to this differentiation. Structures matter, but so do organizations and the actors within them. This study of the West German trade unions will concentrate on both.

A lot of intellectual energy has been spent trying to understand the German phenomenon. There are many compelling reasons for this preoccupation, which to this day shows few signs of abatement. There can be no doubt that Germany's geographic location – in the heart of Europe, at the crossroads between East and West – has been a major factor in the continued interest in this country. The increasingly normalized separation of the two Germanies heightens the significance of the German phenomenon for global politics. There is no reason to believe that this will change at any time in the foreseecable future. Germany's historical traditions, its cultural and scientific achievements, as well as its political conflicts, have all contributed to its uniqueness. This uniqueness, of course, has had both positive and negative ramifications.

For very understandable reasons, it is mainly the negative – since the end of World War II – which have captured the attention of observers concerned with things German. The collapse of the Weimar Republic and the subsequent emergence of the Nazi regime represent momentous events in the history of humanity, let alone Germany and Europe. It is therefore not surprising that virtually all post-war scholarship dealing with Germany remains, at least implicitly, preoccupied with national socialism, its antecedents and legacies. The magnitude of the horrors is still so incomprehensible that any concern – even obsession – with these events and their implications should be not only tolerated but indeed supported. Yet the primacy of national socialism, or what one could call the "Holocaust effect," in the study of virtually anything German has also produced a "crowding out" of phenomena which are unrelated to that aspect of the German past. This often leads to a relative neglect of events which are of far greater importance to the present reality of West German public life.

Largely because of this dominance of the "Holocaust effect," interest in things German among observers in the non-German-speaking world has been confined to political matters in the most immediate sense. Not by chance there exists an array of superb studies in English and French on various aspects of the Federal Republic's political system – such as its state structure and its party configuration – while very few analyses of comparable quality can be found on West Germany's economic arrangements and its network of industrial relations. Time and again one is struck by the supremacy of politics in the study of the Federal Republic at the expense of other areas. This was the case in the mid-1970s when a small number of radicals was accused of endangering the very existence of the republic; it continues to this day when anti-missile demonstrators, radical ecologists and other antinomian manifestations are perceived as destabilizing the democratic order, thus creating another potential Weimar. Although this fear of Weimar is perfectly understandable, it has inadvertently led to a situation in which our perception of the Bonn republic is too much colored by the past. While we must never discount history, it is important to understand the present existence of the Federal Republic on its own terms.

A crucial requirement to that end is a detailed study of what one could term para-political actors and institutions in the Federal Republic. Most notable among them are key interest groups, especially those organizing capital and labor in one form or another. The study at hand will present a comprehensive treatment of trade unions as the major organizational representatives of labor in West Germany since 1945. The unions have been decisive actors in the Federal Republic's economy and its politics. Both of these roles receive detailed attention in this book.

Since the inception of the Federal Republic, the West German economy has been virtually an uninterrupted success story. An extremely stable industrial relations system undoubtedly contributed to this success. Indeed, this system has been widely hailed as a model for labor relations throughout the advanced industrial world, especially in countries with persistent labor problems, such as Great Britain. But like all models – Japan comes immediately to mind – this one has often been mis-interpreted by those who wish to adopt it.

In order for the misunderstandings to be eliminated, three fundamental issues need clarification. The first concerns the question of what governs the conduct of West German industrial relations on the shop floor, in a firm or in an industry. It is important to understand how conflicts are resolved within a factory, how negotiations in an industry are structured, why and when strikes occur, and what practical influence unions have over areas such as employment and technological change.

Once a picture of the system's internal workings has been drawn, one needs to concentrate on explaining the reasons *why* it functions the way it does. This involves an analysis of, among other things, the role of his-torical experience, labor law, the dual system of interest representation pitting works councils against unions, the principles of industrial and unitary unionism and finally the social characteristics of union membership.

The third fundamental issue concerns the future of the West German industrial relations system. The main task here relates to analyzing the unions' reaction to the two-pronged attack of rapid technological change on the one hand and economic crisis characterized by high unemployment and nonexistent growth on the other. While it would be foolish to attempt to predict the future, the unions' behavior since the crisis of 1974–75 permits reasonable assumptions on this score.

Supplementing their role as major actors in the West German economy, the unions have also been important participants in the Federal Republic's polity. Without a doubt, the unions' main contribution in this area has been their deep commitment to the survival of liberal democracy in West Germany. Although occasionally dissatisfied with the policies implemented against them by the government and frequently hoping for an extension of democratic rights beyond the confines of a parliamentary Rechtsstaat, the unions have from the Federal Republic's inception been among the staunchest defenders of the pluralist order. Labor's memory of Weimar, during which its collective resistance succeeded in defending the republic only to contribute later to its eventual downfall by fostering disunity among the working class, continues to inform its political views and actions.

In addition to their support of liberal democracy, other political and social attitudes characterize the unions' activities. To analyze these beliefs, three concerns must be addressed. First, it is important to examine the types of political and social attitudes which the unions have adopted, and to understand the historical origins of these attitudes, their political content, legacies and organizational manifestations. Ultimately, this analysis needs to focus on who determines the unions' official political positions and what kind of intra-union conflicts arise in the process of this attitude formation.

The second concern relates to behavior, especially vis-à-vis the political parties and the state. Regarding their relationship to the former, German unions before 1933 – along with their counterparts in other European countries – maintained a close association along ideological lines, which in fact brought certain unions closer to "their" parties than to other unions. To avoid this potentially internecine intra-class struggle, which in the German case actually contributed to Hitler's rise to power, the West German trade unions united explicitly in one single federation which prides itself on its independence from any political party, yet simultaneously disclaims political neutrality. What are the concrete implications of this arrangement in terms of labor's political behavior? The interaction between the unions and the Social Democratic Party (SPD) has produced some of the most interesting political conflicts and alliances in the Federal Republic. The two institutions continue to overlap without, however, uniting. This has yielded some benefits, as well as handicaps, for West Germany's organized labor movement.

As for the unions' behavior towards the state, one can again learn a great deal from history. The German labor movement developed over a period of nearly one century a particular view of its relationship to the state, a view which continues to influence the actions of West German unions. It is in this context that one has to look at the unions' assessment of legislation and analyze their attitudes towards reform. The republican state existing in West Germany since 1949 has definitely been supported by the unions. But has the state been their ally, their enemy or a neutral arbiter – or perhaps all three rolled into one?

The last fundamental concern in the area of politics centers upon the unions' attitudes and behavior in relation to what one could call the public debate. Priding themselves on being active (i.e. participating) citizens who get involved beyond the narrow issues related to their immediate interests, union members have taken part in virtually all matters of public concern. Unions have participated in debates on such wide-ranging topics as rearmament in the 1950s, the emergency laws and Ostpolitik in the 1960s, the oil embargo and radicalism in the 1970s, and ecology and Euro-missiles in the 1980s. What were the ramifications of these involvements for intra-union politics? How, if at all, did they affect union ideology and union positions on other stands? Did the unions' intervention alter the eventual outcome of these issues?

While it might be valid under certain conditions to speak of the unions as a single entity, it is perhaps even more important to differentiate among unions in order to gain a complete picture of West German labor. The key to understanding labor as a major interest group in the political economy of the Federal Republic lies precisely in being able to discern the different levels of union politics and relate them to their proper arenas of influence and interaction. Whereas certain issues call for an analysis of the German Trade Union Federation (DGB) as a whole, other topics will require a study of particular unions and their concrete strategies. It is important to note that an investigation of the federation alone would not suffice, since many of the powers deployed on a daily basis lie with the seventeen constituent unions. While it may be an oversimplification, it would not be wrong to characterize the federation's primary area of involvement as politics, whereas the activities of the member unions encompass both the political and the economic sphere. Thus the balance of forces among the largest unions within the DGB substantially determines the overall political strategy of the West German labor movement. Since the major member unions assume such a central role in the daily existence of organized labor in the Federal Republic, four chapters of this study are devoted to them.

The first three chapters of the book comprise a general section designed to present the framework and tradition wherein the West German unions operate today. They deal almost exclusively with labor at the federation level. Chapter 1 gives a detailed overview of organized labor in the Federal Republic. While its main concern is to highlight the internal structure of the DGB, it also describes briefly all other labor organizations in West Germany which exist outside this federation. Moreover, it provides some information on the unions' major partners/opponents, the employers' associations. The chapter includes an analysis of the DGB's relations to the major West German parties. It also discusses the federation's relationship to the government in power as well as to the state bureaucracy. Chapter 1 concludes with a brief presentation of a particularly German aspect of labor tradition, namely the business activities of the unions.

The task of Chapter 2 is to shed light on West Germany's confusing legal framework of industrial relations. Emanating from a long tradition of particular interactions among the state, political parties, employers' associations and labor unions, a highly complex and routinized process of legal regulation developed which continues to this day to set rigid parameters for union behavior at the plant level and at the bargaining table. This overarching tendency, which the Germans refer to as Verrechtlichung, is translated here as "juridification." Specifically, the chapter concentrates on analyzing issues such as works constitution (which regulates labor relations on the shop floor), co-determination, collective bargaining, the legal character of contracts, and finally the rules governing strikes as well as lockouts. Chapter 3, the last chapter of this general section, presents a detailed history of the DGB between its founding congress in 1949 and the passage of its third major comprehensive program in 1981. Beginning with the immediate post-World War II period, during which the unions laid the groundwork for their future existence, the analysis concentrates on organized labor's political developments vis-à-vis the state (Allied pre-1949; German thereafter) and the political parties as well as its role in public debate. The chapter also places considerable emphasis on the political conflicts among various constituent unions which have had a major effect on determining the federation's political posture over the years.

The remainder of the book consists of a detailed study of four industrial unions: the metalworkers' union (IG Metall), the chemical workers' union (IG Chemie-Papier-Keramik), the construction workers' union (IG Bau-Steine-Erden) and the printers' union (IG Druck und Papier). There are two reasons why this study focuses on these four to the exclusion of both public sector and other industrial unions. First, one of the foremost concerns of this research has been the role that organized labor has played in West Germany's economic success. The three most important sectors of the Federal Republic's economy have consistently been the metalworking, chemical and construction industries. Together these three areas have accounted for over one-half of West Germany's industrial employment. Moreover, they have contributed a sizeable proportion of the Federal Republic's exports and gross national product. The areas covered by the DGB's remaining industrial unions have simply not assumed comparable importance in the overall context of the West German economy. The same pertains to the public sector unions. In addition, the problems presented by the public sector and public employment in the Federal Republic are markedly different from those found in private industry. It would take another book of equal length to do justice to the situation of public sector unions.

The second important criterion in choosing the four industrial unions was the relative influence of particular unions within the DGB. Also relevant to this analysis were unions which had experienced hardships that in one way or another were characteristic of labor's problems in general. On both these counts, the printers' union, IG Druck und Papier, served as an ideal candidate for study. Because of its illustrious tradition as the oldest German trade union, the printers' organization has consistently exercised a political and intellectual influence within the German labor movement well out of proportion to its size. Of all the unions in the Federal Republic, it has also been the one which has suffered the most due to rapid technological change, starting with the onset of the crisis in the 1970s. By investigating IG Druck und Papier's response to this predicament, one could hope to gauge possible reactions to this problem on the part of other DGB unions in years to come.

The general structure of the four union chapters is similar. Each presents a discussion of the important characteristics of that union's industry and its employers' association. It also provides a brief analysis of the particular union's pre-1933 tradition as well as a more detailed description of the sociology of its membership. Furthermore, the chapters each contain accounts of its post-1949 development. In these summaries an attempt is made to highlight the role of each union as an economic and political actor within its particular industry as well as in the Federal Republic as a whole.

Despite these similarities, each of the industrial union studies has a very different character, reflecting the fundamental differences distinguishing these unions from one another. In this way, the book hopes to qualify the popular image of a monolithic and homogeneous West German labor movement.

Thus, it is not by chance that Chapter 4, dealing with IG Metall, comprises nearly one-third of the entire book. By far the DGB's most important union, IG Metall represents over one-third of the federation's members. In addition to the influence that this union wields as a consequence of its sheer size, it has consistently dominated virtually all aspects of trade union life in the Federal Republic. Very little that has affected West German labor since the beginning of the republic has not in one form or another involved this largest trade union in the non-communist world. Because of IG Metall's position as unquestioned *primus inter pares* within the DGB and its vanguard role in collective bargaining, an account of IG Metall necessarily touches on virtually every important event in West German labor history.

The chapters on the other three unions are more limited in scope. The study of IG Chemie, presented in Chapter 5, concerns itself mainly with the organizational conflicts that have plagued this union throughout much of its existence. Handicapped by severe representational difficulties in West Germany's three chemical giants, BASF, Hoechst and Bayer, this union developed certain compensatory mechanisms whose legacies have involved it in major turmoil, particularly in the late 1970s and early 1980s. This phenomenon created two competing factions within IG Chemie that debated these organizational issues and their implications with much fervor and an equal amount of hostility. In this way, IG Chemie embodies a microcosm of the West German labor movement and its two wings: the "activists" or "reformers" on one side and "accommodationists" or "social partners" on the other.

Chapter 6 examines the construction workers' union, IG Bau-Steine-Erden. The research presented concentrates on the problems faced by a numerically large yet organizationally weak union. IG Bau has never been able to overcome the low levels of unionization in the construction sector. Attempts to combat this deficiency led the union's innovative and charismatic leader Georg Leber to devise an array of particularistic and interest-group-oriented schemes throughout the 1950s and 1960s in order to enhance the attractiveness of IG Bau. This, in turn, led the union into direct conflict with the more collectivist IG Metall. The frequent battles between these two unions, fueled by the personal rivalries of their respective leaders, Georg Leber and Otto Brenner, became the focal point of the disagreements between accommodationists and activists within the DGB.

Chapter 7 deals with the printers' union, IG Druck und Papier. In many ways this union stands in marked contrast to IG Bau. Although always numerically small, it has consistently enjoyed a high level of unionization among the workers belonging to its organizational purview. The case of IG Druck presents a good opportunity to study the effect of well-entrenched, pre-1933 traditions on an important segment of the labor movement. The chapter thus serves to qualify the widely held view that "hour zero" meant a completely new beginning for the German labor movement. Moreover, as already stated, the study of IG Druck raises the issue of the impact of the computer-based, technological revolution on the West German labor movement in general and its traditional "aristocracy" in particular.

The book's conclusion has two purposes. The first is to function as an epilogue which will discuss some key events involving West German labor since the passage of the DGB's new basic program in 1981. The second is to summarize the major findings presented in this volume and to venture some predictions as to the fate of the organized labor movement in the years ahead. To that end, the role of West German unions as major actors in a liberal democracy's polity and economy will be assessed in light of larger theoretical issues. By so doing, the study intends to contribute to a deeper understanding of public life in the Federal Republic of Germany.

# 1 THE STRUCTURE OF THE WEST GERMAN UNION MOVEMENT

## I. WEST GERMAN UNION ORGANIZATIONS

### A. Introductory overview

In the period before 1933 the German union movement was divided along both occupational and political lines. The largest union confederation was the social democratic ADGB (Allgemeiner Deutscher Gewerkschaftsbund – General German Trade Union Federation) which had 4,135,000 members in 1931.[1] The Christian DGB (Deutscher Gewerkschaftsbund – German Trade Union Federation) had 1,292,000 adherents, of which about half were civil servants and white-collar workers. The smallest union confederation was the conservative Gewerkschaftsring (Union Ring) with about 200,000 members. It was popularly referred to as the Hirsch–Duncker confederation after its founders, Max Hirsch and Franz Duncker. In all of these associations, power lay with the member unions rather than the federation, and those unions were mainly organized on occupational lines. The vast majority of blue-collar workers were to be found in the ADGB, whereas the Gewerkschaftsring was a largely white-collar organization. The Christian DGB represented both groups.

Since its inception in the mid-nineteenth century, the social democratic union movement had been led by skilled workers, organized mainly in craft unions. By the turn of the century, a movement was underway to amalgamate related craft unions, and in 1914 seven large unions (metal, construction, transport, wood, textile, government workers, mining) accounted for 70% of the membership in the ADGB's predecessor, the Generalkommission. At the same time 39 smaller craft unions helped block full implementation of industrial unionism within the social democratic union movement.[2] By 1931, as a result of further amalgamations, the total number of ADGB affiliates had been reduced to 30. All of these unions were purely manual-worker organizations. White-collar workers were organized separately in the AFA (Allgemeiner Freier Angestelltenbund – General Free Salaried Staff Association) and civil servants in the ADB (Allgemeiner Deutscher Beamtenbund – General German Civil Servants' Federation).

Although the pre-1933 DGB was officially a "Christian" union federation, its inspiration came from the Catholic workers' movement of the 1890s, and it was effective in organizing Catholics in the metalworking, textile and mining industries. The DGB also included a separate confederation for civil servants, and one for white-collar workers known as the GEDAG (Gesamtverband Deutscher Angestelltenverbände – Overall Association of German Salaried Staffs' Trade Unions). The most important component of the latter was the infamous DHV (Deutschnationaler Handelsgehilfenverband – the German National Clerks' and Shop Assistants' Association), a right-wing union with close ties to the Nazis, which was the largest organization of white-collar workers in Weimar. The presence of the DHV within the pre-war DGB shows how misleading it is to term this federation "Catholic."

After 1933, all trade unions in Germany were eliminated and workers reorganized into the national-socialist-controlled Deutsche Arbeitsfront (DAF – German Labor Front).[3] Although the DAF could not be called a trade union in any meaningful sense, it helped facilitate the creation of industrial unions after 1945 by grouping all workers (both white- and blue-collar) in eighteen Reichsbetriebsgruppen (National Factory Groups) whose organizational areas followed closely those of the sixteen post-war Industriegewerkschaften (industrial unions) of the DGB.

While in exile between 1933 and 1945, most important leaders of both the social democratic and Christian unions agreed that after the war German unions should be reconstructed based on the dual principles of industrial and unitary (non-sectarian) trade unionism. It was decided that both blue- and white-collar workers would be organized together in sixteen industrial unions (Industriegewerkschaften). These unions would then be grouped in a federation which would be independent of all political parties (thus the German term Einheitsgewerkschaft – unitary, non-sectarian trade union). Most of West Germany's union activists supported this plan after 1945, and the result was the creation of sixteen industrial unions and the DGB during the period 1948–50. (For more details see Chapter 3.) A small number of workers, however, could not accept the idea behind the new DGB and thus, contrary to popular belief, the latter is not the only union federation in West Germany.

The first challenge to the nascent DGB came over the issue of industrial unionism. Some white-collar workers and civil servants, many of whom had been members of the social democratic AFA and ADB before 1933, demanded the reconstruction of those organizations after the war. When the DGB refused, the DAG (Deutsche Angestellten Gewerkschaft – German White-Collar Workers' Union) and the DBB (Deutscher Beamten Bund – German Civil Servants' Federation) were formed. In 1951, the DAG had 343,500 members, which represented 35% of all unionized white-collar workers (the remaining 65% being members of DGB unions).[4] By 1981, DAG membership had risen to 494,874, but because of the great increase in white-collar unionization since the 1950s, the DAG now only accounts for about 21% of all white-collar union members.[5] There are few major political or ideological differences between the DGB and the DAG, and most of the latter's top leaders are SPD members, just like the former's.

As for the DBB, it is doubtful whether it should be termed a union federation at all. It does not negotiate with the government since its members are all tenured civil servants (Beamte) for whom collective bargaining is prohibited. It is thus mainly a lobbying organization. In 1981, the DBB had 821,012 members, compared to the 843,485 Beamte who belonged to the DGB.[6]

The only other significant West German union organization outside the DGB is the CGB (Christlicher Gewerkschaftsbund Deutschlands – German Christian Trade Union Federation). The majority of Christian trade unionists of the pre-1933 period supported the creation of a non-sectarian DGB after 1949, though a small number of activists favored a revival of separate unions linked to the new CDU. After the DGB openly supported the SPD in the 1953 Bundestag elections, many CDU supporters threatened to split the new Einheitsgewerkschaft. With the help of Chancellor Adenauer a break was prevented, but a small number of Christian "extremists" left the DGB anyway in 1955 and founded the Christliche Gewerkschaftsbewegung. In 1959 they united with a resuscitated DHV, which had been founded by members of the old far-right union in 1950, to form the Christlicher Gewerkschaftsbund. (See also Chapter 3 for a discussion of these developments.)

Without the support of the CDU, however, such an enterprise was doomed from the start. Although the federation includes eighteen member unions organized in almost exactly the same way as the old pre-war DGB, it has never attracted more than 300,000 members.[7] Its most important member union is the Christian Metal Workers (Christlicher Metallarbeiterverband – CMV), which has been able to elect a few works councilors in some metalworking plants in North Rhine-Westphalia. Despite its impotence, the CGB has proved useful over the years as a lever that can be employed by the CDU and the CSU against the DGB. On several occasions when the latter has taken public positions too close to those of the SPD, leading CDU/CSU politicians like Franz-Josef Strauss have threatened to bring the CGB to life by ordering CDU supporters to join it. (Again, see Chapter 3 for a detailed presentation of such an event.)

Table 1.1 illustrates the relative strength of the four West German union federations at the beginning of 1981:

Table 1.1 *Membership of West German union federations, 1981*

|  | Membership |
| --- | --- |
| DGB | 7,882,527 |
| DBB | 821,012 |
| DAG | 494,874 |
| CGB | 288,170 |
| Total union membership | 9,486,583[8] |

*Source:* Siegfried Mielke (ed.), *Internationales Gewerkschaftshandbuch* (Opladen: Leske & Budrich, 1983), p. 352.

If one includes the DBB membership, this total represents a unionization level of 40.13% for the entire West German workforce.[9] This places the Federal Republic in a middle range between poorly unionized countries like the US and France, and heavily organized ones like Austria, Sweden and Great Britain. (The reason that unionization is not higher in West Germany, despite its strong labor tradition, relates to the legal framework for industrial relations in that country, which will be discussed in Chapter 2.) This 40% unionization level is deceptive, however, since none of the three union organizations outside the DGB has much of an impact on the labor relations in the Federal Republic. It is for this reason that throughout the remainder of this book we will concentrate exclusively on the DGB and its seventeen member unions.

## B. The Deutscher Gewerkschaftsbund

With its almost 8 million members, DGB unions cover one-third (33.35% – 1980) of the West German workforce and 83.1% of all unionized workers.[10] The figure for the entire workforce – both unionized and non-unionized – is lower than the 37–38% levels of the early 1950s, but better than the 29.7% reached in 1969 and 1970, when unionization in West Germany dropped to its lowest levels since the Depression.[11] Appendix 1 lists the seventeen DGB unions and their membership totals at the end of 1983. Several important facts about the DGB can be discerned from this table. First, the member unions can be divided into two broad groups: those organizing workers in the public sector (ÖTV, DPG, GdED, GEW, GdP) and the rest which are concerned with private industry. The five public sector unions confront a series of institutions and problems which are very different from those of the rest of the union movement. It is important to note that the five public sector unions, led by ÖTV, have very close ties among themselves and represent a significant sub-group accounting for 30% of total DGB membership.

A second striking characteristic of the DGB is the enormity of IG Metall, which – comprising in excess of 2.5 million members – is one-third the size of the entire DGB. This is the logical consequence of a strict application of the industrial union principle to metalworking, which, with such industries as autos, steel, machine construction and electronics, constitutes far and away West Germany's largest industrial sector. It should come as no surprise that IG Metall's massive presence – this union is almost four times larger than IG Chemie, the second most important industrial union within the DGB – would create major problems not only in the relations between the DGB and its constituent unions, but also among the member unions themselves, a theme which will recur with some frequency throughout this book.

As one would expect given both German tradition and the West German industrial structure, the majority of DGB members (68%) are blue-collar workers. Of these, 84% are males, so that male blue-collar workers, the traditional core of German labor, account for 57.6% of all DGB members.[12] The percentage of blue-collar workers has been decreasing steadily since the late 1960s, however, as the relative prominence of this group in the West German workforce declines. This has been paralleled by the steady growth of white-collar workers, who accounted for 42.3% of the labor force in 1980 compared to only 28.7% in 1960.[13]

The decline of the male, blue-collar worker has created problems for DGB unions, since they have consistently found it difficult to organize white-collar workers, women and foreign workers. Thus, whereas the unionization level for blue-collar workers is estimated at 48.3%, it is only 17.8% for women and 17.8% for white-collar workers.[14] These last two facts are mutually reinforcing, since about 40% of the DGB's female members are white-collar workers.[15] Given current employment trends in the Federal Republic, the DGB will have to improve its appeal among white-collar workers if it wants to maintain current membership levels, since the number of blue-collar workers will continue to fall both relatively and absolutely in the labor force of the Federal Republic. Yet despite their low organizational levels, white-collar workers and women now each account for about 20% of DGB membership and their importance as interest groups within the unions is on the rise.[16]

## II. THE ORGANIZATION OF EMPLOYERS IN THE FEDERAL REPUBLIC

Before examining the organizational structure of the DGB and its member unions, it is necessary to discuss briefly the unions' "opponents," the employers. This is particularly important since there are three types of business organizations in West Germany and confusion over their respective duties and activities is very common.

The three types of business organizations to be found in the Federal Republic are Wirtschaftsverbände (economic associations), Industrie- und Handelskammern (chambers of commerce) and Arbeitgeberverbände (employers' associations).[17] The economic associations are essentially lobbying organizations. There are thirteen major economic associations in West Germany, the most important of which is the Bundesverband der Deutschen Industrie (BDI – Federal Association of German Industry).[18] The BDI is a federation like the DGB and itself contains 39 industrial associations organized by product groups, such as the Verband der Automobilindustrie (Association of the Automobile Industry) and the Verein Deutscher Maschinenbau-Anstalten (Union of German Machine Construction Works). Each of these individual associations, as well as the BDI itself, lobbies in Bonn for legislation and economic policies favorable to its particular industry. In addition the associations represent the official position of their industries in the media.

The West German Chambers of Commerce, unlike their American counterparts, have since their creation in the nineteenth century always had the character of quasi-etatist institutions. The Chambers are organized on a regional basis, with 81 of them covering the entire Federal Republic. All firms which are liable to pay business taxes (Gewerbesteuern) must, by law, join the local Chamber of Commerce and pay dues to it. Originally, the Prussian state had charged the Chambers with collecting all business taxes and forwarding them to the state administration, but now their duties are confined to activities such as supervising vocational training, granting licenses and inspecting products. All of the regional Chambers are united in the Deutsche Industrie- und Handelstage (DIHT – German Industrial and Commercial Assemblies), which represents their interests in Bonn.

Officially, neither the BDI nor the DIHT has anything to do with the relationship between management and labor. This is the sole responsibility of the employers' associations, which are the unions' bargaining partners in all contract negotiations.[19] There are 56 associations covering all major industries as well as banking and commerce. An important difference when compared to the BDI is that all industries involving metalworking (except steel) – automobile production, machine construction and electronics, for example – are grouped in one employers' association, the Gesamtverband der Metallindustriellen Arbeitgeberverbände (the General Federation of Metal Industry Employers' Associations), commonly known as Gesamtmetall. All 56 industrial associations, as well as 13 Land (state) organizations, are grouped together in the Bundesvereinigung der Deutschen Arbeitgeberverbände (BDA – Federal Confederation of German Employers' Associations). Because of its size and economic importance, Gesamtmetall occupies a position within the BDA analogous to that of IG Metall (its bargaining partner) within the DGB.

The BDA and its member associations have three main areas of activity: social policy, labor law and collective bargaining. The BDA is the official lobby of business on issues involving social security, unemployment and sickness benefits and all other constituent programs of the welfare state. As such, it often takes positions on these issues which are directly opposite to those for which the DGB is lobbying. The BDA also nominates one-third of the members of the independent boards which monitor state social welfare funds. (Selbstverwaltungskörperschaften der Sozialversicherung). In a similar way, the organization sends one representative to sit on the three-member Labor Law Tribunals (Arbeitsgerichte – see Chapter 2 below).

More important than these two functions is the BDA's role in coordinating collective bargaining. As in the DGB, the BDA member associations bargain independently with their trade union counterparts. Unlike the DGB, however, the BDA exercises considerable influence over bargaining through its bargaining committee (Ausschuss zur Koordinierung der Lohn- und Tarifpolitik). It is the job of this committee to ensure that member associations abide by certain bargaining guidelines decreed by the BDA. It was long suspected in union circles that the BDA had drawn up a formal list of concessions which its members were forbidden from granting, such as reducing the work week below 40 hours. The existence of such a list was confirmed when the BDA's so-called Tabu Katalog was leaked to the press in early 1979. (For a discussion of this incident see Chapter 3 below.) Because of its considerable power over member associations, the BDA is often able to "plan" a bargaining round in advance by assigning different functions to different industry groups. Thus the employers can decide centrally where and how to attack the unions, an advantage that the DGB, because of its subservience to its member unions, enjoys to a far lesser extent.

Table 1.2 German Trade Union Federation

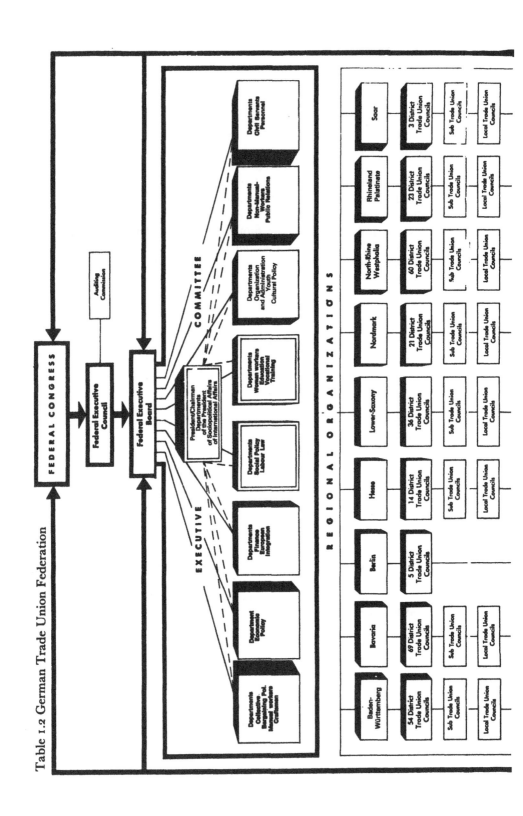

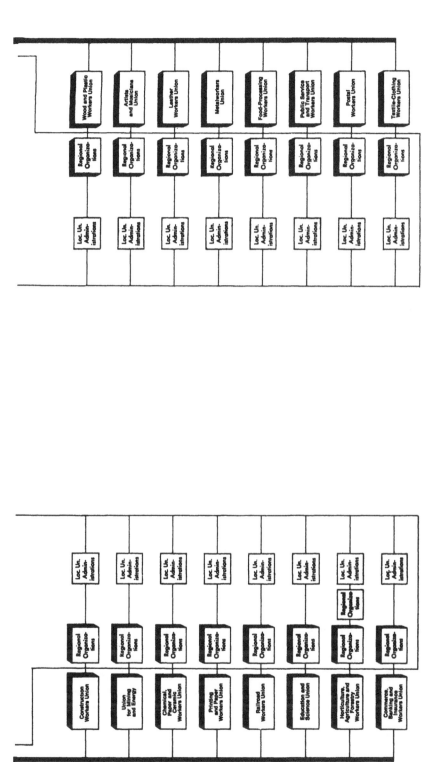

*Source:* Dieter Schuster, *The German Labour Movement – DGB* (Düsseldorf: Deutscher Gewerkschaftsbund, 1973), pp. 120, 121.

## III. THE DGB: A CLOSER LOOK

### A. *The role and internal organization of the DGB*

The DGB is an umbrella organization, which means that its primary function consists of representing the interests of its member unions in all areas of relevance to organized labor. The DGB is first and foremost the voice of labor in Bonn, lobbying for legislation and particular policies in the areas of social welfare (old age pensions, sickness benefits, unemployment insurance), economic affairs (fiscal, monetary and tax policies), social reform (co-determination, labor legislation), education (educational reform), vocational training, and defense and foreign policy (detente, disarmament). In addition to its role as "labor's lobby," the DGB sends representatives to dozens of quasi-state and judicial bodies which are peculiar to the West German governmental system. Lastly, the federation bears responsibility for providing services and coordination to the member unions in the areas of collective bargaining, education, and legal and financial aid.

The organizational structure of the DGB (see table 1.2) resembles closely that of the individual industrial unions.[20] The basic organizational unit at the local level is the DGB county (Kreis), which overlaps almost identically with government counties. In each county, all DGB unions represented therein send delegates to a county delegate meeting (Kreisdelegiertenversammlung) which in turn elects a county executive committee (Kreisvorstand). The leadership of the next highest DGB level, the regional district, can recommend a candidate for the county executive committee to the county delegates, and must give its approval to every candidate who is chosen.

Below the county level are two further DGB bodies, both of which are responsible to the county executive committee. The first are the subsidiary offices (Zweigbüros), set up in rural areas of a county to provide better access to unionists there. The second are the municipal cartels (Ortskartelle), which are DGB offices staffed with at least one full-time official and which are set up in towns populated by at least 200 DGB members. The municipal cartel's main function is to represent DGB positions in local politics. This cannot, of course, take the form of supporting particular candidates, since the DGB maintains a politically nonsectarian posture. A series of general DGB demands is instead addressed to all candidates, and it remains up to the voter to decide which of them will best represent the interests of organized labor. The DGB county executive committee performs a similar duty in the counties, but this level of government lacks major significance in the Federal Republic. The most important duty of the DGB county organization consists in providing legal aid to all union members in cases before the labor courts. This service is particularly crucial for small unions which – unlike IG Metall, ÖTV and other big unions – in many cases do not have their own legal aid departments.[21] In 1981, there were 221 DGB Kreise and 1,351 Ortskartelle.[22] Workers employed full time at these levels comprised the largest group of DGB employees.[23]

Above the counties are the nine DGB regional districts (Landesbezirke). Unlike in many member unions, the DGB regional districts follow fairly closely the Land (state) borders of the Federal Republic. The nine districts are Baden-Württemberg, Bavaria, Berlin, Hesse, Lower Saxony (including Bremen), Nordmark (which includes Schleswig-Holstein and Hamburg), North Rhine-Westphalia, Rhineland-Palatinate and the Saar. The regional districts are administered by a regional district executive committee (Landesbezirksvorstand) which is elected by the delegates at a regional district conference (Landesbezirkskonferenz). As with the counties, delegates are selected by the member unions, and each union is assigned a certain number of delegates in proportion to its size.

Like the DGB Kreis organizations, those at the regional level are involved in two main fields of activity, the first directed towards the member unions and the second towards the local state (Land) government. It is the job of the DGB Landesbezirk to formulate a common position on matters of particular interest to its state in cases such as, for example, the introduction of a nuclear power plant, the continued structural crisis in an important local industry, or a proposal for state educational reform. The Landesbezirk, of course, consults closely with member unions and DGB headquarters at each step in this process. This often entails preparing studies of the problem, then clarifying the DGB position through consultation with leading works councilors and shop stewards, who must present the DGB viewpoint in their plants. Equally important is the selling of the DGB position in the media and in the local Landtag (state assembly). Regional distict officials must have access to the centers of power in the state, and to this end many of them have become Landtag members themselves.

Of the nine regional districts, North Rhine-Westphalia is the largest, accounting for almost one-third (32.7% in 1981) of all DGB members. It is followed by Baden-Württemberg (15.2%), Bavaria (14.1%) and Hesse (8.7%).[24] Since the 1950s, the Federal Republic has experienced a steady industrialization of the south (Hesse, Bavaria, Baden-Württemberg), and since the 1970s this has been accompanied by a serious structural crisis in the traditional industrial areas of the north including the Ruhr, Hamburg and Lower Saxony. As a result, the weight of the southern areas within the labor movement has grown rapidly and will continue to do so in the foreseeable future.[25] Since the south is generally more conservative, and its workers less bound by old social democratic traditions than those in areas like Dortmund, Hamburg and Berlin, this shift could bring about subtle changes in the political character of the DGB.

At the federal level, the DGB congress is the federation's basic legislative body. Congresses took place every two years between 1950 and 1956, and then every three years from 1956 until 1978. At the eleventh congress in 1978, this was again changed, subsequently making all regular DGB congresses quadrennial events. Generally, between 400 and 500 delegates from the seventeen member unions attend each DGB congress. Each union is assigned a given number of delegates proportionate to its size within the federation. The delegates are not elected, but are chosen by the leadership of the member unions. Although the DGB does not publicize this fact, it has been estimated that 300 of the 504 delegates to the 1978 Congress were full-time union officials.[26]

Since each member union sends a certain number of delegates according to its size, and since each union delegation almost always votes as a block, it is possible to draw some general conclusions about the power constellation at DGB conferences and hence within the DGB itself. There have always been two main groups of unions within the DGB, which we have decided to call activists and accommodationists, roughly corresponding to the more general notions of "radicals" and "moderates." This cleavage, based both on political attitudes and on tradition, has been the principal axis along which intra-DGB politics revolved throughout the post-World War II period. In the 1950s and early 1960s the activist wing comprised IG Metall – led by Otto Brenner – IG Chemie, IG Druck, the carpenters' union (Gewerkschaft Holz), and the leatherworkers' union (Gewerkschaft Leder). Their main opponents in the accommodationist camp were the mineworkers' union (IG Bergbau), IG Bau, the textile workers' union (Gewerkschaft Textil-Bekleidung), and the public sector unions, although ÖTV often took an equivocal position between the two factions.[27] As discussed in Chapters 3 and 5 this alignment was to undergo some key developments during the crisis of the 1970s.

Despite the fact that the activist unions accounted for between 40% and 45% of DGB membership from 1950 to 1965,[28] they were only able to exert decisive control over DGB policy for a brief period between 1952 and 1959. From 1959 through the early 1970s, the accommodationists, riding on the coattails of the post-Bad Godesberg SPD, had the upper hand, though never exclusive power, in the DGB. This eminence of the "social partners" within the federation was illustrated by the choice of Ludwig Rosenberg (1962) and later Heinz Oskar Vetter (1969), both clear moderates in the labor movement, to lead the federation. In the 1970s two important changes took place within the DGB's power constellation. IG Chemie moved resolutely from the activist to the accommodationist camp (see Chapter 5), and both ÖTV and the Deutsche Postgewerkschaft (DPG) drifted steadily to the left within the spectrum of DGB politics. This appears to have given the federation a radical majority again by 1981, although throughout the 1970s the situation was closer to a draw between "reformers" and "social partners" than a clear domination of one faction by the other. It is important to point out that the supposed hegemony of IG Metall within the DGB has been something of a myth. Although on most occasions IG Metall has been able to block DGB actions which it opposes, it has by and large never succeeded in imposing its own vision of the DGB in an unmitigated fashion.

Every DGB congress elects a Federal Executive Committee (Geschäfts-führender Vorstand) which actually runs the organization. The Executive Committee consists of a chairman and eight other members, each of whom is responsible for a DGB department (Economic Policy, Social Policy and Collective Bargaining, for example). Between congresses, the Executive Committee is responsible to the DGB Federal Council (Bundesausschuss), which is totally independent of the Congress. Its membership consists of the DGB Executive Committee, the heads of the DGB regional districts and 100 representatives of the member unions apportioned according to their relative size. Thus IG Metall usually nominates 34 representatives, since it accounts for 34% of the DGB membership. The Federal Council meets every three months to review the Executive Committee's actions. The power of this body has led one observer to call it the "de facto chief organ" of the DGB.[29] Its role, which has no equivalent in the member unions, is symbolic of the latter's dominance over the DGB. This dominance by the constituent unions over the DGB is further underscored by the federation's total financial dependence on its members. Each of the member unions contributes 12% of its dues to the federation to finance its operations.

The DGB's main functions at the federation level, headquartered in Düsseldorf, are identical to those of the county and regional district organizations. The federation first and foremost provides services (educational, legal, advisory) to its constituent unions, and lobbies the federal government on all issues of concern to organized labor (social and economic policy and labor legislation, for example). At this juncture we will expand briefly only on the DGB's service functions, leaving its lobbying activities for a later discussion.

Education represents one of the DGB's most important contributions to the daily existence of unionists in West Germany. The federation has the resources to maintain special schools and give generous scholarships to works councilors and other "engaged" workers. These activities have enabled the DGB to win over leading "opinion makers" within the labor force to represent its point of view on the country's shop floors. In addition, the DGB is the only organization able to provide works councilors with the kind of technical training, as well as legal assistance, which they need to carry out their daily duties in supporting the interests of the rank and file. For many workers who have had only limited schooling, the DGB schools furnish the sole opportunity to augment their skills both in a mechanical or instrumental sense and in the larger context of acquiring knowledge.

Another key DGB activity pertains to the support services which the federation provides in the area of collective bargaining. The DGB itself plays no direct role in bargaining, since the signing of contracts has consistently remained the sole and well-guarded prerogative of each constituent union. However, many of the DGB's founders saw "coordination" as the umbrella organization's proper role in collective bargaining, by which they meant the DGB's orchestration of each bargaining round to maximize wage gains. This involves establishing the order in which particular unions would bargain and choosing several of them as trendsetters to determine the terms and tone for the bargaining rounds. This was prima facie not an unrealistic strategy since the BDA has consistently performed similar orchestrations and coordinations among the employers starting in the early 1960s. Yet because of IG Metall's unshakeable opposition to such a construct, which obviously would have entailed some loss in autonomy – and hence power – for the metalworkers' union, this plan was never actualized. Instead, the DGB has had to remain content with providing technical information and other forms of ancillary assistance to its members during the process of collective bargaining.

An important feature of collective bargaining in West Germany is the detailed analysis of the economic situation and recommendations for wage settlements provided by the Federal Economics Ministry, the Council of Economic Advisors (Sachverständigenrat-SVR), and several leading economic research institutes like the DIW (Deutsches Institut für Wirtschaftsforschung – German Economic Research Institute). Many of these organizations offer a point of view implicitly favorable to the employers, and thus can influence public opinion to their benefit during bargaining rounds. In order to counterbalance this bias and provide labor's side of the story, the DGB maintains its own economic research institute, the Wirtschafts- und Sozialwissenschaftliches Institut (Economics and Social Science Institute – WSI). Both the WSI and the DGB's Economics Department furnish member unions with the necessary economic data to make informed wage demands. This is particularly important because, unlike IG Metall, most unions do not have the resources to maintain large-scale economic research facilities. Both the WSI and the DGB's Economics Department are staffed by academic economists who typically have not advanced through the ranks of the union system, which guarantees that they maintain a certain degree of objectivity and independence.

Given the great range in size between the DGB's constituent unions, it should not come as a surprise that the federation regularly has to redistribute resources from the "rich" to the "poor" within the DGB. It does this by exempting unions in financial trouble from their dues payments and by providing assistance to small unions (like IG Druck) that become involved in strikes which they cannot afford. (See the chapter on IG Druck in this volume.) Despite the fears of some, the DGB "aid" has on the whole not led to any increase in the federation's control over the internal affairs of its member unions. The reason for this lies in the DGB's lack of financial leverage over most of its constituent unions, thus robbing the federation of a potentially powerful mechanism of pressure and control. It is significant in this respect that the large unions like IG Metall have consistently blocked all attempts by the DGB to raise the percentage of dues owed by the member unions to the federation.[30]

## B. The DGB, the state and the parties

The most important function of the DGB is undoubtedly its representation of organized labor in the political sphere. This particular role of the federation has three elements: the relationship with the three main political parties (SPD, CDU/CSU and FDP),[31] with the government and with the federal bureaucracy.

The very existence of the DGB as an Einheitsgewerkschaft necessitates its complete and formal independence from any of the country's political parties. Independence, however, does not mean political neutrality, as the unions never tire of reminding anyone who cares to listen. This means that in practice the DGB has a close relationship to social democracy in general and the SPD in particular. Thus, for example, it has been estimated that 82% of the DGB's leading officials are members or sympathizers of the SPD against only 12% for the CDU.[32] Many former union leaders (Georg Leber, Herbert Ehrenberg, Walter Arendt, Hans Matthöffer, Anke Fuchs) have served as ministers, and several others (Hermann Rappe, Ernst Haar, Adolph Schmidt, Werner Vitt) have been SPD Bundestag members and/or important party officials. Finally, the heads of several unions (Karl Hauenschild, IG Chemie; Adolph Schmidt, IG Bergbau) were good friends and unofficial advisors of Chancellor Helmut Schmidt during his chancellorship between 1974 and 1982.

This network of close personal ties between DGB and SPD has misled many into thinking that the relationship between the two organizations is similar to the one between Swedish or British unions and their respective labor parties. Aside from the fact that no financial connections exist between the unions and any political parties in West Germany, the most important difference compared to the Anglo-Swedish situation is that the DGB cannot campaign for or support the SPD during elections. In 1953, acting on SPD instructions, the then head of the DGB Walter Freitag issued an election slogan weakly recommending that workers vote for the Social Democratic Party in the upcoming elections (see details in Chapter 3). This single action led to serious complications within the unitary trade union movement, even briefly threatening its existence. Since that time, the DGB has never dared intervene in political campaigns except in the most innocuous fashion (such as by urging people to vote). Instead, the federation issues so-called Wahlprüfsteine (election guidelines) stating the organization's basic positions and goals. By comparing these lists against the platforms of the parties, the union voter is supposed to be able to decide which of them pursues policies most favorable to labor.

For its part, the SPD has tried to maintain close ties with the DGB unions, especially since the party's Bad Godesberg reforms in 1959. Before its transformation into a Volkspartei, the general feeling among Social Democrats was that there existed little need for a special workers' organization within the SPD since the SPD itself was the workers' party.[33] The SPD concentrated much of its energy on the factory level, where it created SPD factory groups (Betriebsgruppen) to fight the influence of both the CDU and the Communists. As the party began to move towards an active role in government, which in turn necessitated coalitions with the CDU or the FDP, unionists began to feel that their influence over party policy was declining. A clear illustration of this was the split between the SPD and the DGB over the Emergency Law issue throughout much of the 1960s. (See Chapter 3 for a detailed discussion of these events.)

With the participation of the SPD in the Grand Coalition, discussions between the party and the DGB's left wing increased. It was against this background that Otto Brenner, leader of the DGB's most activist union, called for the creation of a special "worker wing" within the SPD in 1967.[34] He probably felt that such an organization would be able to act as the radical "conscience" of the party in power. Brenner's calls were, however, ignored and the attempts of leftist DGB officials like Julius Lehlbach (DGB regional district chairman for Rhineland-Palatinate) to create a workers' wing on their own were torpedoed by the party.[35] It was only in 1972, in the face of the growing intra-party power of the Jusos (the leftist-oriented SPD Youth organization) that the Arbeitsgemeinschaft für Arbeitnehmerfragen

(Working Community for Workers' Issues – AfA) was created by the SPD's leadership as a counterweight to the Young Socialist threat. Just as the party leaders intended, and contrary to the expectations of Brenner and Lehlbach, this "workers' organization" within the SPD has since its inception remained firmly in the hands of the party's apparatchiks and right wing (the "sewer workers" or Kanalarbeiter).

The basic organizational unit of the AfA is the workers' conference (Arbeitnehmerkonferenz) which occurs at the level of the SPD sub-district (Unterbezirk).[36] The conference includes all members of the SPD factory groups as well as all works councilors, shop stewards and union officials from the area who are also SPD members. The members of the workers' conference then elect delegates to a regional (Bezirk) conference and representatives to a state (Land) conference, who in turn elect representatives to a national conference which chooses the AfA executive committee. At the time of this writing the two leaders of the AfA are Helmut Rohde and Hans-Eberhard Urbaniak, both SPD Bundestag members who formerly held minor positions in the unions. Most of the AfA officials in fact seem to be present or former state and local union officials. The AfA sends represetatives to the SPD party congresses and has the right to make proposals to that body, a privilege shared by the Jusos and the SPD women's organization.

In addition to the AfA, the SPD contains a "union" body, the Union Council (Gewerkschaftsrat), founded in 1968 to improve communications between the party of government and the unions.[37] The union council includes the heads of all DGB unions who are SPD members, as well as the head of the DAG and representatives from the DBB. The Union Council has probably exerted greater influence over SPD policies than the AfA, although neither organization has wielded anything like the power generated by informal contacts between key union officials and SPD leaders. The politics of the smoke-filled room has dominated the discourse between the DGB and the SPD and shows few signs of abating, which is not to say that the two bodies have always been in agreement.

As was mentioned earlier, there also exists a small, though significant (10–15%), number of CDU members within the DGB unions. It is an unwritten rule that two of the nine members of the DGB's Executive Committee must belong to the CDU. Moreover, many of the DGB's constituent unions have at least one Christian Democrat among their top leaders, but no CDU member has ever become the head of a DGB union, or of the federation itself.

In line with the tradition of Christian socialism and Catholic worker representation dating to the turn of this century, the CDU always included a workers' wing comparable to the SPD's AfA. It has become traditional for the head of this CDU organization, known as the Social Committees (Sozialausschüsse), to assume the position of labor minister in a CDU-led government. The head of the Social Committees has hitherto always been a DGB union member. Within the CDU, however, the Social Committees are far less influential than the organizations of either big business (the Wirtschaftsrat) or medium-sized and small entrepreneurs (the Mittelstand-ausschuss). Workers in general and DGB unionists in particular have remained the poor cousins within the CDU, despite the importance of working-class votes for this party's continued electoral success, both on the federal and the state levels.

The only party with which the DGB unions have had little or no contact is the FDP. This should come as no surprise, since the FDP has made anti-unionism an important part of its official ideology. By so doing it has attempted to tap the spring of anti-union sentiment among the middle and upper classes in the Federal Republic. Both the FDP's "big business" and "liberal" wings seem to agree on this point, the former for economic reasons and the latter because it sees unions as oligopolistic organizations which impinge on individual freedom. Thus it is quite understandable that no union federation, with the exception of the DBB, has an FDP member on its executive board.[38]

The DGB's relationship with the federal government closely resembles its relationship with the major political parties. The pattern of DGB behavior has varied depending on whether the government is CDU- or SPD-led. The basic demands which organized labor has directed towards the state, however, have changed very little over the last thirty years. The DGB has consistently advocated full employment, continued economic growth, greater social equality for working people, and an expansion of the welfare state. In addition, the federation has called for greater democracy in economic life by means of co-determination (Mitbestimmung), asset formation for workers (Vermögensbildung) and a reform of shop-floor conditions via greater union participation (Betriebsverfassung).

Even though the SPD was out of governmental power between 1949 and 1966, the DGB found a certain amount of sympathy within the CDU for the expansion of social services. The general consensus in West Germany during the 1950s was that the social safety net was too small, and with rapid economic growth the state could provide better and more extensive social benefits. Although many business people in the CDU were ambivalent or hostile regarding such measures, significant reforms in pensions, unemployment benefits and health care were achieved during this period. From the union perspective, however, much more still needed to be done.

In the area of economic democracy the DGB had little success with the CDU governments of the 1950s and early 1960s. After the passage of the co-determination law in the Federal Republic's iron and steel industry in 1951 and the concretization of the Works Constitution Law in 1952 (for both events, see Chapter 3 below), no more progress in this area was possible without the SPD holding governmental power. In the late 1950s, the unions joined the growing chorus of academics and politicians who condemned CDU economic policy as "anachronistic," essentially because it was pre-Keynesian. The DGB thus supported the creation of the Council of Economic Advisors (Sachverständigenrat) in 1962 as an important step towards the modernization of economic policy-making in the Federal Republic.

Once the SPD entered power in 1966 and came to head the government in 1969, the unions made their demands clear in no uncertain terms: Keynesian economic measures, an extension of social benefits, educational reforms (to make the system less "elitist") and an expansion of economic democracy. The first three of these were achieved in large part during the late 1960s and early 1970s, thanks to buoyant economic growth. But due to the controversial nature of economic democracy, the unions were a good deal less successful with this reform. The FDP fought hard, and with much success, to water down union proposals. This further soured the relationship between the DGB and that party.

It seems clear in retrospect that the SPD expected a quid pro quo from the unions in return for the party's attempts to meet basic DGB demands. But here the asymmetrical structure of the West German union movement intervened. Because of the complete independence in collective bargaining of the member unions, there is very little that the DGB itself could offer a government in return for favors. This was illustrated by the case of the Concerted Action, a roundtable of government ministers, union officials and business leaders instituted by the Grand Coalition in 1967. It was hoped that through national discussions of the economic situation, unions could be persuaded to moderate their wage demands in order to keep down inflation. Leaders from key unions like IG Metall and IG Chemie politely attended the meetings, then departed and pursued their own interests in the bargaining rounds, in which they had to heed the pressures of a restive and demanding rank and file. (For details of these developments see Chapter 4 for IG Metall and Chapter 5 for IG Chemie.) The DGB had difficulty explaining to the government and the public that it had little control over its member associations. The federation tried to compensate for this shortcoming by providing strong rhetorical support for the government in seemingly less controversial areas of immediate concern such as foreign policy (viz. the DGB's enthusiastic backing of the government's detente and Ostpolitik).

Under the crisis conditions of the post-1974 period, relations between the DGB and the government became increasingly strained. Social reform and welfare expansion virtually disappeared from the government's agenda and fighting inflation assumed consistently greater importance than combatting unemployment. At times like these, when the aims of the government and organized labor conflict, it becomes clear how limited an influence West German unions have on government policy. The public has often mistakenly interpreted the presence of leading ex-unionists among the SPD's cabinet members as prima-facie evidence for the DGB's power at the state level. Yet it was none other than Hans Matthöfer (IG Metall) and Herbert Ehrenberg (IG Bau) who carried out budget cuts bitterly opposed by the unions. It is important to point out that once an official leaves the union for a career in politics, his/her connection with the union all but ceases. Although the close personal relations between union leaders and SPD ministers have sometimes allowed the former to block or tone down initiatives deemed harmful to labor, the DGB has been able to attain very few of its wishes concerning economic policy, the extension of co-determination and shop-floor reforms since the onset of economic crisis in 1975. This led to major tensions between the SPD and some of the DGB unions at the end of the 1970s, a topic which will receive further attention in Chapter 3.

In summary, labor's post-World War II experience in the Federal Republic seems to have shown that the political "independence" of the unions has undercut their ability to influence the policies of both individual parties and the federal government. Instead of being crucial power brokers within one particular party – like the TUC in the British Labour Party or the LO inside the Swedish Social Democratic Party (SAP) – the West German unions have, in their quest for political independence, become just another interest group. Worse still, organized labor has suffered from a permanent lack of legitimacy since its claims are perceived by both government officials and the general public as intrinsically less valid than those of business, whom many credit with keeping West German industry highly competitive since the 1950s. During the crisis of the late 1970s and early 1980s, the DGB has had to content itself with a defensive role, fighting a rearguard action to protect the gains made by its constituent unions during better times.

There remains yet another area of public activity – though less well known – in which the DGB does have direct influence. This is in the complex world of the Federal Republic's administrative boards, ministerial advisory committees and quasi-governmental institutions.[39] The DGB sends representatives to over 46 committees on special issues (e.g. the Committee on Social Service Reform, the Committee on Youth Problems) which are attached to individual ministries. The DGB also has a seat on twelve administrative boards, such as those of the Federal Post

Office and the Federal Railways. Most importantly, the unions are assigned one-third of the seats (the other two-thirds going to the employers and the state) on the governing bodies responsible for the various social insurance programs (unemployment, sickness and retirement funds). All these arrangements represent a continuation of the old German bureaucratic tradition which seeks to involve the representatives of "organized interests" in the day-to-day functioning of government. Despite the fact that the DGB includes only about 33% of the workforce among its members, its presence on these boards illustrates its de facto recognition by the state as the official representative of labor.

### C. The DGB as a capitalist institution

The German union movement has a long tradition of economic activity. In the period before Bismarck's social legislation of the 1880s, most unions maintained funds which protected their members against sickness, accident and unemployment. As state welfare benefits expanded, unions shifted their emphasis towards providing banking facilities, life insurance and housing for workers. The result of their policy can be seen today in the DGB business empire, which in 1981 was valued at DM 2.7 billion (then about $1.5 billion).[40] Although the significance of these business activities is often exaggerated by the anti-union press, they do deserve to be described briefly here.

The active participation of DGB unions in the Federal Republic's capitalist economy is justified by the union concept of Gemeinwirtschaft (business in the public interest) which arose in the 1920s in close connection with the idea of Wirtschaftsdemokratie (economic democracy).[41] Union-run businesses were to form the core of a future, democratized economy. Until that goal was achieved the firms would serve to keep capitalists "honest." Because union firms were not oriented towards profit, so the theory went, they would be able to keep their prices lower, and thus force their capitalist competitors to do the same. In addition, the union firms would serve as schools of socialism for workers.

With these ideas in mind, the ADGB unions founded on May 31, 1924 the Bank der Arbeiter, Angestellten und Beamten AG (Bank for Workers, Employees and Civil Servants).[42] This institution's descendant in the Federal Republic is the DGB-owned Bank für Gemeinwirtschaft AG (BfG) which is among the ten largest banks in West Germany. A union insurance company had been formed somewhat earlier, in 1912. Today, the union-owned Volksfürsorge Group, which includes five separate companies, comprises the largest insurance enterprise in the FRG and one of the most important in Europe.[43]

Lastly, the unions are owners of a huge housing, real estate and construction firm, the Neue Heimat group. This organization has its roots in the union-led cooperative construction (Bauhütten) and housing movement of the Weimar Republic.[44] The group is divided into the Neue Heimat (NH) and the Neue Heimat Städtebau (NHS).[45] The Neue Heimat is a non-profit (Gemeinnützige) firm involved in housing construction for middle- and lower-income groups while the NHS is a commercial real estate and construction company mainly active in public construction projects. Through its subsidiary Neue Heimat International, the firm has also been involved in large-scale construction abroad, especially in oil-producing countries. The Neue Heimat is purported to be the largest housing and construction group in Europe. In recent years, however, it has been plagued by financial difficulties and corruption scandals which have briefly sapped the DGB's internal morale and marred its image vis-à-vis the West German public. (On these developments see the discussion provided in the conclusion to this volume.)

### D. Conclusion

Throughout its long history, the German trade union movement has often pursued contradictory goals. On the one hand it has hoped to contribute to the radical transformation of an often undemocratic and socially inequitable German society. Yet the unions also recognized quite early that power in Germany has always rested with organized interest groups, and they have consisently sought to win recognition for themselves from the state as the official representatives of labor. After the creation of the Federal Republic, the DGB moderated its ambitions concerning the first goal, and as a reward for so doing has been accepted as part of the West German establishment and a partner in "Modell Deutschland." Its leaders have by and large enjoyed unimpeded access to the highest echelons of power and are often consulted on most matters that directly or indirectly affect working people.

Yet despite its new-found official status, the DGB often appears to be an ineffectual organization, and West German unions in general seem to have trouble converting their numerical strength into concrete gains. Part of the reason for this, as was mentioned above, lies in the fact that official recognition has been bought at the price of political non-alignment. But to understand more fully this paradox of "great strength but insufficient power" we must look beyond membership figures and examine in detail such important areas as West Geman labor law, the history of the DGB, and the workings of the key member unions.

# 2 THE LEGAL FRAMEWORK FOR INDUSTRIAL RELATIONS IN THE FEDERAL REPUBLIC

The legal basis for industrial relations in West Germany is provided by a variety of institutions, laws, court precedents and traditional practices which are expressed in German through the concept of Verrechtlichung (juridification). This framework is crucial for an understanding of the special pattern of behavior which distinguishes West German unions. Yet this aspect of the industrial relations system, perhaps more than any other, has received little attention outside the Federal Republic, in good part due to the often arcane, juridical nature of the subject. The present chapter intends to offer more than just an exercise in comparative jurisprudence, however. After examining the basic features of West German labor law, the analysis below should help provide a picture of how the Federal Republic's industrial relations system functions on a day-to-day basis at the factory, firm or industry level.

Industrial relations in West Germany can be conveniently divided into three areas, each with its own set of norms and institutions. First is collective bargaining, which takes place between unions and employers' associations, usually on the industry level. Bargaining between unions and individual employers (companies) also occurs, although it is far less significant in terms of an appropriate understanding of the legalized nature of capital – labor relations in the Federal Republic. The labor law relevant to this area covers such matters as the bargaining process, contracts, arbitration, strikes and lockouts. The second area pertains to industrial relations on the shop floor. In West Germany this area is regulated primarily by the Works Constitution Law, which defines the institution of the works council and provides for the settlement of disputes originating in the factory. The various laws on co-determination or Mitbestimmung (the right of workers to participate in the decision-making process of their firm) are the principal legislation regulating the third area of industrial relations, which deals with the interaction between a company and its employees.

Thus, the spheres of the industry, the factory and the firm form three separate sub-systems of labor relations in the Federal Republic. West German writers, with only the first two areas in mind, often refer to their country's "dual system of interest representation." In this chapter, these three sub-systems will be differentiated according to their separate legal frameworks. The task, then, will be to determine how the three spheres are related to one another. The Federal Republic's tripartite industrial relations system brings with it both advantages and disadvantages not found in countries such as the United States and Great Britain which have "unitary" frameworks of industrial relations. Before we turn to the discussion of these three sub-systems, however, it will be helpful to put them in their proper historical context by briefly outlining the key developments in juridification which occurred in German industrial relations before 1933.

## I. THE LEGAL FRAMEWORK FOR INDUSTRIAL RELATIONS IN THE KAISERREICH AND WEIMAR

Industrial relations in Wilhelminian Germany were dominated by organized labor's fight for two basic objectives: freedom of coalition and the legal enforceability of contracts. Shortly after the founding of the first German trade union, the cigar workers' in 1865, it appeared as if the state would look favorably on these new associations. The basic business law (Gewerbeordnung) for the North German Confederation of 1869 expressly lifted all restrictive laws on workers' organizations. This clause was then carried over into the new Reich's business law (Reichsgewerbeordnung) after unification in 1871.[1] In 1878, however, the Anti-Socialist Law was passed outlawing workers' associations. All the important socialist unions were banned. In 1890, the Anti-Socialist Law was revoked and freedom of coalition was once again restored, at least in theory. Yet harassment of unions and their members by the authorities continued until World War I. In the famous words of Lujo Brentano: "Workers possess freedom of coalition. If they make use of it, however, they will be punished."[2]

Similar problems confronted unions on the issue of contracts. The basic principles of German law, like those of most Western countries, were based on the idea of the individual and his/her actions and responsibilities vis-à-vis the state. Judges thus had great difficulties in interpreting the actions of *collective* bodies like unions or employers' associations. Judicial opinion on collective bargaining agreements ranged from the view that they had no legal status whatever, to one which held that they were legally binding even for workers or employers who were not organized.[3] The period after 1890 saw an increasing tendency of the courts, as well as of the central government, to intervene as mediators in labor disputes.[4]

Despite this precarious legal position, the number of collective bargaining agreements increased every year through 1914. Most of these contracts were signed in the printing and construction industries.[5] Both sectors were dominated by medium-sized and small firms, which experienced particularly threatening forms of competition either from works operating in the (low-cost) countryside or from the employment of labor at substandard wages. It was therefore in the interest of these firms to cooperate with workers in order to limit low-wage operations in their industries. So-called "organizational agreements" were signed which called on employers to hire only union labor and required unionists to work only for employers paying the contractual wage.

In notable contrast to the situation in industries such as printing and construction, unions failed to make any significant headway in gaining recognition from employers in heavy industry. These employers simply refused to sign contracts and tried to keep labor organizers out of the factories. The dominant pattern of industrial relations before 1914 was therefore one of "sectoral corporatism" practiced in a few industries between skilled worker organizations and medium-sized family firms to the mutual advantage of both sides.[6]

The advent of the Weimar Republic brought five major changes to the German industrial relations system. First, the leaders of heavy industry, fearing revolution, reached an agreement with the leaders of the socialist unions in November 15, 1918. This was the central labor community accord (Zentralarbeitsgemeinschaftsabkommen). In this agreement, the formerly hard-line industrialists recognized the rights of unions to organize in the factories, agreed to contract negotiations, and also introduced the eight-hour day. Second, a collective bargaining law (Tarifvertragsordnung) was passed on December 23, 1918, which made all collective bargaining agreements legally binding. Third, the Weimar Constitution of August 11, 1919 formally guaranteed the right to create "associations for the protection and improvement of labor and economic conditions," i.e. freedom of coalition.[7] Fourth, a national system of special labor courts, the Reichsarbeitsgerichte, was created to decide disputes between labor and management.[8] The courts consisted of one representative each from the unions and the employers' associations and a neutral professional judge. Decisions by the court, most of whose cases involved plant-level disagreements, were reached by a majority vote of the three judges.

The Works Councils Law (Betriebsrätegesetz – BRG) of February 4, 1920 represented the fifth and final important innovation of the Weimar Republic in the area of industrial relations. Under pressure from the revolutionary worker councils movement and mass strikes in March 1919, the authors of the Weimar constitution felt compelled to include a stipulation (Article 165) calling for the creation of workers' councils on the firm, district and national levels.[9] The BRG was the social democratic government's answer to Article 165. It foresaw the election of a workers' council by all workers', both white- and blue-collar, in plants with over 20 employees. The workers' council was to be consulted in all matters affecting the organization of labor in the plant, such as technical innovations, layoffs, expansion, and changes on the shop floor. The council would also give co-determination rights in decisions concerning work time (overtime and short-time), piece rates, vacations, the administration of social benefits and the design of hiring guide-lines.[10] Co-determination in this case meant that if the council disagreed with management's actions in one of these areas, a mediating committee could be summoned, or, if necessary, the case could be brought before a labor court. Despite these important provisions, the powers of the workers' councils were severely limited by their lack of official connection to the unions, whose access to the shop floor was restricted by law. The council was also forbidden to initiate or participate in strike activities and was, in fact, obliged to cooperate with management in order to "protect the plant from unrest."[11] Most of the key elements of the BRG were to surface again in the Federal Republic's Works Constitution Law (Betriebsverfassungsgesetz – BVG) of 1952.

The Revolution of 1918 solved in one stroke all the major problems facing organized labor before 1914, and the German industrial relations system quickly settled into a pattern quite similar to the one existing in West Germany today. On one level, unions signed broad regional or even national contracts with employers' associations. The law interpreted the wage rates set in these contracts as legal minima rather than maxima.[12] A special provision of the Collective Bargaining Law of 1918 allowed the Labor Ministry to extend the contract to all firms and workers in a given industry, even to those not organized in unions or employers' associations. This procedure was termed an Allgemeinverbindlichkeitserklärung (declaration of general applicability). Both unions and employers' associations of that period seem more fragmented than their contemporary counterparts. Yet a general movement was underway to create industrial unions through amalgamations.[13] At another level, workers' councilors regulated the organization of work and hiring and firing in collaboration with management. Labor courts settled disputes. In short, the "dual nature" of German industrial relations was already well established by the 1920s.

Economic and political developments conspired, however, to destroy the equilibrium of this system before it was able to entrench itself in the

Weimar Republic's economy. The rampant inflation of 1923 led the government to introduce binding state arbitration in order to keep wages in line with galloping prices. This meant that the Labor Ministry now had the power to set wages unilaterally if labor and management could not reach an agreement. Believing that the Labor Ministry would be sympathetic to their position, the unions made frequent use of this system during the economic recovery of 1925–26. The unions' expectations were not disappointed. However, when recession returned to plague the German economy again in 1928, the ministry's decisions were no longer so favorable to labor. More important still, the state, labor and management all sought through the binding arbitration process to destroy free collective bargaining long before it was rescinded as part of Chancellor Brüning's attemps to deal with the Depression in 1931.[14]

This practice of trying to set wages via a centralized mechanism was continued by the Nazis, who dissolved all unions in 1933 and reorganized workers in the German Labor Front (Deutsche Arbeitsfront – DAF). So-called labor ombudsmen (Treuhänder der Arbeit) determined wage rates for an entire industry in a given region following consultations with the Labor Ministry. Within the DAF all workers in an industry, both white- and blue-collar, were organized into one of eighteen Reich Labor Communities (Reichsarbeitsgemeinschaften). The old employers' associations remained in existence, but they were forced to centralize and amalgamate into unitary industrial confederations. These innovations by the Nazis undoubtedly facilitated for both management and labor the post-World War II reconstruction of powerful, relatively centralized interest associations organized on an industry-wide basis and empowered to sign contracts encompassing large geographic regions.[15]

## II. INDUSTRIAL RELATIONS AND LABOR LAW IN THE FEDERAL REPUBLIC

### A. The sources of labor law

The legal framework for industrial relations in West Germany provides the "rules" which both unions and employers must respect when pursuing the interests of their members. These rules are derived from four basic sources. The first is the Basic Law (constitution) of the Federal Republic and other laws passed by the Bundestag relating to labor relations, such as the Co-Determination Acts of 1951 and 1976, the Works Constitution Acts of 1952 and 1972 and the Collective Bargaining Agreement Act (Tarifvertragsgesetz) of 1949. Second, contracts signed during collective bargaining also have the force of law. Such contracts are thus sometimes referred to in the German literature as "self-produced labor law" (selbstgeschaffenes Arbeitsrecht).[16] Third, there exists a whole range of "consensual practices" which will be discussed below. These consist of rules which are followed by both unions and employers, either because of tradition or because both sides believe them to be legally binding, even though neither explicit laws nor judicial precedents apply to the issue. A prominent example of this is furnished by the widely held belief during the 1950s that closed-shop agreements were illegal in the Federal Republic, even though no court decision on this subject had been handed down.

Finally, perhaps the most important source today of norms governing labor relations are the decisions of West Germany's labor courts, the Arbeitsgerichte.[17] As was mentioned, a special system of labor courts had been set up in Germany during the Weimar Republic. This system remained in existence during the Nazi period, although it had lost all practical significance.[18] In early 1946, the Allied Control Council passed a law (Law No. 21) which called for the reconstruction of a labor court system. The main provisions of this law were then incorporated into the Federal Republic after its creation in 1949.

The simple labor courts make up the first level of the system. As in Weimar, they consist of a panel of three judges. Two of these represent capital and labor respectively. These representatives are appointed by the labor minister of each state on the basis of lists of suitable candidates submitted by the unions and employers' associations. The candidates need not, and often do not, have any legal training. In addition, the minister appoints a third, "professional", judge to chair each court. This judge is also chosen after consultations with the unions and employers' associations. Decisions of the court are made on the basis of a majority vote of the three judges. Each state also has, as a Court of Appeals, a state Labor Court (Landesarbeitsgericht – LAG), whose composition corresponds to that of the simple labor courts.

Until 1954, the local and state labor courts were the only components of the system. In that year, the federal government created the Federal Labor Court (Bundesarbeitsgericht – BAG) as a "supreme court" for all labor-related cases. The BAG is divided into several separate courts, or "senates," each of which consists of two professional judges, a chairman (who is also a professional judge), and one representative each of capital and labor. All of these judges are appointed by the federal labor minister without consultation with unions or employers' associations. For appeals involving fundamental questions of labor law which call for the establishment of new precedents, a so-called "large senate" (Grosser Senat) of the BAG is formed. It consists of the BAG's chief justice, the eldest chairman of the other BAG senates, four professional judges and two *judges* each representing capital and labor. Again, all appointments are made by the federal labor minister according to the guidelines used for the nomination of all judges in the Federal Republic (Vorschriften des Richterwahlgesetzes). Since professional judges enjoy a majority on all the BAG courts, neither unions nor employers can have much direct effect on their decisions.

Because the Basic Law devotes only one paragraph to unions and because all West German governments have tried to avoid dealing with larger questions of labor law, the interpretations of the BAG since 1955 have played the decisive role in shaping the legal framework for industrial relations. The BAG has based many of its decisions – as we shall see – on a few key theoretical concepts such as Kampfparität (parity of forces) which were developed in legal briefs of the 1950s. Most of its precedents seem entirely consistent with the spirit of German labor law established by the Reich Labor Court during the Weimar Republic. This spirit envisions the role of the courts as ordering industrial relations in such a way as to assure a smooth functioning of the (capitalist) economic system and to maintain social peace. This can best be done, so the BAG believes, by laying down rules for the behavior of both unions and management. Unlike the courts of the Wilhelminian era, the BAG is not anti-union; it views unions rather as key "factors of order" (Ordnungsfaktoren) which must discipline workers who would otherwise not be inclined to follow the "rules" of industrial relations. Since the BAG sees in capital a more reliable source of order than in the unions, it is only natural, given the court's overriding concern with social peace, that its decisions often seem to favor the interests of the former over those of the latter.

## B. The legal status of the unions

It is customary in West Germany to divide labor law into two categories, "individual" labor law and "collective" labor law.[19] The first focuses on the worker and his/her individual rights and interests. It encompasses laws on work safety, hiring and firing, and other matters affecting the worker as an individual. The second category envisions the juridical "actor" not as an individual, but as a collectivity, as members of an interest organization. The legal basis for the overall interpretation of such organizations' role in society derives from Article 9, paragraph 3 of the Federal Republic's Basic Law. It states:

> The right to form associations for the preservation and improvement of work and economic conditions is guaranteed for everyone and for all professions. Agreements which limit this right or attempt to prevent its exercise are invalid, and measures which aim at this are illegal. Measures taken in

accordance with Articles 12a, 35 (paragraphs 2 and 3), 87a (paragraph 4) and 91 [legislation based on the Emergency Laws of 1968] shall not be directed against strikes aimed at preserving or improving work and economic conditions which are led by associations created in accordance with sentence one above.[20]

This paragraph says nothing about unions specifically. The Basic Law never mentions them by name. The popular perception concerning the exact legal status of unions thus emanates from BAG decisions as well as from certain assumptions about the spirit and intent of the Basic Law.[21] Nevertheless, several important points can be understood directly from Article 9, paragraph 3. First, "everyone" and "every profession" has the right to join associations. This means that foreign workers and apprentices, not just adult Germans, can belong to unions. It also means that state employees and civil servants (Beamte) are free to unionize, and employers can form their own associations as well. Lastly, thanks to the third sentence, the right to strike is guaranteed, a significant improvement over the corresponding paragraph in the Weimar Constitution, which did not contain such a clause.

Court decisions and the legal literature specified a number of further conditions which must be met before a coalition can claim legal protection under Article 9, paragraph 3:

- Membership must not be compulsory.
- The coalition must be independent of political parties, churches or the "social opponent" (i.e. employers). Thus "yellow unions" are forbidden.
- The coalition must have a democratic structure.[22]

Since all the trade unions and employers' associations which currently exist in the Federal Republic meet (at least on paper) these criteria, they are considered organizations whose existence and activities are protected under the constitution. The courts have further established conclusively that no one can be discriminated against because of his/her membership or activity in a "protected coalition." Nevertheless, this right has often proved unenforceable in small firms, as can be well imagined.

The major controversy surrounding Article 9, paragraph 3 concerns the question of whether the Basic Law protects "negative coalition freedom" (negative Koalitionsfreiheit) i.e. whether one has the absolute right *not* to join a union. Although it is generally acknowledged by both unions and employers that an individual does have this right (hence the renunciation of the closed shop), the exact practical implications thereof are subject to frequently bitter public debate. Over the past twenty years, the BAG has issued a number of decisions which hold that attempts to negotiate special benefits for union members only, or any contracts which specifically exclude non-union members from certain benefits, are illegal because they infringe the negative coalition freedom of non-unionists. This is so because the "discriminatory" contracts put pressure on workers to join a union (which, of course, is precisely the idea behind them). The issue arose because of the efforts of the textile and construction workers' unions to negotiate such contracts in the early 1960s. Even though this problem has not been definitively settled by the BAG's Grosser Senat, the unions have given up trying to negotiate contracts which would favor their members.

## III. LABOR LAW AND COLLECTIVE BARGAINING

### A. Contracts and the bargaining process

Since the late nineteenth century, wages in Germany have been determined on three different levels. First, unions negotiate contracts with employers' associations setting a broad spectrum of minimum wages for an industry in a large geographical area, typically a state. Details are then completed at the plant level through agreements (formal or informal) between works councils and management. Lastly, the employer concludes an individual contract (Arbeitsvertrag) with each employee. Although the individual contract must meet the stipulations already agreed to by the union and the works council, it may also include special bonuses or a higher pay rate designed to reward employees possessing special skills. Only the first level of wage determination, the legal contract between the employers and the unions, will be discussed here; the other two levels will be considered when we examine more closely the legal organization of the plant later in this chapter.

The Collective Bargaining Law (Tarifvertragsgesetz – TVG) of April 9, 1949 delineates the general framework for all collective bargaining agreements in the Federal Republic. The main stipulations of this law derive from the Tarifvertragsordnung of the Weimar period mentioned earlier. The TVG defines legal contracts as written agreements covering any and all aspects of employment concluded between a union and either an employers' association or an individual firm.[23] Only these three parties, the first two of which are legally defined in Article 9, paragraph 3 of the Basic Law, have the right to sign collective bargaining agreements. This right is known as Tariffähigkeit, or the "ability" to enter into contractual relationships. The latter then are binding for both signatories, which, in the case of agreements between a union and an employers' association, means that all firms belonging to the association must pay contractual wages to unionists in their employ.

This obligation does not extend legally to non-unionists, however, thus in essence permitting an employer to pay unionists and non-unionists in the same plant different wages. To counter this possibility, the TVG allows the Federal Minister of Labor to declare a contract universally binding (allgemeinverbindlich) in a given industry if over 50% of that industry's employers are members of the employers' association which signed the contract (Art. 5, TVG). Like many other aspects of West German labor law, this practice originated in the Weimar Republic.

Although Allgemeinverbindlichkeit appears on paper to be an important instrument for government intervention in labor relations, it has been of little practical importance since 1949. This is best illustrated by the fact that of the 43,500 collective bargaining agreements concluded between 1965 and 1972, only about 500 were declared universally binding.[24] This is the case because a majority of employers pay contractual wages to non-union workers anyway. This seems logical since over 80% of West German employers formally belong to employers' associations. If employers were to pay higher wages to unionists, it would merely furnish a strong encouragement for all other workers to join the union as well. Furthermore, the minority of independent employers would have great difficulties attracting labor if they did not match the contractual wages paid by other firms belonging to the employers' association. Since over 90% of all West German workers earn their living in sectors covered by collective bargaining agreements, it would be fair to say that these agreements regulate the wages and working conditions of the overwhelming majority of employees in the Federal Republic, de facto if not de jure.[25] This situation more than compensates for the fact that only 40% of the country's workforce actually belong to unions as card-carrying members.

The average collective bargaining agreement in West Germany contains two parts, an obligatory and a normative segment.[26] The former comprises agreements between the contract's two signatories on issues such as the resolution of differences over the contract's implementation or interpretation. The task of the normative section of the contract is to decree universal guidelines for pay and working conditions. These attain particular importance by assuming legal status and authority.

One of the most crucial ingredients of the Federal Republic's judicial system of industrial relations centers on the concept of peace obligation (Friedenspflicht), which holds that neither a union nor an employers' association or firm can engage in labor conflict over the terms of a contract which is still in force. Interestingly enough, the TVG fails to make any mention of a peace obligation. Different explanations are offered in the literature for this surprising omission. Erd contends that the German legal concept of contractual loyalty (Vertragstreue) made the idea of a peace *obligation* self-evident to all jurists, and its explicit stipulation in the TVG therefore unnecessary.[27] Däubler claims that the legal difficulties involved in defining precise boundaries for the peace obligation led the TVG's authors to avoid this subject altogether.[28]

Whatever the truth, the key point regarding this matter is that neither the unions nor the employers ever contested the basic idea of a peace obligation, although many questions have been raised over details. A Federal Labor Court decision of 1958 (discussed below) provided a legal basis for customary practice by explicitly confirming the existence of a Friedenspflicht during the life of a contract. Although we will later examine the subject of strike law, suffice it to say at this juncture that the obligation for industrial peace, a concept deeply rooted in traditional German labor law, accounts in large part for the paucity of strikes in the Federal Republic.

Until now, we have spoken of collective bargaining agreements only in general terms. In fact, three different types of agreements exist: the Lohnrahmentarifvertrag (wage framework contract – RTV), the Mantel-tarifvertrag (general framework contract – MTV), and the Lohntarifver-trag (wage contract – LTV).[29] The RTV defines wage and salary groups for a particular industry. It establishes the criteria (training, experience, nature of the job performed, or a combination of all three) which place a worker in a given wage group. More importantly, the RTV also determines the wage rate differentials separating the various wage groups. Most West German industries have between five and eight wage groups for blue-collar workers and between three and five salary groups for white-collar employees.

Differentials are expressed as a percentage (80%, 90%, 110%, etc.) of a base wage, usually the wage rate for a skilled, adult, male worker without special qualifications. In the past, skill differentials were supplemented by age categories (Altersgruppen) and location categories (Ortsgruppen), which were determined respectively by a worker's age and the size of the city where he/she worked. Their purpose originally was to compensate for differences in the cost of living for single vs. married or urban vs. rural workers. However, many of these extra wage categories have since been eliminated. Because of the complexities inherent in framing a wage and salary structure, RTVs are only rarely renegotiated in their entirety. Although minor changes are made frequently, many unions have concluded only one or two complete RTVs for a given industry since 1949.

General framework contracts typically comprise voluminous documents covering all aspects of work time (length of the work week, overtime, vacations), working conditions (manning and training guidelines for different worker groups), special benefits (Christmas and vacation bonuses), and in theory anything else which concerns neither basic wages nor the wage structure. Because of the variety of areas they encompass, MTVs must be very general in character (hence the term "framework"). Details concerning working conditions for particular skill groups are relegated to the contract's so-called appendices (Anhänge) which are negotiated by teams of experts after the MTV itself has been signed. Even with these appendices, however, much of the work of adapting a general framework contract to the specific conditions of a factory's shop floor falls by necessity to the works councils. MTVs are commonly renegotiated every three to five years and they are valid either for the bargaining region of a particular industry or (in the case of small industries) for the entire Federal Republic. Separate contracts are concluded for blue-collar and white-collar workers.

Of the three types of collective bargaining agreements, wage contracts (LTVs) receive the most attention from politicians, the press and the business community. In the Federal Republic, they are normally renegotiated in every industry about once a year, although past wage contracts have run for as little as eight months and as long as two years. As with MTVs, separate accords are reached for manual and clerical employees. In West Germany this is necessary because the former receive a weekly wage, generally calculated by the hour (Lohn), whereas the latter earn a fixed monthly salary (Gehalt).

In most industries, separate wage negotiations occur in each bargaining district. These normally number between eight and twelve for the entire Federal Republic, and their boundaries vaguely approximate those of the eleven federal states (Länder).[30] In the printing and construction industries, wages are negotiated at the national level for the country as a whole. In other industries, district officials of the union start the bargaining process by giving notice that a contract will be reopened several months before its actual expiration date (Kündigung). The union then presents its demands to the local branch of the industry's employers' association. Most often these demands call for a percentage increase in the hourly base wage (Ecklohn). This approach has always had its critics in the labor movement because it leads to money wage increases of different magnitudes in the various age groups, favoring those in higher ones over workers belonging to lower groups. In response, some unions have sought to develop more equitable schemes for their members explicitly designed to help workers in the lower categories. Toward that end they demanded either lump-sum raises (Erhöhungen in festen Beträgen) or combined percentage and lump-sum raises, called "mixed demands" (Mischforderungen) of the form "5% but at least DM 200 per month." This approach has come to be known in German as Sockelpolitik. The wage agreements which emerge amount usually to between 60% and 80% of the original demands. What happens if a settlement cannot be reached through negotiations will be the subject of the next section.

### B. Strikes and lockouts: labor conflict law in West Germany

In notable contrast to the situation in the Weimar Republic, no form of binding or state arbitration exists in West Germany. This is strictly in keeping with the sanctity of the autonomy of collective bargaining (Tarifautonomie) upon which the unions, employers and the state insist. In theory, a union is free to commence strike action against the employers as soon as the old contract expires, thus eliminating the peace obligation. Almost all unions, however, negotiate voluntary arbitration agreements with their respective employers' associations. These vary greatly in detail, but all provide for an extension of the peace obligation until one of the two sides declares that arbitration has failed.

In the next step on the road to conflict, the union organizes a strike vote (Urabstimmung) among its membership in the bargaining district where arbitration has failed. Again there are no legally binding guidelines on strike votes; each union decrees its own procedures in its statutes. Only IG Chemie's bylaws exempt its leadership from the obligation of consulting its members before a strike. In most other unions, 75% of the local membership must approve any industrial action, although in many cases a strike can be ended with the approval of less than 50% of a bargaining district's unionists. Thus union statutes enhance the leadership's ability to call a strike and impede the rank and file from continuing one following a settlement.

In marked contrast to arbitration and strike votes, West German labor law carefully regulates strike activities themselves. The basis for this regulation lies neither in the Basic Law per se, where the word "strike" did not appear until the 1968 Emergency Law amendment, nor in the statutes passed by the Bundestag, but rather in the numerous decisions handed down by the Federal Labor Court (BAG) since its creation in 1954. In a series of opinions, the court has developed a theory of unions and their proper role in West German society which rests on a rather broad interpretation of the spirit of the Basic Law as well as the pre-1933 tradition of labor relations. The BAG's view of the rights and obligations of unions has remained remarkably consistent over the past thirty years.

From the first, the attention of the BAG and its predecessors, the State Labor Courts (LAGs), focused principally on defining the criteria and ground rules for legal labor conflict. Because no new laws were passed concerning strikes and lockouts after the Federal Republic's creation in

1949, it was generally assumed that the three principles which had governed these actions in Weimar still held sway. The first entailed the concept of a peace obligation attached to all valid contracts, as discussed above. The second was the belief that unions had the right to strike and employers the right to lock out after a contract had expired. The third held that individual workers or groups of workers also had the right to strike as long as they had given notice beforehand with respect to their personal labor contracts (Arbeitsverträge). It was also believed that workers had to give their notice even when unions called a strike. This last position can be explained by the fact that during both the Empire and the Weimar Republic strikes were interpreted as falling in the domain of private or individual law (ein individualrechtliches Phänomen).[31] Thus, within the limits stated, both union and "wildcat" strikes as well as lockouts seemed to be permissible. The legality of political strikes remained unclear.

The last issue was to be tested first in the courts of the new republic. In May 1952, IG Druck und Papier called a two-day nationwide newspaper strike to protest the Adenauer government's draft for a new Works Constitution Law. The employers in each of the FRG's states and in West Berlin sued the union for damages incurred through the strike.[32] The cases eventually reached the LAG of each state. The employers hired a number of prominent legal scholars to prepare briefs supporting their contention that the strike was illegal. Most famous among these was the brief written by H. C. Nipperdey, which ultimately provided the theoretical groundwork for the view of unions developed by the BAG after 1954.

Nipperdey's basic contention centered on the view that all strikes which did not meet certain criteria of "social appropriateness' (Sozialadäquanz) and "societal balance" were illegal.[33] This was so, according to the author, because both the Basic Law and the Civil Legal Code (Bürgerliches Gesetzbuch) protected the right of individuals to own and freely operate a business. Since the Basic Law also clearly guaranteed the right to strike, specific rules had to be decreed which would allow the latter right to be preserved without the former being violated. Only if these rules were followed would a strike be "socially appropriate" and hence legal. Nipperdey himself proposed three criteria for "social appropriateness" and "societal balance" which, he implied, could be deduced from the spirit of the Basic Law:[34]

1. The strike must be directed against an employer or an employers' association.
2. It must be a strike over wages or working conditions.
3. The goal of the strike must be the conclusion of a collective bargaining agreement between a union and one or more employers.

Since the newspaper strike violated all of these conditions, it should have, according to Nipperdey, been ruled illegal and the union thus held liable for damages. All of the State Labor Courts, with the exception of the LAG in West Berlin, accepted this line of argument and found for the employers. Thus, even before the creation of the BAG, the West German courts had adopted the notion of Sozialadäquanz and in effect declared political strikes illegal.

It is significant that upon its creation and assumption of duties in late 1954, the Federal Labor Court's first case involved the legal parameters for a strike. The case concerned the question of whether it was necessary for workers engaged in a union-sanctioned strike first to give notice on their individual labor contracts, and whether in response to such a strike an employer could make use of a so-called dismissal lockout (lösende Aussperrung) during which strikers were summarily fired and not rehired.[35] In order to answer these questions, the BAG felt compelled to set forth its own theory of unions and labor conflict. The basic features thereof were drawn from Nipperdey's brief. To quote the most famous passage from what has since come to be known as the 1955 BAG decision (more properly BAG AP n.1 on Art. 9 GG of January 28, 1955):[36]

> Labor conflicts (strikes and lockouts) are on the whole undesirable because they cause economic damage and disturb the social peace which benefits all; but they are admissible in certain circumstances because they are premitted by the Federal Republic's free social order. The interruption of work in the plant as a result of such strikes [those permitted by the FRG's free social order] is socially appropriate [sozialadäquat] because workers and employers must be prepared for such conflicts organized and led by their social partner [i.e. their opposite number] and the free German legal order allows such conflicts as *ultima ratio*. The right to strike and the right to lock out are guaranteed. This is clear from the whole historical development [in Germany] since 1869.

In its decision, the court adopted Nipperdey's argument that only socially appropriate and "balanced" strikes are legal, and it accepted his three conditions for Sozialadäquanz. The BAG further added to these criteria by stating that industrial actions could only involve individuals or groups capable of signing collective bargaining contracts (tariffähige Parteien), and that such actions could only be employed as an ultima ratio or last resort after all possibilities of a negotiated settlement had been exhausted.

In addition to these elaborations, the 1955 BAG decision contained two new and very important elements. The first of these concerned the notion of parity of forces (Kampfparität or Waffengleichheit). In order to justify the legality of the lockout, the court argued that the principle of equality before the law (Art. 3 Basic Law) "does not permit the state ... to treat the weapons of the two social partners [unions and employers] in an unequal manner. The basic principle of equality of weapons, of parity of forces [Kampfparität] pertains."[37] From this principle of parity the BAG concluded not only that lockouts per se were permissible, but also that dismissal lockouts could be used, since only these allowed the employer to impress the full risk of a strike upon a worker. In addition, the employer had to be permitted the freedom to choose whatever form of lockout he/she wished to deploy against a strike.[38]

The second new element in the 1955 BAG decision focused on the court's refusal to submit strikes and lockouts to an interpretation featuring the tenets of individual or private law. Thus the court concluded that it was not necessary for workers participating in a "socially appropriate", union-led strike to give notice concerning their individual labor contract because the legal strike as defined by the court represented fundamentally a *collective* act. Although this interpretation freed the union strike once and for all from the taint of illegality implied by individual law, it also robbed workers of arguments from the latter to justify unofficial or "wildcat" strikes. The BAG drew the logical conclusion from this in its decision of December 20, 1963, when it explicitly declared wildcat strikes illegal. In its ruling, the court stated that the right to strike represented a "dangerous weapon" that could only be entrusted to groups which could "guarantee that strikes will be called only in truly justified cases and which in such cases will follow the rules of combat [Kampfregeln] necessary for the public good. . . . [O]n the workers' side only the unions can fulfill this role."[39]

For the first time the BAG openly referred to unions as "elements of order" (Ordnungsfaktoren) whose job it was to organize and discipline the labor force by obeying the rules decreed by the courts in order to safeguard social peace.[40] This notion of organized labor as an Ordnungsfaktor is one that has continuously been held by the DGB's accommodationist unions led by IG Bau-Steine-Erden.

The basic position of the Federal Labor Court on strikes and lockouts was not to change until 1971. In 1958, the restrictions imposed by the 1955 verdict were tightened even further by an important decision concerning the issue of peace obligation. Prior to the Schleswig-Holstein strike of 1956–57 (see Chapter 4 below), IG Metall called a strike vote before arbitration proceedings had officially been terminated. The court confirmed that a peace obligation existed since IG Metall's arbitration agreement with the employers called for the Friedenspflicht to be extended during the arbitration proceedings. In general, the concept of Friedenspflicht meant, the court contended, that both sides had to desist from any hostile actions (Kampfmassnahmen). The union interpreted this to pertain to full-scale strike activities only, but the BAG ruled that calling a strike vote represented a hostile act because it interfered with the employers' freedom of decision-making by putting undue pressure on them.[41] The BAG found IG Metall guilty of violating the peace obligation and assessed the union damages equal to the losses incurred by the employers as a consequence of IG Metall's illegal action.

In 1971 and again in 1980, the BAG issued new rulings on the lockout which went some distance towards alleviating what many saw as the disproportionate burden imposed on labor by the 1955 decision. In its verdict of 1971, the court introduced the important new idea of "proportionality" (Verhältnismässigkeit). In what amounted to a reversal of its 1955 position, the court contended that:

> The means used in a labor conflict must not exceed what is necessary to achieve the desired goal (a new contract) . . . A labor conflict is thus only legal if and as long as it is conducted according to the rules of a fair fight. It must not aim at the destruction of the other side.[42]

Based on this principle, the BAG concluded that a dismissal lockout did *not* represent a proportionate response to a normal union strike. This weapon could only be used as a means of ending illegal strikes or if a union strike continued for a long period of time and the lockout appeared to be the only way to bring labor back to the bargaining table.[43]

However, the effectiveness of this ruling was called into question during the 1970s by a series of lockouts which seemed to violate the proportionality principle. In 1976, the printing employers locked out 90,000 printers when only 16,000 had been called out on strike, and in 1978 a strike by 80,000 metalworkers was met by a lockout of 120,000 more. (For details see Chapters 7 and 4 respectively.) In response to massive suits by the unions, the BAG handed down a new lockout ruling in 1980. The court attempted to end the controversy once and for all by decreeing the following rules for lockouts analogous to those for strikes:[44]

1. Lockouts could only be called by employers' associations in response to union strikes.
2. Only so-called suspension lockouts were henceforth permitted: workers had to receive their jobs back after the lockout; the burden of proof lay with the employer to show why the workers should not return to their place of employment.
3. The maximum number of workers who could henceforth be locked out in any one bargaining district was *one-quarter* of the total workforce in that industry.

Putting these new tenets into practice, the court concluded that the lockout of 1976 deployed by employers in the printing industry was unlawful as a consequence of its disproportionality. However, the court declared the metal industry's lockout of 1978 legal because "only" 120,000 workers had been locked out, which, out of a total of 500,000 metalworkers in the district, the court did not view as excessive. Despite the fact that the BAG failed to heed the unions' increasingly vocal demand for a total ban on the lockout, this ruling certainly represented a significant victory for organized labor, since it removed many of the advantages granted to employers in 1955. In a sense, the ruling was in keeping with the court's principles of "parity of forces" and "proportionality" since it aimed at restoring the balance of power between capital and labor which had been disrupted in favor of the former since the onset of the economic crisis in 1974–75.

## IV. LABOR LAW AT THE PLANT LEVEL: THE WORKS CONSTITUTION ACT

The Works Constitution Act (Betriebsverfassungsgesetz – BVG) of January 15, 1972 regulates labor relations at the plant level in West Germany.[45] This law replaces the BVG of 1952 which was in turn inspired by the Workers' Council Law (Betriebsrätegesetz) of 1920. The 1952 and 1972 acts are on most points identical and this discussion will therefore concentrate on the latter. The differences between the two center mainly on the formal rights of unions in the plants, and they will receive the necessary attention when this topic is discussed below.

Article 1 of the BVG 1972 states that works councils may be elected in plants with more than five permanent employees. However, the law does not require works councils, and it has been estimated that at most 18.9% of eligible firms actually have such bodies, although this minority accounts for 65.6% of all workers in the private sector.[46] In addition to plants with fewer than five workers, works councils are not permitted in the civil service (which has its own system of worker representation), in religious organizations, and in firms which form part of the mass media. (For this point see the discussion provided in Chapter 7.) A council can be created at the initiative of a plant's employees or of a union represented there. Although all large and most medium-sized plants have works councils, it is hardly surprising that they are to be found less freqeuntly in small firms where workers have reason to fear reprisals if they call for such a body.

The works council is elected to a term of three years by a direct vote of all the plant's permanent employees. The council can consist of from one to thirty members depending on the size of the plant. Blue-collar and white-collar workers must be represented in proportion to their numbers in the factory and minorities such as foreign workers and the handicapped must also have at least one representative each on larger councils. Each of these groups enjoys the privilege of separate elections. In most factories, the various unions (DGB, DAG, CGB), as well as coalitions of independents, present slates or candidate lists for the elections. The council positions are then filled on the basis of strict proportional representation. It is not surprising therefore that DGB union members consistently account for about 80% of all works councilors in the Federal Republic's factories and offices.

The heart of the BVG consists of a set of obligations and restrictions which set fundamental limits on what the works councilors can accomplish. Their most basic duty is to "cooperate with the employer . . . as well as the unions and employers' associations present in the plant for the good of the plant and its workers" (Art. 2, par. 1). To safeguard the internal harmony of the factory, the law strictly forbids councilors from making use of strikes as a means of settling disputes (Art. 74, par. 2). Rather, conflicts are to be resolved by means of an arbitration board (Einigungsstelle) consisting of an equal number of works councilors and employer representatives and a neutral chairman acceptable to both sides. In cases of continued disagreement, decisions of the chairman are binding (Art. 76). Works councilors are further barred from political activity in their official capacity (Art. 74, par. 2). Moreover, they cannot reveal business information to which they are privy after the employer has designated it confidential (Art. 79, par. 1).

The BVG 1972 allows unions a wider official role in plant affairs than did its predecessor in 1952.[47] As in the BVG 1952, the unions have the right to initiate the creation of a works council as well as to contest the results of a works council election (Arts. 16, 19). Union representatives may also attend plant and works council meetings in an advisory capacity (Arts. 31, 46). The new law, however, contains two important changes. First, Article 2 grants union officials unlimited access to a plant as long as management is given prior notice. Second, the revised law permits works councilors to engage in union activities within the plant, thus de facto legalizing open union recruitment on the shop floor (Art. 74, par. 3). In summary, one can say that the BVG 1972 conceives of unions as useful support organizations for the formally independent works councils, but it also subjects them to the same requirement of peaceful cooperation within the plant which circumscribes the works councils' freedom of action.[48]

The works council enjoys two types of rights in its dealings inside the plant.[49] The first of these pertains to Anhörungsrecht or right to be consulted. Before making certain decisions, management must consult with the works council, and the decision can be nullified if management fails to comply with this stipulation. The council has no power to prevent management from carrying out its plans, however. In certain cases the works council can lodge a formal protest if it feels that the employer's actions violate some law or contract. The matter can then be brought before the local labor court which has the final say.

The BVG 1972 invests the works council with rights of co-determination (Mitbestimmung) over a second category of management actions. This means that the employer must gain the approval of the council before he/she can proceed with certain decisions. In case of a dispute between the two sides, the arbitration board (Einigungsstelle) is summoned. Its chairman is obliged to settle all conflicts in a way which best serves the interests of the plant, and hence these decisions have had a tendency to favor management rather than labor.[50] The ban on industrial action imposed on the works council by the Works Constitution Act (Art. 74, par. 2), significantly weakens the council's power of co-determination.

In order that legal standing may be conferred on accords reached by management and the works council concerning various aspects of work in the plant, Article 77 of the BVG empowers both sides to sign plant accords (Betriebsvereinbarungen), which have a legal force similar to contracts. However, Article 77, paragraph 3 of the BVG emphasizes the primacy of collective bargaining agreements between unions and employers by stating that issues of pay or working conditions normally settled in and by them cannot be the subject of a plant accord. Either side can cancel such accords provided three months' notice has been given. The works council can circumvent the restrictions on plant accords by concluding informal plant agreements (Betriebsabsprachen) with management, but these agreements do not enjoy a legally binding character.

The works council's rights of consultation and/or co-determination extend to four areas of factory life: the organization of work, social policy, remunerations, and personnel policy. With regard to the organization of work, the council's approval is necessary for the introduction of overtime or short-time (Kurzarbeit). Moreover, the council co-determines the structure of the working day, including the starting and finishing time of shifts and the spacing of breaks (Art. 87, pars. 2, 3). Works councilors must also make sure that state health and safety regulations are being properly followed. In addition, they negotiate plant accords when necessary in order to fit these regulations to the specific conditions present in their factory.

Perhaps the most important function of the works council regarding work organization involves so-called plant changes (Betriebs-änderungen).[51] Article 111 of the BVG defines these as follows:

1. Reduction or closing down of plant or a significant section thereof.
2. Transfer of the entire plant or sections thereof.

3. Merger with other factories.
4. Significant changes in the organization of the plant, the purpose of the plant, the plant equipment.
5. Introduction of significantly new methods of work or production techniques.

Before taking any of these steps, the employer must inform and consult with the works council. The two sides must then negotiate an "interest equalization plan" (Interessenausgleich) providing for the implementation of the changes in a manner which does justice to the interests of the workforce (Art. 112). If no agreement is attained, the state labor office and/or the plant arbitration board can be summoned by either side to mediate. If differences of opinion still exist, the BVG empowers the employer to implement the changes anyway in the manner he/she sees fit.

Even if no Interessenausgleich can be achieved, however, the employer is still required to compensate workers for any "economic disadvantages" (layoff, transfer or job reclassification) that may result from plant changes, by means of a "social plan" (Sozialplan – Art. 112, par. 1). This normally takes the form of a large lump-sum payment, the size of which varies greatly depending on a worker's age, skill level and number of years worked in the plant. In the case of disagreements between works councils and management, the state labor office and/or the plant arbitration board may again be asked to mediate. This time, though, the arbitration board is charged with drawing up its own social plan if the employer will not agree to one. In addition, an individual worker can sue the firm in labor court if he/she feels the compensation rendered is inadequate.

In the area of social policy, the works council can negotiate extra "plant pensions" (Betriebsrenten) if these have not already been the subject of a collective bargaining agreement. The council is also empowered to supervise administration of the plant pension fund, cafeteria, recreational areas, library, and any other facilities set up for the benefit of the workforce (Art. 87, par. 8).[52]

Article 77, paragraph 3, which forbids plant accords on matters normally covered in collective bargaining agreements, would seem to remove the subject of remuneration from the works council's domain of consultation and co-determination. Yet in practice this is not so. The works council has two principal ways through which it can influence take-home pay in the plant: informal agreements with management and co-determination rights on piece rates and piece-rate compensation.

The take-home pay of a West German worker can be divided into three parts.[53] The first consists of the basic weekly wage set by the union wage contract (Tariflohn). In the case of workers paid according to a pure piece rate, this weekly wage is also guaranteed as long as the workers put in a

40-hour week. Any single worker's actual weekly wage, which is determined by his/her individual labor contract, almost always amounts to a higher sum than the contractual wage rate. The difference between the two is often referred to as an achievement bonus (Leistungszulage).

This difference can result from several different factors. After consultation with the works council, management can agree (most often as a consequence of the general situation in the labor market) to pay the entire workforce a higher basic wage, which is then recorded in everyone's individual labor contract. The next time a union wage contract is signed, however, contractual wages may increase to a level which still remains below the actual wage rate received by workers in a given factory. In this case, management can refuse to increase wages, claiming that the contractual wage level has already been reached. This maneuver, frequently employed during recessions, is known as Anrechnung ("surcharge" but also "acknowledgement"). The only way to prevent this is by having the employer agree to characterize the extra wages included in a worker's Arbeitsvertrag as compensation for a special skill.[54] Union attempts to protect extra wages through so-called effective pay clauses (Effektivklauseln) have generally met with negative verdicts from the Federal Republic's labor courts.[55]

For workers on partial or total piecework, however, there exists another way to receive extra-contractual wages.[56] In piecework a method of work analysis (Arbeitsbewertungsmethode) must first be used to evaluate the actions involved in a certain job. Then a time multiplier (Zeitfaktor) is established which states how much the worker must accomplish in a given unit of time. Lastly, a money multiplier (Geldfaktor), or the piece rate proper, is set. Bonus rates (Prämiensätze) are also issued for work which exceeds the norm. All of these factors together determine a worker's actual weekly wage rate, which can often lie well above the contractual one. Article 87, paragraph 1, no. 11 of the BVG gives the works council full powers of co-determination in all four areas of piece-rate calculation. The results of the works council's negotiations with management can also be decreed in a plant accord and thus become legally protected.

One final element – comprising bonuses for overtime, weekend work, night work, holiday work and the like – contributes to a worker's weekly take-home pay. In industries where such practices are common – printing and steel for example – the union typically negotiates a contract covering these bonuses. In other industries this process is sometimes left to the works council. Once these bonuses have been included, a worker's total gross weekly pay can be calculated. The difference between the average gross weekly pay and the contractual wage rate of a group of workers is referred to in West Germany, as well as in the United States, as the wage gap. The difference between the rate at which gross pay and contractual wages increase in a given year is known as the wage drift. As we shall see, both of these can be quite high in certain industries in the Federal Republic. For the reasons outlined above, works councils contribute significantly to this outcome, thus creating a source of tension between them and the unions.

In addition to its right of consultation concerning layoffs resulting from any plant changes, the works council also retains a say in the hiring, firing and transferring of individual workers.[57] The council can ask management to establish certain universal selection criteria (Auswahlrichtlinien) covering all three cases, but in plants with under 1,000 employees it cannot require this practice (Art. 95). Selection criteria classify workers according to age, wage group, marital status and the like and provide different degrees of job protection (or preferential hiring and firing) on this basis. Selection criteria are subject to the approval of the works council.

Before hiring, firing or transferring a worker, management must consult with the works council (Art. 99). If the council feels that the employer is violating some law or agreement (such as the Auswahlrichtlinien) or is discriminating against a particular worker, it can lodge a formal protest. The case may then be brought before a labor court, which can order an employer to rehire or retransfer a worker and/or pay him/her compensation if it finds the council's objections to be valid (Arts. 99–102). To fire a works council member, management must have the approval of the whole council or, failing that, of the local labor court (Art. 103).

Thus we have seen that despite the limitations imposed by the BVG (no right to strike, priority of union contracts), the position of the works council is a very powerful one. Indeed, constant cooperation on the part of management with the council represents one of the most fundamental prerequisites for the efficient and smooth operation of any large West German factory. Their independent power base in the plant makes works councilors highly influential figures within the unions, and, since approximately 80% of them are union members, they provide organized labor with an important (albeit indirect) say in the day-to-day lives of factory workers and employees.

## V. LABOR LAW AT THE FIRM LEVEL: CO-DETERMINATION

At the present time, four major pieces of legislation provide for four different types of worker participation at the firm level in the Federal Republic: the Works Constitution Act of 1972 (BVG 1972); the Coal, Steel and Iron Co-Determination Law (Montanmitbestimmungsgesetz – MMG) of 1951; the Works Constitution Act of 1952 (BVG 1952); and the

Table 2.1. *Co-determination according to the Co-determination Act of 1951 in the mining, iron and steel industries*

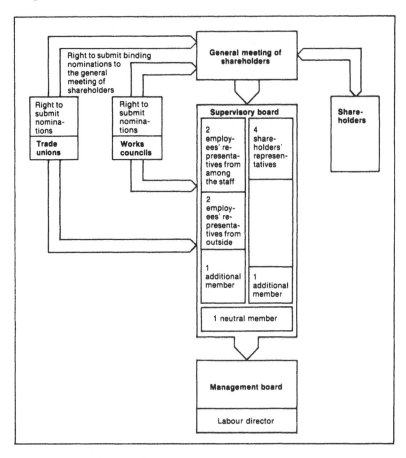

*Source:* The Federal Minister of Labour and Social Affairs, *Co-determination in the Federal Republic of Germany* (Bonn: The Federal Ministry of Labour and Social Affairs, 1976), p. 47.

Co-Determination Law (Mitbestimmungsgesetz – MG) of 1976. The last three of these call for worker representation of various kinds on the supervisory board (Aufsichtsrat) of large companies. The first provides for the creation of a works council on the firm level if a company operates more than one factory.

Article 47 of the BVG 1972 empowers each works council in a firm to send one of its blue-collar and one of its white-collar members to form a company works council (Gesamtbetriebsrat). This new council enjoys the same rights of consultation or co-determination as plant works councils in

Table 2.2. *Co-determination according to the Works Constitution Act of 1952*

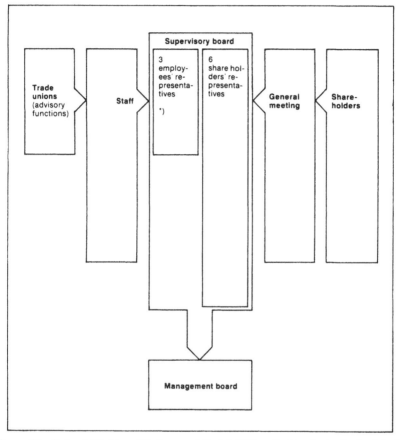

*Source:* The Federal Minister of Labour and Social Affairs, *Co-determination in the Federal Republic of Germany* (Bonn: The Federal Ministry of Labour and Social Affairs, 1976), p. 68.

matters affecting the entire firm or more than one factory. These could include changes in companywide personnel policy, the reorganization and coordination of production involving several plants, a general introduction of new production technology and the like. As on the factory level, management must inform and consult the company works council in all these cases, and the latter can negotiate interest equalization agreements and social plans. The council can also sign company accords (Gesamtbetriebsvereinbarungen) which, like plant accords, have a legally binding character. In addition, Article 107 of the BVG 1972 allows the council to form an economic committee (Wirtschaftsausschuss) which management must keep informed about the economic situation of the company.

Table 2.3. *Co-determination according to the Co-determination Act of 1976 (company with more than 20,000 employees)*

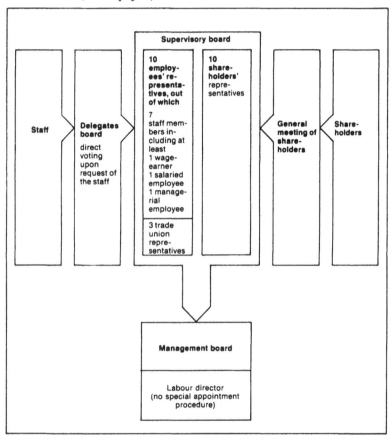

*Source: The Federal Minister of Labour and Social Affairs, Co-determination in the Federal Republic of Germany* (Bonn: The Federal Ministry of Labour and Social Affairs, 1976), p. 14.

Although this body enjoys no formal rights of co-determination, it does allow the various works councils to keep abreast of the "big picture" within the company and receive early warning signals of problems affecting their own factories.

The BVG 1972 provides for a form of worker participation in any firm large enough to have works council. All the other (supplementary) forms of participation in West Germany are restricted to very specific kinds of companies. This pertains especially to the MMG of 1951, which intro-duced so-called parity co-determination (Paritätische Mitbestimmung) on the supervisory boards of all companies with over 2,000 employees engaged in coal mining or in the production (though not in the processing) of iron and steel.[58] (See Table 2.1.) The supervisory board forms part of the tripartite structure of publicly held West German companies (Aktiengesellschaften) established by law.[59] The stockholders' assembly (Hauptver sammlung) of such companies votes for the members comprising the supervisory board, which in turn elects two chief executives, one responsible for business and the other for technical affairs (kaufmännische und technische Angelegenheiten). The day-to-day running of the company is the responsibility of these executives, who need only seek the approval of the supervisory board for major initiatives. The board meets at regular intervals throughout the year to review company policies, and at the close of a business year submits a report and recommendation on dividends to the stockholders' meeting for its approval.[60]

It is clear then that the supervisory board can play a crucial, though by no means decisive, role in the conduct of company affairs. The MMG requires that half of this body (comprising ten, fourteen or twenty members and a chairman, depending on company size) be composed of employee representatives (Arbeitnehmervertreter) in coal and steel firms. Even non-publicly held companies must by law have a supervisory board. In the case of a ten-person board, one of the five employee representatives is named by the blue-collar works councilors on the company works council and one by the white-collar councilors. The DGB, in consultation with any other union federations present in the company, selects two further representatives. Typically, they are leading union officials. The DGB also appoints the last employee representative, although this person may not be a member of any union (MMG, Arts. 6, 8).

The entire supervisory board then elects a neutral chairman. In the case of unresolvable differences between employee and employer representatives over the selection of the chairman, the stockholders' assembly is empowered to name one, although this eventuality has thus far never occurred in practice. The board then proceeds to name the two executives as well as a third, the labor director (Arbeitsdirektor) provided for in the MMG (Art. 13). This additional executive, who is responsible for the firm's personnel policies, cannot be elected without the approval of the employee representatives. In addition to the somewhat circumscribed – but nevertheless important – right of supervising company policy afforded by the presence of union representatives on the board, the power to appoint the Arbeitsdirektor was undoubtedly the most significant gain attained by labor through the MMG. This became amply evident in subsequent years when labor directors developed the important institution of social plans (Sozialpläne) later to be formally incorporated into the BVG 1972.[61]

In the years since 1951, the affected companies have tried numerous legal maneuvers to rid themselves of Montanmitbestimmung.[62] One of these involved the formation of holding companies not directly involved in mining or iron and steel production. Under political pressure from the unions, the federal government in 1956 passed a law (the Montanmitbestimmungsergänzungsgesetz) extending parity co-determination to these companies as well, provided mining or the production of iron or steel accounted for more than 50% of their total revenue. In an important retreat from the MMG, however, this law allowed the selection of the labor director to occur without the approval of the employee representatives.

In 1980, another crisis erupted involving Montanmitbestimmung when Mannesmann AG tried to restructure its internal organization, so that steel would contribute less than 50% of the parent company's sales, thus eliminating the necessity of maintaining parity co-determination in the holding company of this diversifying giant. (For a detailed discussion of the Mannesmann affair see Chapter 3.) Again a law was passed preserving Montanmitbestimmung for six years in firms where iron, steel or coal sales had fallen below 50% of total turnover. Despite these stopgap measures, however, Montanmitbestimmung in any form will by the end of the 1980s apply to only a handful of companies in the entire Federal Republic, thus depriving it of the socio-political significance it may have previously enjoyed.

After the passage of the MMG in 1951, the unions called for the extension of co-determination to all large companies in the Federal Republic. The Works Constitution Act of 1952 actually did this, but not in the way the unions had envisioned. (See Table 2.2.) Articles 76 through 87 of that law called for employee representatives to constitute *one-third* of the members of supervisory boards in all companies with over 500 workers, thus accounting for its seemingly contradictory name "one-third parity co-determination" (Drittelparitätsmitbestimmung). On boards with six members, the firm's workers directly elect one blue-collar and one white-collar representative, both of whom must be regular employees of that particular firm. Should there be nine or more members on the board, the workforce can also elect an "external" representative (i.e. a union official).

Quite understandably this form of co-determination (if one can legitimately call it that) met with universal disapproval from organized labor. For over twenty years, the unions consistently and indefatigably called for the passage of a new, more generous co-determination law comprising the entire West German economy. This finally happened on May 4, 1976. However, the new Mitbestimmungsgesetz (MG) proved to be another major disappointment for labor, since it failed to replicate the gains of even the MMG. (See Table 2.3.) The new law applied to all firms employing more than 2,000 workers. This left the country in effect with three different co-determination systems: Montan in iron, steel and coal companies with over 2,000 employees; MG Mitbestimmung in all other firms with over 2,000 employees; and Drittelparität in firms with between 500 and 2,000 employees. (On the unions' attempts to gain "genuine" co-determination throughout the late 1960s and the first half of the 1970s, and their bitter disappointment with the 1976 co-determination law, see Chapter 3.)

The 1976 law again called for half of the supervisory board members to be employee representatives, but its definition of them and their mode of selection differed substantially from that found in the MMG. First, the employee side had to include one elected representative of the firm's middle management (leitende Angestellte). Second, in boards with six or eight employee representatives, only two could be outside union officials, and on boards with ten representatives only three. Third, the remaining employee representatives (three, five or six, depending on board size) had to be elected directly via a proportional representation system by all the company's employees (except in companies with over 8,000 workers where electors [Wahlmänner] were to be used). This last stipulation made it substantially easier for independents and workers affiliated with non-DGB unions to get onto the supervisory boards. The cumulative effect of all these points in the 1976 law was to undermine the cohesion of the employee side of the board.

Another negative feature of the MG from the unions' point of view was the fact that if two-thirds of the supervisory board cannot agree on a chairman, one can be appointed by the employer representatives alone from among their members (MG Art. 29). Furthermore, if the vote of the board on any matter results in a tie, the chairman has two votes and thus the ultimate power to decide unilaterally (Art. 29). As with the MMG, the board elects a labor director in addition to the other two executives, but the approval of the employee representatives is not required in this selection process. The other duties and powers of the supervisory board are the same as under parity co-determination, with the exception that in this case the employer side can virtually always rely on a de facto majority thanks to the representative of middle management and/or the chairman's tie-breaking second vote. In summary, one can conclude that labor's influence in the 1976 model lies somewhere between that found in the other two co-determination systems (Montan and Drittelparität). A reliable estimate suggests that in the early 1980s about 450 companies in the Federal Republic were subject to the 1976 Mitbestimmungsgesetz.[63]

The above discussion shows that none of the three co-determination models grants a truly significant say to labor in company affairs. The Works Constitution Act in either of its forms is more important in this respect. If real co-determination exists anywhere in West Germany, it does so at the plant level. The great significance attached to Mitbestimmung by the DGB unions over the years can only be properly understood if it is analyzed in the context of labor's overall preoccupation with democratizing the Federal Republic's economy in particular and public life in general. It thus developed into an emotionally charged symbol of organized labor's influence and power in West Germany's political development. As the next chapter will show in some detail, the DGB had a rather hard row to hoe in this difficult process.

# 3 A HISTORY OF THE GERMAN TRADE UNION FEDERATION, DEUTSCHER GEWERKSCHAFTSBUND (DGB): FROM RECONSTRUCTION TO THE THIRD BASIC PROGRAM

## I. THE RECONSTRUCTION PERIOD: 1945–1949

The immediate post-World War II period in Germany was dominated by political uncertainty, societal flux, demographic change and economic dislocation. These four years embodied a crucial juncture for organized labor in that they set the agenda for its subsequent political and economic activities in what became the Federal Republic of Germany.

This is not to say that the events involving organized labor during Germany's reconstruction period predetermined all subsequent developments. Rather, it is merely to state that this early period witnessed the making of critical choices and the formulation of crucial policies which later helped shape the German unions' self-understanding and self-perception as major actors in a liberal democracy with a capitalist economy. In turn, this era also influenced how other actors in the German political economy – notably the state and employers – were to perceive the unions in the political process.

It was Germany's total defeat – so aptly characterized by the term "hour zero" – which made the reconstruction process in that country so different from equivalent endeavors elsewhere in Europe. To be sure, Germany was military defeated and occupied and her economy lay in shambles. More importantly, perhaps, Germany's political institutions had been completely devastated.

In terms of the reconstruction process, this meant that an already difficult task occurred under even more adverse conditions in Germany than elsewhere in Europe. Whereas in France, Great Britain and Italy reconstruction took place under the auspices of an emergency alliance consisting of capital, labor and the state, in Germany the process was complicated by the fact that state power was divided among four occupying nations with conflicting interests and different visions of how they wanted to shape Germany's – and thus Europe's – future. For our purposes it was the United States and Great Britain – with France playing a lesser role – who assumed the position of the state during these crucial four years following Germany's defeat. Both of these powers intervened actively in the formation of what was later to become West Germany's structure of industrial relations, thus playing an important role in shaping the character of organized labor in the new country.

Even before the official surrender of Nazi Germany on VE-Day (May 8, 1945), the Western Allies came into contact with German workers who wanted to organize and reestablish their collective mandate following its destruction by Hitler in 1933. To the surprise of the advancing American forces, a group of German workers and active unionists petitioned the US command in Aachen in March 1945 to be given permission to begin with the rebuilding of a union local in that city.[1] They demanded the displacement and punishment of Nazi collaborators who owned the firms for which they worked and also expressed a desire to start the reconstruction of a Germany based on different principles than the ones which led to the establishment of the Third Reich. Similar developments occurred in many other cities, towns and villages which were liberated by the Allied armies. The content and articulation of the demands varied from place to place, but everywhere workers sought not only to form collective associations in order to begin the much-needed reconstruction of their communities, but also to create a new political and economic order which would prevent a repeat of the events that led to the horrors of the immediate past. These spontaneous grassroots organizations were, according to a British observer, the very first institutions of any kind in the aftermath of Hitler's regime.[2] This early reemergence of organized German workers on the local level even before the war's end corresponded well with General Eisenhower's statement of March 1945 which declared that "circumstances permitting, the German workers will soon be able to unite in democratic unions. The German Labor Front and other formations of Nazi organizations will be dissolved immediately."[3]

One thing seemed quite clear from the beginning. Whatever horrors and humiliation national socialism had inflicted on the German working class and its representatives, it could not obliterate what one of the most astute students of this period called "the organizational miracle."[4] This organizational prowess of the German workers surprised the Allies both because it conveyed that even the Nazis could not destroy the discipline and dedication of the German working class, and because it demonstrated that labor could not be discounted regardless of the form or content of any post-World War II settlement. If German workers had nothing else, they still could organize. By August 1945 when the Allies, led by the British in the north of Germany, officially recognized the newly established unions as legitimate representatives of German workers, nearly one million workers had already been organized. In Lower Saxony alone, for example, 94,000 workers belonged to unions a few weeks after the official ending of the war. By November 1946 there were 1,700,000 union members in the British zone with the figure rising to 2,100,000 by May 1947. During the same period in Bavaria, union membership increased sevenfold from 100,000 to 740,000. By the end of 1948, nearly 5,000,000 German workers – excluding Berlin and the Saarland – had once again become unionized.[5] Barely three years after the end of World War II and fifteen years following the destruction of the independent German labor movement by Hitler, over one-third of Germany's working population was organized in independent trade unions. Pirker's words best summarize the significance of this development for Germany's future as a whole and the labor movement in particular: "The German miracle is above all an organizational miracle, and the rapid reconstruction of the union movement within this development represents ... a part – indeed not an unimportant part – of this organizational miracle."[6]

This organizational savvy of the German working class manifested itself, however, not so much in the top-down, centralized and often overly bureaucratized institutions which later became the hallmark of the West German trade union movement. Rather, organization occurred sporadically on the shop floor, at the plant level and in individual firms. The discrete nature of this grass-roots development was in good part fostered by the division of Germany into four occupied zones, most of which remained fragmented until 1946. Thus, it was mainly the locally developed, indigenous and independent works councils at the factory level which took the first steps in organizing German workers. Two reasons explain the works councils' preeminence at the very beginning of German labor's post-World War II reconstruction: first, by virtue of their position in the factories they assumed organizational responsibility for providing people's most basic needs such as the procuring of food, clothing and shelter. Most scholars of this period, regardless of their political convictions, emphasize the works councils' central position in restarting the production process in Germany's devastated industries. The works councils occupied a strategic position in German industrial life which furnished them with extraordinary powers on the community level.

In addition to providing economic necessities, the works councils filled a political vacuum left as a result of the delegitimation of many employers for supporting the Nazis. Thus, for a brief time – quite analogous to the period following World War I – German labor had the opportunity to restructure German society "from below." As in 1918, no other advanced capitalist country had a similar chance to see its working class transform its political economy in the direction of a democratic socialist formation. But once again this was not to be. A combination of reasons, some internal to the labor movement itself, others involving the constraints imposed on labor by external factors – such as the condition of the German economy, the presence of the Allies and ultimately the reemergence of German capital as the dominant (though this time not exclusionary) social force – again stymied labor's revolutionary potential. This, as we shall see further on, in no way implies that organized labor intended to restore capitalism in Germany. The fact that it could not prevent this restoration and decided ultimately to make the best of it refutes the voluntaristic interpretation which sees organized labor as one of the earliest and most active participants in fostering a capitalist reconstruction in West Germany.[7]

Indeed, if one could point to a single common denominator informing German labor politics at this juncture, it would have to be its anti-capitalism and anti-fascism. The negative memories of Weimar and the legacies of the Third Reich formed important intellectual and experiential bonds for Germany's post-war labor movement and its leaders. Avoiding the pitfalls of Weimar (which had led to the catastrophe of the Third Reich) remained the guiding principle for German labor following the collapse of Hitler's regime. Most labor leaders also shared the commonality of exile, age and ideological affinity. With virtually no exception, Germany's dominant unionists of the reconstruction period had spent the war in Great Britain, Switzerland, the United States or Sweden, were born in the 1880s and were active members of the Social Democratic Party and/or the social democratic trade union federation (ADGB) during the Weimar Republic. These men were deeply marked by the Weimar experience and by subsequent events in German history. For this reason, they sought to reconstruct a new (i.e. non-capitalist) Germany by establishing a labor movement which was different from its Weimar predecessor.

Anti-capitalist and anti-fascist, however, need not be coterminous with revolutionary. A number of analysts of the German labor movement seem at least implicitly to blame the revisionism of these leaders for the eventual system integration of the West German unions.[8] In addition to being too voluntaristic, this view disregards the fact that these leaders were not revolutionaries either by training and conviction or by temperament and experience. By establishing a new labor movement they had hoped to steer a reconstructed Germany away from capitalism towards a vaguely defined version of non-Leninist (i.e. participatory) socialism. That they failed in the latter is not their fault alone. However, their partial success in establishing a united trade union movement meant that capitalism in West Germany could not destroy labor (as happened in the Weimar Republic), thereby substantially enhancing democracy's stability in the Federal Republic.

The main reform that the returning leaders sought for the new labor movement was organizational unity and centralization to counter the fatal splits of labor's Weimar experience. Emigres from Sweden lobbied their colleagues to found a single general union (Allgemeine Gewerkschaft) to which all working people, regardless of rank, salary, job, industry or geography, would belong. This general union would also conduct all negotiations with the employers, both private and public. Whatever sub-divisions there might be – and the advocates of this particular form of union organization left no doubt that the fewer there were the better for the working class – they would simply act as supplementary bodies to the all-encompassing union and never constitute autonomous entities in any respect. While opposed – perhaps not coincidentally – by emigres from the United States, Great Britain and Switzerland, who desired a more decentralized, federated body in which the constituent unions would retain major powers such as that of collective bargaining, the plan for a centralized general union prevailed in late 1945. It was the weighty opinion of Hans Böckler – later to become the German Trade Union Federation's first chairman – that swayed the decision in the direction of the centralized general union.[9] But as a harbinger of things to come, this plan was rejected by the Allied powers, first by the British and later by the Americans. Both Western powers feared that such a centralized, all-encompassing union would give labor too much power, especially in a country where virtually all political institutions were yet to be determined. The Americans in particular feared that such an organization could easily fall under the influence of communist labor leaders and activists.[10] Under British pressure, the German union leaders finally opted for a federated structure of industrial unions in which the overall federation would have limited organizational powers, and matters related to collective bargaining and other forms of grass-roots mobilization would remain the prerogatives of the individual unions.[11] The Americans approved this plan within a few months, and in early 1946 industrial unions in both the British and the American zones of occupied Germany were born.

Total organizational unity eluded the unions, but they did achieve a crucial reform. The establishment of the Einheitsgewerkschaft obliterated political divisions among the organizations and in the representation of workers. Henceforth all wage-earning workers and salaried employees were to belong to one unitary trade union federation, regardless of their political orientation. The Einheitsgewerkschaft and the Industriegewerk-

schaft were to become two of the most important organizational innovations of the post-World War II labor movement. While these gains did not
create the total unity that some leaders had coveted – Pirker for example
sees the defeat of the centralized general union (Allgemeine Gewerkschaft)
as the first in a string of setbacks for organized labor which continued until
the early 1960s – German labor gained official Allied recognition, thereby
also receiving permission to be the German working class's official
representatives vis-à-vis the Allies and the employers. However, the
unions' overall power of representation was still exceedingly limited at the
time since they were forbidden to unite across the zones of Allied
occupation.

Having settled the issue of organization more or less to their satisfaction,
the unions now attempted to implement their ideas about the new
economic and political order which was to enhance democracy and
equality in a new Germany. In this realm, the results proved a lot less
rewarding for organized labor than it had originally hoped. Once again,
with Weimar on their minds, the union leaders argued that political
democracy accompanied by a highly authoritarian economic structure
under the employers' control would, in due course, lead to political
dictatorship, as was the case with the demise of the Weimar Republic. In
this context the unions developed economic and political demands which
essentially aimed at abolishing capitalism in Germany. As Böckler stated
in March 1946: "Political democracy, which we want and for which we
bled for decades, has to have economic democracy as its premise ... The
German workers should not be subjected a second time to events similar to
those of 1920–21 when they were cheated and duped."[12]

The German unions' demands could be clustered into the following
overarching categories: complete de-Nazification of the civil service and all
public agencies; de-Nazification of the upper echelons of German industry;
the socialization of key sectors of the German economy, most notably those
that had been particularly tarnished by their active involvement in Hitler's
war effort, such as steel and iron, chemicals, and the leading banks; and the
socialization of all energy-related industries, especially the coal mines of
the Ruhr area. Lastly, they demanded full-fledged labor participation on a
basis of parity in virtually every aspect of the German economy. This
included labor input "from below" (i.e. at the shop-floor and plant level),
"in the middle" (in the company boardrooms) and "from above" (via
national as well as state-level economic planning agencies which were to
guide – if not totally control and/or own – the major segments of the
German economy).

These labor demands appear quite radical in hindsight, as indeed they
were to an extent. Yet, by the standards of the prevailing Zeitgeist, they

prove to be not much different from the anti-capitalist sentiments which permeated the programmatic statements of virtually every political grouping in Germany at the time. It is important to remember that even the CDU's founding document, the Ahlener Program, states explicitly that "the capitalist system has failed the public and social interests [Lebensinteressen] of the German people. Following the terrible political, economic and social collapse as a consequence of a criminal power-directed politics, only a fundamentally new order can lead to a successful beginning."[13] The program then went on to call for the general socialization of German public life as the only guarantor of human decency and personal justice.

The unions' demands reflected a moderation in form and content which not only revealed the leadership's – as well as membership's – loyal attachment to social democracy in general and the SPD in particular, but also conveyed the caution which the union movement intended to observe as it implemented its radical program. In short, what was to become one of the trademarks of organized labor in West Germany – radical rhetoric accompanied by moderate, often demobilizing, action – had already appeared at this early stage. The wishes of communist unionists and other radical organizers in the middle and lower echelons of the unions for a more comprehensive nationalization of the German economy went unheeded. Moreover, in the tradition of Fritz Naphtali's concept of Wirtschaftsdemokratie – a democratic alternative to Leninism which was developed by the social democratic labor movement in the late 1920s and became the ADGB's official policy in 1928 – the post-World War II successors to the ADGB placed their greatest emphasis on labor participation in the decision-making process of the economy. Thus developed German labor's preoccupation with co-determination (Mitbestimmung), which it hoped to see implemented via a combination of two of its other traditional fixations: on the Social Democratic Party and on helping that party attain state power. As will become clear, neither of these strategies proved particularly successful in winning the unions' participation on a level of full parity in the German economy.

This, however, did not deter them from pushing for Mitbestimmung with all their might beginning in late 1945. At the Klöckner steel works in early 1946 the unions were granted the same number of labor representatives on the supervisory board of the firm as was allotted for the employers. Moreover, a full-time labor director close to the unions assumed a permanent managerial position on the company's executive board concerned with daily operations. Lastly, the responsibilities and rights of the works councils were extended considerably.[14] This plan was the direct precursor to the co-determination implemented in the nation's steel, iron and coal industries best known under the term Montanmitbestimmung.

By 1947, virtually all German steel plants, iron works and coal mines adopted this form of co-determination as their *modus operandi* both for their daily business and their longer-term strategic decisions.

Clearly, this gain was not won without struggle and compromise, both of which ultimately shaped the outcome of the plan. The behavior and attitudes of the unions' major antagonists (the German employers and the Allied powers) influenced the results of Mitbestimmung in terms of its geographic scope and ultimate impact. The German employers would have preferred to avoid yielding any of their often dictatorial powers to labor. But, as already mentioned, their moral and economic position was severely weakened as a consequence of their complicity with Hitler's war machine. Moreover, the large firms – those most likely to witness experiments in co-determination – also faced dismantlement and break-ups at the hand of the Allies during 1946 and 1947. Thus, the curious situation developed in which many employers in the country's steel and coal industries tried to reward their workforce and the respective union for resisting the Allies' attempts to dismantle German plants by agreeing to introduce co-determination. In some places, however, the unions had to resort to strike activities in order to have Mitbestimmung implemented in their respective companies.[15] Wherever instituted by the end of 1947, co-determination resulted from a combination of labor's shop-floor power and capital's desire to unite with the unions against the dismantling measures of the Allies. Co-determination in the German steel and coal industry emanated – at least in part – from a temporary alliance between labor and capital against the Allied occupiers. It also, however, owes its existence to the British Labour government's active interest in this experiment. Thus it is not by chance that full-parity co-determination remained confined to the British zone, while it was never permitted in the areas under American jurisdiction.

It is important to point out that company-level co-determination practiced in Germany's iron and steel industries of the Rhine-Ruhr was perceived by the unions as the first step in a comprehensive democratization of German society as a whole. As to labor's input "from below," the unions faced a difficult structural and political situation due to the presence of the works councils. Structurally, the works councils embodied another form of labor representation on the shop floor where they were the unions' inherent rivals. Politically, many works councilors who had often single-handedly revived worker representation during the immediate post-war period held more radical beliefs than the unions. At this juncture the union leadership responded to this potential challenge "from below" by occasionally deploying tactics of demobilization in order to preserve working-class unity.[16] Lastly, organized labor failed to make headway concerning union participation "from above." On the supra-firm level, the unions were shut out completely, in good part due to the rapid onslaught of the Cold War, which meant a deterioration in virtually all aspects of the unions' existence.

While it would be wrong to blame the Cold War alone for the "freezing" of progressive reforms during the late 1940s, there can be no doubt that this geo-political development represented a formidable obstacle to labor's plans of democratizing Germany. The unions' limited resources were simply no match for the forces which coalesced against labor – both implicitly and explicitly – beginning in late 1947 and lasting well into the early 1950s. With the merger of the British and American zones of occupation into Bizonia in 1947, the cornerstone was laid for a separate Western Germany under American hegemony. Indeed, the formation of Bizonia merely concretized a longstanding inter-Allied development, the increasing predominance of the United States at the expense of its British partner. This, of course, did not bode well for the German labor movement which, although far from having a friend in the British government, most certainly preferred its policies to the openly anti-labor and anti-socialist position of the Americans.

A new ideology emerged concomitantly with the Cold War: anti-communism suddenly became the legitimator of public discourse in the West. The effects of this development on the unions were immense. First and foremost, the Cold War virtually stopped the Allies' attempts to de-Nazify German industry and politics, thereby initiating a rapid process of capital's rehabilitation. This in turn meant that many employers, who previously were eager to come to terms with organized labor in general and their own workforce in particular, could regain the offensive confident that all the powers that be and the Zeitgeist had turned in capital's favor. Second, precisely to avoid being associated too closely with radicalism – especially of the communist sort, which increasingly became identified as the foremost enemy of democracy and "the free world" – the unions were eager to distance themselves from "the communists." This meant the gradual isolation of communist union members at all levels of the organization ultimately leading to their expulsion or marginalization by the early 1950s. Moreover, the Cold War and anti-communism also helped solidify the already predominant social democratic hegemony in the labor movement of what was soon to become West Germany. While a number of unionists still hoped that an all-German labor movement remained possible, the Cold War unquestionably diminished all attempts at unification between the organized labor movement of the Soviet zone and its counterpart in the Western zones. In short, the Cold War and its ideology of anti-communism seriously weakened any reformist potential that organized labor in the western part of Germany had exhibited in 1945 and 1946. This loss of strength occurred via a substantial revival and consolidation of labor's main antagonists (capital and the occupying Allied powers) and a concomitant marginalization of labor's reformist elements and ideas, in favor of a more moderate strategy of acceptance of the status quo.[17]

A major watershed in organized labor's gradual integration into the capitalist reconstruction of Germany's western zones was its acceptance of the Marshall Plan.[18] Already in the latter half of 1947, numerous accommodationist leaders, including Hans Böckler, argued for labor's guarded participation in the American-led European Recovery Program.[19] The dilemma for Böckler was simple: labor could opt to pursue its original plan of a radical restructuring of property and power relations in Germany and thereby, however, risk starvation, or it could join the Marshall Plan and compromise some of its increasingly impractical beliefs.[20] Or as another major labor leader, Fritz Tarnow, aptly phrased the choice: the German labor movement had to decide between the Marshall Plan and the Molotov Plan.[21] By June 1948 there was no doubt that the trade unions in Bizonia would approve the Marshall Plan. At a hastily convened extraordinary union congress in Recklinghausen, a vast majority of the union delegates voted to accept the Marshall Plan. This decision was railroaded through the congress after only eight persons had a chance to voice their opinion on this weighty matter, with only ten minutes allotted to each speaker. Even though five of the eight opposed the unions' acceptance of the Plan, the issue had become moot by then.[22] The congress merely legitimized in public a decision which the inner circle of union leaders had made well before.

A few weeks after Secretary of State Marshall's announcement of the European Recovery Program at Harvard in June 1947, the Economic Council was established in Frankfurt, ostensibly to coordinate and implement economic policy by Germans under Allied supervision. It had become quite clear by the end of the summer of 1947 that this body had assumed the tasks of a quasi-parliament in Bizonia. Indeed, General Lucius Clay, the American High Commissioner in Germany, envisioned the Council's role precisely as a governing body which would gain increasing autonomy from its originators as time and circumstances warranted.[23] As of March 1948, the director of economic policy and all matters related to industrial reconstruction was none other than Ludwig Erhard, formerly Economics Minister in Bavaria and one of Germany's foremost representatives of the Freiburg School of neo-liberal economics. From his inaugural address onwards, Erhard never concealed his belief that the best road to Germany's reconstruction lay in a "social market economy" which emphasized the freedom of the market over any sort of planning. Planning was seen as detrimental to capital formation, which the devastated German economy needed desperately. Toward that end, Erhard and the Council continued to favor a wage and price freeze which had been instituted by the Allies and which, as is usual in such instances, froze wages more consistently than prices.

Moreover, in June 1948, the Economic Council decreed a currency reform which Pirker described in the following manner: "In the history of German capitalism, class divisions had never been more openly and ruthlessly the basis of economic decisions than in the case of the currency reform of 1948."[24] Since it was exclusively a currency reform, the measure obviously favored property owners and people not totally dependent on salaries and wages, such as merchants, entrepreneurs and peasants, over workers and other employees who relied solely on a fixed monetary income. The unions felt deceived and defeated. Although they were aware that currency reform was about to be implemented by the Economic Council, they had hoped that this measure would be accompanied by an "equalization of burden" (Lastenausgleich) which would protect the wage-earning working class from having its monetary income and savings virtually annihilated overnight. In a fashion typical of the unions at that time, they relied almost completely on the Social Democratic Party's presence in the Economic Council to attain an amended version of the currency reform more favorable to workers. The only problem with this strategy was that the SPD had by then lost its leverage in the Council, opting instead for what was termed "practical, constructive opposition."[25] Having pursued a policy of demobilization with the membership, a necessary step in selling the new accommodationist line to the rank and file, the unions were embarrassed in the summer following the currency reform. They failed to bring their own strength to bear, and their reliance on the SPD's quasi-governmental position proved disappointing as well.

When the lifting of price controls in the wake of the currency reform rapidly increased the discrepancy between prices and wages (which remained frozen until October 1948) the workers' situation deteriorated to a degree which the unions could no longer ignore. They called for a general strike to protest the inequities instituted by the measures of the Economic Council and indirectly by the Allies as well. Over nine million workers turned out to demonstrate their displeasure on November 12, 1948, which thus became the largest union-led public action since the prevention of the Kapp Putsch in 1920.[26] Despite this impressive showing, one should remember that the Allies permitted the strike because they were convinced of its tameness, due to its strictly economic character. There is no doubt that this assessment of the German labor movement in 1948 was largely correct. The demonstrators had numerous grievances which they voiced unabashedly. But just like the union leadership, they had by and large begun to accept the existing circumstances. A revolutionary transformation of Bizonia, which was rapidly being integrated into the West, was simply out of the question by late 1948.[27]

Maybe a revolution in Germany following the most devastating war in human history would have been impossible. A destitute, starving, warweary and defeated working class hardly represented the prime candidate for carrying out a successful societal and political transformation. Still, some important "historical moments" were definitely missed by the organized labor movement in the western half of occupied Germany, partly because its leaders were content to "satisfice" rather than attempt to optimize. They wanted some sort of socialism, but were willing to play their role in "organized capitalism" as long as the fundamental structures of liberal democracy were guaranteed, in stark contrast to the situation in the Weimar Republic. Thus, labor emerged from the post-war period controlled and subdued but not defeated.

## II.  THE BATTLE FOR A NEW SOCIAL ORDER: 1949–1953

A little over three months after the official merger of the American, British and French occupation zones into the Federal Republic of Germany, organized labor underwent a parallel development. On October 13, 1949 the trade union federations of the three Allied zones merged at a congress in Munich, thereby forming the new German Trade Union Federation known in German as the Deutscher Gewerkschaftsbund (DGB). Hans Böckler, running unopposed for the chairmanship of this new organization, received 487 votes from the assembled delegates with 59 opposing him and 18 submitting invalid ballots.[28] While certainly an impressive expression of confidence in Böckler as a leader, the relatively high number of negative votes (by German standards) emanated almost exclusively from delegates from the southern parts of the Federal Republic, who seemed a bit concerned by the disproportionately prominent role exerted by unionists from the British zone.[29] The Munich congress finally concretized the dream of many trade unionists haunted by the political divisions of the working class in the Weimar Republic. It established the Einheitsgewerkschaft, the unitary trade union movment which welcomed workers belonging to all "democratic" political organizations and believing in any "democratic" ideology; this, at the time, excluded only national socialists and other elements of the far right, but included communists, a fact which was to change after 1956 when the Federal Constitutional Court ruled the

German Communist Party (KPD) unconstitutional. Comprising nearly 5 million members at its foundation, the DGB federation encompassed sixteen individual unions, most of which could be classified as industrial unions. Each one of the member unions retained its own powers of collective bargaining, membership recruitment, collection of dues and virtually every other aspect of the day-to-day functioning of a labor organization. If one could rather simplistically schematize the division of labor between the DGB federation and its sixteen constituent unions, then it was the former's task to represent labor vis-à-vis society and the state, and the latter's to protect the collective welfare of workers vis-à-vis the employers in the factory and through the process of collective bargaining. Via acceptance of the principle of Industriegewerkschaft, the Munich congress also finalized the other unity cherished by the post-war German labor movement: all workers, regardless of status differences or job classifications, employed by the same company, had to belong to one and the same union. The implementation of the principles of "one plant, one union" and the political inclusivity of the German Trade Union Federation established the Munich congress as a landmark in the annals of German working-class history.[30]

Programmatically, the Munich congress still conveyed German labor's tenacity concerning its radical vision of a just society. The Munich Program of the DGB not only reaffirms the moral validity of the "third way" but argues that it represents the only assurance of a democratic Germany. The founding program of the German Trade Union Federation is a universalistic document, preoccupied as much with the democratic welfare of all Germans as it is with the more immediate concerns of the working class itself. The program barely addresses traditional union concerns such as strategies of collective bargaining and issues regarding social policy, but dwells instead at some length on topics such as economic justice, political participation and democratic reforms. It maintains that economic democracy is an absolute prerequisite for political democracy; the latter without the former constitutes a flawed democracy at best and is prone to collapse into authoritarian rule. The program envisions two major pillars on which this economic democracy would have to be based: the first and more important of the two is co-determination in all its forms – including full-parity labor participation – in all aspects of the economy (i.e. both within the firm and outside it). The second pillar rested on the belief in the necessity of intervening in the market via the socialization of key national industries such as mining, iron and steel, large chemical firms, the energy-producing companies, transportation and banking.[31]

By pushing for the "third way," the Munich Program once again clarified organized labor's conviction that freedom, equality and human dignity could never be attained by a rigidly centralized planning system, such as had become increasingly dominant across the Federal Republic's eastern border in the "other" Germany, to the clear detriment of democracy there. Yet at the same time, the program also distanced itself emphatically from the popular "free market" ideology which was in the process of becoming the hegemonic economic doctrine in West Germany. Indeed, a few weeks before the DGB's founding congress in Munich, the CDU officially rescinded its Ahlener program in which the party challenged the validity of capitalism for Germany, and replaced it with the so-called Düsseldorf guidelines where Erhard's "social market economy" assumed center stage. The CDU's new guidelines represented merely a post-hoc programmatic corroboration of the actual policy of the Economic Council under the leadership of Erhard and with the approval of the Allied powers.[32]

The unions' Munich Program, in contrast, was somewhat outdated. In many ways the document still reflected the hopes and visions which the unions held during the period immediately following the end of World War II and lasting until the outbreak of the Cold War in late 1947. One has the feeling that the Munich Program tried to ignore – perhaps a bit naively – the crucial events of the previous four years. One is struck by the Munich Program's radical bent and socialist overtones. Both in its formulation of co-determination and in its support of public ownership of significant portions of the West German economy, the document clearly reflects a socialist – albeit decidedly anti-Leninist – worldview. The program's overall aim remained the fundamental transformation of German capitalism, something which organized labor hoped to achieve immediately after the war, but which had already grown distant by the late 1940s and became virtually hopeless with the creation of the Federal Republic in 1949. Yet it would be wrong to see this anti-capitalism purely in socialist terms. True to the DGB's nature as an Einheitsgewerkschaft, many of the radical ideas – especially concerning worker participation and the larger aspects of co-determination – also explicitly incorporated elements of Christian socialism and the traditions of radical Catholicism, both of which also rejected the primacy of capitalism as the vehicle for reconstruction in West Germany.[33]

Characteristic of German organized labor's frequent ambivalence and contradictory positions, the Munich Program could perhaps best be labeled anti-capitalist but not anti-systemic. It did not question the validity of the Federal Republic as a political entity, nor did it demand different political arrangements from the parliamentary system which began to rule West Germany in the summer of 1949. It firmly underlined organized labor's long-held belief in the values of liberal democracy and pledged the unions' support for a constitutional order in the Federal Republic. It merely hoped to transform this order into a true democracy by reforming its capitalist structure into an egalitarian system of production characterized by economic democracy and full-parity worker participation. The existing West German system was acceptable to the unions; their program, however, would improve it substantially. Viewed in this perspective, the trade unions' founding program represented as much wishful thinking and homage to bygone traditions as it did a blueprint for concrete union strategies. As to the latter, the unions should have issued a more pragmatic document concentrating on medium-term conflict management.

The first setback for the unions occurred in the formulation of the constitution, the Basic Law.[34] The Basic Law guarantees the freedom to choose one's occupation, and it safeguards each individual's liberty to select a job. It also explicitly forbids any kind of forced labor. Yet, to the chagrin of the unions, it fails to guarantee every citizen's right to work. Furthermore, the Basic Law remains completely silent concerning important aspects of social policy and welfare such as the state's obligation to help the poor and disadvantaged. Lastly, while being very cryptic – indeed quite contradictory – about the role of property and ownership in the Federal Republic, the Basic Law certainly lends itself to an interpretation which holds private ownership as the most fundamental economic and civil right. Although the document does not state a preference for one economic system over any other – thus capitalism enjoys no greater constitutional legitimacy than socialism – the fact that the Basic Law mentions property in numerous prominent places has led to court rulings which came close to the interpretation that capitalism and a free-market economy based on private property are constitutionally anchored.

Labor was particularly perturbed about these points in the Basic Law because they represented a lessening of the protection afforded some of the unions' most likely constituents by the constitutions of some states. Both Hesse and Bavaria, for example, constitutionally guaranteed their citizens the right to work. Some states, including Hesse, explicitly forbade employers to use the lockout under any circumstances. Moreover, other state constitutions contained clauses concerning social policy, worker participation, property rights and even the socialization of some industries, making them a good deal more favorable to organized labor than the Basic Law. This development (whereby the unions were essentially excluded from the constitution) derived largely – according to Pirker and other experts – from the unions' own inertia and lack of interest in constitutional issues.[35] Labor simply failed to recognize the extreme importance of the Basic Law for further court rulings on industrial conflict, and wrote it off as being the primary concern of political parties rather than interest organizations such as trade unions. The union leadership's indifference to the constitutional question could best be illustrated by the fact that this matter was not discussed at the DGB's founding congress in Munich.

Another setback befell the unions on August 14, 1949, when West Germans elected their first parliamentary representatives. Much to organized labor's disappointment, the first Bundestag witnessed the triumph of the bourgeois parties led by Adenauer's CDU and the concomitant defeat of the Social Democrats, who thus were relegated to the benches of the opposition. The election yielded the following results: CDU/CSU 31%, SPD 29.2%, FDP/DVP 11.9%, KPD 5.7%, Bavarian Party 4.2%, German Party 4.0%, Center party 3.1%, Association for Economic Reconstruction 2.9%, with the remainder going to a host of smaller parties.[36] While members of the CDU's labor wing hoped for a grand coalition with the Social Democrats along lines analogous to the trade unions' construct of the Einheitsgewerkschaft, the party's increasingly predominant business representatives preferred a "bourgeois bloc" led by the pro-Western chancellor Konrad Adenauer and dominated by the economic policies of Ludwig Erhard. The CDU's clear choice favoring its capital side to the detriment of its labor orientation proved conclusively that the Ahlener Program had been replaced by the Düsseldorf Program. But the SPD, too, preferred to act as the major opposition rather than compromise its position in a grand coalition with the CDU. In so doing, the Social Democrats did not expect to influence the government over the next four years from the opposition benches, but rather believed that they would appear untainted to the West German voters in 1953 and win, giving them the opportunity to restructure the West German political economy in the direction of democratic socialism. In the meantime, however, organized labor's great hope in parliament lay more or less fallow. The SPD certainly did not possess the power to legislate the reforms desired by the unions. Parliament soon developed into the foremost political institution in the new republic, and from it emanated a wave of attacks on labor's position in West German society. Instead of developing into one of the unions' most reliable supporters, the Bundestag became the prime instigator of the general rollback to which labor and its allies were subjected in the early 1950s. This became especially evident in the battle over Mitbestimmung in 1950–51 and the conflict over a works constitution act, which was eventually passed by the Bundestag in 1952.

At a time when the unions hoped that co-determination, as already practiced in the Federal Republic's iron, steel and coal industries, would be extended to the rest of the West German economy, the employers started a major offensive to rescind Montanmitbestimmung. What the unions anticipated would be a victorious stuggle soon turned into a defensive battle in which organized labor had to muster all its available resources to defend a rather feeble status quo. As mentioned, the unions viewed the co-determination law of 1947, passed under the political and legal aegis of the Allies (especially the British), as a welcome start to a much more ambitious project, the democratization of the German economy and ultimately society as well. This law appeared to the employers, however, as a bothersome interference with their managerial prerogatives over the most fundamental aspects of a capitalist order, the rights and responsibilities connected with the ownership of private property.

The conflict over Montanmitbestimmung dates back to November 1948 when the Allied powers decreed Law No. 75 by which the ultimate decisions concerning property arrangements in Germany's steel, iron and coal industries were to be left to a German government.[37] Having sidestepped perhaps the most controversial question of co-determination, the Allies bequeathed the first West German government a very troublesome issue. Beginning with the establishment of the republic and reinforced by the decisive victory of the bourgeois parties in the Bundestag elections of August 1949, West German capital initiated a major campaign in state and society to rescind Allied laws and conditions in the country's Montan industries and replace them with German ones. Invoking the issue of sovereignty in support of their cause, the employers insisted that a law be passed by the newly constituted Bundestag, which would not only continue to return property confiscated by the Allies to their rightful German owners, but also re-institute German property laws and conduct of management, to replace Allied decrees dating from a period when Germany was not an autonomous state. In May 1950, Allied Law No. 75 was replaced by German Law No. 27 which prohibited further break-ups of existing companies in the Montan area, returned property administered by the Allies to their pre-war German owners and generally legitimized the rehabilitation of many German industrialists whose involvement in Hitler's regime was more than marginal. Moreover, in the wake of this law's "Germanization," it became clear that the co-determination scheme developed under Allied rule would be regarded as an alien construct by the employers and their political supporters, and would have to be replaced by German ways. When it was made public in November 1950 that the economics ministry was working to develop a plan for the West German steel, iron and coal industries in accordance with Law No. 27 which would abolish Montanmitbestimmung, the unions acted with resolve and vigor to defend co-determination. Albeit a highly defensive battle by its very nature, it was to be the unions' only success during the period under consideration and for some time to come.[38]

Labor's ultimate success in rescuing Montanmitbestimmung resulted first and foremost from its unusually swift and convincing mobilization efforts, which sent a clear signal to the employers that the unions would stop at nothing to defend this crucial reform. The two unions directly affected by Montanmitbestimmung, IG Metall and IG Bergbau und Energie, conducted strike votes during December 1951 and January 1952 respectively whose results could not be dismissed by the employers and the government: 96% of the steel and iron workers organized by IG Metall and 92% of the miners belonging to IG Bergbau und Energie voted to strike to defend Montanmitbestimmung in their respective industries. When it became clear during the months of December and January that other DGB unions, with the coordinating help of the federation itself, would lend their support to the two unions, the government scheduled negotiations to reconsider its plan to abolish Montanmitbestimmung.

Almost of equal importance to labor's mobilization on behalf of Montanmitbestimmung was Konrad Adenauer's personal intervention in the dispute. There can be no doubt that Adenauer's active involvement and his close relationship to Hans Böckler – rather than his support for Montanmitbestimmung per se – furthered labor's cause by forcing the employers to moderate their position with their beloved chancellor's prestige on the line.

In an exchange of letters during November and December 1950, Adenauer and Böckler put forth the two views of co-determination in particular and the role of unions in a democratic society in general which were to dominate public debate over industrial relations for much of the 1950s. Essentially, the chancellor argued that parliament had to be the prime locus of politics in a liberal democracy. Unions and other interest groups – although legitimate members of the public community – were not to interfere with the exercise of democracy which consisted in the people electing their parliamentary representatives at constitutionally prescribed intervals. Adenauer conceived of a Rechtsstaat as unimpeded parliamentary rule by which all interest groups – including unions – had to abide if they wanted to remain democratic actors and participants.

Böckler argued that the chancellor's views of democracy were procedurally confined and emphasized form over content. Democracy surely had to mean more than just a periodic journey to a voting booth where one then surrendered political responsibility to a party. For Böckler, democracy necessitated participation on a more regular basis than provided by elections, parties and parliaments. In this context he stressed the content aspect of democracy, and cited worker participation as one of his main examples. Co-determination and unions, to Böckler, far from threatening democracy in a parliamentary system as Adenauer had argued, enhanced the citizenry's participatory responsibilities, thereby adding to the democratic nature of a Rechtsstaat.[39]

Despite the fundamental disagreements between Adenauer and Böckler regarding the nature of democracy and the role of organized labor therein, the chancellor openly supported the DGB chairman in his quest to retain Montanmitbestimmung. Three factors account for Adenauer's position: first, his personal respect and affection for Böckler definitely inclined him to move towards a favorable view of Montanmitbestimmung. Second, Adenauer was aware of the fact that co-determination had its roots in Christian thought, to which he had been close throughout his life. Indeed, he knew that it was around the concept of co-determination and worker participation that the two major traditions of German working-class politics – the socialist/social democratic and the Christian – coalesced following the internecine battles of the Weimar period and the subsequent tragedy of the Third Reich. Co-determination had an integrative role in addition to its participatory one, and this aspect appealed to the chancellor. The continued existence of Montanmitbestimmung seemed as great a concern to the CDU's labor wing as it did to the much larger number of social democratic unionists. However, it was essential to both and as such represented perhaps the most important common bond of the Einheitsgewerkschaft. Adenauer strongly favored this union formation for the long-run stability of the young republic. Third, Adenauer's support of the unions had another pragmatic reason. By the early 1950s, the DGB and most of its constituent unions had become such ardent supporters of Adenauer's foreign policy that they took the unusual move of disagreeing publicly with the SPD.[40] It was not so much the unions' vehement anti-communism which brought them closer to the CDU's foreign policy. After all, one could hardly think of a more explicitly anti-communist politician in the early years of West German politics than Kurt Schumacher, the chairman of the Social Democratic Party. Rather, it was Adenauer's orientation towards the West and his concomitant rejection of the Federal Republic's "eastern option" which much of West Germany's organized labor began to share with the CDU, in notable contrast to the "neutralism" and early "Ostpolitik" of the SPD. With Adenauer's help, the Bundestag psssed the co-determination law on April 10, 1951, maintaining virtually every feature of Montanmitbestimmung as originally decreed by the Allied powers in 1947.

In the meantime a tragedy had shaken the already beleaguered and embattled labor movement. Hans Böckler died unexpectedly on February 16, 1951. His charisma and genuine popularity among the workers and the West German public could not have been matched by anybody at the time, least of all by his unfortunate successor, Christian Fette, who became the second chairman of the DGB after having led the printers' and typesetters' union IG Druck and Papier. Shortly after coming to power, Fette became embroiled in another major showdown between labor on one side and employers and the state on the other: the conflict over a works constitution.

The struggle over the so-called Works Constitution Law (Betriebsverfassungsgesetz) concentrated on what could arguably be called the most essential aspect of working-class politics. The issue was labor's presence on the shop floor and the form of its representational power within West Germany's plants. As such, this complex of issues comprised all areas of labor participation, including the particular format called co-determination. Thus, the battle over Montanmitbestimmung originally represented only a sub-set of the larger problem of labor participation inside West German companies.

As already mentioned, one of the major union aims for the new republic was an extension of parity co-determination from steel, iron and coal to the rest of the West German economy. Toward that end, the unions entered into negotiations with the employers as early as January 1950, hoping to improve labor participation both within and outside the firm. The talks, known as the Hattenheim negotiations, ended disappointingly for the unions three months later. Although the employers agreed to the formation of so-called economic councils (which were to assume merely advisory tasks and consist of an equal number of labor and capital representatives) on the federal and state levels, they refused to yield concerning intra-firm participation by labor.[41] However, the latter dimension of co-determination was by far the more important of the two for the unions, and thus the DGB leadership decided to press matters further. In addition to continuing talks with the employers throughout the spring and summer of 1950, the unions once again demonstrated their "state fixation" by submitting a formal proposal for the reorganization of the West German economy to the federal government, the Bundestag and the Bundesrat (the Federal Council, the "upper house" of the West German bicameral legislature) in the hope that these channels would eventually produce a law providing organized labor with full-parity participation on the plant level.[42] The unions started a series of actions which has remained to this day the single most disappointing struggle in the post-World War II history of German labor.

From the first parliamentary discussion of this issue, held on July 27, 1950, it was clear that the bourgeois parties, led by the single-mindedly pro-business Free Democratic Party, were intent on legislating virtually the opposite of what the unions so desperately wanted. Briefly put, the employers and their parliamentary allies hoped to restrict – even eliminate

– labor's collective power on the shop floor by replacing the presence of unions with that of factory-oriented, syndicalist and highly particularistic works councils. Moreover, the representational power of these works councils would be further curtailed by an elaborate legal system which in essence tied them closer to the welfare of the company than to that of their ostensible clients, the workers. Indeed, these firm-oriented works councils were to become the only legal and official representatives of labor in its daily interaction with capital on the shop floors of West German plants. Far from granting full parity, the bourgeois parties adopted the employers' counter-offer to allow only one-third of a company's advisory board to represent the interests of labor, thus in essence negating any meaningful participation on the part of workers' delegates in the decision-making process.[43]

The unions failed over the next two years to design a comprehensive strategy to counter this devastating turn of affairs. Indeed, virtually every reliable account of this period conveys the image of a disorganized and aimless labor movement which could not make up its mind from one minute to the next. At one point, the leadership tried its luck by lobbying the parties of the Bundestag, only to denounce the legislative process soon thereafter and begin a mobilization of the rank and file. However, this tactic was often retracted before it could yield any tangible results. Only the printers' and typesetters' union managed to conduct a relatively well-organized two-day strike in late May 1952 protesting the imminent passage in the Bundestag of the new Works Constitution Law. (For details of this event see Chapters 2 and 7.) While it is true that the unions' room to maneuver was severely limited by an increasingly anti-labor atmosphere – a direct consequence of the near-hysteric levels that anti-communism had reached in West Germany's public discourse by 1952 – the ultimate passage of such a Works Constitution Law was in good part due to the DGB's failure to design appropriate counter-strategies vis-à-vis the state and the employers.[44] The actual law which passed the Bundestag on July 19, 1952 – a day officially described by the DGB as a "dark moment for democratic development in the Federal Republic" – contained all the union-curtailing measures described above. It banned the unions as the official shop-floor representatives of West German workers. The new representatives, the works councils, were forbidden by law to participate in strikes, prepare other measures which could potentially be detrimental to the welfare of the company, divulge company secrets to outsiders (i.e. unions) and the workers, or compromise their loyalty to their respective employers. In essence, this law confined the power of the works councils to matters of social policy, hiring and firing. With the unions' long-held wish of parity co-determination reduced to an all-but-meaningless one-third of the seats on a company's advisory board, organized labor was further away from economic democracy in 1952 than at any other time in its post-World War II history.[45]

The DGB's performance in this sorry affair was so poor that an unprecedented event occurred at its second congress in September 1952. The delegates voted Christian Fette out of office as chairman of the German Trade Union Federation. A union leader of comparable import- ance had never before – nor has one since – lost his job in a similar fashion. While Fette was an easily identifiable target in the wake of this disaster – and assigning faults to particular people is always simpler than searching for them in the structures and actions of complex organizations – there can be no doubt that the vacillations of the DGB chairman imposed severe leadership problems on organized labor in an hour of great need. Walter Freitag, who had been the head of IG Metall, was elected the DGB's new chairman at the federation's second congress.[46]

The events surrounding the passage of the Works Constitution Law had two additional consequences which further aggravated the unions' already precarious existence. First, they led to a wide-ranging public debate about the role of trade unions in liberal democracy, which – given the conserva- tive Zeitgeist – hardly turned in labor's favor. Conservative legal theorists suggested a number of models designed to curtail the unions' purported power and prevent them from turning a Rechtsstaat into a Gewerkschafts- staat, a frequently cited concept during this period.[47] One of the outcomes of this debate was the establishment of the Federal Labor Court in Kassel in 1954, which – as discussed in Chapter 2 – further restricted the unions' freedom of action by increasing the juridification of an already highly formalized legal interaction between capital and labor.[48]

Second, the episode left the unions in such a bind that they lost confidence in their own strength and scurried for outside help. It is not surprising that to many union leaders at the time – including Walter Freitag – the only available assistance came from labor's trusted ally, the Social Democratic Party. Lacking confidence in its own abilities, the DGB increasingly turned to the SPD to such an extent that during the campaign for the 1953 Bundestag elections the labor federation openly supported the Social Democrats by choosing the thinly veiled slogan "vote for a better Bundestag."[49] This clearly violated one of the most fundamental tenets of the Einheitsgewerkschaft which – while not demanding political neutrality from individual union members – definitely required strict non- partisanship from the organization's official line. Sure enough, this slogan not only incurred the wrath of Konrad Adenauer and other conservatives who now had further evidence of union interference in legislative politics (thus confirming their alarmist vision of the Federal Republic's alleged transformation into a Gewerkschaftsstaat) but it led some CDU unionists to threaten to break away from the DGB since in their opinion the latter had developed into one of the SPD's main "transmission belts," thereby forsaking its mandate as an Einheitsgewerkschaft.[50]

The tension between SPD and CDU unionists continued well into the mid-1950s. In the Bundestag elections of 1953, the SPD suffered heavy losses, in part because of the DGB's open support for the Social Democratic Party, an endorsement which created apprehension among many West German voters, who under different circumstances might have cast their ballots for the Social Democrats. By late 1953 things looked bleak for the DGB. It had lost a major battle with the employers and the state, failed to attain its desired reforms and seen its confidence badly shaken. The DGB seemed finally convinced that if it continued to define as part of its task the fundamental transformation of West German capitalism, it was going to fight a costly and increasingly unpopular battle. The new task facing the unions was to improve the situation at the margin. It was time for the DGB to seek different and less ambitious projects for the years ahead.

## III. THE SEARCH FOR LEADERSHIP AND DIRECTION BETWEEN ACTIVISM AND ACCOMMODATIONISM: 1953-1959

With the SPD's resounding defeat in the Bundestag elections of September 9, 1953, and the DGB's disastrous setback concerning the passage of the Works Constitution Law in the summer of 1952, major reforms for organized labor seemed unattainable with the help of the state. Moreover, it had become quite clear that the unions' desire to form a massive countervailing power (Gegenmacht), with definite socialist overtones, to the steadily solidifying capitalist restoration in the Federal Republic was leading the labor movement towards defeat and marginalization in the political economy of West Germany. An increasingly complacent working class, preoccupied with augmenting its immediate material well-being in a growingly depoliticized culture, seemed an unlikely revolutionary subject. Fewer and fewer workers were moved by the virtues of economic democracy. Instead, they concentrated on increasing their paychecks in order to partake of West Germany's "economic miracle." If the DGB and its constituent unions were not to lose relevance for most workers, as indeed the declining membership figures of the period indicate they were already doing, the labor movement had to reorient its program by emphasizing more immediate, "bread and butter" issues rather than the grand schemes of societal transformation via economic democracy. The DGB's proposal to scale down its program of reform was a necessary solution to organized labor's precarious situation in late 1953. While the DGB clearly did not neglect the "big" issues related to state and society, objective conditions forced it to devise concrete strategies for the here and now.

The full impetus for this reorientation came from Viktor Agartz in the late fall of 1953 through his concept of "expansive wage policy." Using his influence as director of the DGB's research institute, WWI (Wirtschafts-wissenschaftliches Institut der Gewerkschaften, later to be renamed Wirt-schafts- und Sozialwissenschaftliches Institut des DGB – WSI), Agartz argued in a now famous article in the December 1953 issue of the institute's journal that organized labor's primary task consisted in demanding the highest possible wages in every bargaining round with the employers.[51] Agartz's argument comprised three components which in many ways reflected the disposition of most West German unions at the time. Agartz held that labor's expansive wage demands benefitted not only labor but indeed society as a whole. Higher wages would continue to increase consumption, and hence foster full employment and continued economic prosperity. This aspect of Agartz's argument clearly included a Keynesian interpretation of wage policy and its role in a country's economy, especially in its emphasis on generating growth and full employment. The "positive sum" nature of this interpretation of wages helped the unions in their desperate attempt to shed their image as spoilers and trouble-makers, and assisted them in convincing the rest of West German society that the fulfillment of their wage interests was to the benefit of all.

Second, and in logical contradiction to the first point, Agartz's argument about expansive wage policy included a highly particularistic component. Citing the predominantly interest-group-oriented American unions as models, Agartz embraced the latter's "business unionism" as a panacea for the bargaining behavior of West German unions. Unions, after all, were in "business" to maximize the earning power of their members. In failing that, they abdicated perhaps their most important mandate, almost to the point of losing their *raison d'être*. Thus Agartz encouraged unions in the Federal Republic to formulate their wage demands by keeping only the interests of their respective memberships in mind.

This aspect of Agartz's argument corresponded with yet another, Marxist, component. Ultimately, Agartz noted, all wage issues remained power issues. Wage levels reflected the political strength of the working class at a given time in its perennial conflict with capital. It was up to the unions to make certain that the collective strength of labor did not deteriorate. Thus, Agartz concluded, there was a direct link between the organizational power of the working class and the remuneration which it commanded in the economy.[52]

Agartz's article had an immediate impact. It voiced concerns that a number of union activists had contemplated but failed to articulate. "Expansive wage policy" provided some leading unionists with the intellectual framework necessary to derive concrete steps for the reorientation of union strategy. In so-called circles of five, six or ten, union activists met throughout the first half of 1954 to adapt Agartz's argument to union politics.[53] IG Metall's charismatic new leader, Otto Brenner, was particularly intrigued by Agartz's ideas. In them, he saw a possibility of continuing some of the unions' radical traditions as articulated in the DGB's Munich Program, while at the same time conforming labor politics to the reality of capitalism's successes in the mid-1950s. To Brenner, Agartz's essay represented the ideal stepping-stone for a reformulation of union strategies, relying less on grandiose schemes to be implemented with the help of external agents such as political parties and the state, emphasizing instead the unions' autonomous strength in the area of collective bargaining. In this realm Brenner envisioned the possibility of a labor offensive. This theme formed the center-piece of Brenner's keynote address to IG Metall's third congress in August 1954.[54] He demanded that his own union initiate the creation of a short-term "action program" (Aktionsprogramm) which then was to become official DGB policy. Thus began the campaign for the DGB's Aktionsprogramm.

Brenner wasted no time in implementing his ideas. He recognized the opportunity that this issue provided for him to influence the federation's policies via the strength of his union. Shortly after the conclusion of IG Metall's third congress, Brenner and his allies made certain that the Aktionsprogramm would dominate the DGB's third congress held in Frankfurt in October 1954. Indeed, to maximize exposure of his concern, Brenner prevailed upon Viktor Agartz himself to deliver the keynote speech at the federation's congress.

Entitled "Economic Policy and Taxation – Fundamental Issues and Program of the DGB," Agartz delivered a three-hour-long speech touching on virtually every issue relevant to organized labor in West Germany.[55] His speech, interrupted numerous times by thunderous applause from the delegates, demonstrated the peculiar predicament in which the unions found themselves during the mid-1950s. On one hand, Agartz fondly invoked the sweeping radicalism of the DGB's Munich Program and repeatedly extolled the virtues of – and the necessity for – economic democracy and the socialization of key industries. On the other hand, he focused on the bread-and-butter micro-radicalism favored by Otto Brenner which was to form the core of the DGB's new Aktionsprogramm. In this context he mentioned the importance of the 40-hour work week, the implementation of an "active wage policy" (which was a slightly deradicalized version of what formerly was known as "expansive wage policy"), and other reforms to be attained via collection bargaining. Brenner's ploy worked superbly. The combination of his pragmatic activism and Agartz's intellectual radicalism secured the adoption of the Aktionsprogramm by the federation's delegates, thus making this new approach official union strategy. On May Day 1955, the DGB announced the Aktionsprogramm to the rest of the world. Among its main demands were

- the introduction of the 40-hour work week;
- sick pay for blue-collar workers equal to that of white-collar employees;
- equal pay for men and women;
- additional vacation pay and Christmas bonuses;
- extension of co-determination;
- improved standard of living for all through higher wages;
- improved work safety;
- higher job security;
- more and better possibilities for vocational training and education.[56]

While the preamble of this program reaffirms at great length the validity of the unions' founding principles established at the Munich congress in 1949, the very existence of this reminder conveys the fact that most unionists realized that the days when these ideals would once again be relevant to labor were far in the future. The Aktionsprogramm, in notable contrast to the Munich Program, fully accepted the parameters of capitalism. According to the new document, the unions' task was not to transform – or even reform – capitalism, but to maximize labor's gains within it. Co-determination was no longer the vehicle toward economic democracy, but one of a number of means to augment labor's bargaining position vis-à-vis capital. Simply put, the DGB's Aktionsprogramm represented a compromise with reality. In justifying the passage of the Aktionsprogramm nearly 18 months after its announcement, its chief architect, Otto Brenner, explained to the delegates of the DGB's fourth congress the compromise character of the new strategy: on one hand, it upheld the increasingly utopian notion that labor could realize the demands formulated by the Munich Program. On the other hand, it recognized that power relationships in parliament were such that labor could not expect any support from that institution in the foreseeable future. Thus, the necessity arose of finding new channels which relied only on the unions themselves to achieve realistic, short-term goals.[57]

The immediate impact of the Aktionsprogramm was organizational. It not only strengthened Otto Brenner's position in the labor movement, because he was for all intents and purposes the program's originator and main supporter, but it also allocated more power to the constituent unions by emphasizing collective bargaining, which was the exclusive prerogative of each individual union. The new program weakened the DGB and signaled a decisive shift in power away from the federation to its constituent members. It was especially IG Metall, due to its size and prominence in collective bargaining, which profited the most from the Aktionsprogramm. Indeed, it helped IG Metall (partly via the union's active implementation of the program's major terms) to become the un-challenged hegemonic force in the DGB until the federation's congress in 1959. IG Metall's negotiation of the so-called Bremen Accord, which intro-duced the coveted 40-hour work week, and the gruelling 16-week-long strike in Schleswig-Holstein's metal industry to attain sickness benefits for blue-collar workers identical to those enjoyed by their white-collar counterparts, earned IG Metall the respect – as well as envy – of many of its sister unions in the DGB federation. (For more on these events see the detailed discussion of IG Metall in Chapter 4.)

The federation itself encountered difficult times independent of IG Metall's rise to predominance in the wake of the Aktionsprogramm. Ever since Hans Böckler's untimely death, the DGB had suffered from a serious lack of leadership, hitherto perhaps its most important asset and most potent political weapon. Christian Fette, Böckler's successor, endured the ignominious defeat of the Works Constitution Law which led to his dis-missal as described. The DGB's next leader, Walter Freitag, was no more charismatic or resolute than his predecessor. His blunder in openly supporting the SPD's campaign for the 1953 Bundestag elections cost him dearly, especially among unionists belonging to the Christian wing of the labor movement. Freitag never succeeded in regaining the confidence of many disenchanted unionists who identified with the CDU or the other bourgeois parties. Yet he also failed to win the loyalty and respect of the activists around Otto Brenner, thus remaining a lonely and powerless figure, aptly symbolizing the decreasing authority of the federation as a whole. Freitag's successor, Willi Richter, who assumed the DGB's leader-ship at the union's fourth congress held in 1956, asserted no more authority than his predecessors. Conforming to the Zeitgeist, Richter was an expert on social policy, which formed one of the key areas of the unions' new effort as delineated by the Aktionsprogramm. More importantly, Richter was no match for the IG Metall leader, whose interests and ambitions required the presence of a weak DGB leader. In the late 1950s, the leadership problem of the DGB contributed to the centrifugality of West Germany's organized labor movement. Analogies between the DGB and the Holy Roman Empire seemed increasingly accurate. In both, the nominal leader was often a weak, compromise candidate who did not interfere in the affairs of his much more powerful underlings: vassals in the case of the Empire, heads of industrial unions in the case of the DGB.[58]

Another problem for the DGB arose in the wake of its third congress held in the fall of 1954. A number of delegates and union members, virtually all in the Christian camp of the labor movement, were perturbed by Viktor Agartz's keynote address. They vehemently disapproved of its Marxist language and what they considered its inflammatory message. Furthermore, some of the CDU-oriented members of the DGB were also annoyed by the anti-militarist sentiment which dominated this DGB congress perhaps as much as did the discussion concerning the adoption of the Aktionsprogramm. The strong language of a Brenner-led initiative denouncing the impending remilitarization of West Germany particularly irked some conservative union members. By 1955, disaffection with the DGB's alleged radicalism and its closeness to social democracy led a handful of unionists to break away from the DGB and form their own trade union federation called the Christliche Gewerkschaftsbewegung Deutschlands (CGD), renamed Christlicher Gewerkschaftsbund (CGB) in 1959.[59] Yet, the fact that this organization never achieved any significance in West German industrial relations and – more importantly – that it provoked bitter criticism from virtually every political group in the Federal Republic, including the employers' associations, the two churches and the CDU/CSU, attests to the ubiquitous and well-entrenched legitimacy of the Einheitsgewerkschaft in West Germany by the mid-1950s.

While the DGB's reorientation, spurred by the Aktionsprogramm and IG Metall's implementation of it in the bargaining arena, kept organized labor's collective attention away from the state, it would be wrong to interpret this as complacency on the part of the unions regarding the political issues preoccupying West Germany at the time. With the exception of the ultimately insignificant secession by a small minority of Christian unionists, no topic of the period elicited a more spirited discussion and unified response on the part of organized labor than the issue of West Germany's remilitarization in preparation for its joining the North Atlantic Treaty Organization. Still bearing the traumas associated with the Kapp Putsch and deeply suspicious of the profoundly anti-democratic tradition of the old German military establishment, the unions developed an almost instinctive fear of the reintroduction of a major military force in the Federal Republic. Many unionists were convinced at the time that the creation of the Bundeswehr would severely endanger – perhaps even eliminate – the feeble democracy which was gaining stability and legitimacy for the first time in German history.[60] Indeed, the DGB and many members of its constituent unions "unofficially" joined the SPD-initiated "Paulskirche Movement for the Unification of Germany and Against Rearmament", which was a loose association of various extra-parliamentary groups constituted in the spring of 1955. The DGB, while preserving the vehement anti-communism which it had adopted in the early 1950s, changed its attitude somewhat concerning the desirability of West Germany's full integration into the Western alliance, since this would have meant the postponement of German reunification until the distant future. In line with the SPD's thinking at the time, the unions favored a unified Germany free of military attachments to either of the two super-powers.[61]

The unions' shift in position vis-à-vis West Germany's impending NATO membership and reunification can be attributed to several factors: first, none of the top labor leaders had nearly as cordial a relationship with Konrad Adenauer as did Hans Böckler. This in essence meant that the DGB leadership was not as obliged to follow Adenauer's policies, including his unmitigatedly pro-Western orientation. Second, the unions – just like the Social Democratic Party – were still convinced that a unified Germany would strengthen their cause, since it would entail the inclusion of some of organized labor's main bastions located in the German Democratic Republic. Moreover, a unified Germany would have weakened the political position of the Catholics in West Germany's public life. Thus, it was especially the avowed Social Democcrats in the unions who espoused German unification as a desirable political course for the West German labor movement. Third, there can be no doubt that some labor leaders drew a strong connection between West Germany's remilitarization and its integration into the Western alliance. Vehemently opposed to the former, they inevitably became suspicious of the latter. Labor's fear of NATO and West Germany's role therein became even more pronounced during 1957–58 when heated controversy arose concerning the acquisition of atomic weapons for the new Bundeswehr. This met with massive and unified labor opposition.

Although the unions had definitely given up their anti-capitalist reformism of the late 1940s and early 1950s many activists in the DGB still maintained a certain ambivalence about the Federal Republic as it was constituted in the mid-1950s.[62] They mistrusted the state and the employers, both of whom they regarded as unreliable guardians of democracy. For the unions in the mid-1950s, West Germany was a decent place, but one which needed serious improvement in order to win labor's wholehearted support. The unions' ambivalence stemmed partly from their defeats of the early 1950s. However, it also derived from the internal problems, both organizational and strategic, which the DGB and its constituent unions had failed to resolve by the mid- to late 1950s. IG Metall's preeminence in virtually every aspect of the DGB's policy-making was uncontested during this period. Yet this was to change by the end of the decade because of another series of costly intra-DGB battles among some of the largest and most important unions. As usual, these confrontations involved a mixture of personal rivalries, organizational conflicts and ideological disagreements as to what strategies labor should pursue.

Even as the unions, led by IG Metall, were scoring impressive victories during the late 1950s by implementing the Aktionsprogramm through collective bargaining, resentment was growing at DGB headquarters and among many constituent unions towards the giant metalworkers' union and its flamboyant chief, Otto Brenner. (The union was labelled "IG Krawall" [The Trouble Union] at DGB headquarters.) The complaints centered around one issue: in their zeal to put the Aktionsprogramm into effect in the minimum amount of time, Otto Brenner and his union had repeatedly broken union solidarity by dictating a tempo and program which most other unions simply could not follow.[63] IG Metall's accomplishments, while acknowledged by the leaders of most DGB unions, were regarded as burdensome since they placed great pressure on other members to follow the pace dictated by the metalworkers. An informal but determined anti-IG Metall coalition emerged within the DGB by 1958 opposing the union's strategies and, perhaps even more importantly, its leader. Initially headed by Heinrich Gutermuth, the leader of the miners' union (IG Bergbau und Energie), this coalition began a challenge to IG Metall's predominance which eventually went well beyond a personal criticism of Otto Brenner's leadership style. In its opposition to IG Metall, the coalition set out to revise union strategy from top to bottom. In marked contrast to IG Metall's activism and confrontationism, they advocated accommodation and social partnership as the proper strategies for labor. The battle between these two camps within the DGB dominated the federation's congress in 1959 and determined union politics well into the mid-1960s, with its legacy informing conflicts within the West German labor movement to this day.

The controversy between the activists or reformers led by IG Metall and joined by the chemical workers', printers', wood workers' and leather workers' unions on the one hand, and the social partners or accommodationists consisting of the miners', construction workers', textile workers' and public employees' unions on the other, had its antecedents in labor politics of the Weimar Republic when the DGB's social democratic predecessor, the ADGB, witnessed repeated confrontations between the so-called council democrats and the social partners.[64] The former, mainly represented by IG Metall's forerunner, the DMV (Deutscher Metallarbeiter Verband) favored a confrontational strategy vis-à-vis the employers, and demanded worker control of the economy through a series of workers' councils on the plant, firm and regional levels which would regulate both investment and production. The social partners advocated an acommodationist strategy toward both the state and capital. They favored a form of corporatist cooperation among unions, employers and the state in regulating "microeconomic" issues related to collective bargaining, as well as "macroeconomic" ones concerned with the formulation of national economic policy.

Similar problems separated the two wings of the West German labor movement in the late 1950s.[65] IG Metall and its activist allies still believed in the overall validity of the DGB's Munich Program even though they conceded that its fulfillment had to await a more auspicious time. Still, they viewed labor's role in a capitalist society as essentially antinomian. Indeed, it was precisely the unions's position as a Gegenmacht which, according to this view, was the best – perhaps the only – guarantor of a continued democracy under capitalism. While IG Metall's concentration on implementing the terms of the Aktionsprogramm conveyed a sense of pragmatism concerning labor's situation within West German capitalism, it in no way intended to undermine the unions' adversary role vis-à-vis the state and the employers. In the activist view, the Aktionsprogramm was never meant to preempt labor's eventual goals as expressed in the still much revered Munich Program. If anything, the former was to complement the latter.

In notable contrast to the activists, the social partners did not speak about capitalism. To them the Federal Republic had become an ideal democracy, in which labor should participate in an orderly fashion, rather than attempt to expand it via radical schemes such as the Munich Program. Organized labor's role in the Federal Republic, according to this view, was to help "order" the already existing and highly legitimate system so as to facilitate its smooth and democratic operation. The unions were to represent a pillar of support, an Ordnungsfaktor, rather than a source of antagonism and confrontation.[66] In line with their full acceptance of conditions in the Federal Republic, the social partners sought to abolish the Munich Program and replace it with a document much more moderate in tone and content. In particular, the program's call for nationalizations, its radical interpretation of democracy and its quasi-Marxist language bothered the social partners. The most conservative of the accommodationist unions, the construction workers' union (IG Bau-Steine-Erden), was so eager to put Munich behind it that it unilaterally eliminated the nationalization clause from its bylaws as early as 1957, six years prior to the DGB's less comprehensive action in the same direction.

The social partners saw their first chance to weaken IG Metall's hegemony following the Bundestag elections of 1957. The third decisive defeat for the Social Democrats in as many federal parliamentary elections initiated a major reevaluation process in the party as well as in all of social democracy's ancillary areas of influence, which of course included the unions. Adenauer's third convincing victory – which this time even yielded an absolute majority for the Christian Democrats – forced the Social Democrats to consider new paths that might eventually lead to greener pastures. Thus developed the SPD's famous Bad Godesberg reform which, very much to the liking of the social partners among the West German unions, shed social democracy's Marxist past and embraced its Keynesian future. IG Metall's – and especially Otto Brenner's – staunch opposition to the SPD's Godesberg reforms weakened the giant union's intra-DGB position somewhat. While nominally independent of party affiliations, there can be no doubt that a change of such magnitude in the fundamental orientation of the Social Democratic Party had profound theoretical repercussions and practical implications for the DGB and its unions. The SPD's Godesberg policy undoubtedly strengthened the accommodationists within the DGB federation at the direct expense of the activists, most notably IG Metall.

Another event worked in the accommodationists' favor by delivering a crushing blow to IG Metall. The Federal Labor Court ruled at the end of 1958 that IG Metall's sixteen-week-long strike in Schleswig-Holstein in 1956–57 was illegal, and ordered the union to pay over DM 100 million in damages to the employers. Since many observers, both inside and outside the unions, blamed the Court's decision on a tactical error committed by Brenner during the strike, his reputation and that of his union were seriously tarnished.[67] Brenner's room for maneuvering within the DGB was severely limited for the time being, especially since the magnitude of the penalty would have hurt the coffers of any union, even one the size of IG Metall. In short, by intimidating IG Metall, the Federal Labor Court also curtailed the metalworkers' hegemony within the DGB. With its confidence badly shaken, IG Metall led a lackluster bargaining round in 1959, producing only modest gains for its members. This was the long-awaited chance for the social partners to make their move against Brenner and his allies. The opportunity presented itself at the DGB's fifth official congress held in Stuttgart in September 1959.

Although overshadowed by the SPD's impending Bad Godesberg Congress set for October 1959, the DGB's Stuttgart convention also witnessed important milestones in the politics of the West German labor movement. The accommodationists succeeded – against furious resistance by IG Metall and its allies – in persuading the delegates to accept a resolution which called for the establishment of a committee charged with revising the Munich Program by creating a completely new document of equal weight.[68] The committee was then to present the draft of this new "basic program" (Grundsatzprogramm) to the DGB's next congress in 1962, at which point the delegates were to vote on its adoption as the labor movement's definitive guideline. The accommodationists' success in initiating this programmatic reform was in good part due to the appearance of a powerful and charismatic new leader who was Otto Brenner's match in every way. Georg Leber, the young head of the construction workers' union, emerged at the Stuttgart congress as the unchallenged spokesman for the social partners – and Otto Brenner's nemesis. This congress also witnessed the emergence of Ludwig Rosenberg (who would become the DGB's new chairman at the federation's Hanover congress held in 1962). Rosenberg, who was elected the DGB's vice chairman at the Stuttgart congress, had spent thirteen years (1933–46) exiled in England. It was there that he developed into an enthusiastic supporter of Keynesianism, which he long sought to see the West German unions adopt as the official principle for economic policy.

It was not by chance that the Stuttgart congress saw the rise of both Rosenberg and Leber. Each in his own way represented important changes which organized labor was undergoing at the end of the 1950s. But Otto Brenner and his allies could not yet be counted out. The struggle between Brenner and Leber – and Rosenberg's diplomatic interventions between the two – dominated a divided labor movement for the first half of the 1960s.

## IV. THE DGB DIVIDED: 1960–1966

General developments in the West German political economy during the late 1950s and early 1960s made life difficult for the DGB as the prime representative of organized labor. The impressive successes celebrated by capitalism in the Federal Republic at this time led to a stagnation – indeed absolute decline – in union membership. The tight conditions of the labor market caused by the virtual absence of unemployment and the steady growth of the West German economy fueled a prosperity which was unparalleled in all of German history. Employers competed for scarce workers by bidding up their real wages, which at this time often dwarfed the contractual remunerations established in union agreements. In short, many workers who under different conditions might have joined the unions failed to see a reason for doing so. The economic Zeitgeist clearly made the unions seem extraneous to the immediate interests of many workers.

Accompanying this period of economic prosperity was an atmosphere of political conformity which certainly did not help the unions' cause. In addition to the Communist Party (KPD) having been declared unconstitutional in 1956 and the Federal Labor Court's ruling against IG Metall in 1958, there were a number of public events which extinguished the last vestiges of organized labor's radical opposition to the establishment of

West German capitalism. Godesberg attested to the final deradicalization of the West German working class. The political Zeitgeist certainly did not reward engagement on behalf of any potentially antinomian cause. While belonging to a union almost never implied a desire to change existing conditions, the period around 1960 seemed particularly unrewarding and unconducive in political terms for a worker to join organized labor.

In addition to the labor movement's inauspicious position deriving from the booming economy and the highly depoliticized and anti-radical political culture, the unions suffered as a result of major structural changes which had affected West German industry during the early 1960s. Most notable among the "losers" were the miners' union, the woodworkers' union and the textile workers' union. Among the unions discussed in this book, the construction workers' and printers' both lost members in the early 1960s. Other DGB unions, however, gained in membership, mainly as a consequence of structural shifts in the West German economy. The other two organizations subjected to a detailed study in this volume, IG Metall and IG Chemie-Papier-Keramik, both increased their membership throughout the early 1960s. The structural changes of West German industry initiated a major intra-DGB membership flux, altering the character of many relationships among the unions affected.[69] This development exacerbated organized labor's other problems which, although they did not result directly from fluctuations in West Germany's economy or society, originated in the organizational tensions described in the previous section of this chapter.

Especially notable among these intra-labor difficulties were the ongoing disagreements between the activists and the accommodationists concerning fundamental issues of union thought and action. These conflicts often reached a hostile level during the early 1960s, necessitating an institutionalized framework of reconciliation. In addition to the controversies between reformers and social partners, the DGB's subservience to the "vassals" heading the federation's constituent unions furthered the internal centrifugality. Indeed, if there was one area of agreement between activists and accommodationists it was precisely to keep the center merely as a mediator between the two wings, who would ultimately determine union policy. While these organizational difficulties continued to plague the DGB and its unions throughout the 1960s, a number of measures were instituted to counter the potentially detrimental ramifications of the conflict.

In order to make joining unions more attractive to non-organized workers, as well as to increase the retention rate of the organized labor force, the unions offered their existing and prospective members a variety of services and special deals during the late 1950s and early 1960s.[70] All these arrangements aimed to differentiate between unionized and non-unionized workers by helping the former at the direct expense of the latter. Thus, for example, some unions tried to institute advantages for their members by having the employers pay them more than the non-unionized workers in the same industry. Others aimed at quasi-closed-shop solutions where only union members would be offered employment.[71] Virtually every DGB union discussed the implementation of "advantage schemes" and preferential treatments (Vorteilsregelungen) which were explicitly designed to exclude those who, as "freeloaders" (Schwarzfahrer or Schmarotzer), gained all the contractual benefits that the union had achieved without having to bear the burdens and responsibilities of active union membership, such as paying the relatively high membership fees.[72] At this juncture some of the accommodationist unions, led by IG Bau-Steine-Erden, devised elaborate asset formation (Vermögensbildung) schemes for their members on an individual basis. (See Chapter 6 for details.) Conversely, the more collectivist reformers, led by IG Metall and IG Chemie, responded to this predicament by pushing for the implementation of plant-level collective bargaining agreements (betriebsnahe Tarifpolitik) which would enhance the unions' presence on the shop floor at the expense of the powerful works councils, thereby mobilizing organized as well as unorganized workers on the unions' behalf.[73] By instituting this kind of decentralized collective bargaining, its originators hoped that the widespread perception of a cumbersome and distant union bureaucracy would be diminished in favor of a more immediate union presence at the plant level. (See Chapters 4 and 5 on IG Metall and IG Chemie for further details concerning betriebsnahe Tarifpolitik.)

While some of these "advantage schemes" were successfully instituted and later developed into general union policy – such as, for example, IG-Bau-initiated asset formation – others, such as plant-level collective bargaining agreements advocated by IG Metall and IG Chemie, were rarely used in practice. Ultimately, however, the employers' resolve and West Germany's legal and constitutional framework impeded the unions' attempt to favor their members over unorganized workers in a substantial way. It was clearly not in management's interest to augment the unions' power by having them gain more for their members than for others, thereby enhancing the chance of non-organized workers joining the unions. The employers were aided in their opposition by an array of constitutional and legal doctrines ranging from the Basic Law to the Works Constitution Law of 1952, all of which in one form or another forbade favoritism of one party over another, making the closed-shop arrangements and similar "advantage schemes" favored by some unions virtually impossible. Thus, additional union responses were urgently needed.

To that end, the DGB's Stuttgart congress of 1959 empowered the federation and its constituent unions to reorganize their relationship to each other and draft a new union agenda to improve and update the unions' 1949 Munich Program. Regarding the intra-organizational problems of the federation, the congress mandated that by the next DGB congress plans should be worked out that would lead to "a substantial streamlining and coalescing of all union powers and measures."[74] This, however, failed to occur. While the delegates to the DGB's 1962 congress held in Hanover approved new bylaws for the federation, they hardly addressed the major problems of practical coordination between the DGB and its member unions, such as the equalization and administration of financial contributions by each union to the federation, collective strike funds, educational issues, common efforts in public relations, and, most important of all, the formulation and implementation of joint strategies. The bylaws decreed by the DGB's congress in 1962 did in fact entail some centralizing measures, though not the ones intended by the mandate of the Stuttgart convention. Rather than centralizing union power and decision-making, the bylaws merely led to an administrative centralization of the DGB itself. The federation's new statutes diminished the autonomy of the DGB on the state and local levels and upgraded the central administration's position in Düsseldorf. While reducing channels of democratic articulation within the DGB's organizational structure, the bylaws passed in Hanover failed to address the pressing problems of the federation's impaired relationship with its constituent members. These, of course, could never be dealt with adequately by any document, let alone one as formalistic as the bylaws of a large organization. It was not until an extraordinary DGB congress in 1971 that some of the organizational issues raised by the Stuttgart convention were finally resolved.[75]

The creation of a new union program to replace the DGB's founding document of 1949 witnessed the most pronounced conflict ever between the social partners and the activists. This battle raged throughout the early 1960s and had barely abated in 1963 when an extraordinary union congress convened in Düsseldorf to adopt the West German trade unions' second basic program. The program was a meticulous compromise deftly engineered by Ludwig Rosenberg, the DGB's new chairman, between the ideas of Georg Leber and the accommodationists on the one hand, and Otto Brenner and the reformers on the other.

Georg Leber and his colleagues viewed labor as an integrative element (Ordnungsfaktor) in advanced capitalist societies. The leader of IG Bau berated radicals as "advantgardists of the past," as idealists who still clung to the notion of workers as proletarians.[76] This ideology, so Leber believed, was no longer applicable in a free, democratic and prosperous society such as the Federal Republic's, where differences between workers and other social groups had been eliminated, in good part due to the valiant efforts of organized labor over the years. It was simply wrong, Leber argued, for some people "who could not see the forest through the trees ... to hope for a D-Day when capitalism would finally be abolished and freedom and progress would be ready to commence."[77] The essence of modern democracy was its inclusion of all citizens into the political process via the just franchise. Politics was to be conducted by the parties in a parliament whose legitimacy ultimately derived from the voter on election day. If the state governed in such a democratic fashion, it was by definition also a workers' state. The Federal Republic, to the social partners, was everybody's state. As Horst Katzor, a leading member of the railroad workers' union, GdED, stated at his union's congress in 1961: "This state here, this West German Federal Republic, dear friends, is *our* state. ... What is important to me is to defend freedom against all ultras, be they right or left."[78]

Since the state was everybody's state, it also followed for Leber and his colleagues that one had to accept and respect other groups within it. The social partners rejected the notion of classes and instead preferred to speak of interest associations. While these may have occasional differences over policy, they should respect each other. Labor's role in this new order was to improve the standing of its members in a gradual and measured way. It was not to challenge the system of which it had become a welcome and full-fledged partner.[79]

To Brenner and other activists, the Federal Republic represented a genuine Rechtsstaat which the unions were willing and ready to defend. But it was not a panacea, and its political and social arrangements still placed a disproportionate burden on the working class. While not revolutionary, the reformers espoused a modified Marxism which continued to analyze political controversy as class conflict, and perceived economic interaction in terms of an inherently antagonistic relationship between capital and labor. They also viewed production for private profit and its allocation by the free market as the essential dynamo for the system. Since equality of results rather than merely equality of opportunity remained the primary ingredient of democracy for the activists, they continued to view the political economy of the Federal Republic as flawed. Thus, far from believing that a partnership arrangement with the employers would most benefit the working class, the activists still held that a confrontational attitude by labor towards capital would not only benefit the former but in the very process enhance democracy for society as a whole. The reformers viewed both capital and labor as collective entities with conflicting interests rather than as conglomerations of different interest groups who could form permanent partnerships given the proper conciliatory attitude.

Because of this worldview Brenner and his colleagues were staunch opponents of the social partners' asset formation scheme which they regarded as unduly integrationist and coopting, since it was predicated on helping workers as individuals rather than as a collectivity. In short, the activists believed that the major tenets of the Munich Program, though largely unfulfilled, remained valid. The new program for Brenner had to be an improvement (Verbesserung) over the old one, not its "watering down" (Verwässerung).[80]

The stage was set at the DGB's congress in Hanover to work out a compromise between these two positions, which would then yield the labor movement's new basic program. However, the conflict over the so-called emergency laws divided the delegates along activist and accommodationist lines and embroiled them in such heated and extended discussions that they preempted the conclusion of the congress's main task.[81] Therefore, inauguration of this new program was postponed until a special conference held in Düsseldorf in 1963.

The emergency laws consisted of a package of legislation and constitutional amendments which aimed at expanding the government's power in the event of severe internal unrest. The idea for this constitutional revision emanated from the ranks of both the Christian Democratic and Free Democratic parties who felt that the Basic Law, as originally drafted, failed to give the government sufficient executive power in cases of national emergencies. Drafts of the amendment were introduced in the Bundestag in 1960 and 1962. The accommodationists and Godesberg adherents within the SPD quickly realized that this provided a good opportunity for them to underscore the Social Democratic Party's new image by supporting the amendment, while at the same time trying to eliminate some of its harsher provisions. The SPD approved of the emergency laws at this time, at least in theory if not in practice. The unions, on the other hand, split on this issue along expected lines, with IG Metall and the activists bitterly opposing any such constitutional reforms while IG Bau and the social partners basically echoed the SPD's muted support for the emergency laws. Characteristically, the DGB desperately tried to arrange a compromise between the two warring factions.[82]

At the congress itself, both wings summoned their major spokesmen to present their views on the emergency laws to the assembled DGB delegates. Otto Brenner did not shy away from likening the intent and potential effects of the laws to the establishment of a dictatorship in the Federal Republic. In his speech to the Hanover congress as well as in numerous subsequent addresses and articles, Brenner decried the fundamentally undemocratic nature of these laws, especially as far as the unions were concerned, since the laws included anti-strike measures and thereby posed a direct threat to labor's most potent weapon. Brenner and his allies, most of whom were members of IG Chemie, IG Druck und Papier, Gewerkschaft Holz and the public workers' and transport union ÖTV, frequently invoked German history to highlight the legitimacy of their opposition to these laws. In their advocacy of a general strike in case the Bundestag passed the emergency laws, the activists repeatedly referred to the Kapp Putsch in 1920, when it also fell to organized labor to act as defender of a feeble democratic order. The activists also cited the implementation of Article 48 of the Weimar constitution which, they argued, helped destroy the democratic institutions of the first German republic, and paved the way for Nazi dictatorship. Lastly, Brenner and his allies saw these emergency laws as ultimate expressions of a centralized, bureaucratized and dehumanized state whose prime concern was to uphold a mechanistic, technology-oriented and profit-dominated order, rather than the defense of its citizens' democratic rights and privileges.[83]

Leber and his supporters on the other hand, believed that the emergency laws, stripped of their anti-strike measures and their harshest passages concerning the curtailing of civil liberties, would help the Federal Republic – "our state" as it was often called by the social reformers – in defending its democratic order against incursions from any political extreme. In addition to an agreement on normative grounds, the accommodationist unions supported a modified version of the emergency laws as a matter of expediency and pragmatic assessment of political reality. Leber argued in Hanover that it was never going to be a question of *whether* but at best of *how* the emergency laws would be instituted in West Germany. Labor would only hurt its cause if it insisted on a "total no" by taking itself out of political discussion altogether, thereby losing any possibility of influencing the outcome.[84] In addition to Leber's own union, IG Bau, this view received support from the miners', the textile workers', the postal workers' and the railroad workers' unions.

The debate culminated in a vote in which 276 delegates rejected any union support for the emergency laws, while 138 approved such a measure. The unions did, however, show some unity in a later vote on this issue. With only two abstentions, all delegates cast their ballots in favor of conducting a general strike in case the democratic foundations of the republic and the democratic rights of individuals were threatened by the state or anyone else.[85] The DGB's new leader, Ludwig Rosenberg, who personally favored the emergency laws, did his best to represent the wishes of the congress in public, which endeared him to Otto Brenner. Yet, true to Rosenberg's position as mediator between the two wings, Georg Leber and his allies also felt included in the DGB leader's actions.

Over the next six years, organized labor – led almost exclusively by the activist unions IG Metall, IG Chemie and IG Druck und Papier – conducted major activities against the passage of the emergency laws in the Bundestag. As with their tradition of protesting the Federal Republic's re-armament in 1954 and the Bundeswehr's plan to acquire nuclear weapons in 1957, the unions' opposition to the emergency laws became their major activity in the political arena throughout much of the 1960s. It was largely this labor-led protest which forced the SPD to vote against the core of the legislation in 1965, after some of its ancillary segments had already been accepted by the Bundestag.

The debate about the emergency laws once again dominated the next DGB congress held in Berlin in May 1966. Just as in Hanover four years before, the delegates voted to express their dissatisfaction with the laws' incorporation into the legal and constitutional framework of the Federal Republic. The vote this time showed 251 congress participants opposed to the laws, with 182 delegates favoring them.[86] A few months after the Berlin congress, the activist unions joined a number of leading writers, journalists and intellectuals in a demonstration called "Democracy's Emergency." Attended by over 20,000 people from academia, the arts and the activist unions, this "congress' assumed a parallel role to the one played by the "Paulskirche movement" in the disarmament debate of the 1950s. Indeed, it could be viewed as one of the main events of the mid- to late 1960s which spawned West Germany's influential extra-parliamentary new left and its various intellectual heirs of the 1970s and the 1980s.

Nevertheless, the unions' opposition and protest remained largely verbal and programmatic. When the Bundestag passed a softened version of the emergency legislation package in the spring of 1968 with the support of the SPD's parliamentary representatives, including Georg Leber, even the activist unions desisted from taking more serious action than convening another meeting, this time in Dortmund. This gathering was the activists' response to a general call for a march on Bonn which occurred with minimal participation by organized labor, hence remaining virtually an exclusive affair of the Federal Republic's left-leaning intelligentsia.[87] The unions, as Leber had insisted in 1962, could not stop the passage of the emergency laws. They had to be content with issuing one last statement in May 1968 which warned that organized labor would never remain idle in case West German democracy was threatened.[88] The ultimate outcome pleased all parties: Leber and his social partners claimed victory, since a moderated version of the emergency laws had indeed been passed by the Bundestag. Brenner and his activists could always argue that they fought difficult odds against which total victory was almost impossible. Yet the West German labor movement could point with satisfaction to the fact that it had consistently and with large majorities rejected the emergency laws.

While the concrete results were unsatisfactory from the activists' point of view, the process itself led to a moral victory. Ultimately, Rosenberg, too, could rejoice in the outcome, which reflected his efforts at mediation and diplomacy. Rosenberg scored a major coup in successfully keeping both wings of his federation reasonably satisfied. It paled, however, in comparison to his masterpiece, which was the passage of the DGB's new basic program at a special congress in 1963 in Düsseldorf.

The DGB's Düsseldorf Program became the first all-encompassing union document since 1945, delineating in bold strokes organized labor's position on virtually all issues relevant to West German society in the 1960s.[89] Unlike the Munich Program of 1949, the DGB's Düsseldorf Program did not address itself exclusively to topics pertaining to political economy, but also contained a detailed section on social policy and cultural matters, the latter of which included such important items as labor's views on education, research, science and the arts.

In the preamble to this document, the compromises between the DGB's two wings were evident. While the preamble acknowledged the tremendous gains which workers had achieved in the previous years, the document further stated that "injustice in the distribution of income and wealth, dependence on the market and on private economic power, and inequality of educational opportunities have not been overcome."[90] There were other key passages which equally reflected input from either of the two factions. It was undoubtedly the activists who succeeded in placing the following sentences into the program's preamble: "Workers, the vast majority of the population, still remain excluded from the decision-making process over the means of production. Their labor power continues to this day to be their sole source of income."[91] On the other hand, it was probably the social partners who stated that "it continues to be the unions' task to expand the Rechtsstaat and to participate in the democratization of society as a whole. The unions are decisive forces of integration and impel the nation towards further democratic developments in the areas of politics, economics and culture."[92]

While the preamble still had important remnants of the Munich Program, it was largely the body of the program – and especially its economic section – which conveyed the victory of Keynes over Marx, thereby codifying the economic policies which the unions had practiced on a daily basis since the Aktionsprogramm of 1955. The economic section of the Düsseldorf Program was divided into three parts: the basic foundations of economic organization; the aims of economic policy; and the means of implementation. Concerning the first, the new program, like the old, focused on economic co-determination by workers as the basis of a free and humane social order. In contrast to Munich, however, the Düsseldorf

Program sought to accomplish this goal via the institutions of parliamentary democracy.

In the 1949 Munich Program the DGB listed the "socialization of key industries" as one of the prerequisites of a democratic economy. The Düsseldorf Program, in contrast, relegated this to the end of a long list of policy goals. Moreover, replacing "socialization of key industries" was a list of items which looked more like vague aims than fundamental principles:

- To give each individual the highest amount of freedom and responsibility, to let him participate in the formation of the economy on equal terms.
- To guarantee permanent employment suitable to personal needs.
- To achieve a just distribution of income and wealth.
- To facilitate an optimal growth of the economy.
- To impede the abuse of economic power.
- To use planning and competition to arrive at macroeconomic goals.
- To make possible the understanding of economic dependency by publishing appropriate information.

As to the aims of economic policy, the Düsseldorf Program seemed to depart little from its Munich predecessor. It highlighted the importance of full employment and related this goal to steady economic growth, a just distribution of income and wealth, and monetary stability. It also addressed key issues such as the responsibility of the democratic state to halt the abuse of economic power. It pointed to the necessity of price stability without which prior economic planning would be impossible. Price increases, the document argued, primarily affected workers, retired people and others on fixed incomes, and did so unjustly. Given the transformation of the international system and West Germany's increasing integration therein, the Düsseldorf Program emphasized the necessity of international economic cooperation and delineated the positive role the unions might play within the European Economic Community and vis-à-vis the Third World. (The Munich Program, understandably, contained very little on these matters.) Lastly, the new program addressed the area of technological innovation and automation, both of which it regarded as beneficial to the improvement of living standards and to the humanization of work. It warned, however, that rationalization and automation should always be monitored closely lest they endanger jobs.

Concerning the means with which the unions wished to implement their economic policy, the 1963 program reflected in many ways a moderation of the tone and substance of its predecessor from 1949. To begin with, the Düsseldorf Program's position on the issue of economic planning was considerably more moderate than Munich's. The 1949 program associated economic competition with a "chaotic market economy" which could only have adverse effects on workers. The 1963 program insisted on the need for what it called a "macroeconomic planning framework." In a modern, dynamic economy, the securing of full employment, steady economic growth and monetary stability presumed sophisticated economic coordination. To that effect, it was crucial to create a macroeconomic national accounting system which would analyze past and present developments and draw up suggestions for future action. The unions would have to participate in this process. Guidelines on the national budget should become compulsory parameters for the state's economic policies. Planning, in contrast, was envisioned by the 1963 program as only part of a package of "planning and competition." Where the 1949 program spoke of planning alone as an essential vehicle for the democratization of the economy, the 1963 document mentioned planning as only a small part of an overall framework for an otherwise competitive market economy.

The Düsseldorf Program also assumed a moderate posture with regard to the role of the state. The 1963 document asked for a system of "investment guidance" (Investitionslenkung). The unions' position on this issue clearly showed their awareness that the scope and quality of investments represented a key ingredient for the success or failure of a modern economy. It also conveyed their perception that the private and public sector existed as legitimately separate entities. Policies in one inevitably affected the other and therefore required careful coordination. The unions claimed that the basis for investment guidance should be estimates of the needs and demands of individual industries, which should then be published. In this way private investment activities would be influenced via the macroeconomic planning framework, without depriving the individual firm of its final decision as to the quality and scope of its investments. This investment guidance, however, was to involve considerably less rigorous controls than the regulation of capital formation envisioned in the Munich Program of 1949.

The Düsseldorf Program was not a complete retreat, however. It did recommend a number of measures for the democratic control of economic power. For the most part these demands were formulated in rather moderate language. Public investment was to be expanded, the scope for the creation and operation of public corporations (gemeinwirtschaftliche Unternehmen) was to be broadened. The federal budget was to be used to secure full employment and the tax system was to undergo reforms emphasizing direct rather than indirect taxes, with the aim of establishing a system based on the principles of regularity and simplicity. On the subject of co-determination, however, the unions retained the highest degree of continuity from the Munich Program: the existing system of

Montanmitbestimmung was to be expanded to produce full-parity labor representation on the boards of all major firms regardless of their legal status and area of economic activity.

Finally, the new program was decidedly less hostile to rationalization than its predecessor of 1949. Whereas the Munich Program argued that the effects of rationalization in a capitalist economy were inevitably negative and could be countered only by a direct planning mechanism, the Düsseldorf Program of 1963 emphasized the benefits of rationalization as long as adequate safeguards were in place to guarantee job security.[93]

As can be seen from this brief discussion of the Düsseldorf Program's preamble and economic section, many of its formulations were left purposefully vague in order to satisfy both wings of the federation. And that is precisely what happened. While the activists praised the program for having upheld the most sacred principles of the Munich Program, thus conforming to their vision of organized labor as a Gegenmacht in West German society, the social partners claimed victory for exactly the opposite reasons. For them, the Düsseldorf Program testified to the final defeat of Munich's radical legacy, thereby solidifying organized labor's accommodationism. Although both wings hailed the new program as a vindication of their respective beliefs and strategies, it would not be unfair to argue that the social partners gained more via Düsseldorf than their activist colleagues. This was especially true in terms of the unions' relationship to the economy. In this area, the social partners carried the day in good part due to support from Rosenberg and other convinced Keynesians in the DGB. Thus, for example, the much-discussed issue of planning, which had a radical flavor that pleased the activists, had little, if anything, to do with the kind of socialist central planning through nationalization envisaged in the Munich Program of 1949. Rather, Rosenberg and the Keynesians meant by it a kind of medium- and long-term budget planning later introduced by Karl Schiller through the Stability and Growth Law in 1967. In general, most of the Düsseldorf Program's economic demands read like an outline for the reforms Schiller was to introduce four years later.

In the wake of the unions' new basic program, the DGB unveiled a new Aktionsprogramm on May 1, 1965, exactly a decade after the first one was announced.[94] Following a mandate of the DGB's 1962 congress which praised labor's achievements in pursuing the goals delineated by the 1955 Aktionsprogramm, the updated version represented an expansion of union demands, many of which were concretizations of general policies expressed in the Düsseldorf Program. Among the most notable demands of the 1965 Aktionsprogramm were the payment of an extra month bonus (the 13-month year), the right to conclude contracts for individualized asset formation (vermögenswirksame Leistung), four weeks minimum annual vacation, lowering of retirement age, better work-protection plans and greater worker participation in the production process. The latter two demands in particular became increasingly important as the decade came to an end. The first point included relatively sophisticated demands concerning work safety and job protection with respect to increasing automation. There was a direct causal link between the demands of Aktionsprogramm 1965 and IG Metall's collective bargaining agreement concerning protection against rationalization (Rationalisierungsschutzabkommen) which the union negotiated with the employers in 1968.[95] A similarly delayed implementation occurred with the unions' demand for more worker participation on the shop floor. As part of their larger package of Mitbestimmung, this demand received a boost with the prospect of the SPD's entering the government for the first time in the history of the Federal Republic.

The period between 1960 and the creation of the Grand Coalition of the CDU/CSU and the SPD in 1966 represented a turbulent one for the DGB. Various intra-organizational battles shook labor during these few years. With the exception of IG Metall's strike in Baden-Württemberg's metal industry in 1963, which resulted in an ambivalent victory for the union, few industrial actions occurred at this time. (See IG Metall chapter for a detailed discussion of the 1963 metalworker strike in Baden-Württemberg.) A section of the labor movement embraced the liberal–capitalist order in the Federal Republic and became fully integrated into that system. Moreover, this section – the social partners – felt very comfortable with its integration. This was, after all, one of its major aims. The activist unions on the other hand still maintained a critical distance from West Germany's capitalist power centers, even though they, too, learned to accept the legitimacy of the system. Due to the continued antinomy of IG Metall and its allies, the West German trade unions played what one observer called the role of leftwing corrective to an increasingly accommodationist Social Democratic Party and a conservative Zeitgeist in the country as a whole.[96] The activist unions' passionate opposition to the emergency laws and their defense of the ultimate goals of the Munich Program in the discussions surrounding the passage of the DGB's Düsseldorf Program showed the West German public – and especially its increasingly restive intelligentsia – that labor as a Gegenmacht was a necessity for a lively democracy. But as the "radical" unions were actively – though not necessarily consciously – contributing to the creation of West Germany's anti-parliamentary opposition (APO) by continuing to foster a tradition of criticism and dissent in a period of political complacency and cultural conformity, the Social Democratic Party assumed the junior position in the Grand Coalition with the Christian Democrats. Long-awaited opportunities accompanied by unexpected pitfalls became the unions' new reality under this governmental constellation.

## V.   THE UNIONS AND THE GRAND COALITION: 1966–1969

It was the Federal Republic's first serious economic crisis which finally catapulted the Social Democrats towards their long-awaited goal of attaining government power in West Germany. Although the recession which hit the West German economy in 1966–67 looks mild by post-1975 standards, its psychological impact was enormous. It burst the bubble of the economic miracle, provoked the fall of Erhard and his CDU/CSU–FDP coalition and ushered in a CDU/CSU–SPD government committed to a modernization of economic policy along Keynesian lines. Belated in comparison to the post-World War II experiences of many of its European neighbors, the 1966–67 crisis marked the end of neo-liberalism and the beginning of Keynesianism as the dominant economic philosophy and strategy in the Federal Republic.[97]

The SPD's decision to form a government with the Christian Democrats in December 1966 elicited a mixed reaction from the unions. Predictably the social partners, who were closer to the SPD party line, strongly supported the move. The union left, on the other hand, was skeptical, and IG Metall disapproved. However, since the move came at a time of perceived national emergency because of the recession, the entire labor movement – including Otto Brenner's metalworkers – decided to cooperate with the new government's program to revitalize the economy. Two union traditions impelled the DGB and its constituent members to take a step in this direction: the first was organized labor's "republican" belief in liberal democracy, which rallied the unions to the defense of the existing political order in case of a threat. Concomitant with this republicanism, the labor movement's "state fixation" also played a role in convincing it to join forces to fight the crisis. The second tradition which accounted for the unions' move was their closeness to social democracy in general and the SPD in particular. It was this party's modern economic "tool kit" (Instrumentarium) which promised to implement many of the reforms the labor movement had sought since the early 1950s.

While the ascent of social democracy to governmental power undoubtedly provided the political dimension of a successful implementation of Keynesian macroeconomic policy, there were precursors to these developments well before 1966. An important influence in the development of Keynesian economic policy was Karl Schiller, the SPD's leading economic theorist – indeed the architect of Keynesian-style conflict management implemented by the Grand Coalition.[98] The unions' own brand of

Keynesianism, as partly developed by Agartz and subsequently modified by Brenner, had an impact on the Aktionsprogramm of 1955 and had major ripple effects in the discussions on economic policy in the Social Democratic Party as well. The SPD's Godesberg program epitomized the party's Keynesian metamorphosis from its earlier tenets of Marxism.

The unions embraced Keynesianism for three reasons. First, they viewed this economic theory as a vast improvement over the much-disliked policies of the conservative Christian Democrats and especially the neo-liberalism represented by Ludwig Erhard. Second, labor believed that Keynesianism was the economic strategy best suited for a highly complex advanced capitalist society whose problems could not be solved by either Marxism or classical liberalism. Third, it was via Keynesianism and its political corollaries of inclusion that the unions and the party hoped to enable labor to participate in state power.

Ironically, the Erhard era witnessed experimentation with certain Keynesian methods that were later to become the foundation of Schiller's celebrated reforms. With the West German economy facing some inflationary problems in the late 1950s and early 1960s, Keynesians urged Erhard to devise an incomes policy as a way of controlling rising prices. His first hesitant step in this direction came in 1960 with the so-called Blessing Memorandum.[99] The head of the Bundesbank, Karl Blessing, had been asked in 1959 to study the question of wages and recommend a "scientific" guideline for "responsible" wage increases. In January 1960 he presented the government with the Blessing Memorandum, which stated that in order to preserve price stability, wages should not rise more than productivity. He counted on a productivity gain of 3-4% for 1960 and urged that nominal wages be increased by only that amount. Productivity growth, in fact, turned out to be over 7% and so Blessing's credibility was lost. In 1961 and 1962 Erhard returned to his old approach of moral suasion, calling on the unions to moderate their demands – in spite of full employment – for the good of the country. The appeal fell on deaf ears, as industrial wage rates rose at a record pace of 8% in 1961 and 10.4% in 1962, due as much to labor market pressures as to union militancy.[100]

It is hardly surprising that in the face of some of these economic problems, and the evident inability of the government to deal with them, there was a growing consensus in the early 1960s that a change of economic policy was needed. Led by the unions, there was a general demand that "modern" methods of economic management (i.e. Keynesianism) should be implemented on a full-scale basis. As part of this modernization package, the unions clamored for the establishment of an independent body of experts which would advise the government regularly on matters of economic policy. Thus developed the Council of Economic Advisors (Sachverständigenrat, or SVR) which was established by the Bundestag in 1962 and first met in 1963. The SVR, most of whose views remained close to those of the unions and the SPD until the late 1960s, became one of Erhard's most outspoken critics. It strongly urged a thoroughgoing reform of fiscal practice (a national accounts rather than administrative budget, control of state [Länder] spending, and medium-term budget plans, among other measures) as a prerequisite for the introduction of Keynesianism. In addition, the SVR recommended for the first time in its annual report of 1965 constant consultation and regularized discussion among employers, unions and the state on such concepts as "concerted action," "societal accord" and "new social contract," all of which envisioned a quasi-corporatist economic and political order. These mechanisms, the experts believed, would guarantee stability and reduce the mutual mistrust which labor and capital had developed for each other. The council firmly believed that institutionalized cooperation of this kind would represent the best framework for the coordination of a complex capitalist economy.[101]

Although a series of interministerial studies was carried out between 1962 and 1966 investigating ways to improve macroeconomic policy – Erhard even introduced a reform bill in 1966 incorporating many of the changes demanded by the SVR, the SPD and the unions (later to become the Stability and Growth Law under Schiller and the Grand Coalition in 1967) – no major shifts in policy practice occurred before the change of government in December 1966. It was up to Schiller and the SPD to implement some of the Keynesian measures which had been debated in various political bodies of the Federal Republic. To the DGB, the most important reforms were the Stability and Growth Law (Stabilitäts- und Wachstumsgesetz – StWG) and the Concerted Action.

The two were inextricably linked in Schiller's mind and formed the pillars of his Keynesian reforms. It is not by chance that he needed – and received – the unions' cooperation for both of these endeavors. After all, the DGB's Düsseldorf Program made labor's participation in the state's Keynesian-oriented economic policy not only possible but desirable. The Stability and Growth Law, passed by the Bundestag in June 1967, was hailed by the unions as an appropriate and long-overdue change in the country's macroeconomic orientation.[102] Well before the establishment of the SVR in 1962 (and since then as well), the DGB demanded some sort of planning mechanism, the publication of economic evaluations and forecasts at regular intervals, and what could be called a general "technocratization" of the Federal Republic's economic policy in which labor would then have some unspecified but considerable input. The StWG implemented all these reforms. Its main points included the introduction of medium- and long-term budget planning, a greater coordination of federal, state and local spending, and the release of yearly economic reports providing orientation data on future cyclical developments of the economy. Moreover, much to the unions' delight, the law stipulated that the government's economic policies had to correspond to a balanced treatment of the "magic quadrangle" consisting of full employment (perhaps the unions' most persistent concern), the guarantee of steady growth (a close second to full employment in labor's demands), the maintenance of price stability, and finally, the provision for stable exchange rates. In addition, and perhaps most importantly, the federal government was given wide latitude by this law to raise and lower taxes, alter depreciation schedules and block expenditures, all on short notice and without parliamentary approval. Only with the use of such tools could Schiller hope to "fine tune" the economy.[103]

In addition to the parliamentary victory which produced the Stability and Growth Law, Schiller hoped to realize his economic reforms by creating the institution called Concerted Action. The DGB, under the influence of the social partners among its members, advocated labor's participation in such a forum by the fall of 1966 before the establishment of the Grand Coalition. However, it was not until February 14, 1967, that the first round of the Concerted Action met under the chairmanship of Karl Schiller.[104] The idea of the Concerted Action was to establish informal orientation meetings on a regular basis among representatives of the employers, the unions and the state to discuss economic issues which were of interest to all. Schiller had hoped to keep participation confined to a small number of leaders in order to foster discussion and allow an open exchange of opinions.[105]

From the very beginning, the Concerted Action became a major issue of contention within the DGB. There was only one point of unanimous agreement for all unions: the Concerted Action was under no circumstances to interfere in any way with the unions' autonomy of collective bargaining. Since the government, pursuant to the new Stability and Growth Law, issued orientation data which included wage figures that would – according to the government's thinking – be in the best interest of the West German economy as a whole, the unions feared that these data would de facto assume the status of wage guidelines which could severely undermine – if not completely destroy – the unions' method of collective bargaining. As could be expected, it was mainly the accommodationist unions within the DGB, and of course the federation's Keynesian chairman Rosenberg, who were the main supporters of labor's participation in this new quasi-governmental institution. Arguing that the name was an unfortunate misnomer, since there was nothing "concerted" in the sense of agreements among the participants, nor was there any "action" in terms of concrete steps and measures, the proponents of Concerted Action viewed it as a valuable opportunity to voice union concerns at a forum attended by individuals with the power to change matters. Moreover, the formation of Concerted Action meant that for the first time since the creation of the Federal Republic, labor participated on an equal footing with the employers and the state in formulating and implementing major aspects of economic policy. Lastly, the social partners viewed Concerted Action as an institution whose mandate was highly compatible with the objectives of the unions' Düsseldorf Program.[106]

In contrast, many activists feared that no matter how much the official union line insisted on never letting Concerted Action interfere with the unions' bargaining autonomy, the very existence of such an institution and labor's participation therein would inevitably tie the unions to the state's economic policies. Labor's "tie-in" (Einbindung) with the powers-that-be would not necessarily occur in an overt fashion, but rather through moral suasion and covert pressure to behave in a way which would most benefit the "commonweal" (Gemeinwohl) rather than labor's own interests. But it was precisely this "tie-in with the commonweal" (Gemeinwohlbindung) – or perhaps the tie-in with social democracy – that made the activists participate in Concerted Action, while at the same time issuing their verbal protests and reservations. Speaking at IG Metall's congress in 1968, Otto Brenner highlighted the activists' – as well as his own – ambivalence regarding Concerted Action:

> It can never be the task of Concerted Action to tie labor's collective bargaining to so-called wage guidelines, thereby annulling the unions' bargaining autonomy. We will of course continue to conduct our collective bargaining in full knowledge of economic facts and the government's overall aims without, however, surrendering our own decisions and responsibilities. Any attempt to tamper with the unions' bargaining autonomy will meet with the decisive resistance of the entire German union movement.[107]

"The Concerted Action," Brenner continued, "provided an opportunity to discuss the aims of the government's economic policies, to voice one's opinions and debate them with others, without thereby subordinating the unions' opinion to anybody else's"[108] In short, Brenner and the activists remained ambivalent regarding Concerted Action.

With the passage of time, Concerted Action became an increasingly burdensome arrangement for the unions. Already by 1968 and 1969, many union officials had had the unpleasant task of defending labor's participation in Concerted Action to an increasingly restive rank and file which failed to see the tangible benefits for the unions from their participation in this new institution. (Indeed, the passages quoted from Brenner's speech come from a defense of Concerted Action by IG Metall's powerful leader in the face of growing opposition to this arrangement on the part of union delegates.) With many unions – once again following IG Metall's lead – locked into lengthy contracts in the wake of the recession, and the eventual wage gains repeatedly hovering in suspicious proximity to the government's orientation data – dubbed "wage guidelines" – which the unions swore never to follow, Concerted Action's credibility suffered a precipitous decline among the rank and file in the late 1960s. As profits soared in a boom which did not lead to commensurate wage gains, workers conducted unauthorized strikes in September 1969 which were the first of their kind in the history of the Federal Republic. (See the IG Metall chapter on the September strikes of 1969).

As the years progressed, labor's frustration mounted concerning the format of Concerted Action's meetings. Gone were the days of informal chats among a relatively small group of leaders. Now, every session was attended by approximately one hundred people. During the meeting each side would simply read its prepared text with virtually no discussion. Concerted Action had disintegrated into a propaganda forum which permitted the employers, the government and the unions to voice their opinions, with assurances of excellent media coverage the next day. By the early 1970s, the three parties had converted the process of talking to each other to one in which they talked *at* each other.[109] It is with this background in mind that one has to understand the unions' decision in 1977 to leave Concerted Action in protest over the employers' suit challenging the constitutionality of the 1976 Mitbestimmung law.

As to Mitbestimmung, the SPD's participation in government finally gave the unions a chance to resuscitate this favored project. In March 1968, the DGB held a Mitbestimmung conference and called for the extension of co-determination à la Montanmitbestimmung to the largest West German corporations in all industries except coal and steel.[110] Chancellor Kurt Georg Kiesinger responded by setting up a commission of experts, led by Kurt Biedenkopf, to study the problem in detail and make recommendations for future legislation. The Biedenkopf Report was not completed until early 1970 and, by that time, the SPD had become the senior partner in a new coalition with the liberal FDP. One stipulation of their coalition accord was that the problem of Mitbestimmung – which the FDP opposed with considerable vehemence – would not be touched until after the next Bundestag elections scheduled for 1973.[111] In the end, the unions had to wait until 1976 for a new co-determination law which has left them dissatisfied until the time of this writing. (See below in this chapter for a more detailed discussion.)

While little concrete progress was made on the important issue of

Mitbestimmung under the Grand Coalition, the unions did indeed profit from the SPD's participation in this governmental structure via the passage of a very important law, the so-called Arbeitsförderungsgesetz (Work Promotion Law).[112] Not decreed by the Bundestag until June 25, 1969, and thus coming in the twilight of the Grand Coalition's reign, the law very much reflected the unions' desire for an active labor market policy on the part of the state. Foremost among the urgent reforms which the unions demanded during the 1966–67 recession, the Work Promotion Law featured a series of preventive measures anticipating problems related to unemployment. It offered generous reeducation and retraining schemes, on-the-job training and other programs to address the structural imbalances between supply and demand in the labor market of a quickly changing economy. The Work Promotion Law empowered a semi-autonomous, quasi-state agency, the Bundesanstalt für Arbeit (Federal Labor Office) and its 146 local employment agencies to procure appropriate jobs and to function as an employment clearinghouse. It was via this law that the unions succeeded in getting the state to adopt a version of an active manpower policy.

During the last few months of the Grand Coalition, the DGB had to face the arduous process of selecting a new chairman to replace Ludwig Rosenberg, who had reached the mandatory retirement age of 65. Rosenberg was certainly a hard act to follow since he had proved himself to be an excellent mediator between the activists and the accommodationists within the federation. Rosenberg's conciliatory efforts culminated in the formulation and eventual acceptance of the DGB's "new line" as articulated by its Düsseldorf Program of 1963. It was Rosenberg's exceptional diplomatic qualities – in addition to his erudition and intelligence – which made him a highly respected DGB chairman at a crucial time in the federation's history in its relationship to the employers, the state, the political parties (especially the SPD) and, perhaps most important of all, its own constituent unions.[113] While never succeeding in establishing the primacy of the DGB over its 16 member unions, Rosenberg certainly restored the federation's respectability within the West German labor movement.

Once again, the DGB's relationship to its constituent unions dominated the tempestuous selection process of Rosenberg's successor as chairman of the federation. By January 1969, the leaders of most industrial unions, including such powerful ones as IG Metall, IG Chemie and IG Bau-Steine-Erden, had agreed to elect Kurt Gscheidle, a member of the SPD's Bundestag delegation and vice chairman of West Germany's postal workers' union, as the DGB's new chairman at the federation's forthcoming congress in Munich during May of that year. To Brenner and the other dominant "vassals" of the labor movement, Gscheidle seemed an ideal candidate in that he had excellent connections to the Social Democrats and parliament, yet would hardly venture beyond Rosenberg's mediating posture on intra-labor issues. Gscheidle was assumed to be a capable "emperor" who would represent the interests of the empire to the outside world, while at the same time not posing a threat to the comfortable autonomy enjoyed by each of the powerful "vassals."[114] But things turned out differently.

During the early spring of 1969, Gscheidle developed a number of organizational schemes which were intended to strengthen the DGB at the cost of the individual unions. He defended these reforms by arguing that it was increasingly important for organized labor to speak with one voice to parliament and the West German public on matters of such importance as co-determination, the revision of the Works Constitution Law of 1952, asset formation, and the humanization of work. In Gscheidle's view, labor's cause had suffered for too long due to the DGB's weakness, which in turn accentuated the public's awareness of internal disagreements and ideological differences between activists and accommodationists within the unions. Complicating matters, it had become clear that the SPD's top leadership, including Willy Brandt, Helmut Schmidt and Hans-Jürgen Wischnewski, supported Gscheidle because they hoped that his plans would keep the radical unions from drifting even further away from the party, a trend demonstrated by the acrimonious debates over the emergency laws and by the growing disillusionment with Concerted Action among the rank and file of some of the activist unions.[115] Otto Brenner in particular was irate about Gscheidle's reform proposals, and the powerful leader of IG Metall threatened to have his union's delegates cast their ballots against Gscheidle at the DGB congress in May 1969.

The congress was spared a painful showdown by a bizarre incident which eliminated Gscheidle as a viable candidate. While attending an SPD congress in West Berlin, Gscheidle was found in a drunken stupor lying in one of the city's major squares in the middle of the night.[116] This presented a convenient solution to a potentially difficult problem, since virtually all leaders of the unions and the SPD agreed that Gscheidle could not assume the foremost position within the organized labor movement after having suffered such an embarrassment. The "vassals" then quickly proceeded to choose a new "king" who seemed a perfect choice from their standpoint: Heinz Oskar Vetter, deputy chairman of the accommodationist IG Bergbau und Energie and a rather innocuous figure who until then was barely known outside his own miners' union.[117] Indeed, Vetter desisted from introducing major reforms which would strengthen the DGB at the expense of its constituent unions. When he assumed his new post in May 1969, many thought that the unions had again elected a weak person as head of the federation. The subsequent thirteen years of Vetter's reign were to prove them wrong. While Vetter never challenged the much-guarded autonomy of the DGB's member unions, he did in fact make his voice heard both inside and outside the labor movement on virtually every issue pertaining to the unions' existence. In the course of the 1970s, Vetter developed into an influential labor leader whose integrity, concern and activism helped make the DGB an institution respected by the individual unions, the political parties, the employers and the state.

The Grand Coalition came to an end in the fall of 1969. With the SPD becoming the dominant member of a governmental coalition for the first time in the history of the Federal Republic, another new era was to begin for the unions.

## VI.  THE UNIONS AND THE SOCIAL–LIBERAL COALITION, STAGE ONE: 1969–1974

When the SPD under Willy Brandt assumed the senior partnership in a governmental coalition with the Free Democratic Party in the fall of 1969, the unions' hopes could hardly have attained greater heights. Coupled with superb conditions in which there was encouraging economic growth and virtually no unemployment, organized labor's hour finally seemed at hand both in the political arena and in the labor market. However, things proved a good deal more difficult – and ultimately disappointing – for the unions than they had originally envisioned at the end of the 1960s. Despite the auspicious signs, the unions were burdened with an inherent dilemma that had hitherto defied solution for virtually every social democratic labor movement, including the West German. On the one hand, the accession of the SPD to state power meant that, at least to a certain degree, the unions had developed into accomplices and junior partners in "their" party's new government. While this was already partly the case under the Grand Coalition, in which leading unionists – Georg Leber from IG Bau-Steine-Erden being the most prominent among them – assumed high govern-mental positions, this incorporation of the unions into the state developed a fortiori with the SPD becoming the senior partner in the new coalition in Bonn.[118] At the end of 1969, the unions' hopes were twofold: on the one hand, they fully expected the SPD to help them attain major reforms. Foremost on the unions' mind in this context was the extension of the Montanmitbestimmung model to all of West Germany's large firms, with the desire to alter the unfavorable terms of the Works Constitution Law of 1952 a close second. In addition, the unions had a long list of welfare-state-related wishes ranging from an increase in retirement benefits to an improved public health insurance plan. On the other hand, it was mainly the well-organized industrial unions, rather than the DGB, who hoped to be able to translate their newly acquired strength in the labor market into major contractual gains for their members. Many industrial unions, once again led by IG Metall, were eager to harness the sudden restiveness of their rank and file, which had become evident to a completely unsuspecting leadership during the September strikes. On the whole, this period found the unions hopeful and optimistic to a degree which they had not experienced since the late 1940s and very early 1950s.

Contributing to organized labor's expectations during this new era was the prevailing Zeitgeist, appropriately – though with the benefit of hindsight also cynically – labeled "reform euphoria." Years of political drabness and public withdrawal seemed finally to approach their well-deserved end under the dynamic personality of Willy Brandt. A mobilization of virtually every segment of a hitherto complacent West German citizenry ensued in the Federal Republic. In addition to initiating substantial domestic reforms in such areas as education, health, housing and transportation, the SPD-led government completely reoriented West Germany's foreign policy, culminating in the major breakthrough of Ostpolitik.[119] By deflecting attention from the Cold War, which until then had dominated political debate in the Federal Republic, the Social Democratic policies not only contributed to a gradual legitimation of the geopolitical status quo in Europe, but also fostered the acceptance of the German Democratic Republic by a growing number of West German citizens. In addition, the SPD induced an atmosphere of dissent and radical critique within the Federal Republic itself. The SPD's governmental presence enhanced social reforms, yet this very process stimulated forces that wished to go well beyond them. Thus, the SPD inadvertently lent legitimacy to its own critics from the left, by providing them with institutional access to West Germany's "mainstream" politics through the party itself and also through the unions.

Most important among these critics of the SPD was that amorphous student-centered movement called the New Left. Largely spearheaded by the Sozialistischer Deutscher Studentenbund (SDS) – originally the student youth organization of the SPD which was expelled from the party following the SDS's refusal to adhere to the post-Godesberg Keynesian line – the West German New Left, like its counterparts elsewhere, succeeded in politicizing previously taboo areas of public discourse. The New Left's lasting contribution to politics in the Federal Republic lay not so much in its immediate impact, but rather in its organizational, intellectual and sociological legacies. The unions and the SPD, both major targets of the New Left's criticism, were profoundly affected by the ripple effects of the

New Left's activism. It is in this context that one has to view the wide-ranging debates over investment guidance (Investitionslenkung) among the Young Socialists (Jusos) and union economists in the early 1970s, since both groups included influential members of the 1960s' student movement. Other issues addressed by the activist unions within the DGB and the New Left included the Federal Republic's subservient position within the NATO alliance, the domination of the West German print media by the Springer group and the passage of the emergency laws by the Bundestag in 1968.

These developments also had profound effects on the way the unions viewed the world and their role therein. Enthusiastic supporters of the SPD's Ostpolitik (on behalf of which the unions threatened a general strike in April 1972 when the CDU/CSU called for a vote of no confidence in the government), union publications began referring to the DDR by its proper name, rather than as the "Eastern Zone" or the "so-called German Democratic Republic" as they had with few exceptions until this time.[120] Despite the unequivocal rejection of the Soviet-led invasion of Czechoslovakia, the unions began to intensify their contacts with their counterparts in Eastern Europe, including those in the DDR.

An implicit arrangement was to guide the interaction between the unions and the Social Democratic Party following the latter's assumption of the position as senior partner in the new coalition which began to govern in the fall of 1969. The "deal" had two components: in return for holding wage gains to a moderate level (i.e. commensurate to the orientation data issued by the Concerted Action), the SPD would reward the DGB by legislating important reforms. The new SPD-led government hoped to benefit from organized labor's participation in this quasi incomes policy by incorporating the unions into its Keynesian management of the economy. The DGB, in turn, expected the Social Democrats to use their power to enact laws which the unions had long desired.[121] Both were to end up rather disappointed at the conclusion of this period of reform and mobilization in 1974. The eventual outcome of this arrangement can be termed a "double breakdown."

The DGB simply never had the organizational strength vis-à-vis its powerful member unions to deliver its side of the "deal" to the SPD. Fearful of the restive rank and file – which did in fact strike against the leadership's wishes and permission in 1969, 1971 and 1973 – the large industrial unions, once again led by IG Metall, used labor's market power to obtain the highest settlements in the history of the Federal Republic for their respective members. (For details of these important years see chapters on IG Metall and IG Chemie.) But just as the DGB failed to uphold its end of the arrangement due – at least in part – to forces beyond its immediate control, so too did the SPD fall short of fulfilling the unions' wishes. Partly as a consequence of the Social Democrats' dependence on their junior partner, the Free Democrats, the unions failed to obtain some of the crucial reforms for which they yearned, most notably in the areas of co-determination and works constitution.

While gaining important improvements in a number of welfare-state-type areas – such as pension reform, flexibilization of retirement age and the legal equalization of blue- and white-collar workers in case of illness – co-determination seemed to run into major problems from the very beginning of the new government's existence. Indeed, one of the major aspects of the coalition agreement between Social and Free Democrats was that the former were to leave co-determination alone for the time being.[122] In fact, to the great chagrin and disappointment of the unions, Willy Brandt did not mention co-determination in his speech inaugurating the new government.[123] From that moment the unions were put in the unexpected and uncomfortable position of having to nudge the SPD incessantly to get labor a new co-determination law applicable to virtually all of West German industry, which would give labor full parity on the companies' advisory board analogous to Montanmitbestimmung in the coal and steel industries.[124] It was to become a frustrating battle which in the end yielded a good deal less than the unions had hoped in 1969, the onset of the "reform euphoria."

From the very beginning, it was clear that co-determination was going to be one of the most contentious areas between the Social Democrats and the unions on the one hand, and the two coalition partners on the other. The unions wanted nothing short of full-parity labor participation on the advisory boards of all large West German companies, whereas the Free Democrats remained vehemently opposed to any such schemes. The SPD was caught in the middle and hoped that inactivity and passage of time would eventually produce a compromise solution acceptable to both of its "partners."[125] The period under consideration witnessed a proliferation of proposals and counterproposals by all political parties, the employers and the unions, all of which suggested various models of co-determination clearly advocating their particular protagonists' point of view. Much of the debate used the Biedenkopf Report as a reference point. As already mentioned, the unions wasted little time and began putting pressure on the Social Democrats even when the latter were junior partners in the Grand Coalition. Responding to this, Chancellor Kurt Georg Kiesinger appointed a committee chaired by the widely respected legal scholar Kurt Biedenkopf and comprising other leading academics to study all existing forms of co-determination and provide recommendations for reform. In 1970, Biedenkopf submitted a detailed, 400-page document which won the respect of all political parties, the employers and the unions for its meticulous gathering of data and its painstaking efforts in obtaining virtually every available piece of empirical information on this topic.[126]

Concerning the report's recommendations, reactions were a good deal more at odds. Biedenkopf and his colleagues argued for greater labor participation on the Federal Republic's advisory boards than was allowed by the Works Constitution Law of 1952. However, while advocating an extension of labor's presence beyond the one-third decreed by the Works Constitution Law of 1952, the report clearly rejected the unions' and the SPD's proposals for an extension of full-parity co-determination à la Montanmitbestimmung to the rest of West German industry. Three reasons were central to the committee's recommendations: first, the committee felt that such an arrangement would impede efficiency in operating a company. Second, full-parity labor participation in a firm's decision-making would ultimately blur, perhaps even obliterate, existing property relationships. Third, labor participation on such a level would give particular organized interest groups (i.e. unions) undue collective power in the economy, thereby potentially undermining the process and structure of liberal democracy itself. In short, the committee feared – as did many in the Federal Republic – that the extension of full-parity co-determination to all areas of the West German economy would lead to a fundamental transformation – and ultimate deterioration – of the political and economic order.[127]

In the four years following publication of the Biedenkopf Report, a wide-ranging discussion on co-determination ensued involving every political party in the Bundestag, the employers and the unions. For the employers, the Free Democrats and the business wing of the CDU/CSU, the report went too far; whereas for the unions, the SPD and the labor wing of the Christian Democrats, Biedenkopf's recommendations remained well shy of their expectations. A stalemate followed which was not broken until February 1974 when the two parties of the governing coalition submitted a compromise bill to the Bundestag.[128] To the horror of the unions, it featured more characteristics from the FDP's proposal of 1971 than the SPD's from 1968 and the DGB's from 1968 and 1971. By including middle management on the labor side and giving it special status in this representation, by granting management a permanent chairmanship which could always break a tie in its favor via the newly instituted mechanism of a tie-breaking second vote, by abolishing the position of labor director on the company's executive board, and by weakening the power of union-appointed delegates among the labor representatives, the bill clearly bore the FDP's stamp.[129] This was a far cry from the Montan model and had little resemblance to the kind of parity co-determination the unions sought.

The DGB was shocked, yet it continued to hope that a last-ditch effort on its part could change the terms of the bill before it became law. As will become clear in the next section, the unions' hopes remained unfulfilled and the final terms of the law, passed in 1976, were hardly different from those of the 1974 bill.

While Willy Brandt refrained from mentioning co-determination in his inaugural speech in 1969, he did in fact dwell at some length on the necessity for the new government to provide a revision of the 1952 Works Constitution Law. Again, the hopes which the DGB placed in the SPD were ultimately disappointed, though perhaps not as profoundly as in the case of co-determination. Once again, there can be no doubt that the Social Democrats' room to maneuver on behalf of the unions was severely curtailed by their coalition with the Free Democrats. Realistically, the SPD could at best only deliver a compromise solution to the unions which, quite naturally, would fall short of the DGB's expectations. The result of this endeavor was a new Works Constitution Law which has governed daily life in the Federal Republic's plants since 1972.

There can be little doubt that the new version of the law represented a considerable improvement for the unions over its predecessor of 1952.[130] First and foremost, the 1972 law recognized the unions as entities entitled to the collective representation of workers. Moreover, unlike its precursor, it also gave the unions direct access to the shop floor and permitted them to help workers within the plant under certain conditions. Lastly, the new law also increased substantially the individual powers of the nearly 26,000 works councilors who were active on West Germany's shop floors in the early 1970s.[131] It gave them more say in many areas pertaining to personnel issues such as hiring and firing, determination of vacation schedules and vocational education, to mention but a few. The new law also increased the works councilors' voice in matters concerning social policy such as company-related protection plans, health insurance and retirement benefits.[132]

Despite these improvements, the Works Constitution Law of 1972 fell far short of the unions' hopes by not addressing some of the handicaps for labor imposed by the passage of the first Law in 1952. Just like its predecessor from 1952, it aimed at tying the works councilors to their company by demanding that they abide by the so-called duty for peace (Friedenspflicht) and the duty of silence (Schweigepflicht). In short, the new law continued to deny works councilors the right to strike and to divulge information about their employers which could be detrimental to the latter. There could be no doubt that the compromises exacted by the Free Democrats from their senior coalition partners regarding the revision of West Germany's most fundamental rules of industrial relations helped maintain the unions' continued weakness on the country's shop floors.[133]

Despite these disappointments, this period still found the unions by and large in a buoyant mood. Aided by superb conditions in the labor market which yielded exceptionally high wage gains and by the overall reformism which characterized the dominant Zeitgeist, the unions discussed important programmatic innovations. (The optimism of this period stood in notable contrast to the mood of the ensuing years which were characterized by the major economic crisis that gripped the Federal Republic in 1975.) Among the key topics under consideration in the early 1970s were labor's participation in investment decisions at the levels of both the firm and the macroeconomy, problems concerning asset formation for workers and various programs related to improving the quality of work life. It is important to highlight the existence of these intra-union debates sui generis since the very fact that they occurred during this particular period in the DGB's history lends evidence to the unions' hopeful attitudes concerning their future in West Germany. It should be immediately added, however, that characteristically for the fate of many union ideas concerning reforms which emanated from the mobilization period of the early 1970s, few were actually implemented the way their supporters had initially hoped, due to the economic crisis of the mid-1970s.

Regarding the area of investment, one could once again discern a battle between the DGB's two opposing wings. The accommodationists were satisfied by the fact that this issue had already been sufficiently addressed by the DGB's Düsseldorf Program under the heading of "investment guidance." For adherents of this faction, the vagueness of this formulation allowed each union to interpret the concept to its own satisfaction. To the accommodationists, "investment guidance" meant little more than Schiller's Keynesianism aided by quasi-corporatist structures such as the Concerted Action. The activists, on the other hand, eagerly joined the major discussions about "investment guidance" or investment control which took place within the SPD at the time, especially its student-dominated faction of people under 35, called Jusos.[134] For adherents of this wing, labor had to have an active and equal part in investment decisions on the macro and micro levels. The activists believed that only if and when labor was fully informed and consulted regarding investments could a more just and efficient political economy thrive. One of the partially existing – though in the eyes of most activists still woefully inadequate – mechanisms of implementing such labor-controlled investment was full-parity co-determination as practiced in the Federal Republic's steel and coal industries. The activists envisioned that the extension of full-parity co-determination would help implement at least some of the preliminary steps toward labor's equal and active participation in investment decisions in the Federal Republic's large companies. As to labor's input into the macroeconomic investments determining the future of the country's economy, the activists suggested the formation of public "investment councils" in which representatives of capital, labor and the state would decide the appropriate nature and level of important investments. All of this, of course, had to occur with labor as a completely equal participant in all stages of decision-making and control regarding investments.

In the case of asset formation, too, the divisions within the DGB followed a predictable pattern. The accommodationists preferred a law which allowed employers and the unions to sign collective bargaining agreements which permitted the former to pay workers certain sums into special funds\ set aside for each worker who was part of the agreement. Favored by IG Bau-Steine-Erden, this plan of asset formation placed the individual worker at the center of the arrangement. Precisely for this reason, it was vehemently opposed by IG Metall and its allies.[135] The activists criticized this type of asset formation as nothing but deferred wages, thus having no effect on any redistribution of assets in the economy and also adding little to the control of assets on the part of labor as a collectivity. They would have much preferred to see the implementation of some kind of asset formation which resembled the collective approach best known to the industrial world via the Swedish unions' wage-earner funds as formulated in the Meidner Plan.[136]

The discussion concerning the improvement of the quality of work life – also known under the heading of "humanization of work" – flourished in many corners of the DGB during the early 1970s. Culminating in a major conference on the topic organized by the DGB in 1974, debate over this issue comprised virtually every aspect of the unions' growing concern with the adverse effects of rationalization.[137] But in notable contrast to the period after 1975, the unions at this stage were not preoccupied with the "job killing" ramifications of the new technologies. Rather, they wanted to have some input into the overall humanization of the work place, which also entailed exerting influence over the deployment of rationalization measures. In order best to be able to gauge rationalization's effects on a micro and macro level, the unions hoped to persuade the employers and the state of the necessity to create a net of tripartite programs and structures designed to oversee virtually every aspect of technological innovations from the standpoint of their effects on workers and the work process. Lastly, the unions' concern with improving the quality of their members' work lives also began to assume ecological dimensions during this period. Perhaps for the first time ever – given German labor's deep roots in growth-oriented social democracy – humanization of work also entailed a more critical approach on the part of the unions concerning the hitherto unquestioned benefits of economic growth. While it was almost exclusively the quantity of growth which preoccupied organized labor until the early 1970s, interest grew regarding the qualitative aspects of growth within the DGB and its unions. The crudest manifestations of growth purely for growth's sake became a thing of the past in the West German unions' worldview during the early 1970s.

The content of some of these debates also found its way into the DGB's third Aktionsprogramm which was, just like its two predecessors, published on May Day, in this case in 1972.[138] Once again the DGB decided that an update of its medium- and short-term programmatic statements was in order since some of the issues addressed by the 1965 Aktionsprogramm had become moot while new ones arose which lacked programmatic recognition from the trade union federation. Aktionsprogramm 1972 contained numerous innovations and additions which were divided into two groups under the respective rubrics of "demands for changes in societal structures" and "demands for improvement of the quality of life."[139] What follows is a list of the most prominent points of the program appearing in the order of preference assigned to them by the document:

– Less work time (the eight-hour day and the five-day work week with full compensation would have to be extended to every segment of the West German economy. Even shift work should never exceed either of these two limits).

– Longer vacation (an annual vacation of a six-week minimum would have to be introduced in order to protect the health of workers).

– Higher wages and salaries (the most important feature was the DGB's demand for the so-called thirteenth-month bonus, additional holiday pay and vacation money, and the securing of plant-specific benefit plans via collective bargaining agreements or by law).

– A more equitable distribution of assets (to be attained via asset formation schemes).

– An improved and more equitable taxation system accompanied by a better fiscal policy.

– Better job security (under this rubric, the DGB addressed its growing concerns regarding the impact of automation and rationalization on employment).

– Jobs with no danger (here, the unions concretized some aspects of their concerns belonging to the larger complex of "humanization of work").

- Greater social security.

- Improved old-age protection.

- Improved legal protection for workers.

- More and better opportunities for co-determination and worker participation on all levels of the economy.

- A more equitable system of education with less rigid tracking, thus allowing children of workers to have equal access to the country's educational institutions and professional programs.

- An improved and more socially minded housing law with increased protection for renters and further expansion of low-income housing.

- Protection of the environment and greater ecological commitment by the government and the West German public as a whole.[140]

This Aktionsprogramm, just like its two predecessors, presented an overview of the DGB's priorities at this particular juncture in West Germany's history. Very much in the spirit of the times, the program's tone – perhaps even more than its content – reflected the DGB's optimistic and confident state of mind in the early 1970s. The program, in notable contrast to its successor of 1979 which will be discussed below, is filled with lofty expectations and ambitious demands. Moreover, in contrast to its two predecessors and its successor, the program clearly addressed many of its expectations and demands on the state, which at the time – perhaps more than at any other period in the Federal Republic's existence – seemed to be quite favorably disposed to fulfilling some of the organized labor's most pressing needs.[141]

Despite the unions' disappointment regarding the SPD-led government's failure to act on co-determination more favorably and despite the passage of a new Works Constitution Law which also fell short of the unions' expectations, the DGB's enthusiastic support of Willy Brandt's social–liberal coalition hardly diminished during this time. While serious disagreements between unions and party evolved concerning the (non)fulfillment of the tacit "deal," the SPD could continue to count on the DGB's unwavering support in virtually all other areas. There can be no doubt that the unions were upset about not getting the legislation from "their" party for which they had such fervent hopes. The Social Democrats in turn, especially in Karl Schiller's entourage, became increasingly annoyed at the DGB's inability to hold its member unions in line concerning their annual wage gains. Moreover, many labor leaders – especially from the activist faction – began publicly expressing dissatisfaction with the Concerted Action, thus adding strain to the relationship. Yet despite these tensions, the unions continued to support the party's domestic and foreign policies with deeply felt conviction and public enthusiasm. Thus, it was not by chance that the unions threatened to conduct a general strike had the opposition's attempt succeeded in 1972 in toppling the Brandt government because of its vigorously conducted Ostpolitik which culminated in treaties between West Germany and a number of key East European countries.[142] The unions' superb position in the labor market helped the DGB overcome some of the rough edges in its relationship with the SPD, a factor which all but disappeared by the end of the 1970s.

It was the other aspect of the mobilization period which caused some unions internal political difficulties and organizational problems. As already mentioned, a number of "graduates" of the student movement had found their way into the unions by the early 1970s. In addition, important ideas which were first espoused by the extra-parliamentary opposition of the late 1960s carried into established institutions such as the unions and the SPD during the early 1970s. While the accommodationist unions remained largely immune to this "contagion from the left," this was not the case with some of the activist members of the DGB, who – it could be argued – already had a critical tradition which saw labor's role in society as that of a Gegenmacht.

At this juncture the era of mobilization went too far for all unions in the DGB. Frightened by the unconventional nature of political thought and actions advocated by some of these radicals, deeply offended by their constant diatribes against the unions which often characterized the latter as "agents of capitalism" or "traitors to the working class" and perturbed by the radicals' activism in the numerous "wildcat" strikes of the early 1970s, the unions decreed so-called "clauses of incompatibility" (Unvereinbarkeitsklauseln) which made simultaneous membership in a union and a radical leftist organization incompatible.[143] Thus far only reserved for activists of the far right, especially in the Federal Republic's neo-Nazi organizations, the mobilization period created new political realities for the unions in which they felt sufficiently threatened by the radical left to have its members excluded from the unions by declaring them "incompatible" with organized labor's *raison d'être*. While this "incompatibility" included activists in virtually every leftist group which proliferated in the wake of West Germany's student movement of the late 1960s, it notably excluded members of the Federal Republic's Communist Party (Deutsche Kommunistische Partei – DKP) which reconstituted itself in 1968 after its predecessor, the KPD, had been constitutionally banned in 1956. This exception was to cause the unions serious internal and external problems during the economic crisis of the late 1970s, as will be mentioned below.

While the unions still gained very satisfactory wage increases in 1974, a number of events occurred in the course of that year which did not bode well for organized labor during the rest of the decade. The employers' association BDA organized a major offensive against the unions beginning in March 1974. Under the motto "market economy or union state," the employers initiated a massive attack designed to sway public opinion against the unions, who – in the employers' view – were beginning to dominate the country and threaten the very fabric of liberal democracy. The employers' offensive was directed not only against the unions but also against labor's supposedly unbreakable alliance with the Social Democratic Party. Known rather pejoratively as "entanglement" (Verfilzung), the unofficial but close relationship between the unions and the SPD became one of the employers' primary targets in their campaign against the supposed encroachments on democracy by a "union state."[144] The timing of this attack was all the more ironic since it coincided with some serious rifts between the unions and the Social Democratic Party. For, as will be recalled, this was exactly the period when the unions were confronted with the first draft of the Brandt government's compromise bill on co-determination, which was hardly to the DGB's liking. Moreover, the spring of 1974 saw the first strike by public employees in the Federal Republic's history. ÖTV, the largest of the public employees' unions, assumed the unfamiliar role of the DGB's "vanguard" union, displacing IG Metall from its habitual position for the 1974 wage round.[145] In the course of this brief conflict, some bitter feelings developed between the head of the "employers," Chancellor Willy Brandt, and the charismatic leader of ÖTV, Heinz Kluncker. Indeed, since Brandt resigned the chancellorship shortly after this unusual strike, Kluncker remained saddled with the rather derogatory epitaph of "Brandt-killer" for years to come, although it was quite clear from the outset that he and the ÖTV strike had very little, if anything, to do with the popular chancellor's resignation. The fact remains, however, that the Brandt–Kluncker conflict exacerbated already existing tensions between the SPD and the unions.[146] Lastly, 1974 witnessed a number of impressive showings by the conservative opposition in some of the Federal Republic's state elections, thus heralding social democracy's gradual decline from the peak of its political power during the mobilization period of the early 1970s to its nadir in Bundestag elections of March 6, 1983.

By the end of 1974 West German society was at a major turning point (Tendenzwende). The crisis, which had thus far spared West Germany, was about to assume center stage there as well. It was to affect every aspect of West Germany's political economy, including all its major actors, such as parties and interest groups. In terms of our topic, no area of union life remained untouched by the crisis. This pertains as much to labor's relationship with the political parties and the state, as it does to its interaction with the employers. Lastly, it revived certain intra-union disagreements which had temporarily assumed more muted dimensions during the optimistic era of mobilization. In short, as the new chancellor Helmut Schmidt was to put it so aptly in his address to the nation on New Year's Eve 1976–77, "nothing will ever be like it was before 1974."[147]

## VII. THE UNIONS AND THE SOCIAL–LIBERAL COALITION, STAGE TWO: 1975–1981

It could be argued that the last period under consideration in this chapter represented the most difficult and frustrating one for the unions in their post-World War II existence. While the rollback between 1945 and 1949 could legitimately be blamed on superior exogenous forces in the form of the Allied powers, and the defeats of the early 1950s could be attributed to a determined effort of capitalist reconstruction led by a very popular chancellor heading a decidedly anti-labor coalition, the unions' setbacks after 1975, in contrast, offered no immediate culprits. After all, the country continued to be governed by the same SPD-led coalition which – just a few years earlier – had given the unions more hope than any previous government in the history of the Federal Republic. Yet, as we shall see, it was precisely this fact, that, under conditions of economic crisis, exacerbated the unions' frustrations and sense of impotence. What made matters even worse was the unions' full awareness that the status quo was still preferable to any political alternative. This left the unions in a terrible bind: on the one hand, they became increasingly disillusioned with their political partner, while on the other, they could not see any alternatives. This forced the unions to create new strategies, which in turn led to renewed intra-organizational complications and rifts. Ultimately, the severe economic crisis which beset the West German economy in the mid-1970s, led to a crisis of the unions, the SPD, DGB–SPD relations and social democracy as a whole. While this is not to say that this period witnessed labor's disintegration or that the unions suffered only defeats, these six years were fraught with severe, and in many ways still unresolved, problems for the DGB and its constituent unions.

Perhaps no other factor proved to be more detrimental to the unions' existence throughout the crisis than the sudden surge of unemployment in late 1974 and early 1975. Contrary to initial expectations unemployment did not disappear at the end of the decade. Indeed, joblessness intensified well into the 1980s. By 1975, the West German labor market was transformed from one which had less than 1% unemployment and imported millions of workers from Europe's southern periphery, into one in which unemployment became endemic at around 4% for the rest of the 1970s and was to double by the early 1980s.[148] The most immediate ramification for the unions of their sudden weakening in the labor market was their inability to continue exacting wages of the kind they had received under conditions of full employment. In marked contrast to the substantial wage gains attained by all West German unions in 1974, the 1975 bargaining round concluded with pay increases which were dramatically below those achieved in the preceding year. This trend was to continue throughout the rest of the 1970s. Indeed, by the end of the decade the modesty of the unions' wage gains had reached such dimensions that labor's wage share as a percentage of the Federal Republic's gross national product declined to its lowest level since the late 1960s. The unions' impressive pay increases of the first half of the 1970s were all but nullified by the wage restraint exercised throughout the second part of that decade. The doubling of unemployment in the early 1980s led to a further weakening of the unions' bargaining power. While the modest agreements of the late 1970s yielded small – but nevertheless real – wage increases, deteriorating conditions in the labor market forced the unions in the early 1980s to sign contracts which provided pay increases below the level of inflation, thus eroding the earning power of West German workers.[149] The stubborn persistence and sheer magnitude of unemployment presented an existential problem to the unions which they had to counter in the labor market and in the political arena. In order to devise strategies for both areas, the DGB and its constituent unions first had to undertake a thorough analysis of unemployment.

While somewhat schematic, it would not be incorrect to place the DGB's analysis of unemployment into three, overlapping categories: cyclical/ conjunctural, structural and technological. Reflecting the DGB's overall confidence in the Federal Republic's economic performance, particularly under the stewardship of an SPD-led government, the unions largely viewed the crisis and its most detrimental manifestation, unemployment, in cyclical/conjunctural terms. Drawing parallels to the recession of 1966–67, the unions initially believed that unemployment derived from insufficient economic growth, combined with a faulty application of macroeconomic remedies by the government. The crisis, the unions held, was in good part due to deficient demand which resulted from the government's excessive concern with inflation and a concomitant increase in restrictive policies at the behest of the FDP-controlled economics ministry and the independent Bundesbank. The crisis and unemployment were ultimately cyclical in the DGB's view and thus should have been responsive to the implementation of countercyclical measures. This interpretation predominated until 1977 when the DGB finally published its first comprehensive program for full employment, nearly three years after the onset of the crisis, and it continues even to this day to represent a widely held union view concerning the causes of unemployment.[150]

A second source of unemployment which the unions increasingly identified in the late 1970s went beyond the ebbs-and-flows of the business cycle and addressed the structural changes in the international order of production. With the growth in importance of the newly industrializing countries (NICs) and their ability to produce goods which formerly were the mainstay of advanced capitalist countries such as the Federal Republic, certain sectors in the latter experienced increased competitive pressure. Among the most seriously affected industries in West Germany were textiles, shipbuilding and steel. The unions' chief complaint concerning this phenomenon centered on the quasi-permanent nature of the unemployment which it produced. The unions maintained that a portion of the increase in unemployment since 1974 was due to structural changes in certain industries which entailed, in effect, jobs being transferred from the Federal Republic to the NICs. The DGB argued that structural unemployment derived in part from the failure of certain West German goods to be competitive on the world market. But whereas the Federal Republic's industrial leaders blamed high wages for this deficiency, the unions asserted that the fault lay more with management's failure to adapt appropriately to the changing conditions of the world market in certain sectors such as steel and shipbuilding. The unions also blamed capital export as a major contributor to structural unemployment. It had already become an important concern to some weaker unions during the early 1970s. But with West German investment abroad experiencing a substantial annual increase throughout the late 1970s, even the stronger unions voiced their concerns about the adverse effects for West German jobs if these developments continued unabated.[151]

It was the third category, namely technological change, which to the DGB represented the most serious and potentially pernicious cause of unemployment in the late 1970s and beyond. Whereas the West German unions continued to express their traditionally positive attitudes toward technological change and innovation by repeatedly stressing that they were not "machine wreckers," they were frightened by the loss of jobs directly attributable to the introduction of microprocessors and other forms of computerization on a massive scale.[152] Most union publications in the late 1970s discussed at length the adverse effects of those versatile computer chips which the unions tellingly labeled "job killers."[153] It was not only the ever-growing presence of microprocessors in all parts of the Federal Republic's production, but also labor's helplessness in finding appropriate solutions which added to the unions' fears. At least in the case of cyclical and structural unemployment, the DGB could refer to an accepted body of thought. Technological unemployment's major dangers were that workers in all sectors were potentially vulnerable to sudden job losses and that the unions lacked any viable strategies to counter this serious development.[154]

What frightened the DGB most about the seemingly unbridled introduction of technological innovation was the fact that it occurred in an era of little or no macroeconomic growth. It was in this context that some DGB economists developed the "scissors theory" of unemployment.[155] Looking at the relationship between economic production and labor productivity, the theory argued that any form of rationalization as a consequence of technological advance would not cause unemployment as long as growth in production exceeded increases in productivity. This, the DGB submitted, characterized the situation of the West German economy until the crisis of the mid-1970s, thus explaining why the labor movment was by and large never opposed to technological improvements and rationalization per se. However, one of the fundamental aspects of the new crisis in labor's view was the reversal of the relationship between production and productivity, in which the latter appeared to outgrow the former, thus aggravating the unions' precarious situation in the labor market. The DGB feared that increased rationalization as a consequence of the rapidly advancing electronic revolution would further widen the already growing "scissors" between stagnating production and growing labor productivity. Certainly by 1977 the unions had come to recognize that unemployment represented the most serious threat to their well-being.[156] Recognition, however, did not mean passive acceptance. Indeed, if one had to name the single most important preoccupation of West Germany's trade unions since the onset of the crisis in 1975, it would definitely be their struggle against unemployment.

As could be expected given the German labor movement's traditional "state fixation" and its informal but close ties to the Social Democratic Party, the DGB first turned to the SPD-led government for help in this dire situation. The unions demanded a more activist and interventionist posture on the part of the state in battling unemployment. In the DGB's view, the crisis could only be overcome if the state pursued an explicitly reflationary policy replete with a massive increase in public investment, the creation of job programs and a "direct" fiscal policy designed to stimulate economic growth. Rejecting the tight monetary measures proposed by the Bundesbank and the government's preoccupation with inflation, the unions firmly believed that only a concerted effort by the state could lead to a revival in lagging demand, thereby countering at least the cyclical/conjunctural dimensions of unemployment. As to its structural manifestations, the DGB continued to place its primary hopes in the state as well. In addition to the state's "sprinkler" policies which – if properly applied – could help alleviate at least some of the cyclically unemployed, the unions demanded that the state lead the way in designing and implementing "targeted" structural measures which were to benefit especially needy regions and sectors. The unions wanted the government to go beyond the Keynesian instruments of macro-level demand management and establish particular programs in aid of the structurally disadvantaged.[157] In addition to demanding substantial retraining and reeducation programs for technologically "obsolete" workers, and insisting on labor's participation in the conceptualization and implementation of new technologies at all levels ranging from governmental ministries and planning agencies to particular plants, the DGB asked the government to assist the unions in reducing work time by passing legislation permitting earlier retirement and by repealing the existing law – dating from 1938 – which allowed a 72-hour work week. In short, the unions hoped to muster considerable governmental support both on the demand and the supply side in their quest to defeat unemployment and thereby alleviate the most detrimental manifestation of the crisis.[158]

But things were to develop differently. The crisis revived some of the fundamental disagreements between the two coalition partners (the SPD and the FDP) concerning the conduct of economic policy. The social-liberal coalition, was, after all, the creation of a uniquely optimistic boom period in the Federal Republic, during which the two parties' commonalities on cultural matters and areas of foreign policy superseded their vast divergences on the management of the country's economy. The brief era of "reform euphoria" succeeded in pushing these conceptual differences into a temporary background without, however, resolving them in any substantive way. The first phase of the social–liberal coalition was a pact conceived in economic abundance and based on the appearance of political harmony which, in turn, remained highly dependent on continued material prosperity. The crisis abruptly – and, as it eventually turned out, lastingly – disturbed this arrangement between Social and Free Democrats. The Free Democrats, true to their tenets as a party representing a small but wealthy constituency of professionals, managers and other members of the business community, reverted to a crisis interpretation which featured the state as the major culprit and free enterprise as the main victim. As a logical consequence of this analysis, the FDP insisted on the implementation of policies which promised to resolve the crisis via severe curtailments of public expenditures and a concomitant "freeing" of market forces from the fetters of the state. Much, though significantly not all, of the SPD adhered to a diametrically opposite analysis of the crisis, in which the Bundesbank's overly restrictive monetary policies between 1972 and 1974, the problems of international capitalism on a global scale and the particularly ruthless measures of rationalization by West German employers played the most central part. In accord with the unions' wishes, the adherents to this crisis interpretation within the SPD advocated greater state intervention by stimulating demand and by implementing public programs designed to aid ailing sectors of the West German economy. To advocates of these policies, the pursuit of such steps not only represented the logically correct response to lead the Federal Republic out of the crisis, but also the morally compelling answer for Social Democrats to help the most adversely affected victims of the crisis, the growing number of unemployed and under-employed.

In this rift between Free and Social Democrats, which increasingly characterized the politics of economic policy-making in the West German government during the crisis, one man more than anybody assumed the pivotal role of conciliator and leader: Helmut Schmidt. While any chancellor in his/her position as leader of the government becomes the first among equals, Schmidt cut a particularly impressive figure.[159] Schmidt's role is of particular interest to us since no chancellor in the history of West Germany has enjoyed such a close relationship with the DGB and the leaders of its important constituent unions.

Whether by personal conviction, as a consequence of his desire to maintain the coalition with the Free Democrats, or a combination of both, Helmut Schmidt's interpretation of the crisis, its causes and remedies coincided more with the FDP's analyses than with those advanced by his own party, especially its left wing and its academic-dominated youth organization, the Young Socialists (Jusos). His assessment of the appropriate measures to combat the adversities of the crisis also differed substantially from the positions advocated by the DGB and most of its member unions. Schmidt believed that only a policy of austerity by the state could lead to recovery from the crisis. He viewed the entitlement programs which were created and/or expanded during the previous period of economic prosperity as excessive burdens for the West German public to bear in a period of serious structural and cyclical dislocation. Suspicious of stimulating measures, which, in his view, would only endanger price stability while not necessarily producing economic growth, the chancellor abhorred augmenting the already considerable budget deficit (DM 30 billion by the late 1970s) by instituting the unions' reflationary demands. By passing the Haushaltsstrukturgesetz (Budget Structure Law) in 1975, the chancellor introduced one of the most far-reaching and comprehensive austerity packages in the history of the Federal Republic.[160] Hardly any ministry was spared the chancellor's determined cutbacks. For the unions, the Haushaltsstrukturgesetz, accompanied by two previous revisions of the Work Promotion Law of 1969, constituted the first concrete steps towards the implementation of austerity measures at the expense of the labor movement. Its major thrust consisted of initiating severe cutbacks in – even eliminations of – some social and educational services offered by the Work Promotion Law which, as will be recalled, was the first major legislation providing an active manpower policy in West Germany.[161]

Helmut Schmidt succeeded in getting the unions to tolerate, if not applaud, the passage of his austerity measures in the Bundestag. He did this by brilliantly employing a mixture of coercion, persuasion and a genuinely close relationship with some of the unions' most important leaders.[162] Schmidt never tired of reminding the unions that they were hostages to a friendly government. In using this argument, Schmidt appealed not only to the unions' traditionally strong sense of loyalty and "state fixation," but also to their preference for an SPD-led government virtually regardless of the policies which this government pursued in office. Moreover, the chancellor sweetened some of the bitter pills for the unions by pointing to the coalition's junior partner as being mainly responsible for the drastic nature of the government's austerity measures, thus exonerating the Social Democrats. In addition to couching the government's deflationary strategy in the context of "the exigencies of the coalition" (Koalitionszwang), Schmidt also promised to help the unions' cause with other legislation, notably the long-pending co-determination bill.

All of this was made possible by a unique rapport between the chancellor and the leaders of some of the key accommodationist unions. While Willy Brandt was admired by the entire organized labor movement, he never established a strong personal relationship with the union leadership. The latter found him aloof, even a bit haughty, and insufficiently knowledgeable and interested in labor's immediate economic concerns. Schmidt, in contrast, lacked Brandt's charisma but more than compensated for this deficiency in the eyes of many union leaders by being a superb economic expert whose pragmatism, coupled with genuine concern for the average worker, would provide the best combination in defending labor's interests. Schmidt held regular meetings with the union leadership over the years, and repeated visits by union leaders to the chancellor's bungalow must have given the visitor the feeling that he and his union played a crucial role in Schmidt's overall economic strategy. Whether this was actually the case or not remained beside the point, at least until the very end of the SPD–FDP coalition when even Schmidt's rapport with the unions was challenged by open protests, mutual recriminations and general animosity.[163] At the beginning of the crisis there could be no doubt that this arrangement worked. Not only did Schmidt get the unions to keep their protests regarding the passage of the Haushaltsstrukturgesetz to a minimum, but – to the chancellor's delight – the unions held their wage demands to very moderate levels in the 1975 bargaining round. The fact that wage restraint at all costs preoccupied the unions during the first year of the crisis could best be demonstrated by the selection of IG Bau-Stein-Erden, the federation's most accommodationist union, as the DGB's bargaining leader for that round, rather than its habitual vanguard union, IG Metall.[164] At the end of 1975 the unions' hopes regarding government support of labor's cause still remained strong. They were to suffer a severe setback in 1976.

With the Bundestag elections approaching in the fall of 1976, Helmut Schmidt and the Social Democrats felt compelled to reward organized labor in a substantive manner, especially in light of its tolerance of the SPD-led government's austerity measures and labor's obvious restraint on the wage front. By pushing for the passage of the bill on co-determination, the Social Democrats could not have picked a more central and sensitive area in which to assist the unions. The implementation of full-parity co-determination throughout the West German economy was perhaps the most fundamental political goal of the West Geman labor movement. Foiled in this endeavor since the late 1940s and early 1950s, the unions, as will be recalled, placed virtually all their hopes for the attainment of this crucial reform in the SPD's governmental presence. The unions' disappointment concerning the co-determination law of 1976 has to be examined in the context of these exceedingly high expectations determined by a lengthy historical process.

The new co-determination plan which the Bundestag made the law of the land on July 1, 1976, bore heavily the imprint of the FDP to the virtual exclusion of some of the major tenets submitted in earlier drafts by the DGB and the SPD. Indeed, the final law differed only marginally from the proposal submitted to the coalition partners in 1974 which, as already mentioned, reflected much more the desires of the Free Democrats than those of their senior governmental partners and of the unions.[165] Far from fulfilling the DGB's hopes by extending the arrangements of co-determination as practiced in the country's coal and steel industries to all of the West German economy, the new law left no doubt of the employers' continued predominance at the company level. Thus, although there were to be formally an equal number of employer and employee representatives on the supervisory boards of every publicly held company employing more than 2,000 people, the employees' side was to include a representative of the leitende Angestellte (middle management). The unions concluded that since this representative was almost certain to side with the employers, the new law favored capital by reducing labor's de facto representation in the board room. In addition, the board chairman was to be nominated by employer representatives alone and invested with the power of a second vote in the case of deadlock on the board. Furthermore, the labor director who in the 1951 Montanmitbestimmung law was to be nominated solely by the labor representatives on the supervisory board, was, in the 1976 law, to be appointed by the full board, yet another major advantage for the employers. The unions also felt that the new law weakened their organizational presence more than the arrangements of Montanmitbestimmung. Outside union representatives, who formed a majority of the labor side according to the 1951 law, were statutorily assigned a minority position in the 1976 version. Moreover, unlike the provisions of the 1951 law where the union representatives were appointed by union headquarters, the 1976 law stipulated their election by all workers within the firm. Finally, the complex electoral procedures of the 1976 law favored individual and small unaffiliated-group candidacies on the labor side, to the detriment of the DGB unions.[166]

As could be expected, the unions were extremely disappointed with this co-determination law. Yet, once again, the rift between accommodationists and activists came to the fore in the aftermath of the Bundestag's decision. Whereas the former viewed this arrangement as less than perfect and agreed with the DGB's assessment that the law fell short of actual "co-determination," they nevertheless believed that the law represented an improvement over past conditions and thus deserved at least some support from the labor movement. The accommodationists viewed the passage of this law as a direct result of the governmental power of the Social Democratic Party under the astute leadership of Chancellor Helmut Schmidt. To this wing of the labor movement it seemed plausible that due to the exigencies of coalition politics, the SPD could not deliver the kind of co-determination plan which the DGB and the SPD had always desired and for the attainment of which they both still professed to devote their energies. Yet, despite this setback and because of the economic crisis, the accommodationists firmly believed that it was imperative for the labor movement as a whole to maintain its nearly unqualified support for the SPD and Chancellor Schmidt.

For the activists, matters were more complicated. Although they did not advocate any distancing by the unions from the SPD, this wing questioned the magnitude of the gains which the labor movement derived from its close association with the government. Whatever the reasons – inability, unwillingness, or both – the activists increasingly believed that the Schmidt-led coalition simply failed to protect the unions' interests at a time when help from such quarters would have been especially welcome. Although the activists stopped short of calling for any concrete actions by organized labor, developments within some activist unions indicated that a process of estrangement was taking place distancing some members of these unions from Chancellor Schmidt and the SPD. These were the circles which, following the persistence and aggravation of the crisis, ultimately called for union self-reliance independent of – perhaps even in opposition to – an SPD-led government.

Despite the crisis-induced tension between the unions and the social–liberal coalition, Helmut Schmidt continued to court the DGB's favor. He announced on December 16, 1976, in a major speech inaugurating the new government, the implementation of an investment program. Known as ZIP, the German acronym for Zukunftsinvestitionsprogramm (future investment program), this measure was conceived to stimulate domestic demand and decrease unemployment via multi-annual public investments specifically earmarked to improve the Federal Republic's infrastructure. Particular emphasis was to be given to the modernization of transportation, the development of ecologically safer energy systems, the expansion of waterways, the improvement of housing and living conditions, and the continuation of vocational education.[167] The program was to run between 1976 and 1980, and although Schmidt never cited any figures in his address, the magnitude which was originally mentioned hovered around DM 8–10 billion.

Immediately embracing this idea, the DGB wasted little time in contacting the chancellor to express its preferences regarding ZIP. In a letter dated January 20, 1977, and addressed to Chancellor Schmidt, the DGB demanded that the program be significantly more comprehensive by including other sectors of the West German economy as well. To that end, the trade union federation believed that a DM 20 billion budget for ZIP was reasonable. On March 23, 1977, the cabinet established ZIP, allotting about DM 16 billion to this four-year-long investment project.[168]

While obviously happy about this program since it promised to ease unemployment at least in some areas of the West German economy, many in the DGB felt that ZIP was too little too late. In the unions' view, the crisis had succeeded in entrenching itself so deeply into the fabric of West German society that a much greater governmental effort than ZIP was needed if conditions of economic growth and full employment were ever to be restored. ZIP addressed some structural imbalances but failed to alleviate the plight of the "problem groups" consisting mainly of women, the elderly, young entrants into the labor force, the unskilled, foreign workers and workers in depressed sectors and areas. Above all, ZIP was not sufficiently extensive to stimulate macroeconomic growth that would significantly reduce unemployment.

Partly in response to ZIP, but mainly as a result of a failure to recognize the unique nature of this particular crisis, the DGB published a major document in July 1977 entitled "Suggestions Regarding the Restoration of Full Employment."[169] Representing the essential points of the DGB's analysis of and remedies for the crisis – unemployment in particular – the document consists of three parts. Part One, entitled "Acceleration of Qualitative Growth," concentrates on issues such as augmenting state investment by increasing public services, reducing high interest rates which impede both public and private investment, raising the levels of domestic consumption and expanding active manpower policies by the state to increase versatility and improve job qualification among the country's workers, especially those belonging to "problem groups." In this part, the DGB reiterates its demand for concentrated structural policies by the state instead of "sprinkler" remedies which would not be able to reduce unemployment on a permanent basis. Moreover, the DGB makes clear that it will not be deterred from its demands for state assistance by the specter of the growing public deficit's supposedly inflationary nature. Unemployment, the unions asserted, ultimately represents a far greater financial drain and general danger for the commonweal than the public involvement demanded by the DGB.

Part Two of the document, entitled "Social Control of Productivity's Development," focuses exclusively on proposals to curtail the detrimental effects on employment by technological advances. Featured here are some of the DGB's demands concerning the humanization of work both in actuality (i.e. the shop floor) and in its design stages (i.e. the various government ministries and company board rooms). Whereas it would remain up to the unions via collective bargaining agreements and the process of co-determination to intervene in the former, the state would be assigned a major role to assist positively in the latter.

Lastly, in Part Three, the DGB addresses the topic of work-time reduction, an issue which was soon to become perhaps the most divisive in the Federal Republic's industrial relations structure. Starting from the premises that more leisure time permits workers to lead a more humane existence and that shorter work time will also have a beneficial impact on the labor market by necessitating the creation of additional jobs, the document urges the adoption of work-time reduction. Whether via an additional year of mandatory schooling and vocational training, the introduction of work-related sabbaticals, the extension of annual vacation to a minimum of six weeks or the lowering of retirement age to 60 years or below, the DGB favored the introduction of work-time reduction in all possible combinations. The document also demands the abolition of the 1938 law which permitted employers to require workers to put in a virtually limitless amount of overtime per week. While the pamphlet welcomes the introduction of work-time reduction on a yearly, weekly and daily basis, it fails to mention the 35-hour work week, which, only a few months later, was to assume center stage in terms of intra-union controversy for years to come.[170]

Even though the unions received some additional help from the state throughout the rest of the decade and into the early 1980s, the DGB's frustration with the government's austerity measures increased as the crisis continued virtually unabated. Undoubtedly, the unions welcomed projects such as a DM 5 billion investment program spanning a ten-year period to revitalize the depressed Rhine-Ruhr area via job retraining, modernizing the coal industry, industrial diversification and ecological reform, and a DM 500 million job-procurement program passed in 1979 which was to be implemented in those regions suffering from more than 6% unemployment.[171] On the other hand, the DGB was perturbed by the continued imposition of restrictions on the formerly generous Work Promotion Law of 1969, as was the case for example in the summer of 1979 when an administrative decree issued by the quasi-governmental Federal Labor Office in Nuremberg redefined the terms of unemployment forcing the jobless to accept virtually any employment offered to them at the risk of losing their unemployment benefits.[172]

While the DGB's vehement protests against the implication of this decree were successful in that it was withdrawn in its extreme form, further amendments to the Work Promotion Law and other revisions of labor market programs stemming from the reformist heydays of the SPD–FDP coalition weakened the position of the unemployed and thus indirectly that of the unions.[173] Until the demise of the social–liberal coalition in the autumn of 1982, the Schmidt governments basically never rescinded their policy of curtailing the generous entitlements which were instituted by the Brandt-led coalitions during the "reform euphoria" of the early 1970s. Ultimately, Helmut Schmidt succeeded in withstanding pressure from both President Jimmy Carter and the DGB to implement major stimulative programs in order to combat the crisis in West Germany and thereby in the rest of industrialized Western Europe. To the union movement, especially its activist wing, this was a major source of disappointment with the SPD's role in government.

More challenging to the DGB, though perhaps less surprising, than the SPD's failure to be the unions' unequivocal advocate, was the employers' stiffened opposition to labor. While there can be little doubt that the deterioration in union–management relations during the crisis had structural causes, it would be wrong to disregard the role played by particular individuals in heightening the tension between the two "social partners."

Nobody better represented the employers' aggressiveness than the BDA's new leader, Hanns Martin Schleyer. The head of the employers' association since 1974, Schleyer forcefully reorganized this previously weak umbrella association into a centralized, well-coordinated and highly politicized bulwark which guided the employers with a firm hand in their annual battle with the unions and helped industry defend the existing order against encroachments on the freedom of the market by the supposedly growing and "entangled" left.[174]

By the mid-1970s Schleyer and other leading industrialists viewed the SPD, the DGB and many of its member unions as inextricable parts of this "entangled" left. With the continued resilience of the crisis, the employers intensified their ideological offensive against the unions which, as already mentioned, they had begun with their "union state" campaign during the mobilization period of 1973–74.[175] While the content of this campaign was hardly new and indeed harkened back to the 1950s and the era of the Weimar Republic, its intensity in the country's largely conservative press assumed proportions hitherto unseen in the Federal Republic. The employers argued that, if unopposed, the unions would, with the help of other elements of the left, establish a "union state." Such a confrontation, the employers maintained, would jeopardize the democratic institutions of parliament and the social market economy, perhaps the most fundamental pillars of a Rechtsstaat in this view. The unions, according to this argument, had undergone a process of radicalization in the early 1970s which seemed to intensify during the crisis.

There were two parts to the employers' accusation that the unions were about to create a "union state." First the employers attacked the "entanglement" between the SPD, the DGB and its member unions, especially on the leadership level. They felt that the closeness between the Social Democratic Party and the unions on all levels – personal, programmatic and structural – had become so overwhelming that it threatened to transform the politically independent Einheitsgewerkschaft into a partisan union (Richtungsgewerkschaft) under the command of the Social Democratic Party. The second part of the argument reasoned that the increasingly radicalized SPD, dominated by leftwingers, was subverting the unions' political autonomy. Moreover, the employers and the conservative media began to discover communists and other non-Social-Democratic leftists in key union positions. These radicals had succeeded in ensconcing themselves in these offices during the Aufbruchsstimmung (mood of opening) of the late 1960s and the "reform euphoria" of the early 1970s.[176]

The employers received assistance in their campaign against the DGB from the three bourgeois parties – the CDU, CSU and FDP. These parties lent their voice to a wide-ranging debate in the mid-to-late 1970s concerning the possible introduction of a Verbändegesetz (Industrial Relations Act) ostensibly intended to confine the activities and autonomy of all interest groups in order to safeguard parliamentary democracy.[177] Both the Christian and the Free Democrats suggested concrete steps to reform the internal structure and public behavior of interest groups, supposedly to make them conform more to the political conduct of a liberal democratic society. While none of these proposals ever had a chance of becoming law, they added a further edge to an already tense relationship between the unions and the employers.

The height of the conflict was reached in 1979 when an internal CSU paper, mainly authored by the party's Secretary General, Edmund Stoiber, was leaked to the public.[178] Beginning with a detailed discussion of the close "entanglements" between the SPD and the DGB, and then describing the leftward drift of certain unions beyond social democracy, the "Stoiber paper" pondered various measures to counter these developments. One of the solutions suggested by this document was an "Austrianization" of the DGB in which, analogous to the structures of the Austrian Trade Union Federation (ÖGB), groups with official party affiliations would be represented inside the German Trade Union Federation. Another step mentioned by the Stoiber paper to counter the leftward drift of the DGB and its activist members would consist of a massive effort on the part of conservative forces in the Federal Republic to make the miniscule and languishing Christian Trade Union Federation (CGB) into a viable alternative to the DGB. Once again, while none of these suggestions ever left the drawing board and although, following a major public outcry, they were all dismissed by the CSU as notes meant strictly for intraparty consumption, the uneasy relationship between the unions and the employers was further strained by this incident.[179]

Parallel to the employers' ideological offensive against the DGB, West German business also attempted to use the country's court system to proscribe the unions' maneuverability on the shop floor, in company board rooms and ultimately in the process of bargaining. The idea was not to destroy labor via court actions, but rather to weaken its collective resolve by complicating its legal ties with the state by further formalizing this relationship.

The main thrust of this offensive occurred in 1977 when, unexpected by the unions and to their great chagrin, the employers (through twenty-nine employers' associations and nine individual firms) brought a lawsuit challenging the constitutionality of the 1976 Mitbestimmung law.[180] Perhaps more than any other action by the employers during the crisis, this step confirmed to the DGB that the West German business community wanted to use the adverse conditions in the labor market to "roll back" the unions on all fronts, including the crucial one of co-determination. In response to this lawsuit the DGB abandoned the Concerted Action, thus terminating a symbolically important mechanism of conflict management between the two groups.

Ostensibly, the employers' reason for initiating legal action against labor was their view that the new Mitbestimmung law jeopardized stockholders' rights and privileges concerning the fate of private property. In short, the employers based their argument on an alleged sanctification of private property by the Basic Law. Since labor's co-determination in the conduct of company affairs posed a threat to the full sovereignty of owners over their private property, the employers viewed co-determination to be unconstitutional.

It is important to add at this point that the employers never really perceived the emasculated form of co-determination as decreed by the Mitbestimmung law of 1976 to be a threat to their ultimate prerogative over the means of production. Rather, they hoped that the decision by the Federal Constitutional Court in Karlsruhe would set definite legal limits on any further attempts by the unions to promote far-reaching co-determination schemes. Moreover, the employers also calculated that the court's ruling would permit certain interpretations which could potentially help them in their strategy to weaken labor's collective presence inside the Federal Republic's companies.[181]

When the court eventually ruled in 1979, it rejected – to no one's surprise – the employers' suit. Because the 1976 co-determination law fell short of full parity, the court decided that this law did not threaten the prerogatives of employers over investments and property. An essential component of the decision was the fact that the judges viewed capital as enjoying a built-in hegemony because the employers appointed the chairman of the supervisory board, who had the right to cast a second vote in the unlikely event of a tie.[182] The unions reacted to the court's ruling with considerable satisfaction. Yet the decision was not without ambiguities, as indicated by the fact that all protagonists in the dispute were pleased by it.[183] The unions' pleasure was based on the interpretation that the court's ruling did not preclude more extensive Mitbestimmung in the future and that the Basic Law was neutral on questions of property rights. The political parties who had voted for the 1976 law (all four major parties represented in the Bundestag at the time had done so) felt vindicated as well, since the court adjudged the law to be constitutional. The employers, while somewhat disappointed, were able to find comfort in the decision because the court had remained silent concerning the constitutionality of any further expansion of Mitbestimmung. In contrast to the unions, who understood this silence as an invitation to push for full parity co-determination in the future, the employers interpreted it as an indication that the court felt that only the 1976 law was constitutional.[184] Interestingly, and in notable contrast to the generally optimistic interpretation of the official union line, one of the unions' leading legal analysts concurred with the employers' view of the decision in his pessimistic but poignant assessment of the ruling.[185] He argued that the employers' initial hope to have the court's decision address matters of industrial relations beyond the immediate issue of co-determination had largely been realized. Certain passages of the ruling could easily lend themselves to legitimate interventions by the state into areas hitherto more or less under the unions' exclusive autonomy. Furthermore, according to this analyst's interpretation, while the court carefully protected the right of individual workers regarding Mitbestimmung, it was much more restrictive concerning co-determination as a collective right of workers. On the whole, the author concluded, the court viewed Mitbestimmung as an important integrative mechanism for individuals rather than as a participatory scheme of power sharing on the part of a collectivity as represented by unions. Thus, the ruling offered the employers the possibility of decollectivizing industrial conflict by restricting the application of Mitbestimmung to as narrow a level as possible.[186]

While the controversy over the constitutionality of the 1976 Mitbestimmung law represented by far the most prominent example of the employers' strategy to use the courts to narrow labor's scope of action during the crisis, there were a number of other incidents in the late 1970s in which the country's legal system was utilized to intimidate the unions. The frequency and implications of these decisions taken by the courts – especially the Federal Labor Court in Kassel – between 1977 and 1980 came to be regarded by the DGB as part of an "Industrial Relations Act on the installment plan."[187] The common denominator for most of these decisions was the explicit individualization of the worker on the shop floor at the direct expense of the organizational presence of the unions. Taken separately, each of these decisions was hard for the unions to accept. Taken together they made it difficult for the unions to avoid the conclusion that they had become the object of a concerted attack by the employers, through the courts, to limit the unions' shop-floor capacities to resist the degradation of workers' conditions during the crisis.[188] Worse still, these court decisions came at a time when the employers had mounted a major ideological attack against the DGB in the form of the already mentioned "union state" campaign and when West German capital intensified its resolve in the area of collective bargaining with a renewed effort of coordination and centralization as well as a pronounced fondness for the lockout.

One could hardly find more explicit examples of the deterioration of the relationship between capital and labor than the determined use of the lockout by the former and a bolder deployment of the strike by the latter. Even the employers' suit against the co-determination law of 1976 seemed less offensive to the DGB than the massive lockouts which the unions confronted with unprecedented frequency in the late 1970s. Perhaps no other issue united all the DGB unions with such vigor and conviction than the collective battle against the lockout. Few other measures conveyed to them so starkly the employers' ultimate power over the means of production, and by extension over the unions as well. The DGB was determined to do everything it could to curtail, if not – as it preferred – totally eliminate this dangerous weapon at the employers' disposal.[189]

The controversy over the intensified use of lockouts during the crisis began in the spring of 1976 when the employers, countering IG Druck and Papier's strike, locked out over 60,000 printers in more than 700 factories throughout the Federal Republic. It flared up almost exactly two years later when, once again in response to an IG Druck und Paper strike, industrialists in the printing sector locked out 50,000 workers. Overlapping this conflict, employers in Baden-Württemberg's metal industry met IG Metall's strike by locking out 146,000 metalworkers. Lastly, at the end of 1978 and the beginning of 1979, 30,000 steel workers were forcibly kept away from their jobs by the steel industrialists in the Rhine-Ruhr area during IG Metall's strike there.[190]

To the unions, capital's strategy was clear. It involved an increased use of the lockout because the employers hoped to weaken labor's already precarious condition as a consequence of the economic crisis. To the DGB, the lockouts meant three interrelated things: first, they represented an instrument of psychological intimidation, especially in a period burdened by high unemployment and intensified rationalization, since they heightened the already considerable insecurities of workers concerning the stability of their employment. Second, they were intended to demonstrate unmistakably who was the boss. Known in German as the "Herr im Haus" (master of the house) syndrome, the lockout, perhaps more than any other measure, clearly underlines capital's power over the means of production. It demonstrates the employers' ultimate control over the actual access to jobs. Third, lockouts were used to weaken the unions financially.[191] Since West German unions pay strike support to their locked-out members as well, the employers can thus place a heavy burden on union coffers. Indeed, this was the exact scenario in the cases mentioned above. Small IG Druck und Papier was only saved from bankruptcy by an extraordinary amount of financial support from the collective strike fund of all DGB unions and by having been granted a long-term moratorium on payments of its regular membership dues to the DGB. Even mighty IG Metall, the capitalist world's largest individual union, experienced some financial difficulties as a result of having to conduct two strikes while enduring intensive lockouts during the same year. The frequent deployment of lockouts represented a new weapon in the arsenal of the employers which they used with increasing readiness and intensity during the crisis. The DGB had to respond. As could be expected, given the extensively juridified nature of industrial relations in the Federal Republic, it was ultimately a court decision that settled matters, though not to the unions' complete satisfaction.

The Basic Law omits mention of lockouts, as well as strikes. The latter, the DGB argued, were a legal contrivance resulting from a series of decisions reached by the Federal Labor Court, which assumed quasi-constitutional status with the passage of time.[192] Despite massive union protests, however, the legalization of lockouts provided the basis for their widespread use by the employers during the late 1970s. The unions responded to this offensive through labor market action. In order to undercut the legal justification of lockouts, the unions had to turn to the state. Here, again, they met with frustration, despite the SPD's prominent position in government. Anti-lockout legislation, the most desirable way from the DGB's point of view to eliminate the lockout, was stymied by the FDP. Once again, the Free Democrats' vehement anti-unionism and equally strong stand on protecting private property would not allow any such legislation to pass. Even had the FDP been more flexible, important union leaders feared that the use of parliament to stop lockouts would inevitably result in an industrial relations act (Verbändegesetz) which would curtail the right to strike as well.[193] Thus, the DGB was forced to abandon legislative channels and turn all its energies against the lockout into litigation.

As a result of the extensive lockouts which occurred in 1978–79, the DGB and the two immediately affected unions – IG Metall and IG Druck und Papier – initiated mass lawsuits. At least as important as the court actions themselves was the fact that these unions asked every single locked-out worker to sue his/her respective employer for lost wages incurred as a consequence of the lockout. Via these mass actions, the DGB and the two unions succeeded in politicizing an issue of collective grievance which – given the juridified tradition of industrial relations and the general "state fixation" of labor in the Federal Republic – would have previously remained the prerogative of the "apolitical" legal system. The mass lawsuits not only helped raise the political consciousness of those immediately involved, but they also succeeded in disseminating the unions' view regarding lockouts to a public which – on this particular issue – showed a good deal of sympathy and understanding for labor's concerns. Lastly, the unions believed that the rulings by a number of lower courts in labor's favor were directly related to the massive mobilization which the DGB mounted successfully in connection with its legal offensive against the lockouts of the late 1970s.[194] The Federal Labor Court, the ultimate authority on this matter, reached its verdict regarding these lawsuits on June 11, 1980. The decision was greeted by the unions with ambivalence.[195]

While not outlawing lockouts, as the DGB hoped, the court did introduce certain measures which were welcomed by the unions. Lockouts, for example, were not interpreted to be capital's legal equivalent to labor's strike. The court recognized the strike as an integral part of the unions' *raison d'être* and, therefore, judged it to be profoundly different from lockouts due to the employer's controlling position over the means of production, which makes the employer inherently stronger than labor in industrial conflicts. Moreover, the court held that lockouts could not be aimed solely at union members. In addition, the court agreed with the DGB's position that one of the major aims of lockouts was the substantial weakening of union funds. The court thus ruled that the employers could henceforth not initiate a lockout, thereby relegating it from its previously offensive posture to one of pure defense. Lastly, and perhaps most importantly, the court held that lockouts had to occur in a proportional scope to the ongoing strike. In concretizing this point the court found the printing industry guilty of having abused the lockout in a disproportionate manner by locking out many more people than were on strike. Despite these favorable details, the court's verdict represented only a mixed success for the unions since their ultimate hope – the complete and irrevocable elimination of lockouts – remained unfulfilled.[196]

Concomitant with this ruling, the month of June 1980 witnessed yet another attack by the employers on the unions, which the latter viewed as part of capital's rollback strategy. The huge Mannesmann corporation announced a reorganization plan whereby its hitherto autonomous steel-producing company, Mannesmann Hüttenwerke, was to be incorporated into its sole customer, Mannesmann Röhrenwerke, which specialized in the processing of steel received from the Hüttenwerke.[197] While to most people this internal reshuffling seemed a routine procedure often exercised by many outfits of Mannesmann's stature and diversity, to the DGB and some SPD leaders it represented nothing short of an "attack against one of the main pillars of the Federal Republic's social system."[198] The corporation's sole justification for the merger rested on the argument that this measure would save Mannesmann up to DM 50 million per annum. IG Metall and the DGB, however, perceived another reason for Mannesmann's action: to extricate the corporation from the more union-friendly model of Montanmitbestimmung and place it under the jurisdiction of the more capital-friendly co-determination plan defined by the 1976 Mitbestimmung law. Since, according to the proposed reorganization, the corporation would no longer include an independent unit primarily engaged in steel production, Mannesmann would thus leave the steel-producing industry, thereby also legitimately divesting itself of Montanmitbestimmung, which – as will be recalled – pertains only to the areas of steel and coal production.

Although Mannesmann had a long history since the passage of Montanmitbestimmung in 1951 of trying to weaken union presence in the board rooms of the holding company (Mannesmann AG), the renewed attempt to do so by abolishing the autonomy of its steel-producing division was prima facie evidence for the unions of yet another attempt by the employers to weaken labor in the crisis.[199] To the DGB, the Mannesmann affair was a proxy in a much larger frontal attack against labor which included court rulings, the employers' "union state" campaign, the increasing frequency of lockouts and also some political practices of the "bourgeois" parties. By July 1980 the "causa Mannesmann" had become one of the major areas of disagreement between the coalition partners, with the SPD predictably favoring an agreement whereby Montanmitbestimmung would be maintained in the uppermost echelons of the Mannesmann corporation while the FDP strongly defended the corporation's prerogative to pursue any internal reorganization that it wanted.[200] IG Metall and the DGB organized a major conference in July as part of a general mobilization effort in defense of Montanmitbestimmung at Mannesmann. A number of short strikes during the summer clearly conveyed that the "Mannesmann case" was not perceived as an isolated incident by the participants but rather as part of the general employers' offensive against the unions.[201]

With an election imminent in the fall of 1980, the SPD went to some lengths to defend the unions' position while its smaller coalition partner doggedly continued to take Mannesmann's side. It was not until 1981 that this issue was resolved by a compromise between the Free and Social Democrats, which – as had so frequently been the case since the onset of the crisis in the mid-1970s – was hardly to the unions' liking. The most fundamental aspects of a rather complex arrangement called for the continuation of Montanmitbestimmung at Mannesmann AG until 1987 with its permanent disappearance thereafter.[202] Thus, once again the Social Democrats disappointed the DGB by failing to provide the unions with the reforms and legislation they desired and by lacking the wherewithal – or, as a growing number of unionists began to feel, the willingness – to defend them against concerted attacks by employers.

Lastly, capital's offensive against the unions during the crisis also manifested itself in a general deterioration of the quality of work life for workers in the production process and a hardening of positions in virtually all areas of collective bargaining. While there can be little doubt that some employers willfully tried to make the most of labor's weakened position during the crisis, much of the increase in tension between the two "social partners" had structural origins derived from the necessity of remaining competitive in the world market under consistently more difficult circumstances. It is in this context that one has to assess the quickening pace of rationalization to which West Germany employers resorted with unprecedented zeal. The growing use of microelectronics, which is of particular importance to the export-oriented economy of the Federal Republic, began to threaten many jobs. In addition to the unions' quantitative problem of job eliminations, the employers' strategy of rationalization confronted the unions with such qualitative matters as dequalification, further mechanization ("dehumanization") of work and an increasing fragmentation of the work process. The trend towards this quantitative and qualitative deterioration of labor's shop-floor presence during the crisis was further exacerbated as the employers resorted to an intensification of capital export. It was especially the creation of jobs in low-wage countries at the direct expense of employment in the Federal Republic which aroused the unions' ire during a period of already less than optimal conditions.[203] In short, both objective and subjective factors contributed to a substantial worsening of capital–labor relations in the workplace during the late 1970s.

The DGB's suspicion that this deterioration formed an essential part of the employers' general offensive against labor during the crisis was finally corroborated by the appearance in January 1979 of a Tabu Katalog.[204] In existence since 1965 and repeatedly revised since the beginning of the economic crisis in 1975, this Katalog enumerated the BDA's strict guidelines for its members' proper behavior concerning their dealings with labor in the process of collective bargaining. Extending over a number of pages, it set detailed parameters and strict limits for every BDA member regarding such issues as working conditions, work time and work content. The document's firm guidelines clearly aimed at maximizing the employers' control over every phase of their interaction with labor. The Tabu Katalog also served as a concise handbook for the employers' strategy of coordination and centralization in their bargaining with the unions during the crisis. That this "teleguidance" or "remote control mechanism," as the unions called it, was indeed practiced by the BDA and thus represented more than a mere proposal was demonstrated by a controversy involving work-time reduction.[205]

Among the most serious prohibitions of the Tabu Katalog were that no member of the BDA could reduce weekly work time below 40 hours, nor could any firm or association belonging to the BDA offer a vacation package of more than six weeks' duration. When in the summer of 1978 brewers signed a contract with the union representing the workers in that industry (Gewerkschaft Nahrung-Genuss-Gaststätten – NGG) which amounted to a work week under 40 hours, the BDA forced the brewers to rescind the already signed contract and negotiate a new one in which the 40-hour work week was reinstituted in exchange for early retirement plans for elderly workers.[206] Puzzled and angry, the DGB suspected some sort of "teleguidance" on the part of the employers, but no tangible proof was available.

It was not until a few months later that in the course of a major showdown in West Germany's steel industry, in which IG Metall went on strike to attain a reduction in the 40-hour work week, the Tabu Katalog was revealed to the public. While the employers had been busily denouncing the unions for their excessive centralization, internal coordination and gradual undermining of collective bargaining autonomy (Tarifautonomie) – all of which, of course, represented crucial ingredients in the employers' "union state" campaign – it was in fact capital that pursued all these steps with the sole purpose of weakening labor. Yet no one, as far as the DGB could see, seemed particularly concerned about the imminence of an "employers state" ruining the Federal Republic's parliamentary democracy. All of this, of course, left the unions with the feeling that the employers had the edge in virtually every realm in which the two social partners clashed during the difficult period of the late 1970s and early 1980s. Events forced the DGB to undergo a process of strategic reevaluation. A discussion of this development forms the last part of this chapter.

The salience and permanence of three interrelated problems increasingly bothered the unions as the crisis went on: first, the high level of unemployment represented the most severe handicap for organized labor. Second, the Schmidt government's cautious, even reluctant, support for labor left a number of the unions angry and disappointed in light of the few tangible – and, it was felt, mostly inadequate – results which the labor movement could legitimately claim as having derived from "its" party's role as senior member of the governmental coalition. Third, capital's concerted offensive seriously threatened the unions' position both outside and inside West Germany's factory gates. The passionate debates which ensued within the union movement in the quest to find strategies to alleviate some of these pressures led to new steps on labor's part. However, they also contributed to the re-opening of some old intra-union hostilities, hampering the effectiveness of the unions' collective response.

Concerning the latter, the split once again occurred between accommodationist unions and their activist counterparts. While the second group consisted of IG Metall, IG Druck und Papier, the Commerce, Banking and Insurance Workers' Union (HBV) and the Leather Workers' Union (Gewerkschaft Leder), the former group comprised the "gang of five" including IG Chemie, IG Bau, IG Bergbau, the Textile-Clothing Workers' Union (GTB) and the Food-Processing Workers' Union (NGG). In notable contrast to the early 1970s, when IG Chemie found itself among the activists in the DGB, a major aspect of the crisis-induced change within the federation was IG Chemie's conversion to one of the most vocal representatives of the accommodationists by the late 1970s. (For a detailed discussion of IG Chemie's development, see Chapter 5.)

In terms of the formulation and pursuit of counterstrategies to combat the crisis, the accommodationists advocated an even heavier reliance on the state by labor. Emphasizing the traditional ties between the Social Democratic Party and the trade unions, and also giving a lot of credence to the close personal relationship between Chancellor Schmidt and the leaders of the "gang of five," the accommodationist unions pleaded for labor's uncritical support for the SPD. These unions felt that this approach should be the centerpiece of the unions' strategy to counter the adversities of the crisis. This "SPD-and-Schmidt-fixation" assumed such importance among the accommodationists by the late 1970s and early 1980s that their adversaries dubbed them "sewer-worker unions" (Kanalarbeitergewerk-schaften) and/or "chancellor's unions" (Kanzlergewerkschaften).[207] In addition to advocating a political alliance between labor and the SPD's center and right wing, the accommodationists placed a heavy emphasis on early-retirement plans as a way to ease the adversities of the labor market. Almost every union among the "gang of five" had signed collective bargaining agreements with the employers by the early 1980s arranging for early retirement and other flexible work models for their elderly members. Moreover, reflecting these unions' rightward drift and their unabashedly close relationship with the conservative elements of the Social Democratic Party, the "gang of five" made the battle against the supposedly imminent subversion of the labor movement by members of the Communist Party and other radical elements a major priority of union politics during the crisis.[208]

On the whole, the accommodationists opted for an interest-group-oriented solution to the crisis. While some called it "corporatist" or "neo-corporatist" and others described it as an "Americanization" of the West German labor movement, the policy of these unions was first and foremost to defend their membership's interests and only secondarily to be concerned with the plight of other West German workers.[209] In short, the accommodationist wing of the DGB placed its hopes in a countercrisis strategy which emphasized political moderation, heavy reliance on the SPD's "sewer workers," continuation of the close relationship with Chancellor Schmidt, and a particularistic interest-group orientation which favored the core of the working class over its periphery.

The activists on the other hand seemed to undergo a steady process of radicalization during the crisis. This manifested itself in an increasing disillusion with the SPD and Chancellor Helmut Schmidt. While even these unions were wary of publicly criticizing the Social Democratic Party – partly as a consequence of traditional loyalty to the party, partly because of a conviction that no matter how disappointing, the SPD's performance would be better than the CDU's – many leading unionists from the DGB's activist wing expressed considerable disaffection with the government's overly timid policies to counter the crisis. The activist unions distanced themselves from the mainstream of the SPD during the late 1970s and early 1980s without, however, renouncing the traditional ties of the German working class to social democracy.

As a result of this distancing process, the activists began to formulate a strategy of union self-reliance. Far from being a version of radical syndicalism, this step was taken to affirm the unions' disillusionment with the government in power, acknowledge the limits of social democracy and have the unions pick up the slack where the former two structures failed to defend labor's interests. This self-reliance concentrated on making the unions' bargaining power vis-à-vis the employers the centerpiece of labor's strategy to combat the hardships of the crisis. The unions were their own masters in the realm of collective bargaining and did not need to rely on a party, the state or any other outside agent to help in this process. This strategy of self-reliance contained two elements: the first was concerned with strengthening the unions' shop-floor power to counter the hardships imposed by the employers' intensified rationalization measures. The second focused on the introduction of the 35-hour work week which in many ways remained the West German unions' most controversial demand into the middle of the 1980s.

Controversy and conflict surrounded the 35-hour work week from the very beginning of its appearance on the unions' strategic agenda. At IG Metall's turbulent Düsseldorf congress in the fall of 1977, this initiative was finally converted into official union policy by a bare majority following acrimonious debates in which much of the union's leadership – including its chairman Eugen Loderer – and its powerful delegation from the Stuttgart district in Baden-Württemberg opposed this measure.[210] A similar struggle occurred one year later at the DGB's congress when – over the vehement objections of the accommodationist wing – IG Metall and its allies succeeded in making the 35-hour work week an official DGB demand. Supporters of this reform argued that only via a substantial reduction of weekly work time could the DGB contribute to an improvement of the chronically dire situation in the labor market. In addition to having the most powerful employment effect among all forms of work-time reduction, the 35-hour work week – its supporters maintained – also outdistanced other proposals by providing the most favorable possibilities for humanizing work.

While support for the 35-hour work week grew within the DGB in the course of the late 1970s and early 1980s, sufficient reservations as to its feasibility and ultimate benefits for labor lingered in virtually every union – including IG Metall – to make any industrial action on behalf of this goal problematic. This became clear in the steel strike which IG Metall conducted in late 1978 and early 1979.[211] The ambivalence on the part of many unionists was also apparent in the early summer of 1984 when both IG Metall and IG Druck und Papier engaged in lengthy strikes to attain a sizable reduction in the 40-hour work week towards the ultimate goal of its replacement by 35 hours.[212]

Lastly, the activist group also tacitly encouraged increased dialogue between union officials and strategists on the one hand and various left-leaning intellectuals and academics on the other. Since this relationship only fueled the raging controversy about the supposedly subversive activities of radicals and communists in unions – an issue which united employers and DGB accommodationists against the activist unions – the latter had to proceed very gingerly on this matter and chose to do so with virtually no official approval. Indeed, these contacts were not even supported by all leaders of the DGB's activist wing. Yet, despite massive opposition from all sides, the lasting nature of the crisis forced the more adventurous elements among the activist unions to seek help from anybody who was willing to offer it. It is in this context that the so-called Memorandum debates heated up within the DGB during the late 1970s.

Annually published on May Day since 1976 by a number of radical economists originally centered at the University of Bremen but subsequently encompassing all of the Federal Republic, this document gradually developed into the most prominent "counterproposal" to the annual statement on the economy and economic policy published by the highly prestigious and influential Council of Economic Advisors, also known as the "Five Wise Men."[213] With the latter assuming an increasingly rigid advocacy of austerity measures as the crisis continued, the Memorandum became, perhaps *faute de mieux*, a rallying point for all those in the Federal Republic who sought a different solution. At first ignored by the unions because of the prominence of many leftist intellectuals as authors and supporters, the Memoranda enjoyed growing legitimacy as of 1979 when many leading unionists endorsed the Memorandum of that year.[214] The Memoranda thus became annual focal points of the DGB's strategic debates concerning the formulation of economic policy. These documents served as important sounding-boards for the unions' attempts to develop steps against the crisis.

All Memoranda comprised two parts.[215] The first contained a detailed analysis of the causes and manifestations of the crisis. Here, the authors concentrated most of their efforts on explaining the consistently high level of unemployment and the concomitant lack of macroeconomic growth, both subjects close to the unions' heart. The Memoranda argued that in addition to recent advances in rationalization and the exogenous influences of the world market upon the West German economy, contributing factors to the crisis were also to be found in an intensifying process of monopolization and the unchecked pricing power of cartels and large firms in the Federal Republic. The Memoranda's authors maintained that, due to the unchallenged power of the monopolies, their pricing policy – supported by the state's lack of countermeasures, possibly even enhanced by its tax incentives and other subsidies – had increased their profits during the crisis to an extent where these monopolies chose not to invest commensurate to their capabilities and the needs of the West German economy. The Memoranda concluded that the main characteristics of the crisis were excessive profits accompanied by low growth. Sluggish investment was thus not a consequence of insufficient profits.

The second part of the Memoranda concentrated on various policies, strategies and measures which were deemed necessary to counteract the adversities of the crisis. In this section the authors dealt mainly with the unions. Absolutely central were the demands for a consistent increase in consumption via an aggressive wage policy, a progressive and strictly implemented tax policy geared to redistribute the excessive profits of the monopolies, and the increase of direct state expenditures. The Memoranda also advocated the gradual shortening of the work week to 35 hours, the implementation of other work-time-reducing measures such as early retirement and the introduction of an additional mandatory school year, and state policies to ease the burden of job compatibility for labor while simultaneously imposing stricter guidelines on employers by making them hire unemployed workers. Lastly, the Memoranda emphasized the role that institutions such as Mitbestimmung, regional-planning agencies and investment-guidance devices (some still nonexistent) would play in guaranteeing full participation on the part of the unions in the realization of these policies.

While the theoretical propositions put forth in the first part of the

Memoranda initiated major controversies among the Federal Republic's left-wing social scientists and were subjected to considerable criticism by a number of economists, some of whom worked for the unions, the strategies and concrete steps forming the Memoranda's second section gradually began to enjoy the overall support of the unions, particularly those belonging to the DGB's activist wing.[216] Disregarding the Marxist terminology, the unions increasingly began to accept the Memoranda as one of the few public documents which demanded a solution similar to their own to the crisis in the Federal Republic. The integration of the Memoranda into programmatic elements of the DGB's economic thinking could be demonstrated by the fact that by the early 1980s only a few members of the accommodationist unions objected to the document's Marxist language and that it had almost become de rigeur for union intellectuals to sign these annual statements, which they could now do without fear of any organizational reprisal, in contrast to the situation of the late 1970s.[217]

Given the West German trade unions' penchant periodically to formulate programs which give an overview of their position in society, it would have been quite uncharacteristic for the DGB not to respond – via the creation of programs – to so momentous and arduous an event as the crisis afflicting the Federal Republic's economy since the mid-1970s. The peculiarities of this crisis needed to be addressed by the union leadership and discussed in a systematic fashion by the entire organization. The general reevaluation process concerning the areas of collective bargaining, economic policy, the unions' relationship with the state, and their interaction with the parties, especially the SPD, had to be "carried into the organization" as the Germans put it (in die Organisation hineintragen) in order to develop short-term tactics and long-term strategies. Toward this end, the DGB published its fifth Aktionsprogramm in 1979 and its third Basic Program in 1981.[218]

The central point of the former, which, unlike its predecessors, was not published on May Day but appeared instead on June 13, consisted "in realizing short- and medium-term goals for all union activities" under the changing conditions of the crisis.[219] In replacing its predecessor from 1972, the 1979 Aktionsprogramm is an excellent summary of the unions' changed positions, strategies and tactics as a consequence of the dislocations of the intervening period. Following well-established traditions, the changes between the new and the old Aktionsprogramm lie not so much in overt policy shifts but rather in subtle stylistic alterations, rearrangements in the ordering of items and differences in emphasis. Only a careful reading and meticulous side-by-side comparison of the DGB's Aktionsprogramms, in addition to a general knowledge of union policies over the years, will convey the fact that the changes in form also entail considerable divergences in content.[220]

Perhaps the most notable change in emphasis between the two programs is their view of unemployment. Whereas the 1972 Program lists "job security" with little detail and as its fifth item, this concern, accompanied by the demand for guaranteed employment, prominently follows the 1979 Program's preamble as the first point of substance, thus clearly denoting the problem of unemployment as the unions' most serious preoccupation. Moreover, the 16 detailed sub-categories of the "guaranteed employment/job security" demand further corroborate the salience of this issue for the unions.

The mere existence of the second point of the new program, "expansion of collective bargaining autonomy" (Tarifautonomie), highlights the change in conditions for the unions since 1972. Absent from the 1972 Aktionsprogramm, this demand concentrates almost exclusively on lockouts and the DGB's ardent wish to have them unconditionally abolished. Furthermore, this category also includes an extended discussion of "the new – or rather rediscovered – dimension of qualitative collective bargaining" and the growing importance of collective bargaining agreements to areas hitherto covered by state policy and action.

Most important, there is an emphasis throughout the document on the benefits for labor of self-reliance and reducing its traditional orientation towards the state. In the words of a knowledgeable union analyst:

> If one reads the whole text [of the 1979 Aktionsprogramm] in its proper context it becomes clear that in demanding reforms there is a greater emphasis on the unions' own capabilities rather than reliance upon the state for the implementation of demands as had been the case for decades.[221]

Another important difference from the 1972 Aktionsprogramm lies in its successor's repeated reminders of the detrimental nature of rationalization. Specifically, the new Aktionsprogramm does not only discuss rationalization's adverse effects on employment, but also devotes considerable space to related issues such as dequalification and work intensification. Moreover, the program attempts to establish a definite linkage among such phenomena as unemployment, loss of income, deteriorating work conditions, dequalification, the employers' general offensive and the state's inability/reluctance to implement necessary reforms. Unlike its 1972 predecessor, the 1979 Aktionsprogramm makes an attempt to come to terms with the growing interdependence among work, living conditions and the natural environment. It is also in this context, among others, that various forms of work-time reduction, including the 35-hour work week, receive mention.[222]

In sum, the Aktionsprogramm of 1979 incorporated the unions' major experiences since the onset of the crisis. The document's tone and emphasis reflected the shifts in the content of union policies and the arenas of implementation. The Aktionsprogramm's scope was, by its very nature, primarily limited to tactical considerations since its mandate had been to address short- and medium-term problems. Thus, it remained up to the new Basic Program to address changes in the long-term outlook of the unions and delineate the broad framework for the DGB's actions through the decade of the 1980s.

Just like its predecessors of 1949 and 1963, the Basic Program of 1981 addresses virtually every aspect of public life in the Federal Republic and even beyond.[223] Moreover, again like its two forerunners, the new program represents a compromise between the accommodationist and the activist wings of the DGB, large and small unions, those primarily concerned with organizing in private industry and their counterparts in the public sector. Yet, despite these conflicts, which necessarily lend the document an aura of vagueness, a close reading of the Basic Program of 1981 clearly conveys some of the changes which affected the DGB during the 1970s, especially following the onset of the crisis in 1975.

The lengthy preamble of the 1981 Basic Program highlights some important shifts in the unions' political outlook since the adoption of the 1963 Basic Program. The new Düsseldorf Program – the DGB held a special union congress in that city during March 1981 to approve the new Basic Program – omits any mention of Germany's reunification as one of the main preconditions for peaceful order in Europe. Equally interesting is the fact that the new document fails to discuss the capital of Germany, whereas its predecessor still mentioned Berlin in that role. While in and of themselves rather minor points, they nevertheless express a great deal about the change in outlook which informed the DGB's political reality between 1963 and 1981.

The preamble also devotes considerable attention to the two main tenets of the post-World II union movement, namely the industrial and unitary character of West Germany's labor representation. Extolling this as a major historical achievement by contrasting the West German situation to the disastrous consequences of the party-led multi-unionism of the Weimar Republic, the Basic Program of 1981 attests to the unions' worries of seeing their cherished institutionalized unity undermined by the crisis. There can be no doubt that the DGB was worried about the intent of extremists of either political direction to use the crisis in order to undermine the unitary trade union movement. The employers' relentless "union state" attacks, their intensified use of lockouts, their concerted efforts to undermine Mitbestimmung wherever possible and the surfacing of the Tabu Katalog

Katalog alerted the DGB to a definite danger from the right. Moreover, while paling in comparison to this threat against the unitary trade union movement, the DGB also felt less than comfortable with the emergence of certain radical leftist – particularly communist – tendencies among some of its member unions. It is in the context of both of these crisis phenomena that the following passage of the preamble assumed such importance in the intra-union debate which accompanied the adoption of the new program:

> The unitary trade union movement has emerged out of the workers' experiences during the Weimar Republic and the persecutions of Nazi dictatorship. It has combined into one common organization the historical traditions, political directions and ideological currents of the labor movement, especially as constituted by its liberal–socialist [freiheitlich-sozialistisch] and Christian–social [christlich-sozial] components. Any competing unions are rendered completely unnecessary. The internal diversity of opinions guarantees an autonomous and independent political process which articulates the common interests of all workers [Arbeitnehmer]. Political ideologies and directions which want to abuse the unions for their own purposes, are incompatible with the idea of the unitary trade union movement.[224]

This passage of the preamble not only delegitimates any attempts by the Christian right – especially the CSU – to form a viable alternative federation to the DGB on explicitly political lines as had been contemplated in the "Stoiber paper," but it also limits the role of radicals – especially members of the Communist party, DKP – to their marginality in the unions, where their presence as union "members" was tolerated, while the unfolding of their "cadre politics" was not.[225] The program thus justifies the future political direction of the unions by invoking the glories – as well as tragedies – of their past.

The new Basic Program also places great emphasis on a discussion of the Federal Republic's constitution, the Basic Law. In noticeable contrast to the DGB's Düsseldorf Program of 1963 in which the Basic Law was barely mentioned, the new program devotes five lengthy paragraphs in its preamble to the unions' interpretation of the Basic Law's general role vis-à-vis society and the state. In light of important court decisions during the crisis, especially the Federal Constitutional Court's verdict regarding Mitbestimmung, the DGB seems particularly eager to declare in a prominent document that the Basic Law "draws no conclusions regarding the existence of any particular economic order" in the Federal Republic. The Basic Law does, however, in the DGB's view, endorse an economic and social system which recognizes the social responsibilities and collective obligations of capital vis-à-vis the community as a whole. This, for the unions, forms the very essence of a "democratic and social state based on the rule of law" (sozialer Rechtsstaat).[226]

As to the Basic Law's role concerning property, the unions cite the following passages from this document in their Basic Program:

> Property obliges. Its use has to serve the welfare of the general public. Land, natural resources and means of production can be transformed into common property [Gemeineigentum] or other forms of publicly owned property [Gemeinwirtschaft] for the purposes of socialization [Vergesellschaftung].[227]

The DGB's new Basic Program also detects another obligation concerning the Basic Law's stipulation for the continued presence of a sozialer Rechtsstaat in the Federal Republic:

> The sozialer Rechtsstaat contains the permanent mandate not to defend the privilege of the few and to continue upholding the existing power relations, but rather to create the conditions for the enhancement of the personal rights of all people via the introduction and implementation of social reforms.[228]

Although the new Düsseldorf Program, in notable contrast to the medium-term-oriented Aktionsprogramm of 1979, refrains from mentioning such specific items of the employers' offensive as the increased use of the lockout, the Tabu Katalog and the repeated attacks against Mitbestimmung, there can be little doubt that the drafting of this Basic Program was influenced by these measures. Having been subjected to a well-organized offensive by the employers – a process wherein constitutional justifications for the confinement of union activities played a central role – the DGB, not surprisingly, felt a need to display these developments prominently in its most important document.

The unions' experiences during the crisis found their programmatic expression in many of the 30 specific sections which followed the preamble and constitute the bulk of this 28-page document.[229] The most striking difference in comparison with the 1963 Düsseldorf Program consists in the preeminence of concerns such as unemployment, rationalization and humanization of work which dominate every aspect of this program. As to some of the 30 categories, the ones explicitly entitled "Humanization of Work" and "Protection of the Environment" are completely new, thereby highlighting their relatively recent relevance to union politics in particular and West German public discourse in general. Many of the other key sections of the program such as "Control of Economic Power," "Full Employment," "Investment Guidance," "Macroeconomic Planning," "Public Budget, Finance, Tax and Monetary Policy" and "Science and Research," to name but a few, include substantial revisions of their respective predecessors in the 1963 Düsseldorf Program.

The common denominator to most of these changes and additions is in tone and order of appearence in the DGB's new Basic Program. Once again form prevailed over content, indicating perhaps that little in terms of programmatic substance had changed for the unions during the 1970s. Yet it is precisely at the level of nuance that DGB strategic shifts, programmatic preferences and changes in political content become manifest. There can be little doubt that these subtle shifts in tone and emphasis were operative in the creation and formulation of the DGB's Basic Program of 1981 and continued to inform the intra-organizational debate which accompanied the Program's implementation in the early 1980s. Viewed in the context of the Aktionsprogramm of 1979, the resolutions from the union congresses, and the general trajectory of the DGB's concerns during the late 1970s and early 1980s, the 1981 Basic Program represents quite accurately the West German trade unions' state of mind at the beginning of the 1980s. While vague in terms of offering concrete suggestions for the future, the document reflects the painful process of reevaluation upon which the DGB and its constituent unions embarked in the wake of the crisis of the late 1970s. As such, the new Basic Program reconfirms the contention that for organized labor in West Germany "nothing will ever be like it was before 1974."

# 4 VANGUARD OF WEST GERMAN LABOR: THE METALWORKERS' UNION, IG METALL

## INTRODUCTION

Industriegewerkschaft Metall (IG Metall) is not only the DGB's most important member organization, but indeed constitutes the largest labor union in the non-communist world. This union's 2,684,509 members,[1] encompassing a little over one-third of the entire organized West German labor movement, make IG Metall the hegemonic force in post-war developments concerning the working class in the Federal Republic. IG Metall's overall significance pertains not only to its organizational domain, which includes the most crucial sectors of West German industry such as steel, machinery, automobiles and electronics, but also to its leadership position in most areas of union strategy and policy-making. Whether in its role as vanguard for almost every annual wage round, in the formulation of new concepts regarding collective bargaining issues and economic policy, or in the key realms of union–state and union–party relationships, IG Metall represents a first-among-equals within the DGB federation. While a thorough analysis of its activities, strategies and concerns following the end of World War II may not in and of itself entirely explain the course of the West German labor movement since the late 1940s, any account of union politics in the Federal Republic that omits a broad historical presentation of IG Metall's developments would remain woefully inadequate – indeed quite misleading. The task of the following pages will be to offer an encapsulated version of these developments.

The chapter will begin with a relatively detailed overview of some crucial data such as the sociology of the IG Metall membership, the union's organizational components and its collective bargaining system, all of which form the basic framework for a proper contextual analysis of the union's policies and strategies. The remainder of this chapter will assess IG Metall's major activities over the first three decades of its existence. Divided into four analytically distinct periods, each delineating certain visible alterations in the union's policies and strategies, this part of the chapter will highlight IG Metall's developments through the eventful early 1950s, the more complacent decade between 1957 and 1967, and the resurgence of hope and mobilization during the late 1960s and early 1970s. Lastly, it will examine the uncertainties, fears, and guarded optimism which characterize the crisis period of the mid-1970s. The chapter will conclude with tentative evaluations of IG Metall's future role in the West German labor movement and political economy in general.

## I. THE METAL INDUSTRY AND ITS EMPLOYERS' ASSOCIATIONS

### A. The industry

IG Metall commonly refers to its organizational jurisdiction as the Metallindustrie (metal industry), which is in fact a general term for the numerous individual industries that either produce or process metals. Taken together, these industries account for 48% of total sales and 60% of total employment in West German manufacturing.[2] In addition, the 4,321,000 (1981) persons employed in the metal sector represent close to 17% of the entire labor force in the Federal Republic.[3] Metal production and processing truly make up the core of the West German economy and their continued competitiveness on world markets is crucial if the nation's economic successes of the last three decades are to be repeated.

Metal industries fall into two basic categories according to the German industrial classification system.[4] Five of the thirteen industries in the raw materials and production goods sector (Grundstoff- und Produktions-gütergewerbe) manufacture basic metals or metal products which are used by other processing industries. The most prominent metal-producing industry is iron and steel. The investment or capital goods sector (Investitionsgüter produzierendes Gewerbe) consists entirely of metal-processing industries like machinery and motor-vehicle production (cars are considered investment goods). One last metal-processing industry, musical instruments and recreational equipment production, is considered part of the consumer goods sector (Verbrauchsgüter produzierendes Gewerbe).

Of the five production goods industries involving metals, the iron and steel industry is by far the largest and most significant. The other industries are non-ferrous metal production, foundries, cold rolling mills, and wire and wire products, the last four of which are closely tied to raw steel production. The West German steel industry, like its counterparts in all industrialized countries, has suffered over the past decade from a prolonged structural crisis. Despite the fact that the West German industry is by far the most modern and efficient in Europe, 145,000 jobs were lost (from 418,000 to 273,000) between 1960 and 1981[5] as a result of both rationalization efforts and the presence of excess production capacity.

The steel industry in the Federal Republic is highly concentrated, with seven firms accounting for 94.1% of all raw steel production in 1979.[6] These firms were (in descending order of size): Thyssen (Europe's largest steel company), Hoesch, Arbed (a Luxemburg-based firm), Krupp Steel, Klöckner, Mannesmann Steel, and Peine-Salzgitter (state-owned). All these companies produce a range of steel products from raw steel to specialty steel, and Mannesmann is one of the world's largest makers of steel pipes. Most of the companies (Thyssen, Krupp, Hoesch and Mannesmann) have their mills located in the Ruhr Valley, traditional home to German steel, and within the Ruhr, Duisburg and Dortmund are the main production centers. Klöckner owns mills in Bremen (a coastal work), Osnabrück and northern Bavaria, while Peine-Salzgitter is located near the East German border in Lower Saxony. Finally, Arbed is the main producer in the crisis-ridden Saar steel industry. Despite its high visibility and political importance, the steel industry's economic weight when measured in terms of output and employment is significantly less than that of several large metal-processing industries.

All told, there are twelve metal-processing industries represented in the Federal Republic, ranging in size from castings and pressings (43,000 employees in 1981) to machinery (Maschinenbau – 1,023,000 employees). The three dominant industries in this group have traditionally been machinery; electrical equipment, electrical appliances and electronics (948,000); and motor vehicles (787,000), followed by iron and metal wares (such as cutlery) and steel construction (e.g. steel containers, railroad cars). Other important metal-processing industries include aerospace, office equipment and computers, shipbuilding, precision instruments, and watches.[7]

The major strength of the West German economy compared to its European competitors is the former's overwhelming strength in the area of machinery production of every type. West German machine exports played a crucial role in fueling Europe's rapid economic growth after 1949. The importance of foreign sales to this industry is underlined by the fact that its export quota (in percentage of total sales) was 44.8% in 1981.[8] Today Maschinenbau (best expressed by the British term "mechanical engineering") remains the largest industrial employer in the Federal Republic. The "machinery industry," like the "metal industry," is a general category covering over thirty industries producing machinery of different types. The largest of these is the machine tools industry, followed by agricultural machinery, "drive technology" (Antriebstechnik, i.e. motors), office and information technology, and "conveyance technology" (Fördertechnik, i.e. lifts, conveyor belts and elevators).[9]

The machinery industry is characterized by a very low level of concentration; the sector's three largest firms account for about 7% of total employment.[10] The traditional image of the industry as characterized by hundreds of small and medium-sized family firms operating in specialized markets is borne out by the fact that only 426 of Maschinenbau's 5,337 plants (1981) employed more than 500 workers, and the percentage of workers in plants with over 1,000 workers is at 36.7%, well below the average for the investment goods industry as a whole (46.5%).[11]

The largest firms in the industry, Gutehoffnungshütte, DEMAG, Klöckner-Humboldt-Deutz and Gildemeister, generally produce heavy machinery and are located in North Rhine-Westphalia. This state remains the center of the heavy machinery industry and has traditionally led all other states in machinery output and employment. The famous machinery industry of Baden-Württemberg comes second and, along with the Bavarian industry, has been gaining ground on North Rhine-Westphalia in recent years.[12] Machinery production in South Germany presents a picture almost completely the opposite of that in the Rhine-Ruhr area: small and medium-sized firms operating out of small factories producing specialized machinery.

Given the nature of the industry, it is not surprising that skilled male workers make up the heart of the Maschinenbau workforce. Fifty-eight percent of the sector's blue-collar workers are skilled and only 42% semi- or unskilled, an almost exact reversal of the West German industrial average of 40% skilled to 60% semi- and unskilled.[13] As a consequence, the percentage of women and foreign workers (who are mainly unskilled) in the workforce is much lower than the national mean. Because of the sophisticated nature of the technology utilized in much specialized machinery, an above-average percentage (34.6%; industry as a whole: 28.1%) of white-collar workers, and especially technical employees, is required in machine production.[14] In summary, Maschinenbau is an industry dominated by skilled, male, German workers and technicians working for small or medium-sized firms in southern Germany or the Rhine-Ruhr area.

The second largest metal-processing industry, electrical equipment, appliances and electronics (Elektrotechnik or "electro") provides a sharp contrast in almost every way to machinery. It is a highly concentrated industry dominated by several huge companies (Siemens, AEG, Bosch,

Phillips, SEL) producing in very large factories. The three largest firms account for over 30% of both employment and sales in the industry, and 53.8% of its employees work in plants with over 1,000 workers.[15] Thanks to a high degree of automation, a very large percentage of semi- and unskilled workers (71% of all blue-collar workers) can be employed in the production process, and of these, many are women and foreign workers. About 40% of the electro workforce are women, a figure well above the level of 25% for metal processing in general.[16]

Although second to machinery in total employment (1,023,000 to 948,000), the electrical industries are third in total sales, an indicator of the relatively low level of productivity in this sector.[17] Its export quota of 30.1% is also low compared to the average of all investment goods industries (37.3%).[18] Even though electro is classified as part of the latter, its products span several industrial categories. Only 57.5% of the industry's output (1978) comprised investment goods such as electric power equipment, generators, transformers, and computer and communications equipment. A further 24% were consumer products (appliances, consumer electronics) and 18.5% intermediate goods (semi-conductors, electrical parts).[19] Because it requires no special raw materials, the industry is spread throughout the Federal Republic. Baden-Württemberg is the largest electrical producer of all the states (Länder), followed by Bavaria and North Rhine-Westphalia, but other important production sites include West Berlin, Frankfurt and Hanover.[20]

The third prominent industry in metal processing is the motor-vehicle industry with automobile and truck production as its core. The principal West German motor-vehicle producers are well known: Daimler-Benz, BMW, Volkswagen-Audi, Opel (owned by General Motors) and Ford-Germany. These are joined by a number of less prominent companies which specialize in trucks: MAN, Magirus-Deutz and Hanomag. Motor-vehicle production takes place in large plants which are concentrated around a few cities: Stuttgart and Bremen (Daimler-Benz), Munich (BMW, MAN), Rüsselsheim (near Frankfurt) and Bochum (Opel), Wolfsburg (near Hanover) and Kassel (VW) and Cologne (Ford).[21] The importance of large factories in this industry is illustrated by the fact that 83% of its employees work in plants employing more than 1,000 persons, a much higher percentage than in either machine construction or electrical equipment and electronics.[22] As the small number of well-known firms implies, the motor vehicles industry is also very concentrated. It is in fact the most highly concentrated of all the major West German industries, with the ten top companies accounting for about 80% of total sales and 75% of total employment.[23]

Although motor vehicles ranked only third in 1981 in manufacturing employment behind machinery and electrical equipment, its total sales (DM 137 billion) exceeded those of both these industries (DM 125 billion and DM 118 billion respectively).[24] The motor-vehicle export quota of 44% is slightly above the investment goods industry's average (37.3%) and about the same as that of Maschinenbau.[25]

In terms of the makeup of its labor force, motor vehicles occupies a middle position between the two other major metal-processing industries. Although the proportion of blue-collar to white-collar workers (79% to 21%) is much higher than in either Maschinenbau or electro, it is closer to the industrial average (72% to 28%) than either of those two. The motor-vehicle production process relies heavily on a combination of skilled and semi-skilled workers, so that the ratio of skilled to all other blue-collar workers (43% to 57%) is higher than that in electrical equipment (29% to 71%), but below that of the skill-intensive machinery industry (58% to 42%).[26] As in the latter, motor vehicles has very few women in the workforce, but like electrical equipment, foreign workers are numerous, although in this case they are male foreign workers. The picture one can draw of the motor-vehicle industry from these statistics is of skilled or semi-skilled, male, German or foreign workers employed in very large factories near major cities, and working for one of a handful of internationally famous firms.

The distribution of the different metal industries throughout the country had led to contrasting industrial structures in the Federal Republic's two most economically significant states, North Rhine-Westphalia and Baden-Württemberg.[27] The contrast between these two provinces will play a major role in IG Metall's policies, as we shall see. As noted above, North Rhine-Westphalia is the home of West Germany's steel industry, and the machinery industry located there specializes in large-scale heavy machinery production. Because of these two factors, various metal-processing industries like steel-finishing, steel construction (steel containers and boilers), and iron and sheet-metal products are heavily concentrated in this state. This is in notable contrast to Baden-Württemberg, where light machinery, electrical equipment and electronics, and motor vehicles are the principal industries. These three accounted for 81.7% of total metal-industry sales in Baden-Württemberg (1978), as against only 67.5% in North Rhine-Westphalia.[28] The significance of this for IG Metall is that the "heavier" metal-processing industries, and the steel industry itself, have been afflicted by stagnation or decline since at least the mid-1970s, whereas the metal industries of Baden-Württemberg (as well as of neighboring Bavaria) have enjoyed steady growth. There can be no doubt that a shift to the south in West Germany's industrial structure is underway.

## B. The metal industry employers' association

IG Metall's counterpart among the employers' associations is the Gesamt-verband der metallindustriellen Arbeitgeberverbände (United Confeder-ation of Metal Industry Employers' Associations) commonly known as Gesamtmetall.[29] Gesamtmetall is the umbrella organization for the four-teen regional employers' associations which represent all employers in the metal industry of a given region (excluding iron and steel producers and the jewelry, musical instruments and sporting goods industries, all of which have their own separate organizations). In principle, the regional associations act as the collective bargaining partners of IG Metall in their particular areas, while Gesamtmetall is supposed to coordinate the bar-gaining efforts of various regions and act as the metal industry's lobby in Bonn on social and labor legislation. The actual power of Gesamtmetall is, as we shall see, far greater than this official schema implies.

The largest of the regional employers' associations is, not surprisingly, that of North Rhine-Westphalia. It accounts for about 45% of Gesamtmet-all's member firms and 30% of all the employees working in those firms. As in most things, the North Rhine-Westphalia association is followed in importance by that of Baden-Württemberg, in this case the Verband der Metallindustrie Baden-Württemberg (Federation of the Baden-Württem-berg Metal Industry – VMI). Although the VMI contains only 10.3% of all organized metal industry companies, it comprises 17.6% of all their employees. After the VMI, the largest regional associations are those of Bavaria, Hesse and Lower Saxony.[30] Although the Bavarian association is almost as large as the VMI, it is the relationship between the VMI and the Landesverband der metallindustriellen Arbeitgeber Nordrhein-Westfalen (State Federation of Metal Industry Employers of North Rhine-Westpha-lia – LMA-NRW) which dominates Gesamtmetall's internal politics.

The differences between these two associations reflect the divergences in their respective metal industries.[31] Although the VMI, despite its name, actually only represents the metal industry of North Württemberg/North Baden, and thus signs contracts covering IG Metall's bargaining region of that name, it contains within its purview the heart of Baden-Württem-berg's industry, which is built around the motor vehicles, electrical and machine-construction sectors. Of these three, the motor vehicles, and specifically the auto industry, plays the dominant role, since many electrical and machinery companies provide parts and equipment to local auto firms. It is thus commonly claimed that the area's leading auto producer (Daimler-Benz) and leading auto parts supplier (Bosch) play an inordinate role in the VMI's outlook and strategy. In contrast, the LMA-NRW is a huge organization representing generally smaller, less modern companies in the heavier metalworking areas. This might explain why the LMA-NRW has often seemed more immobile and less willing to make concessions than the Mercedes-dominated VMI.[32] This, in turn, is one of the chief reasons why IG Metall has often designated North Württemberg/North Baden its "vanguard" area for industrial action.

Gesamtmetall's most distinctive feature from IG Metall's perspective is the degree to which collective bargaining policy is centralized within that organization. Gesamtmetall's chief organs for collective bargaining coordination are the Tarifpolitischer Ausschuss (Collective Bargaining Committee – TPA) and the Verhandlungskreis (Bargaining Circle – VK).[33] The TPA is composed of the president and vice-president of Gesamtmetall and the presidents and bargaining committee chairmen of the fourteen regional associations. Since this body often proved too ungainly for quick action, the small VK was created in 1977, including only the chairman of the regional bargaining committee and Gesamtmetall's chief officers.

Officially, the TPA and the VK are only supposed to provide background information and a discussion forum for the fourteen independent employers' associations. In practice, however, these bodies largely determine the bargaining strategy of the regional associations through a number of direct and indirect channels. To supplement the preliminary discussion preceding each bargaining round which takes place with the TPA and the VK, Gesamtmetall has the power to lay down guidelines for the coming negotiations which become binding if no regional associations object to them within two weeks of their formulation.[34] Furthermore, if eleven of the fourteen regional associations request it, the VK can meet in the course of bargaining and actively coordinate the various regional negotiating processes.

Finally, Gesamtmetall has in the past carried out negotiations directly on behalf of all the regional associations when requested by the latter to do so. Gesamtmetall creates a Bargaining Commission (Verhandlungskommission) composed of national and regional officials to talk directly with IG Metall.[35] In this case, as in all others, the regional employers' associations must approve any new contracts before they are signed. Yet there can be no doubt that even when these associations bargain independently they must submit to as much, if not more, central direction as the regional bargaining committees of IG Metall. One of the most distinctive features of industrial relations in West Germany is that the employers, who are nominally in competition with one another, are often better organized and more "solidaristic" than the representatives of their workers.

In addition to Gesamtmetall, IG Metall has one other significant bargaining partner, the Arbeitgeberverband Eisen- und Stahlindustrie (Iron and Steel Industry Employers' Association – AGV).[36] This organization serves a peculiar double function as the West German steel industry's political lobby on social and labor legislation and as the bargaining agent for the steel firms in North Rhine-Westphalia and for the Peine-Salzgitter works in Lower Saxony. All of the steel mills in other parts of the Federal Republic (the Saar, Bavaria) negotiate with IG Metall through smaller regional associations.

The AGV's executive committee (Vorstand) mirrors the executive committees of the individual steel firms: one-third of its members are sales directors, one-third technical directors, and one-third labor directors (see the discussion of Montanmitbestimmung in Chapter 2 above). Because of the presence of labor directors chosen by IG Metall on its executive committee, AGV is barred from becoming a full member of the BDA.[37] Nonetheless, relations between the AGV and both Gesamtmetall and the BDA are close, with the former sending a representative as a "guest member" to the boards of both organizations. It is almost certain that bargaining tactics are coordinated with Gesamtmetall and that the AGV had agreed to abide by the BDA Tabu Katalog.[38] This helps explain why the AGV was willing to defend the 40-hour work week, a prominent tenet of the Tabu Katalog, with such vehemence in 1978–79 even though it was under no obligation to do so. (See the discussion below of the 1978–79 steel strike.) Although nominally an independent organization, the AGV must be seen – for IG Metall's purposes – as the "long arm" of Gesamtmetall and the BDA in the steel industry.

## II. IG METALL: SOME BASIC FACTS AND FIGURES

### A. The sociology of IG Metall's membership

IG Metall's approximately 2.7 million members encompass about 35% of the entire DGB membership, thus making this union by far the most important organization within the West German labor movement. Moreover, this union's policies affect the lives of well over one-third of the entire working population in the Federal Republic, since its contractual arrangements in the three categories of its organizational domain – the iron and steel industry, metal processing and the much smaller metal craft sector (Metallhandwerk) – pertain to all workers employed in these industries, whether unionized or not. Thus, in the metal-processing category alone, the working conditions and pay structures of four million West German workers – approximately half of the Federal Republic's entire industrial labor force in 1976 – were determined by IG Metall's contractual agreements with the employers.

In the 1970s, IG Metall's membership grew by approximately 16%, which not only far exceeded the small increases for IG Chemie-Papier-Keramik and IG Bau-Steine-Erden, but also surpassed the 10% average increase in membership for all DGB unions combined.[39] The 1970s saw a 12% rise in IG Metall's organizational level, which by the latter part of the decade yielded a 53% organizational density for IG Metall in all industries belonging to the union's domain.[40] The degree of organizational penetration placed IG Metall approximately in the middle of the seventeen DGB members in terms of unionization.

As to particular developments affecting the various social groups within the union, one could clearly observe a faster rate of growth during the 1970s among the union's "periphery" than among its traditional "core." Thus, female clerical staff employees (Angestellte) increased their membership between 1970 and 1976 by 92%, male employees by 50%, and female workers in general by 40%; male workers – the backbone of IG Metall and the organized labor movement in West Germany – only achieved an 8% growth rate during the same period.[41] However, as the 1979 figures for all four categories show, male blue-collar workers dominate the union in an overwhelming fashion: compared to 2,008,695 male, blue-collar workers, the 276,171 female workers, 295,427 male and 104,216 female, white-collar, salaried employees constitute a clear minority.[42] Blue-collar workers, of course, continue to be better organized (about a 62% degree of unionization) than salaried employees, a group that reached a 28% organizational level by the late 1970s.[43] The rest of IG Metall's membership consists largely of other smaller categories, including artisans and apprentices. Within the two larger occupational categories, however, one could further discern important gender differences, with men in both much better organized than their female counterparts. Yet the major sociological characteristic of the 1970s in terms of IG Metall's changing membership was the steady and continued increase in women and clerical employees within this predominantly male and industrial organization. This shift did not occur solely because of objective changes in the composition of the labor market during the 1970s. Rather, it resulted from subjective crisis behavior on the part of the most peripheral groups within the West German workforce and a conscious response by IG Metall to defend these groups by trying to unionize them as quickly as possible. IG Metall has generally been much more successful in recruiting new members (and avoiding the resignation of veterans) in times of crisis than during more prosperous periods.[44]

Additional sociological patterns are revealed by a brief look at the various industrial sectors within IG Metall's organizational purview. The steel industry has a long tradition of yielding the highest unionization with an overall level of 78.6% (84.4% for blue-collar workers and 59.0% for white-collar employees) in 1975.[45] Next to the steel industry's approximately 239,000 workers, the 2.8 million employed in metal processing assumed greater importance for IG Metall throughout the 1970s since most areas of metal processing continued to grow, whereas steel – suffering under the constraints of a structural crisis with worldwide dimensions – declined during the course of that decade. In the metal-processing sector, the motor-vehicle industry has been by far the most thoroughly unionized sector. Of its 787,000 employees in 1981, 71.5% were unionized. Once again, industrial blue-collar workers far surpassed white-collar employees with levels of union penetration at 80.5% and 40.4% respectively.[46] The machinery industry, with 1,023,000 employees, the second largest of the three metal-processing sectors, showed a much lower degree of unionization than the steel and motor vehicles industries. At 53.8% (66.6% for blue-collar workers, 30% for white-collar employees), this sector's level of organization corresponded fairly closely to the IG Metall average.[47] In electrical equipment, the third major industry within metal processing, IG Metall's presence has been more tenuous. Only 36.5% of the industry's workforce of 948,000 was unionized according to 1975 figures (blue-collar – 45.4%; white-collar – 18.6%).[48] Lastly, the metal-crafts sector (Metallhandwerk) employed 40,000 persons of whom only 32.4% were unionized, with blue-collar workers reaching a level of 41% and other employees a mere 16.3%.[49]

Differences by gender and by occupational category (blue-collar workers vs. clerical employees) have not only permeated the union's rank and file, but also extend to the union's activists. Whereas women succeeded in augmenting their participation on all levels of union politics during the 1970s, they still faced woeful discrimination at the beginning of the 1980s. In the 1976 IG Metall shop-steward elections, only 6.4% of the representatives were blue-collar women, as compared to the blue-collar men's total of 73.4%. The discrepancy – although not as blatant – pertained to the representatives of white-collar employees as well, with the women only reaching the 3.1% mark and the men getting 17.1%.[50] Similar results occurred during the works council elections of 1975 when blue-collar women constituted 5.8% of the representatives (men: 70.5%) while among white-collar employees, women candidates attained 3.1% of the seats with their male colleagues receiving 20.8%.[51] Lastly, the gender composition of the various bargaining commissions (Tarifkommissionen) and the delegates to the union's triannual congresses further exemplifies the vast underrepresentation of women in the organizational structures of IG Metall. At the 1977 union congress only 11.5% of the delegates were women. This, however, compared quite favorably to the two previous congresses in 1971 and 1974, where the percentages of women delegates were a mere 5.5% and 8.2% respectively.[52]

Table 4.1 *Geographic organization of IG Metall*

| Union districts (administrative units within IG Metall) | Bargaining areas (contract-negotiation units within IG Metall) | Federal states |
| --- | --- | --- |
| Hamburg | Hamburg<br>Schleswig-Holstein<br>Unterweser area<br>Northwest areas of Lower Saxony (Northern areas) | Hamburg<br>Schleswig-Holstein<br>Lower Saxony<br>Bremen |
| Hanover | Lower Saxony | Lower Saxony |
| Essen<br>Hagen<br>Cologne<br>Münster | North Rhine-Westphalia | North Rhine-Westphalia |
| Frankfurt | Hesse<br>Rhineland-Palatinate<br>Saarland | Hesse<br>Rhineland-Palatinate<br>Saarland |
| Stuttgart | North Württemberg/North Baden<br>South Württemberg/Hohenzollern<br>South Baden | Baden-Württemberg |
| Munich | Bavaria | Bavaria |
| Berlin | Berlin | Berlin |

*Source:* Projektgruppe Gewerkschaftsforschung, *Rahmenbedingungen*, vol. 1 (Frankfurt am Main: Campus Verlag, 1979), p. 95.

## B. IG Metall's organizational framework

IG Metall's organizational hierarchy can be divided into four inter-dependent levels. At the lowest unit, the shop floor, a number of the union's fundamental interests are formulated and represented by the shop stewards and, unofficially, by the works councilors. The locals form the next unit on the organizational ladder, followed by the union's nine districts, which in turn are directly below the highest stage in IG Metall's organizational hierarchy, the federation. IG Metall's organizational pyramid, encompassing the entire geographic area of the Federal Republic and West Berlin, consisted of nine districts and 166 locals in 1979, with West Berlin officially only attaining the status of a "local" whose de facto activities and importance for the union have always been tantamount to those of any of its nine official districts[53]

The sizes of the locals vary geographically and by membership, ranging from less than 5,000 to in excess of 100,000 members, according to 1979 data. Consequently, district membership and geographic shape have been

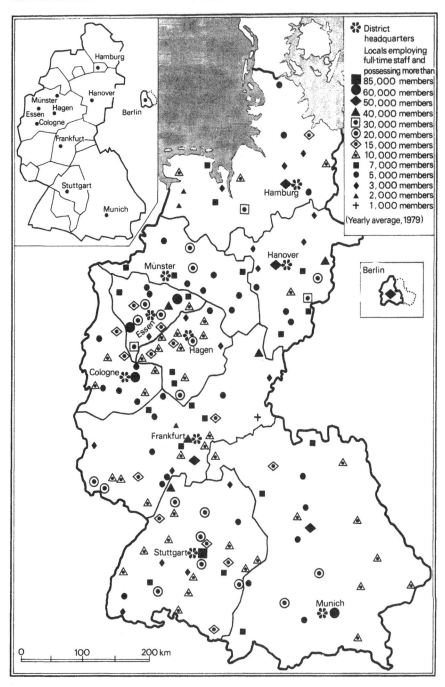

*Figure 1.* IG Metall districts and locals
*Sources:* IG Metall, *Daten–Fakten–Informationen 1985* (Frankfurt: IG Metall, 1985), p. 10; and IG Metall, *Geschäftsbericht 1977 bis 1979* (Frankfurt: IG Metall, 1980), n.p.

*Figure 2.* IG Metall bargaining areas
*Sources:* IG Metall, *Daten–Fakten–Informationen 1977* (Frankfurt: IG Metall, 1977), p. 6; and IG
Metall, *Daten–Fakten–Informationen 1983* (Frankfurt: IG Metall, 1983), p. 8.

far from uniform. To complicate matters, IG Metall districts (administrative units in the union's organizational framework) correspond only vaguely to the geographic and political boundaries of the Federal Republic's individual states. In addition, they do not coincide at all with bargaining areas, within which contract negotiations pertaining to the industries in those areas take place. This geographic discrepancy between union districts and bargaining areas has had a considerable impact on IG Metall's negotiation strategies. It originated in the immediate post-war era, when the bargaining areas were established largely according to the geographic sub-divisions of the employers' associations, whereas the union districts were drawn in response to IG Metall's organizational needs. Table 4.1 and figures 1 and 2 should help clarify these important – and somewhat confusing – distinctions.[54]

Three of the four organizational levels elect both their own political leadership and their representatives for the next higher organizational unit. Three important exceptions to this rule deserve a cursory mention at this point: (1) The delegates to the triannual union congresses come from the political associations of the locals; they are elected on the level of the locals, with one delegate representing 5,000 IG Metall members. (2) All members of the executive committee – the union's leadership – are elected by the delegates to the triannual congresses. (3) The district leadership (nine individual leaders, district secretaries and some of their associates) is appointed by IG Metall's executive committee in Frankfurt and is not elected by the districts' membership. It is thus a crucial mediating body between the union's central leadership and its rank and file in the districts and locals. Often torn in their loyalty between their "constituents" in the district and their employers at IG Metall's head office in Frankfurt, the district leaders have to perform precarious balancing acts in which personal skills, political savvy and charisma are often as important as institutional authority.

The highest legislative and policy-formulating body within IG Metall's organization is the union congress. Held every two years between 1950 and 1962, these meetings became triannual events beginning with the eighth congress in the fall of 1965. An attempt to extend the period between congresses to four years – as a number of unions in the DGB, IG Bau-Steine-Erden and IG Chemie-Papier-Keramik among them, had done – was narrowly defeated in the 1977 and 1980 IG Metall congresses.

The congress sets the guidelines for union policy and determines the parameters of union actions regarding every aspect of IG Metall's activities over the next legislative period of three years. By beginning every congress with a debate on the executive committee's report of its activities over the previous three years, the delegates gain insight into the union's activities, and determine whether the executive committee has fulfilled the mandate decreed by the previous congress. Perhaps more importantly, the delegates are given the chance to initiate changes by supplementing their criticisms of the executive committee's leadership and policy implementation with new suggestions and guidelines for the coming three years.

IG Metall congresses are not rubber-stamp affairs and have in recent years – especially since the onset of the economic crisis – been the scenes of heated controversy, debate and criticism.[55] Congress participants have to vote on hundreds of motions addressing all major issues of the day, ranging from the alteration of job categories to nuclear disarmament. Simple majorities decide the fate of all motions except those which address aspects of IG Metall's bylaws, which require a two-thirds majority.[56] Motions can be introduced by all official organs such as districts, locals, IG Metall's youth or women's sections and, of course, the executive committee itself. A very important "motion commission," representing a cross-section of the union's middle- and upper-level leadership, attaches its recommendations to every motion, urging the congress delegates to approve, reject, alter or table the proposal. Although this commission's suggestions are heeded in the majority of cases by the delegates, there have been numerous crucial exceptions when "revolts" by the delegates rejected the union line and replaced the officially approved motions with their own alternatives, in open defiance of the commission's authority.

After a triannual congress has established the overall framework for IG Metall's policies in the ensuing three years, it is up to the executive committee in Frankfurt to implement the congress's mandate in the day-to-day affairs of the entire union. In this task, the executive committee draws assistance not only from its own extensive staff and from union activists (both full-time and honorary members), but also from the advisory council (Beirat) which acts as the highest constitutive union body between congresses. The executive committee is unquestionably the union's most powerful and influential body. It sets most policy guidelines and determines IG Metall's strategies. Thus, for example, it has the most important voice in determining the priorities and scope of each bargaining round, as well as the right to decide what action is to be taken by which district and/or bargaining area. It therefore has the power to determine when and how to strike should it deem such action to be in the interest of the organization as a whole.

The executive committee consists of eleven full-time and nineteen honorary members, all of whom serve for three-year periods and must stand for election at every congress. Each of the eleven full-timers, including the chairman and his/her deputy, is entrusted with the responsibility of tending to particular areas within the organization. The chairman's concerns include, for example, international relations, economic policy, the press and media, and IG Metall's legal department. His/her deputy is in charge of organizational matters, locals, districts, union publications and personnel issues. In addition to having one member exclusively responsible for collective bargaining problems, IG Metall's executive committee covers issues such as labor market policy, social welfare, works councils, shop stewards, youth and women.

The advisory council serves as IG Metall's highest legislative body between the union's triannual congresses. The council's membership includes, among others, the entire executive committee (both full-time and honorary participants) and leading union activists from the district level. The advisory committee is empowered to convene an "extraordinary congress" and approve all executive committee by-elections which may have occurred between regular congresses. Most important, however, the advisory council serves as an additional sounding-board for the executive committee's policies. It provides the union leadership with added formal and informal help as it deals with difficult issues. The importance of the advisory council's role as "sounding-board" – particularly in the area of collective bargaining – has grown significantly in recent years.

### C. IG Metall's collective bargaining system

The following four structures play the most significant roles in the formulation and implementation of collective bargaining policies and strategies: the executive committee, the district leaders, the regional collective bargaining commissions and the much smaller negotiating committees.[57] The executive committee has in the past dominated all stages and aspects of the collective bargaining process. In addition to having the informal but decisive power and resources to set the tone for contract negotiations, the executive committee exercises formal control over all immediate aspects of the process: cancelling contracts, calling strike votes, and determining where and how to strike. Only IG Metall's triannual congresses, and – in case of a strike – the votes of its participants, have the ability to curtail the executive committee's powers concerning the collective bargaining process.

Among the many tasks facing the district leaders is their role in determining the size and composition of the collective bargaining commissions, which vary considerably by district and bargaining area. Sometimes exceeding one hundred members, all of whom are elected for three-year terms, the commissions' personnel is selected at the level of the locals and is dominated by honorary union activists. Typically, most of the prominent works councilors from the major firms belonging to IG Metall's organizational domain in a particular bargaining area are members of the union's bargaining commission in that area. Although the commissions' formal authority is confined to "consulting' and "counseling," with no official decision-making power over the union's ultimate collective bargaining agreements, their opinions receive careful consideration in the "center's" deliberations. This policy not only reflects the union leadership's necessary respect for the views of its most important local members (i.e. the most active works councilors and shop stewards of the large firms), but also allows the opinions of the union's rank and file to be considered, if not followed.

The bargaining itself is conducted by the negotiating committees of the respective bargaining areas. The committees' members are appointed according to the district leaders' recommendations, and each committee is in fact headed by the district leader himself/herself. These negotiating committees number approximately twenty people, most of whom are full-time union activists and/or key works council members of the area's leading firms. During the advanced stages of the negotiations, the committee's active participants can be reduced to three, the district leader always being one of them. As a rule, the union's formulation of collective bargaining demands consists of a year-long, intricate balancing act where the final terms represent a compromise among IG Metall's varied constituencies.

IG Metall follows a nominally decentralized collective bargaining procedure in which the union concludes separate agreements for its blue- and white-collar workers in each of the independent bargaining areas listed above. Separate contracts are signed for each of the three large production-related areas within IG Metall's organizational purview, namely the iron and steel industry, metal processing and metal crafts. IG Metall also negotiates a special contract with Volkswagen in which actual wages correspond to contractual ones, thus reducing in that company many of the complexities associated with wage gap and wage drift elsewhere in West Germany's metal industry.

There are no formal rules or regulations for the negotiation process itself. Typically one of the parties – usually the union – cancels the contract approximately one month before its expiration date. In most cases, this action is accompanied, or soon followed, by the announcement of the terms desired for the subsequent contract. Meetings between employer representatives and IG Metall's negotiating committees occur in each of the bargaining areas shortly before or soon after the old contract's expiration. Although each bargaining area's negotiating schedule is set up independently, both the union and the employers attempt to gain strategic advantages by manipulating the sequence of negotiations in the bargaining areas to fit their own battle plans. In this way, the crucial concept of a "pilot" or "vanguard" bargaining area developed, whereby the agreements reached in the first area to settle assume a model character for all other IG Metall bargaining areas, which often adopt them with only minor modifications.

If negotiations between the employers and IG Metall fail to result in an agreement, the conflict enters the stage of arbitration. The 1964 arbitration agreement (which was superseded by a new one in 1980 as a direct consequence of rank-and-file disaffection) had the following characteristics: (1) Each bargaining area's arbitration system consisted of two neutral, vote-casting chairmen in addition to two other members, each nominated by the employers and IG Metall respectively. In case the two parties could not agree on nominating two mutually acceptable neutral chairmen, they were then each allowed to name a person of their own choosing. Under either circumstance, both chairmen served a four-year term, with the vote alternating every year. (2) The arbitration process had to be entered into by both parties if either one of the two so desired. (3) Both parties had to observe the usual "labor peace" (Friedenspflicht) demanded by West German labor law throughout the arbitration proceedings. Thus, neither side was permitted to resort to the strike or the lockout until well beyond the actual expiration of the contract. Only after the breakdown of the arbitration process could the union initiate mobilization measures such as warning strikes, temporary work stoppages and, most importantly, the necessary strike vote.

At IG Metall's 1977 congress in Düsseldorf, delegates from the Stuttgart district succeeded in passing a motion which formed the basis for the new arbitration agreement. Its greatest improvements (from the union's point of view) over its 1964 predecessor were the following three provisions: (1) The chairmen of the arbitration committee would not alternate regularly but rather be determined by mutual agreement or by drawing lots. Thus the employers could no longer devise their battle plans in advance according to the political leanings of the respective chairmen. (2) *Both* parties would have to agree to arbitration before it would be required. No one side could force the other to enter the arbitration process, thereby putting an end to the employers' frequently used strategy of prolonging the negotiation proceedings by routinely resorting to lengthy arbitration. (3) Most importantly, the new agreement called for the imposition of a strict limit on the negotiation process – including arbitration. It stipulated a six-week period of conflict resolution – two weeks prior to the old contract's expiration and four weeks thereafter – following which the state of "labor peace" would no longer apply, thereby giving the union the opportunity to engage in strike activities without time-consuming pre-strike rituals, such as strike votes.[58]

As could be expected, IG Metall's strike history has been far from uniform, with industry and region the two most critical factors in determining the frequency, scope and ultimate success of its strikes during the post-war era. Motor vehicles was the most strike-prone industry, leading the field with one-third of the union's strikers and accounting for over 40% of all days lost to strikes within IG Metall's organizational purview.[59] Among the many reasons for the automobile industry's prominence in this category are the high level of unionization of the workforce and the working conditions, characterized by large and concentrated areas of production featuring monotonous, dirty, noisy and often dangerous shiftwork on conveyor belts. The motor-vehicle industry's strong presence in the district of Stuttgart has played a central role in the union's history. This presence made the bargaining area of North Württemberg/North Baden (NW/NB) within IG Metall's Stuttgart district the union's most prominent and innovative area in collective bargaining. Due to the vanguard role of NW/NB for the union's collective bargaining strategy, this discussion will conclude by contrasting NW/NB with North Rhine-Westphalia, IG Metall's and the Federal Republic's largest collective bargaining area. This cursory comparison should lay the groundwork for a better understanding of later passages which highlight NW/NB's eminence as IG Metall's "star" bargaining area.

The most fundamental difference between the two bargaining areas lies in their respective sizes which is closely linked to the relationship between union district and bargaining area in IG Metall. With over one million employees in the metal-processing industry (in addition to those employed in steel and iron), NRW's four districts tower above all other IG Metall bargaining areas in sheer geographic size and number of people. NW/NB, on the other hand, is only one of three bargaining areas within the district of Stuttgart (consult table 4.1 and figures 1 and 2 for clarification). Albeit the biggest and most important among the three, NW/NB still only comprises 550,000 employees in metal processing, and it has no steel industry at all. This substantial discrepancy in size was at the center of IG Metall's choice to overemphasize NW/NB's vanguard role. NRW is simply too big for strike activities given the employers' readiness to respond with extensive lockouts in that bargaining area. Short of banning the lockout or breaking up NRW into smaller bargaining areas – both vigorously and successfully opposed by the employers – IG Metall will have to continue with a no-strike strategy there since the union could probably not afford the enormous costs of either an area strike or a point strike accompanied by a lockout in an area the size of NRW. The paradoxical situation of not being able to strike in its most important bargaining area has plagued IG Metall throughout its post-war history. This has had severe repercussions in the form of defeatism and disillusionment among some of IG Metall's members in NRW.

NW/NB, on the other hand, is small in size but contains a heavy concentration of giant plants belonging to Daimler-Benz, Bosch, SEL and Audi in the Stuttgart, Mannheim and Neckarsulm regions. Organization of the homogeneous membership in this relatively compact area poses no particular problems for the union; nor would strike actions – even if met with the most concerted lockout on the part of the employers – mean prohibitive costs for IG Metall. Frequent mobilization and actual strike experience in the area of NW/NB have led to a high level of organizational efficiency, superb communication between the union leadership and the shop floor and, perhaps most importantly, a confidence on the part of the workers in their own abilities and the ultimate effectiveness of their solidarity via their union's actions.

Another theory accounting for the frequently different union policies and strategies in NW/NB and NRW has been widely debated among experts of industrial relations in the Federal Republic. The argument holds that the IG Metall leadership has always been afraid of a full-blown strike involving the traditionally class-conscious and historically well-organized Rhine-Ruhr workers, who would be less willing than their politically more moderate colleagues in conservative NW/NB to accept the union's "strategy of the calculated strike."[60] In other words, fearing its own rank and file's militancy in the Federal Republic's industrial heartland, IG Metall has pursued a conscious policy of demobilization rather than risk losing control of a potentially volatile situation.

This hypothesis concerning IG Metall's fears of an unruly "red Ruhr" receives further corroboration by the fact that a good portion of the working class in NW/NB regularly votes for the conservative Christian Democratic Party. This is indicated by the sizable margins of that party's victories in each of the post-war elections in the state of Baden-Württemberg, the most concentrated population centers of which are located in IG Metall's bargaining district of NW/NB. Thus, a restrained strategy, which requires that the organization never lose control of "its" rank and file, could be pursued with much greater success in the geographically confined area of NW/NB, with its politically moderate workers, than in the much bigger area of NRW, with its historically more radical working class. Because of NW/NB's conservative political tradition IG Metall could permit its workers there to develop an activist trade union consciousness which has made this bargaining area the union's showcase throughout the land.

These important distinctions between the two bargaining areas – whatever their exact origins – have not only yielded divergent strike activities and collective bargaining aims, but have created substantially different intra-union structures and traditions. NW/NB placed a heavy emphasis on mixed demands (Mischforderungen) in its collective bargaining demands of the 1970s, whereas NRW maintained the conventional approach of direct percentage increases (lineare Prozentualforderungen) during the same period.

Lastly, as one group of authors pointed out, the abundant mobilization and strike experience in NW/NB, and the lack thereof in NRW, have been instrumental in producing superb leadership in the former and somewhat lesser talents in the latter.[61] Although this factor should not be given excessive emphasis, there seems little doubt that capable individuals in key positions can make a difference at the margin. As we will see in subsequent sections of this chapter, in which the highlights of IG Metall's post-war development will be presented, a union's success or failure in a particular endeavor – whether directed toward the political realm or concentrated in the labor market – depends very often on small margins.

## III. ORGANIZED LABOR IN THE GERMAN METALWORKING INDUSTRY BEFORE 1933

Just as IG Metall occupies a highly influential role in the DGB today, its predecessor, the German Metalworkers' Federation (Deutscher Metallarbeiter Verband – DMV), was the most important union in Germany before 1933. The organizational continuity between the two is greater than that of any other DGB member, since the DMV was conceived from the beginning as an industrial union. A brief discussion of the DMV is imperative because many of its experiences formed the basis of IG Metall's present political and social attitudes. Moreover, several of IG Metall's internal conflicts had their percursors in the politics of the DMV.

As in many other German industries, the first unions for metalworking were founded by the Lasallean and Eisenach factions of the social democratic movement in 1868 and 1869 respectively.[62] Almost immediately, a conflict broke out between the Lasallean General German Workers' Association and its metalworkers' union over the refusal by the latter to be simply an arm of the Social Democratic Party. As a result, the Lasallean metalworkers left their association in late 1869 and joined with the Eisenachers to form a unified metalworkers' union, the International Metalworkers (Internationale Metallarbeiterschaft), which in 1873 changed its name to the Metalworkers' Cooperative Union (Metallarbeiter-Gewerksgenossenschaft). The growth of the new organization was very slow, however. When the Anti-Socialist Laws forced its dissolution in 1878, the union numbered only 4,000 members, and was thus not a significant presence in German labor at that time.

During the 1880s, numerous metalworkers' associations on the local level began emerging throughout Germany, and national conventions of these associations met in 1884 and 1888. In June 1891, six months after the Anti-Socialist Laws had expired, metalworkers from throughout Germany met in Frankfurt and founded the Deutscher Metallarbeiter Verband. In a vote on the form of this new organization, the advocates of industrial unionism defeated the defenders of an exclusive craft orientation, thereby making the DMV the first industrial labor union in Germany. Quite naturally, its representatives became the leading advocates of industrial unionism within the social democratic union movement until its dissolution by the Nazis in 1933.

In the first ten years after its founding, the DMV grew steadily. In 1891, it began with 23,205 members, and this number rose to just over 100,000 in 1901.[63] From the very beginning, the core of the union consisted of the skilled mechanics and lathe operators in Germany's machinery industry, which was still organized on semi-artisanal lines in small and medium-sized firms. In 1900 these two categories of workers accounted for 46.5% of the DMV's membership, with most of the remainder composed of other skilled craftsmen such as plumbers and blacksmiths. Less than 12% of the organized metalworkers at this time were unskilled workers or women.[64]

Both the fortunes and the character of the DMV changed substantially with the rapid growth of German industry between 1901 and World War I. In keeping with the general trend within the social democratic labor movement, the union in 1903 gave its approval to collective bargaining as the main instrument for improving the wages and working conditions of its constituents. Until that point the DMV had negotiated only 57 contracts for its members. By 1908 this number increased to 537 contracts with 12,361 firms covering 104,197 workers. In 1913, the last full year before the war, 1,376 collective bargaining agreements were in effect in metalworking, covering 207,472 workers.[65]

This success in contract negotiations was paralleled by a massive increase in DMV membership in the period before 1914. In 1913, the union claimed 554,934 members, a more than fivefold rise over 1901.[66] With the expansion of large factories in the German economy, the percentage of unskilled workers within the organization also rose, to 18.75% in 1912.[67] Unlike unions in many other sectors, the DMV remained relatively untroubled by rivals. By 1914, there were only two small social democratic craft unions left in metalworking (the coppersmiths and the stokers). Both Christian and Hirsch-Duncker metalworkers' unions (founded in 1899 and 1869 respectively) were active in the industry, but they each comprised only about 40,000 members in 1913.[68] Thus of the 33% of Germany's metalworkers who belonged to a union in 1911, over 80% were members of the DMV.[69]

Despite these advances in membership and contractual arrangements, serious problems plagued the DMV before 1914. The most important of these was the uneven pattern in membership development and contract negotiations across Germany. The union's strongholds were in the machinery industries of southern (Baden, Württemberg, northern Bavaria) and central (Saxony, Hesse, Hanover) Germany and Berlin as well as the shipbuilding centers of Hamburg, Bremen and Kiel. However, the DMV was able to make few inroads into the burgeoning electrical equipment industry and virtually none whatsoever into heavy industry (iron and steel, armaments, heavy machinery), which was concentrated in the Ruhr, the Saar and Upper Silesia.[70] The anti-union orientation of Germany's most famous heavy industrial companies (Krupp, Thyssen, Stumm) was legendary. These firms used any conceivable tactic, including blacklists and yellow unions, to keep the DMV outside their factory gates. With few exceptions, these tactics met with success.

Even in those sectors where they were relatively well represented, the metalworkers had trouble conducting successful large-scale strikes. Repeatedly the union had to admit defeat when confronted with employers' associations that were better organized than they. In 1905 the employers responded to strikes in the Berlin electrical and Bavarian metalworking industries with massive lockouts which on both occasions forced the DMV to stop the strikes and order its members back to work. This scenario was repeated in the militant and highly unionized north German shipyards in 1910 and 1913.[71] These defeats, as well as the failure to organize heavy industry, led to the emergence of a radical opposition within the union which attacked the leadership for its timidity and accommodationism.

The support of the DMV leadership for the German war effort served to exacerbate this nascent split within the organization. Led by Robert Dissmann, the opposition group within the DMV became associated with the newly formed USPD after 1917. Its core was in the Berlin armaments industry, with its radical shop stewards who later formed the Revolutionary Shop Stewards Organization led by Richard Müller. This group played an important role in the revolution of November 1918, during which workers' councils were formed in factories throughout the metalworking industry.

At the same time that its membership was engaged in revolutionary activity throughout Germany, the DMV's leadership, along with other social democratic unionists, was in the process of negotiating the Central Labor Community Agreement (Zentralarbeitsgemeinschaftsabkommen) with representatives of heavy industry, which finally brought official recognition to the unions from this sector of the economy. Needless to say, the opposition within the DMV had mixed feelings about this accord.

During the first two post-war meetings of the union in June and October 1919, it became clear that the opposition now represented the overwhelming majority of the membership, and Dissmann was elected the new DMV leader. A split in the organization soon emerged over the future of post-revolutionary Germany, pitting the moderate USPD-dominated executive council against left-wing USPD and KPD sympathizers led by Richard Müller. Dissmann supported a future role for the workers' councils, but he also believed in only a limited socialization of industry, supplemented by co-determination. Müller and his followers called for thoroughgoing socialization of the economy and a wholesale reorganization of industrial relations based exclusively on the workers' councils. The platform outlined by Dissmann in 1919 defines even today the basic ideological position of IG Metall.

With the normalization of the political situation in Germany after 1920, the strength of the radical opposition within the DMV declined. The union now turned to the difficult task of defending the economic interests of its membership, which by that time had grown to over 1,500,000 with the "opening up" of heavy industry. During 1922, the DMV was partially successful in preventing reductions in real wages and increases in the work week in the southern German metal industry. The combination of the French occupation of the Ruhr and runaway inflation in 1923 erased the gains that the DMV had made since 1918. Government policy strengthened the hand of heavy industry while thousands of DMV members lost their jobs in the Rhine and Ruhr areas. By the end of 1923, 23% of the membership was unemployed, and one year later the DMV had lost over half the strength which it possessed barely two years earlier.[72]

The next three years brought a modest economic recovery to Germany, and the union was able to recoup some of its losses of the 1922–24 period. Despite the setbacks suffered during those two years, the DMV continued to be the most important member of the ADGB. Its chairman, Dissmann, aggressively advocated the adoption of the industrial union principle during the discussions on the future of the labor movement which dominated ADGB congresses of the early and mid-1920s. Despite the DMV's numerical weight, it was unable to convince enough other unions of this position for it to become official ADGB policy. The issue assumed lesser urgency after the untimely death of Robert Dissmann in 1926 at the age of 48.

By 1928, the year before the Great Depression began, the DMV had signed collective bargaining agreements covering 43,482 plants and 2.3 million workers.[73] Membership had risen again to 944,000. Yet, unlike in many other sectors of the economy where unions and employers worked together closely, a cooperative relationship had not been established between the DMV and heavy industry. This became all too clear during the wage round in the Ruhr iron and steel industry in late 1928. The employers there reacted to an arbitration award made by the government – and accepted by the union – with a lockout of 215,000 workers which lasted over a month. This was a harbinger of things to come during the next four years. With the support of the Brüning government, employers throughout the country cut wages repeatedly even as unemployment rose dramatically. In 1930, the DMV tried to prevent this through a total strike in the Berlin metalworking industry, but to no avail. Finally, on May 2, 1933 the DMV, along with all other unions, was dissolved by the new Nazi government and many of its leaders were arrested.

As will become clear in the course of this chapter, many of the traits that have characterized IG Metall since 1949 were already present before 1933 in the DMV. The latter's experiences with a group of exceptionally strong and politically very conservative employers led it to develop an official ideology which was conspicuously to the left of that espoused by other German unions. Nevertheless, the employers' strength, as well as the hostility of other ADGB unions towards the DMV, prevented the latter from playing the role within both organized labor and the economy that one would have expected from the union representing Germany's most important industrial sector. For better or worse, the DMV seems to have bequeathed this legacy of ideological radicalism to IG Metall.

## IV. FROM HOPES OF SYSTEM TRANSFORMATION TO AN UNEASY ACCEPTANCE OF CAPITALIST REALITY: 1950–1960

A pervasive preoccupation with the creation of a new social and economic order dominated IG Metall's first official congress, held in Hamburg between September 18 and 22, 1950.[74] Still very much under the adverse effects of National Socialism and its immediate post-war ramifications, the congress pleaded for a fundamental reorganization of every aspect of West German society, including the democratization of the economy as well as the polity. Without the far-reaching introduction of the former, the latter was bound to remain deficient and incomplete. Mitbestimmung represented both the means and the end, the form and the content of this restructuring process.[75] Indeed, certain passages in key speeches at the Hamburg congress indicate that – at least at the time – collective bargaining measures were subordinated to the overall aim of Mitbestimmung. IG Metall and much of the West German labor movement seemed to believe quite sincerely that Mitbestimmung – if fully implemented – would lead to a qualitative transformation of capitalism by infusing it with economic democracy.

Yet, as other passages in the minutes of the congress clearly indicate, realistic assessments of the political climate of the period should have led to a more tempered view of Mitbestimmung's capabilities and the labor movement's potential for changing the course of West German capitalist development.[76] In addition to signs of a concerted employers' offensive in the labor market, the early 1950s witnessed a frontal attack against the unions – especially IG Metall – in the political arena as part of a general defamation of the left. This atmosphere of indiscriminate anti-communism received welcome exogenous support from the Cold War, and was to engulf the internal politics of virtually all DGB unions in a matter of a few years. Indeed, anti-communist and anti-GDR sentiments permeated even IG Metall's publications of the early 1950s, including the minutes of the first union congress.[77]

Thus, from the very beginning, a pronounced ambivalence characterized IG Metall's position within the political economy of the Federal Republic. While consistently trying to cultivate an image as challenger of the system – expressed in the much-used term "Gegenmacht" – IG Metall has with equal tenacity attempted to project itself as a responsible and legitimate actor within the parameters of post-war West German society. Both strains have coexisted since the early 1950s and their contradictory relationship has in some fashion influenced all of IG Metall's policies and strategies, including Mitbestimmung and collective bargaining.

With the passage of the 1951 Mitbestimmung law in the steel and coal industries of the Rhine-Ruhr, IG Metall, with its sister union IG Bergbau und Energie, could claim an important victory on behalf of the entire West German labor movement. The first concrete steps toward a complete democratization of the economy had been undertaken by reforming the board-room structures of some of the Federal Republic's most traditional industrial giants. Yet, at the same time, the passage of this law revealed the severe limitations of IG Metall's potential as a Gegenmacht because of the restoration of the preeminent power of the employers in the new republic. By confining the law's jurisdiction to coal and steel, the employers succeeded in stopping the proliferation of parity-codetermination to the rest of the economy. The extension of Mitbestimmung remains the unions' most elusive goal.[78]

Although IG Metall continued to regard Mitbestimmung and economic democracy as the most essential long-term aim of the labor movement and viewed the existing co-determination program in the country's mining and steel industries as a springboard for short-term policy alternatives, numerous open confrontations with the employers erupted in 1951 emphasizing the continued salience of collective bargaining as the union's most immediate – and most effective – strategy. Among the many strikes occurring that year, the one in Hesse's metal-processing industry deserves attention since it is widely considered to be the first major wage strike in the history of the Federal Republic.[79] IG Metall's ambivalence about acting as a challenger and an agent of order at the same time first became apparent during this early showdown with the employers.

The issues involved in this strike had to do with "turf" and only secondarily with actual wage demands. The employers, seizing the spirit of the times by initiating their rollback of labor, were intent upon "showing the unions who will henceforth determine the tempo of wage developments in the Federal Republic."[80] This hardening of the employers' position corresponded to an increasing resistance on their part (and that of the CDU-led state) to various union-advocated reforms, most notably Mitbestimmung. The time had come for the employers "to put the unions in their place." This strategy included not only the attempt to discredit and delegitimate the strike in the eyes of the public, but also to make its deployment by the unions – and particularly their most powerful representative, IG Metall – as costly and dangerous for labor as possible. To this effect, the employers not only refused to offer any wage raises at the expiration of the old contract, but demanded its extension for a minimum of six months beyond its original time limit. IG Metall's leadership perceived this as a clear provocation which could only be countered by a strike.

IG Metall's publicly stated goals in initiating the Hesse metalworkers' strike in 1951 were to obtain a high proportion of the social product for the working class and to defend real wages. The 10% wage and salary raise demanded by the union in June of 1951 "was to be taken from the profits of the employers" (Unternehmertum).[81] This approach differed radically from the predominant notion that wage restraint was an absolute sine qua non for any viable reconstruction effort, as well as from the DGB's policy of continuing its "constructive cooperation" with the employers regarding wage and price policies through August of that year. The union was serious in pressing the urgency of these issues by making its demand for higher wages the centerpiece of its "battle against profit" and for the "redistribution of the social product."[82] It was looking for the proper bargaining area for a "breakthrough" and eventually settled on Hesse, partly due to that state's constitutional ban on lockouts, and partly as a consequence of the SPD's governing position in Hesse at the time.

IG Metall's demands lacked, however, a commensurate strike strategy. The union's inexperience and fears of a showdown with the employers and Hesse's Social Democratic government led to a less than satisfactory outcome to the strike. The course of the strike revealed the following strategic mistakes which forced the union onto the defensive from the very beginning: Although 30,000 to 40,000 metalworkers in Hesse were called out on strike on the first day (August 24, 1951), the most important metal-processing firms in Kassel and the region's main giant, Opel in Rüsselsheim, continued their regular operations until September 6. Mobilization in these plants was postponed until the middle of the four-week conflict. IG Metall's strategy thus excluded its best-prepared members from actively supporting the union's cause in this crucial industrial action.

An even more destabilizing situation occurred when the union's district leadership permitted many of its locals to conduct special negotiations with individual firms which, by the end of the strike, resulted in the signing of 103 firm-specific contracts affecting approximately 15,000 metalworkers in Hesse.[83] Lastly, the union consented to abide by the arbitration efforts of Hesse's Social Democratic labor minister, in good part as a gesture of loyalty and goodwill toward an SPD-led state government. By submitting to this process, IG Metall surrendered the strategic advantage of not having to face the threat of capital's lockout due to the constitutional ban in Hesse. The recommendation of the arbitrator, a 2.5% wage and salary increase instead of the original 10% demanded by the union, became the final settlement which – as the following figures of the ratification vote clearly illustrate – was quite unpopular among IG Metall's rank and file in Hesse. Of the 79.7% participating in the vote, 63.3% rejected the agreement while 15.5% approved it.[84] The compromise therefore went into full effect, since according to IG Metall's bylaws 75% of the affected members have to reject an agreement in order for a strike to continue. Yet, if one computes the negative votes as a percentage of those voting rather than as a fraction of the total eligible membership in the bargaining area, the figure would have reached 79.2%, an unambiguous statement of disapproval.

Perhaps the greatest shock to the young organized labor movement in the early days of the Federal Republic was the passage of the Works Constitution Law on July 19, 1952, which effectively barred the unions from an official role on the shop floor. Deprived of the very source of their organizational strength and control at the all-important point of production, some unions – including IG Metall – devised new and innovative measures to counter this threat. There is clearly a relation between the unions' – and especially IG Metall's – drastic losses in membership during the 1950s and labor's weakness on the shop floor as a consequence of the 1952 Works Constitution Law.[85]

If IG Metall continued to aspire to the role of system challenger and leader of the DGB's activist wing, then it had to take decisive action countering the obvious threat to its presence on the shop floor. The union introduced shop stewards (Vertrauensleute) in the 1950s as a direct response to the Works Constitution Law.

The position of the Vertrauensleute, who numbered 42,985 in 1956 when first counted by IG Metall,[86] could best be described as ambivalent. Their original mandate, to provide the union with an institutional presence in the plant to counter the works councils' hegemony, has remained unchanged to this day. This mandate was delineated in IG Metall's first "Guidelines for the Vertrauenskörper" published in 1955 and revised in 1973: "The shop stewards are the representatives and spokesmen of all IG Metall members in their area of organizational authority. They represent IG Metall's policies and embody the connection between the organization and the membership."[87]

Given this definition of the shop stewards' role, their concrete tasks have consisted of the following: (1) To represent and strengthen IG Metall at the plant level and on the shop floor. Specifically, this entails disseminating information regarding the union's policies and decisions, stimulating discussions concerning the effects of these actions on the lives of the members in the plant, distributing materials, collecting membership dues (prior to the introduction of the automatic check-off system), procuring new members for the union and publicizing its meetings among all employees. (2) To provide an information network. This includes the systematic attempt to facilitate a "bottom-up" flow of information within IG Metall's organizational structure. Shop stewards have always had to articulate the rank and file's desires and opinions to the union "on the outside" and to the works councils "on the inside." The reverse flow of information has also seen the shop stewards in the unenviable position of mediating between two frequently antagonistic structures of labor representation, the works councils and IG Metall. (3) To aid IG Metall members with their daily chores on the job. Perhaps the most important task for shop stewards has been to inform union members of their rights and duties as delineated in the Works Constitution Law of 1952 and subsequently revised in 1972.

Although IG Metall's original intentions during the 1950s were to have the works councilors' activities controlled by the shop stewards, the institutional constellation at the shop floor and the general political atmosphere of the times usually resulted in the reverse arrangement. The shop stewards, as the legally weaker of the two on the shop floor, developed a greater dependency on the works councilors than vice versa. The shop stewards, frequently in a precarious situation since they were typically appointed for their three-year terms by the union's local administrative offices (Ortsverwaltungen) rather than elected by the plant's unionized rank and file, suffered not only from a lack of power but also from a lack of legitimacy on the shop floor.

Although this basic weakness still remains, the shop stewards have gained substantial ground for themselves and, more importantly, have altered the shop-level discourse throughout IG Metall's organizational domain. This, of course, also implies significant changes within the union's policies and strategies. While IG Metall's introduction of the shop-steward system in the 1950s may have seemed only a desperate defensive measure at the time, one can now conclude with the benefit of hindsight that it introduced a new dimension in the plant-level politics of West Germany's industrial relations system.

Following the debacle of the Hesse strike in 1951 and the shock provided by the passage of the Works Constitution Law in 1952, adversities continued to beset IG Metall. Worthy of mention in this context is the union's strike in Bavaria during the summer of 1954, since it too forced some important strategic alterations in the union's outlook and behavior. Briefly, the issues in the 1954 strike centered on IG Metall's wage demands, which the employers interpreted as a union-led wage offensive in the wake of Agartz's proclamation of "expansive wage policy."[88] (For an extensive discussion of Viktor Agartz's thought and role in the unions see Chapter 3.) The low probability of such a coordinated approach on the union's part could be gauged both by the vehement denials of the existence of such a strategy by Otto Brenner, IG Metall's chairman, and by the union's numerous mistakes and general unpreparedness for this conflict.[89] One eminent scholar's characterization of IG Metall as "stumbling" into the strike as opposed to entering it in a planned and predetermined fashion seems to be borne out by all the stages of this conflict.[90]

No coordinated bargaining strategy lay behind IG Metall's initial demands in its various bargaining areas. Whereas some areas signed contracts before the conflict in Bavaria had even begun, others did so between the strike vote and the actual beginning of the strike, with NRW – IG Metall's largest bargaining area – coming to an agreement with the employers shortly before the end of the strike in Bavaria. This problem of poor timing was accentuated by differences in each area's specific demands. For example, IG Metall's Bavarian demands – raising of the Ecklohn (base wage rate) by 12 pfennigs, 12% salary increases for white-collar workers, raising the allowance for apprentices by DM 10 and a 15% wage increase for all Zeitlöhner (those paid an hourly wage) – were not repeated anywhere else.[91]

Three costly delays before the strike's actual commencement reflected the leadership's vacillation regarding its choice of action: (1) Not until the end of April 1954 did IG Metall cancel the wage and salary contracts which had been due to expire in December 1953; (2) the union's Bavarian leadership took more than a month to schedule the obligatory strike vote following the conclusive failure of negotiations with the employers; (3) ten days elapsed between the strike vote and the union's actual strike measures.[92] Inadequate strike preparations and deficient rank-and-file mobilization resulted from the Bavarian leadership's "mixed messages" of radical rhetoric and timid action. In short, the employers entered the strike better prepared than IG Metall.

IG Metall's weaknesses surfaced on the strike's very first day, August 9, 1954. Rather than concentrate on large plants with a relatively well-organized union membership, IG Metall called for a total strike in Bavaria's metal-processing industry. As a result, the strike quickly collapsed in many small and medium-sized firms. Even in large companies with a sizable union presence, the strike started to crumble due to a lack of preparatory mobilization on the part of IG Metall. With almost no participatory support from the clerical employees, the workers' solidarity began to wane in the first few days of the conflict. The employers used a successful "carrot-and-stick" approach to destroy the already brittle solidarity among the strikers. The "carrots" consisted of numerous plant-specific agreements which undermined the union's position by offering relatively lucrative and immediate wage contracts (eight pfennig raise of the base wage rate and 4% salary increase for clerical employees). The "sticks" entailed the open use of strikebreakers, the intimidation of picketers by photographing them, and in some cases assaulting them physically, refusal to furnish payment for work already performed, the cancellation of leases on company-owned housing and finally the establishment of elaborate blacklists containing all activists, most of whom, in fact, lost their jobs following the strike's conclusion on August 31, 1954.[93]

The final agreement – reached only after the state government's active intervention as a mediator – also reflected the union's defeat in this contest: a ten pfennig rise in the base wage, eight pfennigs more for pieceworkers and a 5–7% salary increase for white-collar employees. In addition, IG Metall had to accept a new wage categorization (Lohngruppenschlüssel) which clearly hurt unskilled and semi-skilled workers by distancing them even further from their skilled colleagues. Whereas an unskilled worker earned 86% of the base wage and his/her semi-skilled colleague 93% prior to the strike, their positions deteriorated to 84% and 90%, respectively. Not surprisingly, 52.8% of the union members voting opposed the settlement at the end of the strike.

The disaster in Bavaria brought home two lessons to the IG Metall leadership. The first was that a coherent bargaining strategy had to be developed before each wage round and then imposed from the center on the various regional union organizations. The second was that an alternative to the "total" strike had to be devised. IG Metall would have occasion to put these lessons into practice beginning in 1956, when the push to implement the DGB's first Aktionsprogramm began. (For a detailed discussion of the Aktionsprogramm see Chapter 3.)

Although the Aktionsprogramm had already been announced before the start of the 1955 wage round in the summer of that year, it seems to have had little effect on the negotiations between IG Metall and the employers in the metal industry. This was due to the fact that many of IG Metall's general framework contracts, which dealt with work time, were not up for renewal until 1956. Also, the unions had agreed that the DGB would first attempt to win the 45-hour work week through direct consultation with the BDA, the major employers' association, and negotiations to that effect continued between the two parties well into 1956. As a result, bargaining in 1955 retained much of the disorganized character of previous years, although IG Metall met less resistance from the employers to wage increases, thanks to buoyant conditions in the economy. From August 1955 until August 1956, standard wage rates rose by 7.6%.[94] IG Metall set the pace for other unions by gaining a 7.4% increase in Baden-Württemberg at the beginning of that year's bargaining round.

In the summer of 1956, with the DGB–BDA talks having broken down, IG Metall began its Aktionsprogramm offensive. Direct negotiations between Brenner and the leaders of Gesamtmetall superseded regional bargaining, and on July 25, 1956 the Bremen Accord was reached whereby the 45-hour work week would be introduced on October 1, 1956 and a pay raise of 1.3% would be granted.[95] This was equivalent to a total hourly wage increase of 8%. Other unions followed IG Metall's lead, and by January 1957 the work week in the Federal Republic had been reduced for 6.8 million workers.[96] The employers' flexibility on this issue was undoubtedly related to the first appearance of tight labor market conditions during the 1956–57 boom, which made employers reluctant to lose workdays through strikes. Brenner added to his 1956 victory at the end of 1957, when another agreement, known as the Bad Soden Accord, was signed by IG Metall and the employers. It provided for a 6% wage increase in 1958 and a further work-time reduction to 44 hours in 1959. Once again this deal was imposed from above on the union's regional bargaining authorities. Moreover, this agreement set the tone for negotiations in other sectors throughout 1958. Having been the most enthusiastic advocate of the Aktionsprogramm among DGB unions, IG Metall helped solidify its role as a "vanguard" within the West German labor movement with its eager application of the program's terms to its bargaining strategy.

As the talks which led to the Bremen Accord were taking place, IG Metall opened its Aktionsprogramm offensive on yet another front. It had been decided that regional bargaining would occur in a specially chosen area parallel to the IG Metall–Gesamtmetall negotiations, with the aim of achieving a breakthrough on some of the Aktionsprogramm's other major demands, such as sick pay, increased vacation time and vacation pay. The Schleswig-Holstein region was designated the "breakthrough point."[97]

Schleswig-Holstein provided an ideal location for the implementation of IG Metall's newly developed strike procedures. First of all, the metalworkers in this bargaining area were predominantly employed in the shipbuilding industry, which was centered in three large urban areas. In all three, IG Metall membership exceeded 70% of all metalworkers, an excellent organizational level for any kind of strike activity. Secondly, Schleswig-Holstein with its 45,000 IG Metall members comprised only 2.5% of the total IG Metall membership, thus making potential costs bearable for the union since the area's small size would not overburden the union's finances even in the case of a lockout or a prolonged strike. Lastly, the shipbuilding industry was enjoying a particularly prosperous period in 1956 with full capacity utilization projected for the following five years.

By focusing on sickness benefits for blue-collar workers as its principal demand in the negotiations for a new general framework contract, IG Metall decided to tackle a problem that should have been solved by the state. Indeed, the SPD had submitted a bill to the Bundestag in 1955 demanding that workers continue to receive a portion of their wages during illness. However, due to the makeup of the legislature at that time, the proposal languished in committee, thus justifying IG Metall's action. With the SPD's exclusion from state power, the centrality of these qualitative reforms lent the Schleswig-Holstein strike additional political overtones and rendered it a "model" for the entire labor movement. In addition, IG Metall's demand for the continuation of pay during illness went to the heart of one of the most complex and still unresolved divisions within the West German working class: that between blue-collar workers (Arbeiter) and white-collar employees (Angestellte). In this case, the union's demand required nothing short of the abolition of such distinctions in certain crucial contractual areas, since white-collar workers had long enjoyed sickness benefits, whereas their blue-collar colleagues lacked them completely.[98]

Following the old contract's expiration at the end of 1955 and protracted, futile negotiations until the fall of 1956, IG Metall decided to initiate its strike activities with the membership's obligatory strike vote held on October 11 and 12, 1956. With 77.5% in favor of the union's demands and its proposed actions, the strike itself began on October 24 of that year. From the very beginning, IG Metall pursued a disciplined course of "flexible escalation," a strategy which entailed the gradual expansion of a point strike to include 38 factories comprising 34,068 strikers at the peak of the conflict on January 11, 1957.[99] The seriousness of the strike, largely due to the unconventionality of IG Metall's demands, could be gauged by the unprecedented solidarity of other DGB unions who actively rallied to IG Metall's support as well as by the employers' united front, supplemented by a common strike fund established in 1956 to aid companies affected by strike activities. The state's early entry as a mediator between the two parties further highlighted the importance of this conflict.

The first attempt at arbitration occurred at the end of November on the state level, as had been the case with the previous two IG Metall strikes of the 1950s. The resulting compromise did not satisfy IG Metall's executive committee or the union's collective bargaining commission in Schleswig-Holstein, which recommended its rejection by the membership. On January 7, 1957, 97.3% of the union's eligible workers complied with this wish by voting against the terms proposed by the arbitrator. The strike continued. At this stage, the federal government in Bonn under the leadership of Konrad Adenauer got involved by arranging a new arbitration process, another first in West German industrial relations. The new agreement, reached at the end of January, contained somewhat more favorable terms, from IG Metall's point of view, than the one resulting from arbitration on the state level in November 1956. Yet it clearly failed to meet many of the leadership's expectations, as demonstrated by the narrow margin of 32 to 30 (with three absentions) favoring ratification in the vote by Schleswig-Holstein's collective bargaining commission. Indeed, when the commission – following IG Metall's statutory procedures – submitted its recommendation to the union's membership, urging it to accept the new agreement, the rank and file rejected the compromise by 76.2% of the district's eligible membership, which meant that the strike had to continue. This rejection was unprecedented in the history of IG Metall and the West German labor movement.

The third and final arbitration process yielded some additional concessions on the part of the employers regarding the level of payment during illness. It seemed to satisfy the strike area's bargaining commission, which this time voted 63 to 3 in favor of ratification. IG Metall's central leadership in Frankfurt, also pleased with the results and eager to end the lengthy conflict, mobilized its most reliable and persuasive officials from around the country and dispatched them to Schleswig-Holstein in a concerted effort to avoid another rejection of the union's recommendation by the strikers. Lest the rank and file once again openly rebuke the leadership, IG Metall officials – according to one source – even went so far as to reduce, occasionally even eliminate, portions of the allowances which were rendered to the strikers by the union in addition to the official strike support stipulated by IG Metall's statute.[100] Still, on February 13, 1957, 57.6% of those eligible to cast a ballot voted to reject the compromise and for a continuation of the strike. Despite this number's obvious significance as a signal of the magnitude of rank-and-file dissatisfaction with the final settlement, it nevertheless fell short of the 75% mark, thus ending the strike. Work had resumed in all of Schleswig-Holstein's metal industry by February 15, 1957.

Although the ratification vote conveyed the widespread displeasure of the union's rank and file with the strike's results, both the outcome and the process of the Schleswig-Holstein strike should be regarded as milestones in IG Metall's collective bargaining history. In spite of the fact that the union did not fully achieve its original goals, it did succeed in getting the employers to pay as much as 90% of net wages for 28 calendar days of illness in some cases, thus securing at least some form of payment for all workers beset by sickness.[101] Further, the new general framework contract in Schleswig-Holstein represented a qualitative innovation in the Federal Republic's collective bargaining system. Not only did a union for the first time organize a strike around demands contained in a general framework contract and thereby depart from the conventional wage and salary strikes of the post-World War II era, but it succeeded in adding social concerns to the predominantly economic issues which were considered "strike-worthy" by the labor movement. Moreover, one should view the subsequent passage of a law stipulating continued wage payments during illness (Lohnfortzahlungsgesetz) as a positive – albeit indirect – result of IG Metall's Schleswig-Holstein strike.

The Schleswig-Holstein strike was to cost Otto Brenner and his colleagues dearly, however. The union committed a legal error by calling a strike vote before negotiations had officially been declared over. The Federal Labor Court interpreted this in October 1958 as a violation of the bargaining partners' peace obligation (Friedenspflicht). In the summer of 1959, the court ordered IG Metall to pay the Schleswig-Holstein branch of Gesamtmetall damages in excess of DM 100 million (then about $23 million). This came as a severe blow to Brenner's reputation, and it had noticeable repercussions on the 1959 wage round, when, for the first time in years, IG Metall surrendered its role as vanguard among the DGB unions. The level of wage rate increases in the metal industry reached only 4.6%, which was 2% lower than the industrial average during that round.[102]

By the late 1950s, the tight labor market had forced most employers to seek additional workers, both West Germans and foreigners, to fill the increasing number of vacant positions in industry. This fierce competition led to a rapidly growing discrepancy between contractual and real pay with wage drift reaching over 20% in industries such as metal processing.[103] The dual nature of worker representation in the industrial relations system lent this development – which was largely induced by the labor market – additional organizational support, further weakening the unions' position in the plants. The objective conditions of the economy furthered the works councils' structural propensity to pursue their own, self-interested, firm-specific syndicalism (Betriebssyndikalismus).

The unions had to react. IG Metall's response was formulated by the head of its collective bargaining division, Fritz Salm, at the union's fifth congress, held in Nuremberg in 1958.[104] Further elaborated in numerous articles, mainly by Salm himself, this collective bargaining strategy set the terms for a strategy of negotiation called 'plant-level collective bargaining policy" (betriebsnahe Tarifpolitik).[105]

This policy tried to attain two related goals of rank-and-file mobilization for the union: first, the weakening of the authority of the works councils by having the shop stewards negotiate plant-level deals during the so-called second wage round; second, the democratization of the union itself by emphasizing a more decentralized and grassroots-oriented decision-making process. The purpose behind the concept of plant-level collective bargaining policy was for IG Metall to regain its organizational momentum during the Wirtschaftswunder (economic miracle). The union hoped to do this by mobilizing its base on the shop floor via a decentralized, firm-level – but nevertheless union-controlled – collective bargaining mechanism.

Plant-level collective bargaining policy was also believed to represent a much-needed decentralization of wage policy. The centralization of IG Metall's decision-making process in the wake of its poorly coordinated collective bargaining strategies of the early 1950s had contributed to the union bureaucracy's aloofness from the rank and file. Although most IG Metall contracts only pertain to a particular collective bargaining area, they often apply over a large geographic region with numerous firms, while providing a common guideline for all industries subject to that contractual arrangement. For example, industries of such varied natures as automobiles, electronics and mechanical engineering are all covered by IG Metall's contracts within the framework of metal processing. In this structure, union-signed contracts can only represent an imperfect common denominator for the union's collective bargaining policies. The industry- and area-specific adjustments and the plant-level specifications remain, given the "dual" framework of labor representation inside West Germany's plants, almost completely the prerogatives of the works councils.

Salm's idea was to counter the union bureaucracy's distance and the works councils' local dominance by implementing plant-level collective bargaining policy. Local union councils, or plant-level collective bargaining commissions, would have complemented the larger, more general and centralized contracts with local ones reflecting the particularities of each decentralized unit.[106] These decentralized bargaining units were to be part of the union, and thus explicitly outside the jurisdiction of the Works Constitution Law. This plan also clearly mandated a strengthening of the union's shop-steward movement and an expansion of the shop stewards' responsibilities and duties into the crucial area of collective bargaining.

It is a telling comment about IG Metall, the West German labor movement and the country's industrial relations structure that except for a failed experiment at Ford in 1960 and IG Chemie's bargaining round of 1970 this strategy of plant-level collective bargaining was never put into practice.[107] (For a discussion of plant-level collective bargaining policy in IG Chemie, see Chapter 5.) In addition to vehement opposition on the part of the employers, Salm's suggested reform was torpedoed by precisely those two structures which it was supposed to change in the first place. Resistance from the works councils – which was expected to some degree by Salm from the very beginning – proved too formidable an obstacle to the proper deployment of this mobilizing strategy.

More importantly, however, the union's own structures helped sabotage this bargaining approach. Both IG Metall's central bureaucracy and its local collective bargaining commissions never actively supported betriebsnahe Tarifpolitik. The bureaucracy feared that deployment of plant-level collective bargaining policy, while clearly designed to strengthen the union's shop-floor presence, could also lead to a loss of its own control over the rank and file. The local bargaining commissions saw their very existence threatened by this proposal, in good part because of the high representation of leading works councilors on every collective bargaining commission. Thus, the formal overlap in personnel between the union and the works councils in key decision-making structures sealed the fate of IG Metall's plant-level collective bargaining strategy in the late 1950s and early 1960s.

## V. FROM THE EARLY 1960s TO THE RECESSION OF 1966–1967: THE UNEASY ACCEPTANCE CONTINUES

By 1960 an important period in the history of the West German labor movement had come to an end. The eleven years since the beginning of the Federal Republic witnessed not only the "big three" strikes discussed above, but many other smaller ones as well. This epoch started out with IG

Metall in the vanguard of the DGB federation and ended with the union even more secure in its status as first among equals within organized labor. Yet IG Metall's role had changed significantly during this period, reflecting the impact on labor of the successful restoration of capitalism in West Germany. The 1950s began with the articulation of IG Metall's vision of a system transformation, a process wherein the union movement – with IG Metall at its helm – would play a central role. Both the end and the means for this transformation were to be furnished by the full implementation of Mitbestimmung. IG Metall's hopes were shattered by various crises which threatened to demoralize – even destroy – the newly founded unitary and industrial labor movement.

Yet the labor movement, led by IG Metall, adapted to the changed situation and held its own under extremely adverse conditions in both the political arena and the labor market. This process of adaptation exacted costs, one of which was the early abandonment of a radical vision and its replacement by a more pragmatic orientation based on the unions' strength in collective bargaining. Given this framework, IG Metall's record was flawed but nevertheless respectable.

The union's actions and attitudes from the early 1960s until the recession of 1966–67 could best be characterized as "conditionally cooperative."[108] IG Metall – unlike some of its sister institutions within the DGB, most notably the construction union IG Bau-Steine-Erden – continued its struggle for the maximization of gains within the existing capitalist system without, however, challenging the legitimacy of this system. IG Metall's acceptance of West Germany's booming capitalist economy did not restrict its activities and capabilities as a union, including the conduct of strikes. Nor did it mean that the union would fully cooperate with the capitalist system. Activism, of which IG Metall was the most ardent advocate within the DGB at the time, entailed precisely an uneasy acceptance of existing conditions, in order to gain as much from the system as possible.

In 1960, the union was able to win back the respect it had lost after the Federal Labor Court's 1958 decision, by signing the Bad Homburg Accord, which called for the phased introduction of the 40-hour week by 1965. One of the Aktionsprogramm's major goals, its attainment clearly represented a victory for the union. In addition, wage increases of 8.5% for 1960 and 5% for 1961 were agreed upon. Once again, IG Metall seemed to have regained its position as pacesetter within the DGB.

A serious threat to this renewed preeminence was posed, however, by the federal government's growing interference in collective bargaining after 1960. In the wake of the inflationary pressures generated by full employment and the threat to West German competitiveness presented by the 1961 revaluation of the Deutsche Mark, influential circles in the Federal

Republic began to call for state control of the unions, unless they adopted a more "reasonable" attitude. Economics Minister Ludwig Erhard refused to go along with this extreme view, but he did use the specter of a West German Taft-Hartley Act to try to pressure IG Metall into assuming a less activist posture in its strategy of collective bargaining. Keynesians meanwhile urged Erhard to devise some kind of incomes policy as a way of controlling inflation, and his first hesitant step in this direction came in 1960 with the "Blessing Memorandum,"[109] whose appeals fell on deaf ears, as industrial wage rates rose at a record pace of 8% in 1961 and 10.4% in 1962, due as much to labor market pressures as to union militancy. (A discussion of this is presented in Chapter 3).

The growing inflationary problem, and the government's apparent inability to deal with it, led Gesamtmetall to the conclusion that a hard line of its own was necessary to break what it saw as a wage–price spiral. The organization's tough new chief, Herbert van Hüllen, decided to confront IG Metall in the 1962 bargaining round.[110] For the first time ever, the employers reopened all their contracts with IG Metall rather than wait for the union to take the first step by demanding a new contract. IG Metall countered with a demand for a 10% wage increase and more vacation time to accompany the work-time reduction of 1½ hours per week already scheduled for 1962 (this added up to an hourly pay rise of 3.5%). Gesamtmetall offered 3%, and a strike vote was taken in the key bargaining region of North Württemberg/North Baden (NW/NB), which IG Metall had chosen as a "breakthrough" district. A confrontation seemed inevitable, but at the last minute Gesamtmetall backed down and granted an increase of 6% plus longer vacations.

An almost identical situation unfolded in 1963, except this time neither side could afford to give in. The economy was in a downturn, but inflation was still increasing, and the federal government urged moderate wage settlements to avoid a recession and to halt inflation. Adopting Blessing's old formula, Erhard recommended wage increases of 3–3.5%, which was equal to the anticipated productivity growth for 1963. (Georg Leber, leader of IG Bau-Steine-Erden and the most prominent advocate of accommodationism, had already done his part "to aid the commonweal" by signing a two-year wage contract in February 1963.) Now all eyes turned to IG Metall.

The employers' uncompromising attitude was clear from the very beginning. Just as in 1962, Gesamtmetall cancelled all existing wage contracts with IG Metall and offered no wage increases for the new agreements. The employers' representatives also demanded a delay in the next phase of work-time reduction and longer life-spans for contracts. Furthermore, they threatened to deploy the lockout in the event of an industrial conflict. In short, Gesamtmetall sought an open confrontation with IG Metall.[111]

Following the cancellations of wage contracts by employers in Baden-Württemberg (February 27, 1963) and North Rhine-Westphalia (March 31, 1963), a string of futile negotiating efforts reaffirmed the two sides' irreconcilable stance: the employers demanded a complete wage freeze, while IG Metall insisted on a minimum increase of 8% in wages and salaries. After the union had undertaken all preparations for conducting strike votes in Baden-Württemberg and NRW respectively, the employers adopted Erhard's recommendation by offering 3–3.5% wage increases, which were rejected by the union. Numerous warning strikes, spontaneous work stoppages and massive demonstrations accompanied the strike votes in both areas, thus lending additional support to the overwhelming numerical approval of the strike by the membership (87.2% of the votes cast in Baden-Württemberg, 83.6% in North Rhine-Westphalia favored some sort of strike action).[112] Just before the strike was set to begin in NW/NB, the IG Metall leadership lowered its demand from 8% to 6% which, in turn, the employers rejected as an insufficient concession. The strike began on April 29, 1963 in Baden-Württemberg, comprising both bargaining areas of North Württemberg/North Baden and South Württemberg/Hohenzollern. Following the Schleswig-Holstein model, the union's central leadership and its Stuttgart district pursued from the very beginning the strategy of a concentrated point strike, focusing on the region's motor-vehicle industry, with actions at factories such as the Daimler-Benz plant in Mannheim. The union's choice to rely on the automobile industry as its vanguard in the strike was based on the well-organized character of its workforce in that sector, a tradition of class consciousness there, and the industry's acute vulnerability due to a boom in car production at the time.[113] By May 1, 1963, the employers had countered IG Metall by locking out 270,000 workers in 420 firms in NW/NB, subsequently followed by an additional lockout of 34,000 in South Württemberg/Hohenzollern on May 5.

At this time the federal government, under the leadership of Ludwig Erhard, assumed the role of ad-hoc mediator. Erhard's efforts culminated in the Bonn Compromise, which ended the strike on May 10, 1963 with the following terms: a 5% wage and salary raise retroactive to April 1 or May 1 (depending on the contract's expiration date); an additional 2% wage and salary increase beginning on April, 1964 lasting until September 30, 1964; and the planned implementation of the next stage of weekly work-time reduction with full pay, beginning January 1, 1964 – as already agreed to by IG Metall and the employers in the Bremen and Bad Homburg contracts.

The strike's outcome can be viewed as unsatisfactory for both parties. The employers clearly failed to obtain their much-desired wage freeze.

They did succeed, however, in further consolidating their centralized collective bargaining mechanism by making the Bonn Compromise the model agreement for all of their bargaining areas in the metal-processing industry. IG Metall, on the other hand, averted the humiliation of having to accept an overt wage freeze. Nevertheless, the final result barely exceeded IG Bau-Steine-Erden's much-maligned 4.9% wage gain. These results could not help but convey the embarrassing fact that, at least as far as this bargaining round was concerned, there was little difference in practice between IG Metall's active wage policy and Leber's accommodationist course of "social partnership."

In the aftermath of the 1963 strike, IG Metall's leadership had to face substantial criticism from the rank and file for not having pressed hard enough for what these critics viewed as the union's legitimate demands. This was especially the case at some automobile plants, notably Daimler-Benz in Mannheim, where radical consciousness had developed around the journal *SoPo* – short for *Sozialistische Politik* – published by the workers.[114] Although about 73% of the eligible rank and file had approved the Bonn Compromise, less than 43% had done so at Daimler. The post-hoc criticism of IG Metall's conduct during the strike centered largely on the union's weak mobilization tactics and its failure to rally the rank and file at an earlier stage of the conflict. Moreover, these critics argued that the union's rationale for the strike was never articulated in political terms and was confined to strict bread-and-butter issues concerning wage and salary increases. The opposition within the union asserted that IG Metall's acceptance of West German capitalism of the early 1960s, and the adherence of the leadership to the notion of a "commonweal" (Allgemeinwohl), stymied any potentially stronger rank-and-file militancy. It was therefore clear to these critics why the conflict in NW/NB developed into what became known as a "TV-strike," during which strikers stayed at home watching television or puttering in the backyard instead of participating in various politicizing activities, such as forming picket lines en masse.

It would be wrong to see the Daimler-Benz *SoPo* criticisms as fruitless or the frustrated concoction of some marginalized radicals. Indeed, the entire strike effort including the obligatory challenges to the nature of its conduct served as a crucial learning experience for IG Metall's membership. The 1963 strike, with all its problems and controversy, laid the groundwork for three pivotal strikes conducted by the union in Baden-Württemberg during the 1970s. Although *SoPo*'s voice may never have been officially acknowledged by the union's leadership, it certainly led to serious soul-searching within IG Metall's top ranks, resulting in some tangible changes in union behavior in the years to come.

Despite these criticisms by activist elements within IG Metall's rank and file, the 1963 strike was interpreted quite differently by the West German public at large. The union's stubborn stance in 1962 and 1963, during a time of growing economic uncertainty, substantially damaged IG Metall's reputation with the public. West Germany's conservative press constantly depicted Otto Brenner as a socialist fanatic who had little concern for the well-being of the country's capitalist economy and the stability of its democratic polity. Even the SPD urged Brenner to avoid a strike in 1963 because such industrial action, it was believed, would threaten the party's new moderate image. The strike was unpopular, and Brenner found himself increasingly isolated. He decided that the union had to cultivate a more moderate, "responsible" image. Gesamtmetall gave him the opportunity in early 1964 when it offered to forget about the DM 38 million which IG Metall still owed the employers in damages as a result of the Schleswig-Holstein strike if Brenner would sign a new arbitration agreement which would make calling strikes more difficult. Brenner gave in.

The 1964–65 and 1966 wage rounds demonstrated IG Metall's moderation. At the end of 1964, the union approved a one-year delay in the introduction of the 40-hour week (scheduled for July 1965) in order not to exacerbate an already extremely tight labor market. In return, a 7.3% wage raise for 1965 and increased vacation time were granted. This agreement, known as the first Erbach Accord, elicited universal praise in political circles. Whether intentional or not, the Accord remained within the guidelines for 1965 issued by the Council of Economic Advisors (SVR) in its first report, which had characterized wage increases of between 7% and 8% as acceptable.[115] In February 1965, following a deadlock in negotiations in the steel industry, an independent arbitrator (Hans Meinhold) justified a wage raise of 7.5% with the argument that wages should increase at a rate equal to the growth in productivity plus inflation. This became known as the "Meinhold formula," and was tacitly accepted by both IG Metall and the employers as the basis for a future cooperative wage policy.

The SVR gave its approval to the Meinhold compromise in its 1965 report,[116] and suggested in the same spirit a wage raise of 6% for 1966. IG Metall opened the new round at the beginning of the year, and the employers again requested that the 40-hour work week be postponed in view of the difficult situation in the labor market. The conciliatory Brenner agreed, and in return won a wage increase of 6% for IG Metall just as the SVR had recommended. The definitive arrival of the 40-hour work week was set for July 1967, and it was to be accompanied by a wage increase of 1.9% for the first six months of that year. Twelve years after its formulation, the major goal of the 1955 Aktionsprogramm was finally to become reality.

Beginning in the early 1960s, IG Metall faced a structural crisis and declining employment in the nation's steel industry. The industry's structural difficulties derived from increasing competition by American, Soviet and above all Japanese steel works in the world market, and from the introduction of important technical innovations. The union responded by calling for the introduction of Sozialpläne (social plans) for which it mobilized the quiet – but nevertheless powerful – mechanism of Montanmitbestimmung.[117] From the announcement of these plans in 1962 until the period of their most frequent use between 1966 and 1968 (and then again following the economic crisis of the mid-1970s), IG Metall's leadership has continually maintained that the implementation of these crucial "cushioning" measures would have been impossible if not for Montanmitbestimmung in the country's steel sector. There is little doubt that IG Metall initially conceived, subsequently negotiated and finally supervised these plans within the general framework of Montanmitbestimmung. These plans thus derived from a structure of industrial relations which exists outside of IG Metall's two conventional channels of interest articulation, the collective bargaining process and the political arena.

The first official Sozialplan signed in 1962 by IG Metall and Rasselstein AG, a steel company jointly owned by the Wolff and Thyssen groups, introduced a new dimension in social policy in the Federal Republic. This agreement included an array of measures designed to ease the adverse consequences of technological change. Specifically, the plan included generous severance pay for workers over 60, other monetary benefits for early retirees according to a seniority plan, and some non-pecuniary incentives.[118] Above all, it provided IG Metall with institutional access.

By gaining access to crucial information regarding technological change and its impact on workers (through their representatives on the full-parity advisory boards), IG Metall was able to soften a potentially damaging blow to the core of its membership. The labor representatives on the advisory boards established close links with the personnel directors and works councilors in the steel firms and together they formulated policies designed to alleviate some of the hardships accompanying technological change. IG Metall's strategies to counter some of the employers' production-related changes were frequently molded in meetings such as those involving personnel directors in the steel industry, which took place during their regular get-togethers in Oberhausen ("the Oberhausen circle").[119] There seems little doubt that such mechanisms would not have existed outside the framework of full-parity Montanmitbestimmung.

> Experience has shown that it is precisely in this realm [structural changes
> and technological developments in the iron and steel industry] that Mitbe-
> stimmung can achieve superb results for the workers if it is properly
> deployed. Thus it was possible to attain social plans in addition to agree-
> ments about technological and organizational measures in numerous firms,
> which clearly protected their workforce from the negative ramifications of
> technological and organizational changes.[120]

Although defensive in nature, IG Metall's social plans – won with the help
of Mitbestimmung for the first time in the early 1960s – laid the foundation
for further developments which were to assume great importance for the
union during the crisis of the 1970s.

In summary, the early 1960s saw IG Metall's ambivalence endure in a
different form and context from that characteristic of the 1950s. Although
the union's strike activities diminished quite drastically after the Schleswig-
Holstein conflict, this alone did not indicate a less determined stance on the
part of the union toward its collective bargaining strategies. These
continued to be guided by the tenets of the 1955 Aktionsprogramm which
were updated by its successor of 1965 and by the concepts of active wage
policy developed in the early 1950s. In addition to relying on its own
bargaining strength, IG Metall employed the mechanism of Mitbestimmung to its advantage in drawing up its Sozialpläne. Lastly, the state
remained inaccessible to IG Metall, just as it had been throughout the
1950s.

Two developments in the latter half of the 1960s catapulted the labor
movement as a whole – and particularly IG Metall – out of a lethargic
phase onto the center stage of political change in the Federal Republic:
the SPD's assumption of state power and a simultaneous process of
repoliticization on the part of West Germany's workers in the wake of the
student revolts. It is to this period of general mobilization in West
German society and IG Metall's role therein that the next section is
devoted.

### VI. FROM THE 1966–1967 RECESSION TO THE 1974–1975 CRISIS: UNION MOBILIZATION AND SOCIAL REFORM

The SPD's decision to form a government with the CDU in December
1966 met with a mixed reaction from the unions. Predictably, the DGB's
accommodationists, who were closer to the SPD party line, strongly
supported the move. Most activists were skeptical, and IG Metall loudly
disapproved. However, since the coalition was formed at a time of perceived national emergency (the 1966–67 recession) Brenner's metalwork-

ers decided to cooperate with the new government's program to revitalize the economy.

The news that Brenner would participate in the Concerted Action came as a surprise to many West Germans. This move fit in well, however, with the moderate image the IG Metall chief had been trying to cultivate since 1964. In the face of the most serious economic crisis since the war and with many of his union's own members threatened with unemployment, Brenner could hardly reject Economic Minister Karl Schiller's request for cooperation in putting the nation back on the path to prosperity. However, Brenner did emphasize repeatedly that the Concerted Action was just a forum for discussion, and in no way limited the freedom of his union's collective bargaining.[121]

The DGB unions, led by IG Metall, did their utmost to support the government's economic policies in the labor market from 1967 through 1969. This was more a result of the weakening of the unions' position due to layoffs and anxiety about the future (engendered by the 1966–67 recession) than of altruism or feelings of solidarity with the government. As the recession deepened, employers began to eliminate many of the non-contractual "extras" which workers received on top of the standard wage rate. This is illustrated by the fact that wage rates rose faster than actual earnings in 1967.[122] The unions could hardly push wage demands at a time when take-home pay was being cut. It is not surprising, then, that in the second half of 1967 many contracts which could have been renegotiated were allowed to continue. Instead, most unions tried to reach informal agreements with employers to stop earnings cuts in exchange for a postponement of new wage bargaining until 1968. An accord signed by IG Metall and Gesamtmetall in October 1967 which postponed negotiations until March 1968 was an example of this trend.[123] As a result of this union weakness, nominal earnings per employed person rose by only 3.2% in 1967, the smallest increase in the Federal Republic's history to that date.

As the economy picked up in early 1968, both Schiller and the SVR recommended wage increases of between 5.5% and 6.5% in order to boost consumer spending and speed the recovery.[124] The unions, however, were still demoralized by the recession and fearful of doing anything that might endanger the upturn. Consequently, labor's wage settlements in 1968 were moderate, with the tone once again set by IG Metall's contract in the metal-processing industry, which was to run for eighteen months and called for a 4% wage rise in 1968. The union justified its modest wage demands by claiming they were necessary to obtain employer approval for the Rationalisierungsschutzabkommen (Rationalization Protection Agreement), which was also signed in 1968. This accord provided protection for

older workers against layoffs caused by technological change, and conveyed a growing interest in "qualitative" issues on the part of IG Metall in
the wake of the 1967 crisis.

By the start of 1969 the economy was booming, and criticism of the
previous year's low wage increases began to mount within the union and
in government circles.[125] IG Metall reacted by convincing Gesamtmetall
to reopen their contract two months early, and a new wage package was
negotiated in August 1969 providing for an 8% pay raise as well as
stepped-up legal protection for union shop stewards (Vertrauensleute).
This increase lay significantly above the 5.5–6.5% which the government
had again recommended for 1969. Trouble arose in early September,
however, when steel industry employers refused to go along with Gesamtmetall in reopening and renegotiating their contracts with IG Metall. As a
result, a marked gap arose between metal-processing industry wages (DM
4.42/hour) and those in the steel industry (DM 3.99/hour) after the August
raises went into effect in metal processing.

The reason for this difference in the employers' response to IG Metall's
overtures lay largely in the contrasting economic conditions of these two
sectors of West German industry. Whereas most major components of
metal processing such as automobiles, electronics and mechanical engineering suffered serious cyclical setbacks during the recession of 1966–67,
none of them experienced the structural dislocation and technological
turmoil of the steel industry and mining as early as the late 1950s. Thus,
while the 1968–69 boom brought a welcome improvement for the metal-
processing industry, it meant a good deal more to the beleaguered steel
sector. Moreover, the two-month difference in the respective expiration
dates of the old contracts might also have contributed to the reaching of a
new agreement in metal processing and the continuation of the status quo
in steel. After all, by entering the new contract in August, the employers in
metal processing "lost" only two remaining months of the old eighteen-
month contracts which were so favorable to them, whereas their counterparts in steel would have had to forego four months on an equally
advantageous arrangement.

Relatively low job security, lagging wages and difficult working conditions characterized the experience of the steelworkers throughout most of
the 1960s. The tremendous boom in the steel industry following the
recession of 1966–67 caught most people by surprise, but failed to alleviate
most of the hardships which had become the norm for the industry's
workers. Indeed, with the exception of job insecurity, which diminished
during the frenzied boom period of 1968–69, all other factors worsened for
the steelworkers. The impressive growth in steel production, which for this
period exceeded that of West German industry as a whole, was largely

achieved without hiring any new workers, thus indicating an even greater intensification of the work process. Worker productivity in the industry reached new heights during these two years, while commensurate wage increases were not forthcoming. With the industry's introduction of disproportionately large price increases (compared to other sectors of the economy) by the fall of 1968 and the announcements of high profits by most steel companies at their annual shareholders' meetings during 1968–69, many steelworkers felt a substantial pay increase was overdue.

Nowhere was this truer than at the Hoesch steel works in Dortmund. Until the fall of 1966, Hoesch workers at the company's Westfalenhütte plant were the wage leaders in the country. By 1969, Hoesch workers made on the average 5% less in hourly wages than their colleagues at other West German steel companies. In the summer of 1969, Hoesch boasted of remarkable profits in its annual letter to stockholders. It was hardly surprising then that in the wake of IG Metall's 8% across-the-board wage agreement in the metal-processing industry, the Hoesch works council demanded a 20 pfennig hourly raise on August 15, 1969 retroactive to August 1. This raise would have yielded an average hourly wage of about DM 4.19, still approximately 20 pfennigs short of the newly attained wages in the metal-processing industry. Management's response on August 25 was a 15 pfennig raise beginning December 1, 1969. The works council rejected this offer on September 1 and demanded renewed negotiations with management. On the morning of September 2, however, the workers refused to resume their regular shifts and began a protest strike on behalf of their demands. Their action preempted both major institutions of collective bargaining within the West German industrial relations system: the unions and the works councils.

The Hoesch workers' surprising initiative soon found numerous imitators across the Federal Republic. Mainly concentrated in the steel industry of North Rhine-Westphalia and the Saar's mining communities, the strikes also reached a steel plant in Bavaria, other steel works in Bremen, shipyard workers in Schleswig-Holstein, miners in Dortmund, workers in the metal-processing industries of the Rhine-Ruhr and Stuttgart areas, and plants in various other industries throughout the country.

The strikes had three distinct – although interdependent – levels of discontent:

1. most early strikes, especially those in the steel industry and in mining, best exemplified by the Hoesch case, had industry–related structural problems as their major catalysts;
2. many subsequent strikes, particularly in metal processing, focused on company-related difficulties, while
3. a third category remained largely preoccupied with plant-level and shop-floor grievances within particular factories.[126]

All strike activities resulted from the workers' high level of discontent due to IG Metall's – and to a lesser extent IG Bergbau und Energie's – inability to increase wages and benefits for their members commensurate with the superboom which the economy enjoyed at the time. However, there were also important local issues, or "internal disproportionalities,"[127] which contributed to the proliferation of work stoppages in September 1969.

IG Metall's response to the wildcat strikes in its organizational domain was swift. Within 24 hours of the Hoesch walkout, talks had begun between the union and the steel employers' association. By establishing its immediate hegemony over the bargaining process, IG Metall was able to protect its overall position, but only provided it show some degree of flexibility and willingness to learn from past mistakes. On September 9, the union submitted a demand for a 14% wage and salary increase in the steel industry. After an 18-hour marathon session with the employers, agreement was reached on Friday, September 12 on a contract specifying an 11% wage and salary increase for all steelworkers, to be paid over a twelve-month period beginning retroactively on September 1. The union also gained three vacation days which were to be added over the ensuing three years. In many plants, the workers succeeded in obtaining further plant-specific benefits, usually in the form of "linear" wage increases ranging from 20 to 70 pfennigs an hour.[128] By the weekend of September 13 and 14, most strike activities had abated.

As to the strike "experience" itself, the only available empirical analysis of these events concluded that although the strikers disapproved of certain policies and strategies on the part of IG Metall and IG Bergbau und Energie, they remained very loyal to these organizations and continued to believe in the overall efficacy and legitimacy of the West German industrial relations system, vehemently rejecting any activities which could have been interpreted as challenging existent political structures.[129] Therefore, the September strikes in the coal and steel industries represented a reaffirmation of classic trade-union consciousness. They were localized struggles involving "bread-and-butter" issues, and they exhibited a definite grass-roots activism without a fundamental criticism of the Federal Republic's political and economic arrangements.

The spontaneous and unauthorized nature of the strikes required new forms of organization and collective action – such as plant occupations, many of which occurred during the walkout. Strike activities which had traditionally been organized and performed by IG Metall – leafletting, picketing, setting up strike crews and communicating demands – suddenly fell to the workers in the steel mills. As a consequence, plant-level structures of labor representation, such as the works councils and the shop-steward networks, played crucial roles during the strikes. Most works *councilors* and shop stewards in the steel industry fully supported the strike.[130] In the rare instances where this was not the case, the workers bypassed this level of institutional representation and set up alternative forms of collective leadership.[131] On the whole, however, these events can be labeled "works councils strikes" since, whether intended to or not, they helped legitimize and strengthen the representational position of the works councils in the steel sector.

This is surprising since works councilors are legally prohibited from conducting strike activities. In fact, all worker-led actions during September 1969 were illegal according to the strict rules governing industrial relations in the Federal Republic. (For a discussion of the main features of this system see Chapter 2.) If only for this fact alone, the initiatives on the part of the workers during this period introduced a new dimension to labor–employer relations. By organizing and carrying out their own wildcat actions the strikers defied the law and their own institutional representatives for the first time since the establishment of the Federal Republic, and they got away with it.

More than any other factor, the absence of – in some cases outright hostility toward – overt political action and the concomitant maintenance of traditional trade-union-like behavior distinguished the West German September strikes from parallel events occurring at around the same time in Italy and France. For example, during the strikes in the Federal Republic there were no reported attempts by the strikers to take over the production process and initiate new, worker-controlled organizational forms, as was frequently the case in Italy and France. One also did not encounter the hostility toward – or active destruction of – private property in West German plants that characterized the work stoppages in other countries, especially Italy. This was, together with the relatively short duration of the strikes, one of the main reasons for the notable absence of police intervention in the West German case.

The strikers perceived their mission strictly in socio-economic terms and focused only on immediate goals. This coincided with the strikers' judgement about the unions' function, which most workers – strikers and non-strikers alike – understood as primarily confined to winning the bread-and-butter reforms associated with collective bargaining. Only 26% of workers surveyed in selected struck factories – as opposed to 29% (!) in a control group of normally functioning plants – expressed any positive views towards the involvement of unions in politics.[132] A further breakdown of the sample reveals that only 7% of the workers – strikers and non-strikers alike – wanted the unions to "exert greater influence on the government and parliament," while only 14% credited the unions with playing an important role in "securing democracy" in the Federal Republic.[133] In addition, 62% of the respondents felt the unions' primary role should be to improve wages, 30% saw their main task as augmenting the existing system of general social welfare, with 27% arguing that the unions' major function was to protect jobs. These figures show that the political consciousness of West German workers, by viewing unions as no more than wage-oriented interest groups, was quite limited in 1969.[134] Politics, to most workers, was still defined in terms of parliament, parties, the government and other institutions of the state, in whose affairs and activities unions ought not involve themselves.

One of the notably "apolitical" steps on the part of the strikers was their distancing – which often bordered on open hostility – from communism and the student left. Repeatedly, one would hear of incidents where workers burned red flags during demonstrations, threatened radical students lest they express their unwelcome support for and solidarity with the strikers, and assaulted film crews from the German Democratic Republic. Most workers voiced at best ambivalent attitudes toward the student demonstrations engulfing West Germany at the same time, and a sizable majority seemed to reject any parallels between the students' and their own efforts. Fourteen percent of the respondents in the above-mentioned survey had wholly negative attitudes towards everything the students represented.[135]

To most workers, political activities were properly confined to the polling booth and had little, if any, relationship to their daily lives on the shop floor. The strikers' mission was clear: rather than try to change or reject the unions – let alone "the system" – they were merely attempting to correct a temporary wrong. By taking matters into their own hands, most strikers felt that their action demonstrated their general discontent with IG Metall's bargaining results over the preceding few years. At the same time, however, there was a widespread belief that the September strikes would shake the union out of its lethargy and return it to its proper function: to defend workers' rights, especially by pursuing a more aggressive wage policy than had been implemented over the previous three years.

In light of these facts, IG Metall's handling of the September strikes seems very insightful. While never appearing overly enthusiastic about the events (for obvious reasons), the union leadership did not denounce the strikers. Instead, IG Metall's strategy was to seize the occasion as quickly as possible, eradicate the sources of trouble responsible for the outbreak of the strikes and try to win the workers back to the fold. For IG Metall the strikes provided both a genuine learning experience and an opportunity to coopt the militancy of the workforce.

The seriousness of IG Metall's intention to make the strikes an important learning experience, which would improve the union's collective bargaining strategies in the early 1970s, could be gauged by the leadership conference on this topic held in January 1970. This meeting was characterized by self-criticism for past mistakes as well as by the attempt to capitalize on the rank and file's mood by redirecting it for the organization's benefit. Otto Brenner said: "We do not want developments similar to the ones we experienced during the spontaneous strikes of last September to recur. From the very beginning, we must be the ones who formulate demands, who push for negotiations and who ultimately conduct them at the right moment."[136] IG Metall's paramount concern was to retain control over every stage of an increasingly volatile process. To that end, the union incorporated into its strategies some of the demands articulated by the strikers during the first two weeks of September 1969.

The main conclusions which the IG Metall leadership drew from the September strikes reflected the workers' concerns. Following is a list of a few of the major changes in the union's collective bargaining strategy, most of which received widespread support during the September strikes of 1969:[137]

1. The bargaining rounds, the conduct of which had undergone a process of increased centralization during the late 1950s and early 1960s, were to assume a more regional character in the early 1970s. Each collective bargaining area was granted a certain autonomy in formulating and implementing its own strategies. These strategies were to reflect the "area-specific" nature of the workers' concerns, without thereby surrendering the central organization's ultimate powers of guidance, coordination and support.

2. The duration of wage and salary contracts was not to exceed twelve months. This new policy guideline reflected the union's recognition of the adverse consequences of having signed 18-month wage and salary agreements (in the spring of 1968). Signing long-term contracts restricted IG Metall's mobility, thereby creating one of the major reasons for the September strikes of 1969.

3. The most important demand in any bargaining round would have to be a wage and salary raise commensurate with the general economic conditions of the time.

4. Each major demand should be supplemented by specific demands particular to the individual bargaining areas. A special emphasis should be given to all attempts aimed at improving methods of wage categorization in order to decrease existing wage differences, thereby improving the position of workers in the lower wage categories.

The last policy guideline had its roots in the September strikes. The strikers did not demand percentage raises – they did not speak of a 14%

wage and salary increase, for example – but rather mentioned absolute figures such as 30, 50 or 70 pfennigs more per hour.[138] The workers' "linear" demands had an egalitarian component which countered the union's percentage demands. The latter had over the years increased the wage differentials between workers in the lower wage categories and those in the higher ones. By accepting the fundamental capitalist premise that wages were to be based on achievement rather than need, IG Metall's wage demands augmented the intra-class stratification of its membership. Critics of the union have argued that this is logical, since the majority of IG Metall's leadership and most of the members of its bargaining committees are skilled workers uninterested in enacting policies which would directly threaten their power and status vis-à-vis their semi- and unskilled colleagues.[139] Thus the "linear" demands of the strikers sought to establish an egalitarianism based on need, which challenged the union's acceptance of an achievement-oriented structure of remuneration.

These official policy guidelines for the union's collective bargaining strategies represented a compromise. As will be shown below, some of the union's bargaining districts combined the more traditional percentage demands with linear ones. This policy of mixed demands (Mischforderungen) played a significant role in the wage rounds of many West German unions during the 1970s. It would be impossible to establish a definitive causal relationship between the September strikes and this development in IG Metall's bargaining strategy. Nevertheless, it seems clear that given the union's sober evaluation of the implications of the strikes, IG Metall policymakers paid close attention to the workers' linear wage demands.

The strikes of September 1969 began a five-year mobilization period during which the West German labor movement won substantial benefits through wage drift, and new gains in the "quality of work life." This period of hope lasted until the onset of the economic crisis in 1974–75, when conditions in the labor market and in the political arena changed.

There were three central reasons for the unions' new labor market strategy in the late 1960s and early 1970s. The first was the booming economy and the concomitant desire on the part of the unions to share in industry's profits, especially given the existence of full employment. Secondly, the unions acted on their traditional belief that wages were one of the major components of economic growth. Thirdly, the unions faced an organizational imperative to respond to a restive rank and file by pursuing a more activist bargaining strategy.

The organizational readiness and competitive spirit which characterized the 1970 bargaining round can only be understood in terms of the powerful ripple effect of the September strikes. The events of that year led to one of the rare moments in the union's history when all components for an exceedingly successful bargaining round were present: a healthy economy; an equally superb situation in most of the industries within IG Metall's purview;[140] a highly mobilized membership; and a union leadership eager to please and intent on avoiding the mistakes of the recent past. The 1970 bargaining round yielded the highest wage and salary gains ever achieved by a union in the history of the Federal Republic.

IG Metall stuck to the guidelines resulting from the soul-searching sessions following the 1969 September strikes.[141] All negotiations took place on a regional level. This decentralization was reflected in the varying demands and differing results for each of the union's bargaining areas which characterized the fall 1970 bargaining round. Wage and salary demands ranged from 12.5% to 18%, with other efforts centered on reducing wage differentials, the introduction of a fully paid thirteenth-month bonus, narrowing the gap between contractually negotiated and actually paid wages, and an attempt to improve the conditions of the most disadvantaged workers by granting them special pay benefits.[142] Over 500,000 workers participated in warning strikes throughout the steel and metal-processing industries. Following the employers' counter-offer of 7% in wage and salary increases in metal processing it took the union leadership only a few weeks to schedule a strike in the bargaining region of North Rhine-Westphalia.

This quick action on the part of the union, eager not to alienate its already restive membership, bore immediate results: the employers agreed to increase pay by 11% in North Rhine-Westphalia's metal industry, provide 12.2% more in wages and 12% more in salary in North Württemberg/North Baden, and 13.5% and 13.0% respectively in South Württemberg/Hohenzollern where over 90% of the IG Metall membership had already voted for a strike.[143] Wage differentials were reduced in all three areas. Aid to vocational programs in the metal industries of all three regions received substantial improvements as part of the agreement. Wage and salary increases in the steel industry hovered between 10% and 13.5%. In addition to winning gains in the remuneration of apprentices and others in vocational training, IG Metall obtained the full payment of a thirteenth-month bonus in the steel sector. All in all, the union's total gains in both wages and salaries reached the impressive level of 24% in the steel industry.[144] Conditions in 1970 rendered it a uniquely successful year for IG Metall.

The peak of the post-1967 boom had been reached by early 1971. The downswing of the fifth post-war cycle began to "cool off" the West German economy, which still boasted virtually no unemployment, a 2.7% rise in real aggregate growth and an increase of 4.5% in capital investments during 1971. Yet these figures paled in comparison with the boom period's high points between 1968 and 1970: 7.3%, 8.2% and 5.8% actual increase in GNP; 8.0% 12.1% and 11.5% for the respective annual increases in capital investments. Most importantly, the second half of 1971 witnessed an inflation rate of 6.4%. The slowdown of the economy started in the machine-tool industry, the core of West Germany's investment goods industry. New orders declined continuously from the second business quarter in 1970, and reached a level by the fourth quarter of 1971 which was 33.5% below that of the first quarter in 1970.[145] It should be added, however, that the actual decline in the production of machine tools over this period amounted only to 5.5% due to the large quantities of back orders which the industry could not fill during the peak of the boom.

A similar pattern of declining orders also beset the automobile industry during the second quarter of 1971 and the electronics industry during the fourth quarter of the same year. Part of this trend has to be attributed to factors beyond the usual cyclical fluctuations of a market economy. The main source of this temporary discomfort was a rapid decline in foreign demand for some West German products, largely as a consequence of repeated revaluations of the D-Mark via its "floating" in May 1971, and shifts in American economic and trade policies during August of that same year. Given the export-dependent nature of the Federal Republic's metal-processing industries, it is not surprising that employers were distressed by these developments, which compounded their existing worries over the general economic slowdown. This relative deterioration in economic conditions accounted for the employers' resolve to challenge IG Metall during the 1971 bargaining round.

Most students of West German industrial relations and union politics – no matter how diverse their opinions – agree that the major impetus (aside from the economic situation) behind the confrontational nature of the 1971 bargaining round in the metal industry was the employers' desire to put IG Metall in its place.[146] The impressive wage gains of the previous two years, which had fully restored labor's overall wage share of the economy (after a loss suffered in the recession of 1966–67) were, in the employers' eyes, the major reasons for the country's excessive inflation (ranging between 5% and 8% during this period) and for a decline in profits. More importantly, however, the employers felt that IG Metall's fate was increasingly determined by a radicalized rank and file which the union leadership would not, or simply could not, control since the September strikes of 1969. The employers watched IG Metall's mobilization with grave concern and decided to confront it as best they could. They vowed to act at the first opportune moment offered by a slowdown in the economy's growth. This moment came in the fall of 1971.

The employers wanted to halt not only IG Metall's mobilization but the political activism engulfing West German society as well. Consequently their offensive went beyond IG Metall's immediate bargaining concerns, aiming at other aspects of the general *Aufbruchsstimmung* dominating political discourse. Gesamtmetall's triannual report of 1968–70, assessing the outlook for the early 1970s, stated:

> The pessimism [of the employers] ... is not only the result of an unfavorable economic outlook. It is at the same time an expression of insecurity and concern regarding the increasing politicization of all economic activity, coupled with incessant attacks against the employers. Various plans and announcements about co-determination, tax reform and the reduction of private profit to increase public wealth are crucial knots in a general web which threatens to strangle all entrepreneurial initiative and leads many employers to wonder whether it still makes sense to undertake risks and continue competing in the market.[147]

IG Metall's situation in 1971 was a difficult one. The union had to perform a precarious balancing act between two potentially contradictory strategies, each of which was tied to a different, but equally legitimate, interest. The first strategy, closely connected to IG Metall's wish to maintain excellent relations with the reform-minded, SPD-led government, required that the union formulate and implement wage policies which reflected "social responsibility," by closely adhering to the government's recommended wage and salary levels and the Concerted Action's orientation data. The second strategy – in clear contrast to the first – aimed at obtaining the highest possible wage settlement for an increasingly restive rank and file. The employers, fully aware of this uncertain union/party/government relationship, tried to alienate one from the others.

During 1971, one could discern numerous junctures at which the SPD used its special relationship with organized labor – IG Metall in particular – to influence the unions' behavior and demands in the coming bargaining rounds. In March, Willy Brandt sent a letter to the DGB's new chairman, Heinz Oskar Vetter, wherein he expressed his hopes – in language similar to that used by the Council of Economic Advisors – that "all concerned parties would demonstrate responsible behavior" in the forthcoming wage and salary rounds.[148] This was followed two months later by the council's own special position paper entitled "On the Cyclical and Monetary Situation in May 1971."[149] In this report, the council pointed out the potential dangers for the West German economy resulting from the inflationary trend. Inflation, the paper concluded, would be fueled by any upward "floating" of the D-Mark and a general instability in the international money markets. The "Five Wise Men" of the council criticized the government for having set a bad precedent for the wage rounds still to be held in 1971 by signing contracts with the public employees' unions in January, yielding wages and salaries which exceeded the government's own orientation data of 7–8%. In May, at a specially convened meeting between the SPD's steering committee and the party's union council (Gewerkschaftsrat) which comprised all top union leaders (including Otto Brenner), Willy Brandt stated that he could not imagine that there would be Social Democrats in leading union positions "who would be inclined to abandon [the party] given the social and political problems facing us."[150]

Concerted Action moved in the beginning of June to further restrict IG Metall's room to maneuver in its upcoming bargaining round. The meeting established the necessity for consolidation and caution to protect the West German economy. Both contractual partners were to contribute to this by exercising wisdom and moderation:

> According to the understanding of all participants, this does not mean a freeze on income, but rather a phase wherein the profit and cost developments reach a level of normalization in the firms and wherein the real increases in income which the workers had attained over the last two years would be secured.[151]

This meeting of the Concerted Action confirmed the government's and its own previous orientation data of 7–8% as "appropriate" wage and salary increases for 1971. These figures were based on an original projection of a 3–4% expected inflation rate, thereby allowing a 3–4% growth in real wages. By mid-June 1971, however, any union settling for 7–8% would merely have recouped the cost-of-living increase without making any substantial gains in real pay, since the inflation rate had reached the 6.5% mark by that time.

Similar developments characterized IG Chemie's strike in the chemical industry. (For a discussion of this conflict see Chapter 5.) The settlement yielded a 7% pay raise, which corresponded to the government's original orientation data for desirable and "appropriate" wage and salary increases for 1971. It also set the general framework for the ensuing struggle between IG Metall and the employers in the metal-processing industry.

In addition to having to heed the government's wishes and counter the employers' renewed resolve, IG Metall had to contend with an increasingly restive membership during the mobilization period of the early 1970s. The tensions within IG Metall burst into the open at the union's tenth congress, held between September 27 and October 2, 1971. Numerous delegates pleaded for a commitment on the part of the union to implement an "active" wage policy in order to continue the real gains won in 1969 and 1970, while others openly demanded IG Metall's withdrawal from the

Concerted Action. Otto Brenner and the rest of the leadership expended much energy in defending the union's support for the new government. Brenner argued:

> We have a social–liberal government which tries to the best of its abilities to master the current economic situation and which under no circumstances wants us to experience a recession similar to the one in 1966 and 1967.[152]

It took the prestige and charisma of Willy Brandt and his keynote speech, during which he emphasized wage restraint, the union's responsibility to the West German economy and its traditional links to Social Democracy, to counter the numerous resolutions calling for a more aggressive bargaining strategy in all aspects of union action.[153]

The 1971 wage round in metal processing began in late August with IG Metall's cancellation of all wage and salary contracts due to expire by the end of September. Following the union's new policy of decentralization and limited regional autonomy in the formulation of bargaining demands, each one of IG Metall's individual bargaining regions set its own goals for the round. Most wage demands hovered between 9% and 11% with many regions also asking for supplementary benefits.[154] The demands in North Württemberg/North Baden centered exclusively on an across-the-board 11% wage and salary increase, whereas in North Rhine-Westphalia the union sought a 9% wage and salary raise in addition to a fully paid thirteenth-month bonus, a benefit which had already been won for the area's steel industry during the 1970 bargaining round.[155]

Following IG Metall's refusal to conduct a centralized bargaining round, the employers resolved to ruin the union's new decentralization approach. Gesamtmetall feared the union's strategy might further enhance the power of an already restive and mobilized rank and file. The employers initiated a two-pronged attack: first, all the employers' bargaining in each of the regions would be conducted by a single group, called a "core commission" (Kernkommission); second, the employers' counterproposals would be designed solely to irritate the union and were not meant to be serious positions for initial bargaining. (Indeed, actual bargaining did not take place for quite some time. Gesamtmetall was obviously not interested in a speedy settlement.)

In the first meeting between IG Metall and Gesamtmetall in Stuttgart on October 6, 1971, the employers made no offer. In the second round of negotiations on October 17, 1971, the employers offered a 4.5% raise to all IG Metall bargaining areas, including NW/NB and NRW. Since inflation was well over 6.0% by then, this offer provided additional evidence for IG Metall that the employers had consciously embarked upon a collision course with the union. Seeing no further point in attempting to negotiate with a recalcitrant opponent IG Metall cancelled all bargaining procedures and entered the arbitration stage with the employers' approval.

The results of arbitration for the NW/NB region were announced on November 2, 1971. They called for a 7.5% wage and salary increase for a contract extending over a seven-month period. Although this percentage was well below the increase sought by IG Metall at the beginning of the bargaining round, the union accepted the terms due to the relatively short duration of the new agreement. The employers, however, rejected the proposal outright. A similar development occurred in NRW two weeks later. There the arbitration process arrived at a 7.3% across-the-board wage and salary increase extending over a twelve-month period. Additionally, 40% of a thirteenth-month bonus was to be paid by the employers. Once again, IG Metall accepted the proposal, but the employers unconditionally rejected it. After similar developments in the bargaining regions of South Württemberg/Hohenzollern, South Baden, Hesse and Hamburg, it was only a question of when and where the union would initiate strike procedures by scheduling a strike vote. The union chose NW/NB, and a vote was taken on November 12. The vote provided a clear mandate – 89.6% of IG Metall's members in the area opted for a strike.

On the 16th of November, IG Metall's leadership in Frankfurt set the beginning of the strike for Monday, November 22, though the union's bargaining committee in NW/NB wanted an earlier date, preferably Friday, November 19.[156] But characteristically for IG Metall – as for most unions in the Federal Republic – the center prevailed over the periphery. On November 17, the employers declared that they would respond to any strike activities with a lockout. Following the threats and counterthreats, the strike began on Monday morning, November 22, 1971, with 55,000 workers staying away from their regular shifts in seven plants in the union's Stuttgart, Esslingen, Mannheim, Heilbronn, Neckarsulm and Heidelberg locals. Just as in 1963, the motor-vehicle industry played from the very beginning a crucial role in IG Metall's strike strategy. Of the seven plants struck, four belonged to Daimler-Benz and two to Audi-NSU. On the next day, IG Metall extended the strike by including 60,000 additional workers in 76 plants throughout the entire bargaining area of NW/NB. In eight of these plants, white-collar clerical employees actively joined in the strike. On the fifth day of the strike, November 26, the employers made good their threats and locked out all workers in plants numbering more than 100 employees. The employers' lockout explicitly excluded white-collar employees. Following the lockout, 360,000 blue- and white-collar workers from 544 plants were in one way or another immediately affected by the conflict in NW/NB.[157]

During the period between November 22 and December 1, there was little contact between IG Metall and Gesamtmetall, as the latter continued to insist on centralized negotiations to include the bargaining area of NRW in addition to the strike-bound region of NW/NB, and the former maintained its position on a decentralized approach respecting the autonomy of each bargaining area. Ultimately, both parties accepted the union-initiated call for a special arbitrator. The arbitrator chosen was the president of the Federal Court of Social Welfare (Bundessozialgericht), who had worked out the compromise between IG Chemie and chemical industry employers following their conflict during the summer of that year. On December 7 the arbitrator presented his proposal to IG Metall and Gesamtmetall: a 7.5% across-the-board pay raise for a twelve-month period and an additional 40% of a thirteenth-month bonus. The employers, however, rejected this suggestion and stuck adamantly to their counter-offer of a 6% wage and salary increase over twelve months with only 20% of a thirteenth-month benefit.

At this point Chancellor Willy Brandt invited the two parties to join him for an urgent meeting in Bonn. The employers hoped that the SPD-led government would impose a settlement on both parties which would be a good deal closer to the employers' offer than the arbitrator's proposal. As one observer put it, "this result, however, simply did not happen. Despite the attempts by [Hanns Martin] Schleyer [then head of the VMI, Gesamtmetall's constituent organization in the NW/NB bargaining area] who based his arguments on the Bundesbank's and the Council of Economic Advisors' positions, and the repeated endeavors on the part of [Karl] Schiller [Economics Minister] and [Hans-Dietrich] Genscher [Interior Minister] to push Brandt to voice his influential opinion, the latter left the room after some time without having made concrete numerical suggestions."[158] Thoroughly frustrated, the employer representatives could only agree to a meeting with their counterparts from IG Metall for yet another bargaining round on the evening of December 8 in Stuttgart.

The events in Stuttgart on December 8 were perhaps the single most decisive factor in determining the conflict's eventual outcome. Over 45,000 people attended a union-organized demonstration, the largest held in Stuttgart since the war. Strikers from all over NW/NB descended upon the city in special trains, buses and automobile convoys. The general atmosphere of the rally was optimistic and confident.[159] Most of the slogans and signs conveyed the widespread conviction among those present that the major issue of this confrontation was the employers' attack upon all progressive forces active in the Federal Republic during the 1970s, including IG Metall, the SPD and Willy Brandt. One speaker at the rally argued, "This is not about percentage points, this is about political power, this is about the federal government." Another concurred, saying, "this is all about power, Messrs. Schleyer and company can boss the blacks [Christian Democrats of CDU/CSU] around much easier than the Brandt government."[160]

The primacy of politics and the closeness between IG Metall and the SPD were the major features of Stuttgart district leader Willi Bleicher's impassioned speech to the 45,000 IG Metall members assembled at the demonstration. Culminating in his now famous exclamation "a Willy Brandt is closer to us than a Rainer Barzel" (then the leading political figure in the CDU/CSU), Bleicher's talk conveyed both in form and content the major sentiments and concerns of a mobilized IG Metall membership.[161] His language, like that of many strike publications, did not shy away from the renewed usage of terms such as "Arbeiterklasse" (working class) and "Grosskapital" (big business) instead of the much more accommodationist "Arbeitnehmer" (employees) and "Arbeitgeber" (employers), which had long ago become commonplace in West Germany's public discourse, including that of the unions.

It was apparently this massive outpouring of solidarity which convinced the employers to alter their position in their meeting with the union leadership scheduled for the evening hours of the same day. As a member of IG Metall's bargaining committee from the NW/NB area mentioned in an interview, Hanns Martin Schleyer expressed genuine surprise at IG Metall's ability to organize a demonstration of this magnitude filled with such enthusiasm and verve.[162] The agreement between the union and the employers was finalized on the evening of December 8 and was officially announced on December 10. It included the following features:

1. A 7.5% across-the-board wage and salary increase for a twelve-month period beginning January 1, 1972.
2. A one-time, lump-sum payment of DM 180 for the months of October, November and December 1971.
3. Partial payment of a thirteenth-month bonus according to the following plan: as of 1972, 10%, 20% or 30% of an average monthly wage or salary; as of 1974, 10%, 20%, 30% or 40% of an average monthly wage or salary depending on the length of employment in the particular company.[163]

Following the ratification of the terms by the union's bargaining commissions in NW/NB, the agreement was presented to the IG Metall rank and file there. On December 14, 1971, the tenth day of the strike, 71.2% of those eligible to vote approved the terms of the agreement, with 20.9% opposing them. This was one of the most convincing expressions ever of support by IG Metall's membership for the conduct and results of a strike. It was only natural that the general features of the contract in NW/NB formed the basis for all other agreements in the metal-processing industry, which were concluded in short order by December 18, 1971.[164]

One can argue that the purely remunerative aspects of this contract were far from sensational, especially given the substantial wage and salary gains of the previous two years and the nearly 7% inflation that plagued the West German economy by late 1971. The employers most certainly failed in their political aim of driving a wedge between IG Metall and the SPD-led government – as well as between the general public and the union – but they fared better in their economic goal of keeping the contract in the lower range of the Concerted Action's orientation data. By granting the lump sum of DM 180 for three months and providing a 7.5% increase throughout the twelve months of 1972, the employers de facto held the union's wage and salary gains to 6.9%, exactly the same figure reached in the settlement of the chemical industry strike six months earlier.

*Handelsblatt*, the leading financial daily in the Federal Republic, accurately summed up the strike's results in the following headline: "The Employers Did Not Do So Poorly After All."[165] The article points to yet another crucial gain for the employers: "Even more important [than the 6.9% gain] for the employers is the fact that by recommending the adoption of the results of the Stuttgart agreement by all other bargaining areas, a step was made in the direction of centralized bargaining."[166]

In its euphoric haste, IG Metall unwittingly did exactly what the employers wanted from the very beginning, and what the union itself was committed to avoid at all costs. A self-imposed centralization "through the back door" clearly violated the quest for greater union democracy in the spirit of the September strikes. Moreover, instead of augmenting regional autonomy as was IG Metall's declared policy following the events of the late 1960s, it exacerbated intra-regional rivalries and resentments such as the one between NW/NB and NRW. All in all, the results of the 1971 bargaining round in the metal-processing industry represented a mixed blessing for IG Metall. It was a sign of the optimism of this period that despite these mixed results and the restiveness of many IG Metall members, few criticisms were levelled at the union's leadership concerning its conduct during the strike. Most in the union believed that on the whole IG Metall had waged a good battle yielding respectable results.

Parallel to these developments in metal processing, IG Metall also conducted negotiations in the steel industry beginning in the fall of 1971. An agreement, however, was not reached until January 14, 1972. From the very start of the negotiation process in October 1971, IG Metall suffered from two handicaps. First, much of the union's organizational energy and strategic concentration was expended on the events in the metal-processing industry, especially the strike in NW/NB. Second, IG Metall was under pressure from the employers in the steel industry to accept a six-month-long wage freeze due to the industry's difficulties at that time.[167] The union refused and made the following demands: 10% wage and salary raises for the 257,000 steelworkers in the bargaining area of NRW; 11% wage and salary increases for the 56,000 remaining steelworkers elsewhere in the Federal Republic; and a raise in apprenticeship allowances with the exact amount differing by areas.[168]

It became even more difficult for the union to continue the bargaining process once the settlement in the metal-processing industry assumed a model character for the increasingly restless steelworkers. In early January 1972, the union's bargaining commission for NRW's steel industry demanded Frankfurt's permission to conduct a strike vote on January 19, 1972. Although granted by IG Metall's central leadership, the issue was rendered moot when an agreement was reached between the union and the employers five days piror to that date. It included the following noteworthy features: a 6.0% wage and salary raise for 286,000 steelworkers, with 27,000 located in special production areas receiving 6.4% or 6.5%; a DM 200 lump sum paid for the period between October 1971 and January 1972; and a 12.5% increase in apprenticeship allowances.[169] The contract was to run for a ten-month period, beginning February 1, 1972 and expiring November 30, 1972. With this contract, IG Metall's wage bargaining round for 1971–72 was largely completed. It was not until late that year that the turbulent 1973 round began its course.

Nineteen seventy-two witnessed a number of important events which had great significance for IG Metall. They included the passage of the revised Works Constitution Law on January 15; the nationwide demonstrations and strikes on April 25, 26 and 27 in favor of the social–liberal coalition's treaties with the Soviet Union and Eastern Europe (Ostverträge); the DGB's new Aktionsprogramm affirmed by the ninth DGB congress held between June 25 and 30; and the Brandt–Scheel government's convincing victory at the polls on November 19. These had implications beyond IG Metall and have thus been discussed in the general DGB section constituting Chapter 3 of this volume. Three remaining events concerned IG Metall more directly.

On April 15, IG Metall's venerable and charismatic leader of nearly twenty years, Otto Brenner, died. No union leader in the Federal Republic's history has achieved equivalent stature or power, and his influence extended well beyond the confines of his own organization. It would not be an exaggeration to regard Otto Brenner as one of the most important figures of West German social democracy. At IG Metall's first and only extraordinary congress held on June 15, 1972, Eugen Loderer, the union's vice chairman, was chosen to assume Brenner's position.[170] Loderer remained at the helm of IG Metall until September 1983 when at the union's fourteenth congress he was succeeded by the union's vice chairman, Hans Mayr.

A second important event specific to IG Metall also occurred in April 1972. Between April 11 and 14, the union held a conference entitled "Task for the Future – Quality of Life."[171] Attended by 1,250 participants, among them dignitaries such as Gustav Heinemann, the Federal Republic's president, three cabinet ministers, foreign guests such as Swedish Prime Minister Olof Palme, and Tony Benn of the British Labour Party, the conference tried to formulate qualitative aims for future union strategy which would supplement the predominance of purely quantitative economic issues.[172] In workshops, small study groups, large plenary sessions and lectures, numerous unionists, academicians and politicians from West Germany and abroad discussed a wide variety of topics which pertained to the enhancement of the "quality of life" both within and outside the plant. Among the issues considered at the conference were the humanization of the work environment itself, which in turn was linked to increased shop-floor democracy, greater worker participation and co-determination on all levels of industrial production. The concept of investment control or investment guidance also received favorable attention from many conference participants. The conference helped IG Metall formulate many of the ideas on quality of work life which were to play an increasingly important role in the union's collective bargaining procedure as the 1970s progressed.

Finally, in 1972 IG Metall had to face for the first time a serious institutional challenge from its rank and file on the issue of works council elections. During the 1972 works council elections, dissident IG Metall members in a number of factories put up opposition candidates to run against the official union slates. This effort, although not widespread, did gain considerable attention in union circles, partly because the challenges occurred in some of West Germany's most prestigious firms and partly because the challengers were successful. The continuity of their presence throughout the 1970s and even into the 1980s – though to a decreasing extent during the latter period – testifies not only to the real needs that these new groups addressed in the works councils of their respective plants, but also to the enduring legacy of the mobilization period.

These often quite diverse opposition groups shared a number of common features. First of all, they evolved because of popular dissatisfaction with IG Metall's official policies, especially in regard to wage demands. The challengers complained about the low level of wage settlements and the union's failure to pursue aggressively either a linear or lump-sum wage policy. Moreover, the challengers felt that IG Metall had abdicated its responsibility to its members by paying too much attention to the SPD's wishes and the Concerted Action's orientation data. Disillusionment with the union's party loyalty led many challengers to abandon the SPD and seek new party allegiances. The rebels presented themselves as "true" unionists who could best represent the interests of the rank and file. They invariably derived their legitimacy from being the most conscientious, diligent and unselfish workers, and their dedication, zeal and competence would restore, they believed, the conditions woefully neglected by IG Metall throughout the late 1960s and early 1970s. As a consequence of the above factors, the challengers won the respect of many of their colleagues.

All these grassroots rebellions occurred in major firms of the metal-processing industry, with a heavy concentration in auto companies including Daimler-Benz, Volkswagen, Ford and Opel. Such actions took place in the 1972 and 1975 works council elections, both of which witnessed an increase in the absolute number of works councilors, in good part due to the revised Works Constitution Law of 1972 (which facilitated the creation of works councils even against the opposition of particular employers).[173] The general atmosphere of mobilization during the 1972 works council elections – which carried over to the 1975, 1978 and even 1981 campaigns – also manifested itself in an impressive gain of voters for IG Metall and all other DGB unions at the direct expense of rival organizations belonging to federations such as the DAG and the CGB.[174] This process seemed especially acute among clerical employees and all white-collar workers. The percentage of white-collar works councilors belonging to IG Metall and other DGB unions increased dramatically throughout the 1970s with simultaneous losses for the DAG, the explicitly white-collar union in the Federal Republic.[175]

The most notable differences among the various opposition campaigns centered around IG Metall's reactions to these challenges. The union responded to the rebels in any of three ways: (1) It expelled them outright. This was the case either when the dissenters belonged to a group of the radical left which IG Metall considered incompatible with union membership or when the new formation defied integration into the old union structure because of serious policy-related incompatibilities. (2) The union allowed the challengers to pursue their candidacy within IG Metall. Typically, this led to two competing IG Metall slates which ultimately would form a synthesis under new terms influenced by the challengers. (3) Lastly, in some instances the rebels succeeded in becoming the "establishment" by deposing the old works councilors and receiving officially recognized IG Metall seats on the works councils. It is the first variation which – significantly – prevailed most often.

The most famous of the 1972 rebellions centered around Daimler-Benz, a company which has played a key role in the union's showcase bargaining area of NW/NB.[176] This involved the so-called *Plakat* group's challenge to the established IG Metall works councilors at the Daimler-Benz factory in Stuttgart-Untertürkheim. The group – which was formed around the newspaper *Plakat* by three veteran shop stewards – received 28% of the total vote in the 1972 works council elections, enough for nine seats. Its members were immediately expelled from the union but have continued their activities, including the publication of their newspaper, up to the time of this writing.

In the view of the dissenters – headed by two German shop stewards, Willi Hoss and Hermann Mühleisen, and their Italian colleague Mario D'Andrea – two interrelated factors led to their opposition. The first had to do with IG Metall's insufficient activism during the mobilization period. The *Plakat* people objected to the union's moderate bargaining results, which they found to be unsatisfactory for assembly-line workers. They blamed this shortcoming on the union's "rigid fixation" on the SPD and thus on the government's concept of commonweal, long a thorn in the side of union radicals. The dissenters also believed that demands for increased democratization and grassroots participation since the 1969 September strikes were opposed by most West German institutions, IG Metall included.[177]

*Plakat's* second cluster of grievances focused on the plant-specific problems at Daimler-Benz's factory in Untertürkheim.[178] The atmosphere at Daimler-Benz was dominated by the same attitude of "social partnership" which, in the view of the dissenters, permeated all levels of union–management relations. This accommodationism, which to the dissenters was tantamount to labor's complete emasculation by management, was supplemented at Daimler-Benz by a "Daimler consciousness" and a widespread "house pride" based on the company's tradition of success since the mid-1950s. This pride in the company was especially strong among a core of highly skilled and highly paid workers who had been carefully nurtured by Daimler-Benz over two decades. This group of workers – overwhelmingly male and German – dominated the works council until 1972. Fluctuations in its composition remained restricted to the selection of successors to deceased or retired works councilors. This coterie of thirty men belonging to Daimler's works council at its plant in Untertürkheim used its preeminence on the shop floor to control the shop stewards. As the *Plakat* group saw this relationship, "the shop stewards were not the works council's partners, they were its errand boys."[179]

Indeed, due to the particular prestige and stature of this plant and its company in the Stuttgart area, the works council led by its chairman Karl Hauff exercised a great deal of influence on IG Metall's locals in the district. Moreover, its relationship to the SPD in the state was unusually close, since Hauff was an SPD delegate to the state legislature.

This convenient combination of a close relationship among the core workers, the highly homogeneous works council, the IG Metall locals, and the SPD excluded unskilled workers, women and over 6,000 foreign workers. With the intensification of labor and the concomitant deterioration of working conditions, the gap between the already privileged and the underprivileged widened. Increases in the quotas of piece-rate work, growing wage gaps and inadequate reimbursement for travel were only three of the many issues which bothered the disenfranchised workers.[180] When the works council failed to react to repeated requests by the affected workers to improve their worsening situation, the *Plakat* group was born to fulfill this need.

The group never intentionally directed its challenge against IG Metall; it was concerned rather with the complacency of the works council. Its demands have always centered on issues such as the reduction of wage gaps, the improvement of working conditions, the moderation of piece rates and other material improvements. After the *Plakat* slate won 28% of the vote in the 1972 works council election, the IG Metall district headquarters in Stuttgart proceeded with the immediate expulsion of Hoss and Mühleisen from the union while D'Andrea was merely reprimanded for his activities.[181] The union has since repeatedly offered to rescind its decision with the proviso that *Plakat* cease all criticisms of the majority group in the works council and stop the publication of its newspaper. Since both requests have met with the dissenters' steadfast refusal, Hoss and his colleagues have never been readmitted to IG Metall.

The 1973 bargaining round started for IG Metall in late 1972 in the steel industry, where the 1972 contracts expired on November 30. IG Metall's bargaining committees in NRW and the Saarland – the two areas comprising most of the country's steel production – formulated the following demands which, in keeping with the union's strategy of decentralization, allowed for regional, even plant-specific, variations: 11% wage and salary increases for most workers and white-collar clerical employees, with members in certain wage and salary categories reaching 12%, and a DM 40 to DM 90 monthly increase for apprentices.[182] During the third bargaining session the employers returned with a 5.6% counterproposal. Following the employers' refusal to change this offer in the fourth session, IG Metall proceeded to initiate strike measures by scheduling a strike vote in NRW's steel industry for December 20 and 21, 1972. Ninety-seven *percent* of the eligible workers voted for a strike. This impressive mandate forced the leadership to set a strike date for January 11, 1973 following the traditional two-week vacation period between December 24 and January 7.

In the quiet of the holiday season, at a time when union members were mainly concerned with family matters, IG Metall's leadership and the steel industry employers signed a contract which caused many of 1973's wildcat strikes. The agreement consisted of an 8.5% wage and salary increase for almost all blue- and white-collar workers in the steel industry.[183] Over 52% of the IG Metall members voted against the contract on January 11 and 12, 1973. This nevertheless meant its acceptance since Paragraph 11 of IG Metall's bylaws states that a contract is valid as long as 25% of those eligible to vote approve its terms.[184]

At the end of January 1973, it became clear that inflation would all but negate the 8.5% pay raise by the early spring. On February 8, 1973, the workers at the three Hoesch steel mills of Westfalenhütte, Phoenix and Union in Dortmund – the same plants as in 1969 – initiated spontaneous strike activities.[185] The steelworkers wanted the 60 pfennig increase in hourly wages contained in IG Metall's original contract demand, rather than the 46 pfennigs to which the 8.5% wage hike amounted.[186] The Hoesch workers received a 60 pfennig raise following their one-day work stoppage. Ten days later, the threat of a massive demonstration by all Hoesch workers in the streets of Dortmund forced management to drop its plan to dismiss the leaders of the 1969 and 1973 wildcat strikes. The Hoesch strikes were followed over the next several months by work stoppages at the Mannesmann works in Duisburg and the Klöckner steel mills in Bremen.[187]

IG Metall's negotiations with the metal-processing industry, which lasted from mid-December 1972 until the end of January 1973, led to results similar to the ones reached in the steel industry. The first agreement was signed in the bargaining area of Schleswig-Holstein on January 5, 1973 and featured a 46 pfennig (8.5%) increase in the base wage.[188] Moreover, IG Metall attained a level of equalization among all regions in the remuneration paid its workers in the lower wage categories. Although a definite improvement, this step still seemed inadequate to a restive rank and file which was worried about inflation and job insecurity resulting from the deployment of new labor-saving rationalization measures.

By April 1973, the first spontaneous work stoppages began to occur in metal processing. Volkswagen experienced its first series of strikes ever, with all six of its plants affected.[189] The major demand of the strikes, which lasted for two days, centered on the increase of the annual bonus, which was to be determined in yearly negotiations between the Volkswagen management and the union's company representatives. The workers insisted on an 8% hike in the bonus for 1973, similar to the raise they attained in 1970 following the September strikes of 1969. Management, however, citing the troubled situation of the company in 1972 and the expected downturn in the automobile industry in 1973, insisted on a 5.35% increase based on gross levels of yearly income. By April 17, the parties attained an agreement which provided a 7% raise in the bonus for 1973 and 1974, to reach 8% at the beginning of 1975.

The month of May saw a nearly fourteenfold increase over the three previous months in the number of companies affected by spontaneous strikes. Work stoppages were registered at 46 plants involving 51,000 workers.[190] It was widely expected that workers in metal processing would try to win through wildcat strikes the bonuses granted their colleagues in the steel industry.

To avoid this eventuality, many firms, led by Daimler-Benz, granted company bonuses to compensate workers for accelerating inflation. These supplemental wage contracts, often signed exclusively at the company level, affected approximately one-quarter of IG Metall's membership. On May 24, 1973, IG Metall and the employers' association of the iron and steel industry agreed to a DM 280 addition (DM 70 each for the months from June through September) to supplement the 8.5% contractually guaranteed pay increase which was being eroded by the 7.9% inflation rate in the spring of that year. The industry was in good part driven to this concession by the steelworkers' reputation for militancy as confirmed by the wildcat strikes of 1969 and 1973. IG Metall's repeated pleas to find a quick solution to the worsening crisis in metal processing along analogous lines met with consistent and steadfast rejection on the part of Gesamt-metall. The union could not exact anything from the employers beyond vague promises of additional plant-level remuneration by the end of August 1973.[191] The West German metal industry suffered through a long and difficult summer that year.

Certain characteristics distinguished the multitude of work stoppages which occurred in July and August of 1973 from previous actions. The most prevalent reason for the non-union-sanctioned work stoppages at more than 100 plants involving over 80,000 strikers was the desire by the workers to regain some of the income they were losing to inflation. In addition to wages, however, the issue of working conditions assumed a hitherto unprecedented centrality. With the economy running at full capacity, many firms introduced a wide range of measures to maximize production. The most common feature of the 1973 strikes were demands to slow down the speed of the assembly line, lower piece-rate quotas, improve the physical conditions of the work environment, and introduce more generous rest periods during working hours. Moreover, in some instances strikers also voiced concern about gaining better job protection in the face of the introduction of labor-saving technologies.

Many of these strikes in the metal-processing industry were either initiated or led by foreign workers and women grouped in the lower wage categories who were disgruntled over the gap between their wage rates and those of their male, German colleagues. Perhaps the single most important factor in determining a particular strike's success or failure was the degree to which these marginal workers received support for their demands from male, German workers. Backing by the works council and/or union shop stewards was also necessary in most cases for a successful strike. In almost every instance where IG Metall distanced itself from the strikers, the actions of the latter were doomed to failure.

It would be wrong to draw the conclusion that the events of spring and summer 1973 failed to touch a responsive chord within IG Metall, despite the union's general hostility to these worker-initiated measures, some of which were – at least indirectly – aimed at the union itself. IG Metall tried to save face by claiming that the roots of the 1973 strikes lay in its own participation in the mobilization process. The activists within the union maintained that the wildcat strikers were inspired by the union's own activism. They cited the successful strike in NW/NB's metal industry in 1971, the consistent gains in membership, the favorable results at the 1972 works council elections, the close ties to a still reform-minded SPD and the increasing preoccupation with qualitative issues concerning the humanization of work, as evidence of this activism. Yet the IG Metall leadership anguished over the fact that the union, as amply demonstrated by the 1973 strike wave in the country's metal industry, had lost initiative and legitimacy in the eyes of its members. It became imperative that both be regained. This would again be achieved in the union's "star" bargaining area of NW/NB in October of that year.

Even the most severe critics of the West German labor movement have readily admitted that IG Metall's battle for the Wage Framework Contract II in the metal industry of NW/NB represented a qualitative departure for the union, in terms of both goals and strategy. It is not by chance that this unique event in IG Metall's history formed the high point of the mobilization period of the early 1970s.

Unlike regular wage contracts, which are usually concluded in one-year intervals with little variation among the numerous IG Metall bargaining areas, general framework contracts and wage framework contracts differ substantially from one region to the next in terms of content and duration. Both types of agreements are usually much more complex in their wording and much longer than wage contracts. This is partly due to the fact that their major task lies in the exact and most minute delineation of the framework wherein the work process of the particular region and industry will occur. Typically, framework contracts include job classifications, the criteria for job categorizations, the exact breakdown of each task into its physical components, and other ergonomic information. Since many of these categories differ by industries – which tend to cluster by regions – the complication in terms of diversity and detail reaches beyond the regional differences to industry-specific stipulations which are typically discussed in lengthy appendices (Anhänge) to the actual contracts. The duration of these contracts is much longer than that of regular wage agreements, with a rough average being five years. However, their de facto duration often extends well beyond the date of expiration, since neither the union nor the employers are usually in a hurry to renegotiate the terms of the old contract.

This was precisely the case with the Wage Framework Contract II (Lohnrahmentarifvertrag II – LRTV II) in NW/NB. Its origins date back to the very first wage framework contract for the bargaining area of NW/NB signed by IG Metall and the employers on April 9, 1948.[192] This wage framework contract was renewed without any changes on December 12, 1953. The only difference between the original document and its renewed form was that instead of a five-year duration, as stipulated by the contract's first signing, the agreement now covered only a three-year period. IG Metall cancelled the contract following proper procedures on December 31, 1956, but a new contract was never negotiated, thus leaving the provisions of the old agreement in force for the next seventeen years. Parts of this wage framework contract were in fact renegotiated throughout the 1960s. Shortly after a strike vote on November 8, 1967 (resulting from a disagreement between IG Metall and the employers concerning the clauses of wage categorization in the contract), an agreement between the two parties was reached. Its codification, however, was removed from the boundaries of the old wage framework contract and instead subsumed under a new agreement called Wage Framework Contract I. However, this new document did not address all of the other issues in the larger wage framework contract still awaiting its renewal. Most importantly, the problem of performance evaluation and the methods of remuneration remained unresolved. These were to be addressed in a new context.

The new agreement, tentatively designated Wage Framework Contract II (LRTV II), reorganized and redefined some of the most fundamental assumptions of West German industry for over 25 years.[193] In fact, it addressed certain conventions which had prevailed in factory production for nearly half a century (since most of the wage framework contracts which were negotiated shortly after World War II followed very closely the guidelines established in the 1920s and subsequently modified in 1932 and

1943–44).[194] The major criteria stipulating wage categories and pay determination had weathered three political regimes and five decades without substantial revision. The concepts developed in the 1920s still pertained to most qualitative aspects of West German industry in the 1970s, at least as far as metal processing was concerned.

The passage of the revised version of the Works Constitution Law in January 1972 provided an immediate impetus for IG Metall to revive negotiations on LRTV II. By augmenting the autonomy of the works councils in the supervision of the work process, the new law provided the unions, at least indirectly, with an improved position on the shop floor. Concretely, this entailed a much greater possibility for IG Metall to control the implementation of its contracts in the day-to-day operations of the plants within its organizational domain. Prior to the passage of the 1972 Works Constitution Law, it would have made little sense for IG Metall to push for serious improvements in this direction since the union simply lacked the necessary leverage on the shop floor to implement such "qualitative" measures in the production process. The post-1972 situation, however, lent itself much more readily to a reevaluation of workplace organization for labor.

IG Metall pursued intensive negotiations on LRTV II in NW/NB beginning in late 1972, but by mid-1973 the talks had stalled. Following the breakdown of negotiations on August 29, 1973, the issues of Wage Framework Contract II were submitted to arbitration. The union presented the following demands to the arbitrator, who, by the luck of the draw, turned out to be the person suggested by IG Metall:

- complete protection from dismissal and loss of income for all workers over 50;

- introduction of paid hourly recreation time of six minutes for assembly-line and piece-rate workers;

- introduction of a paid three-minute break period per hour for using washroom facilities;

- prohibition against dividing the work process on the assembly line into units under 1.5 minutes;

- introduction of more objective criteria for the gathering of data used in the remuneration process;

- a minimum-wage guarantee for piece-rate workers at 140% of their contractual wage level.

Though a good deal more complex and detailed than this brief summary would permit, these highlights of IG Metall's demands convey the general thrust of the union's strategy: to achieve a synthesis of "quantitative" and "qualitative" concerns by safeguarding its members against losses in real wages and the intensification of work.

During the period of arbitration which lasted between September 10 and 20, the membership's enthusiasm for this new conflict manifested itself in the numerous warning strikes throughout the affected area. Over 40,000 workers participated in various forms of work stoppages throughout this ten-day period.[195] On September 20, the arbitrator announced his terms, which included the following revisions of the union's original demands:

- protection from loss of income for workers over 55 with at least one-year tenure in the company of current employment; protection from dismissal for workers over 53 with at least three-years tenure in the company of current employment;

- introduction of fully paid hourly recreation time of six minutes for assembly-line and five minutes for piece-rate workers;

- prohibition of any further division of the work process on the assembly line into smaller units; recognition of the 1.5 minute minimum as the smallest permissible unit of work;

- a minimum-wage guarantee for piece-rate workers at 130% of their contractual wage level.[196]

As to IG Metall's demand concerning the introduction of more objective criteria for the gathering of data to determine the scales of remuneration, the arbitration agreed with the union by addressing some important aspects of the concept of performance. Performance standards were henceforth to be determined by controllable methods which could withstand repeated verification, rather than by traditional forms of categorization.[197]

IG Metall accepted the terms of arbitration on September 21, and the employers rejected them on the 27th. On the following day, both parties agreed that the arbitration effort had failed, thus permitting the union to initiate the necessary steps in preparation for a strike. On October 3, IG Metall's bargaining commission in NW/NB scheduled a strike vote for October 10. Eighty-nine percent of all those eligible voted for a strike. The following day, the NW/NB bargaining commission, pursuant to IG Metall's constitutional guidelines, asked the union's headquarters in Frankfurt for permission to initiate the strike. It began on October 16, 1973 with activities once again concentrating on Daimler-Benz and Bosch plants in the Stuttgart area.[198] This point strike involved 57,000 workers and lasted for five days. On October 21, an agreement was reached, which was ratified three days later by 71.4% of the union's membership in NW/NB. Full production resumed on October 25, and the new Wage Framework Contract II took effect on November 1, 1973.

Here are some of the contract's major features which, according to IG Metall, were among more than 50 items designed to improve working conditions on the shop floor:[199]

- All assembly-line and piece-rate workers receive a minimum of five paid minutes per hour in recreation time.

- Three paid minutes per hour are alotted to the use of washroom facilities.

- Actual work activity per hour is never to exceed 52 minutes.

- All existing units of work cannot be sub-divided further. No unit shall consist of less than 1.5 minutes.

- The income of workers over 55 cannot be reduced, provided the person has been employed by the company for at least one year.

- Workers over the age of 53 cannot be dismissed if they have been employed by the company for at least three years.

- In case of disability due to an accident in the plant or in the process of commuting between the workplace and home, net wages will have to be paid for 78 weeks (instead of merely 6 as was the case prior to this contract).

- For the first two years of employment, all piece-rate workers shall receive wages which amount to 125% of the factory average; thereafter, the rate is to move up to 130%.[200]

- The process of gathering data for the purpose of establishing the system of remuneration will become more objective. Strict rules will regulate all activities connected with this process.

- The works councils will participate in the design of group work and all collective endeavors. Their rights of co-determination on the shop floor also include access to all information which may be construed as pertinent to any changes affecting the workers in the plant.

IG Metall's assessment of the contract's significance was expressed as follows in the union's tenth triannual report submitted to its eleventh congress in September 1974:[201]

> By concluding this contract, we have thus fulfilled the mandate of Decision VI of our last congress in Wiesbaden, especially concerning the two following essential points:
>
> > Work requirements have to correspond to biological limits; they also are subject to social responsibility. The protection of human labor power has to supersede commercial interests at all times.
>
> > Co-determination of the works council has to be secured and augmented via bargaining agreements which pertain to the formation of work and the guidance of the work process.

> We only needed two years to begin to realize these demands. The Wage Framework Contract in North Württemberg/North Baden has stopped the further parcelization of work into monotonous and stultifying tasks without any meaningful content. This is the first step towards a modification of inhuman working conditions.

Few scholars of recent union politics in the Federal Republic would deny the profound importance of this contract. Yet it never went beyond its pioneering character to achieve widespread application in West German industrial relations. The provisions of Wage Framework Contract II barely reached other bargaining areas within IG Metall, let alone the purview of other DGB unions. IG Metall itself attempted few, if any, extensions or improvements of this contract in subsequent years. The economic crisis had by then created an inhospitable atmosphere for union-led reforms similar to the ones attained by IG Metall via this agreement. Above all, the crisis hardened the employers' resistance to union-initiated reforms of such potential importance for the humanization of work on the shop floor.

IG Metall's predicament did not improve during the following year, as the union had to perform delicate balancing acts to reach solutions which would be to everyone's satisfaction. The first of these acts involved the union's perennial attempt to reconcile the SPD-led government's wishes concerning wage levels with the usually much higher wage demands of IG Metall's rank and file. This "see-saw politics" created an unpleasant dilemma for the union: when its demands swung towards one side in a given year, the leadership had to make every effort to appease the other side the next year.[202] Thus developed a pattern during the mobilization period of the early 1970s which frustrated both of IG Metall's constituents – the government and union members – leaving the organization in the unenviable position of satisfying neither. But the general optimism of the era, coupled with economic growth, low unemployment and political reforms helped all involved parties overcome their temporary disappointments.

Things began to change, however, after 1974. Economic constraints started to intensify at the beginning of the year and rank-and-file pressure was more acute than in the previous two years, largely due to the relatively low wage increases attained by IG Metall's 1973 contracts and the wildcat strikes in the summer of that year. This led to the hybrid situation of 1974. The events of 1974 can be categorized as belonging to the crisis period, if the condition of the West German economy is the criterion for judgement. However, when the focus of analysis is IG Metall's bargaining strategy and behavior these events should be considered in the era of mobilization.

The hybrid character of 1974 had its origins in 1973 when the mobilization of a sizable portion of the West German working class encountered a concerted effort by the state to curtail this restiveness, which the government feared would have inflationary effects. By the fall of 1973, West Germany's two most important macroeconomic institutions, the federal ministry of economic affairs and the Bundesbank, initiated deflationary policies, aimed at curtailing public demand and pursuing a course of high interest and tight money supply. The result of these policies was an increase in unemployment. Whereas in September 1973 there were 219,000 unemployed (1.0% of the workforce) and 36,000 laborers on short-time work, the figures had increased to 486,000 (2.2%) and 161,000 by December 1973, and to 562,000 (2.5%) and 256,000 by March 1974.[203] The combined total of the latter two figures represented a higher percentage of workers suffering from un- or underemployment than at any time during the 1966–67 recession.

Since this unemployment was uneven, IG Metall had to reconcile its strategy in those sectors adversely affected by the economic downturn with its policies in areas where the boom continued. Autos and steel were among the prominent representatives of these two trends. In the auto industry, all firms with the exception of Daimler-Benz had dismissed thousands of workers, introduced short-time work on a massive scale and faced a rapidly declining demand for their products by January 1974. The steel industry, however, was still experiencing one of its most impressive post-war booms during the last months of 1973 and the first quarter of 1974.[204] It was thus fortuitous for the union that the 1974 wage round opened with negotiations with the steel industry in late November 1973.

Given the boom conditions in that industry, the steel employers were eager to reach a settlement as quickly as possible, especially since they wanted to avoid a repetition of the wildcat strikes which disrupted production in their industry in 1969 and 1973. A contract was signed for NRW at the end of November 1973 and for the Saarland in the middle of January 1974. In both areas, the union won an 11% wage and salary increase which resulted in a total benefit package of 13–14% counting all the extras in the respective contracts.[205]

The employers in Gesamtmetall, however, refused to accept the steel agreement as a guideline for their upcoming negotiations with IG Metall in the metal-processing industry. Many industrialists tried to use the union's weakened position, which resulted from rising unemployment in this most important sector of the economy, "to teach it a lesson." It was in this context that IG Metall desisted from assuming its habitual vanguard role as the DGB's leader in each annual wage round, surrendering this position to a consortium of unions in the public sector. Led by the DGB's second largest union, the public employees' union (ÖTV), and with the support and cooperation of the railroad workers' union (GdED) and postal employees' union (DPG), the 1974 contract negotiations witnessed the first major public sector strike in the Federal Republic's history. From the very beginning of ÖTV's confrontation with the state, it appeared that both sides were engaged in a "proxy conflict" with ramifications beyond the immediate confines of the public sector. While ÖTV and its two smaller allies waged this conflict on behalf of all DGB unions, the SPD-led federal government was placed in the awkward and uncomfortable position of fighting a proxy battle for West German employers. This situation, among others, led to some highly publicized clashes between Chancellor Willy Brandt and ÖTV's charismatic leader, Heinz Kluncker, who as a consequence of these disagreements was unjustly referred to as "Brandt-killer" following the chancellor's resignation later that year. (For a discussion of this episode see Chapter 3.) After a three-day strike in February involving 560,000 workers in the public sector, an agreement was reached between the parties providing for an 11% wage increase for public employees.

When ÖTV concluded its bargaining round on February 13, 1975, all of IG Metall's contract negotiations were in the arbitration stage. Most of the union's districts submitted demands for a 15–18% wage raise supplemented by an increase in early vacation time totalling 30 paid days.[206] As usual, IG Metall's decentralized demands led Gesamtmetall to form a core bargaining commission (Kernkommission) which appeared at every bargaining area's negotiating table offering an 8.5% wage and salary increase. The first area to receive the arbitrator's verdict was Unterweser (Bremen and Bremerhaven). On February 18, 1974, the arbitrator recommended a 14% wage and salary hike for Unterweser, which was accepted by IG Metall but immediately rejected by the employers.

Then, on February 20, the unexpected happened. IG Metall and the employers accepted the arbitrator's verdict in NRW which entailed considerably less favorable terms for the union than the ones for the Unterweser area. The "NRW model" provided an 11% wage and salary increase for the first ten months of 1974. An additional 2% increase was to be granted for November and December.[207] Following the acceptance of the NRW model with only minimal modifications by most other IG Metall bargaining areas, the Unterweser district was isolated.

The uniqueness of the Unterweser area may explain why the union undermined its own efforts in this conflict.[208] Few other production areas in the Federal Republic have been so completely dependent on a single industry (shipbuilding) as Bremen. Because of this, the potentially adverse economic effects on other areas caused by a strike in Unterweser could remain minimal. Thus, the union risked little disruption to the economy as a whole if it allowed its members in this small area to conduct a strike (which by this time IG Metall's leadership in Frankfurt did not want). Yet mobilization had reached too advanced a stage for the union to renege on its original course of action. Having psychologically prepared Bremen's activist shipyard workers for a conflict, IG Metall felt it would be imprudent to demobilize at such a late date by simply adopting the agreement reached in other bargaining regions. Consequently, on February 28 and March 1, 1974, the union conducted a strike vote. Of those eligible to vote, 88% opted for immediate action. Numerous appeals by the employers to resume negotiations went unheeded. IG Metall was determined to strike and so industrial action began as scheduled with the 6 a.m. shift on March 6, 1974.

From the very beginning of this conflict – the area's first since 1953 – two factors were evident: IG Metall's ambivalence toward the strike action and the employers' strong determination to break the strikers' resolve. There were numerous reports of acts of violence in many of the 67 plants which were involved in the strike. For example, cars were used to drive wedges through some picket lines and a few workers were wounded by various weapons. The employers opted for tactics of violent provocation rather than the more usual and tested method of the lockout. Perhaps their strategy was to create major disruptions by pitting the police force of this Social Democratic bastion – the state of Bremen – against workers from West Germany's most important labor union. Such an occurrence would have placed even further strain on the already tense relationship between the SPD and the DGB, especially the latter's activist wing, of which IG Metall remained the foremost representative.

The union leadership's resolve to conclude a better contract for its Unterweser area than for any of its other bargaining regions was dealt a powerful blow during the course of the strike. The acting head of the pre-strike arbitration process, who had been nominated by the union, suddenly recanted on his own decision and recommended an 11% wage and salary increase commensurate with the agreements reached in the rest of the country's metal-processing industry. This outside intervention infuriated not only the strikers, but also most leading union officials in the area, who maintained as late as March 22 that they would never consent to any agreement below a 14% pay raise. Yet the following results of a "special arbitration" session held two days later became the terms of the new Unterweser contract:[209]

> An 11% wage and salary increase retroactive to January 1, 1974; this was to be supplemented by an additional 1% raise on April 1 and July 1, 1974, respectively.
>
> Two additional days of vacation.
>
> An increase of vacation pay by 50% of an average monthly income.
>
> DM 70 in educational benefits for vocational trainees at all levels.

This agreement was a slightly modified version of the NRW model and thus fell below the terms of the first arbitration for the union's Unterweser area as announced on February 18, 1974. However, the union leadership did not believe this to be true. By adding up all the contract's "quantitative" components, the union arrived at a total percentage of 14.85 which was thus almost 1% over the earlier arbitration's verdict.[210] The central leadership lauded the 14.85% raise as a total victory which could not have been achieved without the three-week-long strike.

While these numerical acrobatics may have been arithmetically correct, they failed to convince the majority of the strikers, including a number of IG Metall officials in the Unterweser area. Many felt cheated and deceived by the union. The overwhelming opinion was that for this agreement a strike of such dimensions had been unnecessary.[211] Indeed, by factoring in the pecuniary losses which every strike participant had to absorb, the additional 0.85% which the IG Metall leadership claimed as such an impressive victory had long been annulled. On March 23, the night before the announcement of the special arbitrator's terms, reliable reports suggested that the union's small bargaining group voted 14 to 8 to reject the proposal and continue with the strike.[212] This decision, however, was overruled by IG Metall's executive committee in Frankfurt. The largely negative reaction to this contract became apparent on March 27, 1974, when 64% of the voting members (or 56.8% of those eligible to vote) rejected it. Falling short of the 75% needed to continue the strike, this vote finalized the conflict in the Unterweser area and also concluded IG Metall's bargaining round for 1974.

While the disillusionment felt by many IG Metall members did not lead to the formation of any new political allegiances on the part of the workers, it contributed to an increasing apathy and skepticism about the efficacy of their traditional representative institutions, the unions.[213] The response by IG Metall members to the 1971 strike in NW/NB's metal industry highlights the difference in atmosphere between the era of mobilization (pre–1974) and the crisis thereafter. Although less favorable in terms of its purely numerical or quantitative gains than the Unterweser contract of 1974, the 1971 strike in Stuttgart's metal industry was considered a stellar success by most union members, whereas the event in Unterweser barely three years later was viewed by the rank and file as an embarrassment and failure. By 1974, the crisis had taken a foothold in the West German economy. That was the major difference affecting the varied perceptions of these two events by many IG Metall unionists. The economic crisis remained a factor in the bargaining rounds throughout the rest of the decade.

## VII. THE CONTINUOUS CRISIS: 1975–1981

In late 1974 and early 1975 IG Metall still held a cyclical interpretation of the crisis. The crisis was not taken as seriously as it should have been since it was perceived as a nasty replay of the cyclical downturn which had caused such havoc in the West German economy in 1966–67. The leadership viewed this crisis as temporary and thus "curable" with the appropriate measures of state-led demand management. When by 1976 unemployment remained virtually unchanged in spite of moderate growth by the economy as a whole, IG Metall's strategists began to appreciate the qualitatively different nature of this crisis. (For some data on this period consult Appendix 8, which gives an economic overview of the Federal Republic.) However, this realization did not yield any solution.

The 1975 wage round still showed some characteristics of the fading mobilization era. In the booming steel industry, IG Metall concluded a favorable contract at the end of 1974. It was to be the last of its kind in what developed a year later into one of the most problem-ridden sectors of the West German economy. In addition to a 14% wage and salary increase, IG Metall demanded four additional vacation days and a qualitative package largely designed to improve working life for older workers. The union won a 9% pay raise and gained two additional vacation days.[214] In terms of the qualitative results, the contract established the virtual impossibility of dismissing any worker over 55. In case of dismissal, however, it guaranteed a severance pay of at least 90% and in many cases 100% of the average wages the worker could have earned, until his/her sixtieth birthday. Lastly, the contract expanded some of the cushioning mechanisms which had existed since the "social plan" arrangements of the early 1960s.

The severity of the crisis could already be gauged by the beginning of 1975 when IG Metall failed to carry over its gains in the steel sector to the metal industry. Indeed, the union assumed such a low profile in this bargaining round that it relinquished its vanguard position, which was taken by IG Bau-Steine-Erden, arguably at this time still the most accommodationist among the DGB's unions. The construction union's 6.6% wage and salary gain, concluded in a new contract five months prior to the expiration of the old one, closely followed the government's orientation data (6–6.5%) and also set the tone for the bargaining rounds of all other unions, including IG Metall. The latter signed a contract with a 6.8% pay increase with no provisions to help workers in lower wage categories via fixed-sum pay increases, as had again been demanded in the three bargaining areas of the Stuttgart district.[215]

In addition to the relatively modest size of the wage and salary raise, the manner in which it was won revealed subtle changes which IG Metall underwent in the wake of the transition from mobilization to crisis. The union pursued a concerted campaign of centralization with the clear intention of augmenting organizational control over the membership. Thus, the district of Hamburg, hitherto consisting of four bargaining areas, was united to form one new bargaining region.[216] Union district and bargaining area merged and became one administrative unit. Another move towards greater centralization occurred when the terms of the settlement reached in the bargaining area of NRW were simply imposed on all other IG Metall bargaining regions by the executive committee's fiat.[217] Decisive steps were taken towards a de facto centralization of IG Metall's wage bargaining throughout the crisis.

In the summer of 1975, the union published a working paper entitled "Defending against Attacks on Already Attained Social Reforms" which represented the first comprehensive response by any West German union to the new challenges facing organized labor as a consequence of the crisis.[218] The document gives an excellent summary of IG Metall's policies from the latter part of the mobilization through the crisis period of the late 1970s. While numerous passages convey the union's disillusionment with many of its conventional strategies (especially its heavy reliance on the state to attain reforms) there are no indications of a clear break with the past. The union's "state fixation," albeit somewhat modified, is very prominent in this document.[219] Yet the article also contains a number of items which point in the opposite direction, toward an expansion of the organizational and political scope of IG Metall's own activities. This resolve anticipated what was to become a distinctive union response to the economic crisis: an increased reliance on union strength.

In 1976, IG Metall's leadership recognized that "things would never be the same again." Showing its growing preoccupation with the crisis, IG Metall hosted a conference in Cologne entitled "Crisis and Reform in Industrial Society."[220] Attended by numerous prominent unionists, academicians, politicians and even some businessmen from West Germany and abroad, the conference attracted considerable publicity as the first public meeting where the crisis and its ramifications for the West German economy and society received serious attention. The importance of this event for IG Metall and the labor movement as a whole lay not so much in its actual results, but in the union's admission to the public and, perhaps more significantly, to itself that it was facing a predicament for which conventional solutions would be inadequate. The conference represented a broadening of the discussion begun in the working paper mentioned above. It legitimized IG Metall's tentative steps into uncharted territory.

The union's attempted strategy of reorientation did not have a direct effect on the bargaining round it conducted in 1976, which differed little from the round in 1975. With the steel industry experiencing a slump, the union made moderate demands in that sector, seeking an 8% across-the-board pay increase as well as minor fringe benefits. Negotiations yielded a 5% pay raise and some support for vocational training for apprentices.[221]

In metal processing, IG Metall also followed the pattern developed one year earlier. Centralization of the union's strategy was evident throughout the entire bargaining round. As in steel, the union demanded an 8% wage and salary increase, extra vacation days and some fringe benefits. Following difficult negotiations over a six-week period, the union concluded a "model contract," which was subsequently adopted by all of IG Metall's regions, in its model bargaining area, NW/NB. The agreement called for a 5.4% pay increase, a DM 110 payment for the months of January, February and March of 1976, some financial assistance for vocational training and a one-day increase of annual vacation time.[222]

In the spring of that year, IG Metall suffered a small but significant embarrassment. The successful strike of the printers' union, IG Druck und Papier, showed IG Metall that willingness to engage in militant action bore positive results in the form of tangible wage gains and other benefits, even under crisis conditions. The fact that this small union dared wage a strike under less than ideal circumstances, and that it signed a respectable contract, including a 6.0% pay increase, encouraged the activists within IG Metall. (For a discussion of the IG Druck strike of 1976 see Chapter 7.) The opinions of this group were to come to the fore within the union in 1977 and especially in 1978.

The year 1977 was a transition period between IG Metall's passive policies of 1975 and 1976, and the stormy era of 1978 and 1979. The 1977 wage round began in late 1976 with negotiations in the steel sector. Because of the industry's troubles, IG Metall decided to temper its demands in that sector's contract negotiations. The union's package, including an 8.5% wage and salary increase, was considerably more modest than the demands submitted to the metal industry a few months later. Nevertheless, numerous warning strikes accompanied the negotiations, which ultimately yielded a 6% pay increase with a number of less important fringe benefits ranging from one additional vacation day to supplementary payments for apprentices and older workers.[223]

Contract negotiations in the metal industry began in January 1977 in a much more charged atmosphere. The metal industry had recouped many of its earlier losses and was well on its way toward a boom. The automobile sector, second largest in the metal industry behind machine tools, but more powerful and politically important due to its high level of concentration and visibility, was buoyant at the beginning of 1977.[224]

IG Metall's leaders were particularly irked by the fact that, at least as they perceived matters, the bulk of the growth over the previous 18 months had been achieved via intensified productivity without any significant creation of jobs.[225] This not only meant that the unions' weakened position in the labor market would continue, but it also implied a deterioration of working conditions on the shop floor. IG Metall's bargaining strategy had to address both of these problems in the not-too-distant future, especially if it was to live up to the union's new emphasis on self-reliance.

From the very beginning, it was clear that IG Metall aimed for a significant pay increase in 1977, not only to improve the material conditions of its members but also to create an added macroeconomic stimulus, which the union hoped would alleviate unemployment. In the fall of 1976, IG Metall officials set the stage for their forthcoming bargaining approach by praising the advantages of stimulating demand for the West German economy.[226] By advocating an intensification of its long-held wage consumption theory, the union was calling into question the mainstream economic policies advocated by the Bundesbank, the Council of Economic Advisors, industry and increasingly the federal government. By formulating wage demands which were explicitly designed to challenge the austerity measures so popular among all economic actors in the Federal Republic at that time, IG Metall assumed the role of an activist countervailing power to most of West Germany's established institutions.

However, a step of this sort entailed some tensions within IG Metall. In addition to the usual disagreements between the union's accommodationists and activists, the crisis revived the latent geographic rivalry between IG Metall's Stuttgart district (responsible for bargaining in NW/NB) and its counterpart in Essen, which was in charge of the union's contracts in NRW. To complicate matters, the geographic cleavage within the union did not correspond to the strategic-political one represented by the division between activists and accommodationists, although, as a consequence of the bargaining rounds in the later 1970s, a widespread view developed both within and outside IG Metall that equated the Stuttgart line with activism and the Essen line with accommodationism.

During the 1977 wage round, the union had to avert an open clash between these two regions, in which Essen proposed a purely quantitative demand package while Stuttgart insisted on qualitative gains. The two regions submitted different demands in line with the divergent union traditions represented by each. Stuttgart concentrated on mixed demands favoring workers in the lower wage categories. Essen, in contrast, demanded an across-the-board 9.5% pay increase.[227] Stuttgart's "egalitarianism" stemmed not only from the presence in that district of the two lowest wage categories, in which workers suffered particularly during the crisis, but also from the luxury of a regional economy enjoying nearly full employment. Still, the union's demands met with opposition in the district itself. Many skilled workers expressed discomfort about IG Metall's "excessive" egalitarianism which threatened, at least indirectly, their privileged position.[228] Reproached once again for not presenting mixed demands, Essen defended itself by arguing that this was unnecessary since the lowest wage category (Wage Group 1) had long been abolished in that area and very few workers were classified as Wage Group 2.[229]

The employers were also divided. The industrialists of the automobile sector were eager to come to a rapid agreement centered on the more straightforward quantitative demands advocated by the Essen line. Finding themselves in the midst of a boom, they wanted to avoid a long, drawn-out negotiation process with IG Metall. The employers belonging to the much more fragmented machine-building industry were eager to hold the line and "teach the union a lesson.'[230] After a number of tense meetings between representatives of IG Metall and the employers the moderates on both sides carried the day. The final contract concluded a 6.9% pay raise in addition to support for vocational training.[231]

The turbulent aftermath of this wage round proved to have a more lasting effect on the subsequent behavior of the two combatants than the actual settlement. On the employers' side, a cleavage developed between the machinery industry, which felt that the contract "brought the union everything; the employers, nothing," and the automobile companies who rejoiced about the speed with which the conflict was resolved.[232] Accusations were leveled within the industry that the automakers had shied away from a showdown and were too "soft" on the union. The employers in the auto sector countered that they had behaved this way because of the boom the industry was experiencing and because of their frequent confrontations in NW/NB with a strike-savvy IG Metall.[233]

The automobile industry's prosperity was the cause of one of the many post-hoc disagreements within IG Metall as well. The workers in the country's automobile plants, a number of which are located in the Stuttgart district, criticized the results of the contract as inadequate and not commensurate with the economic conditions in their sector. Many workers felt the profit explosion warranted at least a 12% pay rise.[234] Moreover, union workers from the Stuttgart district believed that IG Metall's central leadership completely neglected their demands in both form and content. Not only did the contract fall short of the 75% attainment threshold which Otto Brenner had termed the minimum level for a successful settlement, but the union completely ignored qualitative demands which more directly addressed the problems introduced or intensified by the crisis. Intra-union bickering encouraged IG Metall to reevaluate some of its bargaining strategies, structures and aims.

Two events during 1977 helped to encourage the union's rethinking process. In May, IG Metall organized a "Technology Conference," which focused on the necessity for labor to reorient its strategy in light of the structural unemployment caused by technological change.[235] Virtually all lectures and discussions concentrated on the new employment problems and labor market developments brought on by the crisis. The conference also featured for the first time a detailed analysis of new strategies for collective bargaining designed to counter some of the worst manifestations of the crisis. One lecturer explained that the unions should expect only limited assistance from the government. The logical conclusion of the lecture was that it fell to the unions to compensate through collective bargaining for the inevitable losses that the government's austerity measures would entail for labor.[236] The speaker discussed at great length the pros and cons of specific demands such as work-time reduction (daily, weekly, monthly, yearly and lifetime), structural reorganization of the labor process on the shop floor to counter increased rationalization, qualitative control over certain components of the industrial work process, and the implementation of "humanization of work" programs on all levels. The speaker concluded that "collective bargaining contracts will have a chance to be used by imaginative unionists as instruments of social innovation – to find appropriate solutions to the adverse consequences of technological change in the labor market."[237] The Technology Conference placed IG Metall's collective bargaining at the center of attention as the best approach to deal with the crisis. The same conclusion was reached a few months later at the union's twelfth congress held in Düsseldorf in September 1977.

Here, too, the crisis dominated the weeklong proceedings.[238] Problems pertaining to collective bargaining, such as increased work pressure, deterioration of working conditions, rationalization, technological innovation and growing job insecurity, were discussed at length. Many of the official proposals submitted to the congress dealt with various ways to augment union power, especially on the shop floor. Others addressed the complex issue of defending against work intensification, dequalification and unemployment. The most hotly debated strategic point, however, was the demand for the 35-hour work week.[239] A major cleavage erupted between the leadership and the rank-and-file delegates over this issue, with the latter by and large favoring the introduction of the 35-hour work week and the former opposing it. This issue also provoked disagreement between delegates from NRW and their colleagues from NW/NB. The "Stuttgart line" favored longer breaks, a slower work pace and other micro-level approaches to weekly work-time reduction. It wanted IG Metall to place greater emphasis in its collective bargaining strategies on qualitative, control-oriented attempts to counter the growing threats of dequalification, rationalization and deterioration of working life in general.[240] The activists from Stuttgart believed that increased control by labor of work time at the shop level was more effective in securing these improvements than the introduction of the 35-hour work week.

In contrast to this position, the "Essen line," influenced by its large steelworker constituency, pleaded for the 35-hour week as the only viable solution to the adverse effects of rationalization on human health and employment. The steelworkers hoped that a radical reduction of the work week would lead to the establishment of an additional shift in an industry which requires around-the-clock production. To the delegates from NRW, the implementation of the 35-hour week represented the best strategy to fight the specter of steadily increasing unemployment.

Following a bitter showdown which saw a majority of the delegates vote in opposition to the leadership, the 35-hour week was accepted by the congress as official union policy. Measures to defend existing qualifications, as advocated by the Stuttgart line, were also approved. IG Metall succeeded in salvaging a precarious compromise on its collective bargaining policies.

In addition to these strategic issues, the congress debated important tactical matters designed to enhance IG Metall's maneuverability during the increasingly difficult and frequent altercations with the employers. During the 1977 bargaining round, the terms of the old arbitration agreement from 1963 had hindered IG Metall in its preparations for a potential strike. The delegates therefore demanded renegotiation of that agreement. They wanted a new arrangement wherein both parties would have to agree to enter arbitration, the obligation on the union's part to maintain "labor peace" would not extend beyond four weeks following the contract's expiration, and arbitrators would be determined on a case-by-case basis.[241]

Another important tactical debate – also brought on by past experience – centered on the desirability of reducing the size of NRW as a bargaining area by dividing it into several smaller units, perhaps following the contours of the four IG Metall districts.[242] Those arguing for the breakup of NRW advanced the position that the sheer size of this region had become a major liability for the union's collective bargaining strategy, since virtually any strike in NRW would exceed the union's financial capabilities, especially if accompanied by massive lockouts. The union leadership refused to make this demand an official resolution of the congress. In justifying its position, IG Metall's executive committee argued that such a change could never occur without the full cooperation of the employers, who had no interest or desire to change the status quo.

The congress provided an appropriate forum for the articulation of different demands and proposals within the organization. The debates of the congress mirrored similar divisions among West Germany's steel- and metalworkers in the midst of the crisis of the late 1970s, and the ramifications of these debates dominated the ensuing bargaining rounds of 1978 and 1979, perhaps the most taxing and difficult in IG Metall's history.

The 1978 bargaining round started in late 1977 in the steel industry. The union agreed to begin negotiations for a new contract before the old one expired, in order "to adjust to the exceptionally bad economic situation in the steel industry."[243] While this act conveyed a high sense of social responsibility on the part of West Germany's leading union, it was also a tactical move. IG Metall hoped that an early and relatively quick agreement in the depressed steel industry would not in any way influence the upcoming bargaining process in the booming metal-processing sector. The employers' rationale for earlier talks followed the opposite logic. Their aim was to set a precedent for prosperous sectors of the economy by using as a model the relatively modest terms of a settlement attained in one of the country's most severely depressed industrial areas.[244]

However, what was supposed to have been a routine bargaining round turned into a major test of wills between the industry and the union. In addition to a 7% pay increase, IG Metall wanted payment protection for some of its members who had suffered job displacement due to technological innovations. Specifically, IG Metall demanded that every worker who was required to incur a loss in remuneration as a consequence of firm-specific exigencies which placed the worker in a lower-paying job receive his/her previous wages for a minimum of twelve months. Moreover, addressing more fundamental changes, the union asked for a 24-month continuation of previous wages in case of dequalification caused by technological change.[245]

The employers responded by offering a wage freeze for the first six months of the new contract and a 3.5% raise for the subsequent six. They refused to accommodate the union on any of its demands regarding payment protection. Following a series of massive warning strikes at key steel firms such as Mannesmann, Thyssen, Krupp and Hoesch, and the complete breakdown of the negotiations, a special arbitrator proposed the terms for a new contract, which both parties accepted with some reluctance. It entailed a 4% wage and salary increase plus some fringe benefits for apprentices and older workers. As to payment protection, the new contract stipulated that a worker having to occupy a lower-paying job as a consequence of a company-specific exigency be remunerated at his/her previous wage level for at least seven months. Previous to this contract, the corresponding interval was only six weeks. In case of alterations in the work environment due to technological change, the adversely affected workers were to obtain their old wages for twelve months.[246] Again, this interval fell short of IG Metall's original demand for a 24-month period, but doubled the existing six month minimum.

More than any bargaining round since the onset of the crisis, IG Metall's negotiations with the metal industry during the first half of 1978 reflected the union's preoccupation with countering the two greatest hardships of this difficult period: unemployment and rationalization. Both had to be fought with quantitative as well as qualitative measures. In articulating the former, the union leadership argued that only a revival of aggregate demand had any chance of leading the West German economy toward recovery.[247] As it had during the formulation of wage demands for the 1977 bargaining round, IG Metall legitimized its aims by contending that increased wages would yield important macroeconomic benefits as well. The union defended its demand for an 8% across-the-board wage and salary increase as an attempt to protect its members against the adversities of inflation, to guarantee labor's full participation in the recent economic upswing, and to provide a modicum of economic redistribution. Moreover, flaunting its role as a "countervailing power," IG Metall presented its quantitative demands as a progressive challenge to the predominantly conservative economic thinking and austerity-oriented policy-making of virtually all other major institutions in the Federal Republic.

Confronting the rationalization process was the second order of IG Metall's bargaining strategy at the beginning of 1978. Qualitative issues attained central importance during the late 1970s not only because the crisis endangered – or eliminated – existing jobs but also because it threatened the quality of life on the shop floor. In NW/NB's metal industry, for example, a general deterioration of working conditions accompanied by a decline in the relative position of workers could be gauged by a stagnation of the job classification index since the beginning of the crisis.[248] Since a layoff of workers in the lower job categories would raise the overall classification index, the decline of the index meant that people in the higher job categories were adversely affected in some way, either by outright dismissal or by dequalification. Because unskilled workers were more affected by layoffs than the skilled, the latter must have been suffering dequalification. IG Metall's strategy for the 1978 bargaining round aimed at stopping this process of creeping dequalification of the union's core members.

Once again the NW/NB bargaining area of the Stuttgart district received the call to be the union's vanguard in a conflict with the employers. The workers in this region possessed the most extensive strike experience of any in the Federal Republic and it happened that a qualitative contract was awaiting its conclusion there, thus making possible a strike over qualitative issues without violating West Germany's strict strike laws.

Since 1976 IG Metall had been trying to renegotiate the terms of Wage Framework Contract I, which was signed in 1967 and expired in 1974. The original negotiations for a new contract began on an ambitious note since the union sought a fundamental restructuring of the job classification plan in the Stuttgart district's metal industry. As the talks extended over years and the crisis worsened, the union downscaled its initially far-reaching aims and concentrated on more immediate solutions. This resulted in the union's proposal for a "Protective Collective Bargaining Agreement" (Absicherungstarifvertrag – ATV).

The ATV's protective concerns focused on three areas: first, the union sought to defend the income and position of each worker. The union demanded an assurance for every worker that he/she would never be placed in a lower wage or job category than that attained by a certain date (yet to be determined). Regardless of the technological innovation introduced on the shop floor, individuals were to be guaranteed their standard of living. Second, the union sought to buttress this individual form of protection with a collective one. It demanded that the average of each firm's wage and job categorization reached on July 1, 1977 never be undercut in the future. This collective protection was absolutely necessary in the union's view in order to prevent the undermining of individual protection. "Without this collective protection workers could be dismissed, with new ones hired at the same time, who would be placed in lower wage categories; the employers would thus still reach their goal of reducing wage costs via dequalification."[249] The attainment of individual protection without its collective counterpart amounted in IG Metall's view to having a "knife without a handle."[250] Third, IG Metall wanted all firms in the Stuttgart district to be bound contractually to provide annual information to both contracting parties concerning all technological innovations which were to be undertaken and which in any way could affect the production process and the workers' roles therein.

These job-security reforms in the ATV contract addressed prerogatives which had hitherto belonged strictly to the employers. The concepts of both individual and collective protection redefined the conventional notion of "equal pay for equal work." They questioned the validity of the capitalist view of achievement and performance which traditionally were the major factors in assessing remuneration. IG Metall's plan added a social component of protection to the conventional form of categorization, classification and ultimately remuneration. On-the-job performance was no longer to be the sole determinant of the level of payment. Past performance also had to play a major role in assessing job classifications.

This protective program was more comprehenisve than the one reached in the steel industry in early 1978. The latter provided only a monetary cushioning of the adverse effects of rationalization. In contrast, IG Metall's proposal for the protective agreement in the Stuttgart district (the ATV) aimed at a more active confrontation of rationalization by labor at the point of production. By decreeing that previously attained benefits could under no circumstances be reduced or rolled back, this socially responsible form of payment qualified the pure "achievement principle."

In addition to this protection against dequalification and an 8% across-the-board salary increase, IG Metall demanded the abolition of Wage Groups 1 and 2 (the lowest wage categories) by merging them with Wage Group 3.[251] As could be expected the employers were completely unwilling to meet any of the union's demands and thus resorted to counteroffers which the union found unacceptable. IG Metall's situation was further complicated by the continued intra-organizational tension and territorial rivalries between NW/NB and NRW. NRW, in keeping with its position as articulated at the union's twelfth congress, submitted a purely quantitative bargaining demand in the form of an 8% across-the-board pay raise.[252] Unionists in NRW were eager to obtain qualitative reforms in the area of work-time reduction rather than via protection against dequalification. However, the general framework contracts determining work time had not expired in NRW's metal industry at the time, leaving the union paralyzed on this issue. Nevertheless, unionists from NRW, who had built up resentment against IG Metall's leadership in Frankfurt for having ignored them in the union's key conflicts of the past, made it clear to the executive committee that there would be problems if they were again bypassed in favor of their rivals in NW/NB.

The union decided to perform what later turned out to be a costly balancing act. It mobilized in both regions with full force and conducted a strike vote in both areas. With union members in both areas favoring a strike in overwhelming numbers, IG Metall had the mandate to conduct a strike in both or either.[253] Once again, the executive committee chose NW/NB over NRW which, as could be expected, left a considerable residue of resentment in this area against both the union's leadership and the Stuttgart district itself. The executive committee's decision was based on a combination of factors, including NW/NB's strike experience and the greater significance of the issues articulated in the Stuttgart demands. The union's determination to make qualitative issues central to its bargaining strategy during the crisis had to be put into practice if it was to be taken seriously by its members and the employers.

The strike in NW/NB began on March 15, 1978.[254] Following the practice of its three previous strikes in the area (1963, 1971 and 1973), the union again relied on the strategy of point strikes focused on key plants whose workers had "proven" themselves in earlier confrontations.[255] In addition to the workers' strike experience and the union's organizational strength inside the factory gates, IG Metall's selection criteria for "front-line" plants included economic performance and position in the country's web of production. Significantly, the union did not choose its strike locations according to the particular urgency of its contract demands – such as the issue of dequalification. This tactical matter figured prominently in the numerous intra-union criticisms which accompanied the strike's post mortem.

Eighty thousand workers, including 15,000 clerical employees, failed to report to work in 63 plants on the morning of March 15, 1978.[256] All the production sites affected by the strike were within the jurisdiction of the union's Stuttgart local with the exception of one Daimler-Benz factory which belonged to IG Metall's Esslingen local. As in the three earlier strikes, workers in firms such as Daimler-Benz, Bosch and SEL carried the lion's share of the strike. White-collar employees also played an important role. There were almost no incidents in which members of this group became strikebreakers, a frequent occurrence during the previous three strikes conducted by IG Metall in the area.[257]

The employers' reaction was swift. On March 15, the first day of the strike, the decision-making council of the area's metal producers voted 156 to 1 in favor of initiating an area-wide lockout affecting plants with over 1,000 workers.[258] Five days later the employers locked out 146,000 blue-collar workers from 78 plants.[259] By explicitly excluding white-collar employees and clerical staff, the lockout was clearly designed to drive a wedge between the groups involved in the strike. The employers' measure also aimed at imposing a heavy financial burden on IG Metall's coffers. Despite the industry's determination to weaken the union decisively, the impact of this particular lockout was relatively mild compared to previous ones conducted during industrial conflicts in the area. In the lockout accompanying the 1971 strike, for example, the employers had included every plant with more than 100 – rather than 1,000 – employees. Nevertheless, IG Metall felt that the employers in the 1978 lockout had deployed an illegitimate weapon against the union in an unnecessarily injurious way.

Unlike in earlier confrontations, IG Metall decided to fight back. The union's counterattack against the lockouts focused on both the employers and the country's judicial system. Over 30,000 union members sued the employers for loss of wages due to the lockouts.[260] Together with many locked-out printers – whose strike overlapped with IG Metall's – hundreds of metalworkers descended upon the courts in the Stuttgart area, carrying with them their completed complaint forms in huge laundry bins. This represented the first instance in the history of the Federal Republic in which a union organized a politicized and collective response to a lockout. Concomitant with this action, IG Metall extended strike activities to seven more factories, in six of which white-collar employees were called upon to join their blue-collar colleagues. At the peak of the confrontation in late March, 236,000 workers were directly affected by this industrial conflict, either via the strike or via the lockout.[261] By that date, IG Metall had expanded the participation of strikers well beyond the Stuttgart local to include almost the entire NW/NB bargaining area.

In virtually all cases, white-collar employees joined blue-collar workers in the strike, which usually provided the former with their first experience of active participation in a struggle between capital and labor. While IG Metall's organizational efforts to bring blue- and white-collar workers together for this important strike were impressive, white-collar participation in this event could also be attributed to a new "crisis consciousness" which had begun to spread to this group as well. One of the most pervasive manifestations of the crisis in West Germany was the growing awareness on the part of employees that nobody – including hitherto "safe" clerical and staff personnel – was immune to the dangers of technological rationalization.

Despite the union's efforts to mobilize all segments of the workforce, criticism was voiced during and after the strike that IG Metall's elitism reduced rank-and-file participation. Critics argued that this strike – like the previous ones in NW/NB – was essentially a "Funktionärstreik," meaning that it was sustained by the union's officials rather than the members. The latter, many felt, conducted a "Fernsehstreik" (television strike), where large numbers of workers stayed at home and followed the events on the TV news.[262]

The strike ended officially on Thursday, April 6, 1978. With educated estimates of IG Metall's overall costs hovering in the DM 150 million range, this conflict was the union's most expensive to date. Heinz Dürr, then head of VMI, Gesamtmetall's Stuttgart section, estimated a wage loss of DM 350 million, loss in tax revenues of about DM 200 million, and an additional DM 115 million reduction in the contribution to social security.[263] These figures convey the magnitude of the conflict, which continues to be one of the most bitterly contested in the history of the Federal Republic.

The results represented a compromise on both the qualitative and quantitative issues. Through the ATV, IG Metall was able to secure for its members important protection against rationalization. The contract stipulated a three-phased model of job security.[264] The first phase required the employers to announce any potential dequalification and seek alternatives to it. The channel for this information had to be the works councils, whose mandate by law included the conduct of regular meetings with the employers concerning changes in the production process. This phase also envisioned firm-specific agreements to postpone dequalification by employing affected workers elsewhere in the plant and/or provide them with retraining.

In case the measures in phase one failed to prevent dequalification from adversely affecting workers, phase two of the contract would be activated. Basically, this stipulation guaranteed any victim of dequalification his/her previously earned income for up to eighteen months. Following this eighteen-month period, the third phase of the contract would come into play. This required a "soft landing" whereby those initially affected by dequalification would be gradually integrated into their lower job classifications. The contract specified that no blue-collar worker could drop more than two categories in his/her wage classification, while white-collar employees could only be dequalified by one salary category.[265] Moreover, the financial losses involved could only be imposed by withholding pay increases, rather than by making salary cuts.

As for IG Metall's other demands, the union had to make do with the elimination of Wage Group 1 by having all its members reclassified into Wage Group 2 beginning retroactively on January 1, 1978.[266] While the negotiations concerning these qualitative issues dominated much of the public's attention and consumed a great amount of energy on the part of both IG Metall and the employers, bitter struggles accompanied the quantitative aspect of the bargaining round. Eventually, the parties agreed to a 5% across-the-board wage and salary increase retroactive to Januay 1, 1978 and lasting for the entire calendar year.[267] This quantitative gain fell short of IG Metall's expectations. The qualitative segment of the bargaining round represented at least a partial victory for IG Metall. The new rules and regulations placed limits on the unimpeded process of dequalification. They also introduced the concept of need into remuneration, thereby making some inroads into the performance-dominated reward system. The old performance-oriented motto of "equal pay for equal work" no longer pertained exclusively. According to the new terms of this protective contract, an older dequalified worker would obtain higher pay than his/her newly hired colleague for exactly the same job. Age and seniority were given particular consideration in determining remuneration via the ATV.

This protective apparatus nevertheless did not meet the union's original aspirations. Collective protection against dequalification was omitted from the contract, and even the individual protection plan outlined above fell short of an outright moratorium on dequalification. It merely provided a temporary cushioning, which set certain limits on the procedure of rationalization without eliminating its adverse effects. Thus, while the ATV slowed the process of dequalification for the individual worker, it failed to alleviate its consequences, thereby increasing union members' displeasure with the contract.

The conclusion of the negotiations and the signing of contracts in NW/NB did not put an end to the conflict as vocal criticism of the agreement by many workers in NW/NB continued unabated. Workers in NW/NB's booming automobile sector were dissatisfied with the raise because they felt it in no way corresponded to the profits generated by the industry's latest upswing.[268] Moreover, IG Metall's membership reproached the union leadership for having failed to abolish Wage Group 2. This criticism emanated primarily from workers in the electronics industry which employs a large number of unskilled women, most of whom had been classified in either Wage Group 1 or 2. Many women in firms such as Bosch and SEL protested this contractual shortcoming as sexually discriminatory and as providing inadequate protection against future dequalification.[269] This latter point was the most central criticism of the new protective contract. Many rank-and-file members feared that without collective guarantees, individual protection would be ineffective. Because of the contract's limited protection, some workers viewed the entire effort as a failure.[270]

A sense of apprehension characterized the contract's reception in IG Metall's other bargaining areas, none of which had reached agreements of their own by this time. The employers refused to have the whole NW/NB package "transferred" to any of IG Metall's other regions. The contract's qualitative gains remained limited to NW/NB because of a strategic move by the employers to sow discord among the union's ranks and because of resistance by the metal producers in NRW to the Stuttgart agreement, which they saw as inadequate given their more difficult economic situation.

IG Metall had the worst of both worlds. It could not transfer the beneficial aspects of the newly reached agreements to other areas, yet the quantitative dimensions of the contract set a precedent which other areas could not realistically hope to attain. With the exception of the Volkswagen contract in which the union won a 5.9% wage and salary increase following an overwhelming strike vote, all other bargaining areas settled for a 5% pay raise more or less directly dictated by the Stuttgart precedent.[271]

The big loser of this round was undoubtedly NRW. IG Metall's leadership enticed this region with all the necessary preparations for a strike, only to back out at the last moment. Not surprisingly, many IG Metall members in NRW were outraged by their betrayal at the hands of the union executive committee. The words of IG Metall's district secretary in NRW, Kurt Herb, captured the sentiment of many unionists there: "We are perturbed that once again the gunpowder which we have produced here in NRW was used to wage a battle elsewhere."[272] The feelings of deep disappointment and resentment dominated the atmosphere in NRW throughout the year and were an important factor behind the bitter steel strike there in late 1978.

Barely two months after the conclusion of IG Metall's costly strike in the Stuttgart district's metal industry, the union embarked on an equally difficult mission. It set out to force the first major reduction of the work week since the 1960s. To that end, the union canceled on June 30, 1978 its general framework contract in NRW's steel industry. IG Metall was determined to achieve two aims in this bargaining round. First, it eagerly sought to implement the 35-hour work week, one of the crucial mandates of the twelfth union congress and a major component of IG Metall's strategy to counter the effects of the crisis. Second, it wanted to compensate for some of the repeated disappointments suffered by its membership in NRW by achieving a major breakthrough in that district, even at the cost of a taxing strike.

Any account of the strike's background has to begin with at least a cursory overview of the crisis which befell the West German steel industry in late 1974. The 1973–74 period represented an important transitional phase for the steel industry. These two years witnessed a business cycle bifurcated between a superboom in the steel industry and a depression in the construction and auto industries. Steel production was breaking all previous records during 1974, while the automobile industry in the Federal Republic was confronting one of its worst crises in the post-war era. This was reflected in IG Metall's contracts as well, since, as will be recalled, the union obtained higher settlements in steel than in metal processing during that time, a reversal of the situation that had prevailed throughout most of the 1960s and the 1970s.[273]

In 1975, the picture changed dramatically for the world's steel industries, including the Federal Republic's. That year witnessed a drop of 62.5 million tons (8.8%) in worldwide steel production.[274] Most of this slump occurred in the steel industries of the United States and Western Europe, notably Great Britain, France, Belgium and West Germany. In the Federal Republic, the three-year period between 1974 and 1977 – the nadir of the crisis – saw a 26.8% drop in production from 53.2 million tons per annum to 39 million. The decline in 1975 amounted to 24.1%. In 1977, capacity utilization in the West German steel industry declined to 57.6%, the lowest among all leading steel-producing countries in the world at the time. The Federal Republic's steel manufacturers were taking a beating both at home and abroad. Their domestic market share declined from 80% to 70% between 1974 and 1977 while in world exports the West German share fell to 12.2% in 1976 from a high of 17.6% in 1974. Much of this loss occurred due to Japanese and South Korean competition, and the increasing success of small, highly specialized but very efficient steel producers such as the "Bresciani" around the northern Italian city of Brescia.

The effects on employment were equally drastic. Between the beginning of 1975 and the end of 1977, 36,000 steelworkers lost their jobs. Despite the severity of the crisis at that point, it was clear to knowledgeable analysts of the West German steel industry – including the IG Metall leadership – that employment was still too high given the depressed outlook for the industry's future. Moreover, the Federal Republic's steel industry possessed the technological capabilities to push rationalization considerably further, thereby threatening even more jobs. The levels of output required by the market could be reached by raising the capacity utilization of the modern plants via further rationalization while closing the less efficient, more labor-intensive mills. IG Metall feared that this two-pronged attack – productivity increases via rationalization in the core works and layoffs in the marginal ones – could result in an additional loss of 50,000 jobs over the next few years.

IG Metall's response to the steel industry's woes began at an earlier date, and thus forms another important background factor in the eventual industrial action of 1978–79. At the union's steel conference in May 1977, two major policy strategies emerged. The first called for a more vigorous role by the state.[275] Here the union placed its hopes in Strukturpolitik (a vaguely defined collaborative effort on the part of employers, labor and the state to restructure ailing industries) without, however, neglecting the benefits of selective manpower policy, improved retraining programs and state subsidies for troubled firms. The second emphasized IG Metall's new policy of self-reliance. This alternative strategy focused on the reduction of work time through collective bargaining. At this juncture, no particular version of work-time reduction was favored over any other by the union's leaders. The discussion centered as much on early retirement with full pay as it did on a reduction of weekly work time for workers employed in continuous shifts. All proposals concentrated on macro-dimensions rather than, for example, on the introduction of more regularized breaks during working hours. It was clear throughout the conference and in subsequent months that work-time reduction in the steel industry was viewed by IG Metall as mainly a macroeconomic device to increase employment via collective bargaining. While health, safety and other considerations related to the humanization of work entered the intra-union discussion, it was the reduction of work time which dominated the union's strategic planning during the summer of 1977.

In September of that year, only a few months after the steel conference, the 35-hour work week became one of the union's official policy goals, after being passed as a congress resolution supported by the rank and file in spite of the leadership's opposition.[276] The major supporters of this move were workers from the NRW bargaining area, with delegates from the steel industry playing a particularly active role. With the marked deterioration of the employment situation in the steel industry during the winter of 1977-78, work-time reduction for job-saving purposes became increasingly attractive for IG Metall. The opportunity offered itself in the spring of 1978 when the union began to make plans for the steel industry's new general framework contract (which regulates work time). With the old agreement from January 30, 1975 about to expire on June 30, 1978, IG Metall sought to implement the 35-hour work week for the first time in one of Europe's major industries.

The preparation for this key bargaining round resulted in a number of disagreements within the union concerning the optimal strategy and tactics to attain this goal. Rejecting the option of emphasizing the humanization aspects or the employment effects of the 35-hour work week, key segments of the union's steelworkers preferred a different solution altogether. IG Metall members at the three Hoesch works in Dortmund, for example, wanted to see the union push for early retirement (age 55) with full compensation.[277] They argued that this policy would have a more beneficial effect for steelworkers than the 35-hour week with regard to both humanization and employment. While both parties eventually acquiesced in the 35-hour week solution, this dissension left unresolved tensions within the ranks of IG Metall's steelworkers.

An additional complicating factor was that IG Metall's ultimate goals were never clearly articulated by the union leadership. This resulted in a number of misunderstandings and miscalculations both before and during the strike. It was left ambiguous, for example, whether IG Metall wanted to reach the 35-hour week in one step or in small increments over a period of time. The official demand explained only that the union sought a "reduction of weekly work time accompanied by full wage and salary compensation with the *aim* [emphasis added] of reaching a 35-hour work week, possibly even via leisure-time regulations."[278] Had the goal of the industrial action been made more explicit from the outset, the union would have been spared much confusion during the strike and thereafter.

Another point of misunderstanding involved the notion that the 35-hour week was being sought *only* for workers in the steel industry. IG Metall made it quite clear from the beginning of the bargaining round that the 35-hour week was a "steel-specific" demand. But because of the union's predominant position within the DGB, so critical a demand articulated at such a crucial time had to have practical implications for the bargaining strategies of other unions as well. As a result, the union's activities were subject to intense public scrutiny throughout the negotiations, the subsequent strike and its aftermath, which went beyond the already considerable attention routinely accorded to IG Metall's actions by the labor movement and the public at large.

From the day IG Metall cancelled the old general framework contract and submitted its demand for the 35-hour week (June 30, 1978) until the beginning of the strike nearly five months later (November 28), the employers refused to budge. They viewed every union demand as negotiable with one exception: the reduction of the 40-hour week. In spite of IG Metall's insistence that this demand was "steel specific," the employers unconditionally rejected any reforms connected to the shortening of weekly work time. When IG Metall demanded a lengthening of annual vacation time to six weeks instead of the 35-hour work week during its concomitant negotiations in the metal industry, the employers in that industry held firm. Their resolve received a boost from the confusion surrounding the union's demands, in which IG Metall sought one reform from steel and another from the metal-processing industry.

The union suspected soon after the initial negotiations that the steel employers were fighting a "proxy war" for West German capital as a whole. By late August, IG Metall's suspicion was corroborated. In an article about a very unusual occurrence in the brewing industry, where an already signed contract for a 32-hour work week for workers 60 years and older had been rescinded by the West German employers' association (the BDA), the business daily *Handelsblatt* mentioned the existence of a "Tabu Katalog" (taboo catalogue) which delineated certain rules that were not to be broken by any BDA member at the risk of heavy fines or expulsion.[279] One of the main taboos was the reduction of the 40-hour work week in any form.

IG Metall's chances looked dim. What was denied elderly brewery workers represented by one of the most accommodationist unions within the DGB would certainly not be granted to potentially militant workers led by the most activist union in one of the country's foremost industries. (For a discussion of the Tabu Katalog see Chapter 3.)

The fact that the steel industrialists had taken this vanguard position surprised IG Metall, because the association of steel employers (Arbeitgeberverband Eisen-und-Stahlindustrie e.V. – AGV) did not formally belong to the BDA. The initial failure by IG Metall to weigh the steel employers' firm stand on this matter in its caclulations derived from a view of the steel industry as more congenial towards labor than its counterparts in the BDA. IG Metall believed that Montanmitbestimmung had created a special rapport between capital and labor in this industry. All of this changed as a consequence of the events of late 1978 and early 1979.

Montanmitbestimmung had, prior to the summer of 1978, created a sense of fair play between labor and management in the steel sector.[280] Since the conclusion of the first autonomous wage contract in 1955 by the steel industry and IG Metall, negotiations between the two parties had been characterized by moderation, fairness and restraint. It was not by chance that steel – again unlike metal – lacked a formal arbitration procedure. Indeed, with the exception of the 1965 bargaining round – when the arbitration agreement operative in the metal industry was simply adopted by both parties – and the 1977–78 round which, as discussed above, was settled by a special arbitrator, negotiations between IG Metall and the steel industry reached a successful conclusion every year without recourse to arbitration.

At the end of September 1978, a new factor entered the already complex situation. IG Metall was preparing to cancel the wage and salary contracts in NRW's steel industry in routine fashion one month prior to their expiration date on October 31, 1978. This normal procedure suddenly gained added significance because, whether intended or not, a link developed between IG Metall's unresolved qualitative demand for the 35-hour week and its wage demands. IG Metall itself made this link explicit when spokesmen for the bargaining commission explained that the union had desisted from issuing specific figures for its wage demands, because it was waiting for some movement by the employers on the 35-hour work week issue.[281]

Weeks passed, however, without any sign from the AGV that it was ready to negotiate with the union in good faith on work-time reduction. At the end of October, the union finally issued its quantitative demands, which featured a 5% across-the-board wage and salary increase.[282] This passed by a relatively narrow margin in the bargaining commission. The majority on the commission pushed for the acceptance of this low increase, hoping its modesty would induce the employers to make meaningful concessions on qualitative issues. The commission's minority, consisting mainly of activists, opposed this wage demand as inadequate given the projections for the economy's immediate future and in light of an expected improvement in the steel industry.[283]

The industry responded by coopting one of the union's own goals: extended vacation time. The dual strategy pursued by IG Metall whereby it decreed the 35-hour work week to be "steel specific" and demanded longer vacation in the much larger metal-processing sector, was turned against the union by AGV. In addition, on November 7 the employers declared that negotiations on the 35-hour week had failed. This embarrassed IG Metall and forced its hand. More than four months had passed without any sign of progress, and many union members were confused by IG Metall's vacillations concerning work-time reduction. The union's pursuit of a different qualitative strategy in metal processing helped the employers undermine IG Metall's credibility. The union had to act. On November 8, IG Metall began preparations for the first official strike in the German steel industry since the infamous "Ruhreisenstreik" of 1928 which has been credited by many as being one of the causes of the Weimar Republic's fall a few years later.

The employers not only embarrassed the union but succeeded in forcing it to wage a conflict on the industry's schedule and terms. IG Metall was assured the worst possible conditions in which to conduct a strike. The steel industrialists' astute maneuvering, combined with the union's tactical errors and four-month long procrastination, compelled IG Metall to organize a strike in very cold weather and during the pre-holiday and Christmas seasons when production is at its lowest. The strike was thus to occur at a time when it caused the least disruption and involved the smallest cost for the employers. In addition to saving money by forcing the union to strike at a time of low production, the employers would also forego having to pay the traditional Christmas bonuses to striking and locked-out workers. Contrary to the union's intentions, it was IG Metall which was to be financially burdened, by having to support its members throughout the strike. From all points of view the timing of the strike clearly favored the employers over IG Metall.

Moreover, IG Metall's strike preparations were flawed. Union members performed overtime work in many plants up to the beginning of the strike,[284] and in a few instances, overtime production continued at some mills while others were shut down by the work stoppage. The union's poor coordination both before and during the strike resulted from its inexperience with such activity in the NRW steel industry. This handicap was further exacerbated by the lack of adequate pre-strike mobilization. Some warning strikes took place, but on the whole they were disorganized and confined to the local level.

IG Metall's poor strike preparations contrasted markedly with the employers' thorough and meticulous planning. The steel companies, for example, set up a well-endowed mutual-assistance fund to provide financial help to the most needy companies in the event of a strike.[285] The AGV further demonstrated its organizational sophistication by establishing a clearinghouse to coordinate production among all steel firms during a strike so that no company would benefit to the detriment of another. This clearinghouse was also to serve as a distributor of materials among the various steel firms. Moreover, most steel companies – in anticipation of an industrial conflict – had increased their production of sheet steel (hot rolled sheet) since the beginning of the summer in order to stock ample reserves for the booming automobile industry, its major domestic customer.[286] Aware of the fact that IG Metall would try to maximize the impact of its strike by concentrating its efforts on those plants which furnish the largest quantities of supplies to the automobile industry, both the steel and automobile producers – in full coordination with each other – took precautionary measures by stockpiling supplies to overflow levels. The automobile firms made arrangements with foreign steel companies to supply them with all necessary materials in case their regular West German sources could no longer deliver.

IG Metall's conduct of the strike was a significant improvement over the union's flawed preparatory efforts. While mobilization remained inadequate during the lengthy pre-strike period, it became very effective immediately following the strike's official beginning on November 28 at 6 a.m. From the first minutes of the strike until its end on January 8, 1979 – through Christmas and New Year's Day – there were virtually no strikebreakers, even among the white-collar clerical employees.[287] The picket lines were well staffed in spite of the holiday season; this was clearly not a "TV-strike." Daily registration of the strikers required that they be physically present in front of the various factory gates, creating a beneficial ripple effect. With the strike concentrated in steel towns such as Dortmund and Duisburg, the participation of the steelworkers also entailed an unprecedented level of support from the general public. The latter's sympathy for the strikers and involvement with their cause in turn led to an intra-DGB solidarity not experienced since the battles for co-determination and shop-floor representation in the early 1950s and the unions' support for the Brandt government in its defeat of the vote of no confidence in the spring of 1972.

Even after the strike had begun, IG Metall continued to vacillate. The head of the union, Eugen Loderer, announced that the union would be satisfied to gain even a one-hour reduction of the 40-hour week and that the wage demand for a 5% increase was negotiable. However, the union's district secretary from NRW, Kurt Herb, reiterated that its final aim was to force the introduction of a fifth shift by substantially reducing weekly work time and not to improve its members' suntans with more vacation time.[288] These mixed messages, often coming on consecutive days, contrasted sharply with the employers' determination and coordination.

Following the unanimous decision reached in an emergency meeting of the AGV on November 27, one day before the strike, the employers locked out 30,000 workers at six plants.[289]

Three points are noteworthy about this lockout. First, it was the earliest incident of this kind in the areas subject to Montanmitbestimmung. Expert observers suggest that the numerous labor directors – who form part of management in the steel industry but are also invariably close to the union – did not offer much resistance to the employers' decision concerning the lockout.[290] Whatever happened behind the tightly closed doors of the steel company board rooms, there are few indications that the employers' "battle-readiness" was in any way impaired by the presence of labor representatives among the top echelons of managerial decision-making. In short, Montanmitbestimmung and IG Metall's "inside" labor director did not pose obstacles to the employers' maneuverability, including the effective implementation of the lockout.

Second, all six plants chosen for the lockout were relatively marginal to the overall fortunes of the steel sector. Some were operating at a loss, which meant that a lockout simply transferred the labor cost of running an unprofitable factory onto IG Metall through its assistance payments to locked-out workers.[291] Other plants were either small in size or specialized in the production of the kinds of steel which at the time were in low demand.

Third, the lockout was a mild one, especially compared to its counterparts earlier in 1978 in the printing and metal industries. It appeared that the AGV was eager to prove management's claim that the lockout was merely the employers' equivalent to the strike.

The unique nature of this strike and lockout was clear in other ways. For the first time in the history of the Federal Republic, IG Metall officially called for a district-wide solidarity demonstration to take place on December 12, rallying its workers not immediately involved in either the strike or the lockout. The employers responded promptly by claiming that solidarity strikes were illegal and going to court to obtain restraining orders.[292] Some courts – such as the labor court in Düsseldorf – declined to issue a restraining order while others agreed with the employers and forbade non-striking metalworkers to conduct a protest in support of their striking colleagues during official working hours. Despite this legal maneuvering, numerous demonstrations occurred between December 4 and 12, with the largest taking place in Duisburg on December 8.[293] Over 40,000 workers from IG Metall and other DGB unions heard numerous speakers, including Eugen Loderer and Kurt Herb, denounce the employers' use of the lockout.

This theme also dominated one of the most impressive solidarity marches by West German workers since the beginning of the Federal Republic. On December 12, 145,000 workers in 34 cities and towns of North Rhine-Westphalia demonstrated during their regular working hours against the iniquities of the lockout. Neither restraining orders nor threats by employers could stop this massive outpouring of support for the steelworkers. It is significant, however, that the political content of this demonstration was severely limited in scope. The IG Metall- and DGB-sponsored rally carefully focused on one thing alone: opposition to the employers' lockout. It barely addressed the major aim of the steel strike, the 35-hour work week, thereby deftly skirting one of the most controversial and divisive topics within the union and the DGB.

Concomitant with these mobilization measures, IG Metall continued negotiating with the employers. Numerous formal and informal contacts betwen the two parties occurred throughout December, but these meetings yielded no concrete results. The employers, in a brilliant tactical move, convinced IG Metall to accept a political arbitrator who was at the time an ardent opponent of the 35-hour week but otherwise could boast impeccable social democratic and labor-related credentials. The month of December witnessed various interim proposals all of which failed to mention any kind of weekly work-time reduction. Increased vacation time and free shifts seemed to have replaced the 35-hour week as the object of negotiation by Christmas 1978. When word of this substantial change reached the strikers and other steelworkers, demonstrations were organized to protest what many saw as a betrayal of the strike's original goals. Many frustrated strikers began to blame the union's rapid abandonment of the 35-hour work week on the supposed incompetence of the district leader, Kurt Herb. They demanded his ouster and replacement by the Stuttgart district's charismatic secretary, Franz Steinkühler.[294] The level of despair among a significant minority of steelworkers could be gauged by their increasing tendency to vent their anger in ad-hominem attacks against Kurt Herb.

Perhaps in response to rank-and-file pressure, IG Metall expanded the strike by an additional 20,000 workers on January 3, 1979.[295] The employers refrained from responding with a lockout, indicative of their interest in a rapid conclusion of the strike rather than an escalation. On January 7, both parties reached an agreement which brought the conflict to an end. Its main points were:[296]

1. a 4% pay raise over a 15-month period retroactive to November 1, 1978;

2. four additional free shifts for night shift workers as of January 1, 1979;

3. two additional free days for all employees over 50;

4. two additional vacation days for everybody beginning January 1, 1979;

5. one additional vacation day as of 1980;

6. two more free shifts for night shift workers, one free shift for workers over 50, and two additional vacation days for workers under 30 as of 1981;

7. introduction of a 30-day vacation period (six weeks) for everybody as of 1982; and

8. duration of five years for the new general framework contract.

Both parties issued victory statements in the wake of the agreement. The employers rejoiced that the nearly six-week-long strike was finally over. Despite the major concession they had made in granting a substantial increase in paid free time, the employers felt the conflict was well worth their efforts since the union's major aim, the reduction of the 40-hour week, had been foiled. Underscoring the employers' view that preventing IG Metall from breaking the barrier of the 40-hour week was tantamount to maintaining the liberal democratic order in the Federal Republic, the final words of their assessment stated: "The steel industry paid a high price for the restoration of social peace."[297] Despite the employers' desire to emphasize the sacrifices they had made to secure an advantageous settlement, they nevertheless claimed that the contract represented an unconditional victory for them.

IG Metall, of course, argued the exact opposite. Denying the employers' assertion that they had averted weekly work-time reduction, the union viewed the results as a major achievement for the labor movement, because it felt that a fundamental taboo of the employers had finally been violated.[298] The regulations of the new general framework contract yielded time arrangements which totalled less than 40 hours of work per week. Thus, IG Metall concluded in its first post-strike statement, "the 40-hour barrier has been broken."[299]

Many disappointed steelworkers did not share this optimistic evaluation of the strike results. Seldom in IG Metall's history were criticisms of a bargaining result peppered with words such as "betrayal," "defeat" and "ignominy." The critics, focusing on the agreement's deficiencies, argued that only the most arcane arithmetical acrobatics could lead one to believe that a move toward the 35-hour week had occurred. Moreover, many felt that the results split the steelworkers into potentially competing groups benefitting differently from the various vacation and shift arrangements. Lastly, the length of the suggested new general framework contract was condemned. Its five-year duration essentially meant that IG Metall was locked into the 40-hour work week in the steel industry until the end of 1984. Many argued that the contract paid too high a price for a few free shifts and more vacation, especially since the latter arrangements would not yield a substantial increase in jobs, which a growing number of workers recognized as the paramount problem for the 1980s.

The criticisms were not confined to IG Metall's strategy and the results of the contract. Many also voiced strong disagreement with the union's choice of tactics. These complaints centered on IG Metall's indecision as well as its underestimation of the employers' strength and determination. Critics felt that the union's leaders were influenced by an overly optimistic perception of employer attitudes and tolerance for labor, a perception that had become unrealistic as the crisis wore on and as management became increasingly inflexible. The rank and file barraged the union leadership with complaints for months after the conclusion of the strike. This led to one of the most thorough and honest soul-searching efforts ever undertaken by a West German union.

A process of evaluation and assessment occurred involving all levels in the organization. In lengthy meetings held in the union locals of NRW's steel towns, workers debated the strike and its implications long after the contracts had been signed. (Although much of the discussion was sharply critical of the union, it is significant that the high level of rank-and-file mobilization and active worker participation continued after the strike had ended.) Many workers believed that the union's preparatory efforts neglected to provide a clear articulation of the goals of the struggle. Confusion concerning the objectives of the strike dampened the enthusiasm of many actual and would-be strike participants, thereby impeding IG Metall's mobilization efforts. Most of the criticism, of course, centered on the union's failure to attain anything remotely resembling a 35-hour work week.

As noted above, the leadership's initial evaluation of the results of the strike was largely favorable. However, this changed gradually as criticisms began to appear in interviews and informal remarks, which demonstrated that the discontent voiced by the rank and file was echoed, at least in part, by the union leadership. This process culminated at a conference in Braunlage in April 1979 where IG Metall's entire leadership gathered for a four-day-long brainstorming session to discuss the union's crisis-inspired credo of "relying on its own strength."[300] The result was the concept of "new maneuverability" which was henceforth to guide IG Metall's collective bargaining activities. The inspiration for this new idea was furnished by the events of the steel strike.

"New maneuverability" was a strategic response on the part of the union to the increasing militancy, determination and centralization of West German employers in confronting labor – especially its most prominent representative, IG Metall. The strategy also sought to compensate for the decreasing willingness of the government, led by an austerity-oriented Social Democratic chancellor, to carry out reforms and policies favored by the unions. New maneuverability represented a concretization of the lessons IG Metall learned in the course of the crisis. A greater emphasis on collective bargaining was to fill at least part of the gap created by the pro-business attitudes and policies of the SPD–FDP coalition.[301] The new strategy focused particularly on the qualitative areas of collective bargaining, which covered issues increasingly neglected by conservative public policy.

IG Metall also had to develop a set of tactics in response to the employers' aggressiveness. The Braunlage conference listed the following measures as applications of the concept of new maneuverability: better coordination between the executive committee in Frankfurt and the various district leaders in the formulation of collective bargaining demands; more active mobilization at all stages of strike preparation; better communication between the union's functionaries and its shop-floor representatives; increased use of sympathy strikes and other forms of open support for strikers on the part of their non-striking colleagues; and the introduction of a new arbitration agreement in the metal industry (which would abolish many of the advantages gained by the employers in the previous contract signed in 1963 under particularly unfavorable circumstances for IG Metall).[302]

Another of the steel strike's ripple effects was the rapid conclusion of the 1979 bargaining round in the metal industry. Six-week vacations were a less than satisfactory solution to the steel strike, but they met the union's original demands in metal processing. Following the end of the steel strike and the ratification of the new contracts on January 10, it was only a matter of days before the bargaining round in the metal industry came to a mutually satisfactory end. The settlement entailed a 4.3% across-the-board pay increase over a period of thirteen months and – very much in line with IG Metall's wishes – the gradual extension of annual vacation time to six weeks for all metalworkers by the end of 1983.[303] The contract also made the 35-hour work week a completely non-negotiable issue in the metal industry until the end of 1983.

Lastly, the steel strike influenced the bargaining results of almost every other DGB union in 1979. One by one, unions concluded contracts which followed IG Metall's lead in terms of both pay increases and the six-week vacation agreement. Thus, by early summer of 1979, six weeks vacation per annum had become a contractual reality for virtually every West German worker. There can be no doubt that the steel strike had a great deal to do with this beneficial development for the labor movement. The strike and its aftermath gave IG Metall an impetus to start the new decade with renewed vigor and added élan.

The year 1980 began in a promising manner for IG Metall. As Hans Janssen, the executive committee member in charge of collective bargaining, stated, the union "was finally freed from bonds which it had to impose on itself" since 1964.[304] The new arbitration agreement, mandated by the union's Düsseldorf congress of September 1977, finally became reality at the beginning of 1980. Thus ended an episode which began during the aftermath of the Schleswig-Holstein strike in 1957.

The new arbitration agreement represented a substantial improvement for the union. As stipulated by the Düsseldorf congress, arbitration could not be initiated unilaterally but had to be the decision of both parties. Also, instead of having a pair of permanent arbitrators who would alternate yearly, the new agreement called for an ad-hoc approach in which the arbitrator was to be determined in each individual case. Lastly, the requirement to maintain industrial peace during the arbitration process itself was to be abolished.[305] (See above for a more detailed discussion of this agreement.)

IG Metall profitted from this new agreement since its terms fulfilled many of the rank and file's wishes as articulated at the Düsseldorf congress. Specifically, it included the stipulation that four weeks before the expiration of a contract the union's demands had to be presented to the employers. Two weeks later the first round of negotiations would begin. Four weeks after the expiration of the old contract, the union was free to initiate strike procedures. Thus, following a six-week period – from the presentation of new demands to 30 days after the expiration of the old contract – IG Metall had the complete legal freedom to implement its "new maneuverability." There was a built-in incentive for the employers to come to terms during this six-week period.

The 1980 contract negotiations were short and devoid of major controversies. Perhaps in reaction to the discord of the two previous years, the employers and the union aimed for a speedy conclusion of what turned out to be a completely quantitative bargaining round. Disagreement occurred over the so-called social component issue in which the union sought a contract favoring workers in the lower wage categories. With the employers partly willing to concede on this matter, the 1980 contract negotiations ended uneventfully.

The 1981 round, however, witnessed a more complicated scenario. While the negotiations lacked the drama characterizing those of the late 1970s, IG Metall tested for the first time the new arbitration agreement by staging small but frequent work stoppages on a national scale. Just like in the previous year, IG Metall conducted a purely quantitative bargaining round with the foremost aim being an increase in real wages.[306] With the economic crisis returning after a brief respite in 1979, IG Metall believed that the improvement of its membership's living standards was of paramount importance. The union's explicit demand that the contract at least compensate every worker for losses incurred by inflation presaged a collision course with the employers, who sought a wage freeze or "productivity-oriented wage policy" which would grant pay increases to labor only in the amount of the expected growth in productivity for the coming year.[307]

The two sides remained hopelessly deadlocked throughout January and February. In early March, IG Metall began implementing its policy of increased maneuverability. Similar to a hit-and-run action in a military campaign, the battle plan adopted by the union consisted of warning strikes and demonstrations throughout West Germany lasting well into April. Approximately 1.6 million IG Metall members from virtually every union local were involved in some sort of strike activity during the spring of 1981.[308] On April 29, the union and the employers reached a sudden and unexpected agreement in the Stuttgart district. Initially applicable only in the bargaining area of NW/NB, the contract's terms were subsequently adopted with few variations by the union's other areas as well.

During the 1981 bargaining round, the success of new maneuverability demonstrated to the union leadership the mobilizing capacities of this tactical innovation. First, the united and centralized employers front experienced a rare but vehement discord which led to a temporary split between the "doves" from the Stuttgart district and the "hawks" from Hesse and NRW.[309] The piecemeal but steady nature of IG Metall's industrial actions made a unified and concerted response by the employers more difficult. Second, new maneuverability's wide-scale implementation raised the collective consciousness of many IG Metall members. This wage round gave many workers for the first time in their lives a real sense of what it meant to belong to a union and what the process of collective bargaining entailed in daily practice. IG Metall's new maneuverability provided numerous union members outside of NW/NB with a clarification of their relationship to the organization. Even if they produced no other tangible gains, this strategy and the attendant large-scale demonstrations helped solidify a much-needed common bond in a period of increasing uncertainty.

Ultimately, new maneuverability's consciousness-raising dimension led to a rapprochement between the union's leadership and the rank and file, a relationship which had suffered many setbacks in the course of the late 1970s, especially during the steel strike. New maneuverability did not allay all tensions between IG Metall's leadership and its base – and it could not alleviate all intra-organizational rivalries – but it helped to provide West Germany's leading union with a sense of renewed purpose. Both of these psychological factors were significant as the union looked towards a future which would certainly witness more difficult battles with the employers over issues like work-time reduction, humanization of work, rationalization and automation. The introduction of new maneuverability in the 1981 bargaining round could hardly solve IG Metall's problems in the political arena or the labor market, but it left positive impressions on virtually every constituency of this giant union.

# 5 FROM ACTIVISM TO ACCOMMODATION: THE DERADICALIZATION OF THE CHEMICAL WORKERS' UNION, IG CHEMIE-PAPIER-KERAMIK

## INTRODUCTION

Several DGB unions underwent a process of "politicization" during the economic crisis of the mid-1970s. In the case of IG Druck und Papier this development assumed a leftward slant with the more radical elements of the union coming to the fore, while for IG Chemie an opposite trajectory prevailed. In the course of the decade, IG Chemie joined IG Bau-Steine-Erden and IG Bergbau und Energie as a major representative of the West German labor movement's right wing (which we have chosen to call "accommodationist"). What explains this substantial shift in political outlook and direction? What were its organizational origins?

To answer these questions about IG Chemie, the analytic and historical focus of this chapter will concentrate on the union's organizational development and representational dimensions. In the section on IG Metall, heavy emphasis was placed on the union's collective bargaining history, highlighting the strikes which played such a crucial role in the development of that union and the West German labor movement as a whole. In the analysis of IG Chemie, the stress will be placed on organizational issues concerning the union's presence on the shop floor and its implications for intra-union politics. In many ways, the most salient feature of this union has been its internal fragmentation. The division between leftists and rightists and between activists and accommodationists dates back to the early 1950s.

## I. THE CHEMICAL INDUSTRY AND ITS EMPLOYERS' ASSOCIATION

Although the chemical industry was a relative latecomer to the industrialization processes of all Western economies, it quickly made up for lost time. The German chemical industry developed much more rapidly than its competitors in other countries – e.g. Great Britain, the United States and France. The industry also distinguished itself by its export orientation, high propensity toward automation and rapid centralization into larger units of production. These characteristics continued into the Weimar Republic, culminating in the creation of the notorious conglomerate IG Farben in 1925, which was to become the world's dominant chemical concern until its breakup by the Allies after World War II. Centralization, capital-intensive production, automation and export-orientation all required heavy investment and an emphasis on research and development, both trademarks of the industry to this day.[1]

Today, the industries organized by IG Chemie make up a key sector of the West German economy, and include, in addition to the chemical industry proper, the oil-refining, paper-production, rubber-processing, ceramics, glass and plastics industries. Taken together, these industries employed 1,086,000 workers (15% of the total for West German manufacturing) and sold products worth about DM 311 billion (25%) in 1981.[2] The large disparity betwen these two percentages results from the extremely high productivity of many of the industries within IG Chemie's organizational purview, especially oil refining, chemicals and paper production.[3] The central importance of IG Chemie and IG Metall to the economy is underscored by the fact that the industries whose workers they represent account for three-quarters of all employees in West German manufacturing.[4]

The chemical industry with its 565,000 workers and sales of DM 138 billion (1981) is by far the largest of the sectors for which IG Chemie is responsible.[5] Although the machinery, electrical equipment and motor-vehicle industries all employ more people, the chemical industry – thanks to its higher productivity – surpassed all of them in total sales in 1981, making it West Germany's second most important manufacturing industry after food processing according to this criterion.[6] With an export quota of 39.7% (almost the same as that of metal processing), chemicals was also a significant foreign exchange earner.[7]

The industry's major products can be divided into three broad groups: industrial chemicals (25.8% of total chemical production in 1976), intermediate chemical products (47.8%), and chemical consumer goods (26.4%).[8] Industrial chemicals include hydrogen, oxygen, chlorine, sulfuric acid and other standard chemicals as well as organic chemicals like ethylene, propylene and acetylene out of which other chemical products are made. Most of these products – such as fertilizer, plastics and synthetic fibers and rubber – can be found in the second group (intermediate products) along with paint and dye. Finally, the category of chemical consumer goods covers pharmaceuticals, personal hygiene products, soap and detergents, and photographic chemicals.[9] Of all these product groups, the most significant in terms of employment and sales are organic chemicals, pharmaceuticals and synthetic rubber, a substance invented by German chemists.[10]

The chemical industry in Germany has always been dominated by three huge multinational firms: Bayer, Hoechst and BASF. In 1925, these three companies joined together to form the IG Farben trust, the world's largest chemical company. Although the trust was split up after 1945 (see below), the "Big Three" still play a crucial role in both the West German and world chemical markets. The chemical industry is not as concentrated, however, as the attention paid to these three firms would imply. Together they account for just over 25% of total employment and sales in the industry, which places chemicals in eleventh place in terms of overall concentration behind such industries as motor vehicles and electrical equipment.[11]

Large-scale chemical production is located almost entirely in four areas: the Rhine-Ruhr, the Rhine-Main, the Rhine-Neckar and Southeastern Bavaria.[12] The Rhine-Ruhr, which stretches northward from Cologne along the Rhine and then eastward along the Ruhr, is the home of Bayer's two main production facilities in Leverkusen (near Cologne) and Uerdingen (near Krefeld). The Rhine-Main area, centering on Frankfurt, is the headquarters of Hoechst, while BASF is situated in the Rhine-Neckar region around Ludwigshafen. A number of smaller companies use the hydroelectric power abundant in southeastern Bavaria along the Inn River to produce chemical products through electrolysis.[13]

The nature of the chemical production process, with its heavy emphasis on automation, monitoring, and research and development, largely determines the makeup of the industry's workforce. Because production often must take place in very large facilities, it is not surprising that almost two-thirds of all chemical employees work in plants with over 1,000 workers, a figure well above the industrial average of 40%.[14] Also the percentage of white-collar employees is much higher (43%) and that of blue-collar workers much lower (57%) than is usual for West German industry (28% and 72% respectively).[15] Of the white-collar employees, 45% are classified as "technical" as opposed to "clerical and administrative," also an unusually high number.[16]

The composition of the blue-collar labor force exhibits several significant peculiarities. In chemicals, the un- and semi-skilled outnumber skilled workers by 66% to 34% (industrial average: 60% to 40%).[17] The reason behind this is that many of the more complex tasks performed by skilled workers are carried out in the chemical industry by white-collar technicians, while many other jobs like monitoring and packaging can be done by semi- or unskilled workers.[18] Even these simple tasks, however, often require a certain level of linguistic competence in order to follow detailed safety regulations, and this helps explain the below-average presence of foreign workers within the industry. In summary, the structure of the workforce in the chemical industry looks markedly different from that in metal processing and many other industries, where skilled, male, German workers, the traditional core of organized labor, predominate. IG Chemie has thus been faced with the difficult assignment of finding common ground between academically trained technicians and the unskilled, and its difficulties in doing so have plagued the union throughout its history, as we shall see.

The employers' association which organizes firms of the chemical industry is the Arbeitsring der Arbeitgeberverbände der deutschen chemischen Industrie (Consortium of Employers' Associations of the German Chemical Industry – "Arbeitsring").[19] The Arbeitsring covers the same industrial sectors for which IG Chemie is responsible. It is among the most powerful employers' associations in the Federal Republic, since the organizational level among chemical industry employers is estimated at 99%.[20]

Formally, the Arbeitsring functions only as a confederation of the twelve regional employers' associations, which are legally independent. Because of the regional distribution of the chemical industry in West Germany, several regional employers' associations are much more important than others. The three associations which contain Hoechst, Bayer and BASF (Hesse, North Rhine and Rhineland-Palatinate respectively) dominate the Arbeitsring.[21] These three regions have formed a "bargaining community" (Tarifgemeinschaft) which means that they consult closely with each other and coordinate their strategies during bargaining rounds. Because the three regions normally sign contracts one month or more before the other regional employers' associations, their actions set the tone for the entire chemical industry. The independence of the other nine regional employers' associations is further restricted by the Arbeitsring's Coordination Council (Koordinierungsrat) which takes an active part in all contract negotiations. As its name implies, this body coordinates bargaining strategy throughout the chemical industry and in effect forces employers to accept wage guidelines that have previously been determined by the Arbeitsring on the national level. This council even has the power to veto extracontractual wage payments by an individual firm if it feels that they would be disruptive for the industry.[22] Thus, far from being a mere umbrella organization, the Arbeitsring is probably the most centralized employers' association in the Federal Republic, which has consistently given it a major advantage over the often poorly organized chemical workers' union.

Table 5.1  *Organizational level of IG Chemie*[25] *in selected industrial sectors*

|  | Total number of unionized persons | Degree of unionization in % |
| --- | --- | --- |
| chemicals | 295,852 | 47.4 |
| plastics | 27,909 | 44.4 |
| rubber | 55,673 | 67.0 |
| paper | 45,152 | 69.3 |
| glass | 49,125 | 69.8 |
| ceramics | 34,005 | 62.1 |
| fireproof materials | 9,181 | 64.4 |

*Source:* IG Chemie-Papier-Keramik, *Geschäftsbericht 1976 bis 1979* (Hanover: IG Chemie, 1980), pp. 2748.

## II.  IG CHEMIE-PAPIER-KERAMIK

### A. *The sociology of IG Chemie's membership*

With its 657,920 members, IG Chemie-Papier-Keramik is the third-largest DGB union following IG Metall and ÖTV.[23] Founded in Hanover on October 14, 1948, six months before the Federal Republic was officially constituted, this union accounts for approximately 9% of the DGB's total membership.[24]

Table 5.1 illustrates the chemical industry's unquestioned organizational dominance with IG Chemie. It also conveys one of the major problems for the union, a fact which will repeatedly appear in this chapter as IG Chemie's Achilles heel: the union's organizational weakness in its most important industrial sector. This fact has posed the most serious structural impediment to the development of IG Chemie's political power and its bargaining strength.

The overall degree of unionization within IG Chemie hovered around 50% for much of the 1960s and 1970s. In 1975, it reached a level of 54.0% but it slipped slightly to 53.8% by 1979.[26] This level places the density of IG Chemie's unionization well above the DGB's 35%, though not above that of some of the DGB's other major unions, notably IG Metall and IG Bergbau und Energie.

As in the case of the other three industrial unions considered in this study, a sociological breakdown of the membership yields an overrepresentation of male, blue-collar workers at one end of the spectrum and a disproportionately small percentage of female, white-collar workers at the other. Sixty-nine percent of all blue-collar workers in the industries belonging to IG Chemie's organizational domain were unionized in 1979.[27] In stark contrast, only 26.7% of the white-collar clerical employees working in industries belonging to IG Chemie's jurisdiction were members of the union. Given the crucial role played by white-collar workers in the chemical industry, IG Chemie's lack of success in organizing this group has seriously weakened the union.[28]

Nearly 30% of all workers in the Federal Republic's chemical industry work for the Big Three: BASF, Bayer and Hoechst. At these multinational giants – until DuPont's acquisition of Conoco, the three largest chemical companies in the world – the union's presence has been consistently inadequate (for Hoechst and Bayer it actually deteriorated during the 1970s). According to 1977 data, 34.4% of all Hoechst workers were members of IG Chemie, compared to 37.4% at Bayer and 66% at BASF.[29] Disaggregated by blue- and white-collar employees, the figures for Hoechst were 49.8% blue-collar and 14.9% white-collar workers, with the corresponding numbers being 54.5% and 21.8% at Bayer and 82.6% and 43.9% at BASF.[30] If one had to point to a single factor which has caused the most trouble for IG Chemie throughout its post-war history, it would undoubtedly be the union's failure to gain a firmer foothold in two of the three major companies forming what is called "Grosschemie," the big chemical industry.

There is another important area of fragmentation within IG Chemie. The overall category called Angestellte (white-collar employees) has been divided into five distinct sub-groups, each of which represents an official constituency within the union and which at one time or another concluded its own collective bargaining contract with the employers. Of the 434,744 white-collar workers in IG Chemie's organizational domain as of October 1979, 119,810 were unionized (27%).[31] They belonged to the following official categories: foremen, 22,781; technical personnel and non-university-trained engineers, 25,714; chemical and laboratory personnel, 17,273; office clerks, 47,572; and university graduates and post-secondary-degree holders, 6,470.[32] Thus, the union's high concentration of Angestellte has contributed to an internal split which perpetuated a "white-collar mentality" (Angestelltenmentalität), and has hindered IG Chemie's potential for mobilization and intra-union solidarity.

The "white-collar" problem assumed even more acute proportions in the union's most important organizational sector, the chemical industry, and especially at the Big Three multinationals. In entire sections of these firms – especially at Hoechst and Bayer – white-collar employees have to this day remained virtually untouched by the union. Unionization is especially low among clerical, white-collar employees, professionals and para-professionals, a majority of whom are hostile to any attempts by IG Chemie to have them join the organization.

Given these "sociological" difficulties – which derive from production-related, historical and structural factors connected to the evolution of the German chemical industry – IG Chemie has had to devise organizational responses to ensure the union's cohesion, provide an effective shop-floor presence and guarantee a functioning framework for collective bargaining. To this end, IG Chemie has tried to reconcile a high degree of centralization in its decision-making structure with at least a nominal commitment to grassroots democracy. This tension has caused serious intra-organizational debates and political disagreements, including perhaps the most severe intra-union battle within any of the DGB's major industrial unions. At issue was the response to a major question: what organizational structure should IG Chemie adopt as the most expedient *and* democratic during a period of crisis in which the sociological arrangements mentioned above would inevitably cause the union and its members serious problems? This battle – and its ultimate resolution – will be discussed in detail below.

## B. The internal organization of IG Chemie

As with all other unions analyzed in this study, the union congress represents the highest constitutive organ for IG Chemie. Until 1954 congresses were held biannually, while between 1957 (IG Chemie's fourth congress) and 1972 (the ninth congress), they were convened on a triannual basis. As of 1972, congresses have been held every four years; thus, the tenth congress occurred in the fall of 1976 with the eleventh convening exactly four years later in the fall of 1980. The union's executive committee in consultation with the advisory council (Beirat) determines the date, duration and location of each congress. The final decision has to be communicated to every union member at least four months prior to the event.

Delegates are elected in the locals and each delegate represents 1,500 members, but locals with fewer than that are still assured one representative. In the event that the total number of votes in each local is not an exact multiple of 1,500 – and this is virtually always the case – remaining votes from each local are then pooled together and compiled on the union's next highest administrative level, the district. In the union's eight districts, congress delegates are determined in district delegate conferences (Bezirksdelegiertenkonferenz) which give special weights to the traditionally weaker groups in the union such as youth, women and white-collar employees. Each union congress has to be attended by the complete executive committee, all eight district leaders, the chairmen of the national committees for white-collar employees, women and youth, and the chairmen of the national committees for each of the union's industrial groups such as the chemical industry, rubber, paper, plastics and glass.[33]

The congress's main tasks and responsibilities are:
1. to set the overall framework and specific guidelines for the union's activities during the ensuing four-year period;
2. to amend the union's bylaws and statutes;
3. to rule on the hundreds of official demands placed before the congress delegates by various constituencies within the union;
4. to examine the union's financial situation and hear reports from the committees on their activities during the completed legislative period;
5. to dismiss the old executive committee;
6. to elect a new executive committee; and
7. to elect new working committees for the ensuing legislative period.

The congress itself can only exercise its legislative powers with more than half of the delegates present. All decisions are reached by simple majority vote as long as the guidelines do not stipulate a different mode of approval, such as a two-thirds majority vote in the case of certain amendments to the union's bylaws. A deadlock in any voting procedure amounts to a rejection of the issue at hand.

The union's bylaws also provide for the possibility of conducting so-called extraordinary congresses in case of emergency or the necessity to discuss topics of particular importance and urgency for the organization as a whole. One-third of IG Chemie's membership has to request such a congress for it to convene. This demand has to be at both the local and district levels. District leaders have to attend these meetings. The executive committee then has six weeks to convene an extraordinary congress after having obtained the approval of the plenum. The delegates to this special congress are the same as those at the preceding ordinary congress.[34] The tasks of an extraordinary congress include debating the special issues which led to its convening, listening to the executive committee's report on these issues and coming up with suggestions that address the grievances. Only one such extraordinary congress has occurred in IG Chemie's history. It was held on October 30 and 31, 1967 in Hanover, the seat of the union's headquarters. As will be discussed below, the convening of another extraordinary congress was only narrowly averted in the dramatic year of 1979.

In order to counter the lengthy, four-year hiatus between union congresses, IG Chemie's bylaws provide for a so-called Federal Working Congress (Bundesarbeitstagung) to be held every two years between congresses. In sharp contrast to the politicized and election-dominated regular congresses, these gatherings – which include participants from the previous congress – are designed to serve as a forum for debate on pressing issues, without the political ramifications accompanying regular congresses. The executive committee convenes these "working congresses" to discuss new strategies, gauge the membership's reaction to the latest course of events, and enhance the rapport between the union's leadership and its rank and file.

The executive committee, the union's supreme executive organ, is charged with implementing the resolutions passed at the union congresses. The executive committee consists of eight full-time, union-paid members (the Hauptamtliche) and usually nineteen part-time members who – by IG Chemie's statute – have to be employed elsewhere. This latter group (the Ehrenamtliche) consists of active, but non-professional, unionists who perform their non-paid duties strictly as a sevice to the union. The former group consists of the committee's chairman – in effect the union's main functionary and primary political figure – two vice chairmen, the treasurer and four other members, each in charge of specific responsibilities within the organization.[35] For example, one committee member is in charge of collective bargaining issues while others are responsible for co-determination and works constitution, shop stewards, white-collar employees, youth and vocational education, and women. The chairman's organizational concerns include international relations, economic policy, media and public relations, and the overall supervision of IG Chemie's activities in the numerous industrial sectors it organizes.

The union congress elects each member of the executive committee via a simple majority in a secret ballot. In case no candidate obtains the necessary majority on the first ballot, a plurality suffices on the second. The executive committee not only determines the union's overall policies and course of action, but it exercises an additional degree of organizational authority by appointing all district secretaries and other important union personnel on the local level. As in IG Metall, IG Chemie's eight district secretaries and employees are appointed by the executive committee in Hanover and are thus not elected by the union's rank and file in the respective districts. As a consequence, most of the district secretaries seek to please the executive committee, their only official source of legitimation, rather than the regular union members.

IG Chemie's geographic organization consists of eight districts which, unlike IG Metall's, correspond with some degree of accuracy to the states (Länder) of the Federal Republic.[36] (See figure 3.) These districts range in size from the 137,822 IG Chemie members in the largest, North Rhine, to the 50,853 in the smallest, Nordmark-Berlin, according to data from September 30, 1979.[37] While NRW and NW/NB have been IG Metall's most important collective bargaining areas, the three districts where BASF, Hoechst and Bayer have their corporate headquarters and major production facilities have played the leading roles in IG Chemie's

*Figure 3.* IG Chemie regional districts.
*Source:* Hanover, IG Chemie-Papier-Keramik.

*Figure 4.* IG Chemie bargaining areas for the chemical industry.
*Source:* Hanover, IG Chemie-Papier-Keramik.

collective bargaining and internal union politics. Among IG Chemie's twelve bargaining areas covering the chemical industry (see figure 4), by far the three most important are North Rhine (Bayer, with facilities in Leverkusen and Uerdingen), Hesse (Hoechst, with facilities in and around Frankfurt) and Rhineland-Palatinate (BASF with facilities in Ludwigshafen). By having contracts expire one month earlier in these three areas than in the rest of IG Chemie's organizational domain, the union acknowledges the special position assumed by the Big Three in the collective bargaining process. This arrangement renders these three bargaining areas IG Chemie's "vanguard" areas whose settlements usually are transferred to the rest of the chemical industry.[38] Negotiation rounds in each of these areas are attended by union representatives from the other two in order to facilitate coordination among them.[39]

Paradoxically, IG Chemie's three most important organizational districts have comprised the union's weakest bargaining areas, whereas its strongest regions are those where BASF, Hoechst and Bayer have the smallest presence. In contrast to IG Metall, where the "vanguard" area for collective bargaining agreements has usually corresponded to one of the union's most powerful districts, in IG Chemie's case the union has regularly suffered from the considerable disadvantage of having the opposite situation determine its overall bargaining position in the chemical industry.

Between the eight districts and the factories themselves lies one intermediate organizational layer: the union locals. Often described as the backbone of all union activities and the main locus of IG Chemie's organizational power, these 67 units form the most important link between the union and its members on the shop floor. As in the case of the eight districts, the sizes of these locals vary considerably. While one local has more than 40,000 members and another one has in excess of 30,000, two locals comprise fewer than 3,000 members according to data presented to the union's eleventh congress in Mannheim in September 1980. The same report also shows that most locals – fourteen – have between 10,000 and 15,000 members with the next highest frequency being ten locals with between 6,000 and 7,000 members followed by nine locals comprising 7,000 to 8,000 unionists. Whereas some locals have in excess of 70 plants – the Cologne local leads with 90 – other locals, such as Leverkusen and Ludwigshafen, contain as few as eleven plants (which, in the case of these two specific locals, include the two giants, Bayer [Leverkusen] and BASF [Ludwigshafen]).[40]

The executive committee determines the size of the locals and their number. Thus, for example, in 1979 there were 67 locals, down from 70 in 1972–3.[41] According to IG Chemie's statutes, the criteria guiding the executive committee's decisions on the formation of union locals are their "economic and organizational feasibility."[42] One of the basic tenets in setting the boundaries of individual locals pertains to the cohesion of the local economy. IG Chemie's statutes mandate that the executive committee do everything in its power to establish only one local in areas with a relatively homogeneous structure of production.

In sharp contrast to all other DGB unions – especialy IG Metall – IG Chemie's shop stewards constitute the most important means of rank-and-file representation within the organization. The union's bylaws state explicitly that:

> shop stewards are to be elected in every plant. They are to participate in the policy-making process of the union. Shop stewards form the "Vertrauens-leutekörper" [shop stewards' committee] in the plants and have to elect a "Vertrauenskörper" leadership. Rights and duties of the Vertrauenskörper and of its leadership are determined by the guidelines set out by the executive committee for the union's shop stewards. In fulfilling their tasks, the union's shop stewards enjoy the protection of the entire organization.[43]

This passage is all the more significant because it appears under the heading "Scope and Framework [of the locals]" in IG Chemie's bylaws. Clearly, the union sees a direct connection between the role of its shop-stewards and Vertrauenskörper on the one hand and the functioning of its most important organizational unit, the local, on the other.

Unique among all DGB unions, IG Chemie establishes an organizational link between its shop stewards and the union's legislative and delegating bodies, the delegates' councils, which include the elected union representatives in an IG Chemie local. Whereas in most other DGB unions the rank and file elects the members of the delegate councils on the level of the union locals, in IG Chemie's case this task remains the prerogative of the shop stewards.[44]

IG Chemie members vote for shop stewards in shop-steward elections held one year prior to a union congress. (Thus, since 1972, shop-steward elections occur on a quadrennial basis.) These shop stewards, in turn, elect the local delegate council. Every delegate council then votes not only for its own leadership but also participates in elections for representatives to the district council. Finally, and perhaps most significantly, the delegate councils on the union's local level determine who will represent them at the union's all-important congress. Therefore, the composition of the union's congress, its plenum and ultimately its key committees (whose members are elected by the congress) originate with the shop stewards at the plant level and in the locals.

Given this structure of articulation and legitimation, it is quite clear why the existence of "plant-appointed" shop stewards (i.e. shop stewards not elected exclusively by union members) has always been such a bone of contention in IG Chemie's history. The presence of these "plant-appointed", sometimes even non-unionized, shop stewards in 42 of the most important chemical plants within the union's organizational domain has meant that non-unionized chemical workers have exerted a direct influence upon some of the most crucial decision-making bodies in IG Chemie. In 1979, this situation received official union approval via a statutory upgrading of these "plant-appointed" shop stewards in IG Chemie's bylaws. This resulted in the most acerbic and vociferous intra-union conflict in the history of IG Chemie, as will be discussed below.

### C. IG Chemie's bargaining procedures

The last item to be presented in this section concerns the organization of and main institutional participants in IG Chemie's collective bargaining system. Just as in the case of IG Metall, forces of centralization and decentralization exist side by side, sometimes complementing each other, at other times working at cross-purposes. It would be fair to say that in recent years – especially since the mobilization period of the first half of the 1970s and the economic crisis during the latter part of that decade – the centralizing tendencies have come to the fore. Critics within the union feel that this has often occurred at the direct cost of rank-and-file participation and ultimately union democracy.

Unlike IG Metall, where all types of contracts are concluded by the individual bargaining areas, general framework contracts between IG Chemie and the chemical employers have always been signed on a centralized, federal level. Thus, IG Chemie's general framework contracts are negotiated and finalized by the union's executive committee in Hanover and cover the entire chemical industry of the Federal Republic. The wage and salary contracts, on the other hand, are negotiated and concluded on the district level with each of the eight districts having full automony over this process, at least nominally. In practice, quite a bit of intra-district coordination occurs under the guidance of the union's headquarters in Hanover. Moreover, as in the case of IG Metall, IG Chemie also has its vanguard areas which were mentioned above. As a rule, wage and salary contracts for blue- and white-collar workers are signed in one common document.[45]

The most important institutional participants in IG Chemie's collective bargaining process are the executive committee with its special collective bargaining division, the district leaders, the bargaining commissioners, the small negotiating teams engaged in the actual negotiation process and the leader of the negotiation. The executive committee bears responsibility for the conduct of collective bargaining according to the union's statutes. Among its tasks are the coordination of collective bargaining, the issuing of directives, inspection of the terms of already concluded contracts, suggestions for future improvements in the terms of contracts, the conduct of direct negotiations in the case of general framework contracts and representation of the union in arbitration efforts on the federal level. The collective bargaining division of the executive committee is also empowered to enforce all measures of coordination between headquarters and the eight districts in case the executive committee or one of the participating districts deems such actions necessary.[46]

IG Chemie's eight district leaders have an ambiguous position in the process of collective bargaining, like their counterparts in IG Metall. While both the union's statutes and its "guidelines for collective bargaining" make it quite explicit that the district secretaries are employees of the executive committee, both documents also empower these individuals to conclude contracts on their own initiative, determine wage and salary terms and conduct strikes if necessary.[47] Above all, district leaders act as the liaison between the union's top leadership (the executive committee) on the one hand and the district bargaining commissions on the other.

Bargaining commissions are formed according to geographic and industry-specific criteria which constitute the bases of the various contracts. Hence, for the chemical industry there are two types of bargaining commissions: a centrally organized, federal body which is in charge of the general framework contracts, and eight regional commissions that conduct each district's wage and salary negotiations. Until 1971, members of the bargaining commissions were appointed by their locals. Since the 1972 union congress, shop-steward caucuses elect the members of the bargaining commissions who are then approved by the leadership councils of the respective locals. Both professional and non-professional members of the union can be elected to bargaining commissions with the important proviso that the latter maintain a majority at all times.[48] The size of each bargaining commission depends on the size and importance of the particular bargaining area. The head of the commission, the district secretary, leads all the negotiations, although he/she is only an ex-officio member of the commission with a right to speak but not to vote. It is customary to have the leader of the most important local of the district – according to economic criteria – on the commission. Thus the union's rules favor the active participation of locals in the collective bargaining process.

Three sociological and structural characteristics of the bargaining commissions' non-professional members highlight some general trends in the Federal Republic's organized labor movement:[49]

(1) The vast majority of these members are works councilors, usually

from large factories and important firms. Within this set of works councilors the sub-set of works council chairmen is overrepresented.

(2) Although IG Chemie's guidelines for collective bargaining include
an explicit proviso that special considerations be given to women and
youth in the election of commission members, middle-aged men are
overrepresented on most bargaining commissions.

(3) On bargaining commissions with a double mandate for mixed
membership of blue- and white-collar workers, the latter predominate,
once again demonstrating the fact that members of "higher" strata tend to
participate more actively in the political process than their colleagues in
"lower" ones.

In contrast to IG Metall, IG Chemie's bargaining commissions enjoy
full autonomy in making decisions concerning the cancellation of collective
bargaining contracts, the conduct of negotiations and the conclusion of
new agreements. The bargaining commissions' autonomy is structurally
circumscribed, however, by the district leaders' dual role, since they are
empowered to suspend the decisions of the commissions and submit them
to the executive committee for approval.[50]

A negotiating team of five to seven members selected from the larger
bargaining commission conducts the actual face-to-face negotiations. In
the more advanced stages of the negotiating process, this number is
reduced to three. In both groups, the union's position is represented by the
district leader, who is in charge of directing the entire bargaining process.
An experienced member of the bargaining commission who usually comes
from the largest plant in the bargaining area assists the district leader
during the negotiations.[51]

The reality of each bargaining round is a good deal more complex and
confusing than indicated by the union's bylaws and its guidelines for
collective bargaining. The following represents a "typical" bargaining
round conducted by IG Chemie during the 1970s. A few months before the
expiration of the annual wage and salary contracts, the bargaining division
of the executive committee summons all district leaders to Hanover for an
informal discussion of the current situation and the upcoming negotiations
with the employers. At this meeting, certain "coordination guidelines" are
delineated pertaining to such matters as minimum settlement and
maximum demand, the general emphasis of the campaign and tactical
considerations. Armed with coordination guidelines, the district leaders
return to their respective districts and begin the long, often arduous,
process of "selling" this package to the various union notables. It is
incumbent upon the district secretary to defend the union's guidelines in
light of the economic situation in general and that of the chemical industry
in particular, the political climate, IG Chemie's position in the labor

market, and the anticipated reactions of the employers. In presenting his/her case to the bargaining commission, the district secretary can avail himself/herself of a coterie of experts, usually staff members of the executive committee in Hanover or researchers from the DGB's "brain trust," the Wirtschafts- und Sozialwissenschaftliches Institut (WSI).

The district secretary's presentation is followed by an intense discussion of the proposals in the district's locals, on the shop floor of factories and among the members of the bargaining commission. Once each district has reached a conclusion on its demands, inter-district meetings take place in order to coordinate the bargaining round on a strategic and tactical level. In these gatherings, the list of demands is finalized, with the result that all eight districts issue virtually identical demands. Timing and other important matters, such as which district will assume the vanguard role, are also decided among the eight districts at this time. Then the contract negotiations with the employers begin in earnest.

The actual conduct of bargaining rounds seems very ritualized to most West German citizens, including IG Chemie members. Typically, each round begins with a bang as the union accuses the employers of behaving irresponsibly and of committing all sorts of "provocations," and ends with a whimper as IG Chemie follows closely the terms laid down by the DGB's standardbearer, IG Metall.

For many workers, however, especially in the all-important Big Three, the "real" bargaining rounds do not start until the signatures on the new contracts between IG Chemie and the employers' association have already dried. Using the terms of the official contract as a starting point, works councilors begin the so-called second bargaining round in which they try to secure better terms for the workers in their own plants. While such factory-based syndicalism is quite usual in most industrial countries and is fostered by the dual form of labor representation in the Federal Republic, it has assumed greater importance in the chemical industry's Big Three, where IG Chemie has consistently suffered from poor organizational penetration, thus ceding power to the fiefdoms of the works council "princes" or "barons" (known in German as "Betriebsratsfürsten"). This is not to say that IG Chemie's collective bargaining agreements are meaningless. They provide the basic framework and starting point for the "second bargaining round" and establish a common denominator for all the industry's workers, be they employed by large and profitable or small and less prosperous firms.

The last item in need of clarification concerning collective bargaining pertains to arbitration agreements between the employers and the union. This important mechanism (which regulates capital–labor relations after the breakdown of negotiations but before the outbreak of open conflict) is quite different from its counterpart in the metalworking industry. IG Chemie maintains a two-tiered arbitration system with the employers: one on the level of the eight districts for "regional quarrels" and one on the federal level for all other disagreements.[52] The federal tier adjudicates appeals procedures and other impasses which have not been resolved at the district level. Each arbitration board includes six members, three representing capital and three labor. The chairman rotates among these six on a case-by-case basis rather than – as in the metal industry – on an annual one. Arbitration must occur as soon as one of the two parties requests it by declaring that negotiations have failed. Once this request is made, the other party must submit to arbitration and cooperate in the process (Einlassungszwang) as was the case under IG Metall's "old" arbitration agreement of 1964. In addition, the rules stipulate a number of "cooling off" periods at various stages of the arbitration process with the clear intent of forcing both parties to reach an agreement.

What actually happens during sessions of the arbitration boards remains somewhat unclear since they are closed to the public, although minutes are kept for each meeting. In pleading its case, each party is allowed the assistance of outside experts and aides. Simple majority votes decide key issues, although most of the time decisions are reached by a unanimous 6–0 vote. Occasionally, however, one member of the labor side will vote with capital's representatives, yielding a 4 to 2 majority in the latter's favor. This was the case in 1977, for example, when in the course of the arbitration process in the district of North Rhine, IG Chemie's delegate from the executive committee – indeed the head of the committee's section responsible for collective bargaining – voted with the employer representatives and against his two colleagues from the union's North Rhine bargaining area.[53] In the case of a repeated deadlock, arbitration is declared a failure and both parties are free to pursue their preparations for industrial action. If this failure occurs in the context of wage and salary bargaining (i.e. on the district level), however, the process moves automatically to the federal tier, where the same procedure is replicated. Only if this second attempt results in a stalemate are both parties entitled to proceed with a strike or lockout. If the six-member arbitration boards reach an agreement – as they almost invariably do – their terms become final and binding for both parties.[54]

IG Chemie has a very different strike procedure from most DGB unions, most notably IG Metall. Unlike the latter's statutes, IG Chemie's bylaws do not stipulate that a strike vote be held prior to or following a strike. Rather, the executive committee determines all aspects of the union's strike activities, including the timing, scope and location.[55] The IG Chemie leadership can, but does not have to, take the DGB's 75% approval rule into consideration in the preparation of a strike and/or in the ratification of a new contract. The executive committee also determines unilaterally when and under what circumstances a strike should end.[56] In IG Metall's case the district secretaries and above all the bargaining commission are given considerable input and even decision-making power over the union's strike activities. In IG Chemie's situation the executive committee holds a monopoly of authority. In terms of IG Chemie's strike behavior, centralizing tendencies in the union have unquestionably prevailed in the post-World War II period.

## III. IG CHEMIE'S FORERUNNER: THE GERMAN FACTORY WORKERS' CONFEDERATION

A chemical workers' union per se did not exist in pre-1933 Germany. The labor force of this industry was organized in the Verband der Fabrikarbeiter Deutschlands (German Factory Workers' Confederation – VFD) which drew its membership from many other sectors of the economy as well. The history of this union is worthy of a brief examination not only because of its influence on IG Chemie, but also because it occupied a unique place in the early German labor movement as the first organization created by and for unskilled workers.[57]

Before the 1870s, Germany's industrial workforce was dominated by the skilled craftsmen of the metalworking, printing, building and woodworking trades. After unification in 1871, however, a number of new industries appeared requiring production in large, heavily mechanized factories using unskilled labor. These included the nascent chemical industry, which initially produced mainly dyes for the textile industry, as well as the rubber, paper and food-processing (canning) industries. Because none of the traditional trades were represented, the established craft unions at first showed little interest – and sometimes active hostility – towards the factory workers in these sectors. The idea soon arose of combining all unskilled workers – whether in factories, construction or agriculture – into a single union of their own. Thus in 1876 the Verband der Bau-, Fabrik-, Land-, und Handarbeiter (Confederation of Construction, Factory, Agricultural and Manual Workers) was formed as part of the new, united social democratic trade-union movement.

This organization remained small and weak, partly because of the difficulties associated with unionizing the unskilled and partly because the new industries were still fairly small. As a result, the union was unable, in contrast to the powerful printers' and masons' associations, to survive underground after the passage of the Anti-Socialist Law in 1878.

By the end of the 1880s, however, local factory workers' organizations again began to appear in the large German cities. Their focus was mainly on the rubber, margarine, sugar-processing and chemical industries. After the Anti-Socialist Law expired in 1890, these locals joined together to form the Confederation of Factory, Agricultural and Other Industrial Skilled Workers of Germany (Verband der Fabrik-, Land-, und sonstigen gewerblichen Hilfsarbeiter Deutschlands – also called VFD). The union initially numbered 2,460 members, and this rose to 32,000 in 1900, still only a small percentage of the total workforce.[58] As in the 1870s, the unskilled workers' union had little success compared to other German labor organizations. In addition to the reasons cited above, several factors were responsible for this. After 1890, the traditional unions became increasingly interested in the unskilled. Consequently, special unskilled workers' unions were founded in printing and construction which had close ties to the established skilled organizations. Industrial unions also made their appearance in the metal, woodworking and textile industries, and these unions sought to organize both skilled and unskilled workers. In most of the industries where the VFD already had a foothold, the employers were militantly anti-socialist, and they used company unions, paternalism, blacklists and the police to bar the VFD.

Under these conditions it is hardly surprising that the union gained little through either strikes or collective bargaining until well after 1900. For the first decade and a half of its existence, the VFD's efforts centered on jurisdictional battles and boundary disputes with other social democratic unions. Threatened by industrial crypto-craft unionism (unskilled "satellites" of craft associations), the Factory Workers struggled to carve out a place for themselves in the rapidly expanding industrial labor force. After much internal discussion and mediation by the Generalkommission (the umbrella federation of SPD unions), the organizational purview of the VFD was clearly established by 1908. It included the chemical industry, rubber, paper production, margarine and vegetable-oil production, beet-sugar processing, and a number of industries known in Germany as "stones and earth," including potash, cement and brick production. The creation of a separate agricultural workers' union in 1908 by VFD members from that sector further stabilized the organization's internal composition. Nonetheless, individual plants in industries other than those listed above continued to be represented by the VFD up to 1933, so that the Wilhelminian and Weimar labor relations systems remained much closer to the American or British model of overlapping jurisdictions and intra-plant union competition than is generally believed.

In the seven years before World War I, the Factory Workers made their first gains, however modest, in the area of collective bargaining. Eighty-three contracts were signed by the union in 1907, and this number rose to

407 in 1912 and 1,223 in 1913–14.[59] This jump clearly resulted from a public atmosphere favorable to labor, and this mood also caused membership to increase substantially, from about 51,000 in 1904 to over 200,000 in 1913.[60] However, these gains in membership and recognition were very unevenly distributed. The number of contracts signed and workers enlisted in the "stones and earth" and food-processing industries increased significantly, whereas chemicals – the Big Three (BASF, Hoechst, Bayer) in particular – successfully resisted the union.[61] Only 67 contracts, covering fewer than 6,000 workers, were concluded in this key industry in 1913, none of which were with the Big Three.[62] Thus, IG Chemie's subsequent problems with these companies have firm roots in the pre-1914 period.

The aftermath of World War I in Germany brought the famous Zentralarbeitsgemeinschaft agreement in November 1918, in which the employers recognized unions as the legitimate representatives of workers and accepted them as bargaining partners. This accord especially helped organizations like the VFD that had been unable to conclude contracts for most of their members before 1914. During the 1920s, a regularized system of bargaining and contracts was set up throughout the union's organizational domain. By 1929, close to 2,000 contracts covering 1,402,567 workers were in effect.[63] Membership in the VFD also rose spectacularly to 733,000 in 1922, only to fall again because of economic decline to between 400,000 and 500,000 in the late 1920s.[64]

Despite these substantial successes, many of the Factory Workers' old problems continued into the 1920s. Political differences which had always been present within the union were greatly accentuated by the difficult economic conditions of the early 1920s. Communist organizers tried to take advantage of the VFD's traditional weakness in the big chemical plants in order to extend their influence there. The result was a bitter struggle between KPD and VFD members as well as works councilors in BASF, Bayer and Hoechst during 1920 and 1921, a battle which the union won at the cost of weakening its already tenuous position in these firms.

A second threat to the VFD was posed by the trend towards industrial unionism which swept German labor in the early 1920s. A proposal introduced at the 1922 ADGB congress in favor of industrial unionism by the head of the Metal Workers, Robert Dissmann, called for the transformation of the VFD into a chemical workers' union, which would have led to a significant reduction in the former's organizational purview. This danger was averted in 1925 when the ADGB decided to support only voluntary industrial unionism through amalgamations. Despite its opposition to the Dissmann proposal, the VFD moved steadily in the direction of a (broadly defined) industrial unionism and away from its image as the spokesman of only unskilled labor. Attempts were made to organize the growing number of skilled workers within its domain, and this domain was itself greatly expanded through amalgamations with the Wallpaper and Linoleum Workers (1919), the Porcelain and Ceramic Workers (1926) and the Glass Workers (1926).

By the time Hitler dissolved it in 1933, the VFD had been transformed into one of Germany's most important unions, and it operated in a variety of key sectors of the economy. Its position within German labor paralleled closely that of IG Chemie today. Despite the reorganizations undertaken after 1949, IG Chemie was allowed to keep most of the VFD's organizational jurisdiction, with the exception of food processing and some sectors of "stones and earth." Unfortunately, it inherited many of the Factory Workers' problems as well, among which its endemic weakness in organizing effectively within the Big Three chemical companies remains the most troublesome legacy.

## IV.  IG CHEMIE AND POST-WAR RECONSTRUCTION: 1948–1951

From its very foundation on October 14, 1948, the union had to overcome serious adversities. Barely two months after this date, IG Chemie's leader, Otto Heller, a prominent member of the German labor movement and a driving force behind the unification of the chemical unions in the three western zones, died.[65] He was succeeded by Wilhelm Gefeller, who remained at the union's helm for two decades until the eighth congress in the fall of 1969.[66] Together with Otto Brenner of IG Metall, Georg Leber of IG Bau-Steine-Erden, Wilhelm Kummernuss of ÖTV and Ludwig Rosenberg of the DGB, Gefeller continued a tradition of long-serving and charismatic leaders who shaped the character of the West German labor movement.

IG Chemie's organizational domain included industries which were tarnished because of their role in National Socialism. Among the so-called prohibited industries – as designated by the Allies – were many highly developed branches of the chemical industry such as coal-liquefaction and synthetic rubber production. Also, nitrogen and aluminum manufacturing was severely curtailed by the occupation forces. These measures had to be taken quite seriously by an organization such as IG Chemie, many of whose members earned their living by working in those areas of chemical production. The Allied plan to weaken Germany included Demontage or the dismantling of entire plants and industries that were crucial to military production or which had played a particularly heinous role in Hitler's war machine. The steel companies of the Rhine-Ruhr were one major target of the dismantling campaign; the German chemical industry, headed by the heavily implicated giant IG Farben, was another.

IG Chemie, like IG Metall and its predecessors, was compelled to react to the Allied strategy of Demontage. The union's efforts to avoid the dismantling of some of Germany's most crucial chemical production facilities included lobbying by Wilhelm Gefeller of Great Britain's foreign minister Ernest Bevin, and by others in the union's leadership of the American Federation of Labor representative in West Germany.[67] In addition to these "elite" activities, the union also engaged in mass protests for which it mobilized its rank and file and the population at large to resist the Allies' plans. It is noteworthy that the union was very sensitive to the fact that these mass protests and demonstrations could be abused quite easily by various reactionary and neo-fascist elements for their own purposes. Everything possible was done by IG Chemie to minimize the threat from extremist groups which would only have harmed the union's cause and weakened the workers' position in the plants designated for dismantling.[68]

As is well known, little if any of the initially intended dismantling occurred. The Washington agreement of April 1949 listed all the firms, plants and production systems which were to be dismantled and/or discontinued in the three Western sites, but the Petersberg agreement barely six months later (November 1949) rescinded its predecessor's provisions for Demontage.[69] Throughout 1950 and 1951 almost all production facilities were fully reinstated and the "prohibited industries" were by and large permitted to reenter the production process. Dismantling, as originally conceived by the Allies, ceased to be an issue by the end of 1951.

The onset of the Cold War clearly contributed to the Allies' decision not to carry out their original plan of Demontage, though the union's activities both on the "elite" and "mass" levels played a role as well. (Labor's contribution to this effort was duly recognized by capital at the time. In fact, numerous chemical companies sent effusive thank-you notes to the union's leadership.)[70] IG Chemie, like the West German labor movement as a whole, fully expected a reward, in the form of full-parity co-determination. For all large firms in its purview, IG Chemie sought parity co-determination along the lines of the Montan model.[71] The union saw Mitbestimmung as a means to increase economic democracy and worker participation. Since IG Metall and IG Bergbau had acquired Montanmitbestimmung as a consequence of the breakup of the Third Reich's steel and coal cartels, IG Chemie felt it should gain the same advantage from the breakup of IG Farben.

The union movement, represented by both the DGB and IG Chemie, presented its position on IG Farben's proposed breakup in a written declaration submitted to the Allied High Commission in the fall of 1950.[72] While sharing the opposition to breakup that was prevalent throughout West Germany at the time, the union document went one step further by complaining that no mention was made in the proposal of any workers' participation plan in the divestment process and in the daily affairs of IG Farben's designated successor companies.[73] The union document voiced bitter disappointment that the breakup plans failed to offer even an approximation of the Montanmitbestimmung model which had already enjoyed three years of successful implementation in the steel and coal industries of the Rhine and Ruhr areas.

IG Chemie was intent on getting a co-determination program which replicated Montanmitbestimmung for the firms in Grosschemie. This desire was one of the main reasons behind IG Chemie's unconditional support for IG Metall's and IG Bergbau's struggle to maintain Montan-mitbestimmung during the bitter offensive by the employers and the Adenauer government against labor in 1950–51.[74] However, IG Chemie's hopes for an extension of the Montan model to the major firms within its organizational domain were to be denied.

IG Farben's divestiture did not fulfill any of IG Chemie's wishes. First, the giant was indeed broken up. Second, Mitbestimmung was not extended to any of its successor companies (Bayer, BASF and Hoechst). Thus, the position of "labor director" or "personnel director," so crucial to the Montan model, has remained absent from Grosschemie to this day. Moreover, IG Chemie was offered only two of the fifteen seats on each of these companies' advisory boards, which was even fewer than the one-third guaranteed labor by the Works Constitution Law of 1952.[75] In protest over this demeaning decision, all of IG Chemie's works councilors who were asked to serve in these new positions decided to boycott their duties at the request of the union's leadership in Hanover.[76] Lastly, not until the mid-1950s were labor organizing rules – which had already been intro duced in virtually all other segments of West German industry – instituted in IG Farben's Big Three successors. This factor, perhaps more than any other, contributed to the union's weakness in collective bargaining within the Big Three in subsequent years, while at the same time strengthening the power and autonomy of the works councils.

IG Chemie's only consolation at the time was the fact that many small companies, which the union deemed unviable given the market conditions of the chemical industry, merged with larger ones, usually one of the three giants.[77] However, the beating which the union suffered in the late 1940s and early 1950s left its mark during the late 1950s in the form of the union's inability to take advantage of the coming boom in the chemical industry. It was mainly a plant-specific bargaining structure controlled by the works council "barons" that allowed many chemical workers to gain the due rewards of their labor in this period. This was to set a precedent which has continued to handicap the union until the present.

## V. THE DIFFICULT FIFTIES: 1952–1959

Nineteen fifty-two witnessed several events which increased the adversities besetting the union since the late 1940s and, in turn, helped shape developments which have continued to influence IG Chemie's organizational politics to this day. The union suffered two major setbacks which severely weakened IG Chemie vis-à-vis the employers. First, IG Chemie's final hopes for the extension of co-determination were shattered by the passage of the Works Constitution Law by the Bundestag.[78] Second, the chemical industry suffered its worst year since the war, compounding the hardships imposed by the poor showings of the late 1940s.[79]

Both of these events reinforced IG Chemie's defensive tendencies in collective bargaining. As a result, the union concluded contracts between 1952 and 1957 which yielded wage increases for chemical workers far below the national average.[80] This sub-par performance had some serious ramifications for IG Chemie's relationship with its current and potential members. First of all, the union suffered a membership decrease during this time which IG Chemie's leadership construed, perhaps correctly, as a vote of no-confidence in the union. Moreover, in this period the second wage round became institutionalized as a major bargaining mechanism in the chemical industry. It was not by chance that the inadequate collective bargaining agreements concluded by IG Chemie in this era were accompanied by a disproportionately high wage drift compared to the rest of West German industry.[81]

IG Chemie, already seriously handicapped by Allied policy concerning the three successors to IG Farben – the occupying forces had curtailed such basic union rights as collective bargaining and the right to strike – was further weakened on the shop floor following the 1952 Works Constitution Law. Labor's plant-level activities became the de jure and de facto prerogatives of the works councilors who also orchestrated all the second wage rounds. By the mid-1950s, many works councilors became in effect the sole representatives of chemical workers in numerous plants, notably at Bayer, BASF and Hoechst. To many chemical workers, the works council developed into a more powerful institution than the union. It was in this atmosphere that some of the major works councilors at the Big Three turned into veritable "barons" in terms of the power, prestige and patronage they commanded inside the factory gates.

By 1955, it had become incumbent upon the union to counter its growing weakness on the shop floor as the power of the works councils increased. Thus, it was not by chance that the strategy of plant-level collective bargaining (betriebsnahe Tarifpolitik), later picked up by IG Metall, was first developed by IG Chemie. The idea, as articulated in the official union publication *Gewerkschaftpost*, aimed at creating a mechanism which would narrow the large gap between contractual and actual wages while curtailing the autonomy of the works councils in the bargaining process.[82] The union believed that a strategy which was predicated upon the conclusion of plant-level contracts rather than the existing area-wide agreements would enhance its grip on events at specific plants, thereby yielding a more prominent and tangible union presence on the shop floor.

The theory behind plant-level collective bargaining held that contracts concluded at the district level were too all-encompassing and general, because they had, by definition, to accommodate all the district's firms, rich and poor, big and small. To be sure, the existing system served as an equalizer – which was useful given the great diversity among firms – and ensured that in even the smallest, least profitable company of the district, all chemical workers received an adequate wage. Because of this, the old system was viewed as fair and generous, even by the advocates of the new policy. At the same time, however, it was too vague, thus allowing each firm to make special deals with its workers in firm-specific arrangements controlled – on the labor side – by the works councilors. Critics argued that while plant-level collective bargaining would undoubtedly accentuate the differences among plants and thus diminish remunerative equality, the negotiation process would at least be largely controlled by the union. The advocates of this strategy hoped to weaken the shop-floor power of the works council "barons" while at the same time augmenting the union's presence among its constituents.

However, proposals for plant-level collective bargaining in the mid-1950s never went beyond the discussion stage. Having correctly perceived this strategy as inimical to their interests, the works councilors within IG Chemie torpedoed its implementation at the time and have continued to oppose it successfully up to the present. Yet the debate concerning plant-level collective bargaining did have important ramifications in the form of "radicalizing" the union's contractual bargaining demands to a certain degree. IG Chemie soon became, along with IG Metall, one of the most vociferous exponents of the so-called active wage policy developed by Viktor Agartz and made the centerpiece of the DGB's 1955 Aktionsprogramm by IG Metall's leader, Otto Brenner. (For a detailed discussion of this event, see Chapter 3.)

IG Chemie took the tenets of the Aktionsprogramm seriously and reoriented its bargaining strategy to follow this program's more aggressive line.[83] The union demanded higher wage and salary increases with a greater sense of urgency and more resolve. In addition, in accordance with the Aktionsprogramm, the union pushed for shorter work time by aiming to reduce the 48-hour work week and increase annual vacation time.[84] The shortening of work time in all its forms assumed particular urgency for IG Chemie since workers in the chemical industry worked slightly longer on the average than their counterparts in West German industry as a whole.[85] This was true throughout the 1950s and the 1960s and can partly be explained by the high concentration of continuous shift work which forms an integral part of the production process in the chemical industry.[86]

The union's changed approach yielded results. Between 1958 and 1964, the average annual increase in the contracts that IG Chemie signed with the employers was slightly over 8%, thus exceeding the industrial average by 2%.[87] Throughout the 1960s, IG Chemie consistently signed contracts which were slightly higher than the DGB average, thereby making chemical workers one of the highest paid groups in the Federal Republic by the end of that decade.[88] Much of this could not have occurred without the extraordinary economic boom which engulfed the chemical industry for a decade between the mid-1950s and 1960s. After 1958, the union succeeded in eliminating the disparity between the terms of its own contracts and those of other DGB unions, notably IG Metall. However, it failed to bridge the gap between its own contractual gains and the actual amount which the chemical employers paid their workers, especially at Hoechst, Bayer and BASF.

From the mid-1950s onwards, one of IG Chemie's major preoccupations was the issue of work safety. In an industry which requires a number of potentially dangerous and unhealthy processes during its normal course of production, the union is responsible for protecting its members. In the 1950s it became evident that many workers preferred higher paychecks to greater safety and that the works councilors were more than willing to oblige them in their desire, which suited the employers as well. IG Chemie was forced to play the role of guardian and watchdog, making certain that the trade-off between security and remuneration did not tilt completely toward the latter. In so doing, IG Chemie did not shy away from disciplining some particularly lax works councilors whenever the union felt strong enough to reprimand these frequently very powerful shop-floor representatives. Safety became a centerpiece of union concerns in the mid-1950s and has remained so to this day.[89]

In conjunction with the discussion of plant-level collective bargaining and the concern with increased safety at the workplace, IG Chemie had to develop some mechanisms to increase its leverage on the shop floor. It was in this context that the 1950s witnessed the establishment of the shop-steward system within this union. Following the same logic operative at IG Metall during this period, IG Chemie was forced to devise an organizational response to its drastic weakening on the shop floor, especially after the enactment of the Works Constitution Law in 1952. A comprehensive network of shop stewards was designed to furnish union foot soldiers for the trench warfare of the shop floor.

The wing in IG Chemie which advocated the creation and strengthening of the shop stewards to counter the employers could be identified as the activist segment of the union. Collectivist, reform-minded and linked to a relatively radical tradition of the German labor movement, the activists in IG Chemie were particularly concerned by the union's troubles in organizing effectively in the Big Three and the concomitant power and autonomy enjoyed by the works councils in these crucial firms. By the 1950s, this group and its strategy were opposed by many unionized works councilors and by their allies in the union who preferred a course of accommodation, social partnership and collaboration with management. In no other West German union have the different aims and strategies of activists and accommodationists clashed more bitterly over the years than in IG Chemie. Given the organizational peculiarities and controversies over shop-floor representation in this union, one could discern an almost perfect overlap of the activists with the shop steward wing on the one hand and the accommodationists representing IG Chemie's works-councilor faction on the other.

In 1950, IG Chemie could muster only 4,265 shop stewards for its entire organizational domain.[90] By 1959, the number had increased to 10,408.[91] In 1965, it reached 24,997, which meant that there was one shop steward for every 40 employees.[92] Since IG Chemie refrains from publishing data on shop stewards disaggregated by sector, it is impossible to give exact figures for the chemical industry alone. All indications seem to point to a much higher ratio of workers to shop stewards within this industry.[93] Moreover, it has never been a secret that within the chemical industry the union has attained its worst shop-steward representation at the Big Three.

The union ran into serious trouble by the late 1950s over the issue of shop-steward representation. IG Chemie hoped at the time that its shop-steward strategy would significantly strengthen the presence of these union representatives in the chemical industry, which of course could never happen without a strong showing at the Big Three. The employers at BASF, Hoechst and Bayer, however, countered the union's shop-steward strategy by creating shop stewards of their own, so-called company shop stewards (betriebliche Vertrauensleute). Legitimated by company statutes, these company shop stewards were to be elected by all employees, be *they* unionized or not. Moreover, the official mandate given these stewards was one of explicit social partnership since their most important function consisted in mediating among the workers, the works councils and the employers.[94] From IG Chemie's point of view, these company shop stewards were nothing but "early warning systems" for the employers who were interested in hearing about potential trouble spots in time to counter them effectively.[95]

Although over 50% of the company shop stewards since the program's inception have been IG Chemie members, their activities remain by necessity highly circumscribed. First, the fact that they are elected by all workers rather than only unionized ones means that they owe their position to a different constituency than the one which IG Chemie had in mind for its shop-steward strategy. By deriving their legitimacy from all workers, these company shop stewards tend to be politically more compliant and accommodating than their union counterparts. Above all, they are constantly aware of the fact that they owe their position as shop stewards not to the union but to the company.

Second, in certain areas of the three largest companies – especially the research departments and other loci of production dominated by white-collar employees and university-trained personnel – management's strategy of company shop stewards has virtually eliminated the possibility of meaningful representation by IG Chemie. The result was such a poor ratio between union shop stewards and employees (approximately 1:150) that any shop-floor action on the part of IG Chemie has remained all but impossible.[96]

Lastly, this system of company shop stewards has had serious ramifications for the union's internal organization. In particular, the strength of the company shop stewards has forced IG Chemie to take measures which have incorporated non-unionized chemical workers into the union's decision-making process. IG Chemie began to appoint automatically all company shop stewards who were union members to the position of union shop steward as well. Since in IG Chemie – more than in any other DGB union – union shop stewards play major roles in the internal decision-making process of the organization, this procedure of automatic transfer from company to union authority has meant that persons who are elected by non-unionized workers, and thus owe at least partial allegiance to them, have had a say in important union committees and sub-committees. (For further details on this phenomenon see the discussion below.)

Two trends can be discerned concerning the institutionalization of shop stewards in IG Chemie during the 1950s and 1960s. First, the shop stewards were only grudgingly accepted by many in the union during the 1950s. Although most workers in this period saw that union shop stewards were necessary, it was not until 1961 that IG Chemie issued its first official guidelines delineating the shop stewards' tasks and functions,[97] demonstrating that heretofore the shop stewards had not attained numerical importance. Their status was gradually upgraded throughout the 1960s, culminating in 1969 when the shop stewards were officially recognized in the union bylaws as one of the union's four major constituent institutions.

The second trend concerns IG Chemie's balancing act between the shop stewards and the works councilors. While in the early 1950s one can detect a clear bias in union documents favoring the shop stewards' primacy in their competition with the works councilors, this tone changed concomitant with the accommodationist period of the late 1950s and early 1960s.[98] By the mid-1960s, the union was emphasizing the necessity of an equal, symbiotic and mutually supportive relationship between these two structural rivals in pursuit of the common goal of improving the shop-floor representation of all chemical workers. The even-handed approach of the 1960s was carried into the 1970s. However, it could not conceal the antagonisms between these two structures, each of which derived its support from an increasingly polarized and ideologized segment of the union. In the late 1970s, the long-delayed showdown between accommodationists and activists regarding IG Chemie's shop-floor representation threatened to inflict permanent damage on this divided labor organization. (See the discussion below for an elaborate treatment of this controversy.)

## VI.  IG CHEMIE ON THE LEFT: 1960–1969

In notable contrast to the early 1970s when IG Chemie gradually developed into one of the DGB's most conservative unions, throughout the 1960s the union viewed itself – and was in turn perceived by its sister organizations, the employers and the West German public – as leftist and radical. In the 1960s many IG Chemie leaders devoted segments of their speeches to countering the union's image as "the left winger" in the DGB.[99] This political categorization derived from two interrelated phenomena which determined the union's ideological positioning on the spectrum of organized labor throughout the 1960s: first, IG Chemie's relationship to the employers, and second, its role in crucial intra-DGB debates concerning union strategies.

As to the former, the union was labeled "radical" because of its impressive wage gains which, at the time, were higher than those of any other union in the Federal Republic. IG Chemie's biannual report of 1960–62 mentions that "we [IG Chemie] have slowly acquired the reputation in the public's view for being a radical union as a consequence of our successful bargaining strategies and achievements." The document then substantiates this claim by showing that while the average pay increase for labor in all the West German industry was 8.6% for 1960 and 8.5% in 1961, IG Chemie attained 11.5% and 13.2% for its workers during those two years.[100] The fact that some IG Chemie delegates to the union's sixth congress in September 1963 were eager to dispel any notions of communist infiltration of the union also lends evidence to the salience of the union's radicalism at the time, be it purported or real.[101]

The 1963–65 report and speeches at the union's seventh congress in 1966 highlighted the linkage between IG Chemie's wage gains and the union's reputation as radical. The wage increases continued throughout 1966 and 1967, at a time when the economy in the Federal Republic suffered its first significant setback in the post-World War II period. The union's optimism can be gauged from its refusal to acknowledge any downturn in the West German economy, let alone in the chemical industry. Crisis talk, the union's leaders believed in 1966, would prove to be a self-fulfilling prophecy and create a real crisis.[102] The union argued that the gloomy tone used to describe the condition of the West German economy at the time was nothing less than "calculated pessimism" (Zweckpessimismus) by the employers in their strategy to contain labor.[103]

During the 1960s the employers in the chemical industry initiated a concerted offensive to curtail labor's gains, which in good part derived from the latter's advantaged market position. The employers' strategy utilized a two-pronged attack. First, they increased their toughness on the shop floor and made certain that the union's de facto maneuverability within the plants remained circumscribed to the limited channels institutionalized in the 1950s. Management in the chemical industry wanted to make certain that labor's increased power could be "bought off" or "monetarized" on capital's terms, preferably by using the institution of the works councils at direct cost to the union. Under no circumstances was IG Chemie to be allowed to translate its newly gained bargaining power into an increase in shop-floor authority and plant-level control. The employers were ready to sacrifice in "quantity" (monetary remuneration) what they were never willing to relinquish in "quality" (uncontested domination on the shop floor). The employers' strategy was particularly opposed to any of the union's plant-level collective bargaining proposals, one of the major rallying points of the activists in IG Chemie who continued their advocacy of strengthening the shop stewards within the organization.

The employers' strategy also concentrated on increasing coordination and centralization of all their activities with IG Chemie, most importantly collective bargaining. As early as the beginning of the 1960s, the employers in the chemical industry developed a "Tabu Katalog" which imposed rules for dealing with IG Chemie on each member of the employers' association.[104] Severe sanctions such as heavy fines or expulsion were decreed for any infractions of the guidelines. In addition to this enforced intra-capital coordination, the employers tried to streamline collective bargaining negotiations by concluding contracts at the highest possible level. The employers sought to negotiate country-wide "package" agreements which set wage and salary levels, specified the amount of work-time reduction and indicated the quantity of various bonuses as well as severance pay.[105]

While the IG Chemie leadership opposed management's streamlining plans – and the centralizing impact such a scheme would have on the union's own organization – there seems little doubt that the union adopted the form dictated by capital's collective bargaining strategy. Thus the employers' offensive was rewarded with "structural" success, a more substantial and long-term victory than preventing the union from making major strides in a particular wage round. In being forced from the early 1960s to respond to the employers' challenge, IG Chemie experienced an intra-organizational shift in authority over collective bargaining away from the district bargaining commissions to the union executive committee. The union's 1960–62 report mentions that the executive committee had been "intimately" involved in various coordinating measures concerning the union's contract talks in the districts.[106] In the next report (1963–65), one gets the sense of urgency regarding the necessity of coordination in collective bargaining. In response to the measures by the "opposite side", IG Chemie felt it necessary to augment even further the role of the executive committee in the union's wage negotiations.[107]

The shift towards greater centralization caused intra-organizational tensions regarding the future course of the union's negotiating procedure. In the union's 1966–68 report, resistance in many districts to the growing dominance of the executive committee over collective bargaining is noticeable. Critics were equally disturbed about the practice of combining qualitative issues pertaining to general framework contracts with quantitative demands usually articulated in wage and salary contracts, another facet of the overall centralization trend. The union leadership justified its strategy by invoking "the increasingly politicized nature of bargaining rounds and their link to the economic situation of the country as a whole."[108] According to the policymakers in Hanover, the growing complexities facing IG Chemie necessitated greater coordination and more centralized planning on the part of the union's leadership.[109]

Two additional developments concerning collective bargaining worried IG Chemie members during the mid-1960s. First, many believed that the union fell far short of its potential in the 1965 round and settled for inadequate pay increases. Some of the rank and file complained that this centralization was worthless if it could not deliver respectable wage gains, supposedly the most important reason for its implementation. Second and perhaps even more significant was the disillusionment with the union's decision to enter eighteen-month and two-year wage and salary contracts, instead of the customary twelve months. Given the highly legalized nature of the West German industrial relations system and the sanctity of contracts which disallow strike activities during their period of applicability, members of the rank and file and union officials, mainly belonging to the activist wing, believed that IG Chemie had unnecessarily trapped itself, receiving little, if anything, in return.[110]

Concerning the union's position within the DGB, the IG Chemie of the 1950s and 1960s was much closer to the "radical" IG Metall line within the federation than to the accommodationist position advocated by IG Bau-Steine-Erden. Throughout this period, IG Chemie continued to uphold its vigorous belief in the democratic virtue and ultimate necessity of universal co-determination. The union maintained the introduction of a coal-and-steel-like model of co-determination as a centerpiece of its demands and hopes in negotiating with the three chemical giants. Both in speeches at union congresses and in policy statements in the union's newspapers and triannual reports, IG Chemie remained as preoccupied with attaining an extension of "genuine" (i.e. Montan-type) Mitbestimmung as it had been since its defeat on this issue in the early 1950s.[111] For IG Chemie, as for IG Metall and other activist members of the DGB, the economic prosperity and political moderation of that period did not render the inherent value of economic democracy and co-determination obsolete, as the accommodationist unions – notably IG Bau-Steine-Erden – believed.

Furthermore, once again in full accord with IG Metall, IG Chemie lent its enthusiastic support to the strategies and tactics described in the 1955 Aktionsprogramm. To underscore its conviction that this strategy was correct, the union passed a "small" Aktionsprogramm of its own in 1960. This document was specially designed to complement and reinforce the DGB Program with policies specific to the organizational purview of IG Chemie.[112] The "small" Aktionsprogramm emphasized the primacy of collective bargaining in the union's overall strategy. Special attention was given to the reduction of weekly work time, vacations, an active wage policy and better sickness benefits.[113] The primary goal of the program was to strengthen IG Chemie's shop-floor power, countering the factory-level dominance of the works councils.

IG Chemie's initial rejection of asset formation (Vermögensbildung) as a viable strategy for labor was a major factor differentiating it from the accommodationist unions led by IG Bau-Steine-Erden. Just like IG

Metall, IG Chemie responded to this Leber-led initiative with an unequivocal "no."[114] The union viewed the theory behind asset formation as an integral part of the accommodationist package which undermined labor's resolve to pursue an aggressive policy at the bargaining table.

IG Chemie's skepticism concerning the benefits of asset formation was evident in numerous thinly veiled criticisms of Georg Leber and IG Bau-Steine-Erden, particularly in the 1963–65 report. At one point, the document mentions "a clearly recognizable and growing difference in the conduct of collective bargaining among certain unions" which, according to IG Chemie, "necessitates the explicit articulation of each organization's position regarding certain crucial questions."[115] Barely one page later, the reader encounters a categorical rejection of the Leber plan of asset formation by IG Chemie's plenum on the grounds that the scheme "would impede or at least delay by decades true profit sharing by the workers in the sense of augmenting their decision-making powers and representing a genuine form of redistribution of wealth."[116]

Yet, as the 1960s progressed, IG Chemie's profound skepticism concerning asset formation assumed a more ambivalent and instrumental character. While still viewing the whole complex of asset formation as "one of the most controversial chapters in the history of collective bargaining," IG Chemie slowly accepted its validity as long as it in no way interfered with "classical" wage bargaining and only if it went beyond the existing plan of savings incentives decreed by the so-called DM 312 law.[117] At the union's seventh congress in 1966, IG Chemie's executive committee declared its readiness to incorporate asset formation in its overall strategy provided this measure exceeded token gestures which could never lead to a redistribution of wealth.[118] This step clearly distanced IG Chemie from others in the DGB's activist camp, especially IG Metall, which continued to oppose asset formation.

By the end of the decade, IG Chemie had come to accept IG Bau-Steine-Erden's plan of asset formation as a legitimate and essential ingredient of union strategy. Indeed, at the union's eighth congress in 1969, IG Chemie's executive committee not only approved asset formation in general but also agreed to recognize the validity of savings incentives as instruments of collective bargaining.[119] While still insisting on differentiating between "genuine" asset formation and "mere" savings incentives, the executive committee accepted both as official union policy. These initiatives met with severe criticisms from certain activist delegates at the 1969 congress.[120] Throughout the 1960s, the union leadership faced stiff resistance from the shop-steward faction to IG Chemie's gradual departure from radicalism and its journey toward social partnership. Many in IG Chemie remained opposed to the "revisionism" of the DGB's Düsseldorf Program in 1963. But the accommodationist works councilors had both time and the West German political economy on their side. They could sense that ultimately victory would be theirs, though only after a bitter struggle which would leave their side badly shaken.

As the 1960s came to a conclusion, IG Chemie could look back on a decade of major wage gains and overall prosperity for its members. Yet the fundamental differences between the two rival factions dominating the union since the 1950s remained: the activist shop stewards who perceived the primary role of the union as that of a Gegenmacht, and the accommodationist works councilors who saw IG Chemie's major task as being an Ordnungsfaktor.

This arrangement was not an ideal one for the union as it faced the mobilization period of the early 1970s. Many IG Chemie members, alarmed by the centralization of their union's collective bargaining and its accommodationist posture, were frustrated in 1969 because they felt that the union's contracts could have been far superior; nevertheless, few joined the strike waves of September dominated by the country's miners and steelworkers. This did not bode well for the 1970s. Change had to occur both from above and from below.

The turbulence of the union's eighth congress held in September 1969 was a clear sign that the political activism engulfing West German labor did not exclude IG Chemie and its members. For the first time in the union's history, the congress witnessed open and protracted battles involving every weapon in IG Chemie's strategic arsenal. The major showdown came over the union's approach to collective bargaining. As can be expected, the "radicals" pushed for a resurrection of active wage policy coupled with implementation of plant-level collective bargaining. This group, dominated by rank-and-file members and representing the union's shop-steward wing, aimed to decentralize – or in its view "democratize" – the union's collective bargaining strategy which, of course, would also have important implications for IG Chemie's organizational framework. Opposing this group and its policies were the union's organization men, its "apparatchiks," who represented the accommodationist interests of the works councilors. Arguing that the "social partnership" approach which had gained popularity during the 1960s should further be enhanced since it would increase benefits for members, this wing of the union looked askance at the developing radicalism of IG Chemie's shop stewards and their supporters. The acrimonious atmosphere of IG Chemie's eighth congress was an accurate harbinger of the intra-union struggles which were to characterize IG Chemie's politics throughout the 1970s.

## VII. IG CHEMIE AND MOBILIZATION: 1970–1974

The decade of the 1970s can be divided into two halves according to the fortunes of IG Chemie's bargaining strategies, which in turn correspond to the predominance of the policies of one of the union's factions over those of its rival. The period 1970–75 witnessed the ascendancy of the shop-steward wing with its emphasis on shop-floor democracy, increased rank-and-file participation and a more aggressive and decentralized approach to collective bargaining. This phase in IG Chemie's post-World War II history coincided with the general mobilization of West German – indeed European – workers and a superb economic situation accompanied by full employment.

The second half of the decade saw a reversal of the policies which dominated the preceding five years; specifically, this era witnessed a strong centralization of the union's collective bargaining approach. Moreover, IG Chemie's initial demands and the results achieved were far more modest than during the preceding period. Instead of assuming an aggressive posture in dealing with employers and the state, IG Chemie developed into one of the "meekest" and most accommodationist unions within the DGB during the latter part of the 1970s. As one astute observer of IG Chemie described this change: IG Chemie's "loud" collective bargaining approach had changed to a "noiseless one."[121] This period witnessed the triumph of the union's works-councilor wing with its accommodationist view over the activism of the shop-steward faction. Once again, these intra-union developments cannot be separated from events in the country at large. In 1975, the West German economy experienced a crisis which in terms of its duration and structural ramifications was without precedent in the history of the Federal Republic. IG Chemie began the decade in an aggressive and reformist spirit. The 1970s ended with the union as one of the DGB's most outspokenly accommodationist members, preoccupied with defending the status quo.

In the 1970 wage round, IG Chemie decided to put an end to the trend of increasingly centralized bargaining which had characterized labor-management negotiations throughout the 1960s. In response to a restless rank and file and under the influence of the turbulent events at the union's eighth congress, the leadership decided to pursue a decentralized and regional approach in its bargaining with employers. The union sought to implement its long-dormant policy of plant-level collective bargaining in order to gain from the restiveness of its members on the shop floor. To that end, IG Chemie attempted to negotiate a number of plant-specific contracts in some of Hesse's larger chemical companies. Not surprisingly, many works councilors opposed this measure and saw in it a direct challenge to their prerogatives. Works councilors at Hoechst opposed this union initiative with the explicit argument that it would make their own efforts to obtain benefits from the company redundant.[122] While a number of works councilors tried to impede the implementation of this strategy by voicing their opposition in the union's bargaining commission, it nevertheless became policy in Hesse in the early part of 1970.

IG Chemie also had to face the fierce opposition of the employers to its plant-level initiative. The employers were even ready to risk a strike rather than give in to IG Chemie's innovative strategy. The union's eagerness to conduct a decentralized and localized wage round may ultimately have benefitted the employers in Hesse, however. Decentralization, in this case, entailed lack of coordination. Just when IG Chemie was getting its strike preparations into high gear in Hesse, a very favorable contract was concluded in neighboring Rhineland-Palatinate, thereby undermining the efforts by union activists in Hesse.[123] Instead of wanting to strike, a majority of union members in Hesse were quite content to adopt the terms reached in Rhineland-Palatinate for their own district.

Yet the union's decentralized approach can be credited with pressuring the employers into agreeing to the highest wage settlements in the chemical industry in the history of the Federal Republic. Most of the union's bargaining areas accepted 11.5% wage and salary increases following demands for a 14% raise. Hamburg surprised everyone by continuing to hold out for the phased introduction of a thirteenth-month bonus and an absolute wage increase of DM 120 per month for workers in the lower wage categories.[124] Following the failure of all mediation efforts, including the last step at the federal level, a so-called active contractless situation (aktiver tarifloser Zustand) developed in which the union could resort to strike activities without suffering any legal consequences and without having to call a strike vote prior to initiating such action.[125] In this "active contractless situation" IG Chemie conducted a series of localized strikes, the first ones in the chemical industry since Weimar.[126] (All other strikes conducted by IG Chemie in the post-World War II period – including those in 1962, 1963 and 1967 – were in industries of lesser importance such as rubber, glass and paper production.) Even before the union decided to escalate its active contractless situation into a full-fledged area strike comprising the entire Hamburg bargaining region, the employers agreed to IG Chemie's demands. The Hamburg episode boosted the union's confidence and conveyed the impression that its decentralized approach to collective bargaining bore tangible results.

However, one could argue that this optimism was misplaced, especially with the benefit of hindsight which reveals major differences between the bargaining rounds of 1970 and 1971. Understandably, IG Chemie attributed the attainment of its most successful contracts to the union's strategy of decentralized bargaining. However, very satisfying gains were achieved all over the country and thus did not remain confined to Hesse, the only bargaining area where the union had pursued its strategy of plant-level collective bargaining. Therefore, IG Chemie desisted from repeating this policy elsewhere in 1971. It seems that the lucrative nature of the 1970 contracts literally "bought off" IG Chemie's plan to increase the use of plant-level collective bargaining as an alternative strategy to the conventional bargaining relationship with the employers. One could further hypothesize that IG Chemie would have continued to implement its plant-level collective bargaining throughout the early 1970s had the 1970 wage round yielded less spectacular results.

In 1971, IG Chemie encountered a different attitude on the part of the employers than in 1970. Whereas in 1970 the employers were still rattled by the September strikes of 1969, in 1971 they were determined not to grant the union wage concessions of the magnitude of the 1970 agreements. On the whole, 1970 had been a bad year for the chemical industry. While 1968 and 1969 yielded record profits, high investment and overall growth, 1970 found the industry in a slump.[127] Its growth was below the national average and it was suffering from overcapacity partly as a consequence of high investment activity during the preceding two years. Furthermore, wage costs reached record levels in 1970, in part due to the lucrative contract signed by IG Chemie in the spring of that year.[128] Profits were down by the beginning of 1971 and growth remained sluggish. The acute uncertainty in the exchange rates of the capitalist world's currencies at the time created still greater anxiety for most West German employers. The chemical industry, which is heavily export-dependent, feared another revaluation of the Deutsche Mark following such measures in 1961 and 1969. As fate would have it, the Deutsche Mark was once again revalued in May 1971, exactly in the middle of contract negotiations between IG Chemie and the industry.

In short, the situation demanded that the employers exhibit a greater degree of toughness vis-à-vis the union in 1971 than they had in 1970. It was not by chance that the employers' association laid down very strict rules for the proper behavior of all its members throughout the contract talks. Not only were there to be very severe penalties for breaking the ranks of the employers by signing "solo" contracts with IG Chemie, but, in full anticipation of a difficult round, the Arbeitsring established an anti-strike solidarity fund ("Fund for the Securing of Labor Peace") for which each company had to contribute 0.7% of its 1969 wage and salary costs.[129] In addition to these defensive measures, the employers prepared plans of a more offensive nature in the form of various strike-breaking tactics.[130] Even *before* the negotiations were formally under way, a showdown between the union and the employers seemed inevitable given the tense atmosphere.

The wage round began in the middle of February 1971 when IG Chemie cancelled contracts in North Rhine, Hesse and Rhineland-Palatinate which were due to expire on March 31. In North Rhine and Rhineland-Palatinate, IG Chemie's contract demands initially centered on a 12% wage and salary raise and the introduction of the thirteenth-month bonus.[131] In Hesse, the union's demands featured an 11% pay increase and a DM 120 bonus for workers in the lower wage categories.[132] IG Chemie, expecting fierce resistance on the part of the employers in this wage round, formulated its demands with an 8% settlement in mind, which would have corresponded to the government's wage orientation datum of that year.

The revaluation of the Deutsche Mark on May 9 strengthened the employers' already considerable resolve to resist the union. IG Chemie lowered its demands to an 8% pay increase, thereby hoping to gain the employers' cooperation. There were also indications that IG Chemie's leadership was at least partly convinced of the legitimacy of the employers' worry over the potentially adverse consequences of the Deutsche Mark's revaluation for the fortunes of the West German chemical industry. Moreover, the Council of Economic Advisors released a special report at the end of May exhorting the unions to restrain their wage demands in order to restore profit levels which would stimulate sagging investment. While not swayed by the Council's argument, the IG Chemie leadership did not dismiss its recommendations outright, as it did a few years later.

Unimpressed by IG Chemie's reduced demands, the employers maintained their counteroffer from late April calling for a 5% across-the-board pay increase.[133] With a 6.5% inflation rate at the time, this offer remained unacceptable to IG Chemie. As in 1970 though, the union's position was severely compromised by the uncoordinated behavior of its districts. As Hesse and North Rhine were about to announce the failure of the first phase of their mediation efforts with the employers, Rhineland-Palatinate concluded a new contract. The 7.8% pay increase it provided for the period between June 1, 1971 and March 31, 1972 amounted to merely 6.5% when factored over the twelve-month duration of a typical contract.[134] In addition to this pay raise, IG Chemie also attained a phased introduction of the thirteenth-month bonus to be paid in full by the beginning of 1974.

It was the manner of its negotiation more than the particular terms of this contract which dealt a severe blow to IG Chemie's struggle. Once again the union had to conduct complicated negotiations without being able to count on its members at BASF for much-needed support. To add to the union's woes, the IG Chemie leadership of Rhineland-Palatinate justified its actions in terms which the employers found so flattering to their own cause that they reprinted the comments verbatim for their own propagandistic purposes.[135] It seemed as if the union's resolve had been broken and the employers could claim an early victory. Surprisingly, however, this was not to be the case.

The second phase of the wage round began on June 2, when mediation efforts for the North Rhine district failed at the federal level. An escalation of the conflict was now possible. IG Chemie took immediate advantage of this "active contractless situation" by stopping work at major chemical and rubber plants in Cologne on the same day.[136] On each subsequent day, more workers from different plants in the district joined the strike. At first, the work stoppages were largely uncoordinated and depended on the initiatives of the individual plant leadership,, usually made up of works councilors and shop stewards. In order to provide a common spirit of mobilization, IG Chemie's executive committee and the union's district leadership called for a massive demonstration in Cologne on June 8. Attended by over 10,000 IG Chemie members, it showed vividly that a sizable number of supposedly complacent chemical workers was eager to express its will in a collective manner, including by means of various strike activities. Both the employers and IG Chemie were caught by surprise by the turnout at the Cologne demonstration. At the height of the month-long strike period there were a few days when 25,000 chemical workers out of the 200,000 in North Rhine were participating in strike-related activities.[137]

June 14 witnessed the beginning of the third phase of the bargaining round. With mediation having broken down in Hesse, IG Chemie extended its strike activities to include this important district as well. By June 20, fifteen plants with a total of 15,000 workers – out of 100,000 in Hesse's chemical industry – were engaged in the strike. Protest marches were held again in Cologne and all over Hesse throughout mid-June. In both districts, IG Chemie resorted to all forms of strikes ranging from full-scale work stoppages in entire plants to sit-ins, slowdowns, short-term interruptions, lengthening of breaks, late arrivals accompanied by early departures and work-to-rule measures.[138] This active contractless situation was quite conducive to the implementation of annoying guerrilla-type hit-and-run tactics, rather than all-out area strikes in both districts, which IG Chemie simply would not have been able to sustain for any meaningful length of time. A special event in Hesse lent the strikes in that district a unique flavor: for the first time in over 50 years, workers at one of the IG Farben plants stopped production; specifically, 4,000 workers at a Hoechst factory near Frankfurt interrupted their routine for several hours on a work day in late June.[139]

The fourth phase of this bargaining round consisted of a further escalation of IG Chemie's strike activities. On June 22 and 24, negotiations in Hamburg and Westphalia failed to produce results, thus initiating active contractless situations in those two districts as well.[140] Four thousand workers demonstrated in Hamburg, and numerous plants were strike-bound in Westphalia. With the extension of strike activities to these two districts, IG Chemie succeeded in making the showdown a semi-national affair. On June 25, 45,000 workers participated in either demonstrations or various strike activities; on the 29th the number had escalated to 50,000; and on the last day of the month, approximately 38,000 chemical workers refused to perform their regular work.[141]

The strike lasted for nearly one month, which is quite lengthy by the standards of capital–labor relations in West Germany. This was especially surprising in the case of IG Chemie which had conducted only a few short strikes in the post-1945 era, none of which – as already mentioned – were in the chemical industry itself. Indeed, the events of June 1971 represented the first of their kind in the German chemical industry since the early 1920s. Consequently, the federal government, especially the SPD-dominated chancellor's office, became increasingly concerned with the wave of strikes throughout June and began to pressure the two "social partners" to resume negotiations at the bargaining table. Undoubtedly, Willy Brandt's stature in the labor movement and the union's desire to please "their" party in government moved the IG Chemie leadership to comply with this request.

Moreover, IG Chemie's relatively new chairman, Karl Hauenschild, an avid Social Democrat and a prominent member of the SPD's centrist circle, proposed a close alliance between his union and the SPD-led government as the cornerstone of IG Chemie's political strategy. In reality, Hauenschild saw little choice in the matter since the employers – Hauenschild felt – viewed the SPD–labor relationship as a menace which had to be fought on all fronts. It should come as no surprise then that Hauenschild believed that the employers perceived IG Chemie throughout the events of 1971 as a proxy for the SPD-led government. He stated, "I have the feeling that the employers in the chemical industry are trying to provoke a showdown which is directed not only against us, but also against the government. They beat up on the chemical workers and they really mean [to beat up on] Bonn."[142]

On June 3, 1971 the top leadership of IG Chemie and Arbeitsring agreed on contract terms which ended the strike wave. Under the watchful eyes of a special arbitrator appointed by the federal government, and according to the wishes of the SPD-led coalition, the two sides hammered out the following agreement: a 7.8% pay raise beginning retroactively on June 1,

1971 and lasting until March 31, 1972; additionally, each worker was granted a cash payment of DM 60 for April and May 1971, which meant that the annual wage and salary increase turned out to be slightly over 8%. IG Chemie also won the phased introduction of the thirteenth-month bonus, to be fully implemented in all the union's districts by the beginning of 1974. Lastly, the employers desisted from demanding reparation and indemnity payments from the union and also agreed not to take any disciplinary or legal measures against strike participants.[143] Since IG Chemie never conducted a formal strike vote to legitimize its actions during the stoppages, the union was not compelled to submit the new contract to ratification by the rank and file. Thus ended perhaps the most turbulent bargaining round in IG Chemie's post-World War II history. The ramifications of this settlement, however, extended well beyond the usual post-strike evaluations, and exacerbated existing intra-union cleavages during the 1970s.

The strike was both a positive and a negative experience for IG Chemie. Despite its relative inexperience, IG Chemie successfully carried out a 30-day industrial action covering large areas of the country. Moreover, the union had sustained its efforts despite serious adversities. It encountered considerable violence at numerous sites, had to contend with strikebreakers and the police, and ultimately confronted the power of the courts by standing up to various injunctions and temporary restraining orders.[144] The employers' repeated attempts to delegitimize the strike in the eyes of the chemical workers and the public by impugning the legality of the "active contractless situation" failed to intimidate IG Chemie.[145] Credit is also due to the union for its choice of strike maneuvers, which proved very effective. Ultimately, however, the strike deserves to be seen as a victory for the union because it stood up for its rights and refused to yield without a fight, to the surprise of the employers and most everybody else.

On the negative side, disorganization was a major problem. Under no circumstances should Rhineland-Palatinate have broken ranks and concluded a contract of its own when other districts were ready to escalate their activities. This conduct undermined union solidarity, weakened the morale of the members and aided the employers' cause. Moreover, the union was on the whole ill-prepared for the strike. Once the strike was under way, many IG Chemie officials at the district and local levels had no idea what their proper tasks and duties were.[146] Poor preparation and deficient coordination had a demobilizing, indeed paralyzing, effect in many instances when readiness and experience were badly needed for the union's cause. The multitude of strike tactics was also confusing, especially in the absence of firm leadership.

Finally, the lack of a strike vote proved problematic. On one hand it gave the union the freedom associated with an active contractless situation, but it had an adverse effect on the overall mobilization effort. The preparation for the strike vote and the rituals associated with this activity give the union leadership and the rank and file time and perspective to formulate their battle plans. More importantly, however, strike votes reestablish and confirm bonds among all union members, and legitimize the upcoming activity. Given the deeply engrained legalism of West German workers, this act of legitimation should not be discounted in analyzing the significance of the strike vote for union behavior.

The biggest handicap for IG Chemie throughout the strike was its inability to include the Big Three in the events. With BASF gone from the outset, the union's position remained hopeless at Hoechst and Bayer, where its organizational presence has always been well below that at BASF. In addition IG Chemie faced considerable reluctance on the part of key works councilors in the two companies to mobilize workers on the shop floor. The union's decision not to call an official strike vote provided these works councilors and their shop-floor allies, the company shop stewards, with a welcome alibi to boycott all preparations for the strike. They argued that without an appropriate strike vote there was simply no telling whether a sufficient number of workers would support a strike in their plants. The truth, of course, was that these works council "barons" feared that an aborted strike, or any irregularity for that matter, could only hurt their standing with respect to their "clients" (the workers) and their "lords" (the employers).

Many strikers and other union members – including those at Bayer, Hoechst and BASF – resented the cynicism and self-serving behavior of the works councilors and company shop stewards at the Big Three. Their resentment was further exacerbated since there was very little that could be done about the situation short of major structural changes to enhance the organizational presence of IG Chemie within the three chemical giants. The strike had made it clear that the union would be severely handicapped as the representative of chemical workers as long as its shop-floor power in the Big Three remained so precarious. Those who felt dissatisfied with the strike began to aim their criticism at the company shop stewards at Hoechst, Bayer and BASF. This situation had to change if IG Chemie was ever to have a chance to enhance its influence and power in these firms. It was, of course, the activist shop-steward wing of the union which expressed this view. To this group, the strike represented a meager achievement at best.

In marked contrast to this interpretation, the accommodationist works councilor faction of IG Chemie opted for an impassioned defense of the status quo. This wing of the union celebrated the events of 1971 as an unmitigated victory for IG Chemie. Thus, perhaps the most important legacy of the strike was a divisive one. It helped rekindle the rivalry between the union's radical shop-steward faction and its conservative works-councilor wing. This confrontation dominated IG Chemie's intra-organizational politics for the rest of the decade, culminating in a major confrontation in 1979 and 1980.

One reason why organizational questions assumed such salience in the political development of IG Chemie throughout the 1970s was that, comparatively speaking, the crisis which plagued West German industry during the latter half of the decade by and large spared the chemical industry and thus IG Chemie. As a consequence, IG Chemie's activities did not have to address such fundamental and crisis-related issues as the obliteration of an entire profession as in the case of IG Druck (the compositors), or the dequalification offensive which IG Metall had to face from the metal industry. Nor was IG Chemie ever confronted with structural problems comparable to IG Metall's in the steel industry or shipbuilding. This meant that unlike IG Druck und Papier and IG Metall, IG Chemie's planning in the latter half of the 1970s was not consumed with devising strategies to counter serious employment problems within its organizational purview. There is no doubt that the crisis had an effect on IG Chemie's behavior and attitudes in the latter half of the decade, but it is important to point out that the union did not respond so much to an industry-specific crisis – as was the case with IG Metall and IG Druck und Papier – as to the macro-level dislocation plaguing the West German economy at large.

Almost all economic indicators show quite clearly that the chemical industry performed on the average much better than the rest of the economy during the 1970s. This pertains to sales as well as to volume of production and cost structures.[147] The industry also enjoyed a higher rate of labor productivity and witnessed a lower rate of job losses than the economy as a whole. The advantageous situation of the chemical industry between 1970 and 1979 lent additional credence to this sector's reputation as one of the Federal Republic's leading "growth industries."[148] The chemical industry's proportion of West German industry's total sales increased from 9.91% to 11.43% in the span of ten years. In terms of volume of production, the parallel figures were 9.46% and 11.40% respectively.

Lastly, the industry employed a larger percentage of the West German labor force at the end of the 1970s (7.39%) than at the beginning of that decade (6.72%). Despite this generally favorable situation, however, one could clearly discern a difference between the pre-crisis period of the 1970s (1970–74) and the post-crisis era. The latter period witnessed an attempt by the industry to maintain its competitive edge in the world market under deteriorating conditions. This entailed the introduction of increasingly comprehensive measures of rationalization in all aspects of production and the systematic rollback of wages the union had won during better times.

IG Chemie's demands in the first half of the 1970s were consistently much higher than the government's suggested guidelines contained in the so-called orientation data. With the SPD holding senior governmental responsibilities in Bonn, these data became even more important for the SPD-loyal unions, especially the Hauenschild-led IG Chemie. It is in this context that IG Chemie's demands, well in excess of the government's suggested guidelines, represented an act of defiance which in turn seemed almost solely the consequence of the general atmosphere of mobilization among West German workers and the concomitant organizational strength of the activists within this divided union. While the government suggested a 10–11% wage increase in 1970, IG Chemie demanded 14%, which was 33% in excess of the guideline.[149] In 1971, a particularly restive year, IG Chemie's 12% demand exceeded the 7–8% government recommendation by 60%. One year later, the government issued a 6–6.5% guideline which IG Chemie topped by 52% with its 9.5% demand for pay increases. This was followed in 1973 by the union demanding 12% as opposed to the government's guideline of 9–10%, a 26% discrepancy. The mobilization period ended appropriately with IG Chemie's 16.8% demand for wage and salary increase in 1974. This demand exceeded the government's orientation data of 8.5–10% by 82.0%, an all-time record for this union.[150]

In addition to these demands, IG Chemie's bargaining strategy included a commitment to egalitarianism. In all bargaining rounds of this period, the union introduced mechanisms which sought to reduce the remunerative – and thus social – differences among its members by favoring workers in the lower wage categories. Whether in the form of a concerted effort to introduce a systematic, fixed-base wage policy (Sockelpolitik), or to change the existing wage categories by either eliminating the lowest ones or bringing them substantially closer to the higher ones, the union made a sincere attempt to favor its least advantaged members. Because of the gains made during the mobilization period, the increase of contractual wages for women workers substantially outdistanced that of their male colleagues throughout the 1970s.[151] Although major wage differences continue to persist within IG Chemie's membership between men and women, blue- and white-collar workers, skilled and unskilled, the early 1970s were an era in which the union not only showed its awareness of these inqualities but demonstrated that it was trying to improve the situation.

Lastly, IG Chemie's demands also involved a few qualitative issues pertaining to general framework contracts. This group of demands was meant to enhance job security and the quality of work life under increasingly adverse conditions of intensified rationalization. While this process was less acute in the chemical industry than in printing or metal processing, it nevertheless acquired sufficient salience to become a major topic of discussion at IG Chemie's congresses in 1969 and 1972. Rationalization threatened not only the quantity of jobs, but also their quality. An array of countermeasures – both "offensive" and "defensive" – had to be devised to minimize the adverse effects of rationalization on IG Chemie's members.

The defensive measures included various protective devices designed to maintain the prior gains of workers. Among the more prominent were complete job protection for older workers, no loss of pay and status in case of a necessary job change, continued full remuneration during any period of retraining and a comprehensive employment protection plan comprising all existing jobs in the chemical industry.[152] Moreover, IG Chemie demanded a reduction of weekly work time, both to improve the working conditions of its members and to distribute the finite number of jobs in a more equitable way. To that end, the union at its 1972 congress demanded a 40-hour work week as a strict limit in the chemical industry, where at that time 42- and even 45-hour weeks were commonplace.[153] IG Chemie also asked for an extension of annual vacation time as well as an increase in vacation pay.

The union's offensive measures centered on rather vague demands grouped under the headings "humanization of working conditions" and "structural policy." IG Chemie tried to formulate a strategy to counter the adverse effects of rationalization via the introduction of anticipatory and preventive measures introduced jointly by the state, the union and the employers. This quasi-corporatist framework would allow labor and the SPD-led state apparatus to participate in important investment decisions.

The most distinctive feature of IG Chemie's gains between 1970 and 1974 was the yearly contractual increases which continued to exceed the government's orientation data. This contrasts starkly with the post-1975 period when IG Chemie's annual wage increases consistently fell far short of the government's guidelines. With its 11.6% gain in wages and salaries for the 1970 contract, IG Chemie surpassed the government's recommended figure by about 10%.[154] A year later, a pay increase of 7.8% exceeded the orientation data by 4%. In 1972, the union concluded a contract stipulating a 7.3% wage and salary rise which amounted to 17% over the government's guidelines. The 9.9% contract of 1973 exceeded the government's suggestions by 4%. In 1974 the biggest discrepancy occurred between IG Chemie's contractual gains (12.9%) and the government guidelines of 8.5–10%.[155] Never before or since have the union's wage gains exceeded the government's orientation data with such consistency. This development attests to the mobilization period's profound impact on IG Chemie's collective bargaining and the tangible benefits this impact yielded.

## VIII. MODERATION AND INTERNAL CONFLICT: 1975–1981

In all of IG Chemie's activities significant changes occurred after the 1974–75 crisis. In particular, the union's demands were consistently more moderate. Indeed, in two cases, IG Chemie decided not to formulate any wage demands at all and accept whatever the employers offered. The union's reserved attitude and behavior also extended to the qualitative area of general framework contracts where IG Chemie settled for less far-reaching anti-rationalization plans than it had sought in the early 1970s. Most important, however, in three bargaining rounds (late 1974, 1978 and 1979) the union concluded "package deals" in which qualitative demands were readily exchanged for quantitative ones, initiating a process of "monetarization" which eventually became commonplace in this union's collective bargaining approach during the crisis.[156]

The conduct of the negotiations themselves also changed in this period. Decisions were reached with much less participation "from below" and one could observe the annual erosion of the democratic process, the victim of a concerted effort of centralization by the union's leadership. Centralization of decision-making went hand in hand with "package deals" and a consistent effort by the union's center to demobilize the rank and file at every stage of the collective bargaining process.

In 1975, the first full year of economic crisis in the Federal Republic, the union, adhering to its new policy of restraint and moderation, issued no wage and salary demands at all. This occurred in spite of the fact that the SPD-led government had submitted orientation data legitimizing wage increases between 7.5% and 8.5%.[157] One year later IG Chemie demanded an 8.7% wage and salary increase which exceeded the government's suggestions of 6.7–7.5% by 24%. In 1977, the union's demand for a 9% pay increase was 20% in excess of the government's guideline of 7.5%. A similar situation occurred in 1978 when the union's demand for a 7% pay rise exceeded the government's suggestion of 5.5% by 27%. In 1979, IG Chemie repeated its behavior of 1975. Despite the government's suggestion of a 6.5% pay increase for labor, IG Chemie decided not to submit any demands of its own. Just as in 1975, IG Chemie's leadership wanted to underscore its special readiness for accommodation with the employers.

As to the union's qualitative demands, it became clear during the mid-1970s that IG Chemie had resigned itself to replicating with few alterations the major qualitative breakthroughs achieved by its sister unions, particularly IG Metall and IG Druck und Papier. IG Chemie's demands focused increasingly on the defensive aspects of protection against rationalization. This meant an almost exclusive preoccupation with certain forms of job security. Moreover, IG Chemie began to think about the less painful methods of early retirement and dismissals by suggesting various "easing out" plans rather than insisting that all existing jobs be protected. IG Chemie's qualitative demands entailed a veiled economic and job-related "triage": the union would be willing to retire some of its older and more marginal workers with the help of the appropriate cushioning mechanisms, provided that this step would guarantee long-term job security for its core workers.

During its congress of 1976, the union included in its package of proposals a demand for the reduction of weekly work time to 35 hours, but it never paid more than lip-service to this form of work-time reduction in actual contract demands. Whereas for IG Metall and IG Druck und Papier the 35-hour week assumed centrality for all of their qualitative bargaining efforts soon after the onset of the crisis, for IG Chemie this issue remained almost exclusively confined to the realm of programmatic declarations.

During the late 1970s and early 1980s, it was on this issue, among others, that IG Chemie chose to oppose IG Metall's and IG Druck's activism in a pronounced fashion. The 35-hour week had by then divided the DGB unions into those who favored its introduction – and who also happened to represent the DGB's activist unions – on the one hand and those who preferred other arrangements of work-time reduction on the other. IG Chemie played a key role among the latter group, which formed the accommodationist wing of the DGB. Instead of the 35-hour work week, IG Chemie concentrated its endeavors in the realm of work-time reduction almost exclusively on early retirement plans and, to a lesser extent, on increasing vacation time to six weeks per annum.

The growing concern for safety measures added a new dimension to the union's qualitative demands during the crisis. Stunned by the catastrophic chemical disaster at Seveso in northern Italy which had received extensive coverage in the Federal Republic, IG Chemie directed its collective bargaining efforts regarding qualitative issues toward the prevention of similar occurrences in West Germany. Largely because of Seveso, IG Chemie developed a noticeable ecological orientation in its qualitative demands during the latter half of the 1970s.

Both the formulation and the conduct of collective bargaining since 1975 underwent a process of centralization at all levels of the organization. Even the vaguest remnants and legacies of plant-level collective bargaining completely disappeared during this time. Strategy became increasingly the sole prerogative of "experts" at the union's headquarters in Hanover and at various organizational bodies in the districts. Decisions concerning collective bargaining were made by a decreasing number of men at the top of the organization. Once reached, decisions would typically be handed down as *faits accomplis*.

This "top down" decision-making process eliminated virtually all possibility of intra-organizational discussion of important union strategies, while discouraging criticism of the leadership's policies and aims in collective bargaining. Some contract negotiations were conducted in such "silence" that the bargaining commissions themselves – the bodies designated by the union to conduct collective bargaining negotiations – only found out what had happened after the contracts were signed.[158]

In short, a full-scale centralization of IG Chemie's collective bargaining mechanism characterized the crisis period. This entailed a strong concentration of power at the top (i.e. at headquarters), the concomitant loss of power by most regional bargaining commissions, the implementation of quick – almost clandestine – agreements, the collapse of qualitative and quantitative demands into "package deals" to the detriment of both, the discouragement of rank-and-file participation in formulation of union bargaining demands, increasing reliance on experts at headquarters and in the field, and lastly, discouragement of any kind of mobilization on the part of the union, be it in the labor market or the state.

A noticeable decrease in the level of militancy was another indicator of IG Chemie's attempt at demobilization and its reliance on secrecy in its collective bargaining strategy during the late 1970s. Thus, for example, no negotiation for wage and salary contracts ever exceeded 36 days in the post-1975 period, with many contracts signed even more quickly.[159] Only once since 1975 was it necessary to enter the process of arbitration. No strikes were conducted during this period, and only one strike vote was held (in 1977 in the district of Rhineland-Palatinate) leading to no industrial action. The results attained by IG Chemie in this period lent some legitimacy to the criticisms voiced against it by friends and foes alike.

The wage and salary contract which the union concluded in 1975 yielded a 6.8% annual increase, which was 15% below the government's guideline of 7.5–8.5%.[160] This was also one of the years in which IG Chemie did not even formulate an official demand at the beginning of the bargaining round. The 6.1% gain in 1976 was 13% below the government's recommendation, and the 7% pay raise of 1977 fell 7% short of the official ceiling decreed by the government's orientation data. The gap grew larger as the crisis continued. In 1978, the 4.3% pay increase which IG Chemie achieved amounted to 78% of the government's recommendation of a

5.5% annual growth in wages and salaries. One year later, IG Chemie again refrained from formulating any demands at the beginning of the bargaining round, and concluded it with a 4.3% pay increase which was 34% below the government's guideline of 6.5%.[161] The same pattern characterized the wage rounds of 1980 and 1981.

Whereas during the "noisy" period of the early 1970s every contract negotiated by IG Chemie was substantially above the government's orientation data, the exact opposite was true after 1975. Indeed, one of the most distinctive features of the "silent" post-1975 era was its uninterrupted string of low wage gains. The concentration of decision-making power at the "top" of the union during wage rounds thus seems to have correlated inversely with the size of the pay increase.

The union's gains in the qualitative area could hardly have been more modest than its quantitative attainments. Instead of the comprehensive protection against rationalization which the union demanded as part of the new general framework contract, a weak substitute appeared in 1975. Initiated by the employers and two miniscule rival unions in the chemical industry, a so-called Assistance Agency in the Chemical Industry (Unterstützungsverein der chemischen Industrie – UCI) was established and contractually accepted by all parties present in the industry, including IG Chemie. The agency's task was to provide unemployed chemical workers, who had been laid off through no fault of their own and who had worked in the chemical industry without interruption for at least five years, with extra funds to supplement their regular unemployment benefits. It also included special compensatory measures for older workers adversely affected by technological changes in the production process.[162]

Although commendable in its intent, this agency failed to provide what the union had envisioned earlier in the decade as proper protection against rationalization. First and foremost, UCI was unable to prevent any adverse effects of the rationalization process, especially layoffs. The agency did not help the union shape the rationalization process even in its most rudimentary form. As such, it completely lacked any of the "offensive" dimensions which IG Chemie had sought during a more militant period. UCI failed to offer adequate "defensive" mechanisms as well; it provided no retraining or on-the-job compensation to the victims of rationalization.[163]

In addition to its deficient contents, this agency irked many workers because of the way it was created. While nobody in IG Chemie recalled having demanded anything even vaguely akin to this solution, it was suddenly presented by the employers to the union as a *fait accompli*. Many IG Chemie members felt betrayed by the top-down, dictatorial behavior which the union leaders exhibited toward the rank and file, contrasting it with the meek way in which they approached the employers.

This became even more pronounced as the decade drew to an end, with IG Chemie still failing to attain any significant qualitative gains. It either followed in the path of the other unions by adopting a usually weaker variant of their successes, such as the six-week annual vacation which IG Chemie copied from IG Metall following the latter's grueling battle with the steel industry, or it simply remained inactive by accepting the employers' "reforms" and "suggestions" with virutally no changes.[164] During the negotiations for the general framework contract in the spring of 1979, IG Chemie adopted the employers' offer with very few alterations. Changes that the union did demand were insignificant at best.[165]

The only area in which IG Chemie maintained an innovative spirit during the crisis period was – rather tellingly – the development of various asset-formation proposals. As will be recalled, the union – together with IG Metall and in vehement opposition to IG Bau-Steine-Erden – opposed this strategy throughout the mid-1960s as detrimental to collective bargaining, both in spirit and in actual content. By the late 1960s and early 1970s, however, IG Chemie had come around to accepting asset formation as complementary to collective bargaining, albeit still in a subordinate position. As the decade progressed, however, asset formation assumed an increasingly central role in IG Chemie's long-term strategy as a solution to many of the structural problems besetting the chemical industry and the West German economy.

In the late 1970s, IG Chemie devised a number of asset-formation proposals – some of which were later adopted by the DGB as a whole – based on the idea of cooperation with the employers. The most interesting of these plans were the so-called Branchenfonds, or sectoral funds, which, if fully implemented, would provide industry-wide shares for every employee in a given sector.[166] A mechanism was to be developed which could protect every worker in the chemical industry, regardless of whether he/she was employed by a big or small, profitable or non-profitable company. These Branchenfonds, like the "Assistance Agency," were to be maintained by equal contributions from the union and the employers.[167] As such, they represented yet another construct in which the union's activities would be tied to the employers. The very idea of the Branchenfonds – although harboring many egalitarian elements – ultimately conveyed a desire for cooperation with management on the part of the union. Thus, it should be seen as an expression of the overall shift towards an accommodationist posture which IG Chemie experienced after the onset of the crisis in 1975.

This path did not, however, remain unchallenged from within IG Chemie. An increasingly vocal and well-organized opposition to this course formed around the shop-steward wing of the union. This group enjoyed a vigorous growth in membership and received encouragement from the Zeitgeist dominating public discourse in the early 1970s. Following the events of 1969, workers in West Germany became mobilized for the first time since the late 1940s and early 1950s, and even chemical workers joined this bandwagon. (One important result of the mobilization was the strike in 1971. The reformers in the union viewed the strike as a defeat, which they believed to be a direct consequence of the union's weakness due to its complacency and explicitly accommodationist posture.)

The reformers wanted a more activist strategy on the part of IG Chemie. This meant, of course, a more critical position regarding the status quo and a greater emphasis on confrontation than on cooperation. To pursue such a strategy, the activists believed that the union had to undergo important structural changes concerning its shop-floor presence at BASF, Hoechst and Bayer where ultimately the fate of capital–labor relations in the West German chemical industry were decided. They wanted IG Chemie to place a greater emphasis on its shop stewards, to the direct detriment of the union's works councilors. Although the conflict centered ostensibly on a showdown betwen works councilors and shop stewards, IG Chemie's fundamental political orientation was at stake. This conflict, while conceived in the "noisy" and optimistic period of mobilization, came to full fruition during the austere and "silent" era of the crisis.

The lengthy and acerbic struggle between the accommodationists and the activists came to a head in early 1979. Seldom had an intra-union dispute attracted as much attention in the public media as did this confrontation within IG Chemie. It started with an article published on February 20, 1979 in the left-leaning daily *Frankfurter Rundschau* which has consistently enjoyed the reputation as the best-informed major newspaper in the Federal Republic concerning union-related matters.[168] The *Rundschau* piece reported that IG Chemie's executive committee had reached a major decision in a series of meetings – most notably on January 5 and February 9 of that year – to alter the union's bylaws concerning the election and/or appointment of the company shop stewards to official union positions.[169] Rather than undertake this statutory revision – with its serious organizational implications – at the union's next congress in September 1980, the executive committee planned to implement its desired change at a much more restricted forum, the upcoming meeting of the union's advisory council on April 5, 1979.[170] The numerous demonstrations held during March and April in many West German cities during which IG Chemie members demanded that the union leadership increase rank-and-file participation and "return the union to those who really are the union" made clear to the attentive observer that much more was at stake than the legal status of a few sentences in the union's bylaws. Indeed, it was less than commonplace to see union members in the Federal Republic, including relatively high-ranking officials, engaged in active protest against their union's leadership and its policies.

To make matters even more complex, the West German public was informed in the middle of March that IG Chemie's executive committee had fired one of its key officials, the secretary of Hannoversch-Münden, one of the union's traditionally strategic locals.[171] The reason for this highly unusual act had to do with the statutory change proposed by IG Chemie's leadership. The union's executive committee believed that the secretary of the local had overstepped his authority by disseminating materials sent to him by the executive committee pertaining to the upcoming alteration of the bylaws. Not only did IG Chemie's leaders in Hanover see this act as a breach of the fiduciary relationship between the union's executive committee and its employees (the secretaries of the locals) but they were also perturbed by the secretary's personal annotations which accompanied the released materials.

The secretary defended these annotations by stating that as a delegate to the union's congress he had the right to comment on proposed changes in the bylaws.[172] When, after repeated requests by the union leadership, the secretary of Hannoversch-Münden refused to reveal the names of the recipients of his mailing, the executive committee fired him unconditionally. Adding fuel to the fire, all members of the local's council immediately repudiated the leadership's action and demanded the prompt reinstatement of their dismissed secretary.[173] The headquarters in Hanover rejected this demand and the union moved toward a full-scale showdown.

To determine the origins of this conflict – and its ultimate implications – one must examine the role of so-called company shop stewards in the industrial relations of the chemical industry. As discussed above, the German chemical industry has enjoyed a tradition of extreme paternalism and company-based labor protection since the early years of the twentieth century. The large chemical companies sought to keep the unions away from the shop floor. Toward that end, they established elaborate company-dominated housing projects, insurance schemes, welfare programs and, of course, labor organizations, mainly in the form of company-controlled labor unions and shop-floor representatives (i.e. the company shop stewards). It was this thorough and early penetration of the labor side by capital which led to the highly developed cooperation programs and the pervasive ideology of social partnership so characteristic of the chemical industry, on both the company and industry level, throughout the Weimar Republic and up to the present day.[174]

IG Chemie's organizational difficulties date back to this company-orientation and the successful ideological and organizational infiltration by the employers of labor representation on the shop floor. From the very beginning of West Germany's reconstruction era, IG Chemie found it impossible to counter the employers' shop-floor power where it most mattered: the production sites of the Big Three, especially Hoechst and Bayer. When the union established its system of shop stewards in the late 1950s, the three successor companies to IG Farben as well as other major chemical firms responded by strengthening their already powerful shop-floor presence through the creation of an even more extensive network of company shop stewards. This meant that everyone belonging to a particular company was entitled to elect his/her shop steward regardless of unionization on the part of either the candidate or the electorate. The companies tried to bypass IG Chemie's shop-floor presence by creating an organization of their own. The firms envisioned the company shop stewards as complementary to the works councilors, rather than as their rivals, which was the union's original notion in establishing the union-organized shop stewards as IG Chemie's direct representatives on the shop floor. Analysts close to the activist wing within IG Chemie characterized these company shop stewards as "instruments to confine the employees to structures of social partnership."[175] According to these unionists, the presence of the company shop stewards stymied IG Chemie's organizational maneuverability on the shop floor.

IG Chemie had to find a modus vivendi. Since the union had neither the market nor the state power to dislodge these "alien" elements from the nation's plants, it had to adjust to their existence. As late as the latter half of the 1970s, 38 major companies in the West German chemical industry (42 including the other industries in the union's domain such as rubber, glass, paper, etc.) still had the system of company shop stewards as one form of shop-floor representation in addition to the works councils (which, of course, are the primary legal representatives of labor inside West German companies).[176] This means, according to reliable calculations, that approximately one-half of all IG Chemie members employed in the chemical industry elected company shop stewards instead of union ones as late as 1979.[177] Indeed, one-quarter of the union's entire membership worked in companies where all employees – unionized and non-unionized – voted for shop stewards. Thus, in 38 of the biggest chemical firms, the shop-steward structure was de facto determined by the companies and not the union. The electorate consisted of all the employees rather than strictly IG Chemie members, thereby transforming what virtually everywhere else in the industrial relations system was strictly an internal union matter into a company-controlled event.

It so happened that a majority of these company shop stewards were IG Chemie members. (This reflected an empirical reality of shop-floor participation rather than an organizational requirement on the part of the union.) Throughout the years, custom – and IG Chemie's shop-floor weakness – required that the union automatically "appoint" to the position of *union* shop steward every elected company shop steward who happened to be a member of IG Chemie. Thus developed a system in which non-unionized employees acquired potentially crucial input in the union's policies and strategies. This, although true for every member union of the DGB, was a fortiori the case in IG Chemie, where the shop stewards had an even greater role in the decision-making processes and structures of the union. As mentioned above, IG Chemie's shop stewards, rather than the regular union members, have the mandate to vote for the delegates to the union's congresses and also – since 1972 – to elect the members of the union's bargaining commissions. In short, the shop stewards in IG Chemie became crucial organizational conduits for the articulation and legitimation of union policy.

From the late 1950s to the 1970s, IG Chemie practiced this system of shop steward adoption and appointment in 38 of the chemical industry's most important plants. Nevertheless, this mechanism never enjoyed the full legitimacy of inclusion in the union's bylaws. In a sense, IG Chemie's leadership always felt somewhat embarrassed vis-à-vis the other DGB unions and, of course, vis-à-vis a substantial segment of its own rank and file, concerning the existence of this peculiar construct. It is largely for this reason that the union withheld its official blessing from the long-practiced mechanism by excluding it from its bylaws. This changed in early 1979.

The executive committee decided by a 6 to 2 vote during a meeting on April 5, 1979 to amend IG Chemie's bylaws, in order to have the union's statutes correspond to a reality which had existed for nearly three decades on the shop floor of some of the country's leading chemical plants. Both the content of this statutory change and the form of its implementation sufficiently annoyed a large enough minority within IG Chemie to provoke massive protests which had some internecine and lastingly disruptive effects on the union.

The change in content seemed trivial to an outsider who was unfamiliar with its larger implications. The pertinent passage in IG Chemie's bylaws, published in 1977, started with the following sentence: "Shop stewards are to be elected in every factory. They are to particpate in the union's decision-making process and its political life."[178] The executive committee wanted to add the following words: "In every factory shop stewards are to be elected or appointed by the district councils."[179] These few additional words caused members of IG Chemie's activist wing to mobilize an unprecedented protest against a majority of the union and most of its top leaders. The placement of these words in the union's bylaws signified the complete acceptance and legitimation of the company shop stewards as integral elements of the union.

Perhaps even more perturbing to many IG Chemie members than the statutory change itself was the method chosen by the union's executive committee to insert it in the bylaws. Rather than propose it at the union's highest and most open forum (i.e. the congress) thereby ensuring the widest possible debate on this crucial matter, IG Chemie's leaders opted for a cloak-and-dagger action precisely to avoid public exposure. To the union's reformers, the whole affair represented the most egregious act of circumventing union democracy ever undertaken by the more powerful accommodationists. They saw it as the accommodationists' ultimate move to consolidate their power – and thus the status quo – in IG Chemie, at the direct expense of the reformers and their visions for the union.

The roots of the conflict date back to the strike of 1971 and its immediate aftermath. Following IG Chemie's futile attempts to introduce plant-oriented collective bargaining in 1970 and the union's failures in coordinating activities during the strike in the subsequent year, a vocal minority began to place the blame on the company shop stewards at Hoechst, Bayer and BASF. These activists argued that the presence of company shop stewards made it all but impossible for the union to conduct a credible strike in the chemical industry. Encouraged by labor's mobilization efforts, the activists sought to strengthen union power on the shop floor by pushing for a greater role for the union's shop stewards within the organization itself and inside the factories.

At IG Chemie's ninth congress in the fall of 1972, the reformers, led by Paul Plumeyer (who assumed the position of officer in charge of organizational matters and shop stewards on the union's executive committee), aimed their offensive at augmenting the role of shop stewards in the union's decision-making process. Against the wishes of the majority on the executive committee – where Plumeyer and his colleague Werner Vitt were outvoted by the other six members – and against the explicit recommendations of the political program committee, a majority of the union's delegates voted in favor of strengthening the shop stewards' role in formulating IG Chemie's general bargaining strategies and specific wage demands.[180] Moreover, the congress empowered the shop stewards to elect the members of the union's bargaining committees.

As important as the actual resolutions passed by the delegates at this congress were the debates concerning the thorny issues of company shop stewards. The reformers pinned their entire criticism of the union's inability to challenge the employers in a meaningful way on the presence of these "alien" bodies in the midst of IG Chemie's domain. As long as the union proved unable to establish its own independent and autonomous shop-floor representation, it could not develop a viable alternative to the existing strategy of social partnership and cooperation with management. In order to implement the reformers' desire that IG Chemie become an effective "countervailing power," the system of company shop stewards had to be abolished and replaced by a powerful shop steward structure which was completely the union's own.

The accommodationists, representing the union's entrenched bureaucrats and its powerful Big Three works councilors, opposed the activists' demands on the grounds that they would ruin an advantageous situation. The accommodationists accused the reformers of wanting a different union and ultimately a different social order in the Federal Republic. The works council "counts" also opposed the suggested reforms because they directly threatened the status quo on the shop floor, which had given the works councilors privilege and authority. Moreover, it was as a consequence of their positions inside the companies that the works councilors played influential roles inside IG Chemie as well. In this construct, company shop stewards enhanced the works councilors' standing, while the introduction of union shop stewards would present a challenge to the organizational privileges of the councilors. Thus it is hardly surprising that the accommodationists made every effort to prevent the reformers from passing a resolution that would require the union to replace company shop stewards with union ones.[181]

But the debate continued. Two years later, at the union's non-binding "working conference," the delegates once again focused on the shop-steward issue. It was decided at this conference "that company shop stewards were only a transitory solution" and that ultimately the union had to establish union-controlled shop stewards on the shop floor.[182] IG Chemie's quadrennial report submitted to the 1976 congress also gave extensive coverage to this issue. Moreover, fifteen demands from various union locals and districts dealt exclusively with the problem of the shop stewards.

The congress itself was again an acrimonious affair, pitting reformers against accommodationists on issues of union strategy. With the backdrop of the economic crisis, the debates assumed an increased sense of urgency and immediacy in terms of their concrete policy implications for IG Chemie. The activists succeeded in making the congress accept an official resolution addressing the issue of the shop stewards. But the wording of the resolution clearly conveyed the compromises which had to be reached with the accommodationists. It stated that "in consultation with the unionized works councilors and other shop-floor representatives of the union in large companies the situation merits an investigation of how the company shop stewards could be replaced by union ones."[183] The "could" of course was telling. It exonerated the union leadership from having to make this crucial change during the next legislative period between union congresses. Nevertheless, the decision of the tenth congress finally placed the whole issue on the union's official agenda. As of 1976, IG Chemie committed itself to resolving this problem once and for all, albeit at a still unspecified future date.

In 1977, IG Chemie conducted a strike vote in its Rhineland-Palatinate district led by the huge BASF works in Ludwigshafen. Despite the overwhelmingly positive result of the vote in the area as a whole, and a particularly strong showing at BASF, the union decided to call off the strike at the last moment.[184] Once again IG Chemie refused to conduct a strike at one of the Big Three, although its position at BASF was much stronger than at the other two. And once again many union members felt cheated by what they perceived as an overly cautious, even cowardly, union leadership. Many saw the mobilization via the strike vote as futile, and some even assumed sinister motives on the part of the leadership, which had promised much but delivered little.

A year later, the union held one of its mid-term working congresses, wherein the shop-steward issue played a key role. As usual, IG Chemie's two wings clashed on this topic with the activists trying to push the union further than the congress declaration of 1976 and the accommodationists eager to slow things down as much as possible.

The challenge by the activists assumed another dimension that year. They decided to run their own rival candidates to IG Chemie's official entries in some of the key works council elections to be held throughout West Germany in 1978. It was notably at Bayer that the reformers challenged the union's official candidates, some of whom they saw as the most accommodationist "works council counts" within the union. The reformist entries fared exceptionally well. Their "alternative list" won ten out of 25 seats on the works council at Bayer.[185]

The official union candidates and IG Chemie's veterans on the Bayer works council, all of whom belonged to the accommodationist wing of the union, demanded that their rivals be expelled from the union. Indeed, they wanted to initiate court actions against the activist candidates, whom they perceived as incompatible with the unitary trade-union movement because of their political views and their insubordination to the union. However, before it could get that far, IG Chemie's arbitration committee held that these candidates could not be expelled from the union since the existence of two types of shop stewards, company and union, already allowed the presence of more than one union list for works council elections.[186]

The whole episode shocked IG Chemie's leadership. Rival lists at works council elections, if allowed to proliferate in sufficiently large numbers, could have meant the beginning of the end for the union. Lest this dangerous situation be seized by forces hostile to IG Chemie via litigation, the executive committee decided to take matters into its own hands. The committee believed it crucial to give company shop stewards their overdue legitimation by anchoring their existence in the union's bylaws. Thus, there would be no more question concerning company shop stewards and their relationship to the union. This move set the stage for the media events of 1979.

Confronted with massive demonstrations against the union leadership, the executive committee reneged on some of its earlier actions in order to appease the opposition. Thus, the dismissed secretary of the union local in Hannoversch-Münden was reinstated.[187] In addition, the language of the suggested change in the bylaws assumed a more tentative tone. Appointments of company shop stewards to union positions were going to be "the exception" and far from automatic. Indeed, this transfer was only going to occur in cases "where the proper election of union shop stewards by union members was somehow made impossible," whether by forces inside or outside the factory gates.[188]

Nevertheless, a lasting compromise was not achieved. At IG Chemie's eleventh congress in the fall of 1980, the West German public witnessed perhaps the most acrimonious union meeting in recent memory. Personal recriminations overlapped with political disagreements. The accommodationists accused the reformers of trying to make IG Chemie a radical – even subversive – organization which would have little in common with the majority of the union's members. The activists, in turn, reproached the accommodationists for having led the union onto a path of compliance and submission during a period of crisis, when the opposite strategy was urgently needed. Interestingly, but characteristically, each accused the other of having abdicated the mandate of the union and of having violated the sacrosanct tenets of union democracy.

In the end the accommodationists succeeded in purging the major reformer in the union, Paul Plumeyer, and his most important allies. Werner Vitt, Plumeyer's colleague in the voting tandem on the executive committee, barely retained his seat and emerged severely weakened and isolated after the congress. There can be no question that the accommodationists implemented a thorough purge of key activists within IG Chemie. Consequently, the eleventh congress witnessed the final triumph of the accommodationists over their intra-organizational rivals, following a protracted battle for most of the decade. Yet this would be too simplistic a conclusion.

While the reformers lost in terms of "positional" politics and became marginalized in IG Chemie following the union's 1980 congress, they nevertheless gained important programmatic concessions, such as in the controversy over shop stewards. The congress decreed in no uncertain terms that by the end of 1983, company shop stewards would no longer be tolerated within the union's ranks. In other strategic issues as well, the reformers left a strong legacy for IG Chemie as it entered the 1980.

Ultimately, however, the 1980 congress helped establish IG Chemie as one of the most enthusiastic supporters of the DGB's accommodationist wing. On virtually every issue, societal or union-specific, IG Chemie toed the accommodationist line. Despite the union's particularly close ties to the Schmidt faction of the Social Democratic Party, the latter's demise from governmental power and the concomitant weakening of the Schmidt wing within the SPD itself did not change IG Chemie's overall strategy of accommodation. IG Chemie-Papier-Keramik had securely established itself by the middle of the 1980s as the DGB's most outspokenly accommodationist union, advocating strategies with vastly different visions from those favored by IG Metall and its allies in the West German labor movement.

# 6 LEBER'S VANGUARD: THE CONSTRUCTION WORKERS' UNION, IG BAU-STEINE-ERDEN
(written with Thomas C. Ertman)

## INTRODUCTION

The West German construction workers' union, IG Bau-Steine-Erden, occupies a unique place in the Federal Republic's labor history. Unlike construction unions in many other advanced industrial countries, IG Bau has been plagued by chronic organizational weakness. Its membership density has always been the lowest among the major DGB unions. Yet it is precisely this handicap that explains our interest in IG Bau. In an attempt to solve its problems, the union tried, especially in the late 1950s and early 1960s, to develop a new approach to industrial relations which brought it into open conflict with the DGB's dominant force, IG Metall. IG Bau established itself as the leader and chief ideologue of the "social partnership" or accommodationist wing of West German labor, a role which it has only recently learned to share with others in the DGB federation, notably IG Chemie-Papier-Keramik, IG Textil und Beklei-dung, IG Bergbau und Energie and the Gewerkschaft Nahrung-Genuss-Gaststätten.

The main goal of this chapter will be to explain both IG Bau's persistent weakness in the labor market and the kind of organizational response this weakness has called forth. After a discussion of the construction industry and IG Bau's internal structure, the chapter will give a brief history of labor relations in German construction in order to assess the effects of tradition on IG Bau's behavior. A chronological presentation of IG Bau's development since 1950 will follow, giving special emphasis to the Leber period (1955–66) and its lasting effects on the union.

## I. THE CONSTRUCTION INDUSTRY AND ITS EMPLOYERS' ASSOCIATIONS

As in all other industrial countries, the construction industry plays a crucial role in the West German economy. It is estimated that the total value of all construction activities equals about 16% of GDP.[1] Housing construction accounted for 46.8% of this total in 1978, followed by commercial construction at 25.9% and public sector construction at 27.3%.[2] In 1980, 2,040,000 persons were employed in all construction sectors, which amounted to 7.9% of total employment.[3] Construction's importance is further underlined by the fact that in any given year about 60% of all investments eventually flow into this sector.[4]

In the German classification system, construction is sub-divided into a number of industries varying in economic importance. In addition to the Bauhauptgewerbe, or primary construction sector, there are construction finishing (Bauausbaugewerbe), auxiliary construction (Baunebenge-werbe), the construction products industry (Baustoffgewerbe), and the housing service sector typically comprising landlords and architectural firms. Construction finishing covers activities such as painting and plumb-ing, heating and electrical installation. Tasks such as demolition and façade-cleaning are classed as auxiliary construction. Henceforth in this chapter we will mainly be concerned with primary construction, for it is in this area that over 80% of IG Bau's members work. Building construction of all types remains at the heart of the Bauhauptgewerbe, but road-building and bridge- and subway-construction are also important.

As in printing, skilled workers constitute the majority of the labor force in primary construction. Out of a total of 1,190,208 persons employed in this sector in 1978, 666,525 or 56% were skilled workers (including foremen), while only 21.9% constituted semi- or unskilled labor. The percentage of white-collar employees, at 12%, still remains below the industrial average, although it has been steadily rising over the past three decades. The remainder of the workforce consists of apprentices (4.6%) and working owners and their family members.[5] Two other noteworthy characteristics of the labor force in the construction industry have been its large number of foreign workers (Gastarbeiter) and very small number of women. Although 19.1% of all construction workers were Gastarbeiter in 1978, this represents a considerable drop from the 31.2% reached in 1972.[6]

In 1976, there were 58,354 individual firms in primary construction, of which 76% employed fewer than twenty workers. Of the 1,944 firms with more than 100 employees, 73 had between 500 and 1,000, 37 between 1,000 and 5,000 and nine giants more than 5,000 workers. Fifty-eight percent of all construction workers held jobs in firms with under 100 employees, and 22.3% in firms with under 20, showing that small businesses and construction sites dominate this industry. At the other end of the scale, the nine giant companies with over 5,000 workers account for 18.2% of construction's workforce and 28% of its total sales.[7] The largest firms are generally involved in such capital-intensive activities as road-, bridge- and subway-building, as well as large-scale commercial projects like factory construction. Housing construction remains the prerogative of the smaller firms, and it is in this segment of the market that competition has been the fiercest. In summary, construction is characterized by small firm size and low economic concentration, but includes a number of very large firms which dominate certain specialized markets.

Employers in primary construction are organized into two associations, the Zentralverband des Deutschen Baugewerbes (Central Association of German Construction – ZDB) and the Hauptverband der Deutschen Bauindustrie (Main Association of the German Construction Industry – HDB).[8] The difference between these two organizations rests in the fact that the ZDB is a craft association, meaning that its members belong to West Germany's complex system of craft "guilds" (Handwerksinnungen), whereas the HDB is an industrial organization.[9] There are no objective criteria for choosing membership in one or the other association – the decision depends on a firm's self-definition as either craft or industrial and is largely determined by history and tradition. In practice, however, the majority of small and medium-sized firms belong to the ZDB, while most of the large firms are in the HDB. It would not be accurate, though, to call the ZDB an association exclusively of smaller firms, since several of the nation's largest construction companies are also members. Thus, while size can be a useful indicator as to whether a firm belongs to the HDB or the ZDB, it is not a dependable one.

The employers' organizations in the sectors of the industry other than primary construction are very fragmented, with ten separate employers' associations in both construction finishing and auxiliary construction, and 21 in the building materials sector. This results from the fact that the associations are divided on both regional and product lines, thus rendering collective bargaining in these sectors very complex and decentralized.

Finally, it is important to summarize the special characteristics which West German construction shares with the construction industries of most other countries and which present particular problems for a union trying to operate within this industry.

(1) Most construction workers are employed by small, family-owned and -operated firms,

(2) Few, if any, fixed production sites exist in the construction industry. Workers change building projects frequently.

(3) A high rate of labor turnover characterizes the industry, with workers frequently switching employers and often leaving the sector altogether during business downturns.

(4) The weather plays a crucial role in construction. This often leads to intense activity during the summer months and extended layoffs and project interruptions during the winter.

(5) The production process is still by and large of a craft nature. Although the mechanization level in construction has risen steadily since 1949, the industry remains predominantly labor-intensive and thus its productivity level is relatively low (about 10% below the industrial average in 1980).[10] As a result, wage costs assume particular importance, since they represent about 39% of total costs in construction compared to an industrial average of 21-22%.[11]

(6) The industry is especially sensitive to changes in the business cycle, with employment and output fluctuating more markedly than in the economy as a whole.

## II. IG BAU-STEINE-ERDEN: AN OVERVIEW

With its 533,054 members (1981), IG Bau is West Germany's fourth largest union after IG Metall, ÖTV and IG Chemie.[12] IG Bau's organizational area comprises all sectors of construction (including building materials), but, as mentioned, 80% of its members work in primary construction. The union itself divides its organizational purview into three areas – primary construction, finishing construction (incorporating auxiliary construction) and stones and earth (covering building products and quarrying). This last area was, especially in the 1950s, the source of one of the DGB's rare boundary disputes, pitting IG Bau and IG Chemie against each other as the latter contested the right of the former to organize workers in the asbestos and insulation industries. This dispute was only put to rest after mediation by the DGB.

With total employment in construction at 2,040,000 in 1980, IG Bau's membership of 533,054 represents an organizational level of only 26%. Since the union's membership figure also includes about 10,000 retired workers, the real organizational level hovers around 24%, thus making IG Bau the most poorly organized of the major DGB unions. This weakness has plagued the union since its inception. There have been periods when the union's presence among West German construction workers was even more ephemeral than it is today. From an organizational density of 26% in 1950, IG Bau's representation receded to between 17% and 23% in the 1950s and 1960s. It was only with the onset of the economic crisis in 1974 that the union's organizational presence once again reached about 25%, a figure which prevailed with little change until the early 1980s.[13]

A key factor in IG Bau's persistent membership problems is undoubtedly the special character of the construction industry. To this must be added IG Bau's organization as an industrial – rather than a craft – union, as well as certain special features of West German labor law (like the ban on closed or union shops, so important in Britain and the US). Constantly changing production sites, high labor turnover, and the predominance of small family firms all make unionization difficult when it is purely voluntary. In addition, between 20% and 30% of the workforce has consistently been composed of foreign workers since the early 1960s, and their organizational level in the construction industry has never exceeded 9%.[14] Yet these factors do not provide a completely satisfactory explanation, since the construction industry in Austria, whose structure is quite similar to that of the FRG, has a workforce which boasts a 70% level of unionization. As we shall see, IG Bau's representational weakness has played a crucial role in shaping the union's goals and strategy throughout its history. The union's inability to solve this crucial problem has undoubtedly undermined the overall strength of West German labor.

If the area of primary construction is taken alone, IG Bau's organizational density is somewhat higher, at 33%. In addition to the 80% of the union's total membership which work in this sector, about 10% of IG Bau's members are in construction finishing and 8% in building materials and quarrying. Only about 2% of the membership are women, and only 8% white-collar workers, making the union a predominantly blue-collar, male organization. In 1978, there were also about 20,000 foreign workers in the union, mainly Yugoslavs, Turks and Italians.[15] Because IG Bau is very sensitive about its organizational problems, the union releases far less information about its membership than most other DGB unions. It is therefore not possible to offer exact figures on the organizational levels of various skill groups.

The internal structure of IG Bau is fairly similar to that of the other DGB unions already discussed.[16] The union is divided into nine districts: Baden-Württemberg, Bavaria, Hesse, Lower Saxony, Nordmark, North Rhine, Rhineland-Palatinate-Saar, Unterweser-Ems and Westphalia (see Table 6.1). Below these there are 131 locals (Verwaltungsstellen), with West Berlin classified as a special local directly responsible to the union's executive committee based in Frankfurt. The basic organ of membership participation is the membership meeting, which is held periodically to elect the local's executive board as well as to select delegates to the district and national conferences. Each district congress then chooses a district execu-

Table 6.1 *IG Bau districts and locals*

| Districts | Berlin | Baden-Württemberg | Bavaria | Hesse | Lower Saxony | Nordmark | North Rhine | Rhineland-Palatinate-Saar | Unterweser-Ems | Westphalia |
|---|---|---|---|---|---|---|---|---|---|---|
| Locals | (Berlin has no locals) | Balingen | Ansbach | Darmstadt | Braunschweig | Elmshorn (Southwest Holstein) | Aachen | Kaiserslautern (West Palatinate) | Borkum | Bielefeld |
| | | Freiburg | Aschaffenburg | Frankfurt am Main | Celle | Flensburg | Bonn | Koblenz | Bremen | Bocholt |
| | | Singen (Bodensee-Allgäu) | Augsburg | Fulda | Duderstadt | Hamburg | Duisburg | Bad Kreuznach (Nahe-Hunsrück) | Bremerhaven-Wesermarsch | Bochum |
| | | Göppingen | Bamberg | Gelnhausen | Northeim | Husum (North Friesland) | Düsseldorf | Kusel (Westrich und Glantal) | Emden (East Friesland) | Detmold |
| | | Heidelberg | Bayreuth | Giessen | Goslar | Lübeck | Essen | Landau (South Palatinate) | Lingen (Emsland) | Dortmund |
| | | Heilbronn | Coburg | Eschwege-Hersfeld | Göttingen/Holzminden | Kiel | Cologne | Ludwigshafen (Outer Palatinate) | Oldenburg | Gelsenkirchen |
| | | Karlsruhe | Erlangen | Kassel | Hameln | Lüneburg | Krefeld | Mainz | Rotenburg | Gladbeck |
| | | Mannheim | Fürth | Limburg | Hanover | Meldorf (Dithmarschen) | Mönchengladbach & Grenzland | Mayen | Syke-Diepholz | Hagen |
| | | Offenburg | Hof | Marburg | Hildesheim | Neumünster | Mülheim-Oberhausen | Neuwied (Westerwald) | Wilhelmshaven | Hamm |
| | | Reutlingen/Tübingen | Ingolstadt | Wiesbaden | Peine/Wolfsburg | Rendsburg | Wesel (Lower Rhine) | Trier | Norderney | Herford |
| | | Stuttgart | Marktredwitz | Bad Wildungen | Osnabrück | Stade (Lower Elbe) | Solingen-Remscheid | Worms-Eisenberg-Alzey | | Lippstadt |
| | | Schwäbisch Hall | Munich | Friedberg | Stadthagen | Harburg | Wuppertal | Neunkirchen | | Minden |
| | | Ulm | Nuremberg | | Uelzen | | | Saarbrücken | | Münster |
| | | Esslingen | Regensburg | | | | | | | Paderborn |
| | | | Rosenheim | | | | | | | Recklinghausen |
| | | | Straubing | | | | | | | Rheine |
| | | | Schweinfurt | | | | | | | Siegen |
| | | | Würzburg | | | | | | | |
| | | | Passau | | | | | | | |
| | | | Amberg | | | | | | | |
| | | | Kempten | | | | | | | |
| | | | Landshut | | | | | | | |
| | | | Schwandorf | | | | | | | |
| | | | Weilheim | | | | | | | |

*Source:* Frankfurt am Main, IG Bau-Steine-Erden.

tive and the national congress elects the national executive committee, which at present consists of ten members. National congresses took place biannually from 1949 until 1957, when this was changed to a three-year interval. As DGB unions go, IG Bau is very centralized, with all local and district union officials requiring the endorsement of the national leadership. The latter can also remove officials at any time and replace them with its own appointments.

IG Bau's chain of command in the collective bargaining process is also more centralized than in most other unions.[17] Unlike in IG Metall or IG Druck, the collective bargaining committee (Tarifkommission) plays a relatively unimportant role. Recommendations on wage demands and bargaining strategy are made by the national executive committee to the union's advisory council (Beirat), which is composed of the national executive committee itself, the district leaders, and two or three elected representatives from each district. The advisory council then passes on its suggestions to a negotiating committee of four national executive committee members and four regional leaders. By contrast, the collective bargaining committee, made up of 28 representatives elected from the districts, normally meets only to ratify a settlement. IG Bau's bylaws, like those of IG Chemie, contain no specified guidelines for calling or ending a strike. Thus no strike vote is required to initiate industrial action nor is a ratification vote necessary to end a strike. All these measures can be initiated (or dispensed with) at the national executive committee's discretion.

IG Bau has signed a series of arbitration agreements with the HDB and the ZDB since 1950, most recently in March 1979. Under the current system, both sides choose an arbitrator by mutual consent who serves for a term of three years.[18] If negotiations break down at the national level, either side can call on the arbitrator to make an arbitration recommendation, which is non-binding. Strikes are not permitted until such a recommendtion has been rejected by one of the two parties.

Like all other DGB unions, IG Bau concludes both general framework (Manteltarifverträge) and wage (Lohntarifverträge) contracts with various employers' associations (the ZDB and HDB in primary construction). General framework contracts cover issues such as work time, working conditions and vacation, and in construction they often must be particularly detailed in order to include all situations that arise on a building site. These contracts run nominally for about three years, and it has become the practice in primary construction to update or modify these agreements frequently without formally renegotiating them when they expire, as is the case in many other industries. Thus, a national Manteltarifvertrag in construction may actually be in effect for ten years or more with major revisions occurring bi-or triannually. In addition to the single, national, general framework contract for primary construction, IG Bau negotiates separate agreements for all the different sectors of construction finishing, auxiliary construction and the building materials industries.

IG Bau negotiates a central wage contract for the entire Federal Republic covering all blue-collar workers in primary construction. This is the industry's most important single agreement. In central bargaining with the ZDB and HDG, IG Bau sets the construction base wage, which is the hourly pay rate of a skilled mason (known as Wage Group III). After this base rate has been worked out, each of the union's districts signs detailed contracts with the local employers' associations containing a table of all other wage rates calculated according to an agreed system of wage categories and differentials. In 1980, there were seven basic wage categories in primary construction: worker (unskilled), craftsman (semi-skilled), basic skilled worker, advanced skilled worker (skilled worker with two years' experience), special skilled worker, overseer, and work fore-man.[19] Additionally, the pay system originally had four geographic classes (Ortsklassen) in 1950, but these were progressively amalgamated and finally eliminated altogether in 1977.

Wage bargaining in the construction finishing and building materials industries is extremely fragmented compared to its counterpart in primary construction. Contracts are only negotiated on the regional level, and separate agreements must be signed with each employers' association, of which there are ten in construction finishing and twenty-one in building materials. In addition, the union negotiates a national contract for white-collar employees in primary construction and regional contracts for all other sectors of the industry. It is hardly surprising then that the union signed 310 contracts of all types in 1981 alone.[20]

### III. HISTORICAL BACKGROUND: LABOR RELATIONS IN GERMAN CONSTRUCTION

The history of labor relations in the German construction industry before 1933 parallels developments in printing. The building trades boasted the most extensive system of collective bargaining agreements – after printing – in 1914, and the largest number of workers covered by contracts in absolute terms.[21] As in printing, construction was dominated before 1910 by a number of different craft unions, the most important being the masons. Unlike the book printers, however, the masons favored the industrial union principle, and the first labor organization claiming to represent all construction workers was formed in 1911. As we shall see, a cooperative approach to labor relations based on collective bargaining was more controversial in construction, during both the Wilhelminian and Weimar periods, than was the case in printing. This explains why the first national contract for the building trades was not signed until 1910, 37 years after the first conclusion of such a contract in printing.

One can discern four distinct periods in the development of construction unions before 1933. The first, from 1868 to 1878, was the period when the first unions were formed, only to be banned in 1878 because of Bismarck's Anti-Socialist Law. Between 1878 and 1899, various construction unions were re-formed from the bottom up, culminating in the refounding of national unions. From 1899 until 1914, several important unions worked to set up a collective bargaining system that would cover the whole country. The system thus established was progressively dismantled over the next 20 years as a result of World War I and the economic uncertainties of Weimar.

Germany's first construction union was the Gewerksverein der Bauhandwerker, founded in December 1868 by Max Hirsch, a liberal inspired by the example of British trade unions. Although a so-called Hirsch-Duncker (or anti-socialist) union continued to exist in construction until 1921, it never numbered more than a few thousand members. By early 1869 both Lasalleans and Eisenachers had created national masons' and carpenters' unions, but none of these had become very significant by the time all nationwide socialist unions were banned in 1878. Beginning in 1881, important socialist masons' unions began to appear in major cities, most notably Hamburg and Berlin. In the course of the 1880s these unions divided into two camps, normally called the Berlin wing and the Hamburg wing, based on contrasting goals and strategies.

The Hamburg wing under Adolf Daumann was mainly interested in "trade union" issues such as wages and working conditions, and supported the idea of collective bargaining as a means for improving the lot of workers. The Berliners under Gustav Kessler saw the main task of unions as political, in the sense of helping to establish a socialist society. Both wings formed their own national unions after 1890, with the Berliners initially the stronger of the two. But by the late 1890s the Hamburg-inspired Zentralverband der Maurer Deutschlands (Central Union of German Masons – ZMD) was the most powerful union in the construction industry and its successor organizations remained so until 1933.

The ZMD was by no means the only major construction union, however. There were also a large Catholic masons' union, founded 1899, an unskilled workers' union (1889) and important carpenters' and painters' unions, as well as smaller organizations for roofers, glazers, stone workers and potters. In 1907, the ZMD numbered 192,537 members, the unskilled workers' union 70,648, the carpenters 54,395, the Catholic masons 40,135, and the painters 39,009.[22]

Following the formation of a central employers' association in the construction industry in 1899 and the endorsement of collective bargaining at the third congress of free (social democratic) trade unions in that same year, the ZMD started negotiations on the industry's first national contract. An agreement was signed covering Greater Berlin in June 1899 after a fierce lockout by industrialists. A national contract was blocked by elements in the employers' association who were as opposed to collective bargaining as the radical unionists. However, by 1907, 364 local groups among the employers had broken ranks with the national association and signed contracts with local construction unions. Following these developments a national agreement could be worked out by the ZMD in 1908 which specified minimum conditions for all local contracts.[23] When negotiations on a second national contract started in 1909, the masons asked the Catholics, the unskilled workers and the carpenters to join them in the bargaining. The first two accepted, but the carpenters refused because they did not want to collaborate with the Catholics. Negotiations with the employers broke down and the latter locked out 173,400 workers for nearly two months beginning in April 1910. In the end, an agreement was reached which limited the workday to ten hours and set minimum wage rates in several skill categories.

In the lockout's aftermath, the ZMD and the unskilled workers' union decided to join together to form construction's first industrial union, the Deutscher Bauarbeiterverband (German Construction Workers' Union – DBV). In 1914, the DBV was one of the more conservative organizations within the social democratic labor movement. Its leadership showed firm commitment to the strengthening and extension of the collective bargaining system in the areas covered by the union. Not surprisingly, the DBV's leaders supported the formation of the Tarifgemeinschaft with Germany's foremost employers' associations in the wake of the 1918 revolution (see the account in Chapter 2 above). But the experience of war and upheaval had radicalized many construction workers, and a powerful KPD and USPD opposition to the established social democratic leadership emerged at the DBV's 1920 congress. The union's response to this internal dissent was swift and brutal. Two important locals in Saxony were dissolved and over 5,000 communists expelled in January 1921, including the famous leftist intellectual Heinrich Brandler.

With internal opposition eliminated, the union was free to pursue a moderate course. In 1921 it proposed the creation of a vacation pay fund jointly administered with the employers which would allow construction workers to take the vacations normally denied them because of frequent job changes. This was the start of the "Kassenpolitik" (fund politics) which plays a major role in construction's capital–labor relationship to this day. Talks dragged on intermittently for a decade, and an agreement had almost been reached in 1933 when the union was banned by the Nazis.

In late 1922, a number of small craft unions joined the DBV. The new organization changed its name to the Deutscher Baugewerksbund (German Construction Confederation), which became IG Bau's immediate predecessor. The carpenters, Catholic construction workers, painters and stone workers continued to exist outside this industrial union throughout the Weimar period.

With the great inflation of 1923 and the onset of the Depression in 1929, collective bargaining began to lose its effectiveness in Weimar. This was the case even in the generally cooperative atmosphere of the construction industry. Wages came to be increasingly determined by the Reich Wage Office, and free bargaining was eliminated altogether in 1931. On May 3, 1933, trade unions were outlawed by the Nazis, and all construction workers were subsequently organized into a single national socialist industrial union, the Reichsbetriebsgemeinschaft Bau, while building-products and quarry workers were formed into the Reichstarifgemeinschaft Steine und Erden.

This historical sketch has shown that many of the ideas and strategies later championed by IG Bau are in fact deeply rooted in the history of labor relations in German construction. Cooperation and collective bargaining were established early in the industry, although continuous opposition to them existed from a minority of both workers and employers. It was also during Weimar that the DBV set the dubious precedent of dealing harshly with internal dissent. In the 1920s the union began investing its money in the SPD's cooperative housing movement, the forerunner of the DGB-owned Neue Heimat Property Company of the Federal Republic (see Chapter 1). Lastly, it is clear that IG Bau's "fund politics," the innovation for which the union is most famous, was not an original invention of Georg Leber, but had in fact been institutionalized as early as 1921. Thus, just as was the case with all other unions investigated in this study, IG Bau did not arise ex nihilo in 1949 but instead drew on a tradition of labor relations which extended back before the Weimar Republic into Imperial Germany of the nineteenth century.

## IV.  RECONSTRUCTION AND RECOVERY: 1950–1955

As with all other West German labor organizations, the reconstitution of a construction union began from the bottom up.[24] Beginning in August 1945, workers in the American (and later the British) sectors were allowed to form local unions. In most areas, former Social Democratic and Christian Democratic labor activists opted for unitary, non-sectarian industrial unions. The formation of an industrial union for construction was undoubtedly facilitated by the fact that under the Nazis the Reichsarbeits-gemeinschaft Bau had covered the whole sector.

After mid-1946, statewide unions were permitted in all three occupation zones, and separate construction unions were established in Hesse, Würt-temberg, Baden/South Württemberg, South Baden/Bavaria and Rhine-land-Palatinate between June 1946 and July 1947. In the British zone, comprising the key economic regions of North Rhine-Westphalia, Hamburg, Bremen and Lower Saxony, a single zonal construction union emerged in March 1947. The union in the British zone was a powerful organization dominated by members and sympathizers of the German Communist Party (KPD), who had enjoyed a strong influence in the Rhine-Ruhr building trades since the Weimar Republic.[25]

In November 1947 an important step was taken towards the unification of the seven regional unions when a coordinating council for the British and American zones was established in Frankfurt. The council chose the former Hesse district leader of the old Deutscher Baugewerksbund, Jakob Knöss, as its chairman. Knöss's immediate task was to lay the groundwork for a national union. But this was rendered difficult by various factors, including the communist strength in the British zone, restrictions placed on the organizations in the French zone, and the independent attitude of the Bavarian union. Such problems explain why IG Bau was the last DGB union of the original sixteen to be established.[26] A unification congress finally took place in Karlsruhe in October 1949. Knöss was elected the union's first president. All the members of IG Bau's new executive committee were, like Knöss (who was 69), old Weimar trade unionists. The average age of the executive committee's membership was 59, giving the union the DGB's oldest leadership in the early 1950s, a fact which could not help but influence the union's policies.[27] Symptomatic of the union's difficulties at that time was the fact that the Bavarian district was allowed to maintain total financial autonomy vis-à-vis the central office in Frank-furt and that the head of the North Rhine district was the former Communist Reichstag deputy Gerhard Horseling. Horseling remains to this day the only official member of the Communist Party ever to hold high office in a DGB union.

For the moment at least, the communist problem was not the major issue facing the new IG Bau leadership. Rather, difficulties which had plagued German construction workers during the Weimar Republic continued to concern them during the first few years of the new republic. Foremost among these problems were the industry's irregular pattern of employment and the discrimination in pensions, vacations and fringe benefits resulting from this irregularity. Negotiations on a central vacation pay fund

(Urlaubskasse) to deal with the vacation pay problem had been near completion in 1933 when the Nazis came to power. The new regime actually solved the problem in 1936 when the Reich Post Office was designated administrator of construction workers' vacation pay. Employers were to pay the Post Office a certain amount based on the number of people they employed, and workers could pick up their benefits at any branch upon presentation of their employment books. This arrangement was terminated by the Allies in 1945.[28]

In 1948, the construction union in the British zone revived the idea of a joint labor–management vacation fund, and a contract was signed putting this idea into effect on April 8, 1949. By 1951 the fund, called the Beneficial Vacation Fund for the Construction Sector (Gemeinnützige Urlaubskasse des Baugewerbes, or "UK"), had been extended beyond the British zone to the rest of the Federal Republic. This fund, which is still in existence, is administered by a board on which the union and the two employers' associations in the construction industry enjoy 50–50 representation.

Although the issue of vacation pay had been more or less resolved before IG Bau's formal establishment as a union, other important problems continued to demand solutions, chief among them being winter unemployment. As with vacation pay, this too had been addressed by the national socialist government. In 1943 a law on bad-weather compensation was passed which paid construction workers 60% of their net hourly wage for up to 48 days during the winter if they could not work due to weather conditions.[29] On May 26, 1950 the new Federal Minister for Employment annulled this law, thus causing construction workers considerable hardship during the Federal Republic's early reconstruction period. The labor market situation was further aggravated by the high unemployment levels and rapid inflation of the 1950–52 period. Also, many of the refugees and exiles streaming into West Germany from the East sought unskilled or semi-skilled jobs in construction, leading to a downward pressure on wages throughout the industry.

Despite these short-term difficulties, the overall trend in construction assumed an upward trajectory as the huge post-war rebuilding effort began in West Germany. Between 1950 and 1955, the total annual turnover in primary construction more than doubled, from 6 to about 14 million Marks and production rose by 72.6%.[30] As a result, total employment grew from 960,882 in July 1950 to 1,386,210 in July 1955, an increase of 44%.[31]

Despite construction's success in providing employment for many refugees and West Germans displaced from other industries, financial security remained the primary concern for construction workers and their union. The peculiarities of building activities make a social safety net, whether privately or publicly organized, of special importance to such workers. For both fiscal and ideological reasons, the Federal Republic's Christian Democratic government kept welfare benefits to a minimum throughout the 1950s, thus forcing the union to tackle this problem by itself. Two basic approaches were available to IG Bau in the early 1950s. The union could either seek to create new, jointly administered welfare funds with the employers' associations, or it could bargain aggressively to win substantial wage increases which would compensate for irregular employment. These two strategies were by and large mutually exclusive, for once new funds had been established, strikes and confrontations would only jeopardize such institutions and their substantial assets.

That IG Bau had no prior ideological commitment to either approach was best demonstrated by its initial foray into nationwide collective bargaining in 1950.[32] When the first general framework contract for primary construction was signed in April 1950, the 1943 Bad Weather Compensation Law was still in effect. One month later, it was abrogated, and negotiations with the employers began immediately on the creation of a mutually administered fund as a substitute. By July, negotiations had broken down, and IG Bau sought instead to gain substantial wage increases in the ongoing bargaining round to compensate both for high inflation and for the loss of bad-weather benefits. The employers, aware of IG Bau's organizational weakness, refused to give in, and the union was forced to call a strike in August. Although the strike was mostly limited to the prosperous Frankfurt area, it collapsed within two weeks, and IG Bau found itself compelled to accept an arbitration recommendation for a 10% raise, which barely compensated for inflation.[33] Calling a strike in August, a prime month for building activities, proved to be a foolhardy step for the union, since even organized workers (less than one-third of the workforce in primary construction) were unwilling to forego pay checks with the prospect of winter unemployment around the corner.

During the next four years, IG Bau was unwilling, or more likely unable, to cut a forceful figure at the bargaining table. In every wage round the union submitted to arbitration recommendations which fell well short of its initial demands. The lesson that the leadership seemed to draw from these experiences was that a confrontational strategy would be beyond IG Bau's capabilities at that time.[34] As a response to the frustrations and general helplessness which permeated a growing segment of IG Bau at the time, an important faction within the organization began to call for a total reorientation of labor–capital relations in the construction industry, advocating a more cooperative and accommodationist approach between the two. The chief spokesman for this group was the young editor of the union journal *Der Grundstein* and newest member of the executive committee, Georg Leber.

Georg Leber was born in 1920 in Obertiefenbach, a Catholic region in Hesse. He descended from a long line of masons, although he himself had been trained as a salesman.[35] After the war, circumstances forced him to work as a mason, and he joined the Hessian Construction Workers' Union in 1947. By 1949 he was head of the Limburg local, and had already come to the attention of Jakob Knöss. In 1952 Knöss, aware of the need to rejuvenate the aging union leadership, appointed Leber editor of *Der Grundstein*. Within a very short time, Leber had established himself as a dominant figure within IG Bau.

From the very beginning of his career in the union, Leber was deeply convinced that the traditionally antagonistic rhetoric of German industrial relations was anachronistic and ultimately counterproductive both for labor and for society as a whole. For Leber, both unions and employers' associations were "factors of order" (Ordnungsfaktoren) whose constructive behavior was crucial for the smooth functioning of civil society.[36] He had little tolerance for the adversarial tradition between unions and management in a liberal democracy whose political arrangement guaranteed an unprecedented amount of liberty and whose economic system promised affluence for all. Although Leber always favored lobbying the federal government in order to gain advantages for his union and the construction industry as a whole, and never shied away from taking a tough stance at the bargaining table concerning the attainment of tangible gains for his union's members, Leber's vision ultimately advocated a kind of "sectoral corporatism" based on the common interests of workers and employers in the construction industry.

Leber's philosophy was already evident in his first important initiative, a letter sent to the Minister of Labor in July 1953 in which he outlined a solution to the nagging problem of winter unemployment.[37] Leber proposed that 4.5% of the gross wage sum of primary construction be placed in a fund to be administered by the union and the two employers' associations. The Federal Labor Office would then match this sum. Out of the fund, construction workers (regardless of union affiliation) would be paid 80% of their gross wages for any days lost to bad weather between April 1 and September 30, and unemployment benefits for up to 30 days for time lost during the rest of the year.

Many of IG Bau's members immediately recognized that Leber's letter represented the first step in an attempt to reorient the union towards "social partnership." As a result, the organization's future course was the subject of heated debate at IG Bau's second national congress held in October 1953. It was on this occasion that Leber first expounded his accommodationist notion of unions as Ordnungsfaktoren.[38] Although a majority of the congress's delegates supported Leber's ideas, a significant minority, mainly led by communists from the North Rhine district, strongly opposed them. They called on the leadership to pursue an active wage policy aimed at increasing the wage quota under all circumstances, as advocated by Dr. Viktor Agartz of the WWI and IG Metall's new leader, Otto Brenner.

The eventual approval which the IG Bau congress bestowed upon Leber's accommodationist line allowed the leadership to proceed with negotiations on the bad-weather fund. After discussions with the government and employers' associations in early 1954, an agreement was reached which deviated somewhat from Leber's original plan. Nevertheless, the final outcome represented a triumph for IG Bau's charismatic leader. IG Bau and the employers were to create a Wage Compensation Fund (Lohnausgleichskasse – LAK) into which 4% of the total gross wages in primary construction would flow.[39] The Federal Employment Office would not participate in this fund, but would instead pay unemployed construction workers benefits for up to 30 days between October 15 and March 31. These workers would be paid an extra DM 2.50 per day out of the LAK to help close the gap between regular wages and the (then quite meager) unemployment compensation. The creation of the LAK was formalized in a contract signed by IG Bau, the HDB and the ZDB on April 25, 1955. Leber entered labor politics in the Federal Republic with a bang; his accommodationism was here to stay.

## V. THE LEBER ERA: 1955–1966

With the expiration of much of the reconstruction period's special legislation favoring building investments, and the subsequent start of West Germany's second complete business cycle in 1955, conditions in the construction industry began to change. The most striking transformation occurred in the labor market, where shortages of skilled labor developed during the 1955 boom. A foreign-worker recruitment office opened its doors in Italy in 1956, and by 1959, 22% of the workforce in the Federal Republic's construction industry consisted of Gastarbeiter.[40] For the next ten years, growth in the West German economy (and especially in construction) was strong, inflation low, and unemployment almost nonexistent. With the improved economic situation, the Adenauer government moved to upgrade the social security system through reforms in pensions and sickness benefits (1957) and unemployment compensation (1956 and 1959). The implementation of this new economic and social program coincided with Georg Leber's consolidation of power within IG Bau. Although Leber did not actually assume the leadership until 1957, the "Leber era" began in earnest at the union's third congress, held in Munich in September 1955.

IG Bau's third congress witnessed the last confrontation within the organization over the new accommodationist strategy symbolized by the creation of the LAK in April 1955. IG Bau's executive committee and much of its regional leadership supported this course, and wished to complete the organization's transformation into a full-fledged accommodationist union by formally placing Georg Leber, still only the *Grundstein* editor, at its head. Attempts to persuade the 72-year-old Jakob Knöss to retire were, however, unsuccessful, and it was decided to elect Leber vice president instead.[41] However, the fact that Leber gave the congress's keynote address clearly attested to his leadership position within IG Bau and underscored Knöss's status as only the titular head of the union.

In his speech, Leber presented IG Bau's goals for the coming years, based on the DGB Aktionsprogramm of May 1955. He called for a reduction of the work week in construction and an increase in wages and salaries commensurate with economic circumstances, a direct repudiation of the wage policy advocated by IG Metall and the DGB's activist unions which stated that unions should not consider their industry's ability to pay when formulating demands.[42] (Leber was to become even more explicit about his accommodationist wage theory in the early 1960s when he called for a link between wage increases and productivity growth.) Leber proposed the creation of yet another fund with the employers, the Added Assistance Fund (Zusatzversorgungskasse – ZVK), as the final point in IG Bau's program. The ZVK would pay a small monthly pension to all retired construction workers to supplement their state pensions, which were below the national average. These national pensions were inadequate because of the frequent unemployment and job changes which characterized conditions in the construction sector.

In the debate which followed Leber's address, and indeed throughout the congress, an important minority led by KPD sympathizers attacked the union's new course and held up Brenner's IG Metall as an alternative model which, this group believed, would yield the union and its members greater benefits than the accommodationism advocated by Leber.[43] The opposition's seriousness could be properly gauged by the fact that it nominated Karl Jaeckel, a communist leader from the North Rhine district, to run against Knöss for the presidency, a rare challenge among DGB unions. Knöss of course won, but Jaeckel received 65 out of 310 votes, a very respectable showing.[44] This indicates that the opposition group at the congress probably numbered more than 65 delegates, since many activists within IG Bau would have found it difficult to vote against the union's founding father and a venerable representative of 50 years of German labor tradition. In addition to its activities at the union's congresses in the early 1950s, the opposition had tried to practice a more aggressive bargaining policy in its power base of North Rhine. The activists conducted three strikes there between 1951 and 1955 in the construction finishing sector, which was beyond the immediate control of the national leadership.[45]

The congress's approval of Leber's program and its election of Knöss and Leber as leaders did not put an end to the tensions within IG Bau. Indeed, outside political events during the fall of 1955 increased dissension even further. On October 20, 1955, police in North Rhine-Westphalia arrested 50 KPD members because of their contacts with the German Democratic Republic (East Germany).[46] Included among the 50 were five functionaries of IG Bau, one of them Karl Jaeckel. The KPD newspaper *Neue Volkszeitung* printed an account of the incident presenting it as a police attack on IG Bau, a charge which infuriated the union leadership. The executive committee demanded that Gerhard Horseling, district leader of North Rhine, denounce this misrepresentation, which he agreed to do. As a result of his compliance, Horseling was expelled from the KPD on January 11, 1956. Bitter over his explusion, Horseling handed a series of documents to Leber which showed that the heads of nine IG Bau locals in North Rhine were taking orders directly from the KPD and indirectly from the GDR.

This incident provided Leber with a golden opportunity to establish his unchallenged hegemony within the union by not only eliminating communists from leadership positions but concomitantly weakening the intra-organizational presence of other activists who were not members of the KPD but nevertheless disagreed with Leber's accommodationist course. On Sunday, January 15, he called a secret meeting of the union's expanded executive committee and proposed a bold course of action for dealing with the intra-union opposition.[47] The rest of the leadership went along with Leber's plan which dissolved nine of North Rhine's eighteen locals and expelled IG Bau's fifteen top communist functionaries. On the morning of January 16, 44 officials dispatched by the executive committee arrived in North Rhine and removed the designated officials from their offices. Within a few hours, the KPD's power within IG Bau had been broken. As in 1921, the construction workers' union had once again forcibly removed an opposition group from its midst.

It must be said, however, that legitimate fears for the unity of the organization also played a role in the 1956 "purge." In November 1955 a small number of CDU dissidents within the DGB had formed a Christian trade union confederation, and there was widespread concern that the DGB would break apart. (For a detailed discussion of this point see Chapter 3.) This fear was especially great in IG Bau, which had (and still has) a considerable number of CDU sympathizers in its ranks. Overt communist influence and presence within the union was exactly the kind of excuse these Christian Democrats could have seized upon to try to resurrect the old Catholic construction workers' union, thereby ending IG Bau's existence as an Einheitsgewerkschaft.

The big winner in these dramatic events was undoubtedly Georg Leber. News of the purge made headlines in all the West German newspapers the following day, and Leber was hailed as the mastermind behind the operations. The 35-year-old union official became an overnight media celebrity, a position he did not relinquish for over twenty years. With the opposition either eliminated or substantially weakened, Leber was now free to implement his own union philosophy, as well as use his celebrity status to propagate that philosophy within the DGB and West German society as a whole.

Leber's two immediate goals were to sign an arbitration agreement with the employers and to create the ZVK which he had championed at the 1955 congress. The arbitration agreement was concluded as part of a new general framework contract in 1956. It established a permanent arbitration board led by a neutral chairman who could be called on to make non-binding recommendations if negotiations reached an impasse. Leber hoped that the arbitration mechanism would prevent confrontation and reduce tensions during bargaining.

Leber proved equally successful in the case of the ZVK. Talks began with the employers in late 1956, and in January 1957 a draft agreement was drawn up.[48] The ZVK was to be organized like the other jointly administered funds, and six pfennigs were to be deposited in it by the employers for every person-hour worked in primary construction. Workers would then be paid an extra pension upon retirement or disability of up to DM 45 per month depending on years worked in the industry. An official contract governing the fund was signed in October 1957, and the ZVK came into being on January 1, 1958.

As soon as a preliminary agreement had been reached on the ZVK, negotiations began in the 1957 wage round. Leber now had the opportunity to put his views on rational wage bargaining into practice. He had long felt that yearly wage rounds were economically disruptive, and so he offered to sign a longer contract with the employers. In return, he wanted the work week in construction cut to 45 hours beginning April 1, 1957, along with a reasonable wage increase. The employers agreed to Leber's demand on work time and also granted an 8% across-the-board raise (in addition to compensating for the effects of the shorter work week), but the contract was to run for 21 months. It could be reopened if inflation rose above 3.5%.[49] A comparison with IG Metall's Bremen Accord of 1956 illustrates what Leber meant by a "responsible" settlement. IG Metall also won the 45-hour week and an 8% raise, but this was over 15 months instead of 21. Concretely, restraint had produced contracts which were about 1% or 2% lower than IG Metall's. However, the 21-month-long contract backfired on Leber since it had to be reopened and renegotiated in 1958 when inflation reached 5%. Despite this minor problem, Leber had achieved his main purpose, which was to give the West German public and the construction employers concrete proof of his goodwill and moderate accommodationism.

The fall of 1957 was a time of personal triumph for Leber. In order to increase IG Bau's influence in Bonn and his own personal power, he ran for a seat in the Bundestag as an SPD candidate in the September 1957 elections. His victory made him the first major union official to hold a seat in the legislature since Weimar. At this juncture Leber made it amply clear that his ultimate ambitions extended beyond the world of trade unions into the realm of "high politics." Shortly after Leber's electoral success, IG Bau held its fourth national conference in Cologne. This time Knöss did retire, and the 37-year-old Leber finally became the organization's official leader, another important step in his political career.

With the opposition gone, Leber was able to push three initiatives through the Cologne congress with little resistance. The first involved the elimination from the union's charter of a call for the socialization of the construction industry.[50] Leber believed that as long as this clause remained, the employers could never fully trust IG Bau, and a true partnership between labor and management would be impossible. The call for socialization in the union's programs had by this time assumed a largely symbolic character devoid of immediate practical meaning. Nevertheless, its continued presence near the beginning of every DGB union's bylaws conveyed its importance as an integral part of social democratic labor tradition. For this reason, its removal upon the recommendation of the Leber-controlled union executive committee came as a shock to the rest of the labor movement and heralded the arrival of a new approach to union politics in the Federal Republic.

It was also at this congress that Leber first introduced an idea with which he became closely identified: asset formation for workers (Vermögensbildung).[51] Leber believed that the accumulation of assets, whether in the form of property, a house, savings or shares, was the best way for a worker to overcome dependence on his/her own labor and develop a sense of allegiance to democracy and the social market economy. This view complemented Leber's other contention that wage increases alone would never eliminate economic inequalities, because price increases would always hold real wage gains to a minimum. In 1957 Leber had not yet fully worked out his concept of asset formation, but its implementation was approved by the IG Bau congress as a goal for the union.

Leber's third initiative at the 1957 congress concerned winter construction.[52] The arrival of full employment in West Germany in 1955–56 and the strong economic growth since then had stretched construction capacity to the limit. In business and government circles it was feared that building cost increases, caused by shortages, would ignite inflation. One obvious way to raise the industry's capacity was to extend the "construction year" into the winter months of November, December, January and February. In one stroke, the problems concerning capacity and winter unemployment would both be solved. At the 1957 congress, Leber presented a detailed plan for winter construction which called for continued cooperation between the union, employers and federal, state and local government.[53] Government agencies were asked to change their spending habits and award construction contracts throughout the entire calendar year. The employers and the union would study winter construction technology, and the federal government would provide financial inducements to purchase the necessary equipment. Most importantly for the union, the annual wave of firings which always occurred just before Christmas (to avoid paying holiday wages) had to be forbidden.

In February 1958 IG Bau organized a trip to Sweden for a research team to study winter construction techniques there. Leber also persuaded the SPD to introduce a bill in the Bundestag calling for action on this issue. In October 1959, after long discussions in the Bundestag and between the union and employers, a solution was found which satisfied all parties. The empoloyers agreed to stop the Christmas firings, but workers' wages over the holidays would henceforth be paid out of the Wage Compensation Fund (the LAK). The LAK would no longer have to supplement unemployment benefits for construction workers during the winter because state unemployment compensation was to be increased. The government also agreed both to alter its spending practices and provide special low-interest loans to employers to purchase winter construction equipment. As a direct result of these measures, winter unemployment in the industry dropped from 461,000 in 1957–58 to 125,000 in 1959–60. In subsequent years the average fell further to about 35,000.[54]

By the end of the 1950s, most of the problems that the construction workers' union faced at its birth in 1949 had been solved. Winter unemployment had been greatly reduced and the pensions, contractual pay and vacation time of construction workers were now equal to or higher than that of other workers, thanks to the UK, LAK, ZVK and the improved social security system provided by the state. A friendly relationship had been established between IG Bau and the employers' associations, and the union was constantly extolled in the West German media as the model of a responsible labor organization. Why then did IG Bau find itself in a serious crisis in the early 1960s?

Despite Leber's fame and his innovative policies, he failed in the one area that really mattered: he had been unable to persuade more construction workers to join his union. Between 1957 and 1961, IG Bau's membership stagnated at around 425,000, even though employment in its organizational domain had risen by 230,000 workers.[55] As a result, the union's organizational density fell officially from 18.7% to 17%, and in reality shrank to about 15-16%, while remaining approximately 10% higher in primary construction alone.[56] This made IG Bau, despite its rhetoric, by far the weakest organizational representative among the major DGB unions. Thus, new strategies had to be tried to overcome the union's organizational weakness, or else its credibility, and hence influence, would be lost.

The reasons for these membership problems can partly be found in construction's overall situation and that of the economy as a whole between 1959 and 1966, the period of West Germany's third and fourth post-war business cycles. During this time construction was consistently one of the strongest sectors of the economy. Sales more than doubled in primary construction between 1959 and 1965, and during the boom years of 1960 and 1961 alone the volume of construction rose by over 40%.[57] Additionally, construction prices increased by 16% during those two years, and the industry came to be seen by the media and the government as a major contributor to the accelerating inflation of 1961–63.[58]

This rapid rise in construction prices was the result of a shortage of capacity – especially labor power – which had been worsening since full employment arrived in the Federal Republic in 1955–56. The building of the Berlin Wall in 1961 exacerbated the problem by ending the flow of eastern refugees who had been an important source of skilled construction labor since the early 1950s. West Germany had no choice but to begin massive recruitment of foreign workers to solve these labor market problems. In 1957, less than 1% of the workforce in primary construction were foreigners (mainly Austrians and Dutch), but by 1960 this figure had reached 5%. In 1965, 215,000 or 14.8% of the primary construction workers were Gastarbeiter, and their numbers were still rising.[59]

As the number of foreign workers in construction was increasing, two other trends developed in the labor force which were of great significance to IG Bau. Even though conditions in the industry had improved greatly since the 1950s, jobs in construction were still considered less desirable than those in other sectors such as metalworking because of the unpredictability of the weather and the safety problems traditionally associated with the building trades. In the boom years of the early 1960s, skilled construction workers found that they could easily find good jobs in more attractive sectors. Thus they began to leave the industry in significant numbers. The same logic applied to apprentices. Since apprenticeships were readily available in the most attractive areas of the economy, fewer young people were interested in a career in construction, and those that were often exhibited lesser qualifications than previous apprentices. After 1957, the number of apprentices in the construction industry dropped sharply for a decade. In 1954 the industry had 108,407 apprentices; by 1960 the number had decreased to 52,500 just as demand for skilled labor was increasing by leaps and bounds.[60]

In addition to the adverse weather conditions and safety considerations, low wages were a major reason why construction had become unattractive. Although contractual wage rates (Tariflöhne) were among the highest of any industry throughout the 1950s and 1960s, actual earnings, both weekly and yearly, were below the industrial average until 1962, and only slightly above it after 1962.[61] The reason for this was the low level of extra-contractual payments in the industry, which is expressed by the gap between contractual hourly wages and actual hourly earnings (the so-called wage gap). In 1962, this gap was only 6.8%, making construction the sixth lowest out of 48 industries surveyed.[62] Although the gap rose to 17% in 1965 because of labor market pressures, it still lagged far behind the levels of other major industries such as automobiles (68%), machinery (57%) and electronics (47%).[63] Thus, for actual earnings in construction to be equal to those in other top industries, its contractual wage rates had to be considerably higher.

The relatively low wage level in construction can be explained by a number of factors, including intense bidding for construction contracts, guidelines which decreed that actual wages be equal to contractual wages on government projects, and the low pay of unskilled guest workers, who received the minimum permissible by law (and in practice often less). The wage policies of IG Bau in the 1950s also helped contribute to making the pay in the industry unappealing to German skilled workers. Like most other DGB unions, IG Bau tried during this time to narrow the gap between the wages of skilled and unskilled workers in its organizational domain as well as between those employed in large cities and their colleagues working in rural areas.[64] This strategy aimed at making union membership more attractive to the unskilled and to workers living outside the big cities, two groups which West German unions, just like their Weimar predecessors, have had difficulty organizing and continue to up to the present. It was assumed that union loyalty among the skilled was sufficiently strong to survive this "levelling" policy. Extra raises for the lowest-pay groups were negotiated by IG Bau in 1957, 1958, 1961, 1964 and 1967.

Although the reasons for IG Bau's weakness in membership are complex, the changes in the labor market and the structure of the labor force outlined above certainly became key factors in this development after the mid-1950s. In the early part of that decade, membership problems probably had more to do with West German law (the principle of voluntary association as explained in Chapter 2) and the fact that many workers intended to leave the industry (as indeed thousands did) once economic recovery had begun. Also, many of the refugees from the East who found work in the industry bore strong anti-union biases. By the late 1950s the situation had changed. From then on, IG Bau's organizational weakness can be linked to the erosion of the core of West German unions, namely male, German, skilled workers, within the construction industry. The percentage of foreign workers and clerical employees in the labor force in construction rose continuously from the late 1950s at the same time as the percentage of skilled masons and carpenters, the traditionally unionized construction trades, decreased.[65] Worse still, turnover among skilled construction workers remained high for the next two decades, as many of them left for higher-paying jobs. The logical solution to the membership problem was to stabilize the workforce and attract more easily organizable groups by substantially increasing contractual wages.

This, however, was a strategy which Leber chose not to follow, either because he did not recognize the true nature of the problem or (the more likely explanation) because such a move was at odds with his political and ideological views. Leber could hardly present himself as the great moderate union leader who had West Germany's best interests at heart if construction wages were being cited as a major cause of inflation and economic instability. Leber's personal influence with the employers, the CDU-led government and the SPD would decline as a result. He therefore chose an approach to IG Bau's organizational crisis more in keeping with his own worldview.

Leber's strategy was based on two key assumptions. First, he believed that in the political climate of the early 1960s workers were more likely to join unions that were unabashedly accommodationist than those which still clung to the old rhetoric of class conflict and continued to uphold visions of labor as capital's irreconcilable adversary. Thus, in Leber's view, IG Bau (and the DGB as well) had to become more, not less, moderate. Second, Leber felt that his union could no longer allow "free riders" to gain from IG Bau's activities. Union members had to pay heavy dues to the organization for which, Leber believed, they were entitled to enjoy extra benefits in the form of higher wages and fringe benefits. This attitude represented a break with one of the most venerable aspects of German labor tradition, namely the belief that unions were the spokesmen for all workers, whether unionized or not. In addition, the constitutionality under West German labor law of such a "discriminatory" strategy was highly questionable.

At IG Bau's fifth national congress in August 1960 Leber shocked the West German union movement with his polemic against non-unionized free riders. He pointed to the example of Switzerland where non-members had to pay a "solidarity contribution" (Solidaritätsbeitrag) to the union as compensation for gains enjoyed by members and non-members alike. At Leber's urging, the congress approved a resolution calling for the union to begin negotiations with the employers on the issue of extra benefits for IG Bau members and/or penalties for non-members.[66]

The union leadership implemented this resolution on February 3, 1961, when it presented a plan to the ZDB and the HDB for the creation of a mutually administered "Advantage Equalization Fund" (Vorteilsausgleichskasse – VAK). A "solidarity contribution" along Swiss lines would be paid into this fund by all non-unionized construction workers, and the money would then be used for vocational training, scholarships, and vacation and rest facilities which would benefit everyone in the industry. The immediate reaction from both the employers and the other DGB unions was negative, but for opposite reasons.[67] The national employers' association, the BDA, expressed its unequivocal opposition to any unequal treatment of unionized and non-unionized labor, and sent two legal briefs to that effect to the construction employers which stated that the "solidarity contributions" would be unconstitutional since they violated guarantees of free association. The employers opposed this formalized dichotomization since they feared that with the boundaries between unionized and non-unionized clearly drawn, many hitherto unorganized workers would feel compelled to join the union, thereby strengthening labor in the industrial relations system.

The opposition of the DGB unions – particularly among those belonging to the federation's activist wing – to Leber's scheme derived from the traditional attitude that unions were the representatives of the entire West German working class and not only of their actual members. This view saw unions as general organizations of a class rather than, as Leber had insisted, special advocates of a particular interest group.

In the face of this response, IG Bau decided on February 22, 1961 to abandon the VAK idea. In return, the employers agreed to a generous wage settlement in the 1961 round which became known as the Augsburg Accord. From June 1, 1961, wages in primary construction were to be raised by 10.3%, and a schedule was worked out which foresaw the introduction of the 40-hour week with full pay by October 1965. All workers were also to receive a minimum of fifteen days' paid vacation by 1962. Lastly, the employers, at Leber's request, released a bizarre statement which read: "The employers in primary construction recognize IG Bau-Steine-Erden as an element of order (Ordnungsfaktor)."[68] Never was there a clearer expression of the obsession of West German unionists with status and their desire for recognition by management as equals.

The Augsburg Accord did not mean that IG Bau had abandoned the strategy of differentiation, which its critics viewed as a thinly disguised policy of outright discrimination. Talks on the subject with the employers took place intermittently beginning in May 1961. In November, a preliminary agreement was reached between the two sides to set up a new fund called the "Association for the Encouragement of Savings and Rest" (Verein zur Förderung der Spartätigkeit und Erholung). The employers would pay 0.85% of the total wage sum of primary construction to this association, which would then distribute an extra vacation bonus of DM 80 per year to every IG Bau member. IG Bau, the ZDB and the HDB were also to form a common lobby which would represent the interests of the construction industry in Bonn and vis-à-vis the media.

Despite their initial acceptance of this plan, the ZDB and the HDB came under pressure from both the BDA and many of their own members to reject it. A number of employers felt that any kind of differentiation among workers would cause disruptions in the production process. On January 22, 1962, the ZDB and the HDB stated that they had to withdraw their support for the plan. After all the publicity and propaganda that had gone into the notion of "advantage equalization," Leber could not afford to back down without being humiliated. He announced that the union would not sign a wage contract for 1962 until some accord had been reached on this matter. Arbitration began on March 10. The employers offered to introduce a dues-checkoff system to strengthen IG Bau's organization, but Leber felt that this was too extreme a form of cooperation even for him. On March 12, arbitration was declared a failure.

With the expiration of the 1961 wage contract on March 31, 1962, IG Bau was legally free to resort to industrial action, something which it had not done on the national level since the disastrous strike it conducted in 1950. A series of limited warning strikes were called, but, as in 1950, they suffered from poor organization and as a consequence the response by the rank and file remained weak. Leber had no alternative but to return to the bargaining table, and on April 28 the strikes were stopped. On May 18, an accord was reached known as the Wiesbaden Recommendations which provided the basis for a comprehensive settlement in 1962. In a spirit of internal democracy, which was rare for IG Bau, the argument was submitted to the membership for a ratification vote. The union's rank and file approved the terms by a vote of 68.1% to 30.5%.'[69]

The Recommendations represented the first, albeit minor, success for the strategy of differentiation or discrimination. They called for the ZVK to pay an extra pension of up to DM 45 per annum to IG Bau members depending on how long they had been in the union. (The employers had requested – unsuccessfully – that the same extra benefits also be paid to workers who had stayed with the same construction firm for a long period of time, even if they were not union members.) In addition, the union and the employers set up two joint foundations, one to grant scholarships to the orphans of IG Bau members killed on the job and the other to build vacation resorts which would accommodate union members before accepting reservations from other construction workers. This was the full extent of the extra benefits that IG Bau would ever be able to win for its members. Even these small advantages were undermined in 1968 when the Federal Labor Court declared the extra pension payments to former unionists unconstitutional and forbade them immediately. By that time, however, Leber's strategy of differentiation/discrimination had been all but forgotten.

The differentiation campaign was a disaster for IG Bau. Because of its unpopularity in the media and among the general public, Leber succeeded in seriously damaging the positive image which he had spent six years constructing, without attaining any tangible benefits in return such as higher membership or greater organizational strength. He had also greatly strained IG Bau's relationship with both the employers and the other DGB unions. Leber was not conciliatory, however. He sought to retain the ground lost in 1962 both at the fifth national DGB congress and during the 1963 wage round.

Leber believed that a resumption of the anti-radicalism campaign which he had initiated at the DGB's fourth national congress would be the best strategy to restore his blemished image. At that conference, held in Stuttgart in September 1959, Leber called for a strengthening of the DGB at the expense of member unions, especially in wage bargaining, and a revision of the DGB's Basic Program that would eliminate demands for nationalization and other remnants of radical politics. (For the Stuttgart congress, see Chapter 3.) Leber supported a stronger DGB because he thought it would help curb the power of IG Metall. Although IG Metall blocked the attempts to move towards a more powerful DGB, Leber achieved his purpose at the 1959 congress. He forged a cohesive opposition block of accommodationists out of a number of unions (IG Bergbau, Gewerkschaft der Eisenbahner, Deutsche Postgewerkschaft) which had long resented Brenner and his activist ways. In so doing, Leber shattered the public image of a unified trade-union movement. Now, he hoped, it would finally become clear to the West German public that there were good ("responsible") and bad ("irresponsible") unions, and Leber was leader and spokesman of the former.

Leber invoked a similar theme at the DGB's fifth congress. The main issues at this congress, held in October 1962, were the Emergency Laws which the CDU–FDP government was trying to enact, and the revision of the DGB's Basic Program. (For a detailed discussion of both see Chapter 3.) Many conservative Social Democrats thought that the laws should be supported by the SPD in order to buttress the party's newly gained moderate image with the mainstream of the West German electorate. Leber led the attack by the accommodationist unions favoring this position against IG Metall and its activist allies who were totally opposed to the emergency legislation. Although the DGB decided to come out against the Emergency Laws, Leber was able to win many concessions on the draft for the new DGB Basic Program. The aim of socialization was watered down substantially and instead emphasis was placed on Keynesian demand management as the best way to bring about change in the West German economy. (Again, see Chapter 3 on this matter.)

The hostility between Brenner and Leber which had flared at the DGB congress continued during the 1963 wage round.[70] With the economy in a downturn and inflation accelerating, Economics Minister Ludwig Erhard called on the unions to limit wage increases to the rate of expected growth in productivity which was estimated at 3–3.5%. He also asked that scheduled reductions in the work week be postponed in order not to exacerbate the tight situation in the labor market. Lastly, he attacked the annual ritual of wage bargaining, claiming that multi-year contracts helped promote greater economic stability. Otto Brenner resolved to oppose Erhard's bargaining guidelines, and the new head of Gesamtmetall, Herbert van Hüllen, was just as determined to implement them. A major showdown between labor and the employers loomed.

IG Metall made its position clear at the start of the bargaining round by demanding an 8% wage increase and refusing to discuss either the extension of contract duration or the postponement of work-time reduction. (For a detailed discussion of this wage round see Chapter 4.) Faced with an intransigent Gesamtmetall, the metalworkers were gearing up for a major strike in Baden-Württemberg when word came that IG Bau had settled. Leber intentionally undercut IG Metall's position by agreeing to exactly those terms which Brenner's union was fighting. The IG Bau contract was to run for two years and called for a 4.9% wage increase in 1963 followed by 4.8% in 1964. The union claimed that these raises had been calculated on the basis of expected GNP.[71] Finally, a one-hour cut in the work week scheduled for October 1963 was to be delayed until April 1964. There was widespread praise in business and government circles for IG Bau's contract.

It was clear to many trade unionists, however, that Leber had undermined IG Metall's position during a difficult time in order to regain the credibility he had lost vis-à-vis the employers, the government and the public in 1962. Encouraged by the IG Bau settlement, Gesamtmetall was determined to hold the line at 5%, and despite a three-week strike – one of the Federal Republic's bitterest ever – IG Metall could do no better than an agreement which featured a pay increase of exactly 5%. The union was forced to accept the added humiliation of having to delay the introduction of the 40-hour work week after it had pledged to implement this reform during the bargaining round. (For a discussion of these events see Chapter 4.)

Both during and after the 1963 bargaining round, Leber tried to justify his actions by claiming that he was simply applying a new and more scientific formula for calculating wage increases than had hitherto been used in West German labor–management relations. Leber argued that if all wage increases were equal to annual GNP growth plus the rate of inflation, workers would always get their fair share and unions would not be accused of fueling inflation. Confrontational bargaining would end if both labor and management could agree on a scientific method for setting wage increases. Implementing macroeconomic policy would also be easier since wage growth for the coming year could be predicted.[72]

The problem with Leber's vision was that the employers (and Ludwig Erhard) interpreted the GNP formula differently. They opposed any compensation for inflation, since even if this measure did not cause prices to accelerate, it still tended to freeze inflation at existing levels. For workers, Leber's formula meant that they would have to resist taking advantage of a boom or a tight labor market to win large wage increases, a policy which Leber's IG Bau had already been following since the mid-1950s. In effect, the pursuit of collective bargaining according to the GNP formula would have meant labor's permanent "freezing" into its existing share of national income.

Even if this type of wage policy were in the best interest of the country as a whole, it undoubtedly would be detrimental to individual workers. To counter these disadvantages, Leber relied on yet another innovation which turned into one of his pet projects: asset formation for the individual worker (Vermögensbildung). Leber believed that only by accumulating capital could an individual truly attain personal independence. This notion closely paralleled Ludwig Erhard's concept of "people's capitalism." Basically the plan required that the employers pay a certain amount to workers each year above wages and bonuses, which workers had to invest or save rather than spend. This way inflationary consumer spending during periods of economic growth would be dampened, more funds would be available to business for investment, and the individual would gain greater personal economic security. In addition, asset formation offered a convenient way out of the permanent wage–price spiral which in Leber's view posed serious dangers for the West German economy.[73]

IG Bau's 1963 congress approved a resolution urging the union leadership to work out a concrete program for asset formation.[74] In August 1964 the so-called Leber Plan, which had been devised by Leber and a group of outside experts, was announced. According to this proposal the employers were annually to place 1.5% of the wage sum in primary construction into a fund jointly administered by the employers and IG Bau. The fund's assets would then be lent to firms in construction for investment and to workers to buy houses or apartments. All construction workers would hold shares in the fund, but they would not be able to touch either the capital or dividends until they retired, whereupon they could sell the shares. Thus each worker would accumulate a considerable sum of money over 30 or 40 years.[75]

The reactions of politicians in Bonn, both Christian and Social Democratic, to the Leber Plan was very positive. Although the employers also expressed some interest in principle, they opposed Leber's conception of the fund in favor of more voluntaristic forms of asset formation. IG Bau continued negotiation throughout 1964, and a compromise was finally reached on March 4, 1965. The employers agreed to deposit nine pfennigs for every person-hour worked into a special savings account owned by every construction worker, who would contribute two pfennigs and who waived his/her right to touch either the capital or the interest for at least five years. It was estimated that over this period on average about 1,300 DM (then $325) would accrue. Workers had to initiate the process of asset formation themselves. In the first year of the plan's implementation only about half of those eligible responded.[76] Although later expanded and adopted by other unions, asset formation never came close to playing the role in West German labor relations – or the economy – that Leber had envisioned for it. It remained thereafter so closely identified with Georg Leber and his union that virtually any adoption of the plan was rendered impossible due to its highly particularistic nature and its unsuccessful application in the construction sector.

After Georg Leber took over the direction of IG Bau in the 1950s, it was clear that personal, political and ideological considerations were more important to him in choosing a particular strategy than the material welfare of construction workers. Higher wages were what the latter wanted, but Leber passed up the chance to exploit extraordinarily favorable market conditions so as not to undercut his image as the great leader of the DGB's accommodationists. Another reason for Leber's behavior became clear in December 1966. When the SPD entered the Grand

Coalition, Leber abandoned IG Bau and headed for Bonn to assume the post of Minister of Transport. One cannot discount the possibility that Leber was using his prominent role as head of one of the most important West German trade unions to further his own political career. In later years Leber became Minister of Defense, and at one point he even tried to get himself elected President of the Federal Republic. He was never again to play a major role in the trade-union movement.

Whatever he may have achieved as a Social Democratic politician, Leber must be judged on what he did for IG Bau and its members, as well as for the DGB as a whole. Any sober assessment must on balance go against him. Leber seriously undermined labor unity with his attacks on IG Metall, and he tainted that union with an image of irresponsibility which persisted throughout the 1970s and early 1980s. Leber also cast doubts on the claim of West German labor to represent all workers with his polemics against "free riders." By openly encouraging divisions between accommodationist and activist unions within the DGB, he created deep suspicions that continue to plague intra-labor discourse, nearly twenty years after his resignation as leader of IG Bau-Steine-Erden.

As far as IG Bau itself was concerned, Leber failed to correct the union's most serious problem, its permanent organizational weakness. Despite "advantage equalization" and "asset formation," which in hindsight appear to have been little more than gimmickry, IG Bau's organizational level had only risen 2% by 1966. The number of apprentices entering the industry fell sharply after 1957, and actual earnings in construction remained lower than in all other major industries in West Germany. Given these conditions it should come as no surprise that thousands of skilled workers left construction every year during the 1960s. It was left to Leber's successors to deal with these problems which, rather than solving, he had exacerbated.

## VI.  AFTER LEBER: 1967–1981

Following Georg Leber's departure in December 1966, the IG Bau executive committee chose the union's vice president, Rudolf Sperner, as his successor. Sperner remained IG Bau's leader for the next sixteen years, and he guided the union through a difficult period which included three severe recessions and two booms in construction. Sperner slowly moved IG Bau out of the limelight, which was inevitable since the union's notoriety throughout the 1950s and 1960s was inextricably tied to the person of Georg Leber. Throughout the 1970s, IG Bau remained one of the staunchest – though unspectacular – supporters of the DGB's accommodationist wing. Its former leadership role within this group had by this time been decisively usurped by IG Chemie, though this union lacked a leader with the flair and flamboyance of Georg Leber.

When Sperner took over as union leader in December 1966, the construction industry found itself in the midst of West Germany's first serious post-war recession. The combination of budget cuts and high interest rates which brought on the 1966–67 crisis hit construction especially hard. Output declined by 5.5% in primary construction in 1967 and employment dropped by 9.4%.[77] Yet the recession had positive side-effects for IG Bau, in particular the formation of the Grand Coalition. The economic policies which Karl Schiller implemented encompassed much of what IG Bau had been advocating for years

Given its enthusiastic support for the new government, it is not surprising that IG Bau tried to do its part to aid economic recovery. Like many unions, it postponed annual wage increases scheduled for April 1967 until July 1, when the low point of the recession had already passed. A 2.5% wage increase was agreed to from July 1, with an additional 1% to be added on September 1. Although recovery was already well underway by the spring of 1968, the shadow of the recession still hovered over the bargaining tables. IG Bau settled for a 3.5% raise beginning May 1, even though the government had called for increases of 4-5% to boost demand.[78]

IG Bau's attempts to project itself as a model supporter of the new government was dealt a blow in the summer of 1967 when the union was forced to call a strike in the important North Rhine and Westphalia union districts.[79] The strike developed out of an attempt by employers in construction finishing to cut the piece-rate wages of tilelayers, a small but highly organized (95%) group of skilled workers. Taking advantage of the recession, employers wanted to lower piece rates by an average of 44%. The union had no choice but to call a strike, which began on July 10, 1967 and involved about 6,500 workers. The action lasted nine weeks and finally ended when workers voted to accept a piece-rate cut of 5%.

More important than the strike itself was the way IG Bau reacted to it. The union took pains to explain that the strike was not directed against the government, but was forced on the union by employers who had failed to heed the Concerted Action's warnings not to pursue "negative" wage policies. IG Bau emphasized that this incident in no way affected its good relations with the primary construction employers.[80] Also, the union's official publication, Der Grundstein, dispensed with photographs of demonstrations and aggressive rhetoric normally used by other union magazines during strikes. This embarrassed attitude towards its own industrial action stood in sharp contrast to the union's conduct during the next major strike which it called in 1978, as will be discussed below.

By the beginning of 1969, the economic situation in construction had changed completely. Output had increased in real terms by 5.4%, and a boom continued in the industry through 1973, with output rising in real terms by 3.9% in 1969, 7.8% in 1970, 3.4% in 1971 and 6.8% in 1972.[81] Skilled labor shortages were again construction's major problem as many workers who had lost their jobs in 1966–67 never returned, with many others taking advantage of the recovery to switch to other industries. The number of apprentices continued to fall, with the low point reached in 1971 when their were only 26,453 apprentices in construction. (The figure in 1954 had been 103,202.)[82] At the same time, the number of guest workers in primary construction rose sharply as employers found it difficult to hire even unskilled German workers. Foreign labor as a percentage of the workforce in primary construction had declined to a low of only 10.2% in 1967 as thousands went home during the recession. But the figure was back up to an impressive 26.7% in 1971.[83]

Despite the tight labor market situation, IG Bau remained cautious following the recession. The 6.5% wage increase to which the union agreed in April 1969 was criticized as inadequate by many delegates to the union's eighth congress in June of that year, a clear sign that IG Bau was beginning to shed at least some of the Leber legacy.[84] The new leadership began to realize that inadequate pay was one of the factors contributing to the industry's and the union's skilled labor problem. The congress recommended that the differentials between skilled and unskilled wages be raised, both to retain workers already employed in the industry and to attract more apprentices. This measure was to be supplemented by a more aggressive bargaining approach which would take advantage of the ongoing boom in the construction industry. All of these recommendations were decreed in a Working Program (Arbeitsprogramm) published in November 1969.[85] The skilled-labor issue was to be IG Bau's dominant concern over the next decade.

During the early 1970s, IG Bau's leadership finally took steps to alleviate this persistent problem. In February 1970, the Munich Agreement was signed which substantially increased wages in construction. The Agreement provided for a general raise of 2.5% from May 1, 1970. In addition, all workers were henceforth to be paid 2.5% more than their contractual wage rates, as compensation for the disadvantages of construction employment. Lastly, all skilled workers with at least two years' experience were promoted into a new wage category, "advanced skilled worker," which brought with it an additional raise of 2%. This new emphasis on wages continued in 1971 and 1972 when increases of 7.9% and 6.4% respectively were negotiated.[86] Whether as a result of these actions or for other reasons related to the general mobilization of West

German labor at the time, IG Bau's membership rose from 469,953 in 1969 to 522,157 in 1973. The year 1972 also witnessed the first rise in the number of apprentices since the mid-1960s.[87]

In the first half of the 1970s, Rudolf Sperner put great emphasis on cooperation with the SPD–FDP government to solve the problems facing construction. The union lobbied aggressively to keep spending high on government building projects. In 1972, at the union's urging, a special Winter Construction Amendment to the Work Promotion Law of 1969 was passed which included subsidies to employers to encourage winter construction and an extra payment (called "bad-weather money") of DM 2 per hour to all construction workers, covering the period from December through March, to compensate for the adversities of winter building activity.[88]

However, the most important result of union–government cooperation was the reform of vocational training in the construction industry, passed into law by the Bundestag in 1974.[89] The new training system sought to increase the attractiveness of apprenticeship in construction by dividing instruction into the following categories: on-the-job training in a particular skill, general training in other areas of construction, and basic education. The idea was to facilitate skilled-worker mobility within construction so as to discourage switching to other industries, as well as to make vocational instruction more interesting. The new system has been successful, with the number of apprentices in the building trades steadily rising every year since 1972 and reaching 71,496 in 1981 (1971: 26,453).[90]

In 1973, the long boom in construction came to an end, and once again crisis befell the industry. Output dropped 7.5% in 1974 and 5.3% in 1975, while employment in primary construction fell 10.3% and 10.5% respectively in those two years. Unskilled workers bore the brunt of the layoffs, as employers reacted to the downturn by rationalizing and mechanizing production. However, this produced a positive side-effect for IG Bau. Because a majority of unskilled workers (many of them guest workers) were not union members, massive layoffs among their ranks raised IG Bau's organizational level in 1976 above 25% for the first time in a long while. It remained at about this level throughout the latter half of the 1970s and into the 1980s. A modest recovery occurred in the industry in 1976, as output began to rise again, but employment did not increase until 1978. Construction remained relatively strong through 1980, and it was only in 1981 that output and employment again fell sharply.[91]

The 1974–75 crisis had three important consequences for IG Bau which caused the union to reorient its strategy in the late 1970s. The first was the move of the Schmidt government towards restrictive fiscal policies as symbolized by the Budget Structure Law (Haushaltsstrukturgesetz) of

1975. This law, as discussed in Chapter 3, curtailed many of the programs instituted in previous, more prosperous, years by Willy Brandt. Included in the cuts was a portion of the "bad-weather money" paid to construction workers. In general, cooperation with the government was no longer an effective strategy for IG Bau since little, if any, money was available either for additional construction projects or for new social security measures. Consequently IG Bau had to concentrate its efforts on preventing cuts in already existing programs favorable to construction.

A second consequence was that employers took advantage of the economic downturn by severely diminishing the non-contractual pay of construction workers, thus negating the gains IG Bau had made in bargaining during the early 1970s. By 1978, average actual earnings in construction had fallen to twentieth place among West German industries from seventh in 1973.[92] Lastly, as in 1966–67, the crisis initiated an exodus of skilled workers from the industry. This exodus, combined with the slow growth in apprentices, actually led to skilled-worker shortages in the 1970s. At the same time a new phenomenon began to have an important effect on the workforce in the construction industry: increasingly, so-called labor-leasing firms appeared on the market.[93] These firms would "rent" unskilled labor (mainly guest workers) for specific construction jobs. Because the workers were actually employed by the leasing firm, they were not subject to the contracts signed by IG Bau. Clearly the union had to respond to this development.

Given the set of problems facing it in the late 1970s, IG Bau's leadership had only one viable strategy open to it: to concentrate on aggressive collective bargaining in order to protect take-home pay and establish the union's legitimacy as a defender of its members' interests. In addition, pay differentials for skilled workers would have to be increased even further to augment the industry's attractiveness for this group. A major lobbying effort would also have to be undertaken to force a ban on labor-leasing firms.

In 1977, the union signed a contract which accomplished at least some of these goals.[94] Wages were increased by 8.5% and an agreement was reached which called for differentials between pay rates for the skilled and unskilled to be raised progressively over the next three years. During the 1978 wage round, the union had the opportunity to show its new "fighting spirit."[95] Negotiations took place simultaneously on a new general framework contract, where IG Bau demanded longer vacations, and a wage contract, where it asked for higher vacation bonuses and a 7.7% pay rise. Throughout April and May 1978, the union organized nationwide warning strikes. After a compromise had been reached on the two contracts in the Federal Republic, employers in West Berlin refused to accept it, thereby calling forth a full-fledged strike by the union in August of that year. Although this industrial action was minor compared to IG Metall's strikes during the same year, it nevertheless represented a new departure for IG Bau. To underline the importance of this event, the union published a 350-page book on the strike in West Berlin filled with pictures of angry workers.[96] For a brief moment at least, Leber-style accommodationism within IG Bau was eclipsed.

Despite the unspectacular nature of his policies, Sperner was able to lead IG Bau to a number of successes in the 1970s. In 1981, the union reached its highest membership and organizational levels ever, though the latter still remained modest compared to the levels attained by IG Metall, IG Druck and IG Chemie. (It is interesting to note that the level of IG Chemie's organizational representation in the "Big Three" – the union's Achilles heel – quite closely corresponds to IG Bau's overall level of organizational penetration.) The number of apprentices in primary construction also reached its highest point since 1958. The union won substantial wage increases, and proved in 1978 that it was able and willing to conduct large-scale strikes. In 1981 the federal government was persuaded to forbid labor-leasing firms in construction despite considerable opposition from the ZDB and HDB. The average construction worker certainly gained more since Leber's departure in 1966 than during the period when IG Bau occupied center stage in the West German labor movement.

# 7 THE ARISTOCRACY OF LABOR: THE PRINTERS' UNION, IG DRUCK UND PAPIER
## (written with Thomas C. Ertman)

## INTRODUCTION

Although it is one of the DGB's smallest members, the printers' union (IG Druck und Papier) must be included in any comprehensive study of the West German trade-union movement. IG Druck is heir to the longest and one of the most controversial labor traditions in German history. The distinguished history of the printers during the Wilhelminian and Weimar eras inspired the term "labor aristocracy," clearly conveying the substantial influence they and their organization wielded within the unionized labor movement. They have continued to play a disproportionately significant role through the post-World War II era and up to the present day. In the past decade, however, West German printers, like their counterparts the world over, have been confronted by a technological revolution which has threatened the very existence of this "aristocracy." IG Druck's response to this crisis provides an excellent opportunity to analyze how organized labor in the Federal Republic has dealt with technological change.

The electronic revolution in printing and its effect on IG Druck will be only one of several themes developed in this chapter. The history of the printers' union since 1948 illustrates in exemplary fashion many of the fundamental issues which have been explored in this book.

IG Druck was created in 1948 by workers who had been represented since the 1890s by at least four major unions. All of these older printers' organizations were classical craft unions which had consistently opposed the formation of industrial unions, a cause which was being championed by the metalworkers in the 1920s. What then were the mechanisms which allowed these diverse groups of printers to be brought into a single organization after 1948, and how has IG Druck's often fragile internal unity been maintained? The microcosm of IG Druck und Papier reflects some of the problems as well as advantages of the Industriegewerkschaft and the Einheitsgewerkschaft, the two main organizational innovations of the West German labor movement.

The most important forerunner of IG Druck, the German Book Printers' Confederation (founded in 1865), developed a unique approach – which will be discussed below – to both collective bargaining and the problems posed by technological change. This fact naturally raises the issue of continuity in the West German labor movement. One must ask: to what degree has tradition conditioned the behavior of IG Druck? Has today's union drawn upon old response patterns in dealing with crisis situations, or has it developed entirely new strategies better suited to the conditions of the post-war world?

The approach to union–employer relations called "social partnership" – because of its emphasis on collective bargaining, the sanctity of contracts, and arbitration instead of strikes – has been adopted with certain important variations by all West German unions. Indeed, the very attributes which were, until recently, used to describe West Germany's "special" system of labor relations could be applied equally well to the pre-1933 printing industry. What then were the historic preconditions for this accommodationist unionism, and what was the role of the organized printers in this arrangement before and after World War II?

Beginning in the early 1970s the printers were subjected to the dual pressures of an economic and a technological crisis which did not spread with equal force to other segments of industry until the end of that decade. As a result of these pressures, IG Druck abandoned the accommodationist ideology which had brought it considerable success in the 1950s and 1960s and began to present itself as the champion of the DGB's activist wing – rivaling IG Metall – by favoring a more combative posture on the part of the unions vis-à-vis the employers and the state. Is this sudden transformation authentic, and if so, is the crisis of the 1970s sufficient to explain it? Will the process of radicalization which the printers have undergone be repeated in other unions as they face similar problems during the 1980s and beyond? Or will the "new accommodationism" pursued by the chemical workers, as analyzed in Chapter 5, represent a more viable option for West German labor? The crisis moved IG Chemie and IG Druck und Papier to opposite ends of the political spectrum within the DGB. This chapter will present a detailed investigation of the reasons, events and consequences of the latter's new alignment.

This study of the printers' union will begin with a brief sketch of the printing industry, its key technologies, and the nature of its workforce. Although IG Druck also organizes workers in the paper-processing, lampshade- and wallpaper-production industries, this discussion will focus exclusively on its activities in printing because this sector represents by far the most important area of union action. A general overview of the union itself will follow, providing an analysis of the structure of its membership, its internal organization and its collective bargaining procedures.

As the introduction has indicated, the historic tradition which IG Druck inherited is stronger than that of any other West German union. This chapter therefore will provide some background on IG Druck's organizational predecessors, placing special emphasis on factors from the pre-World War II period which influenced union behavior after the war as well. This section will conclude with an analysis, in roughly chronological fashion, of the printers' union's development since 1948. A section on the printing industry and union in the 1950s and 1960s will be followed by one which focuses on the technological and economic crisis of the 1970s and IG Druck's response to them.

## I. THE PRINTING INDUSTRY

Although economically not very significant, the West German printing industry is of immense cultural and political importance. It "manufactures" the country's newspapers, magazines and books, as well as advertising materials, "business papers" (forms, stationary) and printed packaging. Organizationally the industry includes only firms which do the actual printing. Thus, publishing houses and the editorial departments of newspapers and magazines do not formally belong to the industry.

Printing had sales of DM 20.6 billion in 1980, representing about 2% of the total for West German industry.[1] The sector employs approximately 205,000 people, or 2.5% of all industrial workers, which indicates that printing is more labor-intensive than the industrial average.[2] This greater labor intensity means that the printing industry has been burdened with an unusually heavy wage bill. Almost 35% of the sector's sales must go to wages, salaries and fringe benefits, as against an industrial average of only 23.6%.[3] The great significance of the wage bill in printing has, since the nineteenth century, provided the impetus both for rationalization and for agreements seeking to keep wages uniform throughout the entire industry.

Printing has always been a sector where most of the units of production are small. Of the approximately 6,500 printing plants in operation in 1976, 3,612 had fewer than ten employees, and another 2,320 fewer than 50. There were only 154 plants in the Federal Republic with more than 200 workers.[4] In economic terms, however, these 154 plants have consistently dominated the industry. In the late 1970s, they produced 43.7% of the total sales and employed 37% of the industry's workers.[5] These large works have been IG Druck's stronghold, since organization and mobilization in smaller plants is often difficult. Even more important to the union have been the thirteen plants which, in 1976, employed more than 1,000 persons. These "giants," most of which are connected with West Germany's powerful newspaper and magazine chains (Springer, Gruner + Jahr, Bauer, Bertelsmann) have always been trend-setters for the printing industry in both wages and the introduction of new technologies. As will be discussed, most of IG Druck und Papier's important battles of the 1970s involved these companies, at least indirectly.

The printing industry can be broken down into a number of sub-markets, each with its own peculiar characteristics and level of competition. The most important of these sub-markets is the one for newspapers and magazines, which account for 37% of the industry's total sales.[6] The largest national newspaper and magazine chains all have at least one large printing plant where their own publications – and sometimes those of smaller publishers – are produced. The same is true of the large regional newspapers, such as the *Frankfurter Rundschau* or the *Stuttgarter Zeitung*, while smaller newspapers are frequently sent out to be printed. Since the market for newspapers and magazines is highly concentrated, relatively little competition occurs at this level.

Below the giant publisher-owned printing works are a number of large and medium-sized independent printers. All of the 154 largest printing plants in West Germany fall into one of these first two categories. The large independent printers fill huge orders for advertising materials (22% of the printing market), business papers (24%), pre-printed packaging (9%) and books (9%), as well as printing many journals and magazines.[7] Competition for orders is very stiff. The thousands of smaller printing works which comprise the rest of the industry produce a similar range of products, but for a geographically limited clientele. Thus, competition in regional and local markets is fierce. Because of this, many firms have tried to protect themselves by concentrating on items which require special printing techniques, or by building up a long list of standing orders. Nevertheless, it was mainly the small and medium-sized independent printers that were most severely affected by the industry's economic difficulties during the 1970s.

In addition to the printing industry's economic situation, it is essential to know something about the technology involved in order to understand the challenges which IG Druck has faced over the past 30 years. What follows is an account of the "cold type" printing process, which has been used to produce newspapers and magazines since about 1900. In the course of this chapter, the various technical changes which this process has undergone since the mid-1950s will be discussed.

Newspaper printing can be divided into two stages: the production of a printing plate and the printing of the newspaper using that plate.[8] After a reporter has finished an article, a typographical editor puts it into the form which will appear in the newspaper. The editor then passes on the edited copy to a typographer (also called a typesetter or compositor) who works at a Linotype machine. The typographer "types" the article using a keyboard resembling that of a typewriter, and the machine casts it in metal using small lead letters. The article emerges in lines of lead type, hence the machine's name. The lines of type are then brought to the composing room, where a makeup printer positions the various articles to form an entire newspaper page set in lead. A corrector then checks each page for mistakes, with entire lines often needing recasting. Engraved plates containing photographs are also inserted at this time. (The plates are produced by workers call chemographers.) Headlines and advertisements, which use irregular lettering, are added by manual typographers using individual metal letters. When the whole page is complete, a stereotyper takes an impression of it using cardboard or plaster of Paris (or a similar substance). From this mold a metal printing plate of the newspaper page is cast. The plates weigh over 40 pounds and, in the book-printing method (most widely used to produce newspapers, books and business papers, but not magazines), the letters on the plate are raised. In heliogravure printing (used for illustrated and color magazines among other things), the letters are recessed, while in flat printing methods, such as offset or lithography, the plate is an entirely flat surface. Regardless of what method is used, the printing plate is then mounted on the printing press by a printer and his/her assistants. As the papers come off the press, they are folded and cut by machine, but sometimes bundled by hand. The bundles are then loaded onto trucks for delivery.

As this description of newspaper production perhaps indicates, cold type printing requires a wide variety of skilled blue-collar workers, from the typographers and correctors through the makeup printers and stereotypers to the printing press operators themselves. It is not surprising then that the industry contains a high percentage of blue-collar workers in general, and skilled workers in particular, among its labor force. Of all those employed in the industry, 77% are blue-collar, and of these 55% are skilled workers, as compared to an average of only 40% in West German industry.[9] Among white-collar employees, most (61%) are clerical workers, of whom the vast majority are women.[10] Women are also overrepresented, along with foreign workers, among the semi- and unskilled blue-collar employees involved in packaging, loading, cleaning, and assisting skilled workers. In general, however, foreigners play a small role in printing, representing only 6.2% of the workforce, compared to an average of 13.4% in West German manufacturing as a whole.[11] The industry is clearly dominated by German, male, skilled, blue-collar workers, who also constitute the "hard core" of both IG Druck's membership and the West German labor movement at large.

Given the percentage of employees requiring special training, it seems logical that printers have always been among West Germany's most highly paid blue-collar workers (as they have in most other advanced industrial countries). In 1976, the average monthly income of a printing employee was 6.1% above the industrial norm.[12] In 1970, the industry paid the second highest wages in the Federal Republic after oil refining, and in 1976 it still ranked fifth despite the pronounced crisis printing was experiencing at the time.[13] The substantial incomes earned by printers are due not only to high basic wage rates, but also to bonuses for overtime, night and weekend shifts, which are necessary to publish many printed products – such as newspapers and magazines – on schedule.

In summary, printing is an industry of sharp contrasts between the giant printing plants of the media conglomerates on one hand, and the thousands of small works producing for speciality markets on the other; between highly skilled blue-collar workers and clerical white-collar employees; between a privileged core of male German workers and a (relatively) disadvantaged group consisting of women and foreigners.

## II. THE PRINTING UNION AND THE PRINTING EMPLOYERS' ASSOCIATIONS: AN OVERVIEW

### A. IG Druck: sociology and internal organization

IG Druck und Papier (the Printing and Paper Workers' Union), with its 139,000 members (1979), is the twelfth largest DGB union and, as noted earlier, accounts for only about 2% of total DGB membership.[14] IG Druck's organizational level of 45.8% (1978) was significantly higher than the DGB average of about 34%, but still only about half of the 89.1% level which the union boasted in 1949.[15]

Although thus far this discussion has concentrated only on the printing industry, IG Druck's membership is not limited to that sector. The union also represents employees of publishing houses, journalists, writers and workers in the paper-processing and lampshade- and wallpaper-production industries. These areas have played a very minor role in the organization's post-war development though, as membership statistics show. Over 80% of IG Druck's members are employed in printing, as against only 15.7% in paper-processing, the union's next most important organizational domain.[16]

*Figure 5.* IG Druck regional district: Baden-Württemberg
*Source:* Stuttgart, IG Druck und Papier.

*Figure 6.* IG Druck regional district: Bavaria
*Source:* Stuttgart, IG Druck und Papier.

*Figure 7.* IG Druck regional district: Hesse
*Source:* Stuttgart, IG Druck und Papier.

*Figure 8.* IG Druck regional district: North Rhine-Westphalia
*Source:* Stuttgart, IG Druck und Papier

*Figure 9.* IG Druck regional district: Lower Saxony
*Source:* Stuttgart, IG Druck und Papier.

*Figure 10.* IG Druck regional district: Rhineland-Palatinate-Saar
*Source:* Stuttgart, IG Druck und Papier.

*Figure 11.* IG Druck regional district: Nordmark
*Source:* Stuttgart, IG Druck und Papier.

The structure of the printing membership itself will come as no surprise, for it reflects the particular characteristics of the printing workforce enumerated above. Blue-collar workers predominate. Of IG Druck's 132,000 active members in 1975 (that is, total membership minus retirees and the disabled), 78,400, or 70%, were blue-collar workers employed in the printing industry.[17] The organizational level among this group was 57.9%, as opposed to only 18.4% for white-collar printing employees and 32.4% for blue-collar workers in paper-processing.[18] As might be expected, male skilled workers constitute the most important sub-group within the printing workforce as a whole with an organizational level of about 80%.[19] This fact confirms the assumption that skilled workers comprise the "hard core" of union membership in printing. As we shall see, this group dominates all of IG Druck's governing bodies, and thus exercises an overwhelming influence over both the union's internal politics and its strategic goals.

The internal organization of IG Druck is very similar to that of other West German unions, although a somewhat different terminology is used.[20] The lowest level of union organization is the local (Ortsverein), followed by the district (Bezirk), state district (Landesbezirk), and finally the national level, where the union congress (Gewerkschaftstag) constitutes the highest governing body. There are 367 locals throughout the country organized into 51 districts and eight state districts. Six of the latter (Baden-Württemberg, Bavaria, Hesse, North Rhine-Westphalia, Berlin and Lower Saxony) are identical to the West German Länder (states) of the same names. The smaller states of Rhineland-Palatinate and the Saar, as well as Hamburg and Schleswig-Holstein, have been united to form two additional state districts, Rhineland-Palatinate-Saar and Nordmark respectively. Bremen belongs to the union's Lower Saxony district. (See figures 5–11.)

At each level, beginning with the plant, representatives are elected and sent to an assembly at the next higher level. The members of the eight state district assemblies select delegates to the union congress, which has been held every three years since 1958 and occurred at two-year intervals before then. The congress in turn elects an executive committee (Vorstand), headed by a chairman, which runs the union on a daily basis. As we have already noted, certain groups are consistently overrepresented in each of the union's assemblies and at the national congresses. Thus, of the approximately 250 delegates to the congress, about three-quarters are skilled printing workers, with most of them German males.[21] Male, German, white-collar employees also account for a disproportionate number of delegates. Accordingly, unskilled workers have been greatly underrepresented at these congresses. Although they constitute 30% of the union's membership, they fielded only twelve delegates to the 1977 congress. At that congress, there were only 20 women and not a single foreign worker out of a total of 267 delegates. It goes without saying that all the union's chairmen since 1948 have been male, skilled printing workers by training.

In addition to its basic internal structure described above, IG Druck has several organizational peculiarities distinguishing it from other DGB unions. First, plant shop stewards (Vertrauensleute) play a relatively unimportant role in this union. IG Druck counts over 7,000 works councilors among its members, but only about 5,000 shop stewards, a relationship which is reversed in other unions, especially IG Metall and IG Chemie, in both of which the number of shop stewards substantially exceeds the number of works councilors. IG Druck's situation can be explained by the fact that in the small and medium-sized firms which predominate within printing, it is superfluous to have an organizational level in addition to the works councilors'.[22]

Moreover, the 1976 co-determination law plays virtually no role in printing.[23] Most printing firms are too small to fall under the jurisdiction of this law. A special clause contained in both the Works Constitution Law of 1952 and the Co-determination Law of 1976 exempts all media-related companies from co-determination, thereby excluding the large firms. Originating from a view which sees co-determination as potentially endangering the impartiality of the media, this clause, the Tendenzschutz-paragraph, is designed to exclude labor from the advisory boards of the Federal Republic's newspapers, radio stations and television channels. Although several large firms have voluntarily invited IG Druck representatives onto their boards, the abolition of the Tendenzschutzparagraph has been one of the union's major goals during the post-World War II period.

A third and far more significant peculiarity of IG Druck pertains to the presence of semi-autonomous "professional groups" within the union.[24] The practice of dividing the union's membership into different skill groups dates back to the nineteenth century, when the German Book Printers' Confederation was, as the name implies, a confederation of independently organized professional groups (Berufsgruppen) and "sections" (Sparten) in which membership was based on the skilled trade a worker had learned. Thus typographers (both manual and machine), correctors, stereotypers and various types of printers (book printers, lithographers, heliogravurers, for example) all had their own separate sections which represented their members' interest vis-à-vis the union's executive committee in areas of training, work practices and pay. Following IG Druck's formation in 1948, all the sections for skilled workers were retained, and groups which had previously been outside the Book Printers (such as unskilled workers and white-collar employees) formed their own new professional groups similar to those for the skilled workers. However, the skilled-worker sections – especially the Linotype typographers – remained the dominant forces within the union. In 1974, following over 20 years of internal conflict on this issue, the skilled-worker sections were dissolved by the union's executive committee, and all skilled printing workers formed two professional groups (printing plate production and printing) whose powers were strictly limited. This running conflict between different skill groups, which has plagued IG Druck since its creation, will be discussed in greater detail later in the chapter.

### B. Collective bargaining

Employers in the West German printing industry are represented by not one but three employers' associations, the Bundesverband Druck (Federal Printing Association – BVD), the Bundesverband Deutscher Zeitungsverleger (Federal Association of German Newspaper Publishers – BDZV), and the Verband Deutscher Zeitschriftenverleger (Association of German Periodical Publishers – VDZ).[25] As their names imply, the last two groups represent newspaper and magazine and journal publishers respectively, while the first admits only the owners of printing works. Because, as was mentioned earlier, the large newspapers and magazines which dominate the BDZV and the VDZ all possess one or more printing plants, they are members of the BVD as well. The activities of all three organizations have been closely coordinated over the years, with the BVD usually playing the vanguard role in determining the industry's position on wages and social issues.

Because of its heterogeneous makeup, the BVD, like IG Druck, has often been plagued by serious intra-organizational tensions. The main conflicts within this association result from the great disparity of power and financial resources between the large newspaper and magazine groups (Springer, Bauer, Bertelsmann, Gruner + Jahr) which dominate the West German media, and the much smaller independent printing firms which make up the bulk of the BVD's membership. Not surprisingly, these divisions have consistently come to the fore whenever conflicts with IG Druck have erupted, as they did with great frequency during the 1970s.

As in construction, the printing industry's most important contract, the wage contract for blue-collar workers, is negotiated by the union for the entire Federal Republic and West Berlin, rather than on a regional basis as is the case with other unions. This practice dates back to 1873, when the Book Printers negotiated the first collective bargaining agreement covering all skilled printing workers in the Reich. IG Druck bargains directly with

the Bundesverband Druck over both wage and general framework contracts (Manteltarifverträge) for all the industry's production workers. As
in other unions, wage contracts are usually renegotiated on a yearly basis,
while general framework contracts last anywhere from two to five years,
with the longer interval having become the norm in recent years. Contracts
delineating the shop-floor conditions for production workers are by far the
most important for IG Druck because bargaining for all other employee
groups follows the conclusion of these contracts and is therefore heavily
influenced by what is contained in them.

After signing the national manual worker contract with the BVD, the
union negotiates regional contracts with the BDZV and the VDZ concerning all work-related affairs for reporters and clerical employees of
newspapers and magazines. Regional salary contracts are also signed with
the BVD covering white-collar employees in printing plants themselves.
One of IG Druck's longstanding demands has been to have contracts for
white-collar workers negotiated on a national basis as well. This wish has
thus far remained unfulfilled.

Responsibility for the production workers' contract lies with the union
contract commission (Tarifkommission) which usually contains between
40 and 45 members. These include all of the union's national executive
committee officers, the chairmen of the eight state districts and about
twenty representatives elected by the state district congresses. The
contract commission is assisted by a contract committee (Tarifausschuss)
of fourteen people, including technical advisers and delegates from the
state districts. This committee makes recommendations concerning
demands to be presented by the union during negotiations over either wage
or general framework contracts. These recommendations are either
approved or amended by the contract commission. The bargaining process
is carried out by a negotiating committee (Verhandlungskommission) of
ten or eleven people, including the chairman of the executive committee
and several works councilors from the most important printing plants. This
group is selected by the contract commission. When negotiations reach
their final stages, two or three of the union's top officials often engage in
private talks with their counterparts from the employers' association.

Another characteristic of industrial relations in printing which sets it
apart from other sectors is the industry's long history of formal arbitration
arrangements. For many years both before 1933 and after 1948 there were
two arbitration bodies which could be activated in the event of a breakdown in bargaining over national contracts. The first, known as the
Central Arbitration Tribunal (Zentrales Schiedsgericht), could be called
on by either side. Each bargaining party sent an equal number of
representatives (between five and ten) to the tribunal and agreed on a

neutral chairman. Although the arbitration procedure was altered in 1973, this tribunal still remains in existence, but now it must be invoked by both sides and hold its first meeting within 16 days of the breakdown of talks. Arbitration agreements must be approved by a majority of the tribunal's members, thus giving each side veto power. The supposed benefits of this system lie in the fact that a neutral chairman from outside the industry must lead the negotiations, and that no strike can be called before the tribunal recommends a formal settlement, which subsequently has to be rejected.

Before the 1973 arbitration reforms, there was another arbitration tribunal, the Superior Arbitration Office (Oberstes Schlichtungsamt), which was called in case the first attempt at arbitration failed to attain a settlement. The effect of the old arbitration system was to create a long cooling-off period during which union members could not be mobilized and strikes could not be called. Most contract agreements throughout the 1950s and 1960s were reached, as we shall see, with the help of one or both of the arbitration bodies then in use. Although arbitration still exists since the 1973 reforms, strike activity has been substantially facilitated by a considerable shortening of the period during which the peace obligation applies.

## III. LABOR RELATIONS IN THE PRINTING INDUSTRY: THE HISTORICAL BACKGROUND

As in most other European countries, printers were key participants in the development of a trade-union movement in the nineteenth century. From the start, the printers advocated a pragmatic approach to industrial relations which sought to reform, rather than overthrow, the existing social order. The mechanism through which they hoped to achieve this was the collective bargaining agreement.

Although it never ceased to be condemned by the Social Democratic left wing, the printers' accommodationist strategy came to be seen by numerous unions as an effective way to improve the lives of their members. Today the opposition within West German labor between activists led by IG Metall and accommodationists represented by IG Bau centers on disagreements concerning form rather than content, since all unions have now by and large accepted the pragmatic reformism pioneered by the printers over 100 years ago. The pre-1914 German Book Printers' Confederation was thus, along with the Masons' Union (see Chapter 6 above) one of the only unions of that period which resembled a present-day West German trade union in behavior and ideology.

The history of unionism in the printing industry dates back to 1848 when, in the wake of the revolution of that year, printer delegates from throughout Germany met in Mainz to discuss ways to improve their lot.[26] The printers explicitly rejected calls for revolution, and instead drew up a draft for a collective bargaining agreement with the employers which called for higher wages, limits on the number of apprentices (Lehrlingsskala), manning guidelines for the new mechanized printing presses, and the creation of joint contract enforcement and arbitration bodies. All of the main points in the draft of the contract, which was the first of its kind in Germany, remain important concerns of the printers to the present day. Thus, for example, throughout the 1950s, IG Druck blocked increases in the number of apprentices employers could hire in order to preserve a shortage of skilled labor in the industry. The exclusive right of skilled workers to operate new machines was the major issue of the union's strike in the spring of 1978.

Thanks to the reactionary atmosphere which followed the 1848 revolution, the printers had to wait 25 years for their demands to be met. In 1866, they became the second group in Germany (after the cigar workers) to form a union, the German Book Printers' Confederation (Deutscher Buchdrucker Verein – DBV). The union represented all male skilled workers in printing ("book printers" was a term that covered all printers using the raised-letter book printing technique – i.e. those in newspaper and magazine production) and remained the industry's dominant organization until 1933. In 1873, bookbinders and lithographers founded their own separate unions, to be followed in 1898 by the organization of unskilled workers. These were the four basic unions which united to form IG Druck after World War II. The old Book Printers' Confederation lived on after 1948 in the form of IG Druck's skilled-worker sections (Sparten), which continued to exercise what to many appeared a negative influence over the union until their dissolution in 1974.

In 1873, the book printers signed their first wage contract with the printing employers' association, which had been formed in 1869. The contract applied to all skilled workers throughout the Reich, and thus set the pattern for nationwide bargaining which persists to this day. Under the terms of the contract, both sides agreed to form a "collective bargaining community" (Tarifgemeinschaft), which essentially meant that joint committees would supervise the implementation of the contract and arbitrate disputes, thus fulfilling one of the printers' main demands from 25 years earlier. These enforcement bodies became necessary because labor contracts at the time were not yet recognized as legally valid.

The conciliatory attitude of the printing employers, which was sharply criticized by other employer groups, was dictated by the fact that wages represented 60–70% of their total costs in the late nineteenth century. By fixing wage rates for the whole country, it was hoped that wage and price competition among firms could be reduced and the business climate stabilized. Cooperation also came more naturally to this industry because the social distance between (skilled) workers and owners was less than in perhaps any other sector of the German economy. The printers were the "aristocracy of labor" in terms of education and training, and many – if not most – employers were themselves former skilled workers. Both sides were thus able to accept each other as equals. Ultimately, of course, cooperation represented the only sensible option for the employers since the printers possessed special skills essential to the entire production process.

In 1878, not long after the first printing contract was signed, the German government passed the Anti-Socialist laws, which remained in effect until 1890. Many newly formed unions were banned, but the book printers survived by changing their name to the Support Organization of German Book Printers (Unterstützungsverein der Deutschen Buchdrucker – UVDB). During the 1880s, however, a number of reactionary owners gained considerable influence within the printing employers' association and persuaded it to pursue a more confrontational strategy against the union. This was the main cause behind the bitter ten-week nationwide strike which the book printers waged in 1891–92. The printers demanded the introduction of the 9-hour day (53-hour week) which had already become the norm in the printing industries of several other countries. The employers were intransigent, and the ensuing strike was eventually defeated. Rather than radicalize the union, the strike experience seems to have convinced both sides that cooperation was the only way to achieve progress. The employers agreed in 1897 to lower the work week to 54 hours, and it was finally reduced to 53 hours in 1912. Even though it was a failure, the strike of 1891–92 established the printers' reputation as leaders in the fight for work-time reduction, a tradition which continued after 1945, when IG Druck became the first West German union to win the 40-hour week.

In the aftermath of the 1891–92 strike, printers and employers established the second collective bargaining community (Tarifgemeinschaft) in 1896, and it was to last until 1922. The community's wage office not only set wage increases, but also began to negotiate printing prices with the union. Moreover, the employers recognized the workers' right to elect official shop-floor representatives (similar to the future works councilors) who would arbitrate disputes and discuss working conditions with management.

The main concern of large printing employers at this time was competition from provincial printers who did not pay the contractually agreed wage rates and could thus undercut the prices of firms which did so. In an effort to eliminate this "dirty competition," the employers' association negotiated in 1906 an organizational agreement with the book printers according to which employers would hire only union members, and union members would only work for firms belonging to the employers' association and paying contractual wages. In effect, both sides were trying to create a closed-shop situation, one of the rare cases of such an attempt in German labor history. The agreement was successful, mainly because of the high organizational density of the book printers' union (which had again changed its name, this time to the Confederation of German Book Printers – the VdDB – in 1893). By 1914, over 85% of all printing firms were abiding by the contract.[27] This figure is all the more impressive considering the fact that collective bargaining was still the exception in labor relations at the time.

The extraordinary success of the printers' cooperative strategy led to its acceptance by both the socialist labor movement and the state. The social democratic trade-union confederation (which the book printers had joined in 1891) officially recognized collective bargaining agreements as legitimate at its congress in 1899, and a court decision in 1910 stated that such agreements were legally binding (which is not to say that the state was yet willing to enforce them actively).

The most important issue that faced the printers at the turn of the century was precisely the same one confronting them today: technological innovation. In the late 1890s Linotype machines, which had been developed in the United States in 1878, began to appear in Germany. Since manual typographers were one of the most important organizational groups within the book printers' union, this development was frightening indeed. The union conjured up images of thousands of manual typographers being thrown into the streets overnight as Linotype machines operated by unskilled workers rendered skilled printers obsolete. The union began negotiating a contract to cover the introduction of the new machines and demanded that only trained manual typographers be allowed to use them. In addition, the printers asked that the operators of the new equipment be paid wages which were 20% above the contractual rates for all other skilled workers. It was believed that this measure would greatly discourage owners from introducing the new machines. Surprisingly, the employers agreed to all of the union's demands, and a contract was signed in 1900 covering new technology.

The employers' acquiescence can be explained by the fact that the industry and the economy in general were experiencing a boom period which rendered labor particularly scarce. Needless to say, the 20% "bonus" for machine typographers did little to stop the widespread introduction of the new technology, but this arrangement survived both the

Weimar Republic and the Third Reich to become a contentious issue between IG Druck and the industry to this day. The printers saw the 1900 Linotype agreement as one of their greatest victories, and it was to be used, as we shall see, by IG Druck as a model for dealing with the introduction of all new technology after World War II.

With defeat in World War I and the 1918 revolution, the nature of labor relations changed greatly in Germany. Industrialists, fearing nationalization, agreed in 1918 to the formation of a "collective bargaining community" with the social democratic unions, based on the model existing in the printing industry. This arrangement, called the Central Labor Community (Zentrale Arbeitsgemeinschaft) lasted until 1923. The new republican government, in one of its first acts, passed a law recognizing unions as official representatives of the workers and stipulating that all contracts negotiated by these organizations be enforced by the power of the state.

The revolutionary spirit in Germany also led to the appearance in 1919 of an opposition group among the book printers, composed of USPD (the German Independent Social Democratic Party, which broke from the SPD after World War I) and KPD sympathizers. These leftists demanded the creation of a single industrial union for the whole printing industry, but the VdDB vetoed this plan after its membership rejected the measure in a referendum. Instead, a loose federation of the four printing unions, called the Graphical Association (Graphischer Bund), was formed. This cooperation between the various organizations proved essential, as was shown by the fact that when the employers agreed to the first contract for unskilled printing workers in 1921, their wages were fixed as a percentage of the skilled-worker wage rates negotiated by the VdDB. This practice of linking all workers' pay to the skilled worker base rate has remained the defining characteristic of the printing industry's wage structure to the present, and has been a major source of conflict within IG Druck since 1948.

Despite the gains which it brought organized labor, the Weimar Republic was a difficult period for all unions, especially the printers. In 1923, state-administered binding arbitration for all labor disputes was introduced, and this deprived the printers' unions of the collective bargaining autonomy which they had helped establish. The experience of state arbitration, which in effect meant that wages were set unilaterally by the state wage office, led the post-war union movement to ordain collective bargaining autonomy (Tarifautonomie) as its most fundamental guiding principle, as it had always been for the printers. When the Depression arrived in Germany in 1931, the state imposed substantial wage cuts on all workers. Despite their strong organization and long tradition, the printers were powerless against these state actions. Finally, in 1933, the Nazis dissolved all unions and re-formed them into "Reich plant communities" (Reichsbetriebsgemeinschaften) within the national socialist Deutsche Arbeitsfront (DAF). Ironically, the unification of all printing workers into a single organization, the Reichsbetriebsgemeinschaft Druck, was to facilitate the creation of IG Druck as an industrial union 15 years later.

## IV. IG DRUCK UND PAPIER: 1948–1969

### A. The printing industry in the 1950s and 1960s

The two decades between 1950 and 1970 ushered in a period of sustained growth and prosperity for the West German printing industry. Yet the image in the public mind of overwhelming success drew attention away from a number of important structural problems which developed in the printing sector. These problems manifested themselves fully in the 1970s, when the industry, which had previously been considered immune from marked cyclical swings, underwent two recessions within four years.

As did virtually every industry in West Germany, printing experienced an impressive expansion in the two decades following the Currency Reform of 1948. Between 1950 and 1968, printing production tripled, and by 1970 employment, which peaked at 224,100, had more than doubled from 109,800 in 1950.[28] Yet despite the common element of nearly uninterrupted growth, the condition of the industry in the 1950s changed radically in the 1960s.

Printing output rose at an average annual rate of 8.7% between 1950 and 1959, which was slightly below the industrial average of 9.6%.[29] The growth cycles in printing during this decade do not correspond to those either in industry or in the economy as a whole. Whereas the West German economy passed through two complete business cycles, with troughs in 1954 and 1958 and peaks in 1951 and 1955, printing experienced its best years in 1953 (+17.7%), 1954 (+10.5%) and 1958 (+9.1%). In other words, printing flourished during general downturns in the economy as a whole. On the other hand, the industry's two "worst" years came during the booms of 1951 (printing +5.3% vs. GNP +10.4%) and 1959 (+5.5% vs. +7.3%).[30]

One possible explanation for this peculiar cyclical behavior on the part of the printing industry is that during downturns business makes heavier use of advertising to boost sales. But this cannot be the whole story given the fact that the industry's growth pattern was quite different in the 1960s. Unlike during the latter period, the expansion of the 1950s was relatively free of wide swings in either direction, with yearly growth rates almost always fluctuating between 7% and 9%. This can probably be attributed to the extremely diversified nature of printing demand at this time, which was almost evenly divided between the consumer (newspapers, magazines, books), industrial (advertising, packaging) and service (stationery, forms) sectors. In the 1960s, printing became increasingly dependent on advertising for continued growth, and thus became much more directly affected by the industrial business cycle.[31]

At the beginning of the 1950s, printing possessed a labor-intensive, technologically backward production process, which was really only semi-industrial in nature. Its levels of capital stock and productivity were well below the industrial average, and labor costs only remained manageable because of the extremely low wages paid to unskilled workers.[32] Most of the industry's machinery dated from the 1930s or earlier.[33] All this had changed by 1960, however. The printing boom of 1952–53 stretched capacity to the limit and led to massive investment in order to expand the capacity as quickly as possible. Although only one really novel production system – teletypesetting (see below) – was introduced at this juncture, the new equipment, and especially the new printing presses, produced much more efficiently than the older models.

These modernizing investments, while allowing much higher output, also brought with them a heavy financial burden for owners in the printing industry. Work-time reduction and labor shortages also increased costs, and these factors forced many employers between 1955 and 1959 to reduce overhead substantially by reorganizing production, increasing the work pace, and removing older machinery. As a result of these measures, the printing industry was able to raise its productivity to approximately the national industrial average by 1960.[34] For this reason, the 1960s can be called the decade of industrialization in West German printing.

The pattern of growth in printing during the 1960s assumed, as we have mentioned, a much more irregular form. Like industry as a whole, printing passed through two and a half business cycles – the last one ending in 1971 – with peaks in 1960 (+10%), 1964–65 (+6.2 and +6.3%) and 1969 (+11%). The troughs came in 1963 (+3.3%) and 1967 (−0.3%). The downturn in 1967 was slight compared to the plunge taken by the rest of West German industry (−2.8%), but the rebound in 1968–69 was not as strong, with printing growing by 15.7% compared to 21.7% for industry as a whole during the same period. Average annual expansion in printing, however, was 5.8% for the 1960s, slightly above the industrial average of 5.6%.[35]

Despite this relative success, sustained growth could only be achieved at a price. Although printing enjoyed above-average investment in the 1960s, it proved unable to increase its productivity at the same rate as the rest of West German industry.[36] The reasons for this can be traced in part to a drop in investment levels since the 1950s. This was in turn related to slumping profit margins, as wages in general – and especially those of the unskilled – rose steadily throughout the decade. Perhaps more importantly, the technological innovations of the 1960s in printing proved insufficiently "revolutionary" to push productivity levels substantially above those reached in the 1950s. In essence, a technological barrier prevented more rapid productivity growth in the industry. It is true that by the end of the 1960s, most important elements of the new electronic technology of the 1970s – such as computer typesetting and photosetting – had already appeared. However, use of this advanced equipment was still rare in West German printing because its high cost put it beyond the reach of most employers.[37] Moreover, many employers, once they became familiar with the new technology, restrained their investments in anticipation of further improvements and price reductions.

As a result of this lag in the growth of productivity during the 1960s, employers in the printing industry were forced to increase person-hours and hire more workers in order to expand production, instead of relying on improved production techniques, as was the norm in other industries. Thus, whereas hours worked dropped an average of 0.2% per annum between 1960 and 1970 in West German industry as a whole, they rose 0.8% per annum in printing.[38] In order to achieve a comparable increase in production from 1960 to 1968, the printing industry had to hire 15% more workers, while employment in the rest of the economy actually declined. In the short term, this was good news for printing employees and their union, because the industry's tight labor market – especially for skilled workers – drove wages to new heights. By 1970, printing accounted for 2.8% of all hours worked in industry (2.4% in 1960), but produced only 2.4% of total output (2.3% in 1960). Employment reached an all-time high of 224,100 in 1970.[39] But the bubble was bound to burst, since low productivity, high wages and full employment are by and large incompatible in a market economy. The industry and its workers spent the first seven years of the 1970s trying to overcome the structural problems engendered by the "golden" 1960s.

## B. Industrial relations in printing: 1948–1969

### 1. Introduction

The 1950s and 1960s were generally an optimistic period for IG Druck und Papier. Beginning as an entirely new organization in 1948, the union within a short time won substantial gains for its members in both wages and fringe benefits. Despite its size, IG Druck established itself as a pacesetter within West German labor, especially in the area of work-time reduction. Yet the image of unbroken success and intra-organizational harmony often projected by union publications was deceptive. IG Druck was plagued throughout this period by acrimonious conflicts between different membership groups. Many of these tensions dated back to the Weimar Republic and before. An examination of IG Druck's most important activity, collective bargaining, will allow us to determine how the union reacted to these internal challenges as well as to the external hardships posed by technological change and economic expansion during these two decades.

When printing delegates from the three Western occupation zones met in Munich in November 1948, it was not a foregone conclusion that an industrial union would be formed. There was considerable opposition to this idea from a number of quarters.[40] Specialized skill groups like the lithographers, who had had their own union since 1873, were afraid that their interests would be neglected by the dominant book printers within a united organization. The book printers, in turn, felt they had little to gain by joining with the poorly organized but often more radical printing "helpers," as semi- and unskilled workers were called. Both the unskilled and white-collar employees were wary of belonging to a union where skilled blue-collar workers would have a substantial majority which would guarantee them a hegemonic position in any unified organization.

The spirit of the times favored industrial unionism, however, and despite their misgivings the delegates voted to create Industriegewerkschaft Druck und Papier on December 3, 1948. Some of the suspicions of unskilled and white-collar employees concerning the nature of the new union were confirmed when IG Druck's leadership decided to form semi-autonomous professional groups and sectors (see above) to placate rival groups among skilled workers. By tolerating the presence of professional groups in book printing, flat printing and book binding, the union leadership in fact permitted the old pre-war craft organizations to continue their existence within the new IG Druck. The presence of the professional groups represented a retrograde move since unskilled workers would not have a group of their own, even though they had always had their own union. They were to belong to the grouping of skilled workers whom they "assisted." Only after sustained protests by the unskilled workers were they granted their own section within IG Druck in 1952.[41]

Through the collective bargaining process, the union leadership attempted to mediate between the conflicting interests of competing membership groups which the industrial union principle had bound together. In December 1948 IG Druck entered into its first wage negotiations with the recently reconstituted printing industry employers' association. For the time being, the union decided not to tamper with the wage structure, and instead asked for a 30% across-the-board pay increase to compensate for the then-rampant inflation.[42] This demand was quickly rejected by the employers, and a strike vote was called by IG Druck for the beginning of March 1949. Eighty-two percent of the membership endorsed a strike despite the difficult economic situation. Industrial action was averted, however, when IG Druck agreed to a 15% wage rise with no alterations in the wage structure. The union did state that wage rates were to be considered only as minima, and that workers could negotiate extra achievement-related bonuses (Leistungslöhne) individually with their employers. As a result of this decision, the difference between contractual wage rates and actual earnings (known as the "wage gap") increased steadily from 1949 to 1967, thus undermining the efficacy of the collective bargaining process.

The printing wage structure ratified by the March 1949 contract needs to be examined in more detail, because it was the starting point for all later negotiations on that issue. Moreover, the issue of wage structure became a source of heated conflict within IG Druck throughout the 1950s and 1960s. Wage rates in printing at this time were essentially determined by a set of four interlocking categories – skill, sex, age and location of one's workplace (marital status, a category which existed in Weimar, had since been eliminated).

All blue-collar workers were first divided into skilled and unskilled.[43] All skilled workers were paid at the same base rate (called the Ecklohn and set at 100% for the purpose of calculating other wages) except for the correctors, paid 107.5%, and the machine typographers, paid 120% of the base rate. As we have mentioned, the 120% for typographers dated from the contract signed in 1900 which regulated the introduction of the Linotype machine. The correctors received an additional rate of 7.5% in 1925 after complaining about the machine typographers' 120%. This 120% rate for the typographers remained the cause of bad feelings within IG Druck even after the Federal Republic was established in 1949. At every IG Druck congress from 1950 until the 1970s other skilled worker groups demanded that they receive this bonus as well. The debates surrounding the Linotype operators' 120% remuneration rating were often bitter and frequently deflected attention from other intra-organizational problems besetting the union.

Unskilled and semi-skilled workers were sub-divided in 1949 into four categories on the basis of both skill and sex. Semi-skilled males formed the highest wage group (receiving 80% of skilled-worker base pay), followed by unskilled males (76%), semi-skilled females (56%) and finally unskilled females (44%). These blatantly discriminatory groupings violated the

Federal Republic's Basic Law and both the union and the employers were told repeatedly to eliminate them, a task which took nine years.

Within each of the seven basic wage groups, pay was further differentiated according to two additional categories: age (the Altersklassen) and the geographic location of the plant (the Ortsklassen). This meant that workers below the age of 21 (for the unskilled) and with fewer than three years of experience (for the skilled) received less than their group's base wage. The logic behind the Ortsklassen was that in the nineteenth century, and even to some extent in the Weimar Republic, the cost of living in Germany varied according to the size of the city in which one lived. Thus, workers in the largest cities, such as Berlin and Hamburg, were paid their respective group's full wage, while their colleagues in smaller cities received less in proportion to their lower cost of living. The printing industry's 1949 wage structure still contained eleven Ortsklassen, which caused some problems within IG Druck since prices throughout West Germany had become more or less equal.

As a result of this excessive categorization, the 1949 wage structure in printing contained 88 separate pay groups with wage rates ranging from 120% to 24.3% of the skilled-worker base rate, yielding a difference of 520% between top and bottom. In practical terms, this meant that many unskilled workers earned extremely low wages, while their skilled colleagues were among the highest-paid workers in the country. Many unskilled workers felt that if skilled printers represented labor's "aristocracy" then they were its "serfs." The prescribed pay rates for many unskilled wage groups in 1949 were so low that they fell below the minimum wage of 50 pfennigs an hour which had been decreed by the Allies. Thus, the rates of 18 of printing's 88 groups had to be raised to the legal minimum wage in 1949.[44] It should be mentioned that most of these 18 wage groups consisted almost exclusively of female workers, as their semi-official – but clearly pejorative – name, "women's wage groups," conveys.

One more aspect of the printing industry's wage structure – the so-called wage gap – needs consideration. A wage gap has existed in the industry since 1949. It was also present in both the Weimar and Wilhelminian periods. To understand its origins, we must look at how actual take-home pay is calculated in the printing industry.[45] The principles have remained generally the same throughout the history of the Federal Republic and are identical for skilled and unskilled workers, although they do not apply to white-collar employees, who are paid a fixed salary. First, the worker receives the standard hourly wage (Tariflohn) dictated by the wage group to which he/she belongs. After this, workers negotiate their actual weekly wages with the employer, who often is willing to pay more than the

Table 7.1 *Wage rates and bonuses of various skill groups*

| Skill group | Achievement bonus | Actual wage rate |
|---|---|---|
| | % | % |
| heliographic retoucher | 62 | 162 |
| heliographic engraver | 39 | 139 |
| lithographer | 38.5 | 138.5 |
| machine typographer | 13.6 | 136.6 |
| offset printer | 32 | 132 |
| corrector | 14.7 | 122.2 |
| unskilled – highest group | 13.2 | 98.2 |
| unskilled – middle group | 7.7 | 83.2 |
| unskilled – lowest group | 10.4 | 71.4 |

*Source:* Richard Burkhardt, *Ein Kampf ums Menschenrecht* (Stuttgart: IG Druck, 1974), p. 168.

Tariflohn. The difference consists of a so-called achievement wage or bonus (Leistungslohn) which sometimes requires the worker to meet certain production goals before he/she obtains this additional remuneration. In most cases, however, the employers agree to the payment of this bonus because a worker has special skills or performs difficult tasks. The size of the achievement bonuses largely depends on the supply and demand for various categories of workers on the labor market at a given time. A study by IG Druck in 1969 determined the average achievement bonuses, and thus the actual weekly pay rate, for a number of skill groups (see table 7.1).[46] These results show that the "real" wage table in printing looks quite different from the one implied by union-negotiated wage rates. The much-maligned machine typographers pay a penalty for their 120% categorization in that they are accorded lower achievement bonuses, while most unskilled workers earn more than their wage rates would suggest.

In addition to achievement bonuses, two other components contribute to the actual earnings of printers. The first concerns bonuses for overtime and night work, as well as weekend and holiday shifts, which are all of great importance in printing given the nature of the industry's production schedules. IG Druck negotiates these bonuses. In addition, most employers pay their workers Christmas bonuses and sometimes extra vacation money (Urlaubsgeld). In the 1950s, these actions were purely voluntary, but they came to be covered by collective bargaining agreements during the 1960s and 1970s. Thus only the achievement bonuses are entirely free from union influence, and represent that part of the wage gap which IG Druck cannot control. These bonuses are the mechanism through which the labor market makes its greatest direct impact on the wage structure in the printing industry.

As described above, the wage structure in printing presented IG Druck's leadership with several problems which had to be confronted if the union's internal unity was to be preserved. First, something clearly had to be done to improve the situation of the industry's unskilled workers, especially its unskilled women. The gap in remuneration between skilled and unskilled workers had to be reduced by eliminating as many of the age and geographic categories (Alters- and Ortsklassen) as possible, as well as by raising the rates paid to unskilled workers as a percentage of the skilled workers' base rate. But two important obstacles stood in the way of any attempt to equalize wages in the printing industry: the dominance of the union's skilled workers and the wage-gap phenomenon. Practically all skilled-worker groups demanded that their wage rates be lifted from the usual 100% to the 120% earned by the machine typographers, which would of course widen the remuneration gap. At the very least, skilled printers wanted IG Druck to seek special benefits for them which would reflect their exceptionally strong position in the labor market. Also, any effort to narrow the differential between the wages of skilled and unskilled workers would just increase the wage gap, since employers would respond to a slower rise in the contractual wages of hard-to-find skilled workers by simply increasing their achievement bonuses. Conversely, if the union decided to confront the wage-gap issue, which clearly posed a threat to its credibility, the difference between contractual wages of skilled and unskilled workers would have to grow.

Throughout the 1950s and 1960s, IG Druck's leadership reacted in a predictable way to this tangle of problems. The union leadership tried to placate every constituency within the organization and ended up satisfying no one. The contradictory imperatives which the traditional wage structure imposed on IG Druck's collective bargaining activities left all groups feeling slighted, and led to a crisis within the union in the first half of the 1960s. Only in the 1970s, when the wage structure ceased to be the union's main concern, was internal unity more or less restored.

### 2. Collective bargaining in printing: 1949–1969

As soon as the first wage contract was signed in the printing industry in March 1949, IG Druck commenced negotiations on a general framework contract (Manteltarifvertrag).[47] The contract was signed in May 1949, and took effect on July 1 of that year. It provided for a standard work week of 48 hours (although this had little practical relevance in printing) and stipulated twelve to eighteen vacation days per annum depending on the length of the individual worker's employment in a particular firm. The contract also established the Central Arbitration Tribunal (Zentrales Schiedsgericht) to arbitrate bargaining disputes. A second arbitration level – the Superior Arbitration Office – was introduced in 1953. (For a discussion of these two forms of institutionalized arbitration see the appropriate passage above.)

The union's goals for future negotiations included reducing the work week, extending vacations and switching the criterion for vacation length from duration of employment at a given firm to the worker's age. IG Druck was particularly successful in reaching all these goals in the following decade, perhaps because they benefitted, and thus were supported by, all membership groups within the organization. In other key areas covered by general framework contracts, the union intended to maintain traditional control by skilled workers over the number and training of apprentices as well as the manning specifications for the introduction of new equipment. By limiting the number of apprentices and dictating manning requirements, the union hoped to keep the supply of skilled labor tight and thus exact wage increases. This tactic, which had worked in the past for IG Druck's predecessors, continued to bear fruit for the new organization until the 1970s.

The union made its first serious bid to reform substantially the wage structure in September 1949, when it reopened the wage contract signed six months earlier and insisted that the number of geographic categories be reduced from eleven to three.[48] The employers proposed to eliminate seven of the categories, but asked in return that IG Druck drop its demand that contracts for white-collar employees be negotiated on a national level; the union agreed. In order to satisfy one membership group, namely the unskilled workers who suffered most under the Ortsklassen, the leadership chose to slight another group, in this case the clerical and technical employees. This see-saw pattern of rewarding certain groups within the union at the expense of others repeated itself in coming years.

From 1950 through mid-1952, the major problem facing the printers – and all other West German unions – was inflation generated by the economic boom which occurred in the wake of the Korean War. In October 1950, February and June 1951, and February 1952, IG Druck renegotiated its wage contracts in printing to stay even with inflation. The union's demands centered exclusively on pay increases, which it failed to attain in the desired amounts. In October 1950, for example, the union asked for a 15% across-the-board raise, but received only 6%, and in February 1951 it agreed to an increase of 4% after having demanded a 14% pay hike. In June 1951, the union's bargaining was more effective, having attained an 8.9% increase in wages following a demand for 15%. Yet the negotiations of February 1952 brought renewed disappointment to IG Druck. After having demanded a 12.4% pay increase, the union had to make do with 3.1%.[49]

IG Druck's poor record in these wage rounds, and the leadership's apparent unwillingness to consider striking, were particularly disturbing to the rank and file, since the unionization level of the workforce in the printing industry exceeded 80% in the early 1950s, making IG Druck organizationally the strongest trade union in West Germany at that time.[50] It was perhaps to quell this rank-and-file discontent and prove its "fighting ability" (Kampffähigkeit) that IG Druck decided to call a one-day nationwide strike in the newspaper industry in May 1952 to protest the Bundestag's adoption of the new Works Constitution Law. The newspaper employers took the union to court over this action, claiming that the West German constitution forbade political strikes. The courts upheld the employers' view, and IG Druck was ordered to pay compensation equal to the value of lost newspaper production caused by the strike.

Despite IG Druck's lone stand among all DGB unions in actively opposing the Works Constitution Law by strike action, the union leadership came under attack from several quarters during IG Druck's second congress in June 1952.[51] Some delegates wanted a return to the quasi-closed shop which had existed under the Organizational Agreement of 1906. Women demanded an end to wage groups which were blatantly discriminatory, and the unskilled asked that wage increases henceforth be in equal and absolute DM amounts for all workers, since percentage increases automatically widened the wage gap between skilled and unskilled workers. Most importantly, lithographers and flat printers again insisted that their wage rates be raised to the 120% of the machine typographers. This last demand was rejected by the congress, and shortly thereafter many lithographers quit IG Druck and formed a breakaway union of their own. The principle of the industrial union had suffered its first defeat within the DGB. Although the lithographers' union never posed a serious threat to IG Druck, and was eventually reabsorbed into the union in 1965, it served as a continual reminder of the union's fragile internal unity.

The rank-and-file unrest which characterized IG Druck's congress in 1952 had a noticeable effect on the next wage negotiations in printing, which began in October of that year.[52] The union demanded not only a wage increase of 6%, but also the elevation of the highest unskilled wage rate from 80 to 85% of base pay and the elimination of two of the four remaining geographic pay categories (Ortsklassen). The employers were unaccommodating, and the union's claims went to arbitration, where the neutral arbitrator suggested a pay hike of just 2.4%. Instead of passively accepting this recommendation (as it had done in the recent past), the union leadership called a strike vote. Eighty percent of the membership voted in favor of a strike, and the first industrial action on a nationwide scale in printing in over 60 years began on December 6, 1952. Following a nine-day strike, a compromise was reached on December 14, which called for a 4.7% wage increase, a rise in the highest unskilled wage rate to 82.5%, and the elimination of one geographic pay category. The strike could be judged a success in that the final settlement provided substantially better terms than the arbitration award which had been rejected by IG Druck's leadership.

The next major problem confronting the union in the 1950s did not concern wages. A major technological innovation in typesetting was introduced early in the decade, which directly threatened the powerful machine typographers.[53] A new typesetting system which had been developed in the United States, called teletypesetting (or TTS), was first shown in West Germany at the printing machinery fair in August 1954. With TTS, an article is typed into a typewriter-like machine called a perforator which encodes it onto a punched tape. The tape is then fed into a keyboardless Linotype machine, known as a rapid setting machine, which produces the traditional lines of lead type, but at a much faster rate, since the apparatus is no longer manually operated by a typographer. No special typographical knowledge is needed to operate the perforators – and indeed typists seem best suited for the job.

After representatives of IG Druck had evaluated the TTS system, negotiations with the employers began immediately concerning the manning guidelines for the new machines.[54] The union, quite predictably, insisted that only trained machine typographers be allowed to operate both the perforators and the rapid setting machines. IG Druck argued that these workers' special skills would make them better perforator operators, and even agreed to a test in a Hamburg firm where the performance of male typographers on the new equipment would be compared to that of female typists. To the great embarrassment of the union, the latter won the contest.

Because of this outcome, the printers' original demands had to be modified. In an agreement signed on February 4, 1955, machine typographers were granted the exclusive right to operate the rapid setting machines, but would only be given preference over typists on the perforators if they could type a minimum number of words per minute. Since few typographers were interested in operating the perforators in this period of skilled-worker shortages – and even fewer could pass the typing test – most of the new devices were operated by women typists. The union decided to change its tactics, and during a review in 1959 of the 1955 agreement, demanded that all perforator operators, regardless of qualifications, receive the 120% wage rate of the machine typographers.[55] Since labor shortages, especially for qualified workers, were widespread at that time, the employers quickly acceded to this request. Although IG Druck justified this extension of the 120% wage rate with the same argument that had been used in 1900 (namely that the measure would retard the proliferation of new technology), its real purpose was to protect the privilege enjoyed by the machine typographers, which was under constant attack from all of the union's other membership groups. Thus when confronted with its first major technological crisis of the post-war period, IG Druck reverted to its old strategy of manning regulations. That this approach was even partially successful was largely due to booming economic conditions in the Federal Republic rather than to the resourcefulness of the union, as the latter was to discover when it tried to apply the same strategy in the 1970s during the economic crisis.

Two important exogenous events determined the agenda for the wage round in 1955. First, the Federal Labor Court had ruled that sex-based wage groupings were unconstitutional and had to be eliminated as quickly as possible. Second, the DGB's Aktionsprogramm, which contained general collective bargaining goals, such as the 40-hour week and longer vacation time, was released on May 1, 1955. (For a discussion of the DGB's Aktionsprogramm of 1955, see Chapter 3.) Inspired by this document, the printers asked for a reduction in the work week from 48 to 45 hours during the wage negotiations which began in June 1955.[56] The employers, following guidelines decreed by the BDA, rejected all discussion of a shorter work week, and instead offered a 4.2% wage increase accompanied by an improvement of vacation benefits. In addition, management agreed to begin negotiations immediately on a new wage structure concerning the categories for unskilled workers, in order to eliminate sex-based groupings. The union accepted these proposals and hoped that a new wage structure could be formalized by January 1, 1956. In fact, negotiations lasted until January 13, 1958 when a new wage table with five (rather than the previous four) unskilled groupings was approved by both parties. The new categories were to be based strictly on a worker's duties rather than on gender. The wage rates for the new categories were also increased. The five new unskilled and semi-skilled wage groups were:[57]

Group I – no special training – 58% of base pay (formerly 44%)
Group II – six months' experience, some training – 76% (56%)
Group III – minimum one year training – 72.5% (new group)
Group IV – physically heavy work – 82% (76%)
Group V – special skills, responsibility or experience – 85% (82.5%)

Despite this new system, most women workers remained in the two lowest wage groups (I and II).

In the summer of 1956, the West German labor movement's energies were concentrated on the fight for the 45-hour work week. Direct talks on this issue between the DGB and the BDA had failed, and it was anticipated that IG Metall would attempt to force a breakthrough during its collective bargaining negotiations with the employers in the metal industry. IG Druck had opened its annual wage round at the end of May by presenting a demand for a 16.6% pay increase, its highest request ever.[58] The union's leadership felt that aggressive bargaining was necessary because of considerable rank-and-file discontent over the 3.6% and 4.2% settlements of 1954 and 1955 respectively, as well as the rebuff the printers had received the previous year over the 45-hour work week.

No one in West Germany was more surprised than IG Druck itself when the employers in the printing industry countered the union's demand for a 16.6% pay increase by offering to introduce the 45-hour work week beginning October 1, 1956. The employers had obviously received some sort of permission from the BDA to make this major concession. Moreover, many were afraid to run the risk of a strike over IG Druck's 16.6% wage demand in a period of skilled labor shortages accompanied by booming conditions in the printing industry. To "sweeten" the deal, the printing employers granted the union a 5.5% pay increase in addition to the three-hour reduction of the work week which, moreover, was granted with full pay. IG Druck quickly agreed to this package, and on July 10, 1956 became the first West German labor organization to sign a contract on the 45-hour work week. IG Metall reached its Bremen Accord on the same demand two weeks later in an agreement which included only a 1.3% wage increase. (For a discussion of the Bremen Accord, see Chapter 4.) The flexibility of the printing employers on the issue of work-time reduction can be explained not only by this sector's accommodationist tradition of labor–management relations, but also by the fact that the "average" work week (be it 48, 45 or 40 hours) has less practical relevance in printing than in steel manufacturing, for example, because of the fluctuating schedules governing the production of the various forms of printed material.

During the next ten years, the realization of the Aktionsprogramm's goals – the 40-hour work week, longer vacations and higher vacation bonuses – was at the center of IG Druck's collective bargaining activities. The 44-hour week was introduced in January 1, 1959 under the terms of a new general framework contract signed at the end of 1958 by IG Druck and the employers. IG Druck's wage gains of 6.2%, 6.4% and 4.5% attained from 1957 through 1959 respectively were certainly respectable, if not spectacular.[59] In spite of these successes, however, the unresolved problems concerning the wage structure continued to cause considerable unrest within the union. At the printers' fifth congress in September 1959, the delegation from the district of Nordmark demanded the creation of a commission which would develop an entirely new pay structure covering both skilled and unskilled workers.[60] The commission commenced its work in 1961, and was supposed to present its definitive report to the union's 1965 congress. In fact, this contentious issue continued to plague IG Druck until the mid-1970s.

The other familiar complaint raised at the 1959 congress centered on the union's policies favoring skilled at the expense of unskilled workers.[61] Delegates protested the low wage rates that all unskilled workers received. In addition, they objected to the widening gap between the income of skilled and unskilled workers, which they believed to be a consequence of the union's practice of demanding percentage – rather than fixed-sum – pay increases for those in the lower wage categories. During the next wage round, which occurred in 1960, the union arranged for an extra 3% increase to be granted workers in the three lowest skill groups, accompanying the 8.5% general raise received by all workers.[62]

Aggressive bargaining, the usual antidote to membership discontent, also characterized the union's preparations for a new general framework contract, to be negotiated at the end of 1960. IG Druck demanded a phased introduction of the 40-hour work week as well as extended vacations and vacation bonuses amounting to 20% of weekly pay.[63] Surprisingly, the employers met most of the union's demands with little opposition. The 40-hour week would be introduced in steps by October 1, 1965 and annual vacation time was increased, although vacation bonuses had to await the conclusion of the next general framework contract. Once again, IG Druck proved itself a leader in the West German labor movement on the issue of work-time reduction.

The union's success in attaining the 40-hour work week via an innovative phase-in plan undoubtedly emboldened the leadership for the 1961 wage round, in which IG Druck confronted the employers with its biggest demands ever: 17% across-the-board pay increases.[64] An arbitration award of 11.7% in pay increases was voted on by the membership, who only approved the proposal by a disappointing majority of 66.5%. The result showed that despite the union leadership's militant posture after 1960, many members still felt that the organization was not sufficiently exerting itself on their behalf, given the extraordinary boom conditions – and consequent labor shortages – experienced by the West German economy at the time. These labor shortages brought with them a rapid rise in non-contractual wages, and thus widened the wage gap. This was undoubtedly one of the reasons why employers were so willing to raise contractual wage rates by such substantial margins, since these amounts still lagged behind increases in non-contractual wages.

The period from 1961 to 1966 was a difficult one for West German unions. Strong economic growth, full employment and a widening wage gap made trade unions seem superfluous to many workers. This fact was reflected in the plummeting organizational levels which plagued practically all DGB unions at this time, IG Druck included. The latter lost 12,000 members between 1962 and 1964, during a period when employment in printing and paper-processing rose by over 8,000. By 1964, IG Druck's organizational level had sunk to 44%, or less than half of the 89.1% which it had attained in 1949.[65] Union membership of course increased in absolute terms during the 1950s, but it failed to keep pace with the expansion of employment in the industry. The organizational level for male, skilled, printing workers, the union's core, remained fairly constant during this period, but the union failed to attract new members. During the early 1960s the union actually suffered absolute losses among some of its "marginal" constituencies such as unskilled workers, women, non-Germans, white-collar employees and the young.[66] Members of these groups felt consistently slighted by the union's policies. The lack of interest in the union displayed by young workers from all skill groups bore perhaps the most disturbing implications for the organization's future.

IG Druck tried to counter the decline in its membership by negotiating substantial gains in annual wages and fringe benefits. Between 1962 and 1966, the base wage rate in printing rose by 37% (from DM 136 to DM 187 per week) without the union having to resort to a single strike.[67] In the boom years 1962, 1964 and 1965 wage rates increased by 7.6%, 7.8% and 7.1% respectively, and even during the economically weak years of 1963 and 1966 they rose 5% and 5.1%.[68] The new general framework contract, which was concluded in 1965, called for longer vacations and vacation bonuses.[69] On October 1, 1965, IG Druck became the first West German union to attain the 40-hour work week.

It was not the bargaining successes of the DGB unions, but rather the sharp recession besetting the West German economy in 1966–67 which helped the labor movement overcome its organizational malaise and regain some of its popularity with the workers. Although the impact of the crisis was felt less severely in printing than in other industries, employment dropped in that sector by nearly 4,000 in 1967, the first year such a decline had occurred since the 1940s.[70] In 1967, job security suddenly became an issue again, though not solely because of the recession. IG Druck was increasingly concerned by two new production techniques which began to appear in West Germany at this time. Both promised eventually to have an important impact on the printing process and thus on employment in the industry.

The first innovation was photosetting, a technique which allowed printing plates, initially only offset, to be made from a photographic negative of a set text. The negative could be produced directly from a perforator with the help of the second new technique, computer-steered setting. Using this process, a text is typed into a perforator and a computer arranges it into the typographically correct form using one of its programs. The result is fed directly to a photosetting machine which produces the film negative. This new process thus eliminated typesetting in lead. It also completely altered the nature of the makeup printers' and stereotyper's work. In addition, the new technology permitted the automatic setting of headlines and advertisements, tasks which previously were performed by manual typographers.

When this new equipment first reached the Federal Republic, it was extremely expensive and poorly integrated. Consequently, only the largest printers, such as Springer, could afford to purchase it. Therefore, its initial impact on employment was minimal, but the union realized that photosetting could eventually have important implications for its members. During the 1967 wage round, IG Druck decided to forego an annual wage increase and seek instead to defend itself against the new technology's potentially adverse effects by negotiating a rationalization protection accord (Rationalisierungsschutzabkommen). The agreement that was reached in December 1967 obliged the employers to make plans with the works councils for the introduction of all new machinery.[71] The contract committed the employers to make every effort to save the jobs of displaced workers, either by employing them on the new equipment or by finding them positions elsewhere in the plant. If layoffs had to occur, they were to be accompanied by sizable severance payments determined by a worker's skill level and seniority. This accord was the first of its kind in the Federal Republic, yet barely a few years after its conclusion it was deemed inadequate by IG Druck.

The 1966–67 recession brought a fundamental political change to West Germany in the form of the Social Democratic Party's participation in government via the Grand Coalition. This new situation forced the unions to define their positions on a number of crucial political issues, such as the proposed Emergency Laws and the Federal Republic's relations with Eastern Europe. (For a discussion of these events see Chapter 3.) Surprisingly, given its accommodationsist heritage with regard to collective bargaining and shop-floor issues, IG Druck took an unequivocally activist stance on these macropolitical issues, thereby placing the union on the DGB's (and the SPD's) left wing along with IG Metall, a position the two unions were to share increasingly during the economic crisis of the 1970s.[72] The union, like IG Metall, strongly opposed the Emergency Laws and favored a policy of detente towards the German Democratic Republic and Eastern Europe. IG Druck assumed a leadership position among West German unions on the latter issue, establishing contacts with East European – although not East German – unions well before this became a generally accepted practice among other DGB members. Throughout the 1950s and early 1960s, IG Druck's political stands remained consistently close to those of the left (or anti-Bad-Godesberg faction) of the Social Democratic Party. One plausible explanation for this position is that the printers, because of their illustrious tradition and the preeminent role they had played in the pre-1933 labor movement, were less willing than a number of the other unions in the DGB to abandon the major tenets of traditional social democracy, which was precisely what Bad Godesberg aimed to do.

The technological and economic crises which hit the printing industry in the 1970s cemented IG Druck's ties with social democracy's pre-Godesberg positions and extended this identification from political to economic issues as well. Thus the union's emergence in the 1970s as the most activist of all DGB unions was less abrupt and unexpected than most commentators, including the union itself, would have us believe.

## V. IG DRUCK AND THE PRINTING CRISIS: 1969–1981

The 1970s were a difficult time for both the printing industry and its workers. The former was affected simultaneously by a structural crisis and a technological revolution which changed its character extensively between 1969 and 1980. IG Druck responded to this new situation by adopting an activist, often confrontational – and on occasion even militant – strategy, in sharp contrast to its formerly accommodationist and cooperative style. This new strategy, symbolized by the bitter strikes of 1976 and 1978, restored the union to a leading position within the West German labor movement, a prominence which its predecessors had enjoyed before 1914.

This section of the chapter will explain IG Druck's radicalization during the 1970s in the context of both the crisis in the printing industry and political developments within the union itself. Because economic conditions and union response were so closely linked during this time, they will be examined together. For analytic purposes, the years under consideration have been divided into three periods: the onset of the crisis (1969–73); the heart of the crisis (1974–78); and the period of recovery, which for the printing industry began in 1978.

### A. First signs of the crisis: 1969–1973

Although printing was not as severely affected by the recession of 1966–67 as the rest of West German industry, its recovery in 1968–70 also proved less convincing. Printing production declined by only 3% in 1967 and 4,000 jobs (1.8% of the industry's total) disappeared, compared to an employment decline of 6.5% in the economy as a whole. In the ensuing three years, however, industrial production in the Federal Republic rose by 27.9%, while growth in the printing sector lagged behind at 21.3%. In order to accomplish this increase in production, the printing industry hired over 12,000 new workers, thereby pushing employment in this sector to its highest level ever at 224,100, which it reached in 1970. The prosperity ended with a sudden jolt in 1971, when production declined by 0.5% and layoffs began. Although the industry grew again in 1972 and 1973, over 5,000 jobs seemed permanently lost as employment dropped to 219,000 in 1973.[73]

The "mini-crisis" of the early 1970s resulted from the technological lag which printing had experienced in the 1960s. Because little significant labor-saving technology had been developed during this period, growth in the industry after 1968 created a substantial demand for workers. IG Druck took advantage of this situation and the atmosphere of reform euphoria and "Aufbruchsstimmung" by negotiating wage increases totalling 46.3% between 1969 and 1973.[74] Employers invested considerably in 1969 and 1970 in order to expand capacity to keep pace with demand. When demand slackened in 1971, the burden of higher wages and increased investment expenditures exceeded the capacities of many firms, causing numerous bankruptcies.

Two categories of companies were especially affected by the downturn.[75] The first consisted of medium-sized, independent printers employing between 200 and 500 workers. This category represented the segment of the market where competition was fiercest and the loss of one major order could mean a company's permanent ruin. To maintain their competitive edge, firms were compelled to resort to a drastic reduction in prices and/or costs.

The second category included the industry's giants (firms with over 1,000 employees) which were also hurting during this period. While these firms never ran the risk of bankruptcy or serious impairment of their economic activities, their profits certainly suffered as a consequence of the adverse market conditions and high wages which they paid their employees. As a result of this predicament, West Germany's newspaper magnates were eager to introduce the newest production technology from the United States in order to increase productivity, but this could not be done on a large scale in the early 1970s. Although the large firms had already been introducing phototypesetting and computer-controlled setting on a piecemeal basis, they were aware that further technological breakthroughs lay ahead, thus making them reluctant to invest heavily in equipment that would soon be outmoded. Instead they chose to automate tasks such as bundling and loading which typically required the labor of unskilled workers. This explains why the unskilled constituted the majority of printing workers who lost their jobs between 1971 and 1973.[76]

Although this new technology still awaited its large-scale introduction in the Federal Republic's printing industry, many employees in this sector were concerned about the security of their jobs. All realized that a revolution was in the offing, yet none knew for certain what its consequences might be. It was widely believed, however, that machine typographers, as well as stereotypers, correctors and makeup printers, would soon become superfluous. This led employers to reduce greatly the number of apprentices they trained for those jobs. The quantity of apprentices in the industry began declining after 1966 but did not reach its nadir until 1977.[77] This fear of the future, coupled with increased job insecurity, greatly undermined solidarity within the union, because workers from the above-mentioned skill groups, who had hitherto dominated union politics – to the periodic displeasure of many of their colleagues in other job categories – were now facing a problem which other printing workers did not share.

It was against this background of uncertainty and internal disunity that the old question of reforming the wage structure in the printing industry rose once again. A commission had been established in 1959 with the mandate to propose a new wage structure which would eliminate the privileged position of the machine typographers and correctors, thereby putting an end once and for all to their excessive wage rates. Because of the competing demands represented by these two groups and the rest of the workers, both skilled and unskilled, the commission proved unable to agree on a suitable plan until 1968. The proposal called for the creation of eight wage groups, with pay rates ranging from 70% to 130% of the base wage.[78] Broad skill criteria were used to categorize workers, with every unskilled laborer able to receive up to 100% of the base rate and every skilled worker up to 130%.

IG Druck held a special union congress in October 1969 to discuss the plans. Following some bitter debates, they were rejected. Machine typographers and correctors, eager to defend their position of privilege and power, combined forces to defeat the proposal. Curiously, they received support from union radicals who opposed the plan's 60% wage span, calling it inegalitarian, stratifying and divisive. At the 1971 congress IG Druck's leadership presented a new proposal which it clearly wanted the delegates to accept. This plan sought to reduce the number of wage groups to six – with remuneration ranging from 75% to 120% of the base wage rate. Once again this issue engendered heated debate, but the leadership's plan passed in the end – albeit by a vote of only 151 to 87, showing that substantial opposition remained.[79]

The effects of the wage-structure controversy on IG Druck were almost entirely negative. The new plan had little chance of being implemented since the employers seemed quite happy with the old system. Consequently, the entire issue only opened old wounds and created much bitterness inside the union at a time when IG Druck had to face both a structural crisis in the economy and an imminent technological revolution in printing. In combatting these problems, the union's leadership suffered the additional handicap of representing an organization whose constituencies could barely reconcile their conflicting interests. This division had to be countered.

In the wake of the 1971 congress, Leonhard Mahlein, IG Druck's leader, devised a two-pronged approach to deal with his organization's internal discord. First, it was decided that the formal power of the old professional sections (Sparten) within the union had to be broken. These organizations, a legacy of IG Druck's craft heritage, had always served to protect the particularistic interests of one group of skilled workers to the detriment of all others. The typographers were the most powerful of these sections within IG Druck. At the 1974 congress, the union's executive committee succeeded in dissolving the typographer section.[80] In its stead, IG Druck sought to create a "printing plate production professional group" (Berufs-gruppe Druckformherstellung) with far less power.

Second, the leadership decided to unite the union in confronting a common adversary, the employers. Greater activism, in the form of more aggressive rhetoric and a combative bargaining style, would provide members with a clear object for their fears about the future and force them to forget their intra-organizational differences. Only in this context can one explain the union's decision to call a strike during the 1973 wage round after its demand for a 13% wage increase was rejected by the employers.[81] Although the strike affected only a few large firms and lasted just two days, it shocked management since it was the first major work stoppage in the industry in over twenty years. For its efforts, the union received a 10.8% across-the-board pay increase, substantially more than IG Metall's 8.5% of the same year. In retrospect, the 1973 strike can be seen as a dress rehearsal for the larger battles to come.

### B. The crisis of 1974–1978

The deep recession, caused in part by the 1973 oil embargo, hit the printing industry, along with the rest of West German industry, in mid-1974. Given printing's problems during the previous three years, it is hardly surprising that the industry suffered more than other sectors of the economy. In 1974 and 1975 printing production declined by 2.6% and 7.3% respectively, compared with 2% and 6.8% for industry as a whole. By the end of 1975, employment had dropped to 194,500 from 219,000 in 1973. In 1975, the industry's worst year during the crisis, 15,400 jobs were lost.[82] All told, employment in printing declined by 11.5% over a two-year period, compared to the national industrial average of only 9.2%. Thus in 1974–75 printing paid more than adequately for its relatively mild setbacks of 1966–67. After 1975, however, production once again picked up, rising by 7.3% in 1976, 8.4% in 1977 and 2% in 1978.[83] Despite this overall recovery in production, employment dropped another 3.9% in 1976–77[84] and only began to increase again in late 1978, when the crisis, it could be argued, finally ended.

The recession did not affect all sections of the industry equally. In fact, there were three different, though connected, crises besetting printing production at this time. The first was a newspaper crisis, similar to the one occurring simultaneously in the United States.[85] For a number of complex reasons, it had become virtually impossible for many cities to support more than one daily newspaper. Once one newspaper gained a decided advantage in readership over its rival(s), advertisers began to desert the "losers," thus hastening their decline. The economic crisis helped accelerate this process, leading to newspaper bankruptcies or mergers in Hamburg, Berlin, Stuttgart, the cities of the Ruhr region, Hanover and many smaller towns. Since most of these papers owned medium-sized printing plants, typically employing more than 100 people, bankruptcies and mergers translated into substantial job losses for printers.

The second and probably most serious of the three crises affected hundreds of medium-sized independent printers scattered throughout West Germany. As already mentioned, this sector experienced structural problems and fierce competition during the early 1970s. Orders for advertising materials, business papers and printed packaging declined substantially, pushing many firms into insolvency and forcing the rest to cut costs through layoffs. The seriousness of the situation among medium-sized printers is best demonstrated by the fact that 10% of the shops employing between 50 and 500 workers disappeared in 1975 alone. Bankruptcies combined with layoffs resulted in a loss of approximately 12,000 jobs in medium-sized printing firms during 1975. Job losses in these companies thus accounted for over 75% of the total decline in employment suffered by the entire printing industry during that year.[86]

The third crisis, which began in 1975, centered on the technological revolution everybody had anticipated. Starting in 1973 and 1974, several of the country's largest printers, all of whom employed more than 500 workers, decided that the time and the price were right to convert their production to the new, fully integrated, electronic printing technology. In Stuttgart, Hanover and many cities of the Ruhr region, publishers decided to build huge new printing centers using the most up-do-date technology to publish their own papers, in addition to the new ones which they had acquired in the industry's mergers and bankruptcies. Two of the Federal Republic's largest publishing groups (Springer and Gruner + Jahr) also decided at this time to invest generously in a substantial modernization of their massive production facilities. The first of the new printing centers opened at Möhringen outside Stuttgart in January 1976. Several similar centers and reequipped old plants have been brought into operation every year since then.[87]

The main difference between the new integrated systems and the computer-steered setting machines of the late 1960s was the addition of a video terminal (VT) which permits the same person – in theory at least – to write, edit, correct and set an article.[88] A connected photosetting machine then converts the story into a photographic negative which is printed on light-sensitive paper. A makeup printer arranges the stories, along with photos and headlines, onto a page, of which another photo is then taken. (This operation can now also be performed on a VT.) The negative of the entire page is used to produce an offset printing plate. The new system eliminates the need for a separate composition department, since a journalist at a VT could – and in the United States, for example, often does – correct and set his/her own story. In West Germany, however, journalists have resolutely refused to perform this task. Composition departments have thus been retained, although they are equipped with video terminals rather than Linotype or TTS machines.

Had the new computerized printing systems been installed on a large scale throughout the West German printing industry, machine typographers and stereotypers would have become virtually superfluous. As mentioned, however, this did not happen. First of all, as one expert's calculations indicate, the new technology has only proved to be profitable in plants with over 500 workers.[89] Secondly, until very recently, even these plants could only install the new equipment if they used offset or heliogravure printing presses. Thus, many large newspapers – such as the *Frankfurter Allgemeine Zeitung* – which had invested heavily in new book-printing presses in the 1960s and early 1970s, have had to retain the old system until they recover their initial investments. The likelihood of losing one's job in printing due to the introduction of the new technology has consistently been lower than the risk of unemployment brought on by bankruptcies or regular cyclical dislocations. A study by the Federal Labor Office showed that of the 15,400 printing jobs eliminated in 1975, only

1,800 could be traced to technical change of any kind.[90] And as we have indicated, this technological threat has only applied to the 20% of the workforce holding jobs in companies with over 500 employees. Nevertheless, subjective perceptions often outweigh objective realities in terms of their consequences for social action. This was exactly the case with IG Druck, where protecting its members, especially typographers, from the adverse effects of the new technology became the union's overriding concern.

At the height of the recession, IG Druck was not yet in a position to organize major initiatives to protect its members against the potentially detrimental consequences of technical rationalization. Thousands of printers were out of work and many more were afraid they would soon be let go. Machine typographers felt doubly threatened. Yet the organization was still racked by the internal discord which had disrupted the 1974 congress. It was clear that the strategy of focusing the union's attention on a common adversary would have to be pursued even more vigorously if IG Druck was to risk a major battle with the employers over the new technology. In June 1975, IG Druck's leadership moved decisively to implement a more confrontational strategy by removing the conservative editor of the union's bi-weekly magazine *druck und papier* and replacing him with Detlef Hensche, a brilliant left-wing intellectual who had worked in the DGB's policy section but had no previous experience in printing. Hensche proceeded to use his position as editor and member of IG Druck's executive committee to challenge the printing employers in a fashion which old-style union officials would never have dared to try. In so doing he quickly became one of the most controversial figures in the West German labor movement.[91]

IG Druck's move towards an unmitigatedly activist posture quickly became evident during the 1976 contract negotiations.[92] In order to safeguard the still fragile recovery and reduce inflation, the employers had resolved to limit pay increases to about 4%. IG Metall, assuming its traditional role as the DGB's leader during bargaining rounds, countered with demands of between 8% and 8.5%. In late March and early April wage settlements averaging 5.4% were reached in negotiations between IG Metall and the metal industry. The goal of the employers in other industries, supported by the BDA, was to hold the line at 5.4% in their respective areas. Observers in the labor movement fully expected the other unions to follow IG Metall's lead and agree to a wage and salary raise hovering around 5.4%. But IG Druck's executive committee entertained different ideas.

The union's demand for a 9% across-the-board pay increase signaled IG Druck's willingness to do battle with the employers, whose counter-offer of 4.7% was unequivocally rejected by the union. During the arbitration process in April the employers increased their offer to match the 5.4% which had been the BDA's recommended limit. This was to be their final offer. IG Druck, however, insisted that a "six before the decimal point" was an absolute minimum for settlement, even though this meant embarrassing IG Metall and all other DGB unions which had already signed contracts providing smaller gains. Since the BDA firmly supported the printing employers, a strike was inevitable.

On April 27, the union held a strike vote throughout the country, which resulted in an 88.2% approval of industrial action.[93] One day later IG Druck initiated point strikes in 48 of the Federal Republic's largest printing works. The employers were ready. Four hours after the strike began, the BVD, supported by the BDA, called a nationwide lockout in the printing industry, the first in West German history. However, this strategy proved only partially successful. Although the employers locked out approximately 90,000 workers, another 55,000 continued their daily routines.[94] Given the crisis and fierce competition within printing, it is not surprising that many firms refused to comply with the lockout order and maintained their normal production schedules. Under these circumstances, the BVD decided to cut the lockout by half on May 3. In return, IG Druck agreed to end its point strikes and submit to non-binding arbitration under the Social Democratic business leader Walter Hesselbach. The employers could not be convinced, however, to offer more than 5.9%. Since IG Druck had made "a six before the decimal point" its strike slogan, it could not agree to this offer. Opting for further escalation, the union declared a full area strike affecting the whole country on May 6.

While the IG Druck leadership had some difficulty explaining why – with thousands of printers out of work and many firms still threatened with bankruptcy – it resorted to a national strike over a 0.1% wage increase, the length of the strike definitely favored the union's cause. The large newspaper and magazine publishers, who could easily afford to pay wage increases, grew tired of losing millions in advertising revenues in what had become a surrogate battle between the BDA and the DGB. These large firms forced the medium-sized, independent printers, who held the balance of power in the BVD, to return to the negotiating table on May 12. Following two days of talks, a compromise was reached. The union would get its 6% raise as of June 1, and all workers were granted a lump sum of DM 275 for April and May. The total increase amounted to 6.6%. This settlement was approved by IG Druck's membership on May 18 by a narrow margin of 56% to 44%.[95] Thus ended the turbulent 1976 wage round.

If the leadership's main goal was to radicalize and mobilize the union's rank and file, the strike could certainly be termed a success. IG Druck also showed the employers that the union could organize and sustain a nationwide strike, while simultaneously exposing the disunity within the ranks of the Bundesverband Druck. The costs of the strike were very high, however. The union's coffers had been emptied by the lockout, and the employers were convinced that IG Druck would remain incapable for many years of conducting an industrial action of similar magnitude. Moreover, IG Druck's maverick behavior in upstaging other unions accompanied by its increasingly radical rhetoric had created resentment among more moderate unions within the DGB.[96]

Perhaps most importantly, the strike did not foster greater unity within IG Druck itself. Although the old occupational cleavages were forgotten in the heat of battle, an important new division appeared between a large minority of members who felt that the leadership had not gone far enough during the strike and a less vocal majority of unionists who supported the executive committee.[97] The leadership's radical rhetoric had led many members to expect truly radical actions and results. If nothing else, these heightened expectations placed pressure on the IG Druck leadership to legitimize itself by pursuing activist strategies.

No sooner had the 1976 strike ended than IG Druck was faced with the possibility of a major confrontation over the introduction of the new printing technology.[98] The union's goals were twofold. On the one hand, it wanted to protect all machine typographers and other skilled workers from job and/or income loss due to technological change. More importantly, however, IG Druck hoped to impose regulations which would permit only machine typographers to work at the new video terminals. Journalists would be allowed on the new machines only to read and correct their copy. If other union members used the VTs because of a shortage of machine typographers, they were to be paid the machine typographers' wage (120%). IG Druck felt that the Linotype agreement of 1900 and the 1954 accord on TTS machines, both of which included permanent manning rules and protection for skilled workers, were models for solving this new technological crisis.

In September 1975 IG Druck approached the employers seeking an agreement on the new technology. The union presented a series of demands incorporating the two basic goals enumerated above. In addition, they included a stipulation that work on the VTs was not to exceed four hours per day. For almost a year, the employers categorically refused to negotiate. The union decided to expand the range of any potential accord by working together with other unions that would also be affected by the new technology. These included the German White-Collar Workers' Union (DAG) and the journalists' union DJV, both non-DGB members, as well as the DGB's commercial, banking and insurance workers' union

(HBV). As a concession to the DJV, IG Druck agreed to allow journalists to use terminals to typeset their articles if they had previously typed them themselves. In addition, the work week would be limited to 35 hours for anyone using a VT.

In November 1976, the BVD as well as the newspaper and magazine publishers' organizations BDZV and VDZ finally began serious talks with the four unions led by IG Druck. In May 1977, the unions presented a formal proposal incorporating the compromise between IG Druck and the DJV which became the basis for the negotiations with the employers. From the beginning, however, the latter resolutely refused to agree to any permanent staffing rules for the VT. The employers were only willing to allow for temporary guidelines which would protect the jobs and incomes of adversely affected skilled workers. Moreover, they maintained that once these workers had been accommodated, the video terminals could be operated by anyone. Furthermore, the employers intended to consider all new VT workers clerical employees who would be paid accordingly. Lastly, the employers rejected outright the idea of a 35-hour work week for VT workers.

As a result of the fundamental differences separating them, the two sides reached an impasse in the fall of 1977. After arbitration failed in November 1977, the union's "peace obligation" was terminated. Beginning on November 21, IG Druck authorized periodic warning strikes of several hours in about 100 large works. In addition, the union decreed an overtime ban which went into effect immediately. These actions reached a climax on December 23, when a one-day strike was called in the Munich newspaper industry. Despite this mobilization, IG Druck was somewhat hesitant to conduct another large-scale strike so soon after the one in the spring of 1976. In the period between January 20 and 25, 1978, the union's bargaining commission agreed to a compromise whose terms were drafted in the so-called Mayschoss Paper (named after the location where negotiations had been conducted). The compromise included major concessions by the unions on every point. Instead of establishing permanent manning rules, labor agreed that machine typographers and correctors would operate VTs used for correcting but only for a period of five years. VT work would be classified as clerical, and skilled workers would be compensated for the difference between the new clerical salary and their old wages. This, once again, was to last only five years. Short breaks were to occur every hour for VT workers, but the 40-hour work week remained in effect for all.

IG Druck had every intention of accepting the Mayschoss Paper proposal, as did the other unions. However, when its terms were revealed to the newly radicalized printers – who had been stirred for months by the leadership's excessively exhortatory rhetoric and the frequent warning strikes – a storm of protest was unleashed. IG Druck, as well as the DJV, felt compelled to reject the Mayschoss Paper, although the document and its terms were accepted by both the DAG and the HBV. Once again, a strike became inevitable for IG Druck. This time, however, the leadership was less willing to conduct an industrial action than it had been in 1976 since it was aware that the union's coffers were nearly empty.

In order to save money, and in the hope of keeping its membership under control, IG Druck's leadership chose a strategy of gradual escalation of the strike. On February 28, the production workers of four large regional newspapers stayed away from their jobs while warning strikes continued in other firms. The employers responded with a total lockout in Munich beginning on the same day and continued their activities with a two-day national lockout on March 3 and 4. On March 8, IG Druck extended the strike to seven additional large printing firms, and the employers responded on March 14 by further expanding their national lockout and declaring it to be of unlimited duration. On March 15 a strike began in the metal industry of North Württemberg/North Baden. (For a discussion of this strike see Chapter 4.)

With the climate of labor relations deteriorating sharply, the federal government became extremely concerned, just as it had under similar circumstances in 1963. Non-binding political arbitration procedures began under the leadership of the chancellor's adviser Hans-Jürgen Wischnewski (SPD) and the head of the Federal Labor Office, Josef Stingl (CSU). The non-compulsory character of this arbitration was more than counter-balanced by the SPD's and the DGB's pressure on IG Druck to agree to a compromise. On March 19 the union leadership did just that, in effect ending the strike without holding the customary membership ratification vote. The latter action was to cause the IG Druck leadership considerable trouble with some of the union's radical members in the years to come.

The contract which IG Druck accepted did not differ significantly from the terms suggested by the Mayschoss Paper which had appeared two months earlier. It contained the following main points:[99]

1. For a period of eight years, all setting and correcting work on VTs would be performed by skilled printing workers, particularly typographers. This rule could be abrogated if no skilled workers were available or willing to perform these tasks, or if someone already employed at a VT would lose his/her job if replaced by a skilled worker.

2. The entering of texts into the computer had to be performed by skilled workers whose jobs within the firm were eliminated as a

consequence of technological change. Once the supply of such workers from within the firm had been exhausted, clerical employees were entitled to perform this task.

3. All work at VTs was considered clerical work and was to be remunerated accordingly. Workers who were previously paid at the correctors' (107.5%) or machine typographers' (120%) rate would continue to receive their old wages. Other skilled workers would receive a bonus to compensate for the difference between their old wages and their new clerical salaries. These bonuses would be gradually reduced, and ultimately eliminated over a period of six years.

4. Journalists could use VTs only for reading and editing. They were entitled to enter their stories into the computer only if they had previously typed them themselves. Under no circumstances would journalists be required to type another person's story into the computer.

5. Everyone working at VTs was henceforth permitted to take a 5-minute break every hour or a 15-minute break every two hours. The 40-hour work week, however, remained in full force.

Thus, the problem of radical technological change was solved by a compromise which typified the approach of the West German labor movement as well as the general conflict management practiced in the country's industrial relations system. The jobs and incomes of workers affected by the change were largely protected, so that personal hardship would be kept to a minimum. On the other hand, the employers successfully resisted any manning rules which would substantially limit their prerogatives pertaining to the introduction and application of new technology. Even in this area, however, the employers acceded to some of the union's wishes by retaining separate correcting and composing departments, even though, as shown by experience in the United States, this was not technically necessary. It should be added that this latter concession was due as much to pressure from journalists who were reluctant to work with VTs as from skilled workers. The hesitancy – or perhaps inability – of West German unions to impose restrictive work rules – even in such archetypical craft industries as printing – stands in stark contrast to the British and American experiences.

### C. The aftermath: 1978–1980

By late 1978, the printing industry found itself well along the path to recovery. Production rose by 8.3% in 1979 and another 3.6% in 1980. For the first time since 1970 employment also increased, climbing by 4.5% during those two years.[100] To the surprise of many, the industry began complaining about a shortage of skilled workers, including machine typographers, as early as October 1978.[101] This strange turn of events developed as a consequence of three factors. First, almost all medium-sized plants and many large firms continued to use the old production system. Second, virtually everyone had greatly overestimated the pace of technological change, thus causing the number of trained apprentices to drop steadily from 1967 until 1977. Lastly, the development of small, relatively cheap offset printing presses led to a proliferation of new, small, specialized firms after 1974. These companies still needed typographers to set their type.

IG Druck's main concern after 1978 centered quite naturally on the full implementation of the new technology agreement outlined above, commonly called the RTS contract. The union encountered major difficulties in this area.[102] Arguments over interpretation of the contract and the blatant attempts by some firms to circumvent it altogether taxed the union's energies and led to a deterioration of its relations with the employers. This situation resulted in a series of lawsuits brought before the labor courts by both IG Druck and individual works councilors.

During the 1979 wage round, IG Druck tried again to assume the role of the DGB's vanguard, which it had usurped from IG Metall in 1976. Following the latter's aborted struggle to introduce the 35-hour week in the steel industry, IG Druck, in a quixotic act, demanded the same with full compensation for all workers within its contractual purview.[103] But the union was simply too small and too weak to realize a demand of such societal magnitude. In addition, the strikes of 1976 and 1978 left its leadership and members emotionally drained, and its finances seriously depleted. Within two weeks, the printers, following IG Metall's settlement of the steel strike, agreed to six weeks' vacation for all and additional free shifts for older workers.

## EPILOGUE

The relative calm characterizing the three bargaining rounds in the early 1980s could have conveyed the image that IG Druck's fighting spirit of the 1970s had been broken. While continuing its decade-long role as the DGB's most outspokenly radical union on issues ranging from the presence of Communist Party members in the unions to the deployment of intermediate-range nuclear missiles in Europe, IG Druck's activism was muted at the bargaining table and on the shop floor. This was to change, however in the spring and summer of 1984 when IG Druck – in tandem with the other major activist union inside the DGB, IG Metall – embarked on the longest, most difficult and controversial strike in its history to attain the 35-hour work week. While this goal continued to elude the two unions following weeks of bitter struggle, they succeeded in breaking the employers' 40-hour-week barrier which seemed virtually invincible before the strike. Perhaps more importantly this strike seems to have firmly established IG Druck as West German labor's most outspoken representative on matters of radical social change. While this may have added to IG Druck's already considerable woes inside the DGB, vis-à-vis the SPD and the business establishment, there are few indications that the union will change its course in the years to come.[104]

# CONCLUSION

## I. THE PRIMACY OF CONTINUITY

In a period when the unions and labor movements in many large countries of the advanced capitalist world are fighting rapidly deteriorating conditions which may permanently alter their structures and roles in society, the West German unions have enjoyed a continuity in virtually every aspect of their existence.[1] Nevertheless, as amply illustrated by the preceding empirical chapters, continuity in no way implies absence of conflict. As will become evident in the following pages, the road which the trade unions in the Federal Republic are currently traveling represents the rockiest organized labor has encountered since the end of World War II. Yet, despite serious intra-DGB and intra-union divisions, changes in governments at both the federal and state levels, and major alterations in the economy, organized labor has established itself as a stable, predictable and indispensable participant in the Federal Republic's industrial, economic and political life. The DGB and its unions have become permanent pillars of the most enduring and successful democracy ever instituted on German soil, thereby fulfilling perhaps their most important mandate since their creation amidst the rubble left by the darkest episode in German history

As discussed in the preceding chapters, not even the Third Reich with all its external and internal dislocations could sever the continuities between the labor movements of the Weimar and Bonn Republics. While consciously avoiding the mistakes of the former, the post-war labor movement adopted a sufficient number of similarities to allow for a stabilizing continuity. Therefore, the concept of Stunde Null, connoting a complete break with the past and a radical beginning, may be something of a myth for the unions themselves and for students of organized labor in West Germany.

The most important areas of continuity for the post-1945 organized labor movement in the Federal Republic have been the Einheitsgewerkschaft, the Industriegewerkschaft and a highly regularized process of interest intermediation among the state, labor and capital as manifested by the thorough juridification of industrial relations. While some of these constructs originated in the post-World War II period, others claim precursors from the Weimar Republic and even before. For example, the predominance of male, skilled and industrial workers in the trade-union movement predates the Federal Republic. This sociological continuity has clearly borne political implications for labor's stability and predictability up to the present day. Moreover, while fraught with difficulties and tensions, labor's dual system of representation – the works councils on the shop floor and the unions in society at large – has nevertheless provided a routinized form of conflict management between labor and capital since the 1920s.

The unions' preoccupation with economic democracy and other participatory mechanisms also traces its conceptual origins to the Weimar Republic even though it had to await its partial realization in the Federal Republic's co-determination programs. The highly juridified nature of West German industrial relations also owes its longevity in part to the unions' "state fixation" and their concomitant penchant for legal solutions to conflicts. Again, both of these traits hail from the days of the Weimar Republic.

Bonn, however, is not Weimar, and this truism readily applies to the politics of organized labor. Although similarities between the two periods exist, organized labor has had to adapt to new realities. The unions were forced to redefine their relationship to the new country's political parties by forming the Einheitsgewerkschaft. The creation of the unifying Industriegewerkschaft also constituted a major departure from the past. New ways of interacting with the employers and the young state had to be learned, just as contacts among the unions themselves and to the federation had to be established. The unions had to familiarize themselves with certain peculiarities of the country's bargaining system and contractual procedures. Conducting strikes in the new republic entailed an often painful learning experience.

Indeed, as documented in the previous chapters, the unions confronted serious difficulties in virtually every one of these areas throughout the 1950s. As shown by the reaction to their "mistake" of openly backing the SPD for the Bundestag elections of 1953 or the strike debacles suffered by IG Metall around that period, the new conditions required a thorough adjustment effort on the part of the organized labor movement. By and large, however, the unions had successfully completed this process by the late 1950s.

Since that time the unions and their activities have become fully integrated into the functioning of the Federal Republic's economic and political systems. They are major participants in a relatively stable contest and it would be hard to imagine the contemporary Federal Republic without the unions' presence. Corroborating their integration into West German society is the fact that none of the country's other major institutions – not even labor's most outspoken opponents – would like to see the unions disappear from the scene. This, of course, represents one of the fundamental differences between Bonn and Weimar, and also contrasts favorably to other, more antagonistic arrangements elsewhere in the advanced industrial world.

Integration, stability and restrained conflict characterize the unions' position in West German society. They say very little, however, about the costs which the labor movement had to incur to attain this position. Given the trauma of modern German history, the price should be judged a worthwhile and noble investment. Nevertheless, it behooves a study of this kind to look at the challenges – both old and new – which have strained the unions' capacities on the road to systemic integration. The conflicts accompanying continuity are not likely to abate under current conditions. In spite of this, organized labor's prominent position in public affairs will persist, even if at greater costs to the unions themselves than has been the case in the past.

## II. CHALLENGES OLD AND NEW

### A. Contending with the legacies of the past

One of the most profound challenges which the labor movement faced since its revival in the Federal Republic concerns the institutionalization of the Einheitsgewerkschaft. Although this arrangement has given labor the political unity which it so woefully lacked in the Weimar Republic and has prevented it from engaging in internecine warfare based on ideological differences and party affiliations, these very advantages also placed considerable constraints on the unions' leverage as participants in a system dominated by political parties. The Einheitsgewerkschaft has prevented labor from providing overt support to any political parties from which it could demand major legislative favors in return. Thus, while there can be no doubt of the DGB's closeness to the Social Democrats in outlook, history and leadership personnel, the Einheitsgewerkschaft has persistently and effectively prevented the unions from pursuing direct political alliances with the SPD.[2] This arrangement has left the latter relatively independent of its largest constituency which – especially during the crisis of the late 1970s – entailed the implementation of certain policies that were hardly to labor's liking or advantage. In short, the all-encompassing nature of the Einheitsgewerkschaft has prevented the unions from fully translating the weight of their membership into direct political gains for the organization as a whole. The Einheitsgewerkschaft equipped labor in West Germany with great strength but left it simultaneously with insufficient power.

Another old challenge which persists to the present and promises to assume even greater prominence in the future centers around the unions as voluntary organizations. Organized labor has consistently suffered from the "free rider" problem stemming from a constitutional ban on closed-shop arrangements, a prohibition which accords with the unions' self-perception as representatives of *all* workers. By gaining the advantages and benefits accruing to union members, many non-members find it unnecessary to pay the costly membership dues. Given this challenge and that of dual labor representation to be discussed below, it is remarkable that the unions could reach the relatively high organizational level which they have maintained through much of the post-World War II period. Nevertheless, labor remains vulnerable in this area. Just like during the boom of the late 1950s and early 1960s when the abundance of jobs increased wages well beyond the contractual agreements reached by the unions, thereby causing a decline in union membership, similar economic conditions could make the unions seem superfluous and redundant to a growing number of workers. This should be particularly worrisome to the DGB and its constituent organizations since an increasing number of their potential members belong to social strata, occupations and geographic locations where the legacy and tradition of unions as the prime representatives of the working class have already been virtually forgotten. While the "free rider" problem has thus far failed to weaken substantially the unions' organizational presence – largely due to a lingering tradition of labor collectivism among segments of the working class – there can be no guarantee that the small membership losses which the unions have incurred since the beginning of the 1980s will not increase as crisis conditions continue to prevail.

Yet another difficulty for labor in West Germany concerns the constraints placed on the unions' strategic and tactical maneuverability by the juridification of the industrial relations system. As has been argued in the previous section of this conclusion and demonstrated throughout the empirical parts of this volume, juridification helped labor not only to solve day-to-day problems in a routine manner both inside and outside the factory gates – which in other countries often requires disruptive and ad-hoc measures – but it also contributed to making labor a powerful partner in the management of the Federal Republic's political economy. Nevertheless, juridification's restraining qualities have on the whole outweighed the benefits for West German trade unions. Juridification has severely impeded labor's power to mobilize in countless instances ranging from the legal protection given to employers who use the lockout – because of the juridified notion of Kampfparität – to the restrictions on virtually every union initiative including collective bargaining and strikes. While it has thereby undoubtedly contributed to the stability of the system as a whole, juridification has consistently caused labor embarrassment and hardship, and will continue to do so in the years to come.

One of juridification's most consistent challenges to the unions throughout the years has been the dual representation of labor in West Germany. Although it is undeniably true that the substantial overlap between works councilors and active union members renders the problems of dualism less acute in empirical situations, there can be no question that the formalistic separation of these two representative bodies severely circumscribes labor's collective power of representation inside the factories, which in turn necessarily limits the efficacy of its advocacy and protection of the workers.

One example of this concerns West German labor's greatest preoccupation throughout the post-war era, co-determination. The juridified system of industrial relations in the Federal Republic grants the works councils substantial veto power – even anticipatory input – regarding the protection of workers on the shop floor. At the same time, however, the law imposes strict limits on these works councils and their advocacy on behalf of workers which in any way could be construed as political.

With few prospects of a substantial reduction in the high unemployment rate, accompanied by an intensified introduction of new technologies in the production process in virtually all of the Federal Republic's industries, the already considerable power of the works councils may increase even further. Much to the unions' chagrin, the crisis has already led to a number of "mini corporatist" arrangements between certain companies and their works councils emphasizing part-time work, job sharing and flexible work time, all of which are anathema to most West German unions. Collectivist solidarity provided by the unions could become even further eroded by the self-interested attitude on the part of the works councils whose protective actions help only employees in their own plants. Whether this potential development could justifiably be called the "Japanization" or "Americanization" of West German industrial relations is a matter of interpretation.[3] But there can be no doubt that the continued challenge of dualism will assume new dimensions for the unions in the years to come. It will be imperative for them to devise new methods of strengthening solidarity if they want to prevent the disintegration of labor politics from its present national and industrially based collectivism to a sector-specific decentralism dominated by works councils. This scenario becomes even more plausible with the continued weakening of the industrial working class, still the core of union membership and support, and the growing influx of workers who have traditionally remained outside the unions' organization.

Even before the establishment of the Federal Republic, German unions were poorly represented among certain segments of the working class. Typically, unions in both the Weimar and Bonn Republics met with little success in organizing workers employed in non-industrial sectors of the economy: white-collar workers, women, the young, employees of small firms and civil servants. This challenge remained unresolved partly because the large industrial unions of the Federal Republic were not concerned about this issue. Unionization drives to incorporate workers employed in hitherto non-unionized sectors, so common to other advanced industrial countries during the 1960s and 1970s, were infrequent in West Germany. Suffice it to say that the unions' failure or unwillingness to organize workers belonging to "marginal" groups continues to cause dangerous structural weaknesses for labor.

The last of the labor movement's traditional problems and one which shows few signs of abating concerns the ideological split among the unions. The uneasy relationship between progressive or radical elements within organized labor, here referred to as activists, and moderate or system-accepting forces, labeled accommodationist, has informed labor politics since the first substantial organizational articulations on the part of the working class in the nineteenth century. The cleavage between these two factions has varied in intensity ranging from open hostility during the Weimar Republic to respectful disagreement – with occasional flare-ups – in its Bonn successor. One of the major achievements of trade unions in the Federal Republic concerns the adept balancing act with which they have met this perennial challenge. It attests to the high legitimacy enjoyed by the Einheitsgewerkschaft in the eyes of its members, other workers and virtually all important participants in West German politics that the conflict between activists and accommodationists has thus far failed to disrupt the unity of this formally apolitical association. This unity will most likely continue to exist. Nevertheless, developments in the wake of the crisis have led to an intensification of the conflict. New challenges confronting the West German labor movement at present and for the foreseeable future may further exacerbate this longstanding problem of union politics in the Federal Republic.

## B. New challenges for the unions

The first new challenge involves changes in the structure of the economy, most notably sectoral shifts resulting from the decline – in some cases disappearance – of traditional industries such as steel production, coal mining, textile manufacturing, watchmaking and shipbuilding. Accompanying these sectoral problems, geographic areas of the Federal Republic which had been home to many of these industries for decades, have suffered hardships associated with the persistence of high levels of unemployment. The grave social and economic problems of the Ruhr region, the Saar area and Bremen are all inextricably linked to the decline of industries dominating the economies of these areas.

While the first new challenge centered on sectoral shifts in the West German economy, the second pertains to technological innovations inside the country's firms. In a matter of only a few years, the micro-chip revolution has altered virtually every aspect of production in the Federal Republic, as it has in other advanced industrial societies. Until the middle of the 1980s, these far-reaching technological changes displaced primarily unskilled and semi-skilled workers, leaving skilled workers relatively unscathed, in part because they were selected to operate the new technologies. But even this group has begun to suffer job insecurity, since many new methods require fewer workers regardless of skill. Moreover, the trajectory of future developments in the micro-chip revolution seems unlikely to convince management to grant iron clad job security in the years to come.

The third and most pernicious new challenge confronting the unions is unemployment. Resulting in good part from sectoral shifts in the West German economy and the technological transformations of production, unemployment represents by far the most worrisome situation for the DGB. Despite the rather hopeful developments of the mid-1980s in the economy as a whole, little, if any, improvement occurred in the labor market. With the virtual elimination of inflation, the strengthening of an already powerful position in the world market due to the superb performance of West German exports, and an impressive profit explosion, unemployment nevertheless held steady at well over 2 million, reaching a national record of 2.6 million (10.6%) in January 1985. This level of joblessness shows virtually no sign of significant improvement for the future.[4] This scenario reinforced the unions' worries that productivity-led growth contributes little if anything to bettering conditions in employment.

Exacerbating this situation for the unions was the continued influx of young people into the labor market which, due to the delayed appearance of the baby boom in the Federal Republic, is unlikely to diminish until the middle of the 1990s.

Compounding this demographic problem has been the government's persistent unwillingness to initiate expansionary programs which could yield a substantial increase in jobs. Much to the unions' chagrin, the CDU-led coalition has in fact accentuated the austerity measures instituted by the Schmidt governments of the late 1970s and early 1980s. Entitlements have been systematically curtailed, welfare packages reduced, the safety net loosened and programs for vocational training severely limited. These cuts have not only entailed the objective loss of jobs but also created the subjective fear of losing the remaining ones. A noticeable insecurity has affected virtually all workers in the Federal Republic including, for the first time, skilled workers.[5] A comprehensive study sponsored by IG Metall predicts the loss of 160,000 jobs in the electronics, automobile and machine-tool industries by 1990, largely due to automation, and concludes with the dire warning that if left unimpeded the deployment of new technologies could threaten the jobs of 3 to 3.5 million employees in West Germany.[6] The fear and uncertainty among a large and growing number of workers constitutes the least calculable of the new challenges confronting the unions.

The combined impact of these new problems on organized labor in the Federal Republic presents yet another challenge to the DGB and its members. Three words best characterize this situation: segmentation, division and centrifugality. Since the onset of the crisis in the mid-1970s and the deterioration in the labor market during the early 1980s, centrifugal developments have increasingly threatened labor solidarity and unity of purpose. Divisions have deepened between workers in weak and strong sectors, those employed by financially insecure firms and their colleagues in prosperous ones. The differences between blue- and white-collar workers have become more pronounced as have the divisions among workers in competing production units. Above all, there has been a growing separation between the "ins," core workers enjoying relatively high job security, and the "outs," consisting of part-time workers, marginally employed people in highly volatile jobs and the permanently unemployed. These segmentations have enhanced the viability and attractiveness of particularistic, sector-related and even firm-specific remedies, all of which could severely undermine the universalism which has been a major source of union strength. Coupled with a general weakening of working-class culture – which undoubtedly diminishes organizational cohesion and class solidarity – these centrifugal developments threaten the primacy of the unions as the representatives of the West German working class. "Wildcat cooperation" between the works councils and management in prosperous industries to the direct detriment of the peripheral segments of the working class pose a renewed challenge to the DGB and its member unions.[7]

The structural crisis in certain industries and regions has led to a loss in membership among the labor movement's most traditional supporters, and may cause the DGB trouble in the following ways: first, it seems improbable that these unions can fully compensate such losses by recruiting workers from social groups whose members have exhibited resistance to unionization throughout the history of German labor. Second, accompanying this sectoral shift and structural dislocation is a geographic movement which could add to the unions' woes. By being permanently weakened in their traditional bastions of the country's industrial north, the unions have few options but to try their luck at replenishing their diminished ranks with workers from the "high tech" industries, most of which are located in the south around Stuttgart in Baden-Württemberg and Munich in Bavaria. This leads to a third problem. Since many of these workers hail from geographic areas which have consistently yielded impressive electoral majorities for the Christian Democratic parties (CDU and CSU), they may lack the Social Democratic tradition which tied many of their colleagues from the northern industrial regions to the unions. This development may result in shifts in the political expression of the DGB's rank and file which could eventually also have implications for the policies of the union leadership.

In the late 1970s and early 1980s, the unions have been confronted with a hardened and aggressive stance on the part of the employers. As a result of a number of factors such as increased global competition, the growing necessity to modernize under adverse economic conditions, a desire to make the most of the conservative Zeitgeist and labor's impaired market position, the employers have been determined to leave the unions little room to maneuver. While capital never aimed at destroying labor, it certainly has attempted to weaken the unions by trying to contain their power in virtually every arena.

On the shop floor, the employers' challenge to the unions has consisted of a systematic attempt to enhance the power of the works councils by tempting them with firm-specific "deals" to the detriment of the unions' collectivist agreements. This technique of localized flexibility was in good part designed to foster division among the working class. At the bargaining table, the employers pursued a very tough strategy vis-à-vis the unions which resulted in the latter having to accept wage and salary losses in real terms throughout every round in the early 1980s (except that of 1984).

Moreover, the employers would rather initiate major disruptions of the West German economy, incur huge losses and endanger the climate of cooperation and social consensus with labor than concede to the unions on principles such as the reduction of weekly work time. Compare the situation of 1956 when the employers awarded IG Druck and IG Metall a substantial wage raise and three hours of diminished weekly work time without any loss in pay just to avert a strike, with the brutal lockouts and bitter strike activity of 1978–79 and 1984 in the unions' struggle to attain a 90-minute reduction (that remains subject to further constraints on the shop floor).

The employers' determination to weaken the unions is especially disturbing when viewed in conjunction with the Kohl government's frigid relationship with the DGB. That the employers and their most powerful association, the BDA, perceived the conservative–liberal government as "theirs" is conveyed in the words of the government's Labor Minister Norbert Blüm: "I have to make it clear to the employers, that in Bonn the government changed from the SPD to the CDU and not from the DGB to the BDA."[8] The pro-business posture of the federal government has assumed such unabashed proportions that even moderate unionists have begun to speak publicly about the coalition of "capital and cabinet" which has apparently formed an unholy alliance against organized labor.

Relations between the DGB and a federal government in Bonn have rarely been as strained as they are today. It took Chancellor Helmut Kohl over two years following his ascension to power to meet with the head of the DGB in November 1984, a hiatus of unprecedented length. Considering the brevity of this encounter and the coolness in tone, the only surprise is that the meeting occurred at all.[9] Three reasons account for the unions' difficulties with this government: first, while the structure of the Einheitsgewerkschaft prohibits party allegiances by the DGB, it is also clear that the labor movement has always been closer to the SPD than to the CDU. Thus, the very fact that a CDU-led government dominates the political agenda in the Federal Republic places the unions at a disadvantage. The differences may be atmospheric but that does not make them unimportant. For example, the fact that union leaders often are on a first-name basis with Social Democratic chancellors and important cabinet members creates a more congenial and intimate form of communication than has been the case under CDU governments. Helmut Schmidt's relationship to some of the leaders of the accommodationist unions was particularly close, leading to frequent and extensive visits by unionists to the chancellor's bungalow for discussions of topics relevant to labor. Other SPD politicians have also had very close ties to the unions. The independent disposition of the Einheitsgewerkschaft failed to dissolve the informal intimacy between individual members of the Social Democratic Party and the trade unions and never established comparable links between the labor movement and the CDU.

Moreover, CDU-led governments have been more prone to let the market mediate capital–labor relations whereas the Social Democrats attempted to enhance the state's role in this exchange. While labor will by definition remain unsatisfied with the operation of government given West Germany's capitalist framework, capital's victories are likely to be less lopsided in the Social Democratic variant of interest accommodation than under its Christian Democratic counterpart. With politics in consensual democracies like the Federal Republic being a game of appearances and increments, marginal differences of this sort do indeed matter.

Second, the exigencies of a protracted economic crisis under conditions of capitalism will create tensions between unions and the government since their respective objective interests will most likely be at odds, thereby diminishing significantly the importance of the particular government's party affiliations. This was certainly the case in the later years of the Schmidt-led social–liberal coalition which instituted austerity measures that were hardly to the DGB's liking. Indeed, as will be recalled, the unions roundly condemned the Schmidt government's economic policies and in fact organized a major demonstration in Stuttgart in the fall of 1981 protesting "their" party's course of action. Nevertheless, while expressing their displeasure at being hostages to a friendly government, the unions still perceived this government as the lesser of the two evils and never developed the antipathy which they have exhibited toward the Kohl-led CDU–FDP coalition.

In addition to these two structural difficulties contributing to tense relations between the DGB and the government, there exists a third cluster which derives from the first two but exhibits features which seem sui generis to this government, the Zeitgeist and the behavior of some of its members. Beginning with Chancellor Kohl's ill-fated characterization of the unions' demand for the 35-hour work week as "absurd, stupid and imbecilic," and continuing with Count Lambsdorff's description of IG Druck und Papier as "IG Druck und Zensur" (censorship) – implying that IG Druck's radicalism has distanced it from belief in democracy – the government's antipathy towards the unions has repeatedly manifested itself in the antagonistic tone of its statements. To the DGB this stylistic hostility merely corroborates parallel developments in the much more important area of substance. The unions have grown increasingly suspicious that the government seeks an open alliance with the employers against labor. To the unions, evidence abounds. In addition to the government's opposition to the 35-hour work week (which many of its individual functionaries voiced before and during the strikes of 1984), the unions felt that the state under CDU leadership violated the unions' bargaining autonomy, the most important ground rule in West Germany's game of industrial relations. When the Federal Labor Office in Nuremberg reached the unprecedented decision during the strikes to discontinue payments for short-time work to workers who were on temporary layoffs because their firms, though themselves not part of any industrial action, had to reduce or stop production as a consequence of the strikes, the unions experienced one of their most painful moments in recent memory. Although decided by the nominally independent Office, this move constituted, to the DGB's thinking, evidence of governmental support for the employers since an action of such magnitude could never have been taken by the Office's director – a CSU member – without at least the tacit approval of the government. To the unions this signalled the Kohl administration's willingness to assist the employers in their effort to ruin the unions financially by adding a "cold" lockout to the existing "hot" one.[10] The subsequent court decision annulling the Office's fiat failed to convince the DGB that the supposed consensus among all participants in the West German political economy was still intact.

Another example of this anti-union offensive by the CDU/CSU and the FDP is their renewed attempt to introduce legislation expressly designed to weaken the collective representation of workers by DGB unions inside and outside the factory gates. Toward that end a CSU-initiated bill designed to amend the existing Works Constitution Law of 1972 was proposed in the Bundestag, much to he DGB's consternation and chagrin.[11] The bill's main features include an upgrading of the shop-floor powers of the DGB's rivals (the CGB and DAG) to the direct detriment of the DGB, an individualization of the nomination process in works council elections, also aimed at weakening the present intra-company position of DGB unions, and the creation of special committees for white-collar workers which in effect would separate their representation completely from that of their blue-collar colleagues. The Free Democrats, viewing themselves as the political spokesmen of white-collar employees, have traditionally been the main advocates of such an amendment to the Works Constitution Law of 1972. Moreover, the conservative parties have once again begun to allude with some regularity to their traditional desire for the passage of some kind of industrial relations act in the Federal Republic.

The DGB has also been perturbed by the Kohl government's open attempts to exploit existing divisions within the labor movement for its own purposes. In an effort to undermine the legitimacy of the activists' main rallying point, the 35-hour work week, the CDU-led government supported legislation introducing early retirement plans not unlike the ones advocated by the accommodationist wing of the DGB. It is in this context that one has to interpret Chancellor Kohl's address to the delegates of IG Chemie's congress in September 1984. This speech, his official debut as chancellor in establishing personal contact with any union, has to be described, however, as a failure. As demonstrated by the repeated jeers interrupting Kohl's address, IG Chemie delegates did not welcome the chancellor's apperance at the rostrum of their congress even though he advanced views which were designed to strengthen this union's position vis-à-vis its opponents inside the DGB. Although the divisions among DGB unions remain as pronounced as ever, the government's attempts to support the "good" unions in the hope of isolating the "bad" ones have proven clumsy and counterproductive.

Ultimately, of course, the DGB and its member unions continue to begrudge the CDU-led government's failure to take decisive measures against what the unions consider appalling conditions in the labor market. The unions' desperate pleas for government intervention leading to the creation of new jobs have thus far remained completely unheeded. The government's conviction that the best guarantee for an increase in employment rests with an otherwise healthy and steadily growing economy simply cannot accommodate the DGB's wishes for a state-directed employment program. Given the unions' feeble leverage over the Kohl government, it seems unlikely that their hopes in this regard will be fulfilled in the near future.

Despite the chilly relations between the CDU-led government and the organized labor movement, certain improvements are likely to occur, at least in the case of problems where solutions will benefit both parties. The pursuit of a modus vivendi may be of particular importance to the unions since they have confronted yet another political challenge – the crisis of social democracy – which adds to their already considerable difficulties and threatens their traditional self-perception. The problems of the SPD in particular and that of social democracy in general have left a mark on the unions' political reality in the 1980s and beyond.

Social democracy in the Federal Republic, like its counterparts elsewhere in the advanced capitalist world, finds itself at perhaps its most decisive crossroads since 1945.[12] Indeed, the depth of the identity crisis currently afflicting the Social Democrats seems to exceed similar dilemmas which plagued the labor movement's pre-Godesberg existence during the latter part of the 1950s. In marked contrast to social democracy's present predicament, the SPD in the past could gauge with a relatively high degree of certainty what the various implications of policy decisions would be, and, above all, where they would ultimately lead the party and its adherents, including the vast majority of organized workers. Moreover, pre-Godesberg social democracy benefitted from an economy blessed with sustained growth. It could hardly be maintained that its present-day successor enjoys luxuries of a similar kind.

Social democracy's prosperous, and in many ways quite glorious, Bad Godesberg era has come to its irrevocable end. One of the main characteristics of this period was the successful establishment of a Keynesian compact sustained by a political coalition involving much of organized labor and certain key segments of capital. By harnessing the power of growth for the purposes of facilitating private accumulation and the simultaneous expansion of public welfare, the Social Democratic compromise attained a positive-sum result among the major participants in the West German political economy, a situation which ended in the late 1970s and early 1980s. While growth may still appear on occasion as it has in the mid-1980s, it lacks the quantitative vigor which it exhibited between the late 1950s and the mid-1970s. A more negative development from the standpoint of the working class may be the fact that this growth, as already discussed, has increasingly been "decoupled" from the labor market.

Employment and economic growth no longer necessarily coexist, as they did during the Bad Godesberg compact. Their separation comes as a result of increased productivity due to growing rationalization. The strategy which helped social democracy alleviate – if not resolve – the contradictions caused by the "second industrial revolution" is no longer effective as the "third industrial revolution" transforms production in the West German economy. Certain tenets of social democracy have lost relevance since they adhere to an ethic of equality and distributive justice based on macroeconomic growth. Social democracy finds itself in an unenviable predicament. Unlike their main rivals, the Social Democrats enjoy neither certainty of vision nor the necessary political power to implement it should they be given the opportunity to do so in the near future.

Together, the SPD and its allies still represent the most important opposition to the CDU-led government and the conservative Zeitgeist dominating politics in the Federal Republic. In addition, they continue to be the major protectors of those adversely affected by the austerity measures of the conservative–liberal coalition. Yet both the unions and the SPD have to look constantly over their left shoulder, where there now exists a political alternative in the form of the Greens, who simultaneously constitute an important ally of social democracy and its keenest competitor in terms of ideas, policies, strategies and, above all, political support.

Ultimately, social democracy and the SPD may not be spared the bitter choice that they were offered by Richard Löwenthal, one of German social democracy's senior figures and leading accommodationist thinkers, in a much-debated paper entitled "Identity and Future of the SPD."[13] Implicitly acknowledging that the inclusionary model of the post-Godesberg era was over, Löwenthal argued that the SPD had to stop trying to be everything to everybody.[14] The author maintained that the party and social democracy could simply not reconcile the fundamental differences between the values and wishes of an increasingly "post-materialist" intelligentsia on the one hand, and those of a predominantly "materialist" and insecure working class on the other. Löwenthal concluded in no uncertain terms that for social democracy's survival as a major political force in the Federal Republic the SPD had better stop currying favor with the "greening" counterculture and concentrate on regaining the full confidence of its traditional supporters, the industrial working class. In the unresolved dilemma between economy and ecology Löwenthal exhorted the SPD to opt unequivocally for the former, even at the risk of losing some supporters who viewed the salience of the latter as sufficiently important to cast their lot with another party.

The election of March 6, 1983 seemed to corroborate Löwenthal's dire predictions. The SPD lost the vote of nearly two million workers to the CDU, which these workers perceived as being more predictable and competent on the economy. Many of these renegades voted for the Christian Democrats for the first time in their lives.[15] Moreover, this substantial loss to the right occurred in some of social democracy's traditional bastions such as the industrial Rhine-Ruhr area.[16] While this trend lacks finality, as best demonstrated by the return of many of these "materialist" voters and traditional Social Democrats to the SPD in the Hesse and Bremen elections of September 25, 1983 and the party's impressive victories in the Saarland and North Rhine-Westphalia in the spring of 1985, it nevertheless provided a worrisome harbinger of adverse developments which could damage the party's political fortunes for a long time to come.

To worsen matters, the SPD has also been consistently losing voters to the "post-materialist" side of the dilemma, as approximately 750,000 people, primarily young voters, defected to the Greens in the federal elections of March 1983.[17] Unlike the return to the SPD by many of social democracy's "materialist" supporters in subsequent state and local elections, the desertion of social democracy by the Federal Republic's young people, especially those actively concerned with "post-materialist" politics, seems – at least for the foreseeable future – quite irrevocable, thus indeed making them in Willy Brandt's words the SPD's "lost children."

The crisis befalling social democracy – of which its substantial losses in governmental power during the late 1970s and early 1980s have merely been the most visible manifestations – has forced the movement as a whole to devise a new Godesberg. With the old mixture of Keynesianism and faith in the socially beneficial aspects of technological progress severely challenged, it has been incumbent upon the SPD and its allies to design a new paradigm which would essentially perform aggregating functions similar to the Godesberg compact between the late 1950s and its disintegration in the early 1980s. There can be no doubt that the SPD in particular and social democracy in general are in desperate need of a new vision, a new collective charisma and the courage to attempt daring innovations in achieving the much-needed synthesis between ecology and economy.

The first steps were taken when the SPD set up a commission with a clear and wide-ranging mandate to devise a new program by the late 1980s to replace the Godesberg paradigm. At the beginning of 1985, the ghost of the Löwenthal dilemma hovered menacingly over what promised to be a lengthy and arduous process. "Eco-socialists," led by such eminent figures as Erhard Eppler and Johano Strasser, advocated a course which renounced social democracy's hitherto dominant technocratic growth logic, particularly its Godesberg variant. Opposed to this view among members of the commission was an equally influential group of "technocrats" led by Wolfgang Roth and IG Chemie's leader Hermann Rappe, who, although ready to incorporate ecological considerations into social democracy's new guiding principles, maintained the primacy of material expansion as the most fundamental aspect of a successful social democratic policy.[18] With the outcome of this debate completely uncertain at this writing, social democracy's ambivalence and the SPD's vacillations will present another challenge for the unions. Unable to "go it alone," yet sufficiently powerful to avoid being completely dependent on the outcome of this debate and its policy ramifications, the DGB and its member unions will most likely suffer further divisions in their already splintered movement.

Complicating matters, the unions had to confront a completely unexpected series of events which threatened to undermine the legitimacy of the DGB in the eyes of union members and the West German public. In February 1982, the DGB suddenly found itself engulfed by a corruption scandal of unprecedented proportions which challenged the labor movement's impeccable moral credentials, thoroughly embarrassed its leadership and tarnished its reputation as a reformer and defender of the poor. The weekly magazine *Der Spiegel* disclosed in its issue of February 8, 1982 that the leaders of the union-owned construction and housing company, Neue Heimat, had engaged in a number of schemes leading to their personal enrichment.[19] Through the formation of numerous dummy corporations, Neue Heimat's top managers used the market power of Europe's largest construction firm to enhance their personal wealth, sometimes to the direct detriment of the company itself. These arrangements enabled Neue Heimat's chief executive officer, an active unionist and SPD member, to own or co-own 217 apartments in West Berlin and 24 in Hamburg in addition to other real estate, making him a very wealthy individual. To make matters worse, some leading union officials, among them the DGB's head Heinz Oskar Vetter and IG Metall's leader Eugen Loderer, were found to have invested in Neue Heimat-owned buildings in West Berlin as a tax shelter.

While the activities of these union officials were not illegal, they nevertheless represented a scandal of the first order. To the conservative opposition the event provided welcome empirical evidence to support its charges concerning the close and supposedly sinister entanglements (Verfilzung) among the Social Democratic Party, the trade unions and local government officials belonging to both or either. This "red rule of entanglement" (rote Filzokratie) had been one of the main weapons in the conservatives' campaign of "freedom vs. socialism," waged against the SPD and the labor movement since the onset of the crisis in the mid-1970s.

Moreover, in a period when an increasing number of union members had to worry about making ends meet in daily life, some of organized labor's top functionaries publicly discussed six-digit figures which they transferred from one dummy corporation to another. Perhaps even more than the financial inequities, the corruption of a special mandate caused considerable outrage among the rank and file leading to massive renunciations of union membership in the early spring of 1982. After all, the founding idea and continued raison d'être of a union-owned construction and housing company was precisely to provide a socially responsible alternative to corporations solely beholden to the market's profit rationale. As Vetter stated in a televized appearance, this affair involved nothing less than the unions' legitimacy and reputation.

The DGB rose to the occasion. Dismissing much of Neue Heimat's management with little equivocation, it proceeded to purge its own ranks in a fashion unprecedented in both speed and thoroughness. Vetter's designated successor who was to assume the DGB leadership in May 1982 was forced to step aside, making room for an outsider whose reputation was in no way tainted by the Neue Heimat scandal. Ernst Breit, Vetter's successor and until May 1982 the head of the postal workers' union (Deutsche Postgewerkschaft – DPG), fulfilled the one main prerequisite which all his predecessors had had to fulfill as well: he seemed sufficiently innocuous to represent an acceptable compromise between large and small unions, industrial ones and their non-industrial counterparts, and activists and accommodationists. Yet because of the special circumstances of his ascendancy, Breit had to accomplish perhaps an even greater task: he had to be above moral reproach and thereby lend the DGB a renewed sense of honesty and legitimacy.

To everyone's surprise, the Neue Heimat scandal abated with Breit's assumption of the DGB leadership, leaving virtually no negative traces. The unions had succeeded in formulating an effective response to this unexpected and potentially dangerous challenge. In good part due to Ernst Breit's honesty, organizational commitments and convincing leadership qualities, the Neue Heimat incident of 1982 seemed nearly forgotten three years later, providing the unions a rare instance of unmitigated triumph. The magnitude of this success appeared particularly great when contrasted to the mixed results which the unions attained in responding to the multiple challenges confronting them in the 1980s.

## III. UNION RESPONSES TO THE CHALLENGES

Whereas the DGB successfully overcame the Neue Heimat episode and remained completely untainted by the Flick scandal of 1984–85 which tarnished virtually every other established political institution in the Federal Republic, it failed to heal the widening rift within its own ranks. The old cleavage between activists and accommodationists revived with a rarely experienced intensity. Largely centered around the formulation of responses to the adversities confronting labor since the onset of the crisis in the mid-1970s, the disputes between these two factions propelled each of them towards independent – and potentially irreconcilable – strategies of conflict resolution.

Albeit simplistically, the strategies could be divided between those concerned with economic and industrial matters and those focusing on politics. In the industrial sphere the activists have adopted a class-oriented and collectivist approach in contrast to the more interest-group specific, plant-related and particularistic arrangement advocated by the accommodationists. Whereas the former group deliberately resists the centrifugal tendencies threatening the unity of the West German working class, the latter has opted to make the best of this trend by seeking the greatest possible security for its own members. Whether ultimately successful or not, IG Metall and its supporters have designed their strategy to counter what they perceive as an increasing "Americanization" of the West German labor movement and a concomitant "Japanization" of West German industrial relations, both entailing a segmentation of the workforce. No such fears or ambitions have guided the actions of IG Metall's opponents inside the DGB. It is in this context that the issue of work-time reduction became so controversial.

Beginning in the fall of 1977 at IG Metall's Düsseldorf congress, this union became the leading advocate of the 35-hour work week, not only in the Federal Republic but in all of West Europe. Although this demand did

not enjoy unanimous acceptance within the union,[20] IG Metall nevertheless gradually made this issue the centerpiece of its response to the attack
by the employers and the state on the living standard (Besitzstand) of the
working class. Since it was first formulated, this demand was viewed by IG
Metall as the spearhead of the unions' strategy to increase reliance on their
own strength in the wake of the economic crisis. As such, its supporters
have continued to view the 35-hour work week as the most fundamental
expression of organized labor's role as a Gegenmacht in an increasingly
crisis-ridden – and hostile – market economy.

To IG Metall and its allies, particularly IG Druck und Papier, the
importance accorded the struggle for the 35-hour work week seemed
justified for the following reasons: first, this measure would permit the
creation of new jobs, thereby reducing unemployment, the major bane of
the unions' existence in the 1980s. Thus, IG Metall felt that the 35-hour
work week would increase solidarity between employed and unemployed
workers, thereby making it an essential ingredient of the unions' collectivist
countercrisis strategy. The activists viewed this demand as essentially
qualitative. While it contributed little to qualitative improvements in the
work process per se, its collectivist inclusiveness – so its advocates believed
– added qualitative benefits to the lives of the unemployed and other
elements of the working class. Second, by demanding the 35-hour work
week without any loss in remuneration, the activists hoped to implement
one of their traditional beliefs, that the macroeconomic benefits of higher
wages would stimulate consumption. Third, the reduction of the work
week would increase leisure time, which had become important to the
activists in an economy dominated by stressful and monotonous methods
of production. The "quality of work life" or "humanization" aspect of the
35-hour work week definitely played a key role in the activists' advocacy of
this strategy rather than early retirement, a remedy favored by the more
moderate accommodationists. What was the point, the activists argued, of
having workers retire at 58 or 59 when many of them never reached that
age? (This argument played a central role in IG Druck und Papier's strong
support for a shorter work week since only 2.5% of those employed in this
union's organizational domain were 59 years of age or older.) Fourth, the
implementation of the 35-hour work week on a large scale would counter
the proliferation of particularistic segmentations and plant-specific
arrangements which hindered work-time reduction on a micro level.
Activist unions developed a growing antipathy to such measures of
localized decision-making which they regarded as a scheme by the
employers to undermine the collectivism of the unions by taking advantage
of labor's weakened position.[21]

In contrast to the activists, the accommodationists – centered around the "gang of five" comprising IG Chemie-Papier-Keramik, IG Bau-Steine-Erden, IG Bergbau und Energie, Gewerkschaft Nahrung-Genuss-Gaststätten and Gewerkschaft Textil und Bekleidung – advocated early retirement as the best form of work-time reduction under existing circumstances. They based their argument as much on feasibility and expediency as on strategic preferences. Concerning the former, the accommodationists maintained that constellations of power in the Federal Republic made it impossible to have the 35-hour work week implemented in one or two large steps, thereby virtually negating its desired effect of creating additional employment. The incremental reduction of one hour per year would only worsen an already intense production process, benefitting neither employed workers nor the unemployed.

As to the accommodationists' conceptual preferences, they viewed early retirement as the most just settlement for workers who had labored hard for many years.[22] This strategy protected a threatened and deserving group, and if properly instituted – the accommodationists argued – it would also create jobs. In contrast to the 35-hour work week, which could only hurt the competitiveness of West German industry, early retirement, combined with other forms of work-time reduction (such as lengthening the period of compulsory education), provided an ideal solution which did not harm the economy, benefitted deserving workers, offered the possibility of additional employment and above all seemed eminently feasible under existing conditions in West Germany.

In opposition to the activists, the accommodationists were less than impressed with the job-creating possibilities of the 35-hour work week, even when instituted under optimal conditions. In support of their position, the accommodationists also argued that their strategy of work-time reduction enjoyed considerably greater popularity among the workers and the general public than the 35-hour work week. The latter solution suffered from a degree of uncertainty as to its job-creating potential which further impeded its already unlikely realization. Many workers also considered early retirement a far more tangible benefit because they could not make much use of the one hour less per day they would work if the 35-hour week were implemented.

It is important to add that both positions remained hotly contested inside every West German union throughout the late 1970s and early 1980s. In no union was one solution accepted to the complete exclusion of the other. The accommodationists paid lip-service to the validity of the 35-hour work week, just as IG Metall and its allies spoke of early retirement as a valid component of the larger strategy of work-time reduction. The DGB, of course, rose to its mandate as mediator between the two factions, declaring in a number of statements that all forms of work-time reduction were equally necessary and thus deserving of every DGB member's support. Yet, probably in good part due to IG Metall's preeminence, the 35-hour work week gradually emerged as primus inter pares among the various versions of work-time reduction. This, however, in no way diminished its controversial nature within IG Metall itself, among the DGB's constituent unions, in the public debate in the Federal Republic or in the international community.

Seldom in recent memory has a controversy involving West German unions received so much attention from labor movements in Western Europe as IG Metall's seven-week-long strike and IG Druck's thirteen-week struggle for the 35-hour work week waged in the spring and early summer of 1984. For the largest Italian labor union, the left–socialist and communist-dominated Confederatione Generale Italiana de Lavoro (CGIL) to heap praise on a West German union bespeaks a momentous and unusual occasion.

> The most bitter labor struggle in half a century has just been concluded in the Federal Republic of Germany. A wall has been broken: the 40-hour work week. This happened in a country whose economy continues to be the strongest on the continent and whose unions appeared to be gun-shy in the past. This attainment has transformed the trade unions in the Federal Republic of Germany into the vanguard of the labor movement in Europe concerning the rights of workers to a humane work environment and especially in their battle against unemployment.[23]

This conflict, undoubtedly the most controversial and closely followed industrial action in the history of the West German labor movement, highlighted all the problems the unions have confronted in meeting the challenges of the crisis and in devising appropriate responses to its most adverse manifestations.

It should be remembered that the events of 1984 were not IG Metall's first attempt to break the 40-hour work week barrier. In 1979, barely one year after the adoption of this strategy as official union policy by a divided IG Metall congress, the union conducted a bitterly contested six-week-long strike in the steel industry which was the first of its kind in this sector since the notorious "Ruhreisenstreik" of 1928, arguably one of the major harbingers of the Weimar Republic's ignominious end. Despite IG Metall's efforts in that conflict, the union was foiled, and had to accept a consolation prize of six weeks' paid vacation time per annum. With the 40-hour work week safely locked into a five-year-long general framework contract, the union's hands remained tied until 1984. The employers had hoped that by then public opinion in the Federal Republic would be so opposed to the 35-hour work week that it would be impossible for IG

Metall to mobilize a serious offensive based on this issue. By publicly supporting the demand for early retirement and other forms of work-time reduction and by signing a number of contracts featuring such benefits with accommodationist unions, the employers hoped further to delegitimize the 35-hour strategy in the minds of many West German workers, including IG Metall members. The employers' strategy aimed at driving a wedge into an already existing split between the activists and the accommodationists, isolating IG Metall and its radical "appendage" (IG Druck) in the process, and discrediting the activists' demand by questioning its moral integrity and tactical feasibility. Capital's calculation was to prove severely flawed by the spring of 1984.

The employers' mistake derived partly from their genuine aversion to any concession toward the 35-hour work week, which in the course of the early 1980s had developed into an *idèe fixe* beyond its immediate instrumental dimensions, and also from a misreading of IG Metall's determination. The industrialists were also encouraged by the fact that public opinion polls showed a majority of workers favoring other forms of work-time reduction – because workers simply could not envision how the 35-hour work week would help them in their particular firms – and that there was substantial disagreement as to the desirability and feasibility of this demand even within IG Metall. The divisiveness of the 1977 Düsseldorf congress had not faded from memory, nor had the bitterly contested steel strike of 1978–79 which failed to win the union any gains in this direction. Although it was clear at IG Metall's Berlin congress of 1980 and at its subsequent congress in Munich three years later that opposition to the 35-hour work week among the delegates had clearly waned, it still seemed unlikely that the union would risk conducting a strike for this goal upon expiration of the old general framework contract in 1984.

But the employers, the West German public, the DGB's accommodationists and even some constituencies within IG Metall itself were surprised at how the persistent crisis of the early 1980s had toughened the union. Unable to prevent absolute wage losses for its members for three consecutive years, faced with a disadvantageous labor market, terrified by the "job-killing" implications of new technology, and confronted with an SPD in disarray and a hostile government in Bonn, IG Metall reemerged willy-nilly as a leading Gegenmacht in the Federal Republic's political economy. As the two sides drifted apart in the winter and early spring of 1984, it became clear that the employers wanted to isolate IG Metall to the point that the union would not dare begin a strike for fear of being defeated due to large desertions from its own ranks.

To that end, the employers conducted a public relations campaign against the 35-hour work week and IG Metall, the ferocity of which was unprecedented in the history of the Federal Republic. The employers distributed free booklets in trains and set up hundreds of information booths lining the busy shopping malls of the Federal Republic's inner cities denouncing this demand as ruinous to the economy. While the enthusiastic support of the conservative press for the employers was not surprising, the CDU-led government's unbridled opposition to IG Metall's demand, expressed in tones of rarely heard acerbity, constituted a departure from the traditional ritual of pre-contract behavior. With the SPD and the Greens closing ranks behind IG Metall, the battle for the 35-hour work week soon assumed an "overdetermined" character, pitting the "progress-ive" or "irresponsible" opposition spearheaded by IG Metall against the "reactionary" or "responsible" government represented by the employers. Because of the intensity of the conflicts, the 35-hour work week became the most widely discussed and best-known union demand ever articulated in the Federal Republic.

The impasse had worsened to such an extent by April 1984 that some industrial action seemed inevitable. While the union continued to insist on a substantial reduction in weekly work time, the employers adamantly maintained their counteroffer featuring early retirement for older workers and increased flexibility in work-time regulations on the plant level. In early May, IG Metall finally initiated strike action, once again relying on its trusted bargaining area of North Württemberg/North Baden in its Stuttgart district. To the great surprise of the employers and the public – both of whom had assumed that less than the required 75% of the eligible union members would approve their leadership's decision to begin a strike – well over 80% voted in support of industrial action. When the same results occurred a few days later in IG Metall's Hesse district (where the union had not conducted a strike since the early 1950s), the employers were forced to admit that they had underestimated IG Metall's organizational resolve and capabilities.

By conducting strikes in Hesse and North Württemberg/North Baden at the same time, IG Metall shattered a tradition dating back to the union's birth. Never before in its existence had the Federal Republic's most important union gone on strike simultaneously in two of its bargaining areas. With the help of well-targeted point strikes – the union's trademark since the 1950s – IG Metall hoped to incapacitate the major automobile producers with production facilities in these two areas. The success of the union's strategy could be gauged by the employers' enraged response; they immediately called widespread lockouts in both bargaining regions. These direct or "hot" lockouts received added support from "cold" or indirect ones which, as already mentioned, resulted from a controversial decision on the part of the Federal Labor Office's director, who decided not to award short-time work compensation to workers suffering temporary layoffs as a consequence of the strike. This action, while ultimately rescinded by the courts, impaired IG Metall's maneuverability through much of the strike's duration. At the height of the conflict, in the middle of June 1984, well over 400,000 metalworkers were directly or indirectly involved in this industrial conflict.

Nevertheless, the spirit of compromise between the two contestants had not yet been irreparably damaged. Georg Leber, the flamboyant former leader of IG Bau-Steine-Erden and the very embodiment of compromise and accommodationism, was chosen by IG Metall and the employers as special arbitrator for what had become an embarrassing and expensive impasse for both parties.

In addition to his well-known skills as a negotiator, Leber enjoyed IG Metall's confidence because he was a respected member of the Social Democratic Party, a long-time leader of a major DGB union and, most importantly for this particular conflict, a strong believer in the economic necessity and moral validity of all forms of work-time reduction, including the gradual move towards the 35-hour work week. To the employers, Leber represented the ideal accommodationist union leader whose measured views and cautious tactics they urgently needed for a proper conclusion to this struggle.

Leber's compromise, which was announced in late June of 1984, explicitly articulated the credo governing labor–capital relations throughout much of the Federal Republic's history: The agreement had to give full consideration to the workers' social needs and recognize their plight as legitimate. At the same time, however, it had to be cognizant of the demands placed on West German industry in an increasingly competitive world market and avoid measures which could impair capital's international flexibility.

Leber's compromise featured the following major terms: With the 40-hour work week to continue until April 1, 1985, wages and salaries in the metal industry would increase by 3.3% for the period between July 1, 1984 and April 1, 1985. As of the latter date, weekly work time would be set at an average per worker of 38.5 hours. In other words, while certain employees could continue working 40 hours, others would put in only 37 hours to yield a company average of 38.5 hours computed over a two-month period. How this three-hour flexibility would be implemented depended on the negotiations between the management of each company and its works council. The compromise empowered the latter body to monitor the arrangement on a monthly basis to ascertain whether the 38.5 hour average was appropriately implemented. Any deviations would constitute a violation of the contact.

In terms of remuneration, the compromise called for a 3.9% wage and salary increase for everybody starting to work 38.5 hours a week on April 1, 1985. Someone working exactly 38.5 hours as of April 1 would maintain the level of remuneration which he/she earned during the 40-hour work week ending on March 31, 1985, as a consequence of receiving the 3.9% "equalizer." For employees working less than the company average of 38.5 hours per week, further compensation was decreed which would align their level of remuneration with that enjoyed by their colleagues who worked the full 38.5 hours. Those exceeding the new limit had to be paid overtime. These provisions made the 38.5 hour work week the new norm in the Federal Republic's metal industry, contractually replacing its 40-hour predecessor.

In addition to these regulations, every employee was to receive a 2% pay increase beginning April 1, 1985 and extending until March 31, 1986, the expiration date of the entire package. Up to ten hours of overtime work per week and twenty hours per month were permissible, although under special circumstances certain individuals and groups were allowed to exceed this limit. Each worker had the right to receive remuneration for overtime in the form of extra vacations which had to be granted – and taken – within three months of the performed labor. All matters concerning the regulation of overtime work and pay had to occur in consultation with the works council at the company level.

Lastly, the compromise also called for an early retirement plan for elderly workers. Accordingly, 58-year-old workers who had been with the same company for five years or more were allowed to retire at 65% of their gross wages. Workers with twenty years of company loyalty were entitled to 70% of their latest remuneration.[24]

With the ratification votes of both IG Metall bargaining areas largely – though far from convincingly – tallied in favor of the proposed settlement, the bitterest conflict in this union's history ended. IG Metall's leader, Hans Mayr, described the settlement as a victory for millions of workers both in West Germany and Europe, while his counterpart from the employers' association, Wolfram Thiele, praised the final outcome as "historic."[25]

But this "historic compromise" did not conclude strike activities in the Federal Republic that summer. As mentioned, IG Metall's activist partner, IG Druck und Papier, was engaged in a struggle of its own. While echoing the metalworkers' demand for a shorter work week, the printers' union also pushed for an agenda specific to its own needs. IG Druck sought to have the old wage categorization redefined so as to provide more protection and higher remuneration for some of the industry's threatened skilled workers. Moreover, the union wanted to redraft its standing agreement on protection against rationalization, by downplaying its advocacy of defensive responses in favor of more active and interventionist remedies. This, of course, entailed the introduction of co-determination which, as will be recalled, was prohibited in the country's media-related establishments.

From the breakdown of negotiations in late February, it was clear to the IG Druck leadership that it could not again risk a confrontation with the employers in which the latter would resort to lockouts. Thus, the union organized a series of hit-and-run strikes involving a total of 46,000 union members over a thirteen-week period. While this tactic did indeed avoid lockouts, it also reduced the strike's overall effectiveness, since – with the help of modern production methods – most newspapers could assemble at least fragmentary editions with a handful of people. IG Druck could not risk further escalations (such as plant occupations) since it already had to endure being a virtual outcast in the eyes of the printing employers, the employers' federation and the government because of the reputed radicalism of some of its leaders. Less important than IG Metall but even more vociferous, IG Druck found itself in a particularly uncomfortable situation. Even though the union showed every sign of accepting the mediation efforts of the special arbitrator Kurt Biedenkopf, an eminent professor, labor expert and CDU politician, the employers rejected Biedenkopf's proposal, forcing his resignation.[26] Not until the conclusion of the metal-industry strike did the printing employers negotiate seriously with IG Druck. This resulted in an agreement in July which ended the longest industrial conflict in the German printing industry since the nineteenth century.

Although similar to the metal industry's "Leber model" IG Druck's deal with the employers featured some differences worthy of mention: first, rather than adopt the individualization of the metal industry's agreement, wherein one worker might labor 40 hours per week and another in the same plant only 37, the settlement in printing assumed a collective dimension. The contract required everybody in a company to work the same number of hours, averaging 38.5 per week computed on a quarterly, semi-annual or annual basis. In other words, a company as a whole might work 40 hours per person per week for one month, 37 hours the next and 38.5 the third month to attain the average. The contract left it up to specific company arrangements as to which time spans would ultimately be chosen.

Second, the agreement in the printing industry had a longer duration, lasting until March 31, 1987. Third, it included a new wage categorization which elevated a number of skilled workers into higher classifications, thereby increasing their remuneration. Lastly, while failing to attain any anticipatory measures of intervention against the adverse effects of rationalization, the new arrangement added substantial padding to the already considerable cushioning mechanisms.[27]

The strikes highlighted a number of attitudes and practices that have played a crucial role in providing continuity for capital–labor relations in the Federal Republic. Most important among them was the belief in the value of compromise, allowing both parties to claim a victory vis-à-vis their respective constituencies and the West German public. The employers argued that their efforts had been rewarded by the new agreements. They weakened the solidaristic strategy of the unions and augmented the powers of the more compliant works councils by making these institutions officially responsible for implementing the contracts' flexible schemes on the shop floor. Lastly, even as far as the loss of the 40-hour work week was concerned, the employers pointed to the limited duration of the new contracts, which included nothing about further reductions of weekly work time.

The unions could also be jubilant about the results. First and foremost, the employers' rule of "not one minute under 40 hours," which they defended with the explicit endorsement of the CDU-led government, had been defeated. IG Metall and IG Druck broke a barrier which few believed was penetrable before the strikes began, and thereby took a major step on the slow and arduous road towards the 35-hour work week, seven years after this demand began to appear prominently in their programmatic statements. Given the fact that it took from the 1890s until 1919 to reach the eight-hour work day and another 46 years to attain the 40-hour work week, this contract represents a significant achievement.

Second, IG Metall and IG Druck had never before confronted such an explicitly hostile alliance of industry and government, supported by a widely held suspicion on the part of the public – including large numbers of workers – regarding the legitimacy and feasibility of the unions' demands. Despite this formidable opposition, the unions stood firm, and were not afraid to conduct what they knew would be lengthy, costly and perhaps highly divisive strikes. Contrary to the employers' and the government's expectations, the union effort was not timid or poorly organized, and never showed any signs of collapsing.

Third, just as the employers viewed the contracts' silence about any further reduction in weekly work time as prima facie evidence of their success in preventing the implementation of the 35-hour work week, IG Metall and IG Druck saw this as an open invitation to continue their struggle come 1986 and 1987 respectively. Lastly, the strike exhibited an unexpectedly high solidarity among the DGB unions. During the active phases of the industrial conflict, all DGB unions, including the accommodationists, rallied behind their activist rivals with frequent statements of support and a number of large-scale demonstrations. Especially on the local level, both in Hesse and in the Stuttgart area, all unions participated (under the DGB's leadership) in various strike-support activities. With two of their sister organizations engaged in a major struggle against an alliance of employers and CDU-led government, the DGB unions demonstrated convincingly that they could set aside their major differences at least for a short time and fulfill their mandate as the collective representatives of the West German working class. This temporary unity did not, however, relieve the underlying tensions between the two factions, as will be discussed below.

The strike results also posed some major challenges to the unions. Most important among them was the fact that a reduction of 90 minutes in weekly work time hardly seemed sufficient to have any effect in providing desperately needed jobs. Thus, one of the supposed advantages of weekly work-time reduction as opposed to early retirement and other schemes supported by the accommodationists was lost in the empirical reality of the 38.5-hour work week.[28]

In addition, IG Metall had to monitor the tenets of the agreement in an unprecedented fashion. Many union members, including some leaders, recognized that if IG Metall was not careful to provide detailed guidelines for the contract's implementation to works councilors belonging to the union and to its shop stewards, the agreement's company-based flexibility would result in a divisiveness which could permanently damage IG Metall's powers of collective representation.

This "concrete company syndicalism" (betonierter Betriebssyndikalismus), as one observed called the agreement, further contributed to the tendency of the powerful works councilors to make their own "local" deals with management, thereby fostering an atmosphere of "wildcat cooperation."[29] In notable contrast to IG Metall's highly touted though little-used policy of plant-level collective bargaining (betriebsnahe Tarifpolitik), which, as will be recalled, envisioned a localized bargaining strategy controlled by the unions in direct challenge to the works councils, the new agreement threatened to have exactly the opposite effect. Whereas in the former scheme plant-level variations formed part of an official contract between the employers and the union, giving the union the power, particularly via its shop stewards, to control actual implementation, the new agreement put the works councils in charge of adapting the highly flexible terms of this contract to the conditions in their particular companies. In other words, while plant-level collective bargaining sought to strengthen the shop-floor power of unions, the new 38.5-hour contract had the opposite effect by delegating the implementation of plant-specific provisions to the works councils.[30]

Lastly, the strike reactivated public rivalry between activists and accommodationists. While it is true that during the strikes themselves intra-DGB solidarity seemed to work impeccably, especially in the areas most affected by the action, IG Metall remained very bitter about the fact that the "gang of five" had openly and repeatedly spurned the 35-hour work week as a desirable goal for labor, thereby hampering IG Metall's and IG Druck's mobilization efforts and undermining the credibility of their demands. While some members of the IG Metall executive committee acccused the acommodationist unions of holding back in their assistance during the strike, the latter replied no less emphatically that their support for IG Metall's strike activities was genuine.[31] As to their concentration on other work-reduction schemes, the accommodationists argued that it was the prerogative of each union within the DGB to pursue whatever strategy it deemed best for its interests. Only repeated interventions by DGB leader Ernst Breit – who argued that one of the federation's main strengths lay in the diversity of collective bargaining approaches permitted its constituent members, thereby acknowledging the validity of all forms of work-time reduction – helped abate the skirmishing between these two factions.[32]

But the strike and its aftermath only accentuated other differences in the collective bargaining strategies pursued by these two adversaries. On the issue of technological control in connection with the increased pace of rationalization, IG Metall and its allies exhibited at least a surface radicalism by recognizing that labor must play an active role in the formation of what promises to be a substantially altered work environment. While none of the activist unions have thus far succeeded in securing comprehensive contracts to this end, the very fact that they seem concerned with this matter exemplifies the divergent attitudes separating them from their social-partnership-oriented colleagues. The latter have by and large continued to accept management's prerogative on shaping technology in the production process provided that the employers reward labor for its cooperation with comprehensive protection schemes. The more modest ambitions of the acommodationists have thus far been vindicated.

In other aspects of bargaining as well, the strategies of these two wings of the organized labor movment differ. For example, whereas unions belonging to the "gang of five" have more or less openly accepted wage restraint as the most beneficial plan for labor in an economy characterized by crisis and uncertainty, IG Metall and its activist entourage still maintain that the Agartz formula of an active, if not "expansive," wage policy constitutes the unions' best strategy. To that end, the activists have not shied away from mobilizing their membership during bargaining rounds. Whereas most of the accommodationists' negotiations with the employers since the onset of the crisis have been quick and quiet affairs, IG Metall and its allies developed the mobilizing strategy of "new maneuverability" which they have frequently deployed during the early 1980s. With the Federal Labor Court declaring legal all warning strikes conducted as part of labor's "new maneuverability," it would not be surprising to see the activist unions resort to this mobilization tactic in many future bargaining rounds.[33]

Tensions between accommodationists and activists concerning organized labor's strategy in dealing with the state date back to the latter years of the 1970s when the Schmidt government began instituting its austerity measures. Until Schmidt's departure from the seat of power on September 30, 1982, the accommodationist unions were among the government's closest allies within social democracy. Clearly, this close association and "bungalow" relationship changed abruptly with the arrival of Helmut Kohl in Bonn. However, despite icy relations between the unions and the Kohl government, the accommodationist wing of the DGB has repeatedly made it known that it would not oppose the formation of a grand coalition between the CDU and the SPD under the leadership of a chancellor provided by the former party. In other words, the accommodationists' traditional "state fixation" and their equally well-developed emphasis on the importance of unions as "factors of order" helped them create a bridge in their views of the two Helmuts and their respective parties in Bonn.

The activists on the other hand grew increasingly impatient with Helmut Schmidt's policies, although their loyalties to social democracy muted their criticism considerably. By the early 1980s the government's measures had become sufficiently unbearable to the activists to warrant the organization of a major union demonstration protesting Schmidt's austerity package. This disillusionment changed to utter despair and anger with the arrival of the Kohl government in October 1982. Were it not for the accommodationists and the DGB leadership, the West German labor movement would have had virtually no contact with the federal government since the departure of the social–liberal coalition. The activists continue to view the Kohl government with suspicion and fear, thereby preventing an improvement in relations. Firmly opposed to a grand coaliton between the Social and Christian Democrats, the activists have accentuated German labor's other main tradition, to act as a "countervailing power." IG Metall and its allies see their role as embodying the progressive opposition to an increasingly reactionary coalition of employers and government.[34]

In this context, one has to analyze the divisions within the DGB over how to deal with the SPD and the Greens. As responses to recent events demonstrate, there continues to exist a considerable harmony between the DGB unions and the SPD – and increasingly the Greens. For example, in the extensive parliamentary debates concerning the Federal Labor

Office's measure to discontinue payments for short-time work to workers indirectly affected by the strikes of 1984, every speaker belonging to the two opposition parties, the Greens and the SPD, condemned the measure and rallied unequivocally to IG Metall's cause. Conversely, all representatives of the CDU/CSU and FDP who spoke on the issue defended the Office's ruling.[35] In short, acute crises such as the strikes of 1984 and prolonged predicaments such as the Kohl government's persistent refusal to institute major programs to battle unemployment have created an opposition bloc consisting of DGB unions, the SPD and the Greens. But the intra-DGB conflict between activists and accommodationists has clearly influenced organized labor's positions within this opposition bloc and has affected its relationship to the bloc's two other members.

Because of their uncritical acceptance of the logic of growth and its concomitant statism, centralism, incrementalism and technocratic orientation, the accommodationist unions have categorically rejected an alliance with the Greens. Leaders of the "gang of five" unions have been among the most outspoken critics of the Greens and their ancillary social movements, accusing them of being naive dreamers, subversive revolutionaries or, significantly, anti-growth reactionaries. As demonstrated by Hermann Rappe's repeated attacks on the peace movement and by a study commissioned by the food-processing workers' union (NGG) warning West German citizens of the adverse economic consequences of an excessive concern with ecological purity, the accommodationists reject the very *raison d'être* of the Greens as antithetical to an industrial society, and thus to the labor movement.[36] The accommodationists also explicitly oppose any "greening" tendencies within the SPD. This pertains as much to specific positions on issues such as the deployment of medium-range missiles in West Germany as it does to the more general possibility of a "red–green" coalition. The accommodationists deplore social democracy's flirtation with the Greens and view it as detrimental to the party's future viability as a political actor in the Federal Republic. Above all, since this wing of the DGB believes that organized labor's fate in West Germany is inextricably tied to the fortunes of a politically moderate, growth-oriented and statist Social Democratic Party, it vehemently opposes all tendencies which could in any way jeopardize the existence of such an entity.

While it would be wrong to argue that the DGB's activist unions have embraced the Greens as allies, there can be no doubt that a certain thaw bordering on rapprochement has occurred between elements of these two groups. As late as September 1983, inter-union solidarity was sufficiently strong, even between activist IG Metall and accommodationist IG Chemie, for the former to cancel the scheduled appearance at IG Metall's congress of a Green leader who had been expelled from IG Chemie a decade earlier, in order to avoid offending the latter union.[37] Barely one year later, leading members of the metalworkers' union repeatedly expressed laudatory opinions of the Greens, and praised them as a positive force in West German politics. At HBV's congress in November 1984, the delegates of the retail trade, banking and insurance workers' union passed a resolution mandating close collaboration between HBV and the "new social movements". In an interesting parallel to the mobilization period of the late 1960s and early 1970s, when the extra-parliamentary opposition and the student movement – in many ways the Greens' intellectual and structural precursors – established a close relationship with some unions, certain issues of the 1980s have provided common areas of interest and struggle. Like the activists of the 1960s, who embraced investment control and Ostpolitik in quest of such larger ends as enhancement of worker participation and peace, the Greens concentrate their efforts on alleviating unemployment and the abolition of missiles, upholding the same goals as their predecessors. The activist unions, as will be recalled, pride themselves on maintaining a tradition which has been very receptive to these appeals. Thus, when the "red" Greens count the battle against unemployment, uncontrolled introduction of new technologies and lockouts among their very first priorities, most activist unions cannot help but express gratitude.[38] When it also becomes clear to many unionists that their commonalities with the "red" Greens in good part derive from a shared disappointment with accommodationist-style social democracy, the seemingly insurmountable distance separating the two groups appears a lot smaller. Although the activist unions are as hostile to the Greens' cruder forms of no-growth ecologism as their accommodationist colleagues, one can nevertheless detect a growing eco-consciousness among certain unions belonging to the former group. This in no way implies that the activists have resolved the contradictions inherent in the dichotomy between economy and ecology. Rather, one could argue that reformers within the unions have been forced to begin a lengthy process of reflection with regard to ecology and the "new social movements." This sensitization will undoubtedly have a profound influence on social democracy and the SPD.

## IV.  PROSPECTS FOR THE FUTURE

While it is always risky to venture into the realm of prediction, the behavior of the West German labor movement over the next decade provides a topic for speculation which should spare this writer major embarrassment. By and large continuity will prevail. This, however, in no way excludes important changes at the margin. These changes, it is safe to assume, will make life more difficult for unions in the Federal Republic. The coming years will require greater efforts to respond to these challenges, demand more innovative strategies and compromises, and ultimately lead to less stable solutions. This will pertain as much to relations between the two main factions within the federation as to labor's interaction with capital, the political parties and the state. But if the unions' post-1945 history can be used with some accuracy to gauge their future, the unions will make every effort to adapt to changing circumstances.

It is significant, for example, that in the midst of the heightened antagonism between IG Metall and the metal employers surrounding the strike for the 35-hour work week, the two found it not only possible but necessary to initiate an overhaul of the metal industry's vocational training program, which had been based largely on job requirements dating from the 1930s and 1940s.[39] With little fanfare and minimal public reaction, the union and the employers cooperated in the creation of a new apprenticeship program to furnish the metal industry with versatile skilled workers able to perform a multitude of jobs requiring new skills and knowledge. Equally telling is the fact that the employers' association, BDA, and its most powerful constituent member, Gesamtmetall, have been outspoken opponents of the Kohl government's bill to reform the 1972 Works Constitution Law. While the government's reform is aimed at weakening the intra-company presence of the DGB unions at the direct expense of more conservative – and thus presumably more compliant – labor organizations, the employers would rather see the continuation of the status quo than have to deal with the individualized and fragmented shop-floor representation favored by the government. Despite tensions induced by the crisis, there will remain crucial areas of overall consensus between labor and capital in West Germany.[40]

German workers never had a history of machine wrecking and virtually every DGB publication concerning questions of technology and industrialization proudly reaffirms that tradition. This pro-technological attitude will not disappear in the near future, though it is already in the process of undergoing some significant changes.[41] With the growing understanding on the part of a hitherto relatively secure and comfortable working class of the link between the intoduction of new technologies and the persistence of record unemployment, many workers have begun to see technology in the context of power. As an IG Metall program published in 1985 and entitled "Work and Technology – People Must Stay!" put it: technology can fragment work, render it unbearable and destroy it. However, it can also give it new content, lend it additional meaning and enhance human creativity. Which course it follows remains ultimately an issue of political power.[42]

The unions will have to confront issues related to political power in a period when their own is likely to remain impaired. They will continue to depend on the trusted combination of self-reliance and their "state fixation." With the latter option made difficult for them under a CDU-led government and with no major improvements assured even under SPD leadership, the unions' reliance on their own resources looks like the more promising of the two options. The evidence points towards a continuation in this direction with little substantial change.

The accommodationists' self-reliance will continue to accentuate their company-oriented particularism, through which they will defend the interests of their own members to the direct exclusion of other workers. In contrast, the activists seem more intent than ever on reviving the radicalism of the pre-Godesberg 1950s, even hearkening back to the Marxist tones of the DGB's founding program of 1949. All indications point to a continuation of this collectivism by the activists.

The outlook for West German labor and its contribution to democracy in the Federal Republic invites optimism. Ideally, the unions will use the issue of unemployment to establish lasting links with other disadvantaged groups in society, such as women, foreign workers and the young, all of whom are in desperate need of a unifying political structure with respectability and power. By reaching beyond the quantitative view of (un)employment as jobs, and envisioning it in the larger context of control, the unions would be able to provide a much-needed synthesis between ecology and economy. Some of the activists' arguments concerning the 35-hour work week's integrative and collectivist dimensions have already begun to aim in this direction. The pan-party structure of the West German unions would be ideal for such a coalition, since it is hard to imagine the existing party system aggregating such disparate elements in an effective and equitable manner. For this to happen, it is clear that the unions would have to transform their passive independence of parties into an active one, and thereby assume a leadership position in furthering the democratization of the Federal Republic.

Even the worst scenario for organized labor seems at least acceptable in the larger framework of modern German history. For even if the unions degenerate into selfish, particularistic, company-oriented interest groups, they will still find it impossible to neglect their mandate of maintaining the democratic Rechtsstaat in the Federal Republic. The nightmare of the recent past, in which organized labor paid a particularly high price, has rendered even the most compliant of the accommodationist unions into vigilant guardians of West German democracy.

Moreover, labor need not worry. For despite the attacks on the unions by "capital and cabinet" since 1982, Bonn is not Weimar. Unlike in the latter when social democracy and its unions proved the only staatstreu defenders of the republic, the Federal Republic and its institutions enjoy capital's fullest support. There are absolutely no signs of this changing in the foreseeable future.

Ultimately, the heavy burden of Germany's past will remain the most reliable guarantor of stable capital–labor relations in the Federal Republic. The employers and the unions know only too well how horrible things could be – and in fact have been – when rapport between them disintegrates into warfare. If there exists one overriding characteristic of post-war West German labor unions, it is the deep commitment – even obsession – never to allow such a breakdown to occur again.

# Appendix 1   *Membership of DGB Unions, 1983*

| Union | Total | Manual workers (blue-collar workers) | Employees (white-collar workers) | Civil servants | Percentage of DGB membership |
|---|---|---|---|---|---|
| IG Metall, IGM (metalworkers' union) | 2,535,644 | 2,148,262 | 387,382 | — | 32.7 |
| Gew. Öffentliche Dienste Transport und Verkehr, ÖTV (public service and transport workers' union) | 1,173,525 | 575,443 | 510,693 | 87,389 | 15.1 |
| IG Chemie-Papier-Keramik, IG CPK (chemical, paper and ceramic workers' union) | 635,276 | 515,057 | 120,219 | — | 8.2 |
| IG Bau-Steine-Erden, IG BSE (construction workers' union) | 523,129 | 480,817 | 42,312 | — | 6.8 |
| Deutsche Postgewerkschaft, DPG (postal workers' union) | 457,929 | 142,881 | 44,979 | 270,069 | 5.9 |
| Gew. der Eisenbahner Deutschlands, GdED (railroad workers' union) | 379,534 | 189,434 | 7,990 | 182,110 | 4.9 |
| IG Bergbau und Energie, IGBE (mineworkers' union) | 366,328 | 318,423 | 47,676 | 229 | 4.7 |
| Gew. Handel, Banken und Versicherungen, HBV (commerce, banking and insurance workers' union) | 360,372 | 48,234 | 312,138 | — | 4.7 |
| Gew. Textil-Bekleidung, GTB (textile-clothing workers' union) | 263,920 | 238,103 | 25,817 | — | 3.4 |
| Gew. Nahrung-Genuss-Gaststätten, NGG (food-processing workers' union) | 263,525 | 209,870 | 53,655 | — | 3.4 |
| Gew. Erziehung und Wissenschaft GEW (education and science union) | 185,490 | — | 46,749 | 138,741 | 2.4 |
| Gew. der Polizei, GdP (police union) | 167,572 | 9,073 | 16,885 | 141,614 | 2.2 |
| Gew. Holz und Kunststoff, GHK (wood and plastic workers' union) | 149,724 | 139,144 | 10,580 | — | 1.9 |
| IG Druck und Papier, IG DRUPA (printing and paper workers' union) | 144,344 | 112,975 | 31,369 | — | 1.9 |
| Gew. Leder (leather workers' union) | 50,684 | 47,839 | 2,845 | — | 0.7 |
| Gew. Kunst (artists and musicians' union) | 46,668 | — | 46,668 | — | 0.6 |
| Gew. Gartenbau, Land und Forstwirtschaft, GLF (horticulture, agriculture and forestry workers' union) | 42,249 | 36,636 | 2,919 | 2,694 | 0.5 |
| DGB totals | 7,745,913 | 5,212,191 | 1,710,876 | 822,846 | 100.0 |

*Source: Die Quelle*, Vol. 35, no. 5 (May 1984), p. 313.

Appendix 2   *Membership development of DGB since 1950*

| Year | Total membership | Annual change from previous year Absolute | In % | Women | Manual workers (blue-collar workers) | Employees (white-collar workers) | Civil servants |
|---|---|---|---|---|---|---|---|
| 1950 | 5,449,990 | — | — | 840,712 | 4,534,565 | 571,332 | 344,093 |
| 1951 | 5,912,125 | +462,135 | +8.4 | 1,011,436 | 4,924,314 | 626,998 | 360,813 |
| 1952 | 6,004,476 | +92,351 | +1.6 | 1,028,713 | 4,982,564 | 647,632 | 374,280 |
| 1953 | 6,051,221 | +46,745 | +0.8 | 1,046,148 | 5,011,175 | 645,201 | 394,845 |
| 1954 | 6,103,343 | +52,122 | +0.9 | 1,055,213 | 5,052,366 | 641,001 | 409,976 |
| 1955 | 6,104,872 | +1,529 | +0.0 | 1,047,805 | 5,042,365 | 642,340 | 420,167 |
| 1956 | 6,124,547 | +19,675 | +0.3 | 1,043,241 | 5,042,882 | 648,469 | 433,196 |
| 1957 | 6,244,386 | +119,839 | +2.0 | 1,077,652 | 5,113,016 | 675,213 | 456,157 |
| 1958 | 6,331,735 | +87,349 | +1.4 | 1,089,527 | 5,171,657 | 690,724 | 469,354 |
| 1959 | 6,273,741 | −57,994 | −0.9 | 1,070,762 | 5,092,154 | 691,476 | 490,111 |
| 1960 | 6,378,820 | +105,079 | +1.7 | 1,093,607 | 5,144,452 | 721,658 | 512,710 |
| 1961 | 6,382,396 | +3,576 | +0.1 | 1,078,617 | 5 129,706 | 724,200 | 528,490 |
| 1962 | 6,430,428 | +48,032 | +0.8 | 1,058,453 | 5,131,124 | 756,767 | 542,537 |
| 1963 | 6,430,978 | +550 | +0.0 | 1,033,842 | 5,107,985 | 767,110 | 555,883 |
| 1964 | 6,485,471 | +54,493 | +0.8 | 1,022,052 | 5,126,073 | 789,829 | 569,569 |
| 1965 | 6,574,491 | +89,020 | +1.4 | 1,030,185 | 5,157,290 | 835,202 | 581,999 |
| 1966 | 6,537,160 | −37,331 | −0.6 | 1,014,833 | 5,084,552 | 861,160 | 591,448 |
| 1967 | 6,407,733 | −129,427 | −2.0 | 976,793 | 4,922,721 | 878,982 | 606,030 |
| 1968 | 6,375,972 | −31,761 | −0.5 | 971,590 | 4,863,591 | 896,492 | 615,889 |
| 1969 | 6,482,390 | +106,418 | +1.7 | 984,074 | 4,926,943 | 930,233 | 625,214 |
| 1970 | 6,712,547 | +230,157 | +3.6 | 1,027,150 | 5,088,713 | 986,112 | 637,722 |
| 1971 | 6,868,662 | +156,115 | +2.3 | 1,050,488 | 5,153,000 | 1,065,550 | 650,112 |
| 1972 | 6,985,548 | +116,886 | +1.7 | 1,115,266 | 5,188,890 | 1,140,803 | 655,855 |
| 1973 | 7,167,523 | +181,975 | +2.6 | 1,179,762 | 5,286,964 | 1,206,152 | 674,407 |
| 1974 | 7,405,760 | +238,237 | +3.3 | 1,284,500 | 5,416,282 | 1,313,586 | 675,892 |
| 1975 | 7,364,912 | −40,848 | −0.6 | 1,313,021 | 5,310,435 | 1,381,774 | 672,703 |
| 1976 | 7,400,021 | +35,109 | +0.5 | 1,353,958 | 5,265,983 | 1,435,724 | 698,314 |
| 1977 | 7,470,967 | +70,946 | +1.0 | 1,402,643 | 5,289,361 | 1,483,241 | 698,365 |
| 1978 | 7,751,523 | +280,556 | +3.8 | 1,482,349 | 5,370,488 | 1,548,947 | 832,088 |
| 1979 | 7,843,565 | +92,042 | +1.2 | 1,540,832 | 5,387,356 | 1,609,960 | 846,249 |
| 1980 | 7,882,527 | +38,962 | +0.5 | 1,596,274 | 5,376,454 | 1,658,121 | 847,952 |
| 1981 | 7,957,512 | +74,985 | +1.0 | 1,650,773 | 5,410,578 | 1,703,449 | 843,485 |
| 1982 | 7,849,003 | −108,509 | −1.4 | 1,649,399 | 5,319,430 | 1,701,657 | 827,916 |
| 1983 | 7,745,913 | −103,090 | −1.3 | 1,644,770 | 5,212,191 | 1,710,876 | 822,846 |

*Sources*: Reinhard Jühe, Horst-Udo Niedenhoff and Wolfgang Pege, *Gewerkschaften in der Bundesrepublik Deutschland* (Cologne: Deutscher Instituts Verlag, 1977), p. 62; Deutscher Gewerkschaftsbund, *Geschäftsbericht 1978 bis 1981* (Düsseldorf: Deutscher Gewerkschaftsbund, 1982), pp. 465–468; *Die Quelle*, Vol. 33, no. 4 (April 1982), pp. 247, 249; *Die Quelle*, Vol. 34, no. 5 (May 1983), pp. 317, 319; and *Die Quelle*, Vol. 35, no. 5 (May 1984), pp. 313–314.

Appendix 3 *Membership development of IG Metall since 1950*

| Year | Total membership | Annual change from previous year Absolute | In % | Women | Manual workers (blue-collar workers) | Employees (white-collar workers) | Civil servants |
|---|---|---|---|---|---|---|---|
| 1950 | 1,290,670 | — | — | 135,579 | 1,199,202 | 91,468 | — |
| 1951 | 1,528,121 | +237,451 | +18.4 | 175,250 | 1,422,345 | 105,776 | — |
| 1952 | 1,580,467 | +52,346 | +3.4 | 183,440 | 1,469,834 | 110,633 | — |
| 1953 | 1,604,140 | +23,673 | +1.5 | 186,928 | 1,491,850 | 112,290 | — |
| 1954 | 1,658,298 | +54,158 | +3.4 | 200,089 | 1,549,304 | 108,994 | — |
| 1955 | 1,657,840 | −458 | −0.0 | 199,782 | 1,541,827 | 116,013 | — |
| 1956 | 1,660,913 | +3,073 | +0.2 | 204,786 | 1,542,947 | 117,966 | — |
| 1957 | 1,720,120 | +59,207 | +3.6 | 218,391 | 1,594,551 | 125,569 | — |
| 1958 | 1,762,438 | +42,318 | +2.5 | 216,428 | 1,635,894 | 126,544 | — |
| 1959 | 1,750,475 | −11,963 | −0.7 | 215,066 | 1,623,252 | 127,223 | — |
| 1960 | 1,842,818 | +92,343 | +5.3 | 226,667 | 1,705,929 | 136,889 | — |
| 1961 | 1,849,572 | +6,754 | +0.4 | 214,920 | 1,712,157 | 137,415 | — |
| 1962 | 1,903,690 | +54,118 | +2.9 | 218,897 | 1,756,979 | 146,711 | — |
| 1963 | 1,895,802 | −7,888 | −0.4 | 214,271 | 1,742,226 | 153,576 | — |
| 1964 | 1,936,676 | +40,874 | +2.2 | 208,453 | 1,773,773 | 162,903 | — |
| 1965 | 2,011,313 | +74,637 | +3.9 | 214,673 | 1,829,880 | 181,433 | — |
| 1966 | 2,023,891 | +12,578 | +0.6 | 213,253 | 1,832,857 | 191,034 | — |
| 1967 | 1,957,946 | −65,945 | −3.3 | 197,412 | 1,763,191 | 194,755 | — |
| 1968 | 1,964,684 | +6,738 | +0.3 | 197,634 | 1,767,668 | 197,016 | — |
| 1969 | 2,070,980 | +106,296 | +5.4 | 208,340 | 1,858,021 | 212,959 | — |
| 1970 | 2,223,467 | +152,487 | +7.4 | 226,951 | 1,985,022 | 238,445 | — |
| 1971 | 2,312,294 | +88,827 | +4.0 | 245,672 | 2,047,887 | 264,407 | — |
| 1972 | 2,354,975 | +42,681 | +1.8 | 267,739 | 2,070,423 | 284,552 | — |
| 1973 | 2,640,697 | +105,772 | +4.5 | 302,005 | 2,141,279 | 319,418 | — |
| 1974 | 2,593,480 | +132,783 | +5.4 | 343,302 | 2,248,233 | 345,247 | — |
| 1975 | 2,556,184 | −37,296 | −1.4 | 337,614 | 2,206,168 | 350,016 | — |
| 1976 | 2,581,340 | +25,156 | +1.0 | 340,812 | 2,205,463 | 375,877 | — |
| 1977 | 2,624,388 | +43,048 | +1.7 | 355,621 | 2,238,245 | 386,143 | — |
| 1978 | 2,680,798 | +56,410 | +2.1 | 379,824 | 2,286,403 | 394,395 | — |
| 1979 | 2,684,509 | +3,711 | +0.1 | 380,387 | 2,284,866 | 399,643 | — |
| 1980 | 2,622,267 | −62,242 | −2.3 | 369,963 | 2,234,361 | 387,906 | — |
| 1981 | 2,622,069 | −198 | −0.0 | 376,908 | 2,234,247 | 387,822 | — |
| 1982 | 2,576,471 | −45,598 | −1.7 | 369,273 | 2,189,279 | 387,192 | — |
| 1983 | 2,535,644 | −40,827 | −1.6 | 361,981 | 2,148,262 | 387,382 | — |

*Sources*: Reinhard Jühe, Horst-Udo Niedenhoff, and Wolfgang Pege, *Gewerkschaften in der Bundesrepublik Deutschland* (Cologne: Deutscher Instituts Verlag, 1977), p. 74; Deutscher Gewerkschaftsbund, *Geschäftsbericht 1978 bis 1981* (Düsseldorf: Deutscher Gewerkschaftsbund, 1982), pp. 465–468; *Die Quelle*, Vol. 33, no. 4 (April 1982), pp. 247, 249; *Die Quelle*, Vol. 34, no. 5 (May 1983), pp. 317, 319; and *Die Quelle*, Vol. 35, no. 5 (May 1984), pp. 313–314.

Appendix 4  *Membership development of IG Chemie-Papier-Keramik since 1950*

| Year | Total membership | Annual change from previous year Absolute | In % | Women | Manual workers (blue-collar workers) | Employees (white-collar workers) | Civil servants |
|------|------|------|------|------|------|------|------|
| 1950 | 394,774 | — | — | 84,253 | 359,883 | 34,891 | — |
| 1951 | 452,684 | +57,910 | +14.7 | 100,856 | 413,478 | 39,206 | — |
| 1952 | 463,790 | +11,106 | +2.5 | 101,772 | 422,562 | 41,228 | — |
| 1953 | 451,650 | −12,140 | −2.6 | 98,588 | 415,916 | 35,734 | — |
| 1954 | 449,334 | −2,316 | −0.5 | 99,552 | 414,764 | 34,570 | — |
| 1955 | 456,576 | +7,242 | +1.6 | 100,258 | 442,066 | 34,510 | — |
| 1956 | 473,617 | +17,041 | +3.7 | 104,292 | 439,068 | 34,549 | — |
| 1957 | 485,413 | +11,796 | +2.5 | 104,410 | 449,577 | 35,836 | — |
| 1958 | 510,102 | +24,689 | +5.1 | 109,973 | 472,551 | 37,551 | — |
| 1959 | 510,611 | +509 | +0.1 | 107,864 | 472,423 | 38,188 | — |
| 1960 | 519,641 | +9,030 | +1.8 | 107,882 | 479,641 | 40,000 | — |
| 1961 | 524,737 | +5,096 | +1.0 | 103,813 | 482,147 | 42,590 | — |
| 1962 | 526,565 | +1,828 | +0.4 | 101,860 | 476,713 | 49,852 | — |
| 1963 | 523,334 | −3,231 | −0.6 | 99,119 | 471,853 | 51,481 | — |
| 1964 | 533,699 | +10,365 | +2.0 | 97,849 | 477,807 | 55,892 | — |
| 1965 | 542,160 | +8,461 | +1.6 | 97,328 | 481,890 | 60,270 | — |
| 1966 | 537,434 | −4,726 | −0.9 | 93,015 | 474,907 | 62,527 | — |
| 1967 | 527,834 | −9,600 | −1.8 | 87,869 | 462,733 | 65,101 | — |
| 1968 | 533,814 | +5,980 | +1.1 | 88,620 | 467,871 | 65,943 | — |
| 1969 | 552,552 | +18,738 | +3.5 | 91,577 | 482,170 | 70,382 | — |
| 1970 | 598,831 | +46,279 | +8.4 | 100,004 | 519,092 | 79,739 | — |
| 1971 | 613,057 | +14,226 | +2.4 | 103,599 | 526,095 | 86,962 | — |
| 1972 | 626,771 | +13,714 | +2.2 | 108,340 | 533,266 | 93,505 | — |
| 1973 | 645,178 | +18,407 | +2.9 | 113,032 | 545,665 | 99,513 | — |
| 1974 | 655,703 | +10,525 | +1.6 | 116,158 | 550,004 | 105,699 | — |
| 1975 | 644,271 | −11,432 | −1.7 | 114,162 | 533,557 | 110,714 | — |
| 1976 | 643,390 | −881 | −0.1 | 114,132 | 530,055 | 113,335 | — |
| 1977 | 651,037 | +7,647 | +1.2 | 117,278 | 534,443 | 116,594 | — |
| 1978 | 650,675 | −362 | −0.1 | 119,045 | 531,591 | 119,084 | — |
| 1979 | 657,920 | +7,245 | +1.1 | 122,129 | 538,110 | 119,810 | — |
| 1980 | 660,973 | +3,053 | +0.5 | 123,680 | 540,774 | 120,199 | — |
| 1981 | 654,633 | −6,340 | −1.0 | 123,705 | 534,252 | 120,381 | — |
| 1982 | 643,079 | −11,554 | −1.8 | 121,889 | 523,297 | 119,782 | — |
| 1983 | 635,276 | −7,803 | −1.2 | 120,197 | 515,057 | 120,219 | — |

*Sources:* Reinhard Jühe, Horst-Udo Niedenhoff and Wolfgang Pege, *Gewerkschaften in der Bundesrepublik Deutschland* (Cologne: Deutscher Instituts Verlag, 1977), p. 65; Deutscher Gewerkschaftsbund, *Geschäftsbericht 1978 bis 1981* (Düsseldorf: Deutscher Gewerkschaftsbund, 1982), pp. 465–468; *Die Quelle*, Vol. 33, no. 4 (April 1982), pp. 247, 249; *Die Quelle*, Vol. 34, no. 5 (May 1983), pp. 317, 319; and *Die Quelle*, Vol. 35, no. 5 (May 1984), pp. 313–314.

Appendix 5 *Membership development of IG Bau-Steine-Erden since 1950*

| Year | Total membership | Annual change from previous year Absolute | In % | Women | Manual workers (blue-collar workers) | Employees (white-collar workers) | Civil servants |
|------|------|------|------|------|------|------|------|
| 1950 | 389,470 | — | — | 5,534 | 376,071 | 13,399 | — |
| 1951 | 432,918 | +43,448 | +11.2 | 6,536 | 415,621 | 17,297 | — |
| 1952 | 410,346 | −22,572 | −5.2 | 4,874 | 394,729 | 15,617 | — |
| 1953 | 422,825 | +12,479 | +3.1 | 4,573 | 404,342 | 18,483 | — |
| 1954 | 441,712 | +18,887 | +4.5 | 4,274 | 424,814 | 16,898 | — |
| 1955 | 443,295 | +1,583 | +0.4 | 4,088 | 426,769 | 16,526 | — |
| 1956 | 443,568 | +273 | +0.1 | 3,512 | 427,716 | 15,852 | — |
| 1957 | 443,724 | +156 | +0.1 | 3,712 | 428,164 | 15,560 | — |
| 1958 | 425,977 | −17,747 | −3.9 | 3,519 | 411,199 | 14,778 | — |
| 1959 | 425,140 | −837 | −0.2 | 4,069 | 409,840 | 15,300 | — |
| 1960 | 425,835 | +695 | +0.2 | 4,287 | 410,121 | 15,714 | — |
| 1961 | 425,978 | +143 | +0.1 | 4,298 | 410,788 | 15,190 | — |
| 1962 | 443,583 | +17,605 | +4.1 | 4,375 | 426,774 | 16,809 | — |
| 1963 | 476,923 | +33,340 | +7.5 | 3,989 | 459,276 | 17,647 | — |
| 1964 | 502,918 | +25,995 | +5.5 | 3,713 | 483,606 | 19,312 | — |
| 1965 | 509,725 | +6,807 | +1.3 | 3,790 | 488,543 | 21,182 | — |
| 1966 | 514,360 | +4,635 | +0.9 | 3,884 | 491,685 | 22,671 | 4 |
| 1967 | 509,300 | −5,060 | −1.0 | 3,863 | 486,439 | 22,861 | — |
| 1968 | 503,388 | −5,912 | −1.2 | 3,834 | 476,615 | 26,773 | — |
| 1969 | 496,593 | −6,435 | −1.3 | 4,195 | 467,583 | 29,367 | 3 |
| 1970 | 504,230 | +7,277 | +1.5 | 4,736 | 475,701 | 28,529 | — |
| 1971 | 511,699 | +7,469 | +1.5 | 4,821 | 482,696 | 29,003 | — |
| 1972 | 520,879 | +9,180 | +1.8 | 5,067 | 488,362 | 32,517 | — |
| 1973 | 522,157 | +1,278 | +0.2 | 6,123 | 488,177 | 33,980 | — |
| 1974 | 517,902 | −4,255 | −0.8 | 7,345 | 478,566 | 39,336 | — |
| 1975 | 509,422 | −8,480 | −1.6 | 8.903 | 469,197 | 40,225 | — |
| 1976 | 504,548 | −4,874 | −1.0 | 10,983 | 463,085 | 41,463 | — |
| 1977 | 500,244 | −4,304 | −0.9 | 12,855 | 458,990 | 41,254 | — |
| 1978 | 517,842 | +17,598 | +3.5 | 14,265 | 473,041 | 44,801 | — |
| 1979 | 525,591 | +7,749 | +1.5 | 15,506 | 479,807 | 45,784 | — |
| 1980 | 533,054 | +7,463 | +1.4 | 17,918 | 487,218 | 45,836 | — |
| 1981 | 537,737 | +4,683 | +0.9 | 20,240 | 493,832 | 43,905 | — |
| 1982 | 530,960 | −6,777 | −1.3 | 22,419 | 487,771 | 43,189 | — |
| 1983 | 523,129 | −7,831 | −1.5 | 24,265 | 480,817 | 42,312 | — |

*Sources*: Reinhard Jühe, Horst-Udo Niedenhoff and Wolfgang Pege, *Gewerkschaften in der Bundesrepublik Deutschland* (Cologne: Deutscher Instituts Verlag, 1977), p. 63; Deutscher Gewerkschaftsbund, *Geschäftsbericht 1978 bis 1981* (Düsseldorf: Deutscher Gewerkschaftsbund, 1982), pp. 465–468; *Die Quelle*, Vol. 33, no. 4 (April 1982), pp. 247, 249; *Die Quelle*, Vol. 34, no. 5 (May 1983), pp. 317, 319; and *Die Quelle*, Vol. 35, no. 5 (May 1984), pp. 313–314.

Appendix 6 *Membership development of IG Druck und Papier since 1950*

| Year | Total membership | Annual change from previous year Absolute | In % | Women | Manual workers (blue-collar workers) | Employees (white-collar workers) | Civil servants |
|------|------|------|------|------|------|------|------|
| 1950 | 129,089 | — | — | 33,497 | 122,141 | 6,948 | — |
| 1951 | 137,083 | +7,994 | +6.2 | 36,593 | 129,501 | 7,582 | — |
| 1952 | 131,793 | −2,290 | −1.7 | 35,815 | 125,053 | 6,740 | — |
| 1953 | 129,879 | −1,914 | −1.5 | 34,738 | 123,962 | 5,917 | — |
| 1954 | 130,042 | +163 | +0.1 | 34,491 | 124,422 | 5,620 | — |
| 1955 | 130,815 | +773 | +0.6 | 33,811 | 124,843 | 5,972 | — |
| 1956 | 133,430 | +2,615 | +2.0 | 34,416 | 127,479 | 5,951 | — |
| 1957 | 137,099 | +3,669 | +2.8 | 34,311 | 131,013 | 6,086 | — |
| 1958 | 140,472 | +3,373 | +2.5 | 34,502 | 134,371 | 6,101 | — |
| 1959 | 141,189 | +717 | +0.5 | 32,738 | 134,847 | 6,342 | — |
| 1960 | 140,908 | −281 | −0.2 | 30,025 | 134,824 | 6,084 | — |
| 1961 | 143,924 | +3,016 | +2.1 | 29,413 | 137,346 | 6,578 | — |
| 1962 | 145,887 | +1,963 | +1.4 | 29,354 | 138,749 | 7,138 | — |
| 1963 | 145,415 | −472 | −0.3 | 27,569 | 137,626 | 7,789 | — |
| 1964 | 144,560 | −855 | −0.6 | 25,956 | 136,136 | 8,424 | — |
| 1965 | 148,592 | +4,032 | +2.8 | 25,524 | 140,809 | 7,783 | — |
| 1966 | 145,786 | −2,806 | −1.9 | 25,455 | 137,795 | 7,991 | — |
| 1967 | 143,555 | −2,231 | −1.5 | 24,178 | 134,921 | 8,634 | — |
| 1968 | 140,511 | −3,044 | −2.1 | 22,530 | 129,013 | 11,498 | — |
| 1969 | 143,357 | +2,847 | +2.0 | 22,775 | 134,442 | 8,915 | — |
| 1970 | 148,325 | +4,968 | +3.5 | 23,403 | 138,458 | 9,867 | — |
| 1971 | 150,831 | +2,506 | +1.7 | 24,791 | 139,506 | 11,325 | — |
| 1972 | 153,407 | +2,576 | +1.7 | 29,160 | 139,438 | 13,969 | — |
| 1973 | 160,062 | +6,655 | +4.3 | 27,412 | 144,939 | 15,123 | — |
| 1974 | 164,465 | +4,403 | +2.8 | 29,051 | 147,762 | 16,703 | — |
| 1975 | 157,985 | −6,480 | −3.9 | 28,312 | 140,271 | 17,714 | — |
| 1976 | 158,180 | +195 | +0.1 | 29,349 | 139,864 | 18,316 | — |
| 1977 | 152,256 | −5,924 | −3.7 | 28,729 | 133,934 | 18,322 | — |
| 1978 | 145,980 | −6,276 | −4.1 | 27,547 | 127,710 | 18,270 | — |
| 1979 | 139,069 | −6,911 | −4.7 | 26,989 | 116,859 | 22,210 | — |
| 1980 | 143,970 | +4,901 | +3.5 | 29,930 | 118,824 | 25,546 | — |
| 1981 | 151,796 | +7,826 | +5.4 | 33,730 | 122,428 | 29,368 | — |
| 1982 | 145,271 | −6,525 | −4.3 | 33,106 | 118,486 | 26,785 | — |
| 1983 | 144,344 | −927 | −0.6 | 32,924 | 112,975 | 31,369 | — |

*Sources*: Reinhard Jühe, Horst-Udo Niedenhoff and Wolfgang Pege, *Gewerkschaften in der Bundesrepublik Deutschland* (Cologne: Deutscher Instituts Verlag, 1977), p. 66; Deutscher Gewerkschaftsbund, *Geschäftsbericht 1978 bis 1981* (Düsseldorf: Deutscher Gewerkschaftsbund, 1982), pp. 465–468; *Die Quelle*, Vol. 33, no. 4 (April 1982), pp. 247, 249; *Die Quelle*, Vol. 34, no. 5 (May 1983), pp. 317, 319; and *Die Quelle*, Vol. 35, no. 5 (May 1984), pp. 313–314.

Appendix 7 *National product of the Federal Republic of Germany 1950 to 1982 (% change)*

| Year | Gross National Product | | | Use of GNP (real change) | | | | Distribution of GNP (nominal change) | |
|---|---|---|---|---|---|---|---|---|---|
| | Total in bill. DM (1 bill. = 1,000,000,000) | Change | | Personal consumption | Fixed capital formation | | Exports | Gross income from employment | Property and entre- preneurial income |
| | | Nominal | Real | | Machinery and equipment | Construc- tion | | | |
| 1950 | 98.1 | — | — | — | — | — | — | — | — |
| 1951 | 120.0 | +22.3 | +10.4 | +7.9 | +9.5 | +2.4 | +35.7 | +21.3 | +21.1 |
| 1952 | 137.0 | +14.2 | +8.9 | +9.2 | +7.0 | +9.9 | +12.8 | +11.5 | +16.0 |
| 1953 | 147.7 | +7.8 | +8.2 | +11.0 | +10.0 | +21.9 | +16.1 | +10.4 | +4.1 |
| 1954 | 158.6 | +7.4 | +7.4 | +6.1 | +18.2 | +9.1 | +24.0 | +9.3 | +5.1 |
| 1955 | 181.4 | +14.4 | +12.0 | +10.4 | +25.0 | +17.9 | +16.7 | +14.0 | +16.6 |
| 1956 | 200.5 | +10.5 | +7.3 | +8.8 | +5.4 | +11.0 | +15.2 | +12.1 | +9.5 |
| 1957 | 218.5 | +9.0 | +5.7 | +6.2 | −2.3 | +1.4 | +16.0 | +9.7 | +9.0 |
| 1958 | 234.3 | +7.2 | +3.7 | +5.1 | +6.2 | +2.9 | +4.8 | +8.5 | +4.7 |
| 1959 | 254.9 | +8.8 | +7.3 | +5.7 | +12.0 | +11.6 | +12.6 | +7.1 | +10.2 |
| 1960[a] | 284.7 | +11.7 | +9.0 | +8.0 | +17.6 | +5.2 | +13.0 | +12.2 | +11.6 |
| 1961 | 331.4 | +9.4 | +4.9 | +6.0 | +12.0 | +4.9 | +3.6 | +12.8 | +2.2 |
| 1962 | 360.5 | +8.8 | +4.4 | +5.4 | +8.0 | +2.9 | +3.2 | +10.6 | +4.0 |
| 1963 | 382.1 | +6.0 | +3.0 | +2.9 | +0.5 | +1.6 | +7.6 | +7.3 | +2.7 |
| 1964 | 419.6 | +9.8 | +6.6 | +5.0 | +8.0 | +12.9 | +8.1 | +9.3 | +10.8 |
| 1965 | 458.2 | +9.2 | +5.5 | +6.9 | +7.7 | +3.5 | +6.5 | +10.9 | +7.1 |
| 1966 | 487.4 | +6.4 | +2.5 | +2.9 | −1.2 | +2.4 | +10.3 | +7.7 | +2.7 |
| 1967 | 493.7 | +1.3 | −0.1 | +1.0 | −7.4 | −6.5 | +7.3 | −0.1 | +0.8 |
| 1968 | 535.2 | +8.4 | +6.5 | +4.5 | +7.3 | +2.5 | +13.3 | +7.4 | +5.8 |
| 1969 | 597.7 | +11.7 | +7.9 | +7.9 | +23.0 | +4.3 | +10.9 | +12.5 | +6.0 |
| 1970 | 679.0 | +13.6 | +5.9 | +7.3 | +17.7 | +6.7 | +7.2 | +18.1 | +9.5 |
| 1971 | 756.0 | +11.3 | +3.3 | +5.2 | +5.9 | +6.8 | +6.1 | +13.0 | +6.4 |
| 1972 | 827.2 | +9.4 | +3.6 | +4.0 | −1.0 | +6.3 | +6.4 | +9.9 | +7.6 |
| 1973 | 920.1 | +11.2 | +4.9 | +2.5 | +0.8 | −0.2 | +11.5 | +13.5 | +7.5 |
| 1974 | 986.9 | +7.3 | +0.4 | +0.3 | −10.2 | −9.8 | +11.8 | +10.1 | +0.1 |
| 1975 | 1,032.9 | +4.9 | −1.8 | +3.1 | +0.4 | −6.9 | −6.0 | +4.1 | +4.4 |
| 1976 | 1,127.9 | +8.7 | +5.3 | +3.4 | +6.5 | +3.6 | +11.5 | +7.3 | +15.2 |
| 1977 | 1,200.6 | +6.7 | +2.8 | +3.5 | +7.7 | +1.3 | +4.3 | +6.9 | +6.0 |
| 1978 | 1,290.7 | +7.5 | +3.6 | +4.0 | +8.2 | +2.9 | +4.1 | +6.7 | +9.1 |
| 1979 | 1,398.2 | +8.3 | +4.4 | +3.3 | +9.5 | +7.6 | +5.8 | +7.7 | +8.3 |
| 1980 | 1,484.2 | +6.4 | +1.8 | +1.5 | +2.5 | +3.7 | +5.8 | +8.3 | −1.2 |
| 1981 | 1,543.1 | +4.0 | −0.2 | −1.2 | −3.4 | −4.2 | +8.5 | +4.7 | −0.7 |
| 1982 | 1,600.0 | +3.7 | −1.1 | −2.3 | −7.2 | −4.5 | +3.5 | +2.3 | +6.7 |

[a] Until 1960 without Saarland and Berlin, from 1961 incl. Saarland and Berlin.
*Source*: Dresdner Bank, *Statistical Survey – Supplement to Economic Quarterly* (April 1983), p. 1.

Appendix 8  *Labor market[a] of the Federal Republic of Germany 1950 to 1982*

| Year | Working population | | | Wage and salary earners | | | Unemployed, short-time workers, vacancies | | | |
|---|---|---|---|---|---|---|---|---|---|---|
| | Total population | Total | Self-employed and assisting family members | Total | in industry except construction[b] | foreigners | Unemployed | Unemployment ratio[c] | Short-time workers | Job vacancies |
| | (in mill.) | (in mill.) | (in mill.) | (in mill.) | (in mill.) | (in mill.) | (in 1,000) | (in %) | (in 1,000) | (in 1,000) |
| 1950 | 50.2 | 20.4 | 6.4 | 13.8 | 4.9 | — | 1,580 | 8.5 | — | 116 |
| 1951 | 50.5 | 20.9 | 6.3 | 14.6 | 5.5 | — | 1,432 | 7.5 | 93 | 117 |
| 1952 | 50.9 | 21.3 | 6.2 | 15.7 | 5.7 | — | 1,383 | 7.1 | 125 | 118 |
| 1953 | 51.4 | 21.8 | 6.2 | 16.3 | 5.9 | — | 1,263 | 6.4 | 83 | 126 |
| 1954 | 51.9 | 22.4 | 6.1 | 17.1 | 6.3 | 0.1 | 1,228 | 6.0 | 56 | 140 |
| 1955 | 52.4 | 23.2 | 6.1 | 18.0 | 6.8 | 0.1 | 935 | 5.1 | 25 | 203 |
| 1956 | 53.0 | 23.8 | 6.0 | 18.9 | 7.3 | 0.1 | 767 | 4.0 | 25 | 222 |
| 1957 | 53.7 | 25.3 | 6.1 | 19.5 | 7.5 | 0.1 | 759 | 3.7 | 19 | 227 |
| 1958 | 54.3 | 25.5 | 6.1 | 19.7 | 7.7 | 0.1 | 769 | 3.7 | 55 | 226 |
| 1959 | 54.9 | 25.8 | 6.0 | 20.6 | 7.7 | 0.2 | 540 | 2.6 | 26 | 291 |
| 1960 | 55.4 | 26.2 | 6.0 | 20.3 | 8.1 | 0.3 | 271 | 1.3 | 3 | 465 |
| 1961 | 56.2 | 26.6 | 5.9 | 20.7 | 8.3 | 0.5 | 181 | 0.8 | 3 | 552 |
| 1962 | 56.9 | 26.7 | 5.7 | 21.0 | 8.3 | 0.6 | 155 | 0.7 | 4 | 574 |
| 1963 | 57.6 | 26.7 | 5.5 | 21.3 | 8.3 | 0.8 | 186 | 0.8 | 11 | 555 |
| 1964 | 58.3 | 26.8 | 5.3 | 21.5 | 8.3 | 0.9 | 169 | 0.8 | 2 | 609 |
| 1965 | 59.0 | 26.9 | 5.1 | 21.8 | 8.5 | 1.1 | 147 | 0.7 | 1 | 649 |
| 1966 | 59.6 | 26.8 | 5.0 | 21.8 | 8.4 | 1.2 | 161 | 0.7 | 16 | 540 |
| 1967 | 59.9 | 26.0 | 4.9 | 21.1 | 7.9 | 1.0 | 459 | 2.1 | 143 | 302 |
| 1968 | 60.2 | 26.0 | 4.8 | 21.2 | 7.9 | 1.0 | 323 | 1.5 | 10 | 488 |
| 1969 | 60.8 | 26.4 | 4.6 | 21.8 | 8.3 | 1.4 | 179 | 0.9 | 1 | 747 |
| 1970 | 60.7 | 26.7 | 4.4 | 22.2 | 8.6 | 1.8 | 149 | 0.7 | 10 | 795 |
| 1971 | 61.3 | 26.8 | 4.2 | 22.4 | 8.8 | 2.1 | 185 | 0.9 | 86 | 648 |
| 1972 | 61.7 | 26.7 | 4.1 | 22.6 | 8.6 | 2.3 | 246 | 1.1 | 76 | 546 |
| 1973 | 62.0 | 26.9 | 4.0 | 22.9 | 8.7 | 2.5 | 273 | 1.3 | 44 | 572 |
| 1974 | 62.1 | 26.6 | 3.9 | 22.6 | 8.5 | 2.3 | 582 | 2.6 | 292 | 315 |
| 1975 | 61.8 | 25.8 | 3.8 | 22.0 | 7.9 | 2.1 | 1,074 | 4.7 | 773 | 236 |
| 1976 | 61.5 | 25.6 | 3.7 | 21.9 | 7.7 | 1.9 | 1,060 | 4.6 | 277 | 235 |
| 1977 | 61.4 | 25.5 | 3.5 | 22.0 | 7.6 | 1.9 | 1,030 | 4.5 | 231 | 231 |
| 1978 | 61.3 | 25.7 | 3.4 | 22.3 | 7.6 | 1.9 | 993 | 4.3 | 191 | 245 |
| 1979 | 61.4 | 26.0 | 3.4 | 22.7 | 7.6 | 1.9 | 876 | 3.8 | 88 | 304 |
| 1980 | 61.7 | 26.3 | 3.3 | 23.0 | 7.7 | 2.0 | 889 | 3.8 | 137 | 308 |
| 1981 | 61.7 | 26.1 | 3.2 | 22.8 | 7.5 | 1.9 | 1,272 | 5.5 | 347 | 208 |
| 1982 | 61.6 | 25.6 | 3.2 | 22.4 | 7.2 | 1.8 | 1,833 | 7.6 | 606 | 105 |

[a] Yearly averages – until 1956 excl. Berlin, population from 1950 incl. Berlin.

[b] Up to 1970: industrial enterprises with 10 or more employees; from 1971: all enterprises of companies with 20 or more employees (including producing craft enterprises).

[c] Until 1965: unemployed as a ratio of wage and salary earners (employees, workers, officials and unemployed); from 1966: unemployed as a ratio of employed wage and salary earners (incl. established officials, excl. armed forces) according to microcensus.

*Source:* Dresdner Bank, *Statistical Survey – Supplement to Economic Quarterly* (April 1983), p. 3.

Appendix 9  Personal income and savings[a] in the Federal Republic of Germany 1950 to 1982

| Year | Wages and salaries per employed person (net earnings) Total economy | Wages and salaries per employed person (net earnings) Industry (incl. construct industry) | Gross hourly earnings of male workers in industry in DM | Wages and salaries (gross) | Wages and salaries (net) | Pensions | Mass incomes | Disposable income[bc] DM bill. | Personal consumption DM bill. | Savings[bc] DM bill. | savings ratio[d] in % |
|---|---|---|---|---|---|---|---|---|---|---|---|
| 1950 | — | — | 1.38 | — | — | — | — | 65.0 | 62.9 | 2.1 | 3.2 |
| 1951 | +14.1 | +16.5 | 1.59 | +21.5 | +19.5 | +10.9 | +17.7 | 75.4 | 73.1 | 2.4 | 3.1 |
| 1952 | +7.8 | +7.1 | 1.71 | +11.4 | +10.5 | +17.1 | +12.2 | 85.7 | 81.2 | 4.5 | 5.3 |
| 1953 | +6.0 | +4.2 | 1.79 | +10.2 | +10.6 | +10.5 | +10.4 | 94.5 | 88.7 | 5.7 | 6.0 |
| 1954 | +5.2 | +3.7 | 1.84 | +9.4 | +9.8 | +5.5 | +8.8 | 101.6 | 94.6 | 7.0 | 6.9 |
| 1955 | +7.9 | +6.5 | 1.96 | +13.8 | +13.6 | +12.4 | +13.3 | 113.3 | 106.1 | 7.2 | 6.4 |
| 1956 | +8.1 | +7.9 | 2.17 | +12.1 | +11.6 | +11.5 | +11.7 | 125.3 | 118.0 | 7.3 | 5.8 |
| 1957 | +5.0 | +4.3 | 2.36 | +8.2 | +8.8 | +22.8 | +12.2 | 140.0 | 128.5 | 11.4 | 8.2 |
| 1958 | +6.7 | +6.3 | 2.51 | +7.9 | +6.9 | +13.1 | +8.4 | 151.6 | 138.4 | 13.2 | 8.7 |
| 1959 | +5.4 | +5.7 | 2.64 | +7.4 | +7.6 | +3.0 | +6.5 | 162.4 | 147.7 | 14.7 | 9.0 |
| 1960 | +9.3 | +9.8 | 2.88 | +12.5 | +11.0 | +4.1 | +9.1 | 187.9 | 171.8 | 16.0 | 8.5 |
| 1961 | +10.2 | +10.2 | 3.17 | +12.8 | +11.9 | +8.9 | +11.1 | 206.8 | 188.3 | 18.5 | 8.9 |
| 1962 | +9.2 | +10.0 | 3.53 | +10.8 | +10.2 | +9.6 | +9.9 | 224.0 | 204.8 | 19.2 | 8.6 |
| 1963 | +6.2 | +6.5 | 3.79 | +7.3 | +6.8 | +6.4 | +6.7 | 240.4 | 216.8 | 23.6 | 9.8 |
| 1964 | +9.0 | +10.7 | 4.15 | +10.1 | +9.5 | +10.1 | +9.4 | 263.1 | 233.5 | 29.6 | 11.3 |
| 1965 | +9.1 | +9.0 | 4.54 | +10.5 | +11.4 | +12.1 | +11.9 | 293.4 | 257.6 | 35.8 | 12.2 |
| 1966 | +7.3 | +7.2 | 4.84 | +7.3 | +5.9 | +9.5 | +6.8 | 311.3 | 275.1 | 36.2 | 11.6 |
| 1967 | +3.3 | +2.7 | 4.99 | ±0.0 | -0.5 | +9.9 | +1.9 | 318.6 | 282.6 | 36.0 | 11.3 |
| 1968 | +6.2 | +7.6 | 5.18 | +6.8 | +5.4 | +5.0 | +5.2 | 343.6 | 300.8 | 42.9 | 12.5 |
| 1969 | +9.2 | +9.6 | 5.71 | +12.2 | +10.3 | +8.2 | +9.6 | 381.9 | 330.8 | 51.1 | 13.4 |
| 1970 | +14.7 | +16.7 | 6.49 | +17.4 | +14.8 | +8.4 | +13.6 | 427.0 | 367.6 | 59.5 | 13.9 |
| 1971 | +11.8 | +10.8 | 7.25 | +12.6 | +10.6 | +11.8 | +10.8 | 472.3 | 407.8 | 64.5 | 13.7 |
| 1972 | +9.0 | +9.7 | 7.89 | +9.1 | +9.1 | +13.4 | +10.4 | 525.8 | 447.8 | 78.1 | 14.8 |
| 1973 | +12.0 | +11.3 | 8.76 | +12.6 | +8.9 | +11.7 | +9.8 | 573.3 | 491.7 | 81.6 | 14.2 |
| 1974 | +11.4 | +11.5 | 9.68 | +9.4 | +7.8 | +14.9 | +10.3 | 622.9 | 527.6 | 95.4 | 15.3 |
| 1975 | +7.2 | +7.5 | 10.40 | +3.4 | +3.6 | +23.1 | +9.4 | 682.4 | 576.5 | 107.8 | 15.8 |
| 1976 | +7.0 | +8.3 | 11.08 | +6.7 | +4.2 | +7.4 | +5.1 | 726.7 | 624.7 | 104.8 | 14.4 |
| 1977 | +6.9 | +6.7 | 11.89 | +6.8 | +5.6 | +7.1 | +6.1 | 766.0 | 662.6 | 103.4 | 13.5 |
| 1978 | +5.5 | +5.5 | 12.50 | +6.8 | +8.0 | +5.9 | +7.3 | 816.1 | 713.9 | 109.7 | 12.5 |
| 1979 | +6.6 | +6.5 | 13.20 | +7.8 | +8.3 | +5.8 | +7.4 | 881.6 | 766.4 | 122.5 | 13.2 |
| 1980 | +5.5 | +7.1 | 14.16 | +8.2 | +6.7 | +6.6 | +6.5 | 948.0 | 821.6 | 126.4 | 13.3 |
| 1981 | +4.8 | +5.3 | 14.94 | +4.3 | +3.9 | +8.0 | +5.0 | 998.0 | 860.9 | 138.1 | 13.3 |
| 1982 | +4.2 | +4.7 | 15.60[f] | +2.2 | +1.2 | +5.5 | +2.4 | 1,054.0 | 899.4 | 154.6 | 14.0[f] |

a Last four columns: 1950–59 excl. Saarland and Berlin.
b Without retained profits
c Of private households.
d Savings as percentage of disposable income.
e January–October
f January–June
Source: Dresdner Bank, Statistical Survey – Supplement to Economic Quarterly (April 1983), p. 7.

Appendix 10  *Wages and productivity per person (% change)*

| Year | Gross wages per employed person | | Productivity (real) (GDP per employed person) |
|------|---------|------|------|
|      | Nominal | Real |      |
| 1951 | +16.3 | +8.0 | +7.7 |
| 1952 | +7.9 | +5.7 | +6.9 |
| 1953 | +5.9 | +7.8 | +5.7 |
| 1954 | +5.2 | +5.0 | +4.9 |
| 1955 | +7.9 | +6.2 | +8.0 |
| 1956 | +8.0 | +5.4 | +4.4 |
| 1957 | +5.2 | +3.1 | +3.4 |
| 1958 | +6.7 | +4.4 | +3.2 |
| 1959 | +5.5 | +4.5 | +6.4 |
| 1960 | +9.4 | +7.9 | +7.1 |
| 1961 | +10.2 | +7.7 | +4.2 |
| 1962 | +9.0 | +5.8 | +3.3 |
| 1963 | +6.1 | +3.0 | +3.0 |
| 1964 | +8.9 | +6.5 | +6.3 |
| 1965 | +9.0 | +5.4 | +4.9 |
| 1966 | +7.2 | +3.6 | +3.1 |
| 1967 | +3.2 | +1.8 | +2.9 |
| 1968 | +6.1 | +4.5 | +6.9 |
| 1969 | +9.2 | +6.2 | +6.2 |
| 1970 | +14.7 | +10.6 | +4.4 |
| 1971 | +11.9 | +6.2 | +2.7 |
| 1972 | +9.4 | +3.4 | +3.8 |
| 1973 | +11.9 | +5.0 | +5.0 |
| 1974 | +11.0 | +3.7 | +2.8 |
| 1975 | +7.1 | +1.0 | +1.9 |
| 1976 | +7.7 | +3.1 | +7.0 |
| 1977 | +7.0 | +3.5 | +3.2 |
| 1978 | +5.3 | +3.2 | +2.7 |
| 1979 | +5.9 | +1.8 | +3.2 |
| 1980 | +6.6 | +0.7 | +1.1 |
| 1981 | +5.6 | +0.3 | +0.7 |

*Sources*: Joachim Bergmann, Otto Jacobi and Walther Müller-Jentsch, *Gewerkschaften in der Bundesrepublik: Gewerkschaftliche Lohnpolitik zwischen Mitgliederinteressen und ökonomischen Systemzwängen*, third edition (Frankfurt am Main/New York: Campus Verlag, 1979), pp. 450, 455; SVR, *Herausforderung von Aussen* (Stuttgart: Kohlhammer, 1979), p. 80; idem, *Investieren für mehr Beschäftigung* (Stuttgart: Kohlhammer, 1981), p. 76.

# NOTES

## 1. THE STRUCTURE OF THE WEST GERMAN UNION MOVEMENT

1 Figures on Weimar union membership are from Siegfried Mielke (ed.), *Internationales Gewerkschaftshandbuch* (Opladen: Leske & Budrich, 1983), pp. 341–342. Mielke also provides a good summary of Germany union organization before 1933. See also Gerard Braunthal, *Socialist Labor and Politics in Weimar Germany: The General Federation of German Trade Unions* (Hamden, Conn.: Archon Books, 1978), pp. 84–94.

2 Mielke, p. 345. Also Braunthal, *Socialist Labor*, pp. 87–88, 99–101.

3 On labor organizations during the national socialist dictatorship, see Lutz Unterseher, "Kollektives Arbeitsrecht und Tarifsystem", unpublished PhD dissertation, Frankfurt University, 1975, pp. 86–93; also Hans-Gerd Schumann, *Nationalsozialismus und Arbeiterbewegung: Die Vernichtung der deutschen Gewerkschaften und der Aufbau der "Deutschen Arbeitsfront"* (Hanover: Goedel, 1958); and Timothy Mason, *Sozialpolitik im Dritten Reich* (Opladen: Westdeutscher Verlag, 1977).

4 Reinhard Jühe, Horst-Udo Niedenhoff and Wolfgang Pege, *Gewerkschaften in der Bundesrepublik Deutschland: Daten, Fakten, Strukturen* (Cologne: Deutscher Instituts Verlag, 1977), pp. 62, 113.

5 Mielke, *Internationales Gewerkschaftshandbuch*, pp. 352–353.

6 Ibid.

7 Jühe et al. *Gewerkschaften*, p. 352.

8 Mielke, *Internationales Gewerkschaftshandbuch*, p. 352.

9 Ibid., p. 351.

10 Ibid.

11 Jühe, et al. *Gewerkschaften*, p. 62.

12 Deutscher Gewerkschaftsbund, *Geschäftsbericht des Bundesvorstandes des Deutschen Gewerkschaftsbundes 1978 bis 1981* (Düsseldorf: DGB, 1981), p. 468.

13 Mielke, *Internationales Gewerkschaftshandbuch*, p. 352.

14 Jühe et al., *Gewerkschaften*, p. 28.

15 DGB, *Geschäftsbericht 1978 bis 1981*, p. 468.

16 Ibid.

17 On business organizations in West Germany, see Walter Simon, *Macht und Herrschaft der Unternehmerverbände BDI, BDA und DIHT im ökonomischen und politischen System der BRD* (Cologne: Pahl-Rugenstein Verlag, 1976).

18 On the BDI, see Gerard Braunthal, *The Federation of German Industry in Politics* (Ithaca: Cornell University Press, 1965).

19 On the organization of employers' associations see Bundesvereinigung der Deutschen Arbeitgeberverbände and Deutscher Gewerkschaftsbund (eds.), *Über die Verbände: eine*

*synoptische Selbstdarstellung der Tarifvertragsparteien* (Wiesbaden: Universum Verlagsanstalt, 1978).

20 For a critical discussion of the DGB organizational structure, see Manfred Wilke, *Die Funktionäre* (Munich: R. Piper & Co. Verlag, 1979), pp. 53ff.

21 Ibid., p. 56.

22 Mielke, *Internationales Gewerkschaftshandbuch*, p. 347.

23 Wilke, *Die Funktionäre*, p. 52.

24 DGB, *Geschäftsbericht 1978 bis 1981*, p. 472.

25 In 1950, Hesse, Baden-Württemberg and Bavaria accounted for 35% of DGB membership, against 38% in 1980. See Jühe et al., *Gewerkschaften*, p. 79, and DGB *Geschäftsbericht 1978 bis 1981*, p. 472.

26 Wilke, *Die Funktionäre*, p. 108.

27 See the chapter "Ideologische Richtungen im DGB" in Frank Deppe, Jutta von Freyberg, Christof Kievenheim, Regine Meyer and Frank Werkmeister, *Kritik der Mitbestimmung: Partnerschaft oder Klassenkampf?* (Frankfurt am Main: Suhrkamp Verlag, 1969).

28 Jühe et al., *Gewerkschaften*, pp. 62–78, own calculations.

29 Horst Föhr, *Willensbildung in den Gewerkschaften und Grundgesetz* (Berlin: Schweitzer Verlag, 1974), p. 73.

30 Wilke, *Die Funktionäre*, p. 78.

31 Since the bulk of our research ends with events in 1981 when the new political party, the Greens, was not yet enjoying any representation on the federal level and was barely existent in state and local politics, we have decided to limit our discussion of the unions' relationship to this new political entity to some general remarks in the conclusion of this volume.

32 Mielke, *Internationales Gewerkschaftshandbuch*, p. 374.

33 On the relationship between unions and the SPD after 1949, as well as the creation of the AfA, see Hella Kastendiek, *Arbeitnehmer in der SPD* (Berlin: Verlag Die Arbeitswelt, 1978), esp. pp. 19ff.

34 Ibid., p. 43.

35 Ibid., pp. 46ff.

36 On the organization of the AfA, see ibid, pp. 98ff.

37 Ibid., p. 65.

38 Mielke, *Internationales Gewerkschaftshandbuch*, p. 374.

39 On this point see Wilke, *Die Funktionäre*, pp. 96–102.

40 DGB, *Geschäftsbericht 1978 bis 1981*, p. 644. All dollar amounts in US dollars.

41 For the concept of Wirtschaftsdemokratie, see Fritz Naphtali, *Wirtschaftsdemokratie: Ihr Wesen, Weg und Ziel* (Berlin: Verlagsgesellschaft des ADGB, 1928); and Rudolf Kuda, "Das Konzept der Wirtschaftsdemokratie" in Heinz O. Vetter (ed.), *Vom Sozialistengesetz zur Mitbestimmung* (Cologne: Bund Verlag, 1975), pp. 253–276.

42 Kurt Hirche, *Die Wirtschaftsunternehmen der Gewerkschaften* (Düsseldorf: Econ-Verlag, 1966), p. 49.

43 Ibid., pp. 651–653.

44 Ibid., pp. 63–64.

45 See the article in *Der Spiegel*, Vol. 36, no. 6 (February 8, 1982) entitled "Gut getarnt im Dickicht der Firmen."

## 2. THE LEGAL FRAMEWORK FOR INDUSTRIAL RELATIONS IN THE FEDERAL REPUBLIC

1 Wolfgang Däubler, *Das Arbeitsrecht*, fifth edition (Hamburg: Rowohlt, 1982), p. 44.

2 As quoted in ibid., p. 48.

3 Ibid., p. 46.

4 See the example of the construction industry cited in Karl-Gustav Werner, *Organisation und Politik der Gewerkschaften und Arbeitgeberverbände in der deutschen Bauwirtschaft* (Berlin: Duncker & Humblot, 1968), pp. 70, 74ff.

5 Peter Ullman, *Tarifverträge und Tarifpolitik in Deutschland bis 1914* (Frankfurt am Main: Peter Lang, 1977), pp. 97–100.
6 See the more detailed discussions of labor relations before 1914 in the various industrial union chapters below.
7 Quoted in Däubler, *Das Arbeitsrecht*, p. 49.
8 On the labor courts in Weimar see Lutz Unterseher, "Kollektives Arbeitsrecht und Tarifsystem," unpublished PhD dissertation, Frankfurt University, 1975, pp. 75–82.
9 Däubler, *Das Arbeitsrecht*, pp. 225–226. We decided to translate the Betriebsrätegesetz of 1920 and the Betriebsrat of the Weimar Republic as "Workers' Council Law" and "Workers' Council" respectively to distinguish them from the post-World War II situation in which we chose to translate the Betriebsverfassungsgesetz and the Betriebsrat as "Works Constitution Law" and "Works Council."
10 Ibid., pp. 226–227.
11 Ibid., p. 227.
12 Unterseher, *Kollektives Arbeitsrecht*, p. 67.
13 Gerard Braunthal, *Socialist Labor and Politics in Weimar Germany: The General Federation of German Trade Unions* (Hamden, Conn.: Archon Books, 1978), pp. 99–101.
14 See Unterseher's discussion of Zwangsschlichtung in *Kollektives Arbeitsrecht*, pp. 70–74.
15 On the organization of industrial relations under national socialism see ibid., pp. 86–93; also the general works by Hans Gerd Schumann, *Nationalsozialismus und Gewerkschaftsbewegung: Die Vernichtung der deutschen Gewerkschaftsbewegung und der Aufbau der "Deutschen Arbeitsfront"* (Hanover: Goedel, 1958); and Timothy Mason, *Sozialpolitik im Dritten Reich* (Opladen: Westdeutscher Verlag, 1977)
16 Däubler, *Das Arbeitsrecht*, p. 31.
17 On the labor court system in the Federal Republic, see Xenia Rajewsky, *Arbeitskampfrecht in der Bundesrepublik* (Frankfurt am Main: Suhrkamp, 1970), pp. 24–28. Also Unterseher, *Kollektives Arbeitsrecht*, pp. 120–130.
18 Unterseher, *Kollektives Arbeitsrecht*, p. 93.
19 Däubler, *Das Arbeitsrecht*, p. 41.
20 *Grundgesetz für die Bundesrepublik Deutschland vom 23. Mai 1949 mit Ergänzungen nach dem Stand vom 12. April 1972*, Article 9, paragraph 3.
21 The interpretation of Art. 9, par. 3 as well as the discussion of court decisions related to it are based on Däubler, *Das Arbeitsrecht*, pp. 52–69.
22 Ibid., pp. 55–57.
23 *Tarifvertragsgesetz vom 9. April 1949*, Articles 1 and 2. For the complete text of the TVG, see the labor law collection *Betriebsverfassungsgesetz und Wahlordnung* (Munich: Beck Verlag, 1978), pp. 264–270.
24 Willy Brandt (ed.), *Materialien zum Bericht zur Lage der Nation 1972*, Bundesdrucksache VI/3080, p. 178.
25 OECD, *Collective Bargaining and Government Policy in 10 OECD Countries* (Paris: OECD, 1979), p. 60.
26 For a comprehensive discussion of collective bargaining agreements in West Germany, see Ulrich Zachert, *Tarifvertrag: Eine problemorientierte Einführung* (Cologne: Bund Verlag, 1979). Also Däubler, *Das Arbeitsrecht*, pp. 72–84.
27 Rainer Erd, *Verrechtlichung industrieller Konflikte* (Frankfurt am Main: Campus Verlag, 1978), p. 231.
28 Däubler, *Das Arbeitsrecht*, p. 88.
29 Ibid., pp. 75–76.
30 For an illustration of the numerous variations in bargaining procedure among DGB unions, see the industrial union chapters.
31 Erd, *Verrechtlichung*, pp. 186–187.
32 For an account of the newspaper strike cases and the briefs prepared for them, see Rajewsky, *Arbeitskampfrecht*, pp. 36–51.
33 Ibid., pp. 44–47.
34 Ibid., p. 46.
35 For the background of the case and the text of the BAG decisions see Ulrich Zachert,

Maria Metzke and Wolfgang Hamer, *Die Aussperrung* (Cologne: Bund Verlag, 1978), pp. 2–13.

36 As quoted in ibid., pp. 5–6.

37 Ibid., p. 7.

38 Ibid., p. 10.

39 As quoted in Erd, *Verrechtlichung*, p. 188.

40 Rajewsky, *Arbeitskampfrecht*, p. 76.

41 Ibid., pp. 70–71.

42 Zachert et al., *Die Aussperrung*, p. 55. The complete text can be found in ibid., pp. 54–66.

43 Ibid., pp. 61–62.

44 Däubler, *Das Arbeitsrecht*, pp. 188–189.

45 The complete text of the BVG 1972 can be found in *Betriebsverfassung und Wahlordnung* (Munich: Beck Verlag, 1978). Throughout this discussion, the text of the BVG 1972 will be cited by article and paragraph according to this edition.

46 Däubler, *Dar Arbeitsrecht*, p. 237.

47 Erd, *Verrechtlichung*, pp. 31, 38.

48 Ibid., p. 37.

49 Däubler, *Das Arbeitsrecht*, pp. 276–277.

50 Erd, *Verrechtlichung*, p. 85.

51 See also ibid., pp. 80–84, and Däubler, *Das Arbeitsrecht*, pp. 322–328.

52 Däubler, *Das Arbeitsrecht*, p. 295.

53 Richard Burkhardt, *Ein Kampf ums Menschenrecht* (Stuttgart: IG Druck, 1974), p. 167. Burkhardt analyzes the components of pay using the typical remunerations of printing workers.

54 Ibid.

55 See Erd, *Verrechtlichung*, pp. 47–58.

56 See the discussion in Eckhart Teschner, *Lohnpolitik im Betrieb* (Frankfurt am Main: Campus, 1977), pp. 12–15. This is the standard work on plant-level wage determination.

57 Erd, *Verrechtlichung*, pp. 69–80. On recent changes in job protection law and practice in the wake of the 1974–75 and 1979–80 recessions, see idem., "Gesetzlicher Kündigungsschutz und Wirtschaftskrise" in *Kritische Justiz*, Vol. 15, no. 4 (1982), pp. 367–382.

58 For the background of the passage of the 1951 MMG and the 1976 MG, see Chapter 3. Full texts and interpretations of all the co-determination laws can be found in Der Bundesminister für Arbeit und Sozialordnung (ed.), *Mitbestimmung* (Bonn: Ministerium für Arbeit und Sozialordnung, 1970). An English edition of this book is also printed by the West German government. Our citations of these laws are based on this edition. For a critical assessment of Mitbestimmung, see the essays found in Deppe et al., *Kritik der Mitbestimmung*.

59 Däubler, *Das Arbeitsrecht*, p. 357.

60 Ibid., pp. 359–364.

61 Ibid., p. 363.

62 Ibid., pp. 387–388.

63 Ibid., p. 379.

### 3. A HISTORY OF THE GERMAN TRADE UNION FEDERATION

1 Frank Deppe, Georg Fülberth and Jürgen Harrer (eds.), *Geschichte der deutschen Gewerkschaftsbewegung* (Cologne: Pahl-Rugenstein, 1978), p. 282; see also Dieter Schuster, *Die deutsche Gewerkschaftsbewegung DGB* (Düsseldorf: DGB Bundesvorstand, 1976), p. 73. Schuster cites two other gatherings of unionists at a very early stage, one in Hamburg on May 11, 1945 and another in Hanover on May 14, 1945.

2 The British historian Raymond Ebsworth as cited in Eberhard Schmidt, *Die verhinderte Neuordnung 1945–1952* (Frankfurt am Main: Europäische Verlagsanstalt, 1977), p. 25.

3 General Dwight D. Eisenhower as cited in ibid., p. 25.

4 Theo Pirker, *Die blinde Macht: Die Gewerkschaftsbewegung in der Bundesrepublik* (Berlin: Olle & Wolter, 1979), Vol. 1, pp. 21, 22.

5  Figures are from ibid., pp. 23, 24; and also Schuster, *Die deutsche Gewerkschaftsbewegung*, p. 74.
6  Pirker, *Die blinde Macht*, p. 22.
7  As the most prominent representatives of this voluntaristic interpretation of organized labor's active participation in the reconstruction of a capitalist West Germany, see Eberhard Schmidt, *Die verhinderte Neuordnung*, Theo Pirker, *Die blinde Macht*, Vols. 1 and 2; Lutz Niethammer, "Entscheidung für den Westen – Die Gewerkschaften im Nachkriegsdeutschland" in Heinz O. Vetter (ed.), *Aus der Geschichte lernen – Die Zukunft gestalten; Dreissig Jahre DGB* (Cologne: Bund Verlag, 1980), pp. 224–234; and Richard Detje, *Von der Westzone zum Kalten Krieg: Restauration und Gewerkschaftspolitik im Nachkriegsdeutschland* (Hamburg: VSA-Verlag, 1982).
8  The most prominent analysts pursuing, at least partially, this argumentation are Frank Deppe, Theo Pirker, Eberhard Schmidt and Lutz Niethammer.
9  For a superb biography of Hans Böckler see Ulrich Borsdorf, *Hans Böckler: Arbeit und Leben eines Gewerkschafters von 1875 bis 1945* (Cologne: Bund Verlag, 1982).
10  Deppe et al., *Geschichte*, p. 286; and Schmidt, *Die verhinderte Neuordnung*, pp. 44, 45.
11  Deppe et al., *Geschichte*, p. 285; Schmidt, *Die verhinderte Neuordnung*, p. 41; and Pirker, *Die blinde Macht*, pp. 45–47. This seems a bit ironic, since the British unions are by and large not structured along industrial lines and lack the organizational centralization that even these industrial unions in Germany were going to exhibit.
12  As quoted in Schmidt, *Die verhinderte Neuordnung*, p. 68; and also in Frank Deppe, Jutta von Freyberg, Christof Kievenheim, Regine Meyer and Frank Werkmeister, *Kritik der Mitbestimmung: Partnerschaft oder Klassenkampf?* (Frankfurt am Main; Suhrkamp, 1969), p. 83.
13  "Das Ahlener Wirtschaftsprogramm für Nordrhein-Westfalen vom 3, Februar 1947," in Rainer Kunz, Herber Maier and Theo Stammen (eds.), *Programme der politischen Parteien in der Bundesrepublik* (Munich: Verlag C. H. Beck, 1975), p. 127.
14  Schmidt, *Die verhinderte Neuordnung*, p. 74.
15  Both Deppe and Schmidt give useful accounts of two strikes which occurred at this time, the first at Bode-Panzer in Hanover in November 1946 and the second at Miele in Bielefeld in April/May 1947. See Deppe et al., *Geschichte*, p. 292; and Schmidt, *Die verhinderte Neuordnung*, pp. 91, 94.
16  Deppe, Pirker and Schmidt attach considerable significance to this point. Deppe et al., *Geschichte*, p. 299; Pirker, *Die blinde Macht*, pp. 54, 55; and Schmidt, pp. 94–96.
17  Arno Klönne, *Die deutsche Arbeiterbewegung: Geschichte – Ziele – Wirkungen* (Düsseldorf: Eugen Diederichs Verlag, 1980), pp. 292–294.
18  On the Marshall Plan as part of the general reconstruction of a capitalist economic order in what was to become the Federal Republic of Germany, see the excellent discussion provided by Dirk Berg-Schlosser, "Die Konstituierung des Wirtschaftssystems" in Josef Becker, Theo Stammen and Peter Waldman (eds.), *Vorgeschichte der Bundesrepublik Deutschland: Zwischen Kapitulation und Grundgesetz* (Munich: Wilhelm Fink Verlag, 1979), pp. 93–121.
19  Pirker, *Die blinde Macht*, pp. 85–87; Deppe et al., *Geschichte*, pp. 312, 313; and Schmidt, *Die verhinderte Neuordnung*, pp. 114–124.
20  Schmidt, *Die verhinderte Neuordnung*, p. 116.
21  Ibid., p. 115.
22  Ibid., pp. 117, 118; and Pirker, *Die blinde Macht*, p. 94.
23  Schmidt, *Die verhinderte Neuordnung*, pp. 126, 127.
24  Pirker, *Die blinde Macht*, p. 98.
25  As quoted in Schmidt, *Die verhinderte Neuordnung*, p. 128.
26  Deppe et al., *Geschichte*, p. 316. For an excellent study of the strike on November 12, 1948, its antecedents and surrounding events, see Gerhard Beier, *Der Demonstrations-und Generalstreik vom 12. November 1948: Im Zusammenhang mit der parlamentarischen Entwicklung Westdeutschlands* (Frankfurt am Main: Europäische Verlagsanstalt, 1975).
27  Thus, for example, the Western powers had made Germany a member of the Organization for European Economic Cooperation (OEEC) as early as April 1948. See Schmidt, *Die verhinderte Neuordnung*, p. 112.

28 Deutscher Gewerkschaftsbund, *Protokoll des Gründungskongresses des deutschen Gewerkschaftsbundes, München, 12.–14. Oktober 1949* (Cologne: Bund Verlag, 1950), pp. 126ff.

29 Schmidt, *Die verhinderte Neuordnung*, p. 166.

30 Schuster, *Die deutsche Gewerkschaftsbewegung*, pp. 79–84; Helga Grebing, *Geschichte der deutschen Arbeiterbewegung* (Munich: Deutscher Taschenbuch Verlag, 1966), pp. 253–258.

31 Deutscher Gewerkschaftsbund, *Protokoll 1949*, pp. 318–323; Deppe et al., *Geschichte*, pp. 320–326; Hans Limmer, *Die deutsche Gewerkschaftsbewegung* (Munich: Günter Olzog Verlag, 1970), pp. 78–83; and Hans-Adam Pfromm, *Das neue DGB-Grundsatzprogramm: Einführung und Kommentar* (Munich: Günter Olzog Verlag, 1982), pp. 162–171.

32 For the Düsseldorf guidelines see "Düsseldorfer Leitsätze vom 15. Juli 1949" in Kunz et al., *Programme*, pp. 131–140.

33 Deutscher Gewerkschaftsbund, *Protokoll 1949*, pp. 318–323; Schuster, *Die deutsche Gewerkschaftsbewegung*, pp. 84–86; Limmer, *Die deutsche Gewerkschaftsbewegung*, pp. 78–83; Deppe et al., *Geschichte*, pp. 320–326; Grebing, *Geschichte*, pp. 256, 257; and Pfromm, *Das neue DGB-Grundsatzprogramm*, pp. 162–171.

34 For a complete text and analysis of the Basic Law, see Jürgen Seifert (ed.), *Grundgesetz und Restauration* (Neuwied: Luchterhand, 1977). On the relation between the Basic Law and the Federal Republic's industrial relations system, see Chapter 2 above.

35 Pirker, *Die blinde Macht*, pp. 129–134; Limmer, *Die deutsche Gewerkschaftsbewegung*, p. 87; and Schmidt, *Die verhinderte Neuordnung*, p. 168.

36 Bernhard Vogel, Dieter Hohlen and Rainer-Olaf Schultze (eds.), *Wahlen in Deutschland* (Berlin: De Gruyter, 1971), p. 306.

37 Deppe et al., *Geschichte*, p. 335; Schmidt, *Die verhinderte Neuordnung*, p. 176; and Deppe et al., *Kritik*, pp. 96, 97.

38 Deppe et al., *Kritik*, pp. 58–94; Schmidt, *Die verhinderte Neuordnung*, pp. 182–192; Deppe et al., *Geschichte*, pp. 333–346. For a particularly critical view of this episode see Horst Thum, *Mitbestimmung in der Montanindustrie: Der Mythos vom Sieg der Gewerkschaften* (Stuttgart: Deutsche Verlagsanstalt, 1982).

39 For the Adenauer–Böckler exchange see Pirker, *Die blinde Macht*, pp. 188–195.

40 Deppe, in particular, attaches great significance to the DGB's pro-Western views on foreign policy at this juncture. See Deppe et al., *Geschichte*, pp. 328, 329.

41 Schmidt, *Die verhinderte Neuordnung*, pp. 194, 195; and Deppe et al., *Geschichte*, pp. 340, 341.

42 Deutscher Gewerkschaftsbund, *Vorschläge des DGB zur Neuordnung der deutschen Wirtschaft* (Düsseldorf: DGB, 1950).

43 Pirker, *Die blinde Macht*, pp. 278–284; Limmer, *Die deutsche Gewerkschaftsbewegung*, pp. 89–93; Schmidt, *Die verhinderte Neuordnung*, pp. 194–201; and Schuster, *Die deutsche Gewerkschaftsbewegung*, pp. 88, 89.

44 On the unions' confusion and vacillation in this struggle, see Schmidt, *Die verhinderte Neuordnung*, pp. 201–218; Deppe et al., *Geschichte*, pp. 342, 343; and Pirker, *Die blinde Macht*, pp. 247–260. An excellent account of the anti-communist Zeitgeist and its influence in this conflict can be found in Wolfgang Hirsch-Weber, *Gewerkschaften in der Politik: Von der Massenstreikdebatte zum Kampf um das Mitbestimmungsrecht* (Cologne: Westdeutscher Verlag, 1959), pp. 95–113.

45 For the 1952 Works Constitution Law see *Betriebsverfassungsgesetz und Wahlordnung* (Munich: C. H. Beck Verlag, 1978); for a very useful graphic presentation of labor's one-third-parity participation scheme according to the 1952 Works Constitution Law, see Der Bundesminister für Arbeit und Sozialordnung, *Mitbestimmung* (Bonn: Bundesministerium für Arbeit und Sozialordnung, 1979), pp. 57–62.

46 For the controversy surrounding Christian Fette see Deutscher Gewerkschaftsbund, *Protokoll – 2. Ordentlicher Bundeskongress Berlin, 13. bis 17. Oktober 1952* (Düsseldorf: DGB, 1953), pp. 118, 119, 129, 156–159, 160. Also Pirker, *Die blinde Macht*, pp. 288–290.

47 On this ideological offensive against the union, see Pirker's last chapter in his first volume, *Die blinde Macht*, pp. 291–316; also Limmer, *Die deutsche Gewerkschaftsbewegung*, pp. 91–93; and Klönne, *Die deutsche Arbeiterbewegung*, pp. 297–315.

48 On the conservative role of juridification during the restoration period of the Federal Republic see Roderich Wahsner, "Das Arbeitskartell: Die Restauration des kapitalisti-

schen Arbeitsrechts in Westdeutschland nach 1945" in *Kritische Justiz*, Vol. 7, no. 4 (1974), pp. 369–386. The process of juridification at the time was part of a larger debate on the proper role of unions in a liberal democracy. As such, this represented a harbinger of what was to become known as the "union state" (Gewerkschaftsstaat) campaign by the employers against the DGB in the course of the 1970s. On the debate of the 1950s, see Götz Briefs, *Zwischen Kapitalismus und Syndikalismus: Die Gewerkschaften am Scheideweg* (Munich: L. Lehnen, 1952); idem, *Das Gewerkschaftsproblem gestern und heute* (Frankfurt am Main: Knapp, 1955). Briefs was perhaps the most prominent conservative theorist at the time who warned of the dangers which necessarily would emanate in every liberal democracy from essentially non-democratic interest groups, particularly those representing labor. For a similar analysis see Günter Triesch, *Die Macht der Funktionäre: Macht und Verantwortung der Gewerkschaften* (Düsseldorf: K. Rauch,. 1956). For the opposite argument see Wolfgang Abendroth, *Die deutschen Gewerkschaften: Weg demokratischer Integration* (Heidelberg: Wolfgang Rothe Verlag, 1955). It is interesting to note that Abendroth, although providing a classical Marxist analysis of the German trade union movement prior to World War II and the developments in West Germany between 1945 and 1953, refrains from representing the unions as having sold out to capitalism or the "system" in one form or another. Rather, he links the union movement to the democratization process and sees its continued existence as the guarantor for the maintenance of the first successful liberal democracy in modern German history. Thus, he differs considerably in his assessment of the unions as contributors to democracy from those of such prominent authors also belonging to the West German left as Theo Pirker, Eberhard Schmidt, Lutz Niethammer, Arno Klönne and even Frank Deppe, who is one of Wolfgang Abendroth's most eminent and prolific students of union politics and the working class in the Federal Republic. For other arguments in this debate see the summary provided by Evelies Mayer in her book *Theorien zum Funktionswandel der Gewerkschaften* (Frankfurt am Main: Europäische Verlagsanstalt, 1973). See also the following articles in *Gewerkschaftliche Monatshefte*: Theo Pirker, "Gewerkschaften am Scheidewege" in *Gewerkschaftliche Monatshefte*, Vol. 3, no. 12 (December 1952), pp. 708–713; idem, "Die Gewerkschaft als politische Organisation" in *Gewerkschaftliche Monatshefte*, Vol. 3, no. 2 (February 1952), pp. 76–79; idem, "Staatsautorität und pluralistische Ordnung" in *Gewerkschaftliche Monatshefte*, Vol. 3, no. 10 (October 1952), pp. 577–583; Dolf Sternberger, "Parlamentarismus, Parteien, Verbände" in *Gewerkschaftliche Monatshefte*, Vol. 3, no. 8 (August 1952), pp. 473–477; Alfred Weber, "Staat und gewerkschaftliche Aktion" in *Gewerkschaftliche Monatshefte*, Vol. 3, no. 8 (August 1952), pp. 478–481; Wolfgang Abendroth, "Zur Funktion der Gewerkschaften in der westdeutschen Demokratie" in *Gewerkschaftliche Monatshefte*, Vol. 3, no. 11 (November 1952), pp. 641–648; Franz Grosse, "Die Gewerkschaften in den westlichen Demokratien" in *Gewerkschaftliche Monatshefte*, Vol. 3, No. 8 (August 1952), pp. 450–457; Viktor Agartz, "Zur Situation der Gewerkschaften im liberal-kapitalistischen Staat" in *Gewerkschaftliche Monatshefte*, Vol. 3, no. 8 (August 1952), pp. 464–468; and Otto Stammer, "Gesellschaftliche Entwicklungsperspektiven und pluralitäre Demokratie" in *Gewerkschaftliche Monatshefte*, Vol. 12, no. 10 (October 1961), pp. 577–583.

49 On the Bundestag elections and the DGB, see Schuster, *Die deutsche Gewerkschaftsbewegung*, pp. 89, 90; and Limmer, *Die deutsche Gewerkschaftsbewegung*, pp. 93–95.

50 On the problems of the unitary trade-union movement's neutrality and subsequent developments, see Limmer, *Die deutsche Gewerkschaftsbewegung*, pp. 97, 98; and Schuster, *Die deutsche Gewerkschaftsbewegung*, p. 90.

51 Viktor Agartz, "Expansive Lohpolitik" in *Mitteilungen des Wirtschaftswissenschaftlichen Institutes der Gewerkschaften*, Vol. 6, no. 12 (December 1953), pp. 245–247.

52 In addition to the article entitled "Expansive Lohpolitik" these ideas were expressed in many of Agartz's speeches and writings beginning with his "Socialist Economic Policy" delivered at the SPD's annual party congress in 1946. There can be no doubt that Viktor Agartz was among the most influential theorists in social democratic and union circles following the end of World War II until his demotion from the directorship of the WWI in late 1955. See Viktor Agartz, *Wirtschaft, Lohn Gewerkschaft: Ausgewählte Schriften* (Berlin: Verlag Die Arbeitswelt, 1982); Volker Gransow and Michael Krätke, *Viktor Agartz:*

*Gewerkschaften und Wirtschaftspolitik* (Berlin: Verlag Die Arbeitswelt, 1978); and Viktor Agartz, *Gewerkschaft und Arbeiterklasse* (Munich: Trikont Verlag, 1971).

53 On these circles, see William Graf, *The German Left since 1945* (New York: Oleander, 1976), pp. 123, 124.

54 Otto Brenner, "Die Aufgaben unserer Gewerkschaft in der gegenwärtigen Situation" in Industriegewerkschaft Metall, *Protokoll über den 3. ordentlichen Gewerkschaftstag der IG Metall, Hannover, 13.–18. September, 1954* (Frankfurt am Main: IG Metall, 1955), pp. 268–287.

55 Viktor Agartz, "Wirtschafts- und Steuerpolitik: Grundsätze und Programm des DGB" in Deutscher Gewerkschaftsbund, *Protokoll – 3. Ordentlicher Bundeskongress, Frankfurt a.M., 4. bis 9. Oktober, 1954* (Düsseldorf: DGB, 1955), pp. 423–468.

56 Schuster, *Die deutsche Gewerkschaftsbewegung*, pp. 91, 92; and Limmer, *Die deutsche Gewerkschaftsbewegung*, pp. 95, 96.

57 As quoted in Limmer, *Die deutsche Gewerkschaftsbewegung*, p. 96; and more extensively in Pirker, *Die blinde Macht*, Vol. 2, pp. 161–164.

58 On this analogy between the DGB and the Holy Roman Empire emphasizing the weakness of the titular head in relation to the powerful vassals, see the article "Der Vize-Komplex" in *Der Spiegel*, Vol. 13, no. 36 (September 2, 1959); see also the cartoon "Richters Rüstung: Für Stammesherzöge zu klein" in *Der Spiegel*, Vol. 16, no. 36 (September 5, 1962).

59 On the CGD/CGB respectively, see Limmer, *Die deutsche Gewerkschaftsbewegung*, p. 98; Schuster, *Die deutsche Gewerkschaftsbewegung*, p. 90; and Siegfried Mielke and Fritz Vilmar "Bundesrepublik Deutschland (BRD)" in Siegfried Mielke (ed.), *Internationales Gewerkschaftshandbuch* (Opladen: Leske und Budrich, 1982), pp. 337–384. Chapter 1 of this volume provides a brief description of this organization.

60 Otto Kirchheimer, "West German Trade Unions: Their Domestic and Foreign Policies" (Santa Monica: The Rand Corporation, April 1, 1956, unpublished research memorandum), pp. 83–95.

61 Ibid., pp. 95–106.

62 This point comes out beautifully in Kirchheimer's insightful analysis of the West German trade unions, especially pp. iii–vi, 99–106 and 137–140.

63 The term "IG Krawall" is mentioned in an article entitled "Die Meisterringer" published in *Der Spiegel*, Vol. 12, no. 39 (September 24, 1958). Two further articles in *Der Spiegel* also emphasize IG Metall's – and especially Otto Brenner's – problems with other unions in the DGB. "Bremse für Brenner" in *Der Spiegel*, Vol. 12, no. 3 (January 15, 1958); and "Otto der Gusseiserne" in *Der Spiegel*, vol. 13, no. 45 (November 4, 1959).

64 On divisions within the ADGB after 1918, see Limmer, *Die deutsche Gewerkschaftsbewegung*, pp. 50–54; and Deppe et al., *Geschichte*, pp. 170–179. On the ADGB in general, see Gerard Braunthal, *Socialist Labor and Politics in Weimar Germany* (Hamden, Conn.: Archon, 1978).

65 For an exellent summary of the different ideologies which have characterized these two wings in the DGB, see the chapter entitled "Ideologische Richtungen im DGB" in Deppe et al., *Kritik*, pp. 222–234.

66 This dichotomy of the unions' representing a *Gegenmacht* or *Ordnungsfaktor* has influenced much of the debate on labor in the Federal Republic, both within and outside the unions. For an important book in which these two concepts are featured, see Eberhard Schmidt, *Ordnungsfaktor oder Gegenmacht: Die politische Rolle der Gewerkschaften* (Frankfurt am Main: Suhrkamp, 1971).

67 See "Otto der Gusseiserne" in *Der Spiegel*, November 4, 1958.

68 Schuster, *Die deutsche Gewerkschaftsbewegung*, pp. 92, 93; and Pirker, *Die blinde Macht*, Vol. 2, pp. 296–310.

69 On this intra-DGB flux and some organizational problems arising from a net loss in membership, see Deppe et al., *Geschichte*, pp. 384–389.

70 On this service orientation of the unions, see Deppe et al., *Geschichte*, pp. 385, 386.

71 "Nur für Organisierte" in *Der Spiegel* Vol. 13, no. 37 (September 16, 1959).

72 For the most detailed study of these "advantage schemes" or "preferential treatments" on a union-by-union basis, see Rolf Seitenzahl, Ulrich Zachert and Heinz-Dieter Pütz, *Vorteilsregelungen für Gewerkschaftsmitglieder* (Cologne: Bund Verlag, 1976).

73 On betriebsnahe Tarifpolitik see Ulrich Kulke, *Betriebsnahe Tarifpolitik zur Stärkung der gewerkschaftlichen Basis* (Berlin: Verlag Die Arbeitswelt, 1977); Eberhard Schmidt, "Zur Strategie der betriebsnahen Tarifpolitik" in Otto Jacobi, Walther Müller-Jentsch and Eberhard Schmidt (eds.), *Gewerkschaften und Klassenkampf - Kritisches Jahrbuch '72* (Frankfurt am Main: Fischer Verlag, 1972), pp. 145–161; and Otto Jacobi, "Tarifpolitische Konzeption der westdeutschen Gewerkschaften" in Otto Jacobi, Walther Müller-Jentsch and Eberhard Schmidt, *Gewerkschaften und Klassenkampf - Kritisches Jahrbuch '74* (Frankfurt am Main: Fischer Verlag, 1974), pp. 149–160.

74 As quoted in Schuster, *Die deutsche Gewerkschaftsbewegung*, p. 100.

75 On this aspect of the 1962 congress, see Limmer, *Die deutsche Gewerkschaftsbewegung*, pp. 103–105; and Schuster, *Die deutsche Gewerkschaftsbewegung*, pp. 100, 101.

76 As quoted in Deppe et al., *Geschichte*, p. 339.

77 As quoted in Deppe et al., *Kritik*, p. 222; also in Limmer, *Die deutsche Gewerkschaftsbewegung*, p. 106.

78 As quoted in Deppe et al., *Kritik*, pp. 223, 224. This emphasis is in the original.

79 Leber's and the accommodationists' position is well summarized in Deppe et al., *Kritik*, 222–227; Deppe et al., *Geschichte*, pp. 398, 399; and Limmer, *Die deutsche Gewerkschaftsbewegung*, p. 106.

80 As quoted in Limmer, *Die deutsche Gewerkschaftsbewegung*, p. 105. Brenner's and the activists' position is well summarized in Deppe et al., *Kritik*, 227–234; Deppe et al., *Geschichte*, pp. 400, 401; and Limmer, *Die deutsche Gewerkschaftsbewegung*, p. 105.

81 Schuster, *Die deutsche Gewerkschaftsbewegung*, pp. 101–103.

82 On this particular intra-DGB debate and the unions' relationship to the Emergency Laws in general, see Eberhard Schmidt, *Ordnungsfaktor*, pp. 64–69; Deppe et al., *Geschichte*, pp. 406–409; "Gewisse Unruhe" in *Der Spiegel*, Vol. 20, no. 21 (May 16, 1966); and "Rohe Eier" in *Der Spiegel*, Vol. 21, no. 12 (March 13, 1967).

83 This summary of the activists' opposition to the Emergency Laws, including their appeal to such emotion-laden subjects in German history as the Kapp Putsch in 1920 and the role of Article 48 of the Weimar Constitution, is based on Deppe et al., *Geschichte*, pp. 406, 407.

84 As quoted in Schuster, *Die deutsche Gewerkschaftsbewegung*, p. 101.

85 Schuster, *Die deutsche Gewerkschaftsbewegung*, pp. 101, 102.

86 "Gweisse Unruhe" in *Der Spiegel*, May 16, 1966; and Schuster, *Die deutsche Gewerkschaftsbewegung*, p. 102.

87 Schmidt, *Ordnungsfaktor*, pp. 68, 69; and Deppe et al., *Geschichte*, pp. 407, 408.

88 As quoted in Limmer, *Die deutsche Gewerkschaftsbewegung*, pp. 120, 121.

89 Limmer, in particular, emphasizes the comprehensive nature of this program in his analysis of the DGB's second Basic Program. See Limmer, *Die deutsche Gewerkschaftsbewegung*, p. 107. The DGB's Düsseldorf Program of 1963 has been published in a number of forms. Most prominent among them has been a pamphlet published by the DGB entitled *Grundsatzprogramm des Deutschen Gewerkschaftsbundes* (Düsseldorf: DGB, n.d.). However, the program has also appeared in two widely available volumes by eminent union members and experts. See Gerhard Leminsky and Bernd Otto, *Politik und Programmatik des Deutschen Gewerkschaftsbundes* (Cologne: Bund Verlag, 1974), first edition, pp. 45–62; and Hans-Adam Pfromm, *Das neue DGB-Grundsatzprogramm: Einführung und Kommentar* (Munich: Günter Olzog Verlag, 1982), pp. 172–203. All subsequent citations of the Basic Program will be from the Pfromm volume.

90 Pfromm, *Das neue DGB-Grundsatzprogramm*, p. 174.

91 Ibid., p. 174.

92 Ibid., p. 173.

93 The preceding presentation of the DGB's 1963 Basic Program established in Düsseldorf and the comparisons with its Munich predecessor of 1949 are based on the published versions of each program as they appear in Pfromm, *Das neue DGB-Grundsatzprogramm*, pp. 162–171 (Munich Program), and pp. 172–203 (Düsseldorf Program).

94 For the entire *Aktionsprogramm* of 1965, see Pfromm, *Das neue DGB-Grundsatzprogramm*, pp. 205–208.

95 Limmer provides a detailed interpretation of the DGB's 1965 *Aktionsprogramm* in light of

its particular points regarding rationalization and automation. See Limmer, *Die deutsche Gewerkschaftsbewegung*, pp. 113–115.

96  Deppe et al., *Geschichte*, p. 403.

97  Good analyses of this period can be found in Elmar Altvater, Jürgen Hoffmann and Willi Semmler, *Vom Wirtschaftswunder zur Wirtschaftskrise* (Berlin: Olle & Wolter, 1908); Karl Neumann, *Konjunktur und Konjunkturpolitik* (Frankfurt am Main: Europäische Verlagsanstalt, 1972); and Jürgen Krack and Karl Neumann, *Konjunktur, Krise, Wirtschaftspolitik* (Frankfurt am Main: Europäische Verlagsanstalt, 1978).

98  Among his most important speeches of that period was one entitled "Lebensfragen der deutschen Volkswirtschaft" held at IG Metall's second congress in Stuttgart in September 1952. See Karl Schiller, "Lebensfragen der deutschen Volkswirtschaft" in Industriegewerkschaft Metall, *Niederschrift der Verhandlungen des 2. ordentlichen Gewerkschaftstages der Industriegewerkschaft Metall für die Bundesrepublik Deutschland in Stuttgart vom 15. bis 20. September 1952* (Frankfurt am Main: IG Metall, n.d.), pp. 213–227.

99  The Blessing Memorandum is discussed in Robert Flanagan and Lloyd Ulman, *Wage Restraint: A Study of Incomes Policy in Western Europe* (Berkeley: University of California Press, 1971), p. 185.

100  For these data see Dresdner Bank, Statistical Survey (supplement to *Economic Quarterly*), July 1981.

101  Sachverständigenrat, *Jahresgutachten 1965 – Stabilisierung ohne Stagnation* (Stuttgart: W. Kohlhammer, 1956), par. 187–192.

102  On the Stability and Growth Law and its relationship to the DGB, see Limmer, *Die deutsche Gewerkschaftsbewegung*, pp. 122–126; Deppe et al., *Geschichte*, pp. 414–418; and Joachim Bergmann, Otto Jacobi and Walther Müller-Jentsch, *Gewerkschaften in der Bundesrepublik*, third edition (Frankfurt am Main: Campus Verlag, 1979), pp. 91–96.

103  See "Gesetz zur Förderung der Stabilität und des Wachstums der Wirtschaft vom 8.6.1967" in *Bundesgesetzblatt* 1967, Part I, pp. 582ff.

104  Bergmann et al., *Gewerkschaften*, p. 99.

105  On the Concerted Action see Rolf Seitenzahl, *Einkommenspolitik durch Konzertierte Aktion und Orientierungsdaten* (Cologne: Bund Verlag, 1974); Hermann Adam, *Der Kampf um Löhne und Gewinne* (Cologne: Bund Verlag, 1976), second edition, esp. pp. 70–75; and Hermann Adam, *Die Konzertierte Aktion in der Bundesrepublik* (Cologne: Bund Verlag, 1970).

106  This view is presented in Adam, *Der Kampf*, pp. 70–75.

107  Otto Brenner, "Sicherheit und Fortschritt durch eine starke IG Metall" in Industriegewerkschaft Metall, *Protokoll des 9. ordentlichen Gewerkschaftstages der IG Metall, München, 2. bis 7. September, 1968* (Frankfurt am Main: IG Metall, n.d.), p. 216.

108  Ibid., p. 215.

109  Seitenzahl, *Einkommenspolitik*, pp. 158–160.

110  Schuster, *Die deutsche Gewerkschaftsbewegung*, p. 105; for the exact scheme formulated by the DGB at this conference held in Cologne on March 12, 1968, see Erhard Kassler, "Stationen zu einem ungeliebten Gesetz" in *Das Mitbestimmungsgespräch* (January 1976), p. 4.

111  "Die Zeit läuft" in *Der Spiegel*, Vol. 27, no. 24 (June 11, 1973).

112  *Arbeitsförderungsgesetz (AFG)* (Neuwied: Luchterhand Verlag, 1978), pp. 151–284.

113  On Rosenberg's diplomatic qualities and his keen sense for compromise, see two interviews with *Der Spiegel* which Rosenberg granted in the 1960s; "Wo alle sich verrückt benehmen" in *Der Spiegel*, Vol. 16, no. 18 (May 2, 1962); and "Zerreissproben noch und noch" in *Der Spiegel*, Vol. 21, no. 12 (March 13, 1967).

114  "Problem vor Torschluss" in *Der Spiegel*, Vol. 23, no. 4 (January 20, 1969); and "Lieber Schwächer" in *Der Spiegel*, Vol. 23, no. 9 (February 24, 1969).

115  "Wir haben einen" in *Der Spiegel*, Vol. 23, no. 15 (April 7, 1969).

116  "Nachts auf der Strasse" in *Der Spiegel*, Vol. 23, no. 12 (March 17, 1969).

117  "Wir haben einen" in *Der Spiegel*, April 7, 1969.

118  For an excellent analysis of the union's traditional "state fixation" which received an added dimension with the SPD's assumption of senior leadership of the government see

Bodo Zeuner, "'Solidarität' mit der SPD order Solidarität der Klasse? Zur SPD-Bindung der DGB-Gewerkschaften" in *Prokla*, Vol. 6, no. 1 (1977), pp. 1–32. For two good historical analyses of these developments in the German labor movement up to the late 1960s and early 1970s see Jutta von Freyberg, George Fülberth, Jürgen Harrer, Bärbel Hebel-Kunze, Heinz-Gerd Hofschen, Erich Ott and Gerhard Stuby, *Geschichte der deutschen Sozialdemokratie 1863–1975* (Cologne: Pahl-Rugenstein Verlag, 1977), second edition; and Arno Klönne, *Die deutsche Arbeiterbewegung.*

119 On Willy Brandt and *Ostpolitik* see David Binder, *The Other German – Willy Brandt's Life and Times* (Washington: New Republic Book Company, 1975).

120 Compare, for example, IG Metall's anti-GDR attitude in the early 1960s (*Protokoll 1962*, pp. 78, 79) to its acceptance of Ostpolitik in the 1970s: *Geschäftsbericht 1971 bis 1973*, pp. 15–16; *Geschäftsbericht 1974 bis 1976*, p. 15; and *Geschäftsbericht 1977 bis 1979*, pp. 17–20. On Ostpolitik see also DGB, *Geschäftsbericht 1969 bis 1971*, introduction, and *Geschäftsbericht 1972 bis 1974*, pp. 4–6.

121 The DGB was rather explicit about its expectations vis-à-vis the SPD's position in the state as the following statement indicates: "The DGB expects that the new federal government will pay greater attention than has been the case in the past to the needs of the workers who with their families represent more than 80 percent of the Federal Republic's population." As quoted in Gerard Braunthal, *The West German Social Democrats, 1969–1982: Profile of a Party in Power* (Boulder: Westview Press, 1983), p. 118.

122 Braunthal, *The West German Social Democrats*, p. 117.

123 Deppe et al., *Geschichte*, p. 447.

124 Schuster, *Die deutsche Gewerkschaftsbewegung*, pp. 104–108; Kassler, "Stationen zu einem ungeliebten Gesetz," pp. 3, 4; and Leminsky and Otto, *Politik*, pp. 147–155.

125 A series of articles in *Der Spiegel* between 1969 and 1974 provides an excellent overview of the intricacies and complexities of the debates on *Mitbestimmung* among the FDP, the SPD and the DGB. Some of the articles are: "Miese Dialektik," *Der Spiegel*, Vol. 23, no. 42 (October 13, 1969); "Wenig dran rühren," *Der Spiegel*, Vol. 24, no. 6 (February 2, 1970); "Nicht stöpseln," *Der Spiegel*, Vol. 24, no. 41 (October 10, 1970); "Noch einige Runden," *Der Spiegel*, Vol. 27, no. 37 (September 10, 1973); "Die Nagelprobe," *Der Spiegel*, Vol. 27, no. 46 (November 12, 1973); "Epochaler Vorgang," *Der Spiegel*, Vol. 28, no. 5 (January 28, 1974); "Gar nicht vereinbart," *Der Spiegel*, Vol. 28, no. 6 (February 4, 1974); "Jetzt kommt's zum Schwur," *Der Spiegel*, Vol. 28, no. 9 (February 25, 1974); "Denkbar eng," *Der Spiegel*, Vol. 28, no. 11 (March 11, 1974); "Fragwürdige Methoden," *Der Spiegel*, Vol. 28, no. 14 (April 1, 1974). Three interviews are of particular interest: one with Willi Michels of IG Metall, another with Kurt Biedenkopf who chaired the commission appointed by Chancellor Kurt Georg Kiesinger to work out an extended scheme of co-determination, and a third with Friedhelm Farthmann, formerly a director of the DGB's research institute WSI and subsequently an important cabinet member of the SPD-dominated government of the Federal Republic's most important state, North Rhine-Westphalia. "Das lassen wir uns nicht abhandeln," *Der Spiegel*, Vol. 24, no. 6 (February 2, 1970) (Michels interview); "Der Begriff glatte Parität ist irreführend," *Der Spiegel*, Vol. 27, no. 46 (November 12, 1973) (Biedenkopf interview); and "Aus SPD-Sicht untragbar," *Der Spiegel*, Vol. 28, no. 9 (February 25, 1974) (Farthmann interview).

126 For the Biedenkopf report see *Mitbestimmung im Unternehmen. Bericht der Sachverständigenkommission zur Auswertung der Erfahrungen bei der Mitbestimmung*, Bundesdrucksache VI/304.

127 Schuster, *Die deutsche Gewerkschaftsbewegung*, p. 106; Deppe et al., *Geschichte*, p. 448; "Wenig dran rühren" in *Der Spiegel*, February 2, 1970; and "Miese Dialektik" in *Der Spiegel*, October 13, 1969.

128 Kassler, "Stationen zu einem ungeliebten Gesetz," p. 5.

129 Ibid.

130 See Gerd Siebert and Barbara Degen, *Betriebsverfassungsgesetz '72: Kommentiert für die Praxis* (Frankfurt am Main: Nachrichten Verlags-Gesellschaft, 1979), fourth edition, pp. 27–371.

131 Siebert and Degen, *Betriebsverfassungsgesetz*, pp. 7–26; Deppe et al., *Geschichte*, p. 439; Leminsky and Otto, *Politik*, pp. 123–130; and "Nicht stöpseln" in *Der Spiegel*, October 5, 1970.

132 Siebert and Degen, *Betriebsverfassungsgesetz*, pp. 7–26; and Deppe et al., *Geschichte*, p. 439.

133 For a list of the constraining dimensions of the 1972 Works Constitution Law, see Siebert and Degen, *Betriebsverfassungsgesetz*, pp. 17, 18; for a good discussion of these dimensions which were already quite apparent during the parliamentary debates in the Bundestag and the various drafts of the eventual legislation, see "Zum Wohl" in *Der Spiegel*, Vol. 25, no. 5 (January 25, 1971).

134 On the Jusos' involvement in this debate over a general radicalization of economic policy on the part of the SPD left, see Wolfgang Roth (ed.), *Investitionslenkung: Ergebnisse einer Diskussion zwischen jungen Unternehmern und Sozialdemokraten zum Problem von Markt und Lenkung* (Reinbek: Rowahlt, 1976); Horst Heidermann (ed.), *Langzeitprogramm 3, Jungsozialisten: Kritische Stellungnahme zum Problem einer gesellschaftspolitischen Langzeitplanung* (Bonn-Bad Godesberg: Verlag Neue Gesellschaft, 1973); and Rudolf Scharping and Friedhelm Wollner (eds.), *Demokratischer Sozialismus und Langzeitprogramm* (Reinbek: Rowohlt, 1973). For a representative sample of the activist union view on investment controls, see Industriegewerkschaft Metall, *Geschäftsbericht 1971 bis 1973* (Frankfurt am Main: IG Metall, n.d.), pp. 104–112. For a very useful intra-union discussion on "investment guidance" presenting different views on the subject within the DGB, see the entire August 1974 issue of *WSI-Mitteilungen* entitled "Schwerpunktthema: Investitionslenkung"; *WSI-Mitteilungen*, Vol. 27, no. 8 (August 1974).

135 IG Metall in fact organized the publication of an entire book opposing the kind of asset formation which the accommodationists advocated. It was appropriately entitled "No to Asset Formation." See Karl Pitz (ed.), *Das Nein zur Vermögensbildung: Gewerkschaftliche Argumente und Alternativen zur Vermögensbildung* (Reinbek: Rowohlt, 1974).

136 For a good presentation of the Meidner Plan see Andrew Martin, "Trade Unions in Sweden: Strategic Responses to Change and Crisis" in Peter Gourevitch et al., *Unions and Economic Crisis: Britain, West Germany and Sweden* (London: George Allen & Unwin, 1984), pp. 272–275.

137 See Heinz Oskar Vetter (ed.), *Humanisierung der Arbeit als gesellschaftspolitische und gewerkschaftliche Aufgabe: Protokoll der DGB-Konferenz vom 16. und 17. Mai 1974 in München* (Frankfurt am Main: Europäische Verlagsanstalt, 1974). For some excellent samples regarding the unions' lasting interest in this matter into the early 1980s, see Gerhard Leminsky, "Humanisierung der Arbeit aus eigener Kraft"; Frieder Naschold, "Humanisierung der Arbeit zwischen Staat und Gewerkschaften"; and Willi Pöhler, "Staatliche Förderung für die Verbesserung der Arbeits-und Lebensqualität," all in *Gewerkschaftliche Monatshefte*, Vol. 31, no. 4 (April 1980).

138 See Pfromm, *Das neue DGB-Grundsatzprogramm*, pp. 209–214; Leminsky and Otto, *Politik*, pp. 63–65; and Schuster, *Die deutsche Gewerkschaftsbewegung*, pp. 109–113. For an excellent analysis of the DGB's 1972 *Aktionsprogramm*, especially in comparison to its successor of 1979, see Gerhard Leminsky, "Zum neuen Aktionsprogramm des DGB" in *Gewerkschaftliche Monatshefte*, Vol. 30, no. 12 (December 1979), pp. 745–754.

139 Schuster, *Die deutsche Gewerkschaftsbewegung*, pp. 109, 110.

140 All of the above is in Pfromm, *Das neue DGB-Grundsatzprogramm*, pp. 209–214.

141 Leminsky, "Zum neuen Aktionsprogramm des DGB," pp. 745–754.

142 On the mobilization by the unions – especially the activists – on April 25, 26 and 27, 1972 (on two days preceding the decisive vote in the Bundestag and on the day itself), see Kurt Steinhaus, *Streiks in der Bundesrepublik 1966–1974* (Frankfurt am Main: Verlag Marxistische Blätter, 1975), pp. 104–109.

143 This sudden change in the political climate of the early 1970s is quite remarkable. Thus, for example, as late as in its documentation of the 1968–1970 period, IG Metall's biannual report to its 1971 congress only talks about "right radicalism." See IG Metall, *Geschäftsbericht 1968 bis 1970*, pp. 19–21. However, the next report to the 1974 congress concentrates almost exclusively on leftist groups which had become active among workers, especially during the numerous strikes of the early 1970s. See IG Metall,

*Geschäftsbericht 1971 bis 1973*, pp. 22–26. Rather than calling this section "right radicalism" as it had done in the past, IG Metall labeled this part of the document "political extremism." This heading appears again in the subsequent report to IG Metall's Düsseldorf congress of 1977. See the section entitled "Politischer Extremismus" in IG Metall, *Geschäftsbericht 1974 bis 1976*, pp. 24–27. Here, the union resumes its attacks on right radicalism and goes to some length to denounce extremism of both the left and the right, declaring them incompatible with union membership. In a passage denouncing one of the many Maoist groups which were active on the fringes of the West German left at the time, IG Metall quotes from one of this group's documents in which the group exhorts Maoists to vote for Franz Josef Strauss and Alfred Dregger in order to form "the broadest possible united front against the contemporary Hitlers in Moscow." See IG Metall, *Geschäftsbericht 1974 bis 1976*, p. 27. Clearly, IG Metall used this passage to ridicule the politics of these extremists by discrediting their judgement and maturity. However, it also provided IG Metall with prima facie evidence of one of the DGB's longest-held tenets, that ultimately the extreme right and the extreme left were not only very similar in form and content but represented equally unacceptable views and activities for organized labor. For a radical critique on the unions' "clauses of incompatibility" see the encyclopedic volume of analysis and documentation entitled *Rotbuch zu den Gewerkschaftsausschlüssen* (Hamburg: J. Reents Verlag, 1978).

144 On the employers' "union state" campaign and its effect on the DGB, see the two special issues of *WSI-Mitteilungen* edited by Rolf Seitenzahl and entitled "Gewerkschaftsstaat oder Unternehmerstaat": *WSI-Mitteilungen*, Vol. 29, no. 8 (August 1976), and *WSI-Mitteilungen*, Vol. 30, no. 12 (December 1977); see also Detlef Perner, "Herr S. und der Popanz 'Gewerkschaftsstaat'" in *Vorgänge – Zeitschrift für Gesellschaftspolitik* (May 1978), pp. 85–92.

145 Accounts of the ÖTV strike can be found in Heinz Hauser, "Der Streik im öffentlichen Dienst 1974" in Otto Jacobi, Walther Müller-Jentsch and Eberhard Schmidt, *Gewerkschaften und Klassenkampf*, pp. 101–115; and Kurt Steinhaus, *Streiks*, pp. 147–154.

146 See "Streik: 'Wir sind keine impotenten Freier'" in *Der Spiegel*, Vol. 28, no. 6 (February 4, 1974); and "Willy Brandt: 'Ihr lasst mich alle allein'" in *Der Spiegel*, Vol. 28, no. 8 (February 18, 1974).

147 As quoted in Frank Deppe, *Autonomie und Integration: Materialien zur Gewerkschaftsanalyse* (Marburg: Verlag Arbeiterbewegung und Gesellschaftswissenschaft, 1979), p. 7.

148 See Dresdner Bank, Statistical Survey (supplement to *Economic Quarterly*), July 1981; also OECD, *Economic Surveys: Germany* (Paris: OECD, 1984), pp. 11–13.

149 The preceding information comes from a number of sources: Ingrid Kurz-Scherf, "Tarifpolitik und Arbeitskämpfe" in Michael Kittner (ed.), *Gewerkschaftsjahrbuch 1984: Daten–Fakten–Analysen* (Cologne: Bund Verlag, 1984), p. 91; Ulrich Billerbeck, Christoph Deutschmann, Rainer Erd, Rudi Schmiede and Edwin Schudlich, *Neuorientierung der Tarifpolitik? Veränderungen im Verhältnis zwischen Lohn- und Manteltarifpolitik in den siebziger Jahren* (Frankfurt am Main: Campus Verlag, 1982), pp. 133, 134, 285, 363, 472, 613 and 615; Norbert Koten, Karl-Heinz Ketterer and Rainer Vollmer, "The political and social factors of Germany's stabilization performance," paper prepared for Brookings Project on the Politics and Sociology of Global Inflation, 1980, pp. 69, 70; and Jeffrey Sachs, "Wage, profits and macroeconomic adjustment in the 1970s: A comparative study", paper presented at Conference of the Brookings Panel on Economic Activity, Massachusetts Institute of Technology, Cambridge, Massachusetts, October 1979, pp. 18–25.

150 For the DGB's full employment program see DGB, *Vorschläge des DGB zur Wiederherstellung der Vollbeschäftigung* (Düsseldorf: DGB, 1977). For some representative points regarding the cyclical/conjunctural arguments of the unions' analysis of the crisis see, for example, Deutscher Gewerkschaftsbund, *Geschäftsbericht 1975 bis 1977* (Düsseldorf: DGB, n.d.), pp. 336–341.

151 Some of the major arguments concerning the unions' worries about structural imbalances in the West German and global economies can be found in a two-volume publication emanating from a conference organized by IG Metall betwen May 17 and 19, 1976, in Cologne, entitled "Crisis and reform in industrial society." See Industriegewerk-

schaft Metall, *Krise und Reform in der Industriegesellschaft* (Frankfurt am Main: Europäische Verlagsanstalt, 1976), 2 volumes; see also Günter Pehl, "Eine neue internationale Arbeitsteilung setzt sich durch" in *Die Quelle*, Vol. 29, no. 5 (May 1978), pp. 275–277; Karl Buschmann, "Probleme der internationalen Arbeitsteilung in der Textil und Bekleidungsindustrie" in *Gewerkschaftliche Monatshefte*, Vol. 29, no. 6 (June 1978), pp. 355–367; and Klaus Busch, "Fuhrt Kapitalexport zu Arbeitsplatzexport?," *WSI-Mitteilungen*, Vol. 32, no. 9 (September 1979), pp. 493–501.

152 Here is a typical passage from the DGB publication delineating the unions' ambivalent view towards rationalization: "In the past, the DGB has welcomed the results of rationalization and technical change insofar as it was ensured that by raising work productivity, it was also possible to improve workers' social conditions and no negative effects occurred at their expense.... Should those with ... responsibility fail to do away with mass unemployment, the trade union position on rationalization and technical change would have to be critically rethought." *DGB Report*, no. 13/3, 1978, pp. 5, 6.

153 On the term "job killers", and a representative discussion of this syndrome since the crisis of the mid-1970s, see Peter Kalmbach, "Rationalisierung, neue Technologien, und Beschäftigung" in *Gewerkschaftliche Monatshefte*, Vol. 29, no. 8 (August 1978), pp. 455–467.

154 The unions did, however, address the issue of technological change and rationalization in connection with strategies concerning the humanization of work. By the late 1970s and early 1980s, there were a number of interesting ideas advanced in union publications concerning possible union measures to counter the most adverse effects of technological change. For this, see the entire issue of *Gewerkschaftliche Monatshefte*, Vol. 31, no. 4 (April 1980).

155 The most eminent representative of the "scissors theory" of unemployment among union economists has been Rudolf Henschel, the leading and most senior staff economist in the federation's economic policy section in Düsseldorf. Among his relevant writings on this topic are: "Eine Problemskizze aus gewerkschaftlicher Sicht", unpublished manuscript, May 4, 1979; "Die gewerkschaftliche Kritik am Memorandum '79" in *Gewerkschaftliche Monatshefte*, Vol. 31, no. 2 (February 1980), pp. 109–116; "Arbeitslosigkeit: Folge einseitig quantitativ orientierter Wachstumspolitik" in *WSI-Mitteilungen* Vol. 33, no. 4 (April 1980), pp. 206–216; and "Memorandum '80 ist eine gute Grundlage für die weitere Diskussion" in *Die Quelle*, Vol. 30, no. 6 (June 1980), pp. 332, 333.

156 See the DGB's pamphlet *Vorschläge des DGB zur Wiederherstellung der Vollbeschäftigung* in which the federation delineated its program for the restoration of full employment in the West German economy.

157 Indeed, it is interesting to note that the German translation of the inter-European union paper *Keynes Plus* bears the title *Über Keynes hinaus* which literally translates into English as "beyond Keynes." See Clas-Erik Odhner, *Participatory Economics of Keynes Plus* (Stockholm: n.p., 1978); and Europäisches Gewerkschaftsinstitut, *Über Keynes hinaus: Gestaltung der Wirtschaftspolitik durch Alternativen* (Brussels: n.p., 1978).

158 For a representative summary of all these points, see Deutscher Gewerkschaftsbund, *Geschäftsbericht 1978 bis 1981* (Düsseldorf: DGB, n.d.), pp. 55–142 and 365–394.

159 As the rest of Europe and the United States tumbled from one crisis situation to another during the late 1970s, the comparatively mild manifestations of problems in the Federal Republic at that time inspired admiration of West Germany's overall performance under the leadership of Helmut Schmidt by many analysts in the West. Schmidt's and the SPD's election slogan of 1976 – "Modell Deutschland" – had become accepted by journalists and scholars alike as an appropriate characterization of Schmidt's leadership at the helm of a surprisingly stable ship. For three scholarly collections on "Modell Deutschland," see Wilfrid Kohl and Giorgio Basevi (eds.), *West Germany: A European and Global Power* (Lexington, Mass.: D.C. Heath & Co., 1980); Andrei S. Markovits (ed.), *The Political Economy of West Germany: Modell Deutschland* (New York: Praeger, 1982); and William Patterson and Gordon Smith (eds.), *The West German Model: Perspectives on a Stable State* (London: Frank Cass, 1981). For a representative journalistic account of West Germany's characterization as a "model," see "Germany:

The Model Nation?" in *Newsweek* (European edition), September 27, 1976. On Helmut Schmidt's leadership role, see "Helmut Schmidt: Asserting Germany's New Leadership" in *The New York Times Magazine*, September 21, 1980; and "A Talk with Helmut Schmidt" in *The New York Times Magazine*, September 16, 1984.

160 The official title of the Budget Structure Law is "Massnahmen zur Verbesserung der Haushaltsstruktur". It was published officially by the government in September 1975. See *Bulletin* (Bonn: Presse-und-Informationsamt der Bundersregierung, September 1975).

161 On the governmental cutbacks in the labor market during the crisis via budgetary restrictions and legal measures, see Hans Pfriem and Hartmut Seifert, "Funktion und Formwandel von Arbeitsmarktpolitik: Vom System positiver Anreize zu einer systematisierten Kontroll-und Sanktionspraxis" in *WSI-Mitteilungen*, Vol. 32, no. 2 (February 1979), pp. 68–79; and Hartmut Seifert, *Öffentliche Arbeitsmarktpolitik in der Bundesrepublik Deutschland: Zur Entwicklung der Arbeitsmarktpolitik im Verhältnis von Steuerungsaufgabe und Anpassungsfunktion* (Cologne: Bund Verlag, 1984).

162 A brief but excellent characterization of Helmut Schmidt's good rapport with the DGB leadership can be found in Gerard Braunthal, *The West German Social Democrats*, p. 114. Braunthal cites Willy Brandt's alleged remark that "Helmut Schmidt has three coalition partners, the DGB, the FDP, and the SPD – in that order."

163 When in November 1981 the Bundestag passed yet another of Chancellor Schmidt's austerity measures, IG Metall's Stuttgart district organized a major anti-government rally which was attended by over 70,000 metalworkers. This represented one of the very few incidents in the history of the Federal Republic where officially organized union demonstrations protested actions undertaken by the Social Democratic Party. It is interesting to note, however, that the official union press – while vehemently attacking the government's austerity package – refrained from mentioning the Stuttgart demonstration. This pertains also to IG Metall's two major publications, its bi-weekly newpaper *metall* and its monthly magazine *Der Gewerkschafter*. On the demonstration see Richard Ullmer, "Sparpolitik und Beschäftigungsprogramme" in *express*, Vol. 19, no. 12 (December 15, 1981), p. 3.

164 Otto Jacobi, "Tarifpolitik in der Wirtschaftskrise 1974/75" in Jacobi et al., *Gewerkschaften und Klassenkampf*, p. 103.

165 Erhard Kassler, "Stationen zu einem ungeliebten Gesetz," pp. 3–15.

166 On *Mitbestimmung '76* see Federal Ministry of Labour and Social Affairs, *Co-determination* (Bonn: Bundesministerium für Arbeit und Sozialordnung, 1976), pp. 7–45; also German edition, *Mitbestimmung* (Bonn: Bundesministerium für Arbeit und Sozialordnung, 1978), pp. 29–48.

167 Deutscher Gewerkschaftsbund, *Das Programm für Zukunftsinvestitionen der Bundesregierung vom Frühjahr 1977* (Düsseldorf: DGB, 1978), pp. 11–15.

168 Ibid., p. 11.

169 See the already mentioned DGB pamphlet *Vorschläge des DGB zur Wiederherstellung der Vollbeschäftigung*.

170 All of the above information stems from *Vorschläge des DGB zur Wiederherstellung der Vollbeschäftigung*.

171 "Hilfe für Regionen mit mehr als sechs Prozent Arbeitslosen" in *Frankfurter Rundschau*, June 17, 1979; "Bonner Arbeitsmarktprogramm kommt an" in *Süddeutsche Zeitung*, August 8, 1979; IG Metall, *Geschäftsbericht 1977 bis 1979*, pp. 71, 77–79; Der Bundesminister für Arbeit und Sozialordnung, *Arbeitsmarktpolitisches Programm der Bundesregierung für Regionen mit besonderen Beschäftigungsproblemen* (Bonn: Bundesministerium für Arbeit und Sozialordnung, 1979); "Problemgebiete des Arbeitsmarktes holen auf" in *Frankfurter Rundschau*, April 22, 1980; and Franz Heinrichs, "Neues Leben auf den Halden?" in *metall*, May 30, 1979.

172 See *Dienstblatt der Bundesanstalt für Arbeit*, Runderlass 230/78.

173 "Welche Arbeit zumutbar ist, soll im Einzelfall geprüft werden," in *Frankfurter Rundschau*, May 17, 1979; "Einigung der Koalitionspartner", in *Handelsblatt*, May 17, 1979; Norbert

Möller-Lücking, "AFG-Regierungsentwurf wird den Aufgaben nicht gerecht" in *Die Quelle*, Vol. 30, no. 2 (February 1979), pp. 112–113; and Gerd Muhr, "Was bringt die 5. Novelle zum Arbeitsförderungsgesetz?" in *Die Quelle*, Vol. 30, no. 7–8 (July/August 1979), pp. 424–425.

174 See "Fast einen Tobsuchtsanfall" in *Der Spiegel*, March 3, 1975; and Walter Simon, *Macht und Herrschaft der Unternehmerverbände BDI, BDA und DIHT im ökonomischen und politischen System der BRD* (Cologne: Pahl-Rugenstein Verlag, 1976), pp. 110–122.

175 On the "union state" campaign see the two special issues of *WSI-Mitteilungen* from August 1976 and December 1977 mentioned in note 144. See also Detlef Perner, "Herr S. und der Popanz 'Gewerkschaftsstaat'" mentioned in the same note. For two excellent articles on this topic, see also Iring Fetscher, "'Gewerkschaftsstaat' und Freiheit" in Ulrich Borsdorf, Hans O. Hemmer, Gerhard Leminsky and Heinz Markmann (eds.), *Gewerkschaftliche Politik: Reform aus Solidarität* (Cologne: Bund Verlag, 1977), pp. 127–134; and Hans-Hermann Hartwich, "Organizationsmacht gegen Kapitalmacht – Die Gewerkschaften in der Innenstruktur der Bundesrepublik" in ibid., pp. 80–108.

176 For two prototypical examples advancing the argument of the supposed subversion – Unterwanderung – of the unions by radical leftists and communists, see Ernst Günter Vetter, "Die Roten sind auf dem Marsch" in *Frankfurter Allgemeine Zeitung*, April 21, 1979; and Die Heimliche Volksfront" in *Frankfurter Allgemeine Zeitung*, July 9, 1979.

177 In addition to the materials on the "union state" which are also relevant to this topic, see Fritz W. Scharpf, *Autonome Gewerkschaften und staatliche Wirtschaftspolitik: Probleme einer Verbändegesetzgebung* (Cologne; Europäische Verlagsanstalt, 1978); Siegfried Balduin and Hermann Unterhinninghofen, "Zur Diskussion um ein Verbändegesetz" in *WSI-Mitteilungen* Vol. 30, no. 12 (December 1977), pp. 56–67; Ernst-Wolfgang Böckenförde, "Die politische Funktion wirtschaftlich-sozialer Verbände und Interessenträger in der sozialstaatlichen Demokratie: Eine Beitrag zum Problem der 'Regierbarkeit'" in *Der Staat*, Vol. 15, no. 4 (Fall 1976), pp. 457–483; and "Wes Brot ich ess', des Lied ich sing" in *metall*, Vol. 36, no. 13 (June 22, 1984), pp. 16, 17.

178 For a very thorough collection of materials concerning the CSU's paper and the ensuing debate, see Industriegewerkschaft Metall (ed.), *Spalte und Herrsche: F. J. Strauss und die Einheitsgewerkschaft* (Frankfurt am Main: IG Metall, n.d.); Frank Deppe, Detlef Hensche, Mechtild Jansen und Witich Rossmann, *Strauss und die Gewerkschaften: Texte, Materialien, Dokumente* (Cologne: Pahl-Rugenstein Verlag, 1980); and virtually the entire issue of IG Metall's newspaper *metall* from July 18, 1979.

179 All of the above points are discussed in detail in IG Metall (ed.), *Spalte und Herrsche* and also in Deppe et al., *Strauss und die Gewerkschaften*.

180 "Das Mitbestimmungsgesetz ist verfassungsmässig" in *Frankfurter Allgemeine Zeitung*, March 2, 1979; DGB, *Geschäftsbericht 1975 bis 1977*, pp. 29–33, and IG Metall, *Geschäftsbericht 1977 bis 1979*, p. 31.

181 For some of these ideas, see two superb articles written by the two leading legal experts within the union movement: Michael Kittner, "Zur verfassungsrechtlichen Zukunft von Reformpolitik, Mitbestimmung und Gewerkschaftsfreiheit" in *Gewerkschaftliche Monatshefte*, Vol. 30, no. 6 (June 1979), pp. 321–342; and Ulrich Zachert, "Mitbestimmung ohne Gewerkschaften?" in *Gewerkschaftliche Monatshefte*, Vol. 30, no. 6 (June 1979), pp. 342–346.

182 See the Court's decision in *Blick durch die Wirtschaft*, March 5, 1979; and "Im Namen des Volkes" in *Das Mitbestimmungsgespräch*, Vol. 25, no. 3 (March 1979), pp. 63–86.

183 "Worum es in Karlsruhe ging" in *Frankfurter Rundschau*, March 2, 1979; "Für alle etwas" in *Frankfurter Allgemeine Zeitung*, March 2, 1979; and "Nach dem Karlsruher Urteil: Alle sind erleichtert" in *Die Welt*, March 2, 1979.

184 See *DGB Nachrichten-Dienst*, March 7, 1979; the *Frankfurter Rundschau*, *Süddeutsche Zeitung* and *Frankfurter Allgemeine Zeitung* of March 3, 1979; *Die Quelle* of March and April 1979; the "Dokumentation" section of the *Gewerkschaftliche Umschau*, No. 2, 1979; and IG Metall, *Geschäftsbericht 1977–79*, pp. 31-34

185 Michael Kittner, "Zur verfassungsrechtlichen Zukunft."

186 Ibid.

187 For this term –Verbändegesetz auf Raten – see Ulrich Zachert, "Mittbestimmung ohne Gewerkschaften?," p. 346.

188 The outcome of three cases which were ultimately adjudicated by the Federal Labor Court in Kassel particularly irked the unions. In the first instance, the Court held that the union would not be permitted to conduct shop-steward elections on company premises, even during breaks. In the second case, the Court decided that the wearing of union emblems on company-owned protective helmets was not permissible. Lastly, the Court reached a very complex decision which – while not explicitly forbidding the distribution of union literature on company premises – made such action a good deal more difficult than had been previously the case. See Ulrich Zachert, "Mitbestimmung ohne Gewerkschaften?," pp. 342–346.

189 The seriousness of this issue for the DGB can be gauged by the vast quantity of published material which has appeared on lockouts. No other topic – with the exception of co-determination – has preoccupied the DGB to such an extent since the onset of the crisis in the mid-1970s as lockouts and their prevention. Following is a very selective list of the most important publications representing the DGB's point of view: Michael Kittner, *Verbot der Aussperrung: 7 Fragen – 70 Antworten* (Frankfurt: IG Metall, n.d.); Manfred Bobke, *Gewerkschaften und Aussperrung: Eine Analyse gewerkschaftlicher Strategien und Rechtsargumentationen gegen die Aussperrung* (Cologne: Bund Verlag, 1982); Hans Hermann Wohlgemuth, *Staatseingriff und Arbeitskampf: Zur Kritik der herrschenden Arbeitskampfdoktrin* (Cologne: Europäische Verlagsanstalt, 1977); Karl-Jürgen Bieback (ed.), *Streikfreiheit und Aussperrungsverbot: Zur Diskussion einer gewerkschaftlichen Forderung* (Neuwied: Luchterhand Verlag, 1979); and Ulrich Zachert, Maria Metzge and Wolfgang Hamer, *Die Aussperrung: Zur rechtlichen Zulässigkeit und praktischen Durchsetzungsmöglichkeit eines Aussperrungsverbots* (Cologne: Bund Verlag, 1979), second edition.

190 On the printers' strike of 1976 see "Druckerstreik 1976" in Rainer Duhm and Ulrich Müchenberger (eds.), *Arbeitskampf im Alltag: Wie man sich wehrt und warum* (Berlin: Rotbuch Verlag, 1977), pp. 11–36; on the printers' strike of 1978 see Walther Müller-Jentsch, "Der Arbeitskampf in der Druckindustrie" in Otto Jacobi, Walther Müller-Jentsch and Eberhard Schmidt (ed.), *Arbeiterinteressen gegen Sozialpartnerschaft: Kritisches Gewerkschaftsjahrbuch 1978/79* (Berlin: Rotbuch Verlag, 1979), pp. 10–23; on IG Metall's strike in Baden-Württemberg's metal industry see Eckart Hildebrandt, "Der Tarifkampf in der metallverarbeitenden Industrie 1978" in ibid., pp. 60–63; on IG Metall's steel strike later that year see Willi Dzielak, Wolfgang Hindrichs, Helmut Martens and Walter Schophaus, *Arbeitskampf um Arbeitsplätze: Der Tarifkonflikt 1978/79 in der Stahlindustrie* (Frankfurt am Main: Campus Verlag, 1980). All three of these strikes receive ample coverage in the chapters on IG Metall and IG Druck und Papier in this volume.

191 Karl-Heinz Janzen, "Aussperrung – Klassenkampf von oben oder legales Arbeitskampfmittel?" in *Der Gewerkschafter*, Vol. 26, no. 9 (September 1978), pp. 21–28; Ulrich Zachert, "Aussperrung und Gewerkschaften" in *Gewerkschaftliche Monatshefte* Vol. 29, no. 5 (May 1978), pp. 280–289; and Hans Hermann Wohlgemuth, "Zur Auseinandersetzung um die Aussperrung" in *Gewerkschaftliche Monatshefte*, Vol. 30, no. 3 (March 1979), pp. 145–152.

192 See Manfred Bobke, *Gewerkschaften und Aussperrung*, pp. 1–17, 21–27; Otto Ernst Kempen, "Zur Vorgeschichte der Aussperrungsrechtsprechung des Bundesarbeitsgerichts seit 1945" in Karl-Jürgen Bieback (ed.), *Streikfreiheit und Aussperrungsverbot*, pp. 184–199; Henner Wolter, "Aussperrung und Verhältnismässigkeit – Kritik des 'obersten Gebots' des Arbeitskampfrechts" in ibid., pp. 224–251; Gerhard Müller, "Fragen zum Arbeitskampfrecht nach dem Beschluss des Grossen Senats des Bundesarbeitsgerichts vom 21, April 1971" in *Gewerkschaftliche Monatshefte*, Vol. 23, no. 5 (May 1972), pp. 273–286; Lorenz Schwegler, "Streikrecht und Rechtsprechung: Zum politischen Charakter des sogenannten Arbeitskampfrechts nach dem Beschluss des Grossen Senats des BAG vom 21.4.1971" in *Gewerkschaftliche Monatshefte*, Vol. 23, no. 5 (May 1972), pp. 299–309; and Michael Kittner, "Parität im Arbeitskampf? Überlegungen zur For-

derung nach dem Verbot der Aussperrung" in *Gewerkschaftliche Monatshefte*, Vol. 24, no. 2 (February 1973), pp. 91–104.

193 See the statements by Eugen Loderer, IG Metall's chairman, in his article "Aussperrung verbieten" in *metall*, April 19, 1979, p. 17.

194 See Hans Hermann Wohlgemuth, "Zur Auseinandersetzung um die Aussperrung," pp. 147–152.

195 See "Kampf gegen Aussperrung geht bis zum Verbot weiter" in *Welt der Arbeit*, June 12, 1980; and "Gemeinsame Erklärung des DGB, der IG Metall und der IG Druck" in *Die Neue*, June 13, 1980.

196 See Manfred Bobke, *Gewerkschaften und Aussperrung*, pp. 81–113; and Ulrich Zachert, "Gewerkschaftliche Autonomie und rechtliche Rahmenbedingungen: Die Aussperrung im Spektrum der Einschränkung von Gewerkschaftsrechten" in *Gewerkschaftliche Monatshefte*, Vol. 31, no. 5 (May 1980), pp. 293–302.

197 See "Ausstieg aus der Montanmitbestimmung?" in *Frankfurter Rundschau*, June 6, 1980; on the Mannesmann controversy, see IG Metall's excellent documentation in IG Metall, *Der Angriff: Mannesmann gegen Mitbestimmung* (Frankfurt am Main: IG Metall, n.d.).

198 See the speeches by Eugen Loderer and Rudolf Judith at IG Metall's special "Mannesmann conference" held in Dortmund on July 3, 1980; Eugen Loderer, "Die Montanmitbestimmung – Faustpfand der Wirtschaftsdemokratie"; and Rudolf Judith, "Montanmitbestimmung in Gefahr," speeches presented to the IG Metall Iron and Steel Conference, Dortmund, July 3, 1980; also "IG Metall will Montanmitbestimmung nicht ausmerzen lassen" in *Frankfurter Rundschau*, June 18, 1980. Herbert Wehner, the venerable leader of the SPD's parliamentary delegation and with Helmut Schmidt and Willy Brandt one of the Social Democrats' "big three," saw Mannesmann's action as an "assault on the nerves of the republic." See "... rührt am Nerv der Republik" in *Frankfurter Rundschau*, June 18, 1980.

199 "Montanmitbestimmung mit allen Mitteln verteidigen" in *Frankfurter Allgemeine Zeitung*, June 12, 1980; "Die IG Metall will nötigenfalls kämpfen" in *Handelsblatt*, July 4/5, 1980; "Stahlbetriebsräte reden offen von Streik" in *Frankfurter Rundschau*, July 23, 1980.

200 On the SPD's support of the union position see "SPD will Mannesmann durchkreuzen" in *Süddeutsche Zeitung*, June 18, 1980; "Schmidt: Hände weg von Montanmitbestimmung" in *Handelsblatt*, July 7, 1980; and "Wehner: Gruppenantrag nicht taktisch gemeint" in *Frankfurter Rundschau*, July 3, 1980. On the FDP's opposition to a "Lex Mannesmann," see "Genscher droht mit Koalitionsbruch" in *Frankfurter Rundschau*, August 15, 1980; "FDP will die Zustimmung verweigern" in *Frankfurter Rundschau*, June 24, 1980; and "Koalitionsstreit über Mitbestimmung verschärft" in *Süddeutsche Zeitung*, June 28/29, 1980.

201 On DGB and other inter-union solidarity with IG Metall's plight in the Mannesmann affair, see "Drohung des DGB" in *Handelsblatt*, July 17, 1980; "Gewerkschaften beraten über Abwehrmassnahmen" in *Frankfurter Allgemeine Zeitung*, July 17, 1980; "Vetter zieht Parallelen zu Weimar" in *Frankfurter Allgemeine Zeitung*, June 28, 1980; "ÖTV voll hinter Mitbestimmung" in *Frankfurter Rundschau*, July 15, 1980; and "Fall Mannesmann soll kein Reinfall werden" in *Frankfurter Rundschau*, July 2, 1980.

202 German Information Center, New York, *Relay from Bonn: The Week in Germany*, February 6, 1981.

203 See Pehl, "Eine neue internationale Arbeitsteilung," and Busch, "Führt Kapitalexport."

204 For the text of the Tabu Katalog see "Die Tabus der Arbeitgeber: So sieht die Widerstandslinie gegen die Gewerkschaften aus" in *Die Zeit*, January 26, 1979; and "der tabu-katalog der unternehmer" in *druck und papier*, Vol. 117, no. 3 (January 29, 1979), pp. 8–11.

205 For examples of the unions' interpretation of the Tabu Katalog as a "remote-control mechanism" for the employers' collective bargaining strategies, see "Neue Wege der Tarifpolitik" in *metall*, May 2, 1979; "Wir haben Zeichen gesetzt" in *Der Gewerkschafter*, Vol. 27, no. 5 (May 1979), pp. 21–26; and Martin Heiss, "Tabu Katalog fügt der Allgemeinheit Schaden zu" in *Die Quelle*, Vol. 30, no. 2 (February 1979), pp. 93, 94.

206 See Gerhard Gerlach, "Tarifbewegungen, Arbeitskämpfe und tarifvertragliche Arbeitsbedingungen im Jahre 1978" in *WSI-Mitteilungen*, Vol. 32, no. 3 (March 1979), pp. 132–
144; Gerhard Gerlach, "Neuere tarifpolitische Strategien der Gewerkschaften in der
BRD zur Sicherung von Arbeitsplätzen und Besitzständen" in *WSI-Mitteilungen*, Vol. 32,
no. 4 (April 1979), pp. 221–227; Klaus Pickhaus and Witich Rossmann, *Streik und
Aussperrung '78: Hafen – Druck – Metall* (Frankfurt am Main: Nachrichten Verlag, 1978),
p. 70; and Gert Hautsch and Bernd Semmler, *Stahlstreik und Tarifrunde 78/79* (Frankfurt
am Main: Institut für Marxistische Studien und Forschungen, 1979), pp. 13, 14.

207 The right-wing faction of the SPD, a number of important party "apparatchiks" and
middle-level "organization men" have been dubbed "sewer works" by their opponents
for their excessive interest in orderly conditions and power within the party at the
expense of ideological purity. Much closer to Helmut Schmidt than to Willy Brandt, the
"Kanalarbeiter" have been characterized by their criticis as "'mouse-grey' backben-
chers who after their parliamentary work prefer to drink beer, gorge themselves, and play
skat in a smoke-filled restaurant" rather than "engage in political discussion." (For these
passages see Gerard Braunthal, *The West German Social Democrats*, p. 208.) In short, the
"sewer workers" within the SPD proper and in the labor movement as a whole
represented the pragmatic, bread-and-butter accommodationism which had traditionally assumed a central position in the development of German social democracy. The
accommodationist wing of the DGB, comprising the "gang of five" in the late 1970s,
developed an increasing affinity for Chancellor Schmidt and the "sewer workers" as the
crisis continued unabated in the Federal Republic.

208 It would be well beyond the scope of this chapter to give a full account of the West
German Communist Party's role vis-à-vis the unions. Suffice it to say that the Deutsche
Kommunistische Partei (DKP), which was reconstituted in 1968 after its predecessor,
the KPD, had been declared unconstitutional in 1957, exerted a strong presence in
certain unions during the latter half of the 1970s. Recognizing the futility of its electoral
activities which yielded consistently abysmal results and rejecting any form of violent or
clandestine strategy against the existing parliamentary order, the DKP's activism within
certain unions represented the sole possibility for the party to lend at least some
significance to its existence. Moreover, the party also opted for this approach because it
regarded the unions as the only institutions within West German capitalism capable of
initiating and implementing social change. Indeed, in viewing the DGB and its
constituent unions as the only effective organizations of the West German working class,
the DKP pursued from the very beginning an exceedingly pro-DGB line which bordered
on subservience with one major exception: the DGB's traditional ties to the SPD. In
attempting to woo the organized working class away from its strong SPD-allegiance,
DKP activists within the unions gradually developed into model "organization men" on
the rank-and-file level. Their unselfish behavior often met with great success among
workers who welcomed the activism of these people not because they belonged to the
DKP but in spite of it. By the end of the 1970s, the situation had become sufficiently
widespread in some of the activist unions to incur the wrath of the SPD-dominated
leadership, especially at the DGB and its accommodationist members. The intra-union
tensions reached such dimensions by 1979 that leading union officials accused the DKP
of infiltrating the unions in order to make them the party's transmission belt of Leninist
dogma. In short, the "subversion" theme, so readily used by the employers and the
conservative media in their attacks against labor, also found its enthusiastic supporters
within the union movement itself. The issue was complicated by the fact that part of the
DKP's pro-DGB strategy entailed active denunciations by the communists of other
leftists within the unions who – unlike the DKP's members – were personae non gratae
according to the union's "clauses of incompatibility." Thus, in addition to the SPD vs.
DKP rivalry there was a concomitant DKP vs. "undogmatic leftist" tension which
intensified considerably in the last few years of the 1970s.

The first area of major conflict concerned the interpretation of union history,
particularly the very sensitive era of the last few years of the Weimar Republic. Central to
the debate was a widely used and very thorough book on the history of the German labor

movement authored by a number of historians from the University of Marburg, whose history department had a reputation for representing views which were close to – though not identical with – those advocated by the DKP. The book, whose detailed documentation of the post-World War II period was extensively used in the writing of this chapter, was edited by Frank Deppe, Georg Fülberth and Jürgen Harrer, and entitled *Geschichte der deutschen Gewerkschaftsbewegung*. Published by the Cologne-based firm of Pahl-Rugenstein, which has specialized in publishing studies in the social sciences and history that expounded views bearing similarities to the ones put forth by the DKP, the book aroused immediate suspicions on the part of many an accommodationsist union leader by virtue of the institutional affiliation of its authors and the reputation of its publisher. The book's severe criticism of the labor movement's social democratic leadership and its close alliance with the SPD during the Weimar Republic irked many DGB leaders. Accompanied by the book's virtual silence on the divisive strategies pursued by the Communist Party (KPD) within the union movement during the latter years of the Weimar Republic, the Deppe et al. volume served as prima facie evidence for many unionists that the DKP and its intellectual allies were trying to use a one-sided interpretation of history to make a negative statement about the continued ties between the SPD and the labor movement during the Bonn Republic as well. The reaction to the book and its larger implications was wide-ranging and engaged the interest of many unionists as well as a number of leftist intellectuals. For the three most authoritative attacks against the book emanating from the official union press see Manfred Scharrer, "Eine die Geschichte verfälschende 'Gewerkschaftsgeschichte'" in *Die Quelle*, Vol. 29, no. 11 (November 1978), pp. 606–608; Gerhard Beier, "Leninisten führten die Feder" in *ÖTV-Magazin*, no. 3 (March 1979), pp. 33–37; and Hermann Weber, "Kommunistische Gewerkschaftspolitik in der Weimarer Republik" in *ÖTV-Magazin*, no. 4 (April 1979), pp. 39–42. See also "'Hier wird Geschichte gefälscht' – Kritik aus der ÖTV an Historikern aus Marburg" in *Frankfurter Allgemeine Zeitung*, April 10, 1979. For the "undogmatic left's" intermediate position on this important debate, see Edgar Weick, "Aus der Geschichte lernen" in *express*, Vol. 17, no. 4 (April 23, 1979), pp. 8, 9; Peter von Örtzen "Wie lässt sich Geschichtsschreibung im DKP-Stil messen?" in *Frankfurter Rundschau*, April 11, 1979; and "Zwei Linien und ein roter Faden" in *Frankfurter Rundschau*, October 6, 1979. The issue was sufficiently important and divisive for the DGB to organize a major conference on the matter with all sides invited to present their views. While the Munich conference held on the 13th and 14th of October 1979 eliminated some of the sharper edges of the underlying hostilities, it failed to alleviate them completely, and they thus continue to linger. See "Mit den Experten konnten die Veteranen nichts anfangen" in *Frankfurter Rundschau*, October 15, 1979; "Das Signal zum Widerstand blieb aus" Part One published in *Frankfurter Rundschau*, October 13, 1979 and Part Two published in *Frankfurter Rundschau*, October 18, 1979. The DGB also published the proceedings of the conference in Heinz O. Vetter (ed.), *Aus der Geschichte lernen – die Zukunft gestalten: Dreissig Jahre DGB*. See note 7 above.

The Deppe et al. book would most likely not have become such an issue of contention had it not been for the fact that it was adopted in many union schools' curricula, thereby giving it extensive exposure. The form and content of youth education within the unions represented the second area of intra-union conflict involving the DKP. The controversy gained public attention over the so-called "Oberurseler Papier" in which union leaders from the DGB's education center in Oberursel, just outside of Frankfurt, accused the DKP and its supporters of trying to undermine the existing political conditions within the unions, with the aim of making them subservient to the DKP. It is important to point out that the main author of the Oberurseler paper, the director of the DGB's education center in Oberursel, Hinrich Ötjen, perceived himself as a member of the independent or "undogmatic" left and professed to be as critical of the SPD-dominated union establishment as were his major targets in the paper. The ensuing intra-DGB feuds were very heated, resulting in further exacerbations of the already considerable differences between accommodationist and activist unions within the federation. The activist unions led by IG Metall and IG Druck und Papier vowed never to send any of their young officials to a

DGB-run education center whose director engaged in red-baiting. The accommodationists led by IG Bergbau und Energie and IG Chemie-Papier-Keramik embraced the paper's accusations and viewed it as an excellent corroboration of their long-held fears concerning the DKP's "cadre politics" designed to undermine the existing union structures solely for the party's benefit. Thus, an interesting anti-DKP alliance developed within the labor movement in which right-wing social democrats and "sewer workers" joined independent leftists, often of a very radical sort, in opposing the communists' operations, which remained almost exclusively confined to the activist unions. It is quite clear that the two members of this tenuous alliance opposed the DKP's presence within West Germany's trade unions for very different reasons. For the Oberurseler Papier, see "Erst Posten erobern und dann gegen kritik abschotten" in the documentation section of the *Frankfurter Rundschau*, May 5 and May 7, 1979. For the most pronounced statements by the accommodationists on this matter, see "Kommunisten an 'Knotenpunkten' in der DGB-Jugend fest verankert? Die DGB-Bundesjugendschule warnt vor DKP-Einflüssen" in *Einheit*, April 1, 1979; and "Kampf um Teewasser organisieren; Lenin: Mit vielen Kniffen an die Macht" in *Einheit*, May 1, 1979. For one of the most acerbic replies within the labor movement to the accusation of the DKP's allegedly subversive tactics and strategy see "Auf Dreck muss geklotzt werden" in *Frankfurter Rundschau*, April 25, 1979. For IG Metall's irritated response to the accusations implicitly leveled at it and other activist unions by the accommodationists see "IG Metall wirft DGB-Bundesjugendschule Diffamierung vor" in *Frankfurter Rundschau*, January 4, 1980; "IG Metall-Jugend will Härte" in *Frankfurter Rundschau*, January 3, 1980; "Vom Stolz über das Abfangen antiautoritärer Tendenzen" in *Frankfurter Rundschau*, January 12, 1980; and "Preiss; 'In der Gewerkschaft zählt nicht das Trennende, sondern die Solidarität'" in *Die Neue*, May 16, 1979. For good documentation on the direct debate between accommodationsists and activists regarding this matter see "'Schmuddelige Kampagne gegen Kommunisten'" in *Frankfurter Allgemeine Zeitung*, April 26, 1979; "'Bild von der Gewerkschaftsjugend hängt schief links'" in *Frankfurter Rundschau*, June 1, 1979; "Vorwurf der Verniedlichung kommunistischer Ziele gegen Detlef Hensche" in *Frankfurter Rundschau*, September 29, 1979; "Schon einmal dienten Feindbilder dazu, Verfolgungen einzuleiten" in *Frankfurter Rundschau*, October 22, 1979; and "Der Unterwanderweg ist lang" in *Der Spiegel*, January 14, 1980. The most comprehensive treatment of all these matters regarding the DKP's role in the education of union youth, the interpretation of labor history and the intra-labor battles between activists and accommodationists can be found in Ossip K. Flechtheim, Wolfgang Rudzio, Fritz Vilmar and Manfred Wilke, *Der Marsch der DKP durch die Institutionen: Sowjetmarxistische Einflussstrategien und Ideologien* (Frankfurt am Main: Fischer Verlag, 1980). As can be readily gauged from the title of this book, its authors are extremely critical of the DKP and its numerous sympathizers among the activist wing of the DGB, and find the communist presence in the unions worrisome and counterproductive. The book represents a joint effort by the ephemeral anti-DKP coalition consisting of right-wing social democrats and "undogmatic" – i.e. non-communist – leftists.

The third area of union politics in which the DKP's existence played a crucial role during the crisis of the late 1970s was the formulation of economic policy. Centered around the so-called "Memorandum" which was originally published by a number of radical economists with DKP leanings at the University of Bremen, the debates once again concerned both the form and content of the Communist Party's engagement in union affairs during the crisis. In this case too there existed a coalition of right-wing social democrats and non-communist radicals who opposed the Memorandum's strategies for diametrically opposite reasons. Furthermore, once again this uneasy alliance faced the bulk of the DGB's activist wing comprising IG Metall and IG Druck und Papier, who not only favored the annual publication of the Memoranda but also seemed untroubled by the DKP sympathies of some of its main authors. For the Memorandum debates and their documentation see the discussion in this chapter.

209 On the notion of the "Americanization" of the West German labor movement as the

consequence of the crisis, see Jürgen Hoffmann, "'Amerikanisierung' der deutschen Gewerkschaftsbewegung? Probleme der gewerkschaftlichen Politik in der Bundesrepublik unter den Bedingungen des wirtschaftlichen Strukturwandels" in *Gewerkschaftliche Monatshefte*, Vol. 32, no. 7 (July 1981), pp. 418–433. For an analysis of the unions' corporatist crisis strategies, including IG Metall's and others' belonging to the activist wing, see Jürgen Hoffmann, "Einheitsgewerkschaft oder 'korporatistische Blockbildung'? Probleme einer solidarischen Interessenvertretungspolitik in der ökonomischen Krise der Bundesrepublik" in *Prokla*, Vol. 11, no. 2 (1981), pp. 6–26.

210  See the debates surrounding "decision no. 12" at the congress in Industriegewerkschaft Metall, *Tagesprotokoll des 12. ordentlichen Gewerkschaftstages der IG Metall in Düsseldorf vom 18. bis 24. September 1977* (Frankfurt am Main: IG Metall, 1977),, pp. 285–383, esp. pp. 315–323 and 377–381; for the final version of "decision no. 12" as it was accepted by the congress's delegates see idem, *Entschliessungen, Anträge, Materialien: Zwölfter ordentlicher Gewerkschaftstag der Industriegewerkschaft Metall für die Bundesrepublik Deutschland in Düsseldorf vom 18. bis 24. September 1977* (Frankfurt am Main: IG Metall, 1979), pp. 327–329.

211  For the steel strike see Dzielak et al., *Arbeitskampf um Arbeitsplätze*; Hausch and Semmler, *Stahlstreik*; and Industriegewerkschaft Metall (ed.), *Der Arbeitskampf in der Eisen- und Stahlindustrie von Nordrhein-Westfalen, Osnabrück, Bremen, Dillenburg und Niederscheiden (1978/79)* (Frankfurt am Main: IG Metall, n.d.). For a detailed analysis of the steel strike, see the chapter on IG Metall in this volume.

212  For the strikes conducted by IG Metall and IG Druck und Papier in the spring and summer of 1984, see the entire issue of *Gewerkschaftliche Monatshefte*, Vol. 35, no. 7 (July 1984); and the entire issues of *Die Quelle*, Vol. 35, no. 5 (May 1984), no. 6 (June 1984) and no. 7/8 (July/August 1984). The events of 1984 are also discussed in the Conclusion of this volume.

213  For an assessment of the Memorandum's growth in intellectual stature and political significance within the debate on economic policy see "Mehr als linkes Gequassel" in *Die Zeit*, May 4, 1979.

214  For the Memorandum of 1979 see "Vorrang für die Vollbeschäftigung – Alternativen der Wirtschaftspolitik" in *Blätter für deutsche und internationale Politik*, Vol. 24, no. 5 (May 1979), pp. 614–633. Once again form and appearance assumed greater significance in an already polarized intra-labor atmosphere than substance and content. The very fact that "Memorandum 1979" appeared in a journal which was published by Pahl-Rugenstein and often served as an intellectual forum for authors with DKP-oriented sympathies was sufficient for many union leaders to denounce the document regardless of its message. This negative attitude toward "Memorandum 1979" was especially prominent among the leading circles of the DGB's accommodationist unions. That form prevailed over content could best be demonstrated by the fact that "Memorandum 1978," which advocated a strategy similar to that proposed by its immediate successor and provided a virtually identical analysis of the West German economy's ills, met with almost no resistance from the DGB leadership. In addition to lacking the numerous signatures of active union members and officials as was the case with "Memorandum 1979," "Memorandum 1978" was published by the union-owned publisher "Bund Verlag," rather than a journal belonging to an outfit with known sympathies for the Communist Party. For the Memorandum of 1978 see Arbeitsgruppe "Alternative Wirtschaftspolitik," *Memorandum: Alternativen der Wirtschaftspolitik* (Cologne: Bund Verlag, 1978).

215  See the example "Memorandum 1980," Arbeitsgruppe "Alternative Wirtschaftspolitik," *Memorandum: Gegen konservative Formierung – Alternativen der Wirtschaftspolitik* (Cologne: Bund Verlag, 1980).

216  Two recurring points in the Memoranda – one theoretical and one strategic – irked many otherwise sympathetic economists and led to a lively response by a number of intellectuals belonging to that unlikely coalition of right-wing social democrats and members of the "undogmatic left." Many objected to the Memoranda's analysis which emphasized excessive profits as one of the main reasons for the economic crisis. A number of radical authors criticized the Memoranda's particular care to subordinate any

measures to the existing union structure, thereby avoiding potential challenges to the unions as presently constituted. Some critics of these documents were particularly perturbed by the Memoranda's cautious prescriptions and what they perceived as an overt attempt on the part of the Memoranda's authors to curry favor with the DGB's activist unions, notably IG Metall, by mouthing the latter's policies and using Marxist terminology. For these criticisms of the Memoranda see Elmar Altvater, Jürgen Hoffmann and Carlos Maya, "Konzentration als Ursache von Profitratendifferenzen? Eine Auseinandersetzung mit der These vom positiven Zusammenhang zwischen Konzentration und Profitraten im 'Memorandum'" in *WSI-Mitteilungen*, Vol. 33, no. 4 (April 1980), pp. 196–206; and Elmar Altvater and Jürgen Hoffmann, unpublished letter to Rudolf Hickell and Axel Zerdick, two of the leading authors and originators of the Memoranda, Berlin, April 30, 1980. For a very controversial criticism of "Memorandum 1979" emanating from the DGB's leading economic journal *WSI-Mitteilungen* see "Zum Memorandum '79" in *WSI-Mitteilungen*, Vol. 32, no. 6 (June 1979), pp. 294–297. This article incurred the wrath of the DGB's activist wing, particularly IG Metall, since it partly voiced the opinion of the accommodationists, although it also contained major attacks on the Memorandum from the left which, to the activists, represented a dangerous sign of adventurism and political immaturity.

217 See for example the DGB chairman's stern circular to the federation's district and local offices in May 1979: Heinz Oskar Vetter, "Brief an die DGB-Landesbezirke und DGB-Kreise von dem DGB-Bundesvorstand," May 29, 1979, unpublished document. See also the DGB's critical position vis-à-vis "Memorandum '79 – Eine Bewertung aus gewerkschaftlicher Sicht" in *Wirtschaftspolitische Informationen*, no. 3, June 15, 1979, pp. 1–7. The DGB's chief economist, Rudolf Henschel, also published an influential article criticizing "Memorandum 1979": Rudolf Henschel, "Die gewerkschaftliche Kritik am Memorandum '79" in *Gewerkschaftliche Monatshefte*, Vol. 31, no. 2 (February 1980), pp. 109–116. But barely four months later the same Rudolf Henschel had virtually nothing but praise for "Memorandum 1980"; see Rudolf Henschel, "Memorandum '80 ist eine gute Grundlage für die weitere Diskussion" in *Die Quelle*, Vol. 31, no. 6 (June 1980), pp. 332, 333.

218 For the Aktionsprogramm of 1979 see Pfromm, *Das neue Grundsatzprogramm*, pp. 215–226; for the Grundsatzprogramm of 1981 see Leminsky and Otto, *Politik und Programmatik des Deutschen Gewerkschaftsbundes*, second edition, pp. 34–59.

219 Heinz Oskar Vetter, "Aktionsprogramm '79 ist eine Aufgabe für alle" in *Die Quelle*, Vol. 30, no. 7/8 (July/August 1979), pp. 387, 388. This article by the DGB's leader precedes the publication of the Aktionsprogramm of 1979 which appears as "DGB-Aktionsprogramm '79" on pp. 389–395 of the same issue of *Die Quelle*.

220 On this importance of different nuances in tone which convey subtle changes in content see Gerhard Leminsky, "Zum neuen Aktionsprogramm des DGB" in *Gewerkschaftliche Monatshefte*, Vol. 30, no. 12 (December 1979), pp. 745–754. Leminsky writes: "A close analysis will show that the new Aktionsprogramm of 1979 does not provide fundamentally new goals; rather, it summarizes on the level of an Aktionsprogramm all developments experienced by the unions in their practice of the last few years. Put differently: The Aktionsprogramm catches up with concrete union politics. Nevertheless, this summary of demands delineates important changes, because it clearly highlights shifts in policy considerations – only, of course, if one sees them in a larger context." See p. 746 of the article by Leminsky.

221 Ibid., pp. 748, 749.

222 All of the above information on the DGB's Aktionsprogramm of 1979 stems from Pfromm, *Das neue Grundsatzprogramm*, pp. 215–226 and "DGB-Aktionsprogramm '79" in *Die Quelle*, pp. 389–395.

223 For the Basic Program of 1981 see Leminsky and Otto, *Politik*, pp. 34–59. For a detailed paragraph-by-paragraph commentary of the DGB's 1981 Basic Program see Pfromm, *Das neue Grundsatzprogramm*, pp. 18–161, and the entire issue of *Gewerkschaftliche Monatshefte*, Vol. 31, no. 1 (January 1980) which consists of articles by Heinz Oskar Vetter,

Volker Jung and a side-by-side comparison of the DGB's two Basic Programs from 1963 and 1981. For a very useful and meticulously compiled commentary on the 1981 Basic Program in a larger historical, political and economic context see Günter Arndt, Frank Deppe, Werner Petschick and Klaus Pickshaus (eds.), *DGB Programm '81 untersucht für die Praxis* (Frankfurt am Main: Nachrichten Verlag, 1981).

224 Leminsky and Otto, *Politik*, p. 36.

225 This interpretation receives special emphasis in Heinz Oskar Vetter's influential article published in January 1980 in *Gewerkschaftliche Monatshefte* strategically timed to have the maximum impact on the intra-union debates concerning the upcoming congress in Düsseldorf which was to finalize the new Basic Program. See Heinz Oskar Vetter, "Zum Beginn der Diskussion um ein neues Grundsatzprogramm' in *Gewerkschaftliche Monatshefte*, Vol. 31, no. 1 (January 1980), pp. 1–12.

226 Leminsky and Otto, *Politik*, p. 35.

227 Ibid.

228 Ibid.

229 The Basic Program is a 28-page document in brochure form which has been distributed to every DGB member in the Federal Republic and continues to be the most widely available version of this important union document. See Deutscher Gewerkschaftsbund, *Grundsatzprogramm des Deutschen Gewerkschaftsbundes* (Düsseldorf: DGB, n.d.).

## 4. VANGUARD OF WEST GERMAN LABOR: THE METALWORKERS' UNION

1 This was the membership figure as of December 31, 1979, reported in the union's triannual account submitted to every union congress. See Industriegewerkschaft Metall, *Geschäftsbericht 1977 bis 1979* (Frankfurt am Main: IG Metall, 1980), p. 175.

2 Statistisches Bundesamt, *Statistisches Jahrbuch des Statistischen Bundesamtes 1982* (Bonn: Statistiches Bundesamt, 1983), pp. 175, 1980; own calculations.

3 Ibid.; also Dresdner Bank, *Statistical Survey*, Supplement to *Economic Quarterly* (April 1983), p. 3; own calculations.

4 Statistisches Bundesamt, *Statistisches Jahrbuch 1982*, p. 175.

5 Josef Esser, Wolfgang Fach and Werner Väth, *Krisenregulierung* (Frankfurt am Main: Suhrkamp, 1983), pp. 45, 46; see the general discussion of the world steel crisis in ibid., pp. 22–47; and in Willi Dzielak, Wolfgang Hindrichs, Helmut Martens and Walter Schophaus, *Arbeitskampf um Arbeitsplätze: Der Tarifkonflikt 1978/79 in der Stahlindustrie* (Frankfurt am Main: Campus Verlag, 1981), pp. 44–85.

6 Esser et al., *Krisenregulierung*, p. 38.

7 Statistisches Bundesamt, *Statistisches Jahrbuch 1982*, p. 175.

8 Ibid., p. 181.

9 Projektgruppe Gewerkschaftsforschung, *Rahmenbedingungen der Tarifpolitik*, 3 volumes (Frankfurt am Main: Campus Verlag, 1979), Vol. 2, p. 16. On the major sectors in machine construction, see Industriegewerkschaft Metall, *Strukturwandel in der Metallindustrie* (Frankfurt am Main: IG Metall, 1977), pp. 49–87.

10 Projektgruppe Gewerkschaftsforschung, *Rahmenbedingungen*, Vol. 2, p. 16.

11 Ibid., p. 10; Statitisches Bundesamt, *Statistisches Jahrbuch 1982*, p. 176.

12 Verband Deutscher Maschinen- und Anlagenbau, *Statistisches Handbuch für den Maschinenbau – Ausgabe 1982* (Frankfurt am Main: VDMA, 1983), p. 14.

13 Statistics on labor-force composition are taken from Projektgruppe Gewerkschaftsforschung, *Rahmenbedingungen*, Vol. 2, pp. 107–108, 279–282.

14 Ibid., pp. 279–280.

15 Ibid., pp. 10, 14–15.

16 Ibid., pp. 108–110, 279–282.

17 Statistisches Bundesamt, *Statistisches Jahrbuch*, p. 180.

18 Ibid., p. 181.

19 Institut für Bilanzforschung, *Die Elektroindustrie in der Bundesrepublik Deutschland* (Frankfurt am Main: IBF, 1979), p. 5.

20 Michael Breitenacher, Klaus-Dieter Knörndel, Hans Schedl and Lothar Scholz, *Elektrotechnische Industrie* (Berlin: Duncker & Humblot, 1979), p. 33.

21 Achim Diekmann, *Die Automobilindustrie in der Bundesrepublik Deutschland* (Cologne: Deutscher Instituts Verlag, 1979), p. 22.

22 Projektgruppe Gewerkschaftsforschung, *Rahmenbedingungen*, Vol. 2, p. 10.

23 Ibid., p. 12.

24 Statistisches Bundesamt, *Statistisches Jahrbuch 1982*, pp. 175, 180.

25 Ibid., p. 181.

26 Ibid., pp. 107–110, 279–282.

27 See the discussion in Willi Dzielak, Wolfgang Hindrichs and Helmut Martens, *Den Besitzstand sichern! Der Tarifkonflikt 1978 in der Metallindustrie Baden-Württembergs* (Frankfurt am Main: Campus Verlag, 1979), pp. 37–39.

28 Ibid., p. 37.

29 The discussion of Gesamtmetall is based on Projektgruppe Gewerkschaftsforschung, *Rahmenbedingungen*, Vol. 1, pp. 73–81; and on Dzielak et al., *Den Besitzstand*, pp. 28–36.

30 Figures on the size of Gesamtmetall's regional associations are from Projektgruppe Gewerkschaftsforschung, *Rahmenbedingungen*, Vol. 1, p. 75.

31 On the differences between the two regions, see Dzielak et al., *Den Besitzstand*, p. 37.

32 During the 1976 bargaining round, for example, the VMI was seen to have pushed through policies which favored the interests of the large auto firms to the detriment of small and medium-sized firms in other industries and regions. See ibid., pp. 34–36.

33 On Gesamtmetall's bargaining practices, see ibid., pp. 31–32. See also the more detailed, but older, discussion in Claus Noé, *Gebändigter Klassenkampf: Tarifautonomie in der BRD* (Berlin: Duncker & Humblot, 1970).

34 Noé, *Gebändigter Klassenkampf*, p. 188.

35 Dzielak et al., *Den Besitzstand*, p. 32.

36 On the AGV, see Dzielak et al., *Arbeitskampf*, pp. 66–70.

37 In the aftermath of the 1978–79 strike, there was talk about changing the AGV's statutes to get around this. See ibid., p. 70.

38 Ibid., p. 69.

39 Projektgruppe Gewerkschaftsforschung, *Rahmenbedingungen*, Vol. 1, p. 93.

40 Ibid.

41 Ibid., p. 94.

42 IG Metall, *Geschäftsbericht 1977 bis 1979*, p. 174.

43 Projektgruppe Gewerkschaftsforschung, *Rahmenbedingungen*, Vol. 1, p. 95.

44 Ibid., p. 96.

45 Ibid., p. 105.

46 Ibid.

47 Ibid.

48 Ibid.

49 Ibid.

50 Ibid., p. 109.

51 Ibid., p. 111.

52 Ibid., p. 112.

53 IG Metall, *Geschäftsbericht 1977 bis 1979*, pp. 144, 145.

54 Projektgruppe Gewerkschaftsforschung, *Rahmenbedingungen*, Vol. 1, p. 84.

55 On this point, see the minutes of the union's twelfth congress held in Düsseldorf from September 18 to September 24, 1977, published in Industriegewerkschaft Metall, *Protokoll 12. ordentlicher Gewerkschaftstag der IG Metall für die Bundesrepublik Deutschland, Stadthalle Düsseldorf, 18 September bis 24. September 1977* (Frankfurt am Main: IG Metall, 1978).

56 The union's bylaws as of January 1, 1981 are contained in: Industriegewerkschaft Metall, *Satzung* (Frankfurt am Main: IG Metall, 1981).

57 On IG Metall's collective bargaining practices, see the discussion in Projektgruppe Gewerkschaftsforschung, *Rahmenbedingungen*, Vol. 1, pp. 85–92.

58 A good critique of this new arbitration agreement can be found in Rainer Erd, "Neues Schlichtungsabkommen: Konzentration und Zentralisierung der Tarifverhandlungen in der Metallindustrie", *express*, Vol. 17, no. 12 (December 13, 1979), p. 6. Erd argues that although this new agreement gives IG Metall important latitude for maneuver during the bargaining rounds, it also has a centralizing effect which will make future bargaining rounds between the employers and the union much more predictable and calculable for both sides. Thus, the new arbitration agreement lends additional support to a "corporatist" interpretation of West German industrial relations, of which Rainer Erd is one of the most prominent exponents.

59 Projektgruppe Gewerkschaftsforschung, *Rahmenbedingungen*, Vol. 1, p. 99.

60 On IG Metall's "strategy of the calculated strike," see Dietrich Hoss, *Die Krise des "Institutionalisierten Klassenkampfes": Metallarbeiterstreik in Baden-Württemberg* (Frankfurt am Main: Europäische Verlaganstalt, 1974), pp. 65, 66.

61 See Willi Dzielak et al., *Den Besitzstand*, p. 28.

62 Our account of the history of IG Metall's predecessor organizations is based principally on the following two works: Industriegewerkschaft Metall, *90 Jahre Industriegewerkschaft 1891 bis 1981: Von Deutschen Metallarbeiter-Verband zur Industriegewerkschaft Metall* (Cologne: Bund-Verlag, 1981); and Lothar Wentzel, *Inflation und Arbeitskämpfe* (Hanover: SOAK-Verlag, 1981).

63 IG Metall, *90 Jahre*, p. 536.

64 Wentzel, *Inflation*, p. 16.

65 Peter Ullmann, *Tarifverträge und Tarifpolitik in Deutschland bis 1914* (Frankfurt am Main: Peter Lang, 1977), pp. 221–225.

66 IG Metall, *90 Jahre*, p. 536.

67 Wentzel, *Inflation*, p. 16.

68 IG Metall, *90 Jahre*, p. 536.

69 Wentzel, *Inflation*, p. 18.

70 Ibid., pp. 18–21.

71 On these strikes, see ibid., pp. 21–22.

72 IG Metall, *90 Jahre*, pp. 241, 536.

73 Ibid., p. 268.

74 See the minutes of the first IG Metall congress, Industriegewerkschaft Metall, *Niederschrift der Verhandlungen des 1. ordentlichen Gewerkschaftstages der Industriegewerkschaft Metall für die Bundesrepublik Deutschland im Gewerkschaftshaus Hamburg von 18. bis 22. September 1950* (Frankfurt am Main: IG Metall, 1951).

75 On Mitbestimmung, see ibid., especially pp. 311–327.

76 Ibid., p. 307.

77 Ibid., p. 73.

78 For a complete discussion of Mitbestimmung, see Chapters 2 and 3.

79 For IG Metall's official account of the Hesse strike, see *Geschäftsbericht 1950 bis 1952* (Frankfurt am Main: IG Metall, 1953), pp. 125–127; for a more detailed and critical discussion of this event, see Joachim Bergmann, Otto Jacobi and Walther Müller-Jentsch, *Gewerkschaften in der Bundesrepublik*, third edition (Frankfurt am Main: Campus Verlag, 1979), pp. 264–269; and Theo Pirker, *Die blinde Macht: Die Gewerkschaftsbewegung in der Bundesrepublik* (Berlin: Olle & Wolter, 1979), Vol. 1, pp. 226–229.

80 Pirker, *Die blinde Macht*, Vol. 1, p. 226.

81 *metall*, Vol. 3, no. 17 (August 29, 1951), p. 1.

82 Industriegewerkschaft Metall, *Der Grosse Streik in der Hessischen Metallindustrie vom 27. August bis 22. September 1951* (Frankfurt am Main: IG Metall, 1951), p. 24.

83 IG Metall, *Geschäftsbericht 1950 bis 52*, p. 125.

84 Ibid., p. 127.

85 Consult the IG Metall membership table at Appendix 3 for details.

86 Manfred Weiss, *Gewerkschaftliche Vertrauensleute: Tarifvertragliche Verbesserungen ihrer Arbeit im Betrieb* (Frankfurt am Main: Europäische Verlagsanstalt, 1978), p. 96. See also Eberhard Schmidt, "Die Auseinandersetzung um die Rolle der Vertrauensleute in der IG Metall" in Otto Jacobi, Walther Müller-Jentsch and Eberhard Schmidt (eds.), *Gewerkschaften und*

*Klassenkampf: Kritisches Jahrbuch '74* (Frankfurt am Main: Fischer Verlag, 1974), pp. 130–145.

87 Weiss, *Gewerkschaftliche Vertrauensleute*, p. 83.

88 Bergmann et al., *Gewerkschaften*, p. 269.

89 For the best account of this strike, see Pirker, *Die blinde Macht*, Vol. 2, pp. 109–115.

90 Ibid., pp. 115, 122.

91 Pirker, *Die blinde Macht*, p. 116; Bergmann et al., *Gewerkschaften*, p. 269; and Industriegewerkschaft Metall, *Geschäftsbericht 1954 bis 1955* (Frankfurt am Main: IG Metall, 1956), p. 83.

92 IG Metall, *Geschäftsbericht 1954 bis 1955*, pp. 83, 84.

93 Ibid., p. 85.

94 William Fellner, *The Problem of Rising Prices* (Paris: OEEC, 1961), p. 327.

95 For a concise overview of IG Metall's wage bargaining rounds from 1951 through 1974, see Bergmann et al., *Gewerkschaften*, pp. 231–256.

96 Fellner, *The Problem*, p. 343.

97 On the 1956–57 Schleswig-Holstein strike, see Pirker, *Die blinde Macht*, Vol. 2, pp. 212–222; the articles which appeared in Issues 3, 4, 6 and 7 of *Der Spiegel* in 1957; and Bergmann et al., *Gewerkschaften*, pp. 277–284.

98 Industriegewerkschaft Metall, *Geschäftsbericht 1956 bis 1957* (Frankfurt am Main: IG Metall, 1958), p. 92.

99 Ibid., p. 93.

100 Rainer Kalbitz, "Biographie über den Streik in Schleswig-Holstein 1956/57," unpublished thesis, Bochum, 1969, p. 83.

101 IG Metall, *Geschäftsbericht 1956 bis 1957*, p. 94.

101 Fellner, *The Problem*, pp. 348–350.

103 Industriegewerkschaft Metall, *Geschäftsbericht 1960 bis 1961* (Frankfurt am Main: IG Metall, 1962), pp. 38, 48.

104 Industriegewerkschaft Metall, *Protokoll: 5. ordentlicher Gewerkschaftstag der Industriegewerkschaft Metall für die Bundesrepublik Deutschland; Nürnberg, vom 15. bis 20. September 1958* (Frankfurt am Main: IG Metall, 1959), pp. 128–135.

105 Fritz Salm, "Betriebsnahe Tarifpolitik tut not" in *Der Gewerkschafter*, Vol. 6, no. 8 (August 1958); "Betriebsnahe Tarifverträge" in *Der Gewerkschafter*, Vol. 6, no. 9/10 (September/October 1958), pp. 1–2; "Dringliche Aufgaben unserer Tarifpolitik" in ibid., pp. 30–31; "Betriebsnahe Tarifverträge, Teile 1–4" in *Der Gewerkschafter*, Vol. 9, nos. 8–11 (August, September, October, November 1961); and Bergmann et al., *Gewerkschaften*, pp. 196–201, 212–218.

106 IG Metall, *Protokoll 1958*, pp. 128–155.

107 Bergmann et al., *Gewerkschaften*, pp. 216–218.

108 Ibid., p. 232.

109 The Blessing Memorandum is discussed in Robert Flanagan and Lloyd Ulman, *Wage Restraint: A Study of Incomes Policy in West Europe* (Berkeley: University of California Press, 1981), p. 185.

110 For details of Gesamtmetall's new "confrontationalist" strategy, see Hoss, *Die Krise*, pp. 83–99.

111 The 1963 Baden-Württemberg strike is the subject of both Hoss's *Die Krise des Institutionalisierten Klassenkampfes* and Claus Noé's *Gebändigter Klassenkampf: Tarifautonomie in der Bundesrepublik Deutschland* (Berlin: Duncker & Humblot, 1970); there is a good summary of the conflict in Bergmann et al., *Gewerkschaften*, pp. 284–294.

112 Industriegewerkschaft Metall, *Geschäftsbericht 1962, 1963 and 1964* (Frankfurt am Main: IG Metall, 1965), p. 130.

113 Ibid., pp. 44–45.

114 Hoss, *Die Krise*, pp. 119, 120, 167.

115 Sachverständigenrat zur Begutachtung der gesamtwirtschaftlichen Entwicklung, *Jahresgutachten 1964*, Bundesdrucksache IV/2890, paragraph 235.

116 Ibid., paragraph 98.

117 "Social plans" are agreements worked out between the union, the works council and a

single firm, and regulate large-scale layoffs or plant closures. They stipulate who will lose his or her job and usually provide for substantial severance pay for all workers so affected. On Sozialpläne, see: Wolfgang Wenzel, "Zur Entwicklung und Geschichte von Sozialplänen in der Bundesrepublik Deutschland" in Autorengemeinschaft (ed.), *Sozialpolitik in der Eisen- und Stahlindustrie: Mit Ausgewählten Sozialplänen* (Cologne: Bund Verlag, 1979), pp. 14 ff.

118 Ibid., pp. 18–19.

119 Ibid., p. 23.

120 Ibid., p. 21.

121 See the interviews with Brenner that appeared in *Der Spiegel*, Vol. 21, no. 14, (March 27, 1967), and Vol. 23, no. 21 (May 19, 1969), as well as in Leo Brawand (ed.), *Wohin steuert die deutsche Wirtschaft* (Munich: Verlag Karl Desch, 1971), pp. 158–180.

122 See the table of wage drift in Helmut Arndt (ed.), *Lohnpolitik und Einkommensverteilung* (Berlin: Duncker & Humblot, 1969), p. 487.

123 "Wer mault, muss gehen" in *Der Spiegel*, Vol. 21, no. 24 (June 5, 1967); and "Rosen um Mitternacht" in *Der Spiegel*, Vol. 21, no. 45 (October 30, 1967).

124 See *Der Spiegel* articles: "Vorschuss auf den Mai," Vol. 21, no. 49 (November 27, 1967), and "Mut zur Pflicht," Vol. 23, nos. 1–2 (January 6, 1969); also Sachverständigenrat zur Begutachtung der gesamtwirtschaftlichen Entwicklung, *Im Sog des Booms* (Stuttgart: W. Kohlhammer, 1969), pp. 25–27.

125 An extensive account of the background to the "September Strikes" of 1969 is provided by Eberhard Schmidt, *Ordnungsfaktor oder Gegenmacht: Die Politische Rolle der Gewerkschaften* (Frankfurt am Main: Suhrkamp, 1971), pp. 58–80, which also provides a day-by-day account of the strikes themselves. The definitive study of the causes and effects of the strikes is Michael Schumann, Frank Gerlach, Albert Gschlössl and Petra Milhoffer, *Am Beispiel der Septemberstreiks – Anfang der Rekonstruktionsperiode der Arbeiterklasse?* (Frankfurt am Main: Europäische Verlagsanstalt, 1971). This is often referred to as the "SOFI" study, since it was carried out by the Soziologisches Forschungsinstitut (SOFI) in Göttingen. Our account of the strikes is mainly based on these works, since IG Metall's internal publications are (understandably) not very forthcoming on the subject.

126 Schmidt, *Ordnungsfaktor*, pp. 115–116; Schumann et al., *Am Beispiel*, pp. 46–48.

127 Schumann et al., *Am Beispiel*, p. 7.

128 Schmidt, *Ordnungsfaktor*, pp. 81–104.

129 Schumann et al., *Am Beispiel*, pp. 58–77 and 140–158; and Schmidt, *Ordnungsfaktor*, pp. 117, 123–142.

130 Schmidt, *Ordnungsfaktor*, pp. 125, 136, 137, 151, 152; Kurt Steinhaus, *Streiks in der Bundesrepublik 1966–1974* (Frankfurt am Main: Verlag Marxistische Blätter, 1975), pp. 64 and 75.

131 Schmidt, *Ordungsfaktor*, pp. 117–123.

132 Schumann et al., *Am Beispiel*, p. 143.

133 Ibid., p. 60.

134 Ibid.

135 Ibid., pp. 145–147.

136 *Der Gewerkschafter*, Special Issue 2A, Vol. 18, no. 2 (February 1970), pp. 3ff.

137 Industriegewerkschaft Metall, *Geschäftsbericht 1968 bis 1970* (Frankfurt am Main: IG Metall, 1970), p. 121.

138 Schmidt, *Ordnungsfaktor*, p. 123.

139 Ibid.

140 IG Metall, *Geschäftsbericht 1968 bis 1970*, pp. 56–63.

141 Ibid., p. 121; and Steinhaus, *Streiks*, p. 73.

142 IG Metall, *Geschäftsbericht 1968 bis 1970*, pp. 121–122.

143 Ibid., p. 122.

144 Ibid.

145 Dietrich Hoss, "Zum Verhältnis von gewerkschaftlichen Kampf und Sozialdemokratie: Der Metallarbeiterstreik in Baden-Württemberg 1971" in Rainer Deppe, Richard Herding and Dietrich Hoss, *Sozialdemokratie und Klassenkonflikte: Metallarbeiterstreik – Betriebskonflikt – Mieterkampf* (Frankfurt am Main: Campus Verlag, 1978), p. 38.

146 Dietrich Hoss, "Zum Verhältnis," pp. 39–43, 55, 60, 61; Bergmann et al., *Gewerkschaften*, pp. 310–311; Steinhaus, *Streiks*, pp. 93–95; and Regine Meyer, *Streik und Aussperrung in der Metallindustrie* (Marburg: Verlag Arbeitsbewegung und Gesellschaftswissenschaft, 1977), pp. 211–232, 293.

147 Gesamtverband der Metallindustriellen Arbeitgeberverbände, *Geschäftsbericht 1968 bis 1970* (Frankfurt; Gesamtmetall, 1971), p. 22.

148 *Frankfurter Rundschau*, March 30, 1971.

149 Sachverständigenrat zur Begutachtung der gesamtwirtschaftlichen Entwicklung, *Jahresgutachten 1971*, Bundesdrucksache VI/2847 (Bonn: n.p., 1971), Appendix: "Sondergutachten vom 24.5.1971."

150 *Frankfurter Rundschau*, May 18, 1971.

151 As quoted in Bergmann et al., *Gewerkschaften*, p. 311.

152 Industriegewerkschaft Metall, *Protokoll: 10. ordentlicher Gewerkschaftstag der Industriegewerkschaft Metall für die Bundesrepublik Deutschland, Rhein-Main-Halle, Wiesbaden, 27. September bis 2. October 1971* (Frankfurt am Main: IG Metall, 1972), p. 387.

153 For Brandt's speech to the congress, see ibid., pp. 14–48.

154 Meyer, *Streik und Aussperrung*, pp. 251–255.

155 The best overall accounts of the 1971 strike, which we have drawn upon here to supplement internal union documents and press materials, are those found in Hoss, "Zum Verhältnis," and Meyer, *Streik und Aussperrung*.

156 Bergmann et al., *Gewerkschaften*, p. 313.

157 Steinhaus, *Streiks*, p. 97.

158 Hoss, "Zum Verhältnis," p. 77.

159 Ibid., p. 78.

160 Ibid., p. 79.

161 IG Metall, "Streik-Nachrichten," December 9, 1971.

162 Hoss, "Zum Verhältnis," p. 79.

163 Industriegewerkschaft Metall, *Geschäftsbericht 1971 bis 1973* (Frankfurt am Main: IG Metall, 1974), p. 104.

164 Ibid.

165 As quoted in Steinhaus, *Streiks*, p. 102.

166 As quoted in ibid., pp. 102, 103.

167 IG Metall *Geschäftsbericht 1971 bis 1973*, p. 119.

168 Ibid., p. 123.

169 Ibid., p. 120.

170 See the special conference protocols and minutes of the extraordinary union congress held in Otto Brenner's memory and to elect a new leadership team: *Protokoll – Ausserordentlicher Gewerkschaftstag der Industriegewerkschaft Metall für die Bundesrepublik Deutschland, Sheraton-Hotel, München, 10. Juni 1972* (Frankfurt am Main: IG Metall, 1972).

171 IG Metall, *Aufgabe Zukunft – Qualität des Lebens* (Frankfurt: Europäische Verlagsanstalt, 1972). This is Volume 9 in the series "Zukunft der Gewerkschaften."

172 IG Metall, *Geschäftsbericht 1971 bis 1973*, pp. 18, 53.

173 "Betriebsratswahlen 1972," in Otto Jacobi, Walther Müller-Jentsch and Eberhard Schmidt (eds.), *Gewerkschaften und Klassenkampf: Kritisches Jahrbuch '73* (Frankfurt am Main: Fischer Verlag, 1973), p. 43.

174 Industriegewerkschaft Metall, *Geschäftsbericht 1974 bis 1976* (Frankfurt am Main: IG Metall, 1977), pp. 351–354; idem, *Geschäftsbericht 1971 bis 1973*, pp. 234–236; idem, *Geschäftsbericht 1977 bis 1979*, pp. 253–256.

175 IG Metall, *Geschäftsbericht 1974 bis 1976*, pp. 351–354; idem, *Geschäftsbericht 1971 bis 1973*, pp. 234–236; idem, *Geschäftsbericht 1977 bis 1979*, pp. 253–256.

176 See "Betriebsratswahlen bei Daimler-Benz" in Jacobi et al., *Kritisches Jahrbuch '73*, pp. 45–52; also "Betriebsratswahlen bei Daimler-Benz Stuttgart" in Otto Jacobi, Walther Müller-Jentsch and Eberhard Schmidt *Gewerkschaften und Klassenkampf: Kritisches Jahrbuch '75* (Frankfurt am Main: Fischer Verlag, 1975), pp. 72–75.

177 "Betriebsratswahlen bei Daimler-Benz," pp. 45–59.

178 Ibid., p. 46–47.

179 Ibid., p. 46.
180 Ibid., pp. 47, 48.
181 Ibid., p. 51.
182 IG Metall, *Geschäftsbericht 1971 bis 1974*, pp. 148, 154.
183 Ibid., pp. 149, 154, 155.
184 Ibid., p. 149. It is important to note that the union's document does not provide the information as to how many of the eligible members rejected the terms of the contract. For this datum, see Walther Müller-Jentsch, "Die spontane Streikbewegung 1973," in Jacobi et al., *Kritisches Jahrbuch '74*, p. 46.
185 Steinhaus, *Streiks*, p. 116.
186 Ibid.
187 Ibid.; see also "Streiks bei Mannesmann, Duisburg" in Jacobi et al., *Kritisches Jahrbuch '74*, pp. 55–71, esp. pp. 56–65.
188 IG Metall, *Geschäftsbericht 1971 bis 1973*, pp. 149, 155, 156.
189 Klaus Gülden and Horst Peter, "VW: Krisenlösung durch Entlassungen" in Otto Jacobi et al., *Kritisches Jahrbuch '75*, pp. 38–40.
190 Müller-Jentsch, "Spontane Streikbewegung," p. 47.
191 IG Metall, *Geschäftsbericht 1971 bis 1973*, p. 147.
192 "Zeittafel" in Industriegewerkschaft Metall (ed.), *Werktage werden besser* (Cologne: Europäische Verlagsanstalt, 1977), p. 155. The "Zeittafel" is a chronological list of events surrounding the strike for Wage Framework Contract II in NW/NB. It can be found on pp. 155–158 in the volume *Werktage werden besser*.
193 Reimar Birkwald, "Menschengerechte Arbeitswelt," pp. 95–100; and Lothar Zimmermann, "Der Kampf," pp. 65–71; both in *Werktage werden besser*.
194 Birkwald, "Menschengerechte Arbeitswelt," p. 95.
195 Steinhaus, *Streiks*, p. 138.
196 Ibid.
197 IG Metall, *Geschäftsbericht 1971 bis 1973*, pp. 177.
198 Ibid., p. 199.
199 Ibid., p. 177. The entire text of LRTV II can also be found in *Werktage werden besser*, pp. 174–192.
200 Note the difference in wording between IG Metall's original demand and the arbitrator's verdict on the one hand, and the final agreement on the other. Whereas the first two talk about percentages based on the "contractual wage levels" of each individual piece-rate worker, the final formulation of the pertinent passage in Wage Framework Contract II mentions percentages based on "factory average." Steinhaus explains the differences between IG Metall's and the arbitrator's versions on one hand and the final outcome on the other in the following manner: "IG Metall had demanded an individual minimum guarantee of 140% of the contractual wage level, with the arbitrator suggesting 130%. Now, the final percentage rate was not only below both of these figures due to its incrementalization by different time periods. The most decisive fact was that the minimum guarantee in the final version was not related to the income of the individual worker, but rather to the factory average of real wages. This variant was more complicated and less understandable than the previous two, and above all it meant that real wage increases [i.e. above and beyond the gains stipulated by the annual wage and salary contracts negotiated by the union] would only be granted in the rarest of circumstances." See Steinhaus, *Streiks*, p. 141.
201 IG Metall, *Geschäftsbericht 1971 bis 1973*, pp. 177.
202 On the notion of "see-saw" politics in West German industrial relations, see Bergmann et al., *Gewerkschaften*, pp. 86–106.
203 Walther Müller-Jentsch, "Wirtschaftskrise und Gewerkschaftspolitik" in Jacobi et al., *Kritisches Jahrbuch '75*, p. 12.
204 Steinhaus, *Streiks*, pp. 145–146.
205 Ibid.
206 IG Metall, *Geschäftsbericht 1974 bis 1976*, pp. 128, 129.
207 Ibid., pp. 130, 131.

208 On the 1974 Unterweser strike and its backround, see the exhaustive study Forschungs-gruppe "Metallarbeiterstreik," *Streik und Arbeiterbewusstsein: Bericht über eine sozialwissen-schaftliche Untersuchung des Metallarbeiterstreiks im Unterwesergebiet 1974* (Bremen: Research monograph of the University of Bremen, 1978), upon which our account of these events is based.
209 Ibid., pp. 26–27.
210 Ibid., p. 29.
211 Ibid., p. 30.
212 Dietrich Eissegg, "Der Streik der Metallarbeiter im Unterwesergebiet 1974," in Jacobi et al., *Kritisches Jahrbuch '74*, p. 125.
213 Ibid., pp. 127–128.
214 IG Metall, *Geschäftsbericht 1974 bis 1976*, p. 134.
215 Ibid., pp. 138, 139.
216 Otto Jacobi, "Tarifpolitik in der Wirtschaftskrise 1974/75," in Jacobi et al., *Kritisches Jahrbuch '75*, p. 103.
217 Ibid.
218 "Die Angriffe auf die soziale Sicherung abwehren!," *metall*, Vol. 27, no. 19 (September 25, 1975), p. 2.
219 Ibid. For a discussion of IG Metall's continued "state fixation" in this document see Otto Jacobi and Walther Müller-Jentsch, "Gewerkschaftliche Tarifpolitik in der Wirt-schaftskrise," in Rainer Duhm and Ulrich Mückenberger (eds.), *Arbeitskampf im Krisenall-tag: Wie man sich wehrt und warum* (Berlin: Rotbuch Verlag, 1977), pp. 42–44.
220 IG Metall, *Krise und Reform in der Industriegesellschaft*, Vol. 1: Materialien, Vol. 2: Protokolle (Frankfurt am Main: Europäische Verlagsanstalt, 1976).
221 IG Metall, *Geschäftsbericht 1974 bis 1976*, p. 141.
222 Ibid.
223 IG Metall, *Geschäftsbericht 1977 bis 1979*, p. 144.
224 Willi Dzielak et al., *Den Besitzstand*, pp. 38, 39.
225 IG Metall, *Geschäftsbericht 1977 bis 1979*, p. 505.
226 Projektgruppe Gewerkschaftsforschung, *Tarifpolitik 1977* (Frankfurt am Main: Campus Verlag, 1978), p. 73.
227 IG Metall, *Geschäftsbericht 1977 bis 1979*, p. 511.
228 Projektgruppe Gewerkschaftsforschung, *Tarifpolitik 1977*, pp. 82, 83.
229 Projektgruppe Gewerkschaftsforschung, *Tarifpolitik 1978* (Frankfurt am Main: Campus Verlag, 1979), pp. 44, 45.
230 *Tarifpolitik 1977*, p. 112.
231 Dzielak et al., *Den Besitzstand*, p. 36.
232 Projektgruppe Gewerkschaftsforschung, *Tarifpolitik 1977*, p. 112.
233 Ibid., p. 114.
234 Ibid., pp. 107, 108.
235 IG Metall, *Strukturelle Arbeitslosigkeit durch technologischen Wandel? Referate, gehalten auf der Technologie-Tagung der IG Metall, 24./25. Mai 1977, Frankfurt am Main* (Frankfurt am Main: IG Metall, 1977).
236 Hans Pornschlegel, "Tarifpolitische Perspektiven des technologischen Wandels" in ibid., pp. 103–124.
237 Ibid., p. 124.
238 See IG Metall, *Entschliessungen – Anträge – Materialien: 12. ordentlicher Gewerkschaftstag der IG Metall für die Bundesrepublik Deutschland, Stadthalle Düsseldorf, 18. bis 24. September 1977 Protokoll 1977* (Frankfurt am Main: IG Metall, 1978).
239 Ibid., pp. 313–324.
240 Ibid., pp. 561–575.
241 Ibid., pp. 610–615.
242 IG Metall, *Protokoll 1977*, pp. 312, 313.
243 IG Metall, *Geschäftsbericht 1977 bis 1979*, p. 548.
244 Projektgruppe Gewerkschaftsforschung, *Tarifpolitik 1978*, p. 71.
245 IG Metall, *Geschäftsbericht 1977 bis 1979*, p. 549.

246 Ibid., pp. 522, 553.
247 Projektgruppe Gewerkschaftsforschung, *Tarifpolitik 1978*, pp. 27–29.
248 Ibid., p. 64.
249 Eckart Hildebrand, "Der Tarifkampf in der metallverarbeitenden Industrie, 1978," in Otto Jacobi, Walther Müller-Jentsch and Eberhard Schmidt (eds), *Arbeiterinteressen gegen Sozialpartnerschaft – Kritisches Gewerkschaftsjahrbuch 1978/79* (Berlin: Rotbuch, 1979), p. 66.
250 Quoted in Dzielak et al., *Den Besitzstand*, p. 59.
251 IG Metall, *Geschäftsbericht 1977 bis 1979*, pp. 521, 524, 532.
252 Ibid., p. 531.
253 Ibid., pp. 522, 526.
254 The best secondary sources on the strike are Dzielak et al., *Den Besitzstand*, and Projektgruppe Gewerkschaftsforschung, *Tarifpolitik 1978*.
255 IG Metall, *Geschäftsbericht 1977 bis 1979*, p. 522.
256 Ibid.
257 Klaus Pickshaus and Witich Rossmann, *Streik und Ausperung '78* (Frankfurt: Nachrichten Verlag, 1978), p. 58.
258 Projektgruppe Gewerkschaftsforschung, *Tarifpolitik 1978*, p. 93.
259 IG Metall, *Geschäftsbericht 1977 bis 1979*, p. 522.
260 Ibid.
261 Ibid.
262 Projektgruppe Gewerkschaftsforschung, *Tarifpolitik 1978*, p. 92.
263 Ibid., p. 94.
264 IG Metall, *Geschäftsbericht 1977 bis 1979*, p. 523.
265 Ibid., p. 537.
266 Ibid., p. 534.
267 Ibid.
268 Projektgruppe Gewerkschaftsforschung, *Tarifpolitik 1978*, p. 109.
269 Ibid.
270 Ibid., pp. 97, 98, 110.
271 IG Metall, *Geschäftsbericht 1977 bis 1979*, p. 534.
272 As quoted in *Handelsblatt*, April 17, 1978.
273 IG Metall, *Geschäftsbericht 1974 bis 1976*, pp. 134, 140.
274 The statistics cited in the next two paragraphs, as well as the overall characterization of the steel crisis, are taken from Dzielak et al., *Arbeitskampf*, pp. 49–57, 218.
275 IG Metall, *Zur Situation bei Eisen und Stahl, 27. Mai 1977 – Dortmund: Referate, Diskussionsbeiträge, Dokumente* (Frankfurt: IG Metall, n.d.). pp. 7–25.
276 This was the famous – or notorious – Resolution No. 12 passed at the twelfth IG Metall congress in Düsseldorf held between the 18th and the 24th of September, 1977. For the resolution see "Entschliessung 12 des 12. ordentlichen Gewerkschaftstages der IG Metall in Düsseldorf (18.-24. September 1977)" in IG Metall, *Der Arbeitskampf in der Eisen- und Stahlindustrie* (Frankfurt: IG Metall, n.d.), pp. 22, 23. It is also reprinted in IG Metall, Bezirksleitung Münster, *44 Tage Arbeitskampf: Dokumentation über die Tarifauseinandersetzung 1978/1979* (Münster: IG Metall, 1979), pp. 36, 37. For an excellent excerpt of the actual discussions concerning the 35-hour work week on the floor of the Düsseldorf conference, see "Protokollauszug: IG Metall Gewerkschaftstag Sept. '77: zur 35-Std.-Woche" in Revier-Redaktion, *Streikwinter: Der Stahlarbeiterstreik 1978/79 – Eine Dokumentation* (Duisburg: Revier-Redaktion, 1979), pp. 24–30.
277 Dzielak et al., *Arbeitskampf*, pp. 96–99.
278 IG Metall, *Der Arbeitskampf*, p. 11.
279 Dzielak et al., *Arbeitskampf*, pp. 21, 22.
280 On the history of labor relations in the West German steel industry, see ibid., pp. 70–82.
281 *Westfälische Rundschau*, September 30, 1978.
282 IG Metall, *Geschäftsbericht 1977 bis 1979*, p. 556.
283 Dzielak et al., *Arbeitskampf*, p. 23.
284 Helmut Martens, "Der Streik um die 35-Stunden-Woche in der Stahlindustrie 1978/79," in Otto Jacobi, Eberhard Schmidt and Walther Müller-Jentsch (eds.),

*Arbeitskampf um Arbeitszeit: Kritisches Gewerkschaftsjahrbuch 1979/80* (Berlin: Rotbuch Verlag, 1979), p. 15.
285 Dzielak et al., *Arbeitskampf*, p. 29.
286 Ibid., p. 133.
287 Gert Hautsch and Bernd Semmler, *Stahlstreik und Tarifrunde 78/79* (Frankfurt: Institut für Marxistische Studien und Forschungen, 1979), pp. 33, 36.
288 *Süddeutsche Zeitung*, December 1, 1978.
289 "Chronologie der Tarifauseinandersetzung" in *Der Gewerkschafter*, Vol. 27, no. 1 (January 1979), p. 7.
290 Dzielak et al., *Arbeitskampf*, p. 28.
291 Ibid., pp. 29–30.
292 On these legal moves, see ibid., pp. 30–32.
293 "Chronologie der Tarifauseinandersetzung."
294 Martens, "Der Streik," p. 24.
295 Dzielak et al., *Arbeitskampf*, p. 38; IG Metall, *Der Arbeitskampf*, p. 16; "Chronologie" in *Der Gewerkschafter*, p. 7.
296 IG Metall, *Geschäftsbericht 1977 bis 1979*, pp. 557, 585–586.
297 Quoted in Dzielak et al., *Arbeitskampf*, p. 41.
298 IG Metall, *Geschäftsbericht 1977 bis 1979*, pp. 557–559.
299 IG Metall, *Streik-Nachrichten*, No. 31.
300 The results were summarized in two articles: "Neue Wege der Tarifpolitik" in *metall*, Vol. 31, no. 9 (May 2, 1979), pp. 6–7; and "Wir haben Zeichen gesetzt" in *Der Gewerkschafter*, Vol. 27, no. 5 (May 1979), pp. 21–26.
301 IG Metall, *Geschäftsbericht 1977 bis 1979*, pp. 90–93.
302 Ibid., p. 602; Hans Janssen, "Unsere Handlungsmöglichkeiten erweitert" in *Der Gewerkschafter*, December 1979, p. 1; and Wolf-Gunter Brügmann, "IG Metall – von Fesseln befreit" in *Frankfurter Rundschau*, March 17, 1981.
303 IG Metall, *Geschäftsbericht 1977 bis 1979*, pp. 557–558, 568–569.
304 Wolf-Gunter Brügmann, "IG Metall."
305 See the discussion on arbitration on pp. 000–00 above.
306 "Ziel für 1981: Einkommen sichern" in *metall*, Vol. 32, no. 20 (November 5, 1980), p. 9.
307 Hans Janssen, "Arbeitgeberstrategie: Minderung der Realeinkommen" in *Der Gewerkschafter*, Vol. 29, no. 1 (January 1981), p. 4.
308 Hans Janssen, "Unsere Aktionen gehen weiter" in *Der Gewerkschafter*, Vol. 29, no. 4 (April 1981), p. 2.
309 Hans Janssen, "Die Fronten werder härter: Tarifbewegung 1981 im Rückblick" in *Der Gewerkschafter*, Vol. 29, no. 7 (July 1981), pp. 4–5.

## 5. FROM ACTIVISM TO ACCOMMODATION: THE DERADICALIZATION OF THE CHEMICAL WORKERS' UNION

1 A short historical overview of the chemical industry can be found in Willi Dzielak, Wolfgang Hindrichs, Helmut Martens, Verena Stanislawski and Wolfram Wassermann, *Belegschaften und Gewerkschaften im Streik* (Frankfurt am Main: Campus Verlag, 198), pp. 51ff.
2 Statistisches Bundesamt, *Jahrbuch des Statistischen Bundesamtes 1982* (Bonn: Statistisches Bundesamt, 1983), pp. 175, 180; own calculations.
3 Ibid., p. 181.
4 Ibid., pp. 175, 180; own calculations.
5 Ibid.
6 Ibid.
7 Ibid., p. 181.
8 Projektgruppe Gewerkschaftsforschung, *Rahmenbedingungen der Tarifpolitik*, 3 volumes (Frankfurt am Main: Campus Verlag, 1979), Vol. 2, p. 304.
9 "Branchenanalyse Chemische Industrie" in *WSI-Mitteilungen*, Vol. 26, no. 6 (June 1973), p. 214.

10  Ibid.
11  Projektgruppe Gewerkschaftsforschung, *Rahmenbedingungen*, Vol. 2, p. 298.
12  Fritz Böllhoff, *Die wirtschaftliche Bedeutung der chemischen Industrie in sektoraler und regionaler Hinsicht* (Münster: Deutsches Übersee-Institut, 1968), p. 97.
13  Ibid.
14  Projektgruppe Gewerkschaftsforschung, *Rahmenbedingungen*, Vol. 2, pp. 298–299.
15  Ibid., p. 438.
16  Ibid., pp. 359–360.
17  Ibid., p. 440.
18  Dzielak et al., *Belegschaften*, p. 60.
19  Our account of the Arbeitsring is based on Projektgruppe Gewerkschaftsforschung, *Rahmenbedingungen*, Vol. 2, pp. 117–127; see also Dzielak et al., *Belegschaften*, pp. 68–71.
20  Projektgruppe Gewerkschaftsforschung, *Rahmenbedingungen*, Vol. 2, p. 118.
21  Ibid., p. 119.
22  Ibid., p. 124.
23  "Bericht: Der 11. ordentliche Gewerkschaftstag der IG Chemie-Papier-Keramik (IGCPK) vom 7. bis 13. September 1980 in Mannheim" in *Gewerkschaftliche Monatshefte*, Vol. 13, no. 11 (November 1980), p. 758.
24  Projektgruppe Gewerkschaftsforschung, *Rahmenbedingungen*, Vol. 1, p. 128.
25  Industriegewerkschaft Chemie-Papier-Keramik, *Geschäftsbericht 1976 bis 1979* (Hanover: IG Chemie, 1980), pp. 274–278; and also "Bericht: Der 11. ordentliche Gewerkschaftstag," p. 760.
26  "Bericht: Der 11. ordentliche Gewerkschaftstag," p. 758.
27  Ibid.
28  Ibid.
29  Projektgruppe Gewerkschaftsforschung, *Rahmenbedingungen*, Vol. 1, p. 137.
30  Ibid.
31  IG Chemie, *Geschäftsbericht 1976 bis 1979*, p. 158 (figures for whole industry employment) and p. 247 (figures for degree of organization).
32  Ibid., p. 247.
33  Industriegewerkschaft Chemie-Papier-Keramik, *Satzung der Industriegewerkschaft Chemie-Papier-Keramik gültig ab 1.1.1977 [Satzung '77]* (Hanover: IG Chemie, 1977), pp. 68–69.
34  Ibid., pp. 69–70.
35  Ibid., pp. 64ff.
36  Projektgruppe Gewerkschaftsforschung, *Rahmenbedingungen*, Vol. 1, p. 129.
37  IG Chemie, *Geschäftsbericht 1976 bis 1979*, pp. 268–269.
38  Projektgruppe Gewerkschaftsforschung, *Rahmenbedingungen*, Vol. 1, p. 133.
39  Ibid.
40  IG Chemie, *Geschäftsbericht 1976 bis 1979*, pp. 254–257.
41  Industriegewerkschaft Chemie-Papier-Keramik, *Geschäftsbericht 1972 bis 1975* (Hanover: IG Chemie, 1976), pp. 260–261; and idem, *Geschäftsbericht 1976 bis 1979*, p. 249.
42  IG Chemie, *Satzung '77*, p. 48.
43  IG Chemie, *Satzung '77*, "Aufbau der Gewerkschaften: die Verwaltungsstellen," section 35, paragraph 2, p. 48. Vertrauenskörper literally means "trusted body" or "body of trust." Shop stewards in German are called Vertrauensleute. The Vertrauenskörper is a body comprising both the shop stewards and the works councilors of a given plant. As such, it encompasses both representatives of the workers on the shop floor: the "official" and "legally recognized" works councillors and the union-bound shop stewards.
44  Ibid., pp. 80–87.
45  Projektgruppe Gewerkschaftsforschung, *Rahmenbedingungen*, Vol. 1, p. 130.
46  For a complete discussion of the institutional actors, see ibid., pp. 130–135; on the role of the executive committee, see Industriegewerkschaft Chemie-Papier-Keramik, *Richtlinien für die Tarifarbeit* (Hanover: IG Chemie, 1973), p. 3.
47  For example, see the section "Tarifzuständigkeit, paragraph 2: Bezirke" in section 3 of ibid., pp. 4–5.
48  Projektgruppe Gewerkschaftsforschung, *Rahmenbedingungen*, Vol. 1, p. 131.

49 Ibid.
50 Ibid., p. 132.
51 Ibid., p. 133.
52 On the arbitration procedures, see ibid., pp. 134–135.
53 Ibid., p. 135.
54 Ibid.
55 IG Chemie, *Satzung '77*, section 15, p. 25.
56 Ibid., section 20, pp. 28–29.
57 The only extensive account of the Fabrikarbeiterverband and its history is the book prepared by the union for its fortieth anniversary in 1930: Der Verband der Fabrikarbeiter Deutschlands, *Festschrift zur Erinnerung an die Gründung und den 40-jährigen Kampf* (Hanover: Vorstand des Verbandes der Fabrikarbeiter Deutschlands, 1930); see also the summary in Dzielak et al., *Belegschaften*, pp. 64–68. Our overview of the VFD is based on these two sources.
58 VFD, *Festschrift*, p. 133.
59 Ibid., pp. 168, 170, 171.
60 Ibid., p. 113.
61 Ibid., pp. 170–171; also Peter Ullmann, *Tarifverträge und Tarifpolitik in Deutschland bis 1914* (Frankfurt: Peter Lang, 1977).
62 Ullman, *Tarifverträge*, p. 225.
63 VFD, *Festschrift*, p. 174.
64 Ibid., p. 113.
65 Industriegewerkschaft Chemie-Papier-Keramik, *Geschäftsbericht 1948 bis 1950* (Hanover: IG Chemie, 1951), p. 5.
66 See discussion in ibid., p. 7. See also Industriegewerkschaft Chemie-Papier-Keramik, *Jahrbuch 1949–1950* (Hanover: IG Chemie, 1951), pp. 19–20.
67 See discussion in IG Chemie, *Jahrbuch 1949–1950*, p. 20.
68 IG Chemie, *Geschäftsbericht 1948 bis 1950*, pp. 7–9; IG Chemie, *Jahrbuch 1949–1950*, p. 20.
69 IG Chemie, Jahrbuch 1949–1950, pp. 20–21.
70 Ibid., pp. 21–23.
71 Industriegewerkschaft Chemie-Papier-Keramik, *Geschäftsbericht 1950 bis 1952* (Hanover: IG Chemie, 1953), p. 14.
72 A clear statement of this may be found in ibid., pp. 11–15.
73 IG Chemie, *Jahrbuch 1949–1950*, pp. 25–27.
74 See the sympathetic discussion of Montanmitbestimmung in Industriegewerkschaft Chemie-Papier-Keramik, *Jahrbuch 1951* (Hanover: IG Chemie, 1952), pp. 21–23.
75 For the details of the breakup and on union representation, see ibid., pp. 26–35; and also IG Chemie, *Geschäftsbericht 1950 bis 1952*, pp. 11–15.
76 IG Chemie, *Geschäftsbericht 1950 bis 1952*, p. 15.
77 Ibid., p. 14.
78 In general, for union reaction, see Industriegewerkschaft Chemie-Papier-Keramik, *Jahrbuch 1952* (Hanover: IG Chemie, 1953), pp. 32–41.
79 See ibid., pp. 47–78, for the union's own account of economic development in West Germany during this period.
80 For a brief account of collective bargaining during these years, see Dzielak et al., *Belegschaften*, pp. 82–86.
81 Ibid., p. 86.
82 Articles appeared in the April and June issues (no. 4 and no. 6) of the *Gewerkschaftspost* in 1955. See Industriegewerkschaft Chemie-Papier-Keramik, *Geschäftsbericht 1952 bis 1954* (Hanover: IG Chemie, 1955), pp. 147ff; and Dzielak et al., *Belegschaften*, pp. 77–78, 82–83.
83 Industriegewerkschaft Chemie-Papier-Keramik, *Geschäftsbericht 1954 bis 1956* (Hanover: IG Chemie, 1957), p. 7; Dzielak et al., *Belegschaften*, pp. 75–77, 82–83.
84 IG Chemie, *Geschäftsbericht 1954 bis 1956*, pp. 7–8.
85 See the union's own comparisons to other industries in ibid., pp. 22–23.
86 Ibid., pp. 23, 151–152.
87 Dzielak et al., *Belegschaften*, p. 83 and Table 5 on page 537.

88 See Table 5 in ibid., p. 537.

89 On IG Chemie-Papier-Keramik's early concern for safety issues, see IG Chemie, *Geschäftsbericht 1954 bis 1956*, pp. 30–32; and idem, *Geschäftsbericht 1957 bis 1959* (Hanover: IG Chemie, 1960), pp. 76–80.

90 Dzielak et al., *Belegschaften*, p. 119.

91 Industriegewerkschaft Chemie-Papier-Keramik, *Geschäftsbericht 1960 bis 1962* (Hanover: IG Chemie, 1963), p. 261.

92 Dzielak et al., *Belegschaften*, p. 119.

93 Some of the possible indications are discussed in ibid., pp. 119–120.

94 Dzielak et al., discuss these company shop stewards in ibid., p. 120; the role of the Vertrauensleute in keeping channels of communication open between workers, works councils and employers is discussed in the interesting article by Loke Mernizka and Siegfried Dreher, "Stellung und Aufgaben gewerkschaftlicher Vertrauensleute" in Otto Jacobi, Walther Müller-Jentsch and Eberhard Schmidt (eds.), *Gewerkschaften und Klassenkampf: Kritisches Jahrbuch 1972* (Frankfurt: Fischer, 1972), pp. 162–164.

95 Cited in Otto Jacobi and Hans Günter Lang, "Anpassung und Zentralisierung: zur Entwicklung in der IG Chemie" in Otto Jacobi, Walther Müller-Jentsch and Eberhard Schmidt (eds.), *Arbeitskampf um Arbeitszeit: Kritisches Jahrbuch 1980* (Berlin: Rotbuch, 1980), p. 190.

96 Dzielak et al., *Belegschaften*, p. 120.

97 Ibid.

98 Ibid., p. 121.

99 For example, see the speeches by Karl Kuepper (pp. 53–58) and Wilhelm Gefeller (pp. 277–307) in Industriegewerkschaft Chemie-Papier-Keramik, *Protokoll der Verhandlungen des 6. ordentlichen Gewerkschaftstages der Industriegewerkschaft Chemie-Papier-Keramik vom 22. bis 27. September 1963 in Wiesbaden* (Hanover: IG Chemie, 1964).

100 The quote and the figures may be found in IG Chemie, *Geschäftsbericht 1960 bis 1962*, p. 360.

101 Gefeller discussed the problem (so called) of "communist infiltration" in his above-mentioned address in IG Chemie, *Protokoll 1963*, pp. 279ff.

102 In particular, see the remarks made by Kuepper (pp. 66–74) and Gefeller (pp. 282–302) in Industriegewerkschaft Chemie-Papier-Keramik, *Protokoll: 7. Ordentlicher Gewerkschaftstag in Dortmund 1966* (Hanover: IG Chemie, 1976).

103 See Gefeller's address in ibid., p. 288.

104 Industriegewerkschaft Chemie-Papier-Keramik, *Geschäftsbericht 1963 bis 1965* (Hanover: IG Chemie, 1966), pp. 313–315; and Dzielak et al., *Belegschaften*, pp. 70–71.

105 Dzielak et al., *Belegschaften*, pp. 83–84.

106 IG Chemie, *Geschäftsbericht 1960 bis 1962*, pp. 346–348.

107 IG Chemie, *Geschäftsbericht 1963 bis 1965*, pp. 321–323.

108 IG Chemie, *Geschäftsbericht 1966 bis 1968* (Hanover: IG Chemie, 1969), pp. 256–257.

109 Ibid., p. 257.

110 Dzielak et al., *Belegschaften*, p. 84 and note 51 on p. 555.

111 For a representative view, see Gefeller's remarks in IG Chemie, *Protokoll 1963* pp. 295–299.

112 IG Chemie, *Geschäftsbericht 1960 bis 1962*, pp. 5–7.

113 Ibid.

114 See the address by Gefeller in IG Chemie, *Protokoll 1963*, pp. 278ff.

115 IG Chemie, *Geschäftsbericht 1963 bis 1965*, p. 319.

116 Ibid., p. 320.

117 IG Chemie, *Geschäftsbericht 1966 bis 1968*, p. 263.

118 Ibid.; and IG Chemie, *Protokoll 1966*, p. 290.

119 Dzielak et al., *Belegschaften*, p. 80.

120 Ibid.; for elevation to official policy, see Industriegewerkschaft Chemie-Papier-Keramik, *Geschäftsbericht 1969 bis 1971* (Hanover: IG Chemie, 1972), p. 312; for earlier developments of the debate see *Geschäftsbericht 1966 bis 1968*, p. 263.

121 Edwin Schudlich, "'Tarifpolitik ohne Kampfgeschrei': Die Tarifbeziehungen in der

chemischen Industrie 1970–1979" in Ulrich Billerbeck, Christoph Deutschmann, Rainer Erd, Rudi Schmiede and Edwin Schudlich (eds.), *Neuorientierung der Tarifpolitik?* (Frankfurt: Campus Verlag, 1982), p. 284.

122 Dzielak et al., *Belegschaften*, pp. 84–85.

123 Ibid., p. 85; and Otto Jacobi, "Streik der Chemiearbeiter 1971" in Jacobi et al., *Kritisches Jahrbuch 1972*, pp. 28–44.

124 Dzielak et al., *Belegschaften*, p. 85.

125 Ibid., pp. 85–86.

126 Ibid., p. 86.

127 Jacobi, "Streik der Chemiearbeiter," pp. 34ff.

128 These wage agreements were the highest in post-World War II history; see ibid., p. 30.

129 Kurt Steinhaus, *Streiks in der Bundesrepublik, 1966–1974* (Frankfurt: Verlag Marxistische Blätter, 1975), p. 86.

130 Steinhaus, *Streiks*, pp. 86–87; Dzielak et al., *Belegschaften*, p. 136.

131 Dzielak et al., *Belegschaften*, p. 137.

132 Ibid.

133 Jacobi, "Streik der Chemiearbeiter," pp. 34–35; Dzielak et al., *Belegschaften*, p. 138.

134 Dzielak et al., *Belegschaften*, p. 139; Jacobi, "Streik der Chemiearbeiter," pp. 35–36; Steinhaus, *Streiks*, p. 87.

135 Jacobi, "Streik der Chemiearbeiter," p. 36.

136 Ibid.; also Dzielak et al., *Belegschaften*, p. 139.

137 Jacobi, "Streik der Chemiearbeiter," p. 36.

138 Ibid., p. 37.

139 Steinhaus, *Streiks*, p. 93.

140 Dzielak et al., *Belegschaften*, pp. 147–149.

141 Steinhaus, *Streiks*, p. 90.

142 Der Spiegel, Vol. 27, no. 21 (June 28, 1971) – as quoted in Dzielak et al., *Belegschaften*, p. 151.

143 Dzielak et al., *Belegschaften*, pp. 153–154.

144 For highlights of strike violence, see Dzielak et al., *Belegschaften*, pp. 144–155; see also Jacobi, "Streik der Chemiearbeiter," p. 38.

145 Dzielak et al., *Belegschaften*, pp. 142, 147.

146 Ibid., pp. 140–141.

147 For general overviews of chemical industry performance up to 1975, see Projektgruppe Gewerkschaftsforschung, *Rahmenbedingungen der Tarifpolitik*, Vol. 2, pp. 308–321; for entire decade, see Schudlich, "'Tarifpolitik ohne Kampfgeschrei,'" pp. 273–281.

148 Projektgruppe Gewerkschaftsforschung, *Rahmenbedingungen*, Vol. 2; Schudlich, "'Tarifpolitik,'" p. 276.

149 See table in Schudlich, "'Tarifpolitik,'" p. 285.

150 Ibid.

151 Ibid., pp. 286–287.

152 For discussion of rationalization in the 1969 and 1972 congresses, see Industriegewerkschaft Chemie-Papier-Keramik, *Protokoll: 8. ordentlicher Gewerkschaftstag Wiesbaden – 31. August bis 6. September 1969* (Hanover: IG Chemie, 1970), p. 186; and idem, *Protokoll: 9. ordentlicher Gewerkschaftstag Dortmund – 17. bis 22. September 1972* (Hanover: IG Chemie, 1973), p. 132. For defensive countermeasures, see the discussion in Schudlich, "'Tarifpolitik,'" p. 296; and in Jacobi and Lang "Anpassung und Zentralisierung," pp. 192–204.

153 Schudlich, "'Tarifpolitik,'" pp. 298–300.

154 Ibid., p. 285.

155 Ibid.

156 Schudlich, "'Tarifpolitik,'" pp. 291–293 and 302–305; Jacobi and Lang, "Anpassung und Zentralisierung," pp. 202–204.

157 Schudlich, "'Tarifpolitik,'" pp. 285.

158 Jacobi and Lang, "Anpassung und Zentralisierung," p. 203; Schudlich "'Tarifpolitik,'" pp. 292, 293.

159 Schudlich, "'Tarifpolitik,'" p. 292.

160  Ibid.

161  Ibid.

162  Jacobi and Lang, "Anpassung und Zentralisierung," p. 199; Schudlich, "'Tarifpolitik,'" pp. 291–293.

163  Jacobi and Lang, "Anpassung und Zentralisierung," p. 199.

164  The passivity and cooperativeness of IG Chemie is a major theme in ibid., esp. pp. 194–201, and in Schudlich, "'Tarifpolitik,'" pp. 291–293.

165  Jacobi and Lang, "Anpassung und Zentralisierung," pp. 199–200.

166  Manfred Krüper, "Muster für einen Branchenfonds" in Gewerkschaftliche Umschau, No. 6, November/December 1978, pp. 6–7.

167  Ibid.

168  "IG Chemie Vorstand möchte umstrittene Praxis zementieren" in Frankfurter Rundschau, February 20, 1979.

169  Ibid.; and Jacobi and Lang, "Anpassung und Zentralisierung," pp. 188–194.

170  Frankfurter Rundschau, "IG Chemie Vorstand möchte"; and Jacobi and Lang, "Anpassung und Zentralisierung," pp. 188–194.

171  The official was Ferdinand Patschkowski; an early press account of the firing and its repercussions may be found in the Frankfurter Rundschau, "Ruf nach Rücktritt des IG Chemie-Chefs Hauenschild wird laut," March 26, 1979.

172  Ibid.

173  Ibid.

174  See the discussion in Dzielak et al., Belegschaften, pp. 64–68.

175  Jacobi and Lang, "Anpassung und Zentralisierung," p. 190.

176  Ibid.

177  Erwin Schudlich, "Das System der 'Betrieblichen' Vertrauensleute in der Chemischen Industrie – Seine Funktion und seine Problematik für die Politik der Industriegewerkschaft Chemie-Papier-Keramik," unpublished manuscript, Frankfurt, 1979, p. 7.

178  IG Chemie, Satzung '77 p. 80.

179  Jacobi and Lang, "Anpassung und Zentralisierung," p. 193; and Frankfurter Rundschau, "IG Chemie Vorstand möchte."

180  This 6–2 split of the executive committee continued with great consistency throughout much of the 1970s, especially with regard to issues of organizational reform. See also Otto Jacobi, "Innerverbandliche Stellung der Vertauensleute in der IG Chemie-Papier-Keramik" in Otto Jacobi, Walther Müller-Jentsch and Eberhard Schmidt (eds.), Gewerkschaften und Klassenkampf: Kritisches Jahrbuch 1973 (Frankfurt: Fischer, 1973), p. 88.

181  "IG Chemie: Auf dem Weg zu einer gelben Gewerkschaft?," express, Vol. 17, no. 4 (April 23, 1979), p. 4.

182  Ibid.

183  IG Chemie, Geschäftsbericht 1976 bis 1979, pp. 299–303; see also Jacobi and Lang, "Anpassung und Zentralisierung," pp. 188–194.

184  Projektgruppe Gewerkschaftsforschung, Tarifpolitik 1978 (Frankfurt: Campus Verlag, 1980), pp. 143–186.

185  Edeltraud Remell, "Bruderzwist im Haus Hauenschild" in Vorwärts, No. 16 (April 12, 1979), p. 19.

186  Ibid.

187  "Wille zur Kollegialität in der IG Chemie bekundet" in Frankfurter Rundschau, April 19, 1979.

188  Jacobi and Lang, "Anpassung und Zentralisierung," p. 193.

## 6. LEBER'S VANGUARD: THE CONSTRUCTION WORKERS' UNION

1  Wolfgang Richter (ed.), Bauarbeit in der Bundesrepublik (Cologne: Pahl-Rugenstein Verlag, 1981), p. 27.

2  Industriegewerkschaft Bau-Steine-Erden, Geschäftsbericht 1975 bis 1978 (Frankfurt am Main: IG Bau-Steine-Erden, 1979), p. 45.

3  Sachverständigenrat zur Begutachtung der gesamtwirtschaftlichen Entwicklung, Investi-

*eren für mehr Beschäftigung; Jahresgutachten 1981–82* (Stuttgart: Kohlhammer, 1982), Appendix VI, table 17.

4 Richter, *Bauarbeit*, p. 27.

5 IG Bau, *Geschaftsbericht 1975 bis 1978*, p. 48.

6 Ibid.

7 Ibid., p. 53; Richter, *Bauarbeit*, p. 49.

8 For a discussion of the construction employers' associations see: Karl-Gustav Werner, *Organisation und Politik der Gewerkschaften und der Arbeitgeberverbände in der deutschen Bauwirtschaft* (Berlin: Duncker & Humbolt, 1968), pp. 186–206.

9 On the difference between "Handwerk" and "Industrie" organizations see Detlef Perner, *Mitbestimmung im Handwerk? Die politische und soziale Funktion der Handwerkskammern im Geflecht der Unternehmerorganisationen* (Cologne: Bund Verlag, 1983). Perner's detailed study is the best account of "Handwerk" as an organizational arrangement in the West German economy.

10 SVR, *Jahresgutachten 1981/82*, Appendix VI, table 24.

11 IG Bau, *Geschäftsbericht 1975 bis 1978*, p. 52.

12 For the exact figures, see Appendix 1.

13 Our own calculations based on figures in various *Geschäftsberichte* of IG Bau.

14 Hermann Bayer, Wolfgang Streeck and EckbertTreu, *Die westdeutsche Gewerkschaftsbewegung in Zahlen* (Königstein: Anton Hain, 1981), p. 31.

15 IG Bau, *Geschäftsbericht 1975 bis 1978*, p. 227.

16 On the internal organization of IG Bau, see Werner, *Organisation und Politik*, pp. 206–234.

17 Walther Müller-Jentsch and Wolfgang Streeck, "Industriegewerkschaft Bau-Steine-Erden" (unpublished manuscript, Frankfurt am Main, 1970), pp. 11ff.

18 IG Bau, *Geschäftsbericht 1975 bis 1978*, pp. 135–137.

19 Industriegewerkschaft Bau-Steine-Erden, *Geschäftsbericht 1979 bis 1981* (Frankfurt am Main: IG Bau, 1982), p. 355.

20 Ibid., p. 455.

21 Our account of the history of labor relations in German construction is based on Werner, *Organisation*, pp. 11–166; and Peter Ullman, *Tarifverträge und Tarifpolitik in Deutschland bis 1914* (Frankfurt: Peter Lang, 1977), pp. 75–97.

22 Werner, *Organisation*, p. 111.

23 Ibid., p. 85.

24 Our account of IG Bau's history from the 1940s until 1981 is based on the union's own *Geschäftsberichte* and Werner, *Organisation*. When other sources are used they will be noted.

25 "Eure Bruderhand" in *Der Spiegel*, Vol. 10, no. 4 (January 25, 1956), pp. 17–18.

26 The seventeenth DGB member, the police officers' union, joined the labor federation in the spring of 1978.

27 Werner, *Organisation*, p. 224.

28 Ibid., p. 275.

29 Ibid., p. 285.

30 Zentralverband des deutschen Baugewerbes, *Jahrbuch des deutschen Baugewerbes 1966* (n.p.: ZDB, 1967), p. 72; Industriegewerkschaft Bau-Steine-Erden, *Geschäftsbericht 1955 bis 1956* (Frankfurt: IG Bau, 1957), p. 57.

31 Zentralverband des deutschen Baugewerbes, *Jahrbuch 1956* (n.p.: ZDB, 1957), p. 498.

32 Our account of IG Bau bargaining rounds is drawn exclusively from its *Geschäftsberichte* unless otherwise noted.

33 Doris Nolle, "IG Bau-Steine-Erden 1949–1957 – Die Entwicklung zu einer kooperativen Gewerkschaft" in Claudio Pozzoli (ed.), *Grenzen gewerkschaftlicher Politik* (Frankfurt: Fischer, 1978), pp. 32–33; Industriegewerkschaft Bau-Steine-Erden, *Jahrbuch 1951/52* (Frankfurt: IG Bau, 1953), pp. 51–52.

34 Nolle, "IG Bau-Steine-Erden," pp. 33–34; Müller-Jentsch and Streeck, *Industriegewerkschaft*, p. 14.

35 Werner, *Organisation*, pp. 224–226.

36 See the interview with Leber, "Die Gewerkschaft is kein Turnverein" in *Der Spiegel*, Vol. 16, no. 3 (January 17, 1962).

37 Werner, *Organisation*, p. 284.
38 Ibid., p. 276; on the 1953 congress also Nolle, "IG Bau-Steine-Erden," pp. 34–35.
39 Werner, *Organisation*, p. 287.
40 ZDB, *Jahrbuch 1966*, p. 65.
41 Werner, *Organisation*, p. 223.
42 Industriegewerkschaft Bau-Steine-Erden, *Protokoll des 3. ordentlichen Gewerkschaftstages 1955* (Frankfurt: IG Bau, 1956), pp. 470–493.
43 Ibid., pp. 501–503.
44 Ibid., p. 620.
45 Nolle, "IG Bau-Steine-Erden," p. 37.
46 "Eure Bruderhand" in *Der Spiegel*, Vol. 10, no. 4 (January 25, 1956), pp. 17–18.
47 Ibid.; see also IG Bau's own account of this affair in IG Bau, *Geschäftsbericht 1955 bis 1956*, pp. 18–38.
48 On the creation of the ZVK, see Werner, *Organisation*, pp. 279–283.
49 Industriegewerkschaft Bau-Steine-Erden, *Geschäftsbericht 1957 bis 1959* (Frankfurt: IG Bau, 1960), pp. 129, 131–132.
50 See the debate on this issue in IG Bau, *Protokoll des 4. ordentlichen Gewerkschaftstages 1957* (Frankfurt: IG Bau, 1958), pp. 460ff; also Müller-Jentsch and Streeck, *Industriegewerkschaft*, pp. 46–48.
51 On Vermögensbildung, see Werner, *Organisation*, pp. 332–343.
52 On winter construction, see ibid., pp. 283–303.
53 IG Bau, *Protokoll 1957*, pp. 467–471.
54 Werner, *Organisation*, p. 296.
55 ZDB, *Jahrbuch 1966*, p. 72.
56 Werner, *Organisation*, p. 211; own calculations.
57 Industriegewerkschaft Bau-Steine-Erden, *Geschäftsbericht 1960 bis 1962* (Frankfurt: IG Bau, 1963), p. 19.
58 Ibid., p. 34.
59 Walther Müller-Jentsch, "IG Bau-Steine-Erden: Juniorpartner der Bauindustrie" in Otto Jacobi, Walther Müller-Jentsch and Eberhard Schmidt (eds.), *Gewerkschaften und Klassenkampf: Kritisches Jahrbuch 1973* (Frankfurt: Fischer, 1973), p. 103.
60 IG Bau-Steine-Erden, *Geschäftsbericht 1953 bis 1954* (Frankfurt: IG Bau, 1955), p. 31, and *Geschäftsbericht 1960 bis 1962*, p. 24.
61 Müller-Jentsch and Streeck, *Industriegewerkschaft*, p. 25.
62 Wolf-Rainer Roloff, *Interpretation und Analyse der lohn-und sozialpolitischen Zielsetzung der Industriegewerkschaft Bau-Steine-Erden* (Hilden: Selbstverlag Dr. Roloff, 1971), p. 140.
63 Müller-Jentsch and Streeck, *Industriegewerkschaft*, p. 25.
64 Roloff, *Interpretation*, pp. 105, 108.
65 ZDB, *Jahrbuch 1956*, p. 498; and Richter, *Bauarbeit*, p. 147.
66 Industriegewerkschaft Bau-Steine-Erden, *Protokoll über den 5. ordentlichen Gewerkschaftstag 1960* (Frankfurt: IG Bau, 1960), pp. 254–262; also Werner, *Organisation*, pp. 303–321.
67 Werner, *Organisation*, pp. 306–308.
68 IG Bau, *Geschäftsbericht 1960 bis 1962*, pp. 75–76.
69 Werner, *Organisation*, pp. 312–321; the text of the Recommendations can be found in IG Bau, *Geschäftsbericht 1960 bis 1962*, pp. 77–80.
70 "Die Leber-Party" in *Der Spiegel*, Vol. 17, no. 13 (March 27, 1963).
71 Industriegewerkschaft Bau-Steine-Erden, *Geschäftsbericht 1963 bis 1965* (Frankfurt: IG Bau, 1966), p. 22.
72 IG Bau-Stein-Erden, *Protokoll über den 6. ordentlichen Gewerkschaftstag 1963* (Frankfurt: IG Bau, 1963), pp. 235–239.
73 Ibid., pp. 239–243; Werner, *Organisation*, pp. 332–343.
74 During this congress, Leber also staged an impressive display of his enormous influence within the labor movement and the Federal Republic by getting US President John F. Kennedy to address IG Bau's membership. This was an unprecedented achievement among West German unions. IG Bau-Steine-Erden, *Protokoll über den 6. ordentlichen Gewerkschaftstag 1963* (Frankfurt: IG Bau, 1963).

75 Werner, *Organisation*, p. 334.
76 Ibid., pp. 340–341.
77 Industriegewerkschaft Bau-Steine-Erden, *Geschäftsbericht 1966 bis 1968* (Frankfurt: IG Bau, 1969), pp. 33, 39.
78 Ibid., pp. 236–239.
79 "Mit körperlicher Kraft" in *Der Spiegel*, Vol. 21, no. 34 (August 14, 1967); also Joachim Bergmann, Otto Jacobi and Walther Müller-Jentsch, *Gewerkschaften in der Bundesrepublik*, third edition (Frankfurt: Campus Verlag, 1979), pp. 294–297.
80 Bergmann et al., *Gewerkschaften*, p. 298.
81 See the reports on the construction industry in Industriegewerkschaft Bau-Steine-Erden, *Geschäftsbericht 1969 bis 1971* (Frankfurt: IG Bau, 1972), p. 29; idem, *Geschäftsbericht 1972 bis 1974* (Frankfurt: IG Bau, 1975), p. 44.
82 IG Bau, *Geschäftsbericht 1969 bis 1971*, p. 43; *Geschäftsbericht 1953 bis 1954*, p. 31.
83 Müller-Jentsch, "IG Bau-Steine-Erden," p. 103.
84 Ibid., p. 108.
85 The text of the Program can be found in IG Bau, *Geschäftsbericht 1969 bis 1971* pp. i–vii.
86 IG Bau, *Geschäftsbericht 1969 bis 1971*, pp. 212–214; *Geschäftsbericht 1972 bis 1974*, p. 282.
87 IG Bau, *Geschäftsbericht 1966 bis 1968*, p. 42; *Geschäftsbericht 1972 bis 1974*, pp. 52, 180.
88 IG Bau, *Geschäftsbericht 1972 bis 1974*, pp. 516–518.
89 Ibid., pp. 587–589.
90 Industriegewerkschaft Bau-Steine-Erden, *Geschäftsbericht 1979 bis 1981* (Frankfurt: IG Bau, 1982), p. 46.
91 IG Bau, *Geschäftsbericht 1975 bis 1978*, pp. 45, 48c; *Geschäftsbericht 1979 bis 1981*, pp. 42, 46.
92 IG Bau, *Geschäftsbericht 1975 bis 1978*, p. 334.
93 IG Bau, *Geschäftsbericht 1979 bis 1981*, pp. 13–15.
94 IG Bau, *Geschäftsbericht 1975 bis 1978*, pp. 327–332.
95 Ibid., pp. 333–379.
96 Industriegewerkschaft Bau-Steine-Erden, *Dokumentation der Solidarität* (Frankfurt: IG Bau, 1979).

## 7. THE ARISTOCRACY OF LABOR: THE PRINTERS' UNION

1 "Druckgewerbe sieht schwarz" in *Frankfurter Rundschau*, February 18, 1981.
2 Official statistics give employment in printing as 174,000 in 1983 ("Druckindustrie spürt nichts vom Aufschwung" in *Frankfurter Rundschau*, June 14, 1983). However, this only includes employees in printing works with more than 20 workers. A study in the late 1970s showed that about 31,000 persons were employed in works smaller than this: Manfred Lahner and Regina Grabiszewski, "Auswirkungen technischer Änderungen in der Druckerei- und Vervielfältigungsindustrie" in *Mitteilungen aus der Arbeitsmarkt- und Berufsforschung*, Vol. 4, 1977. We have therefore estimated total employment as 205,000.
3 Ulrich Billerbeck, Christoph Deutschmann, Rainer Erd, Rudi Schmiede and Edwin Schudlich, *Neuorientierung der Tarifpolitik* (Frankfurt am Main: Campus Verlag, 1982), p. 357.
4 Hugo Reister, *Profite gegen Bleisatz* (Berlin: Verlag die Arbeitswelt, 1980), p. 174.
5 Ibid.
6 Ibid., p. 12.
7 Ibid.
8 For a description of both the new computer-controlled printing process and the old "cold type" method which it replaced, see "The Times Enters a New Era of Electronic Printing" in *New York Times*, July 3, 1978.
9 Projektgruppe Gewerkschaftsforschung, *Rahmenbedingungen der Tarifpolitik* (Frankfurt am Main: Campus Verlag, 1979), Vol. 2, p. 510.
10 Ibid., pp. 510–511.
11 Ibid., p. 592.
12 Ibid., p. 472.
13 Ibid., pp. 472–473.

14 Industriegewerkschaft Druck und Papier, *Geschäftsbericht 1977 bis 1980* (Stuttgart: IG Druck, 1981), p. 284.
15 Billerbeck et al., *Neuorientierung*, p. 458; Hellmut G. Haasis, "Kritik und Alternative gewerkschaftlicher Tarifpolitik am Beispiel der Industriegewerkschaft Druck und Papier" in Paul Mattick (ed.), *Beiträge zur Kritik des Geldes* (Frankfurt am Main: Suhrkamp, 1976), p. 274.
16 Projektgruppe Gewerkschaftsforschung, *Rahmenbedingungen*, Vol. 1, p. 183.
17 Ibid., pp. 181, 183.
18 Ibid., p. 183.
19 Ibid., p. 174.
20 For a description of IG Druck's internal organization, see Projektgruppe Gewerkschaftsforschung, *Rahmenbedingungen*, Vol. 1, pp. 166–172.
21 Ibid., p. 190.
22 Ibid., p. 176.
23 IG Druck, *Geschäftsbericht 1977 bis 80*, pp. 233–234.
24 On Berufsgruppen and Sparten, see Claudia Weber, "Die Handlungsbedeutung von Konfliktverarbeitungsmustern unter sich verändernden sozio-ökonomischen Bedingungen," unpublished manuscript, Institut zur Erforschung sozialer Chancen, Cologne, May, 1980, pp. 70–77.
25 On bargaining and employers' associations, see Projektgruppe Gewerkschaftsforschung, *Rahmenbedingungen*, Vol. 1, pp. 168–172. Our account of both is based on this source.
26 This short history of labor relations in printing before 1945 is drawn from Richard Burkhardt, *Ein Kampf ums Menschenrecht* (Stuttgart: IG Druck, 1974); and Peter Ullmann, *Tarifverträge und Tarifpolitik in Deutschland bis 1914* (Frankfurt am Main: Peter Lang, 1977).
27 Burkhardt, *Ein Kampf*, p. 68.
28 Reister, *Profite*, pp. 156–157.
29 Ibid., p. 156.
30 Ibid.
31 Ibid., p. 12.
32 Ibid., pp. 26, 28.
33 Ibid., p. 161.
34 Ibid., pp. 18–19, 32.
35 All figures from ibid., p. 156.
36 Ibid., p. 36.
37 Ibid., p. 65.
38 Martin Osterland, Wilfried Deppe, Frank Gerlach, Ulrich Mergner, Klaus Pelte and Manfred Schlösser, *Materialien zur Lebens- und Arbeitssituation der Industriearbeiter in der BRD* (Frankfurt am Main: EVA, 1973), table 17.
39 Klaus Grefermann, *Papierverarbeitung und Druckerei-Industrie aus der Sicht der siebziger Jahre* (Berlin: Duncker & Humblot, 1973), p. 65; Reister, *Profite*, p. 157.
40 Reister, *Profite*, p. 94.
41 Weber, "Die Handlungsbedeutung," p. 77.
42 Industriegewerkschaft Druck und Papier, *Geschäftsbericht 1948 bis 1950*, (Stuttgart: IG Druck, 1951), pp. 43–51.
43 For the details of the 1949 wage structure, see Burkhardt, *Ein Kampf*, pp. 159–160.
44 Ibid., p. 159.
45 Ibid., pp. 167–170.
46 Ibid., p. 168.
47 Ibid., p. 122.
48 IG Druck, *Geschäftsbericht 1948 bis 1950*, pp. 53–60.
49 IG Druck, *Geschäftsbericht 1950 bis 1952* (Stuttgart: IG Druck, 1952), p. 17; Burkhardt, *Ein Kampf*, p. 210; Reister, *Profite*, pp. 95–96. To highlight IG Druck's deficient results at the time, one could examine them in relation to the Bremen formula discussed in the chapter on IG Metall. As will be recalled, Otto Brenner decreed that a bargaining round was successful for labor if it attained three-fourths of its original demand. It should be noted, however, that Brenner conceived this formula much later, during a period of economic

growth accompanied by virtually no unemployment. Moreover, Brenner intended this formula to apply first and foremost to his own organization, IG Metall.

50 Industriegewerkschaft Druck und Papier, *Geschäftsbericht 1956 bis 1959* (Stuttgatt, IG Druck, 1959), p. 57.

51 Burkhardt, *Ein Kampf*, pp. 140–141, 146; Reister, *Profite*, p. 105.

52 Burkhardt, *Ein Kampf*, pp. 139–140.

53 On the introduction of the TTS system and its ramifications, see Walther Müller-Jentsch and Rainer Erd, "Innovation in the Printing Industry in the Federal Republic," Research Paper of the Anglo-German Foundation for the Study of Industrial Society, no. Bo179/4E, pp. 33–36.

54 Industriegewerkschaft Druck und Papier, *Geschäftsbericht 1954 bis 1956* (Stuttgart: IG Druck, 1956), pp. 46–48, 194–195.

55 Industriegewerkschaft Druck und Papier, *Geschäftsbericht 1956 bis 1959* (Stuttgart: IG Druck, 1959), pp. 113–114, 290–292.

56 On the 1955 round see IG Druck, *Geschäftsbericht 1954 bis 1956*, pp. 60–74.

57 IG Druck, *Geschäftsbericht 1954 bis 1956*, p. 133.

58 On the 1956 round see IG Druck, *Geschäftsbericht 1954 bis 1956*, pp. 81–90.

59 Burkhardt, *Ein Kampf*, p. 210.

60 Industriegewerkschaft Druck und Papier, *Protokoll vom 5. ordentlichen Gewerkschaftstag vom 20. bis 26. September 1959 in Hannover* (Stuttgart: IG Druck, 1959), p. 57.

61 Ibid., pp. 490–492, 504–507.

62 On the 1960 round see Industriegewerkschaft Druck und Papier, *Geschäftsbericht 1959 bis 1962* (Stuttgart: IG Druck, 1963), pp. 129–135.

63 Ibid., pp. 104–110.

64 On the 1961 round, see ibid., pp. 139–147.

65 Industriegewerkschaft Druck und Papier, *Geschäftsbericht 1962 bis 1965* (Stuttgart: IG Druck 1966), pp. 74, 100.

66 Ibid., pp. 73–79.

67 IG Druck, *Geschäftsbericht 1959 bis 1962*, p. 148; *Geschäftsbericht 1965 bis 1968* (Stuttgart: IG Druck, 1969), p. 328.

68 Burkhardt, *Ein Kampf*, p. 310.

69 IG Druck, *Geschäftsbericht 1962 bis 1965*, pp. 152–153.

70 Reister, *Profite*, p. 157.

71 IG Druck, *Geschäftsbericht 1965 bis 1968*, pp. 318–322.

72 Ibid., pp. 11–21.

73 All these figures from Reister, *Profite*, pp. 156–157.

74 Burkhardt, *Ein Kampf*, pp. 210–211.

75 Reister, *Profite*, pp. 58–61.

76 Ibid., pp. 50, 55.

77 IG Druck, *Geschäftsbericht 1977 bis 1980*, p. 141.

78 Burkhardt, *Ein Kampf*, p. 172.

79 Ibid., p. 173. For the text of the proposal, see Industrigewerkschaft Druck und Papier, *Protokoll – 9. ordentlicher Gewerkschaftstag Industriegewerkschaft Druck und Papier – Nürnberg 1971* (Stuttgart: IG Druck, 1972), pp. 87–92. For almost twenty years, this proposal remained a dead letter as other concerns occupied IG Druck. In the early 1980s, however, interest in wage structure reform reemerged. See Erwin Ferkmann, "Bilanz des Arbeitskampfes 1984," in Gewerkschaftliche Monatshefte, Vol. 35, no. 11 (November 1984).

80 See the debate on the dissolution in Industriegewerkschaft Druck und Papier, *Protokoll – 10. ordentlicher Gewerkschaftstag Industriegewerkschaft Druck und Papier – Hamburg 1974* (Stuttgart: IG Druck, 1975), pp. 486–503.

81 Burkhardt, *Ein Kampf*, pp. 153–154.

82 Lahner and Grabiszewski, "Auswirkungen," p. 524; Reister, *Profite*, p. 157.

83 Billerbeck et al., *Neuorientierung*, p. 446.

84 Reister, *Profite*, p. 157.

85 "Zusammenbrüche in ungeahnt kurzer Zeit" in *Der Spiegel*, Vol. 29, no. 6 (February 3, 1975).

86  Lahner and Grabiszewski, "Auswirkungen," p. 550.
87  On Stuttgart-Möhringen, see Billerbeck et al., *Neuorientierung*, pp. 433–443. Also Ulf Kadritzke and Dieter Ostendorp, "Beweglich sein fürs Kapital. Das 'Stuttgarter Modell' der Rationalisierung und Arbeitsplatzvernichtung in der Zeitungsproduktion" in Otto Jacobi, Walther Müller-Jentsch and Eberhard Schmidt (eds.), *Gewerkschaftspolitik in der Krise* (Berlin: Rotbuch, 1979). A contrasting case which details the introduction of the new technology in a large Gruner + Jahr plant can be found in Billerbeck et al., *Neuorientierung*, pp. 415–437. See also "Computer werden Kündigungen schreiben" in *Der Spiegel*, Vol. 30, no. 20/21 (May 17, 1976).
88  "The Times Enters a New Era of Electronic Printing" in *New York Times*, July 3, 1978.
89  Reister, *Profite*, p. 64.
90  Lahner and Grabiszewski, "Auswirkungen," p. 524.
91  See "Das Gefährliche an Detlef" in *Wirtschaftswoche*, no. 12, 1978 (March 17); and the interview with Hensche in *Der Spiegel*, Vol. 32, no. 25 (June 19, 1978).
92  On the 1976 strike and its background, see Industriegewerkschaft Druck und Papier, *Geschäftsbericht 1974 bis 1977* (Stuttgart: IG Druck, 1977), pp. 81–90; Projektgruppe Gewerkschaftsforschung, *Tarifpolitik unter Krisenbedingungen*, Forschungsbericht des Instituts für Sozialforschung, Frankfurt am Main, 1977; Rainer Erd, "Der Kampf um die 6 vor dem Komma" in Rainer Duhm and Ulrich Mückenberger (eds), *Arbeitskampf im Krisenalltag* (Berlin: Rotbuch Verlag, 1977).
93  IG Druck, *Geschäftsbericht 1974 bis 1977*, p. 84.
94  Ibid., p. 85.
95  Ibid., p. 87.
96  Projektgruppe Gewerkschaftsforschung, *Tarifpolitik*, pp. 218–219.
97  Ibid., pp. 216–218.
98  On the 1978 strike and its background, see IG Druck, *Geschäftsbericht 1977 bis 1980*, pp. 76–80; Projektgruppe Gewerkschaftsforschung, *Tarifpolitik 1978: Lohnpolitische Kooperation und Absicherungskämpfe* (Frankfurt am Main: Campus, 1979), pp. 187–276; Walther Müller-Jentsch, "Der Arbeitskampf in der Druckindustrie 1978" in O. Jacobi, W. Müller-Jentsch and E. Schmidt (eds.), *Arbeiterinteressen gegen Sozialpartnerschaft* (Berlin: Rotbuch Verlag, 1979).
99  For a complete text of the RTS contract, see Projektgruppe Gewerkschaftsforschung, *Tarifpolitik 1978*, pp. 249–276.
100  IG Druck, *Geschäftsbericht 1977 bis 1980*, p. 100; Dresdner Bank, *Statistical Survey*, July 1981, p. 2.
101  "Gern behilflich" in *Der Spiegel*, Vol. 32, no. 42 (October 16, 1978).
102  Billerbeck et al., *Neuorientierung*, pp. 383–385.
103  Ibid., pp. 395–396.
104  As this work goes to press, IG Druck has agreed in principle to unite with several smaller unions representing artists and TV and radio employees to form a "media union," to be called IG Medien-Druck und Papier, Publisistik und Kunst. See *druck und papier*, special issue, December 10, 1984. At a specially convened union congress in June 1985, IG Druck delegates voted unanimously to work towards the creation of such a union by the late 1980s, largely to counter employment problems in the increasingly concentrated world of media, print or otherwise. See articles and cover story "Auf Kurs zur Mediengewerkschaft: Volle Kraft voraus" in *druck und papier*, Vol. 123, no. 12 (June 10, 1985).

### CONCLUSION

1  For some good analyses of developments among the labor movements of advanced capitalist countries in the 1980s, see the issue of *Prokla* entitled "Gewerkschaftsbewegung am Ende? Eine internationale Bilanz"; *Prokla*, Vol. 14, no. 1 (Spring 1984). In addition to two different interpretations of the West German situation, this publication contains articles on the unions in Italy, France, Sweden, Great Britain and the United States. For an excellent presentation of labor's problems in West Europe in the crisis of the 1980s, see

Wolfgang Lecher, "Gewerkschaften in Europa: Zwischen Resignation und Widerstand" in *Aus Politik und Zeitgeschichte*, December 22, 1984, pp. 29–46. *Aus Politik und Zeitgeschichte* is the supplement of the weekly newspaper *Dar Parlament*. For a good contrast between the relative continuity in labor's existence in the Federal Republic and the severe, mostly negative, changes elsewhere in Europe, see the three-part series on European unions in *The New York Times* written by R. W. Apple, Jr., that paper's London correspondent. "Sharp Dip in Power and Influence Hampers Labor Unions in Europe," *New York Times*, January 20, 1985; "West German Unions: An Atypical Success Story," *New York Times*, January 21, 1985; and "British Unions Hunting for Path Back to Glory," *New York Times*, January 22, 1985.

2 This structurally distanced relationship between the DGB and the SPD becomes especially noticeable when compared to similar traditions in Great Britain, Sweden and Austria where in each case – though with significant variations – the respective union federations enjoy much closer official ties with their country's social democratic parties.

3 The concepts of "Japanization" and "Americanization" have been used with increased frequency by prominent analysts of West German labor to describe its pursuit of particularistic, company-oriented settlements akin to the Japanese "company unions" or the American interest-group-type labor organizations, in contrast to the German labor movement's tradition of collectivist and class-directed representation. See Jürgen Hoffmann, "'Amerikanisierung' der deutschen Gewerkschaftsbewegung? Probleme der gewerkschaftlichen Politik in der Bundesrepublik unter den Bedingungen des wirtschaftlichen Strukturwandels" in *Gewerkschaftliche Monatshefte*, Vol. 32, no. 7 (July 1981), pp. 418–433; idem, "Einheitsgewerkschaft oder 'korporatistische Blockbildung'? Probleme einer solidarischen Interessenvertretungspolitik in der ökonomischen Krise der Bundesrepublik" in *Prokla*, Vol. 11, no. 2 (Summer 1981), pp. 6–26. See also the editorial by the *Prokla* collective "Editorial: Gewerkschaftsbewegung am Ende?" in *Prokla*, Vol. 14, no. 1 (Spring 1984), pp. 3–9. Moreover, the extensive writings of Wolfgang Streeck and Josef Esser address this topic in a thought-provoking fashion, though from very different normative perspectives.

4 "Arbeitslosenzahl auf höchstem Stand seit 1948" in *Frankfurter Rundschau*, February 5, 1985.

5 For the most convincing and thorough studies concerning the insecurities of workers during the crisis and the rise of an existential fear even among hitherto relatively secure skilled workers, see the three volumes on workers' consciousness compiled under the leadership of Rainer Zoll at the University of Bremen. Rainer Zoll (ed.), *Arbeiterbewusstsein in der Wirtschaftskrise* (Cologne; Bund Verlag, 1981); idem (ed.), *Die Arbeitslosen, die könnt' ich alle erschiessen!* (Cologne: Bund Verlag, 1984); and idem (ed.), *Hauptsache, ich habe meine Arbeit* (Frankfurt: Edition Suhrkamp, 1984).

6 Industriegewerkschaft Metall, *Maschinen wollen sie – nur Menschen nicht: Rationalisierung in der Metallwirtschaft* (Frankfurt: IG Metall, 1983).

7 For the term "wildcat cooperation" and an excellent study of this company-oriented syndicalism or egoism (Betriebsegoismus) in the crisis-ridden economy of the Federal Republic, see Wolfgang Streeck, "Neo-corporatist Industrial Relations and the Economic Crisis in West Germany" in John H. Goldthorpe (ed.), *Order and Conflict in Contemporary Capitalism: Studies in the Political Economy of Western European Nations* (Oxford: Clarendon Press, 1984), pp. 291–314.

8 As quoted in *Der Spiegel*. "Gewerkschaften: Die zwei auf neuem Kurs" in *Der Spiegel*, Vol. 38, no. 29 (July 16, 1984).

9 Despite the meeting between Chancellor Kohl and Chairman Breit in July 1985 and the subsequent conference involving union leaders, cabinet members and top representatives of the business community on September 5, 1985, relations between the unions and the conservative government remain tense. Most labor leaders retain their deep-seated suspicion of the Chancellor and his cabinet, in good part due to the government's inability – or unwillingness – to institute far-reaching economic measures to mitigate the country's high level of unemployment. Another area of union concern centers on organized labor's fierce opposition to the government's attempts to introduce changes in the 1972 Works

Constitution Law, which the unions felt would harm the shop-floor representation enjoyed by DGB members. Mainly under the FDP's influence – and aided, paradoxically, by the Greens, who submitted a related bill – the proposals aim at encouraging the formation of splinter groups among blue-collar workers as well as among representatives of middle management (leitende Angestellte), an effort clearly designed to weaken the DGB. While the Greens hoped that their reform would facilitate the representation of various radical and unconventional elements which had been denied the benefits of unionization, the FDP's ambitions aimed in exactly the opposite political direction. For a good juxtaposition of the 1972 Works Constitution Law and the government's proposed reforms see "Novellierung der Betriebsverfassung: Änderungsabsichten der CDU/CSU–FDP-Koalition" in Der Gewerkschafter, Vol. 33, no. 7–8 (July, August 1985), pp. 2–3.

10 This episode erupted on May 18, 1984 when the head of the Federal Labor Office, Heinrich Franke, issued a letter to the regional offices instructing them to cease paying short-time assistance to any metalworker indirectly affected by the strike. Franke's justification centered on the interpretation that by demanding the 35-hour work week in every single one of its bargaining areas, IG Metall had basically conducted a nationwide campaign on this issue, although it actually only conducted strikes in Hesse and Baden-Württemberg. Since the union was engaged in a supra-regional battle, so Franke reasoned, it had to assume supra-regional responsibilities which in this case would have meant paying strike support to those of its members who had become indirect participants in the conflict of being rendered idle in areas and industries affected by the strike. The financial burdens imposed on IG Metall by this decree were prohibitive. IG Metall and the DGB reacted immediately to the Franke decree by taking the Office to court. However, it was not until June 22, 1984 that the first court decision held for IG Metall, thereby forcing the Federal Labor Office to resume payment of short-term work compensation to all those indirectly affected by the strike. To the unions, the introduction of this new dimension to industrial conflict – what they called "cold lockout" – signaled a serious violation of the Federal Labor Office's mandate of strict neutrality. To the DGB, the SPD and the Greens, this episode represented prima-facie evidence that the CDU-led government had become an open partner in the employers' offensive against labor. To the employers, the CDU, CSU and FDP the Franke decree restored impartiality to the Federal Labor Office. What to the unions and their allies seemed an egregious breach of impartiality, to the employers and their political friends meant the reestablishment of neutrality on the part of a key parapublic actor. For a detailed documentation of the Franke decree, the unions' declarations, the court decisions and the parliamentary debates, see the entire issue of Gewerkschaftliche Monatshefte, Vol. 35, no. 7 (July 1984).

11 "Schwere Kiste" in Der Spiegel, Vol. 38, no. 50 (December 10, 1984); and "Sozialer Frieden in Berieben ist bedroht durch die Pläne der Koalition zur Verschlechterung des Betriebsverfassungsgesetzes" in Gewerkschaftspost, Vol. 36, no. 2 (February 1985), pp. 1–2.

12 On this topic, see Bodo Zeuner (ed.). Genossen, was nun? Bilanz und Pespektiven sozialdemokratischer Politik (Hamburg: Konkret Literatur Verlag, 1983); Klaus Thüsing, Arno Klönne and Karl-Ludwig Hesse (eds.), Zukunft SPD: Aussichten linker Politik in der Sozialdemokratie (Hamburg: VSA-Verlag, 1981); Peter Glotz, "Zur aktuellen Situation der SPD" in Association for the Study of German Politics (ASGP) Journal, no. 9 (Autumn 1984), pp. 9–21.

13 Richard Löwenthal, "Identität und Zukunft der SPD" in Gewerkschaftliche Umschau, January/February 1982, pp. I–IV, part of a special section entitled "umschau dokumentation." Some of these ideas have also appeared in Richard Löwenthal, Social Change and Cultural Crisis (New York: Columbia University Press, 1984), especially in the chapter entitled "Beyond the 'Social Democratic Consensus,'" pp. 164–183.

14 On the one hand Löwenthal implicitly acknowledges that the Godesberg era, which transformed the SPD into a modern "catch-all party," is over. Yet his article pleads precisely for a vigorous revival of the "catch-all party" ideology, which the author fears is threatened by a renewed form of radicalism which would marginalize the SPD as did the SPD's Marxism of the pre-Godesberg era. The concept of the "catch-all party" comes from Otto Kirchheimer who developed it on the basis of his intimate knowledge of the

SPD. Kirchheimer of course decried the SPD's development from what he called a class-mass party (which he identified with substance) to a catch-all party, which he saw as mainly preoccupied with appearance. See Otto Kirchheimer, "The Transformation of the Western European Party Systems" in Joseph LaPalombara and Myron Weiner (eds.), *Political Parties and Political Development* (Princeton: Princeton University Press, 1966), pp. 177–200.

15 While there can be no doubt of social democracy's electoral vulnerability, especially among its young supporters who have shown increasing propensities for a "greenward" drift and among its working-class core which has demonstrated some sympathies for the CDU, it is interesting to note that there also exist good indications of stable support for the SPD among its traditional voters. Thus, for example, barely six months following the desertion of the party by a large number of skilled workers in the Bundestag elections of March 6, 1983, the SPD won the overwhelming support of this group in the state elections of Hesse and Bremen on September 25, 1983. Indeed, there were signs that in particularly crisis-torn areas, such as the shipyards of Bremen, workers once again viewed the SPD as the last and most reliable resort. On this phenomenon, see Andrei S. Markovits, "The Legislative Elections of September 25, 1983: Some Thoughts and Interpretations" in *German Studies Newsletter*, Vol. 1, no. 1 (Winter 1983), pp. 10–13.

16 Ursula Feist, Hubert Krieger and Pavel Uttitz, "Das Wahlverhalten der Arbeiter bei der Bundestagswahl 1983" in *Gewerkschaftliche Monatshefte*, Vol. 34, no. 7 (July 1983), pp. 414–427.

17 Ursula Feist and Klaus Liepelt, "Die Wahl zum Machtwechsel: Neuformierung der Wählerschaft oder Wählerkoalition aus Hoffnung – Eine Analyse der Bundestagswahl vom 6. März 1983" in *Journal für Sozialforschung*, Vol. 23, no. 3 (Summer 1983), pp. 287–310.

18 "Ökologischer TÜV" in *Der Spiegel*, Vol. 39, no. 2 (January 7, 1985).

19 "Neue Heimat: Die dunklen Geschäfte von Vietor und Genossen" (cover story) in *Der Spiegel*, Vol. 36, no. 6 (February 8, 1981). The next issue of *Der Spiegel* published on February 15, 1982 continued featuring the Neue Heimat affair as its cover story. While one week later the story disappeared from the magazine's cover, it still received ample coverage inside the issue.

20 As will be recalled, it was mainly the Essen contingent within the union that favored the adoption of the 35-hour week as IG Metall's main strategy of collective bargaining during the late 1970s and 1980s. At the time that this intra-union debate arose with all its ferocity at the union's Düsseldorf congress in 1977, the more activist Stuttgart representatives advocated further micro-level reforms and controls by labor along the lines of the Wage Framework Contract II concluded in that district in 1973. Indeed, the next two strikes conducted by IG Metall in bargaining areas within each of these two districts featured separate strategies. Thus, the metalworkers' strike in North Württemberg/North Baden in the spring of 1978 centered on micro-level qualitative issues, while the steel strike in NRW later that year concentrated exclusively on the attainment of the 35-hour work week. In little over five years there had occurred an intra-union shift of sufficient magnitude to allow IG Metall to conduct its most difficult industrial action concerning the 35-hour week in a bargaining area whose workers in the not too distant past had seen that demand as secondary to their desire that the union exert greater control over matters of technological change, rationalization and job allocation on the shop floor.

21 For a comprehensive summary of all arguments in favor of work-time reduction, especially the 35-hour work week, see Hans Mayr and Hans Janssen (eds.), *Perspektiven der Arbeitszeitverkürzung: Wissenschaftler und Gewerkschafter zur 35-Stunden-Woche* (Cologne; Bund Verlag, 1984); and most articles in *Die Mitbestimmung*, Vol. 30, no. 1 (January 1984), and Vol. 30, no. 9 (September 1984).

22 For the best summaries favoring early retirement as opposed to the 35-hour work week, see *Die Mitbestimmung*, Vol. 30, no. 6 (June 1984).

23 As quoted in Lecher, "Gewerkschaften in Europa," p. 33.

24 For a good summary of the agreement between IG Metall and the employers see Dieter Benthien, "Durchbruch geschafft – Tor zur 35-Stunden-Woche aufgestossen" in *Die*

*Quelle*, Vol. 35, no. 7/8 (July/August 1984), pp. 390–392; Ingrid Kurz-Scherf, "Tarifliche Arbeitszeit in Bewegung" in *WSI-Mitteilungen*, Vol. 37, no. 9 (September 1984), pp. 513–526; idem, *Arbeitszeit im Umbruch: Analyse und Dokumentation der neuen tariflichen Arbeitszeitbestimmungen* (Düsseldorf: WSI, 1984); this document represents far and away the most thorough compilation of all forms of worktime reduction. Lastly, the entire issue of *Gewerkschaftliche Monatshefte*, Vol. 35, no. 7 (July 1984) contains not only a detailed chronology of the strike, its antecedents and its aftermath, but also all the offers and counteroffers which led to the "Leber model."

25 For the characterizations of the strike and its results by these two important men, and a generally informed evaluation of the "Leber model," see "Pflock im Neuland" in *Der Spiegel*, Vol. 38, no. 27 (July 2, 1984). See also the excellent account by Hans Mayr, "Der Kampf um die 35-Stunden-Woche: Erfahrungen und Schlussfolgerungen aus der Tarifbewegung 1984" in *Gewerkschaftliche Monatshefte*, Vol. 35, no. 11 (November 1984), pp. 661–671.

26 Biedenkopf's resignation resulted from major pressures against his valiant mediation efforts not only by the printing employers but also by the employers' federation BDA and possibly even the Kohl government itself. See "Wollen uns fertigmachen" in *Der Spiegel*, Vol. 38, no. 26 (June 25, 1984); and Gerd Elvers, "Entscheidung oder Hängepartie: Aspekte des Arbeitskampfes 1984" in *Gewerkschaftliche Monatshefte*, Vol. 35, no. 11 (November 1984), pp. 683–689.

27 For a good summary of all aspects of IG Druck und Papier's 13-week-long strike, see Erwin Ferlemann, "Bilanz des Arbeitskampfes 1984 – Aus der Sicht der IG Druck und Papier" in *Gewerkschaftliche Monatshefte*, Vol. 35, no. 11 (November 1984), pp. 671–683. For a special assessment of the new wage categorization and its concrete effects on IG Druck's members, see Rolf Walther, "Jeder zweite besser eingruppiert!" in *druck und papier*, Vol. 123, no. 1 (January 7, 1985), p. 12.

28 One year after the strike settlement, this worry seems largely unfounded. Aided by the export-led boom in the Federal Republic's automobile and machine-tool industries, employment in the sectors affected by IG Metall's settlement has in fact increased. There is no doubt that at least part of this increase can be attributed to the reduction of the work week. Most preliminary findings of a number of empirical studies investigating the job-creating and/or job-retaining dimensions of IG Metall's pathbreaking contract seem to bear out the union's optimistic and confident claims.

29 The author is indebted to Volker Bahl from the DGB's head office in Rhineland-Palatinate for the term "betonierter Betriebssyndikalismus" which has been translated as "concrete company syndicalism." The term "wildcat cooperation" is used following Wolfgang Streeck's definition in his already cited article "Neo-Corporatist Industrial Relations and the Economic Crisis in West Germany" which is among the finest in a long line of insightful articles by Streeck on "mini-corporatist" arrangements in West German industrial relations.

30 The unions' worries about the proper implementation of these terms can be gauged in "Prediger in der Wüste" in *Der Spiegel*, Vol. 38, no. 47 (November 19, 1984). Some of the Federal Republic's largest automobile plants such as Daimler, BMW and Opel arrived at schemes based on the 38.5-hour work week which in fact promised to create additional jobs by forcing the employers to hire more workers. See "Bei Daimler flexible Arbeitszeiten" in *Frankfurter Rundschau*, February 15, 1985; and "Umsetzung der 38.5-Stunden-Woche; Beispiele, Modelle, Argumente" in *express*, Vol. 23, no. 2 (February 11, 1985), pp. 1–6.

31 The accommodationist unions' support for IG Metall's and IG Druck's strike varied from district to district, even from local to local. Thus there were a number of instances where – under the aegis of the DGB – considerable support by workers belonging to the accommodationist unions was accorded the struggle waged by their activist colleagues. However, cases also occurred where solidarity for the strikers was sparse at best. As to the official line, a perusal of all publications emanating from the headquarters of the accommodationist unions revealed at least tacit support for IG Metall's and IG Druck's struggle. See for example the cover story of IG Bau's *Der Grundstein* of June 1984 in which

three villainous-looking men depicting the Kohl-led government, the Federal Institute of Labor and the employers sit on a worker's neck trying to crush him to the ground. The story is entitled "Solidarität mit den Streikenden: Regierung, Bundesanstalt für Arbeit und Unternehmer sitzen dem Arbeitnehmer im Nacken" in *Der Grundstein*, Vol. 35, no. 6 (June 1984).

32  For a sample of this intra-DGB sniping between activists and accommodationists on this issue, see "IG Metall rügt andere Gewerkschaften im DGB" in *Frankfurter Rundschau*, August 31, 1984; and "IG Bau sieht keine Spaltung" in *Frankfurter Rundschau*, September 13, 1984.

33  "Warnstreiks sind Rechtens" in *Frankfurter Rundschau*, September 13, 1984.

34  See Erwin Ferlemann and Hans Jannsen (eds.), *Existenz sichern, Arbeit ändern, Leben gestalten* (Hamburg: VSA-Verlag, 1985).

35  See "Aktuelle Stunde im Bundestag zur 'Lage im Arbeitskampf' vom 25. Mai 1984" in *Gewerkschaftliche Monatshefte*, Vol. 35, no. 7 (July 1984), pp. 425–435.

36  "Schwankerei ist nicht am Platz: Spiegel-Interview mit dem IG Chemie Vorsitzenden Hermann Rappe über Friedensbewegung und SPD" in *Der Spiegel*, Vol. 37, no. 26 (June 27, 1983); Rappe compared the Greens' vision of the Federal Republic to the unpopular Morgenthau Plan which wanted to render Germany an agricultural – thus backward and powerless – society. See "An Morgenthau erinnert" in *Frankfurter Rundschau*, January 21, 1985; and "Ein beispielhafter Streit über Schadstoffe in Lebensmitteln" in *Frankfurter Rundschau*, December 28, 1984. For the most pronounced statement by a leading accommodationist against any union alliance with the Greens, see Hermann Rappe, "Fur eine klare Abgrenzung der Gewerkschaften von den Grünen" in *Gewerkschaftliche Umschau*, January/February 1985 as part of a special section entitled "umschau dokumentation."

37  Every West German union typically extends an invitation to all of the country's major political parties to send a representative to address the union's delegates at the congress. IG Metall followed this custom in 1983, asking the new Green Party to send a speaker as well. The Greens chose Rainer Trampert, one of their best orators and then a major member of the Green Party's executive council. When IG Metall found out that Trampert had been expelled from IG Chemie in 1974 for having criticized his union's policies at his firm, Texaco, the Greens were asked to send someone in Trampert's stead. Neither organization budged, thus leaving the Greens without a speaker at IG Metall's 1983 congress.

   The DGB's official relationship to the Green's remained troubled well into the middle of the 1980s. At the DGB's major academic conference "Full Employment, Co-determination, Shaping of Technology" held between March 26 and 28, 1985 in Cologne, the closing plenary session saw eminent delegates from all political parties represented in the Bundestag – except the Greens – discuss these topics with union representatives. The DGB's executive committee decided at the last minute to cancel without explanation its already extended invitation to the representative of the Green Party.

38  A good example of the discrepancy between agreeing with the Greens' aims but fearing their direct tactics pertains to their introduction of a bill in the Bundestag which would categorically forbid any kind of lockout. See "Gesetzentwurf der Fraktion DIE GRÜNEN IM BUNDESTAG zum Verbot der Aussperrung vom 18. June 1984" in *Gewerkschaftliche Monatshefte*, Vol. 35, no. 7 (July 1984), pp. 442–445. While on the one hand this elated the DGB since no other party seemed to have the courage to do it, it also worried the unions because such a bill could easily lead to a counterbill by the conservative forces demanding restrictions on the unions, especially concerning their maneuverability in deploying their ultimate weapon, the strike.

39  "Der Maschinenschlosser wird bald zum alten Eisen gehören" in *Frankfurter Rundschau*, October 25, 1984.

40  See "Unternehmerpräsident gibt Koalition einen Korb: Gegen Änderung des Betriebsverfassungsgesetzes" in *Frankfurter Rundschau*, March 26, 1985; "Hinter 'Gesprächspartnerschaft' veschanzt" in *Frankfurter Allgemeine Zeitung*, March 27, 1985; and Ernst Günter Vetter, "Rauchzeichen der Partnerschaft" in *Frankfurter Allgemeine Zeitung*, March 27, 1985. As already argued, the employers have steadfastly sided with the unions against the government's attempts to reform the 1972 Works Constitution Law. For a discussion of

this controversial topic, see Wolfgang Schneider, "Novellierung des Betriebsverfassungs-gesetzes: Angriff auf die Vertretungsstrukturen der Arbeitnehmer," in *Gewerkschaftliche Monatshefte*, Vol. 36, no. 8 (August 1985), pp. 502–506. Yet, on another important issue of contention – the so-called "strike paragraph" – there occurred a shift in alliances with the unions favoring the status quo, the government maintaining a posture of distance and detachment, and the employers clamoring for revision. In the wake of the controversy over the "cold" lockouts which accompanied the strikes in 1984, the employers have demanded a major revision of paragraph 116 of the 1969 Works Constitution Law which, in its new version, would explicitly absolve the Federal Labor Office from paying any assistance to workers indirectly affected by a "hot" confrontation between labor and capital. Such a revision would clearly weaken the unions since they then would be compelled to assume support payments not only to their members who are directly involved in a strike but also to those indirectly affected by any industrial action. Even unions with IG Metall's resources would not be able to sustain a conflict for any length of time under these circumstances. See, for example, "Bonn will den Streikparagraphen vorerst nicht antasten" in *Frankfurter Allgemeine Zeitung*, August 16, 1985; and "Die Wurzel allen Übels liegt in der unbestimmten Gesetzesformulierung" in *Handelsblatt*, August 16, 17, 1985.

41  For a strong statement endorsing industrialization and its absolute necessity for the preservation of employment, see the DGB's position as articulated in "Keine industrie-feindliche Politik mit den Gewerkschaften" in *Die Quelle*, Vol. 36, no. 2 (February 1985), pp. 67–68. Despite the statement's pro-technological overtone, the article constantly mentions the necessity to save the environment and is accompanied by a picture of a garbage dump, a clear symbol of one of industrialization's most unpleasant costs.

Yet another unmistakable sign of the growing ecological orientation even among some of the DGB's most ardently pro-growth and pro-technology unions can be gauged by IG Bau-Steine-Erden's new emphasis on the benefits of ecological involvement for labor in creating jobs. The union has started a massive campaign under the slogan "construction +protection of the environment = jobs" which is designed to involve unemployed construction workers in ecologically sound construction projects. See, for example, the cover story of *Der Grundstein*, Vol. 36, no. 2 (February 1985) entitled "Bauen + Umweltschutz = Arbeitsplätze." This otherwise rather conservative union and charter member of the accommodationist "gang of five" has become one of the most vocal advocates of a merger between ecology and economy. See "Umweltschutz schafft Arbeitsplätze," the cover story of *Der Grundstein*, Vol. 36, no. 4 (April 1985) and similar articles in subsequent issues of this union's official monthly publication. See also the article by the union's chairman, Konrad Carl, "Bauen und Umwelt – Herausforderung unserer Zeit" in *Die Mitbestimmung*, Vol. 31, nos. 4–5 (April–May 1985), pp. 133–135.

It is clear that severe job losses pushed this union towards its newly gained ecological awareness. This in part also pertains to other unions and the DGB. Thus it is not by chance that the federation published a widely distributed and very comprehensive program in April 1985 entitled "Ecology and Qualitative Growth" in which the job-creating dimensions of ecology receive special consideration. The zero-sum relation-ship between ecology and economy, thus far one of the labor movement's major tenets, seems to be undergoing a gradual process of erosion. See DGB, *Umweltschutz und Qualitatives Wachstum: Bekämpfung der Arbeitslosigkeit und Beschleunigung des Qualitativen Wachstums durch mehr Umweltschutz* (Düsseldorf: DGB, 1985); and Marie-Luise Weinberger, "Die Grünen: Vom Mythos zur Erstarrung?" in *Gewerkschaftliche Monatshefte*, Vol. 36, no. 8 (August 1985), pp. 489–501.

This cautious merger of the hitherto seemingly incompatible dimensions of "economy" and "ecology" corresponds to the SPD's shift in this direction. The Social Democrats have begun to view ecology and economy as inextricable and necessary for progressive reform in an advanced industrial society. The SPD's change assumed major strategic proportions for the party in a two-day conference held on March 23 and 24, 1985 in Dortmund and tellingly called "Work and Environment." See "SPD versucht den 'Brückenschlag': Arbeitsplatzsicherung und Umweltschutz nicht mehr als Gegensatz" in *Frankfurter Rundschau*, March 25, 1985.

Lastly, it is interesting to note that the unions have increasingly begun to speak about "technologischer Wandel" (technological change) instead of "technologischer Fortschritt' (technological progress). The latter clearly conveys a more positive attitude towards technology which was further reinforced by its frequent joint appearance with the term "sozialer Fortschritt" (social progress). "Technologischer Wandel," on the other hand, portrays a much more ambivalent and cautious disposition. The union's and the SPD's new sensitivity vis-à-vis ecology has led to interesting alliances inside the labor movement. A case in point involved a position paper co-authored by the leading accommodationist inside the DGB, IG Chemie chairman Hermann Rappe, and one of the most vocal and charismatic leaders of the activists, IG Metall's vice-chairman Franz Steinkühler. See Hermann Rappe and Franz Steinkühler, "Hohe Wachstumsraten sind kein Ziel an sich" in the "Dokumentation" section of the *Frankfurter Rundschau*, May 2, 1985.

42 Industriegewerkschaft Metall, *Arbeit und Technik – Der Mensch muss bleiben!* (Frankfurt: IG Metall, 1985). This is the title and official publication of IG Metall's first "Aktionsprogramm" in which the union tries to develop strategic measures and tactical steps to counter the negative consequences of rationalization and technological change in favor of a more humane form of production for the rest of the 1980s. Conveying the importance which IG Metall has attached to the social consequences of rapid technological change, both inside and outside the factory gates, is the fact that the union also published an English-language version of this pamphlet, under the title *Work and Technology – People Must Stay!* (Frankfurt: IG Metall, 1985), thus hoping to gain attention beyond the German-speaking world. See also Industriegewerkschaft Metall, *Technikentwicklung: Gestaltung ist machbar* (Frankfurt: IG Metall, 1984).

# Bibliography

A. *Books and documents*

Abendroth, Wolfgang. *Die deutschen Gewerkschaften: Weg demokratischer Integration.* Heidelberg: Wolfgang Rothe Verlag, 1955.

Abendroth, Wolfgang, Anton-Andreas Guha and Gerhard Brosius. *Gewerkschaften und Frieden.* Frankfurt am Main: Nachrichten-Verlag, 1982.

Abosch, Heinz. *The Menace of the Miracle.* New York: Monthly Review Press, 1983.

Achten, Udo, Karl-Jürgen Bieback, Wolfgang Däubler, Christoph Schminck-Gustavus, Gerhard Stuby and Ulrich Zachert. *Recht auf Arbeit – Eine politische Herausforderung.* Demokratie und Rechtsstaat, Vol. 38. Neuwied: Hermann Luchterhand Verlag, 1978.

Adam, Hermann. *Der Kampf um Löhne und Gewinne.* Cologne: Bund Verlag, 1976.

*Die Konzertierte Aktion in der Bundesrepublik.* Cologne: Bund Verlag, 1970.

AFL–CIO, ed. *German-American Trade Union Solidarity in the Struggle Against Fascism.* Washington DC/Düsseldorf: AFL/CIO, DGB, 1985.

Agartz, Viktor, *Gewerkschaft und Arbeiterklasse: Die ideologischen und soziologischen Wandlungen in der westdeutschen Arbeiterbewegung.* Edited by Lutz Ziegenblad. Munich: C. Trikont Verlag, 1971.

—. *Wirtschaft, Lohn, Gewerkschaft: Ausgewählte Schriften.* Schriftenreihe Gewerkschaftspolitische Studien, Vol. 17. Berlin: Verlag Die Arbeitswelt, 1982.

Allen, Christopher. "Structural and Technological Change in West Germany: Employer and Trade Union Responses in the Chemical and Automobile Industry." Unpublished PhD dissertation, Brandeis University, 1983.

Altmann, Norbert, Günter Bechtle, and Burkart Lutz. *Betrieb-Technik-Arbeit,* Frankfurt am Main/New York: Campus Verlag, 1978.

Altaver, Elmar, Jürgen Hoffmann and Willi Semmler. *Vom Wirtschaftswunder zur Wirtschaftskrise: Ökonomie und Politik in der Bundesrepublik.* Berlin: Verlag Olle & Wolter, 1979.

Altvater, Elmar, Kurt Hübner and Michael Stanger. *Alternative Wirtschaftspolitik jenseits des Keynesianismus.* Opladen: Westdeutscher Verlag, 1983.

*Arbeitsförderungsgesetz (AFG)*. Neuwied; Luchterhand Verlag, 1978.

Arbeitsgruppe "Alternative Wirtschaftspolitik." *Memorandum: Alternativen der Wirtschaftspolitik*. Cologne: Bund Verlag, 1978.

—. *Memorandum: Gegen konservative Formierung – Alternativen der Wirtschaftspolitik*. Cologne: Bund Verlag, 1978.

—. *Memorandum '82: Qualitatives Wachstum statt Gewinnförderung – Alternativen der Wirtschaftspolitik*. Marburg: Kontaktanschrift Arbeitsgruppe Alternative Wirtschaftspolitik, 1982.

Argument-Sonderbände. *Gewerkschaften im Klassenkampf. Die Entwicklung der Gewerkschaftsbewegung in Westeuropa*. Berlin: Argument-Verlag, 1974.

Arndt, Günter, Frank Deppe, Werner Petschick and Klaus Pickhaus, ed. *DGB Programm '81 untersucht für die Praxis*. Frankfurt: Nachrichten-Verlag, 1981.

Arndt, Helmut, ed. *Lohnpolitik und Einkommensverteilung*. Berlin: Duncker & Humblot, 1969.

*Aufgabe Zukunft: Qualität des Lebens*. Vol. 9 of Zukunft der Gewerkschaften. Frankfurt am Main/Cologne: Europäische Verlagsanstalt, 1974.

Autorengemeinschaft. *Sozialplanpolitik in der Eisen und Stahlindustrie*. Reihe: Qualifizierte Mitbestimmung in Theorie und Praxis. Cologne: Bund Verlag, 1979.

Bahl, Volker. *Staatliche Politik am Beispiel der Kohle*. Frankfurt am Main: Campus Verlag, 1977.

Bandholz, Emil. *Zwischen Godesberg und Grossindustrie oder wo steht die SPD?* Reinbek-Hamburg: Rowohlt Verlag, 1971.

Barkin, Solomon, ed. *Worker Militancy and its Consequences, 1965/75: New Directions in Western Industrial Relations*. New York: Praeger, 1975.

Bayer, Hermann, Wolfgang Streeck and Eckbert Treu. *Die westdeutsche Gewerkschaftsbewegung in Zahlen*. Sozialwissenschaft und Praxis Schriften des Wissenschaftszentrums Berlin, Vol. 36. Königstein/Ts: Verlag Anton Hain, 1981.

Becker, Hans, Otto Brenner, Rudolf Judith, Eugen Loderer, Franz Ludwig, Wolfgang Spieker and Heinz Oskar Vetter. *Montanmitbestimmung: Geschichte, Idee, Wirklichkeit*. Cologne: Bund Verlag, 1979.

Becker, Josef, Theo Stammen and Peter Waldmann, eds. *Vorgeschichte der Bundesrepublik Deutschland: Zwischen Kapitulation und Grundgesetz*. Munich: Wilhelm Fink Verlag, 1979.

Beier, Gerhard. *Der Demonstrations- und Generalstreik vom 12. November 1948*. Frankfurt am Main: Europäische Verlagsanstalt, 1975.

Bergmann, Joachim, ed. *Beiträge zur Soziologie der Gewerkschaften*. Frankfurt am Main: Suhrkamp, 1979.

Bergmann, Joachim, Otto Jacobi and Walther Müller-Jentsch. *Gewerkschaften in der Bundesrepublik: Gewerkschaftliche Lohnpolitik zwischen Mitgliederinteressen und ökonomischen Systemzwängen*. Studienreihe des Instituts für Sozialforschung, Frankfurt am Main. Frankfurt am Main/Cologne; Europäische Verlagsanstalt, 1975, first edition.

—. *Gewerkschaften in der Bundesrepublik: Gewerkschaftliche Lohnpolitik zwischen Mitgliederinteressen und ökonomischen Systemzwängen*. Studienreihe des Instituts für Sozialforschung, Frankfurt am Main. Frankfurt am Main: Aspekte Verlag, 1976, second edition

—. *Gewerkschaften in der Bundesrepublik: Gewerkschaftliche Lohnpolitik zwischen Mitglieder*

*interessen und ökonomischen Systemzwängen.* Studienreihe des Instituts für Sozialforschung, Frankfurt am Main. Frankfurt am Main/New York: Campus
Verlag, 1979, third edition.

Bergmann, Joachim and Walther Müller-Jentsch. *Gewerkschaften in der Bundesrepublik: Gewerkschaftliche Lohnpolitik im Bewusstsein der Funktionäre.* Studienreihe
des Instituts für Sozialforschung, Frankfurt am Main. Frankfurt am Main:
Aspekte Verlag, 1977.

Bernd, Otto. *Gewerkschaftsbewegung in Deutschland.* Cologne: Bund Verlag, 1975.

*Bertriebsverfassungsgesetz und Wahlordnung.* Munich: Verlag, C. H. Beck, 1978.

Beyme, Klaus von. *Challenge to Power: Trade Unions and Industrial Relations in Capitalist
Countries.* London/Beverly Hills: Sage Publications, 1980.

—. *Gewerkschaften und Arbeitsbeziehungen in kapitalistischen Ländern.* Munich:
R. Piper & Co. Verlag, 1977.

Bieback, Karl Jürgen, Hans-Joachim Böhlk, Detlef Hensche, Otto-Ernst
Kempen, Jacob Moneta, Ulrich Mückenberger, Roderich Wahsner, Horst
Weigand, Hans-Hermann Wohlgemuth and Henner Wolter. *Streikfreiheit und
Aussperrungsverbot: Zur Diskussion einer gewerkschaftlichen Forderung.* "Demokra-
tie und Rechtsstaat," Vol. 42. Neuwied/Darmstadt: Luchterhand Verlag,
1979.

Biedenkopf, Kurt. *Mitbestimmung im Unternehemen. Bericht der Sachverständigenkommission zur Auswertung der Erfahrungen bei der Mitbestimmung.* Bonn: Bundesdrucksache VI/304, 1970.

Billerbeck, Ulrich, Christoph Deutschmann, Rainer Erd, Rudi Schmiede and
Edwin Schudlich (Projektgruppe Gewerkschaftsforschung). *Neuorientierung der
Tarifpolitik? Veränderungen im Verhältnis zwischen Lohn- und Mantelarifpolitik in den
siebziger Jahren.* Forschungsberichte des Instituts für Sozialforschung,
Frankfurt am Main. Frankfurt am Main/New York: Campus Verlag, 1982.

Billerbeck, Ulrich, Rainer Erd, Otto Jacobi and Edwin Schudlich (Projektgruppe
Gewerkschaftsforschung). *Korporatismus und gewerkschaftliche Interessenvertretung.*
Frankfurt am Main/New York: Campus Verlag, 1982.

Binder, David. *The Other German – Willy Brandt's Life and Times.* Washington: New
Republic Book Company, 1975.

Binkelmann, Peter, and Irmtraut Schneller, *Berufsbildungsreform in der betrieblichen
Praxis.* Frankfurt am Main/Munich: Aspekte Verlag, 1975.

Birkner, Ulrich, Rainer Campmann, Peter Rischbach, Horst Kammrad, Wolfgang
Röhrer and Oskar Schammidatus, eds. *Schichtarbeit: Schicht und Nachtarbeiter-
Report.* Frankfurt am Main: Fischer Taschenbuch Verlag, 1973.

Bischoff, Joachim, Robert Gath, Werner Jütte, Maria Kurbjuhn, Christoph Lieber
and Klaus Schardt. *Marxistische Gewerkschaftstheorie.* West Berlin: Verlag für
das Studium der Arbeiterbewegung, 1976.

Boarman, Patrick M. *Germany's Economic Dilemma: Inflation and the Balance of
Payments.* New Haven/London: Yale University Press, 1964.

Bobke, Manfred. *Arbeitsrecht im Arbeitskampf.* Düsseldorf: WSI, 1985.

—. *Gewerkschaften und Aussperrung.* WSI-Studie zur Wirtschafts und
Sozialforschung. Cologne: Bund Verlag, 1982.

Böllhoff, Fritz. *Die wirtschaftliche Bedeutung der chemischen Industrie in sektoraler und
regionaler Hinsicht.* Münster: Deutsches Übersee Institute, 1968.

Bölling, Klaus. *Die letzten 30 Tage des Kanzlers Helmut Schmidt: Ein Tagebuch.* Hamburg: Rohwolt, 1982.

Borsdorf, Ulrich. *Askpekte der Mitbestimmung.* WSI Arbeitsmaterialien 7. Düsseldorf: WSI, 1985.

*Hans Böckler: Arbeit und Leben eines Gewerkschafters von 1875 bis 1945.* Cologne: Bund Verlag, 1982.

Borsdorf, Ulrich, and Hans O. Hemmer, eds. *Gewerkschaften-Wissenschaft-Mitbestimmung.* Cologne: Bund Verlag, 1979.

Borsdorf, Ulrich, Hans O. Hemmer, Gerhard Leminsky and Heinz Markmann, eds. *Gewerkschaftliche Politik: Reform aus Solidarität: Zum 60. Geburtstag von Heinz O. Vetter.* Cologne: Bund Verlag, 1977.

Borsdorf, Ulrich, Hans O. Hemmer and Martin Martiny, eds. *Grundlagen der Einheitsgewerkschaft: Historische Dokumente und Materialien.* Cologne: Europäische Verlagsanstalt, 1977.

Bosch, Gerhard. *Arbeitsplatzverlust: Die sozialen Folgen einer Betriebsstillegung.* Frankfurt am Main: Campus Verlag, 1978.

—. *Wie demokratisch sind Gewerkschaften? Eine empirische Untersuchung der Willensbildung auf den Gewerkschaftstagen 1968 und 1971 der Industriegewerkschaft Metall.* Gewerkschaftspolitische Studien, Vol. 6. Berlin: Verlag Die Arbeitswelt, 1974.

Bosch, Gerhard, Hartmut Seifert and Bernd-Georg Spies. *Arbeitsmarktpolitik und gewerkschaftliche Interessenvertretung.* Cologne: Bund Verlag, 1984.

Bosse, Ulrich. *Ein Betrieb macht dicht ... Werksschliessung im Kalletal: Betriebsstillegungen – Zentrales Problem gewerkschaftlicher Politik.* Offenbach: Verlag 2000, 1978.

Brammerts, Hermann, Gerhard Gerlach and Norbert Trautwein. *Lernen in der Gewerkschaft: Beiträge aus dem DGB-Projekt "Mitbestimmung und politische Bildung."* Frankfurt am Main: Europäische Verlagsanstalt, 1976.

Brandt, Gerhard, Otto Jacobi and Walther Müller-Jentsch (Projektgruppe Gewerkschaftsforschung). *Anpassung an die Krise: Gewerkschaften in den siebziger Jahren.* Frankfurt am Main/New York: Campus Verlag, 1982.

Brandt, Gerhard, Bernard Kündig, Zissis Papadimitriou and Jutta Thomae. *Computer und Arbeitsprozess: Eine arbeitssoziologische Untersuchung der Auswirkungen des Computereinsatzes in ausgewählten Betriebsabteilungen der Stahlindustrie und des Bankgewerbes.* Forschungsberichte des Instituts für Sozialforschung. Frankfurt am Main: Campus Verlag, 1978.

Braunthal, Gerard. *The Federation of German Industry in Politics.* Ithaca: Cornell University Press, 1965.

—. *Socialist Labor and Politics in Weimar Germany: The General Federation of German Trade Unions.* Hamden, Conn.: Archon Book, 1978.

—. *The West German Social Democrats, 1969–1982: Profile of a Party in Power.* Boulder, Colo.: Westview Press, 1983.

Brawand, Leo, ed. *Wohin steuert die deutsche Wirtschaft?* Munich: Verlag Karl Desch, 1971.

Brehm, Horst, and Gerd Pohl, eds. *Interessenvertretung durch Information: Handbuch für Arbeitnehmervertreter.* Cologne: Bund Verlag, 1978.

Breitenacher, Michael, Klaus-Dieter Knörndel, Hans Schedl and Lothar Scholz. *Elektrotechnische Industrie.* Berlin: Duncker & Humblot, 1974.

Briefs, Götz. *Das Gewerkschaftsproblem gestern und heute.* Frankfurt am Main: Knapp, 1955.

—. *Gewerkschaftsprobleme in unserer Zeit: Beiträge zur Standortbestimmung.* Frankfurt am Main: Fritz Knapp Verlag, 1968.

—. *Zwischen Kapitalismus und Syndikalismus: Die Gewerkschaften am Scheideweg.* Munich: L. Lehnen, 1952.

Brock, Adolf, ed. *Gewerkschaften am Kreuzweg: Ausgewählte Beiträge aus den "Arbeitsheften der Sozialwissenschaftlichen Vereinigung."* Berlin: Verlag Die Arbeitswelt, 1973.

Brock, Adolf, Wolfgang Hindrichs, Reinhard Hoffmann, Willi Pöhler and Olaf Sund. *Die Interessenvertretung der Arbeitneher im Betrieb.* Theorie und Praxis der Gewerkschaften, Themenkreis Betrieb, Vol. 3. Cologne: Europäische Verlagsanstalt, 1969.

Buhbe, Matthes, Klaus Gretschmann, Sabine Hilmer, Erich Hödl, Hans-Helmut Kotz, Gernot Müller and Joachim Wagner. *Krisenverschärfung durch Angebotspolitik.* Cologne: Bund Verlag, 1984.

Bundesminister für Arbeit und Sozialordung. *Arbeitsmarkpolitisches Programm der Bundesregierung für Regionen mit besonderen Beschäftigungsproblemen.* Bonn: Bundesministerium für Arbeit und Sozialordnung, 1979.

—. *Mitbestimmung.* Bonn: Bundesministerium für Arbeit und Sozialordnung, 1979.

—. *Reform der Betriebsverfassung: Erläuterungen, Gesetz, Wahlordnung.* Bonn: Bundesministerium für Arbeit und Sozialordung, 1971.

Burkhardt, Richard. *Ein Kampf ums Menschenrecht: Hundert Jahre Tarifpolitik der Industriegewerkschaft Druck und Papier und ihrer Vorgängerorganisationen seit dem Jahre 1873.* Stuttgart: Industriegewerkschaft Druck und Papier, Hauptvorstand, 1974.

Cerny, Karl H., ed. *Germany at the Polls: The Bundestag Election of 1976101.* Washington, DC: American Enterprise Institute for Public Policy Research, 1978.

Childs, David. *From Schumacher to Brandt: The Story of German Socialism 1945–1965.* Oxford: Pergamon Press, 1966.

Crouch, Colin, and Alessandro Pizzorno, eds. *The Resurgence of Class Conflict in Western Europe Since 1968, Vol. 1 – National Studies.* New York: Holmes & Meier Publishers, 1978.

Crouch, Colin, and Alessandro Pizzorno, eds. *The Resurgence of Class Conflict in Western Europe Since 1968, Vol. 2 – Comparative Analyses.* New York: Holmes & Meier Publishers, 1978.

Cullingford, E.C.M. *Trade Unions in West Germany.* Boulder, Colo.: Westview Press, 1976.

Dähne, Eberhard, and Klaus Priester. *Arbeitsbedingungen und gewerkschaftlicher Kampf; Materialien zur Entwicklung der Arbeitsbedingungen und zur Diskussion um die "Humanisierung der Arbeit" in der BRD.* Informationsbericht No. 20. Frankfurt am Main: Institut für Marxistische Studien und Forschungen, 1978.

Dahrendorf, Ralf. *Das Mitbestimmungsproblem in der deutschen Sozialforschung.* Munich: R. Piper & Co. Verlag, 1965.

Däubler, Wolfgang. *Das Arbeitsrecht.* Reinbek-Hamburg: Rowholt Taschenbuch Verlag, 1976.

—. *Gewerkschaftsrechts im Betrieb: Argumentationshilfen für die Praxis in Betrieb und Verwaltung*. Neuwied: Hermann Luchterhand Verlag, 1978.

—. *Das Grundrecht auf Mitbestimmung und seine Realisierung durch tarifvertragliche Begründung von Beteiligungsrechten*. Frankfurt am Main: Europäische Verlagsanstalt, 1973.

Deppe, Frank. *Autonomie und Integration: Materialien zur Gewerkschaftsanalyse*. Schriftenreihe für Sozialgeschichte und Arbeiterbewegung, Vol. 9. Marburg: Verlag Arbeiterbewegung und Gesellschaftswissenschaft, 1979.

—. *Das Bewusstsein der Arbeiter: Studien zur politischen Soziologie des Arbeiterbewusstseins*. Cologne: Pahl-Rugenstein Verlag, 1971.

Deppe, Frank, Jutta von Feyberg, Christof Kievenheim, Regine Meyer and Frank Werkmeister. *Kritik der Mitbestimmung: Partnerschaft oder Klassenkampf?* Frankfurt am Main: Suhrkamp Verlag, 1969.

Deppe, Frank, Georg Fülberth and Jürgen Harrer, eds. *Geschichte der deutschen Gewerkschaftsbewegung*. Cologne: Pahl-Rugenstein Verlag, 1977.

Deppe, Frank, Detlef Hensche, Mechtild Jansen and Witich Rossmann. *Strauss und die Gewerkschaften: Texte, Materialien, Dokumente*. Cologne: Pahl-Rugenstein Verlag, 1980.

Deppe, Frank, Helmut Lange and Peter Lothar, eds. *Die neue Arbeiterklasse: Technische Intelligenz und Gewerkschaften im organisierten Kapitalismus*. Frankfurt am Main: Europäische Verlagsanstalt, 1970.

Deppe, Rainer, Richard Herding and Dietrich Hoss. *Sozialdemokratie und Klassenkonflikte: Metallarbeiterstreik – Bertriebskonflikt – Mieterkampf*. Studienreihe des Instituts für Sozialforschung, Frankfurt am Main. Frankfurt am Main/New York: Campus Verlag, 1978.

de Schweinitz, Dorothea. *Labor–Management Consultation in the Factory*. Honolulu: University of Hawaii Press, 1966.

Detje, Richard. *Von der Westzone zum kalten Krieg: Restauration und Gewerkschaftspolitik im Nachkriegsdeutschland*. Hamburg: VSA-Verlag, 1982.

Deutscher Gewerkschaftsbund. *Entwurf eines Gesetzes über die Mitbestimmung der Arbeitnehmer in Grossunternehmen und Grosskonzernen*. Schriftenreihe Mitbestimmung. Düsseldorf: DGB, n.d.

—. *Gesamtwirtschaftliche Mitbestimmung–Unverzichtbarer Bestandteil einer Politik der wirtschaftlichen und gesellschaftlichen Krise*. Schriftenreihe Mitbestimmung, No. 6. Düsselforf, DGB, n.d.

—. *Geschäftsbericht 1969 bis 1971*. Düsseldorf: DBG, 1972.

—. *Geschäftsbericht 1971 bis 1973*. Düsseldorf: DBG, 1974.

—. *Geschäftsbericht 1972 bis 1974*. Düsseldorf: DBG, 1975.

—. *Geschäftsbericht 1974 bis 1976*. Düsseldorf: DBG, 1977.

—. *Geschäftsbericht 1975 bis 1977*. Düsseldorf: DBG, 1978.

—. *Geschäftsbericht 1977 bis 1979*. Düsseldorf: DBG, 1980.

—. *Geschäftsbericht 1978 bis 1981*. Düsseldorf: DBG, 1982.

—. *Grundsätze des Deutschen Gewerkschaftsbundes zur Weiterentwicklung des Betriebsverfassungsrechts*. Schriftenreihe Mitbestimmung, nos. 1–2. Düsseldorf: DGB, 1983.

—. *Grundsatzprogramm des Deutschen Gewerkschaftsbundes*. Düsseldorf: DGB, n.d.

—. *Das Programm für Zukunftsinvestitionen der Bundesregierung vom Frühjahr 1977.* Düsseldorf: Deutscher Gewerkschaftsbund, 1978.

—. *Protokoll des Gründungskongresses des deutschen Gewerkschaftsbundes, München, 12.–14. Oktober 1949.* Cologne: Bund Verlag, 1950.

—. *Protokoll – 2. ordentlicher Bundeskongress Berlin, 13. bis 17. Oktober 1952.* Düsseldorf, n.d.

—. *Thesen des Deutschen Gewerkschaftsbundes zur Mitbestimmung in öffentlich-rechtlichen Unternehmen und Einrichtungen.* Schriftenreihe Mitbestimmung, no. 4. Düsseldorf: DGB, 1983.

—. *Umweltschultz und qualitatives Wachstum.* Düsseldorf: DGB, 1985.

—. *Vorschläge des DGB zur Neuordnung der deutschen Wirtschaft.* Düsseldorf: DGB, 1950.

—. *Vorschläge des DGB zur Wiederherstellung der Vollbeschäftigung.* Düsseldorf: DGB, 1977.

Deutscher Gewerkschaftsbund and WSI. *Regionale Beschäftigungspolitik und gewerkschaftliche Interessenvertretung: Fachtagung von DGB und WSI.* Düsseldorf: n.p., 1985.

Deutsches Institut für Wirtschaftsforschung. *Enquete über die Bauwirtschaft* (im Auftrage des Bundesministers für Wirtschaft), Vol. 1. Berlin: DIW 1973.

—. *Enquete über die Bauwirtschaft.* (im Auftrage des Bundesministers für Wirtschaft), Vol. 3. Berlin: DIW, 1973.

Diekmann, Achim. *Die Automobilindustrie in der Bundesrepublik Deutschland.* Cologne: Deutscher Instituts Verlag, 1979.

*Dienstblatt der Bundesanstalt für Arbeit.* Runderlass 230/78. Nuremberg: Bundesanstalt für Arbeit, 1978.

Dohse, Knuth, *Ausländische Arbeiter und bürgerlicher Staat.* Königstein/Ts: Verlag Anton Hain, 1981.

Dohse, Knuth, Ulrich Jürgens and Harald Russig, eds. *Ältere Arbeitnehmer zwischen Unternehmensinteressen und Sozialpolitik.* Frankfurt am Main: Campus Verlag, 1982.

—. *Statussicherung im Industriebetrieb: Alternative Regelungsansätze im internationalen Vergleich.* Arbeitsberichte des Wissenschaftszentrums Berlin, Internationales Institut für Vergleichende Gesellschaftsforschung/Arbeitspolitik. Frankfurt am Main: Campus Verlag, 1982.

Doleschal, Reinhard, and Rainer Dombois, eds. *Wohin läuft VW?* Reinbek bei Hamburg: Rowohlt Taschenbuch Verlag, 1982.

Dombois, Rainer, and Heiner Heseler. *Polnische und deutsche Seehäfen im Vergleich: Eine Studie über die Hafenarbeit in unterschiedlichen Gesellschaftssystemen am Beispiel der norddeutschen Seehäfen und der Häfen Gdansk und Gdynia.* Forschungsberichte der zentralen wissenschaftlichen Einrichtung 'Arbeit und Betrieb.' Bremen: Universität Bremen, 1980.

Duhm, Rainer, and Ulrich Mückenberger, eds. *Arbeitskampf im Krisenalltag: Wie man sich wehrt und warum.* Berlin: Rotbuch Verlag, 1977.

Duhm, Rainer, and Harald Wieser, eds. *Krise und Gegenwehr: Ein Arbeitsbuch zum politischen Alltag in den Betrieben.* Berlin: Rotbuch Verlag, 1975.

Düll, Klaus, Dieter Sauer, Irmtraut Schneller and Norbert Altmann. *Öffentliche Dienstleistungen und technologischer Fortschritt.* Vols. 1–2. Frankfurt am Main/ Munich: Aspekte Verlag 1976.

Dzielak, Willi, Wolfgang Hindrichs, Helmut Martens and Walter Schophaus. *Arbeitskampf um Arbeitsplätze: Der Tarifkonflikt 1978/79 in der Stahlindustrie.* Forschungsberichte aus dem Landesinstitut Sozialforschungsstelle Dortmund. Frankfurt am Main/New York: Campus Verlag, 1981.

Dzielak, Willi, Wolfgang Hindrichs, Helmut Martens, Verena Stanislawski and Wolfram Wassermann. *Belegschaften und Gewerkschaft im Streik: Am Beispiel der chemischen Industrie.* Untersuchungen der Sozialforschungsstelle Dortmund. Frankfurt am Main/New York: Campus Verlag, 1978.

Dzielak, Willi, Wolfgang Hindrichs and Helmut Martens. *Den Besitzstand sichern! Der Tarifkonflikt 1978 in der Metallindustrie Baden Württembergs.* Forschungsberichte aus dem Landesinstitut Sozialforschungsstelle Dortmund. Frankfurt am Main/New York: Campus Verlag, 1979.

Ebbinghausen, Rolf, and Friedrich Tiemann, eds. *Das Ende der Arbeiterbewegung in Deutschland?* Opladen: Westdeutscher Verlag, 1984.

Ehrenberg, Herbert, and Anke Fuchs. *Sozialstaat und Freiheit: Von der Zunkunft des Sozialstaats.* Frankfurt am Main: Suhrkamp Verlag, 1980.

Erd, Rainer. *Verrechtlichung industrieller Konflikte: Normative Rahmenbedingungen des dualen Systems der Interessenvertretung.* Projektgruppe Gewerkschaftsforschung. Frankfurt am Main/New York: Campus Verlag, 1978.

Esser, Josef. *Gewerkschaften in der Krise: Die Anpassung der deutschen Gewerkschaften an neue Weltmarktbedingungen.* Frankfurt am Main: Suhrkamp Verlag, 1982.

Esser, Josef, Wolfgang Fach and Werner Väth. *Krisenregulierung: Zur politischen Durchsetzung ökonomischer Zwänge.* Frankfurt am Main: Suhrkamp Verlag, 1983.

Europäisches Gewerkschaftsinstitut. *Über Keynes hinaus: Gestaltung der Wirtschaftspolitik durch Alternativen.* Brussels: n.p., 1978.

Federal Employment Institute. *Employment Policy in Germany – Challenges and Concepts for the 1980s.* Nuremberg: Bundesanstalt für Arbeit, 1978.

Federal Ministry of Labour and Social Affairs. *Codetermination.* Bonn: Bundesministerium für Arbeit und Sozialordnung, 1976.

Fellner, William, Mitton Gilbert, Bent Hansen, Richard Kahn, Friedrich Lutz and Dieter deWolff. *The Problem of Rising Prices.* Paris: OEEC, 1961.

Ferlemann, Erwin, and Hans Janssen, eds. *Existenz sichern, Arbeit ändern, Leben gestalten.* Hamburg: VSA-Verlag, 1985.

Flanagan, Robert, and Lloyd Ulman. *Wage Restraint: A Study of Incomes Policy in Western Europe.* Berkeley University of California Press, 1981.

Flechtheim, Ossip, Wolfgang Rudzio, Fritz Vilmar and Manfred Wilke. *Der Marsch der DKP durch die Institutionen: Sowjetmarxistische Einflusstrategien und Ideologien.* Frankfurt am Main: Fischer Taschenbuch Verlag, 1980.

Föhr, Horst. *Willensbildung in den Gewerkschaften und Grundgesetz.* Berlin: Schweitzer Verlag, 1974.

Forschergruppe "Metallerstreik '74." *Streik und Arbeiterbewusstsein: Bericht über eine sozialwissenschaftliche Untersuchung des Metallstreiks im Unterwesergebiet 1974.* Bremen: Universität Bremen, 1978.

Freyberg, Jutta von, George Fülberth, Jürgen Harrer, Bärbel Hebel-Kunze,

Heinz-Gerd Hofschen, Erich Ott and Gerhard Stuby. *Geschichte der deutschen Sozialdemokratie 1886–1975.* Cologne: Pahl-Rugenstein Verlag, 1977, second edition.

Funke, Hajo, Brigitte Geisller and Peter Thoma, eds. *Industriearbeit und Gesundheitsverschleiss: Diskussion und Ergebnisse der Tagung: "Sicherheit am Arbeitsplatz und Unfallschutz."* Frankfurt am Main: Europäische Verlagsanstalt, 1974.

Furlong, James, *Labor in the Boardroom: The Peaceful Revolution.* Princeton, NJ: Dow Jones Books, 1977.

Gehrcke, Wolfgang, ed. *Die Schlacht um 35 Stunden: Die Stahlkocher und ihr Streik.* Dortmund: Weltkreis-Verlag, 1979.

Glastetter, Werner, *Die Stellung der Bundesrepublik Deutschland in der Weltwirtschaft.* Cologne: Bund Verlag, 1973.

Glotz, Peter, *Die Beweglichkeit des Tankers: Die Sozialdemokratie zwischen Staat und neuen sozialen Bewegungen.* Munich: Bertelsmann Verlag, 1982.

Götz, Christian. *Heinz Oskar Vetter.* Cologne: Europäische Verlagsanstalt, 1977.

Gourevitch, Peter, Stephen Bornstein, George Ross, Andrew Martin, Andrei Markovits and Christopher Allen. *Unions and Economic Crisis: Britain, West Germany and Sweden.* London: George Allen & Unwin, 1984.

Graf, William. *The German Left Since 1945.* New York: Oleander, 1976.

Gransow, Volker, and Michael Krätke. *Viktor Agartz: Gewerkschaften und Wirtschaftspolitik.* Gewerkschaftspolitische Studien, Vol. 12. Berlin: Verlag Die Arbeitswelt, 1978.

Grebing, Helga. *Geschichte der deutschen Arbeiterbewegung.* Munich: Deutscher Taschenbuch Verlag, 1966, second edition.

Grefermann, Klaus. *Papierverarbeitung und Druckerei-Industrie aus der Sicht der siebziger Jahre.* Berlin: Duncker & Humblot, 1973.

Gross, Hermann, Margarete Steinrücke, Horst Tholfus and Claudia Weber. *Die Tarifbewegung 1976 in der Druckindustrie: Dokumentation und Interpretation.* Institut zur Erforschung Sozialer Chancen, Bericht No. 9. Cologne: Verein zur Förderung des Instituts zur Erforschung Sozialer Chancen e.V., 1976.

Gülden, Kalus, Wolfgang Kruty and Ingrid Krutz-Ahling. *Humanisierung der Arbeit? Ansätze zur Veränderung von Form und Inhalt industrieller Arbeit.* Gewerkschaftspolitische Studien, Vol. 3. Berlin: Verlag Die Arbeitswelt, 1973.

Gülden, Klaus. *Mitbestimmung in der Wirtschaftskrise: Fallstudie über die Stillegung eines Walzwerks.* Gewerkschaftspolitische Studien, Vol. 10. Berlin: Verlag Die Arbeitswelt, 1968.

Güthe, Bernd, and Klaus Pickshaus. *Der Arbeitskampf in der Druckindustrie im Frühjahr 1976.* Soziale Bewegungen, Analyse und Dokumentation des IMSF, Nachrichten-Reihe 5. Frankfurt am Main: Nachrichten-Verlag, 1976.

Hartrich, Edwin. *The Fourth and Richest Reich: How the Germans Conquered the Postwar World.* New York: MacMillan Publishing Co., 1980.

Hauff, Volker, and Fritz W. Scharpf. *Modernisierung der Volkswirtschaft: Technologiepolitik als Strukturpolitik.* Frankfurt am Main: Europäische Verlagsanstalt, 1975.

Hautsch, Gert, Jörg Huffschmid, Winfried Schwarz and Peter Wiener. *Arbeitskämpfe '77.* Soziale Bewegungen, Analyse und Dokumentation des IMSF, Nachrichten-Reihe 12. Frankfurt am Main: Nachrichten-Verlag, 1978.

Hautsch, Gert, and Bernd Semmler. *Stahlstreik und Tariffrunde 78–79.* Soziale

Bewegungen, Analyse und Dokumentation des IMSF, no. 7. Frankfurt am Main: Institut für Marxistische Studien und Forschungen, 1979.

Hautsch, Gert, Gerhard Hess, Johannes Henrich von Heiseler and Klaus Pickshaus. *Tarifbewegungen und Arbeitskämpfe 1976–77*. Soziale Bewegungen, Analyse und Dokumentation des IMSF, Nachrichten-Reihe 8. Frankfurt am Main: Nachrichten-Verlag, 1977.

Heidermann, Horst, ed. *Langzeitprogramm 3, Jungsozialisten: Kritische Stellungnahme zum Problem einer gesellschaftspolitischen Langzeitplanung*. Bonn/Bad-Godesberg: Verlag Neue Gesellschaft, 1973.

Herbig, Rudolf. *Notizen aus der Sozial-Wirtschafts- und Gewerkschaftsgeschichte vom 14. Jahrhundert bis zur Gegenwart*. Düsseldorf: Bundesvorstand des Deutschen Gewerkschaftsbundes (DGB), 1978.

Hildebrandt, Eckart, and Werner Olle. *Ihr Kampf ist unser Kampf: Ursachen, Verlauf und Perspektiven der Ausländerstreiks 1973 in der BRD, Teil 1*. Reihe Betrieb und Gewerkschaft. Offenbach: Verlag 2000, 1975.

Hirche, Kurt, *Die Wirtschaftsunternehmen der Gewerkschaften*. Düsseldorf: Econ-Verlag, 1966.

Hirsch, Joachim. *Die öffentlichen Funktionen der Gewerkschaften: Eine Untersuchung zur Autonomie sozialer Verbände in der modernen Verfassungsordnung*. Stuttgart: Ernst Klett Verlag, 1966.

Hirsch-Weber, Wolfgang. *Gewerkschaften in der Politik: Von der Massenstreikdebatte zum Kampf um das Mitbestimmungsrecht*. Cologne: Westdeutscher Verlag, 1959.

Hofmann, Rolf. *Welt-Chemiewirtschaft*. Opladen: Westdeutscher Verlag, 1975.

Hohlen, Dieter, Rainer-Olaf Schultze and Bernard Vogel, eds. *Wahlen in Deutschland*. Berlin: De Gruyter, 1971.

Hoss, Dietrich. *Die Krise des "Institutionalisierten Klassenkampfes": Metallarbeiterstreik in Baden-Württemberg*. Studienreihe des Instituts für Sozialforschung, Vol. 2. Frankfurt am Main/Cologne: Europäische Verlagsanstalt, 1974.

Huss, Herman, and Eberhard Schmidt, eds. *Kooperation und Mitbestimmung: Überlegungen zur innerbetrieblichen Mitbestimmung*. Frankfurt am Main: Europäische Verlagsanstalt, 1972.

IG Bau-Steine-Erden. *Dokumentation der Solidarität*. Frankfurt am Main: IG Bau, n.d.

—. *Geschäftsbericht 1953 bis 1954*. Frankfurt am Main: IG Bau, 1955.

—. *Geschäftsbericht 1955 bis 1956*. Frankfurt am Main: IG Bau, 1957.

—. *Geschäftsbericht 1960 bis 1962*. Frankfurt am Main: IG Bau, 1963.

—. *Geschäftsbericht 1966 bis 1968*. Frankfurt am Main: IG Bau, 1969.

—. *Geschäftsbericht 1969 bis 1971*. Frankfurt am Main: IG Bau, 1972.

—. *Geschäftsbericht 1972 bis 1974*. Frankfurt am Main: IG Bau, 1975.

—. *Geschäftsbericht 1975 bis 1978*. Frankfurt am Main: IG Bau, 1979.

—. *Geschäftsbericht 1979 bis 1981*. Frankfurt am Main: IG Bau, 1982.

—. *Protokoll des. 3. Ordentlichen Gewerkschaftstages 1955*.

IG Chemie-Papier-Keramik. *Geschäftsbericht 1949 bis 1950*. Hanover: IG Chemie, 1951.

—. *Geschäftsbericht 1950 bis 1952*. Hanover: IG Chemie, 1953.

—. *Geschäftsbericht 1952 bis 1954*. Hanover: IG Chemie, 1955.

—. *Geschäftsbericht 1954 bis 1956*. Hanover: IG Chemie, 1957.

—. *Geschäftsbericht 1957 bis 1959*. Hanover: IG Chemie, 1960.

—. *Geschäftsbericht 1960 bis 1962.* Hanover: IG Chemie 1963.

—. *Geschäftsbericht 1963 bis 1965.* Hanover: IG Chemie, 1966.

—. *Geschäftsbericht 1966 bis 1968.* Hanover: IG Chemie, 1969.

—. *Geschäftsbericht 1969 bis 1971.* Hanover: IG Chemie, 1972.

—. *Geschäftsbericht 1972 bis 1975.* Hanover: IG Chemie, 1976.

—. *Geschäftsbericht 1976 bis 1979.* Hanover: IG Chemie, 1980.

—. *Jahrbuch 1949–1950.* Hanover: IG Chemie, 1951.

—. *Jahrbuch 1951.* Hanover: IG Chemie, 1952.

—. *Jahrbuch 1952.* Hanover: IG Chemie, 1953.

—. *Protokoll 1963.* Hanover: IG Chemie, 1964.

—. *Protokoll 1966.* Hanover: IG Chemie, 1967.

—. *Protokoll 1969.* Hanover: IG Chemie, 1970.

—. *Protokoll 1972.* Hanover: IG Chemie, 1973.

—. *"Richtlinien für die Tarifarbeit."* Special publication, n.p., n.d.

—. *Satzung '77.* Hanover: IG Chemie, 1978.

IG Druck and Papier. *Analyse des Arbeitskampfes 1976 in der Druckindustrie.* Schriften-reihe der Industriegewerkschaft Druck und Papier, no 27. Stuttgart: Industriegewerkschaft Druck und Papier, Hauptvorstand, 1977.

—. *Geschäftsbericht 1948 bis 1950.* Stuttgart: IG Druck, 1951.

—. *Geschäftsbericht 1959 bis 1962.* Stuttgart: IG Druck, 1963.

—. *Geschäftsbericht 1962 bis 1965.* Stuttgart: IG Druck, 1966.

—. *Geschäftsbericht 1965 bis 1968.* Stuttgart: IG Druck, 1969.

—. *Geschäftsbericht 1974 bis 1977.* Stuttgart: IG Druck, 1978.

—. *Geschäftsbericht 1977 bis 1980.* Stuttgart: IG Druck, 1981.

IG Metall. *Der Angriff: Mannesmann gegen Mitbestimmung.* Frankfurt am Main: IG Metall, n.d.

—. *Arbeit und Technik – Der Mensch muss bleiben.* Frankfurt am Main: IG Metall, 1985.

—. *Die Arbeit der Vertauensleute.* Frankfurt am Main: IG Metall, 1976.

—. *Aufgabe Zukunft – Qualität des Lebens.* Reihe "Zukunft der Gewerkschaften," Vol. 9. Frankfurt am Main: Europäische Verlagsanstalt, 1972.

—. *Dokumentation. Der Arbeitskampf in der Eisen- und Stahlindustrie von Nordrhein-Westfalen, Osnarbrück, Bremen, Dillenburg und Niederschelden (1978/79).* Frankfurt am Main: IG Metall, 1979.

—. *Dokumentation. IG Metall – 30 Jahre soziale Gegenmacht: Gedenkveranstaltung zur dreissigjährigen Wiederkehr des Vereinigungs-Verbandstages in Lüdenscheid.* Frankfurt am Main: IG Metall, 1979.

—. *Dokumentation. Streik der Metaller in Schleswig-Holstein 1956/57.* Frankfurt am Main: IG Metall, 1978.

—. *Dokumentation über die Tarifauseinandersetzung 1978/79: Bezirkskonferenz in Dülmen, 4. Mai 1979.* Münster: Bezirksleitung der IG Metall, 1979.

—. *Dokumentation. Wir kämpfen um unsere Arbeitsplätze: Dokumentation der Belegschaft DEMAG-Kunststofftechnik, Kalldorf (Lippe) 1969–1975.* Münster: Bezirksleitung der IG Metall, 1975.

—. *Entschliessungen, Anträge, Materialien: 12. ordentlicher Gewerkschaftstag der Industriegewerkschaft Metall für die Bundesrepublik Deutschland in Düsseldorf vom 18. bis 24. September 1977.* Frankfurt am Main: IG Metall, 1979.

—. *Fünfundsiebzig Jahre Industriegewerkschaft 1891 bis 1966: Vom Deutschen Metallarbeiter-Verband zur Industriegewerkschaft Metall.* Frankfurt am Main: Europäische Verlagsanstalt, 1966.

—. *Geschäftsbericht 1950 bis 1952.* Frankfurt am Main: IG Metall, 1953.

—. *Geschäftsbericht 1954 bis 1955.* Frankfurt am Main: IG Metall, 1956.

—. *Geschäftsbericht 1955 bis 1957.* Frankfurt am Main: IG Metall, 1958.

—. *Geschäftsbericht 1960 bis 1961.* Frankfurt am Main: IG Metall, 1962.

—. *Geschäftsbericht 1961 bis 1962.* Frankfurt am Main: IG Metall, 1963.

—. *Geschäftsbericht 1962, 1963 und 1964.* Frankfurt am Main: IG Metall, 1965.

—. *Geschäftsbericht 1968 bis 1970.* Frankfurt am Main: IG Metall, 1971.

—. *Geschäftsbericht 1971 bis 1973.* Frankfurt am Main: IG Metall, 1974.

—. *Geschäftsbericht 1974 bis 1976.* Frankfurt am Main: IG Metall, 1977.

—. *Geschäftsbericht 1977 bis 1979.* Frankfurt am Main: IG Metall, 1980.

—. *Der Grosse Streik in der hessischen Metallindustrie vom 27. August bis 22. September 1951.* Frankfurt am Main: Europäische Verlagsanstalt, 1951.

—. *Handbuch für die Vertrauensleute der IG Metall.* Frankfurt am Main: IG Metall, 1973.

—. *Krise und Reform in der Industriegesellschaft.* Vol. 1: Materialien, Vol. 2: Protokolle. Frankfurt am Main: Europäische Verlagsanstalt, 1976.

—. *Maschinen wollen sie nur – Menschen nicht: Rationalisierung in der Metallwirtschaft.* Frankfurt am Main: IG Metall, 1983.

—. *90 Jahre Industriegewerkschaft 1891 bis 1981: Vom Deutschen Metallarbeiter-Verband zur Industriegewerkschaft Metall.* Cologne: Bund Verlag, 1981.

—. *Niederschrift der Verhandlungen des 1. ordentlichen Gewerkschaftstages der Industriegewerkschaft Metall für die Bundesrepublik Deutschland im Gewerkschaftshaus Hamburg von 18. bis 22. September 1950.* Frankfurt am Main: IG Metall, 1950.

—. *Personalplanung und Betriebsrat.* Schriftenreihe der IG Metall 65. Frankfurt am Main: IG Metall, 1976.

—. *Protokoll – 5. ordentlicher Gewerkschaftstag der Industriegewerkschaft Metall für die Bundesrepublik Deutschland; Nürnberg, vom. 15. bis 20. September 1958.* Frankfurt am Main: IG Metall, 1959.

—. *Protokoll – 10. ordentlicher Gewerkschaftstag der Industriegewerkschaft Metall für die Bundesrepublik Deutschland; Rhein-Main-Halle, Wiesbaden, 27. September bis 2. Oktober 1971.* Frankfurt am Main: IG Metall, 1972.

—. *Protokoll – Ausserordentlicher Gewerkschaftstag der Industriegewerkschaft Metall für die Bundesrepublik Deutschland; Sheraton-Hotel, München, 10. Juni 1972.* Frankfurt am Main: IG Metall, 1973.

—. *Satzung.* Frankfurt am Main: IG Metall, 1981.

—. *Spalte und Herrsche: Franz Josef Strauss und die Einheitsgewerkschaft.* Frankfurt am Main: IG Metall, n.d.

—. *Stahlpolitisches Programm der IG Metall.* Frankfurt am Main: IG Metall, 1985.

—. *Strukturelle Arbeitslosigkeit durch technologischen Wandel? Referate, gehalten auf der Technologie-Tagung der IG Metall, 24./25. Mai 1977.* Schriftenreihe der IG Metall 72. Frankfurt am Main. IG Metall, 1977.

—. *Strukturwandel in der Metallindustrie: Analytische und konzeptionelle Ansätze der IG Metall zur Strukturpolitik 1975 bis 1977.* Frankfurt am Main: IG Metall, 1977.

—. *Tagesprotokoll des 12. ordentlichen Gewerkschaftstages der IG Metall in Düsseldorf vom 18. bis 24. September 1977.* Frankfurt am Main: IG Metall, 1977.

—. *44 Tage Arbeitskampf: Dokumentation über die Tarifauseinandersetzung 1978–79.* Münster: Bezirksleitung der IG Metall, 1979.

—. *Technikentwicklung: Gestaltung ist machbar.* Frankfurt am Main: IG Metall, 1984.

—. *Werktage werden besser: Der Kampf um den Lohnrahmentarifvertrag II in Nordwürttemberg/Nordbaden.* Cologne: Europäische Verlagsanstalt, 1977.

—. *Work and Technology: People Must Stay!* Frankfurt am Main: IG Metall, 1985.

—. *Zur Situation bei Eisen und Stahl, 27. Mai 1977, Dortmund: Referate, Diskussionsbeiträge, Dokumente.* Frankfurt am Main: IG Metall, 1977.

Institut für Bilanzforschung. *Die Elektroindustrie in der Bundesrepublik Deutschland.* Frankfurt am Main: IBF, 1979.

Institut für Marxistische Studien und Forschungen (IMSF), ed. *DGB wohin? Dokumente zur Programm-Diskussion.* Frankfurt am Main: Nachrichten-Verlag, 1978.

—. *Gewerkschaften und Rationalisierung in der BRD.* Frankfurt am Main: Verlag Marxistische Blätter, 1973.

Institut für Sozialforschung. *Gesellschaftliche Arbeit und Rationalisierung.* Opladen: Westdeutscher Verlag, 1981.

Institut für Sozialwissenschaftliche Forschung. *Arbeiten 1965 bis 1979.* Munich: ISF, 1979.

Institut für Zukunftsforschung, ed. *Ausländer oder Deutsche.* Cologne: Bund Verlag, 1981.

Jacobi, Otto, Walther Müller-Jentsch and Eberhard Schmidt, eds. *Arbeiterinteressen gegen Sozialpartnerschaft: Kritisches Gewerkschaftsjahrbuch 1978/79.* Berlin: Rotbuch Verlag, 1979.

—. *Arbeitskampf um Arbeitszeit: Kritisches Gewerkschaftsjahrbuch 1979–80.* Berlin: Rotbuch Verlag, 1979.

—. *Gewerkschaften und Klassenkampf: Kritisches Jahrbuch 1972.* Frankfurt am Main: Fischer Taschenbuch Verlag, 1972.

—. *Gewerkschaften und Klassenkampf: Kritisches Jahrbuch 1973.* Frankfurt am Main: Fischer Taschenbuch Verlag, 1973.

—. *Gewerkschaften und Klassenkampf: Kritisches Jahrbuch 1974.* Frankfurt am Main: Fischer Taschenbuch Verlag, 1974.

—. *Gewerkschaften und Klassenkampf: Kritisches Jahrbuch 1975.* Frankfurt am Main: Fischer Taschenbuch Verlag, 1975.

—. *Gewerkschaftspolitik in der Krise: Kritisches Gewerkschaftsjahrbuch 1977–78.* Berlin: Rotbuch Verlag, 1978.

—. *Moderne Zeiten – Alte Rezepte: Kritisches Gewerkschaftsjahrbuch 1980–81.* Berlin: Rotbuch Verlag, 1980.

—. *Starker Arm am kurzen Hebel: Kritisches Gewerkschaftsjahrbuch, 1981–82.* Berlin: Rotbuch Verlag, 1981.

Jacobs, Eric. *European Trade Unionism.* London: Croom Helm, 1973.

Jaeggi, Urs. *Kapital und Arbeit in der Bundesrepublik: Elemente einer gesamtgesellschaftlichen Analyse.* Frankfurt am Main: Fischer Taschenbuch Verlag, 1973.

Judith, Rudolf, ed. *25 Jahre Montanmitbestimmung: Reden und Dokumente*. Frankfurt am Main: IG Metall, 1976.

—. *Die Krise der Stahlindustrie – Krise einer Region. Das Beispiel Saarland*. Reihe: Qualifizierte Mitbestimmung in Theorie und Praxis. Cologne: Bund Verlag, 1980.

Jühe, Reinhard, Horst-Udo Niedenhoff and Wolfgang Pege. *Gewerkschaften in der Bundesrepublik Deutschland: Daten, Fakten, Strukturen*. Cologne: Deutscher Instituts-Verlag, 1977.

Jung, Werner, and Ulrich Laube. *Die alleingelassenen Belegschaften: Betriebsvereinbarungen und gewerkschaftliche Tarifpolitik*. Gewerkschaftspolitische Studien, Vol. 9. Berlin: Verlag Die Arbeitswelt, 1977.

Jürgens, Ulrich and Frieder Naschold, eds. *Arbeitspolitik*. Opladen: Westdeutscher Verlag, 1984.

Kalbitz, Rainer. *Aussperrungen in der Bundesrepublik: Die vergessenen Konflikte*. Schriftenreihe der Otto Brenner Stiftung 14. Cologne/Frankfurt am Main: Europäische Verlagsanstalt, 1979.

—. "Biographie über den Streik in Schleswig-Holstein 1956–57." Unpublished Master's thesis. University of Bochum, 1969.

Kassalow, Everett M. *Trade Unions and Industrial Relation: An International Comparison*. New York: Random House, 1969.

Kastendiek, Hella. *Arbeitnehmer in der SPD: Herausbildung und Funktion der Arbeitsgemeinschaft für Arbeitnehmerfragen (AfA)*. Berlin: Verlag Die Arbeitswelt, 1978.

Katzenstein, Peter, ed. *Between Power and Plenty: Foreign Economic Policies of Advanced Industrial States*. Madison, Wisc.: The University of Wisconsin Press, 1978.

Kendall, Walter. *The Labour Movement in Europe*. London: Allen Lane, 1975.

Kern, Horst, and Michael Schumann. *Das Ende der Arbeitsteilung? Rationalisierung in der industriellen Produktion*. Munich: Verlag C. H. Beck, 1984.

—. *Industriearbeit und Arbeiterbewusstsein*. Frankfurt am Main: Suhrkamp Verlag, 1977.

—. *Industriearbeit und Arbeiterbewusstsein, Teil I*. Frankfurt am Main: Europäische Verlagsanstalt, 1970.

—. *Industriearbeit und Arbeiterbewusstsein, Teil II*. Frankfurt am Main: Europäische Verlagsanstalt, 1970.

—. *Der soziale Prozess bei technischen Umstellungen*. Frankfurt am Main: Europäische Verlagsanstalt, 1972.

Kindleberger, Charles P. *Europe's Postwar Growth: The Role of Labor Supply*. Cambridge, Mass.: Harvard University Press, 1967.

Kirchheimer, Otto. "West Geman Trade Unions: Their Domestic and Foreign Policies." Santa Monica: unpublished research memorandum, The Rand Corporation, April 1, 1956.

Kittner, Michael. *Arbeits- und Sozialordnung*. Cologne: Bund Verlag, 1978.

—, ed. *Gewerkschaftsjahrbuch 1984: Daten-Fakten-Analysen*. Cologne: Bund Verlag, 1984.

—, ed. *Streik und Aussperrung: Protokoll der wissenschaftlichen Veranstaltung der Industriegewerkschaft Metall vom 13. bis 15. September 1973 in München*. Schriftenreihe der Otto Brenner Stiftung 3. Frankfurt am Main: Europäische Verlagsanstalt, 1973.

—. *Verbot der Aussperrung: 7 Fragen – 70 Antworten.* Frankfurt am Main: IG Metall, n.d.

Klönne, Arno. *Die deutsche Arbeiterbewegung: Geschichte-Ziele-Wirkungen.* Düsseldorf: Eugen Diederichs Verlag, 1980.

Kohl, Wilfrid, and Giorgio Basevi, eds. *West Germany: A European and Global Power.* Lexington, Mass.: D. C. Heath and Co., 1980.

Krack, Jürgen, and Karl Neumann. *Konjunktur, Krise, Wirtschaftspolitik.* Frankfurt am Main: Europäische Verlagsanstalt, 1978.

Kräling, Klaus, Thomas Krüger, Renate Müller, Hannes Schröder and Helmut Völkel. *Bestrafte Solidarität: Drucker und Journalisten im gewerkschaftlichen Kampf.* Schriftenreihe Kritische Gewerkschaftspolitik, Vol. 6. Berlin: Verlag Die Arbeitswelt, 1973.

Küchle, Hartmut. *Theoretische und empirische Voraussetzungen quantifizierter Konjunkturprognosen.* Cologne: Bund Verlag, 1979.

Kulke, Ulrich. *Betriebsnahe Tarifpolitik zur Stärkung der gewerkschaftlichen Basis.* Gewerkschaftspolitische Studien, Vol. 11. Berlin: Verlag Die Arbeitswelt, 1977.

Kunz, Rainer, Herbert Maier and Theo Stammen, eds. *Programme der politischen Parteien in der Bundesrepublik.* Munich: Verlag C. H. Beck, 1975.

Kurz-Sherf, Ingrid. *Arbeitszeit im Umbruch: Analyse und Dokumentation der neuen tariflichen Arbeitszeitbestimmungen.* Düsseldorf: WSI, 1984.

—. *Der Kampf hat sich gelohnt.* Düsseldorf: WSI, 1984.

Langkau, Jochen, and Claus Kohler, eds. *Wirtschaftspolitik und wirtschaftliche Entwicklung.* Bonn: Verlag Neue Gesellschaft, 1985.

Lecher, Wolfgang. *Gewerkschaften im Europa der Krise: Zur Zentralisierung und Dezentralisierung gewerkschaftlicher Organisation und Politik in sechs Ländern der Europäischen Gemeinschaft.* WSI-Studie zur Wirtschafts und Sozialforschung. Cologne: Bund Verlag, 1981.

—. *Stand und Perspektiven von Arbeitnehmerbeteiligung und Mitbestimmung in Europa.* WSI Arbeitsmaterialien 6. Düsseldorf: WSI, 1985.

Ledwohn, Josef, and Heinz Seeger, eds. *Gewerkschaften – Standort und Perspektive.* Frankfurt am Main: Nachrichten-Verlag, 1971.

Leminsky, Gerhard, and Bernd Otto. *Politik und Programmatik des Deutschen Gewerkschaftsbundes.* Cologne: Bund Verlag, 1974, first edition.

—. *Politik und Programmatik des Deutschen Gewerkschaftsbundes.* Cologne: Bund Verlag, 1984, second edition.

Lenhardt, Anne, and Gerhard Weiss. *Stahlkrise an der Saar – Ein Kampf um Arbeitsplätze.* Soziale Bewegungen, Analyse und Dokumentation des IMSF, Nachrichten-Reihe 11, Frankfurt am Main: Nachrichten-Verlag, 1978.

Limmer, Hans. *Die deutsche Gewerkschaftsbewegung.* Munich: Günter Olzog Verlag, 1966.

Linz Storch de Gracia, Juan J. "The Social Bases of West German Politics." Unpublished PhD dissertation, Columbia University, 1959.

Loderer, Eugen. *Einheitsgewerkschaft: Solidarisches Handeln – Soziale Gegenmacht.* Schriftenreihe der IG Metall 86. Frankfurt am Main: IG Metall, 1980.

Loesch, Achim von. *Die gemeinwirtschaftlichen Unternehmen der deutschen Gewerkschaften: Entstehung – Funktionen – Probleme.* Cologne: Bund Verlag, 1979.

Löwenthal, Richard. *Social Change and Cultural Crisis.* New York: Columbia University Press, 1984.

Lutz, Burkart. *Betriebliche Personalplanung zwischen Unternehmensplanung und Personalpolitik.* Frankfurt am Main: Campus Verlag, 1979.

——. *Krise des Lohnanreizes: Ein empirisch-historischer Beitrag zum Wandel der Formen betrieblicher Herrschaft am Beispiel der deutschen Stahlindustie.* Frankfurt am Main/ Cologne: Europäische Verlagsanstalt, 1975.

——. *Personalplanung in der gewerblichen Wirtschaft der Bundesrepublik.* Frankfurt am Main: Campus Verlag, 1979.

Lutz, Burkart, Klaus Düll, Guido Kammerer and Dieter Kreuz. *Rationalisierung und Mechanisierung im öffentlichen Dienst: Ein Gutachten für die Gewerkschaft ÖTV.* Munich: Carl Hanser Verlag, 1970.

Maase, Mira, Werner Sengenberger and Friedrich Weltz. *Weiterbildung – Aktionsfeld für den Betriebsrat? Eine Studie über Arbeitnehmerinteressen und betriebliche Personalpolitik.* Munich: Institut für Sozialwissenschaftliche Forschung, 1975.

Mahlein, Leonhard. *Rationalisierung – sichere Arbeitsplätze – menschenwürdige Arbeitsbedingungen: Zum Arbeitskampf in der Druckindustrie 1978.* Schriftenreihe der Industriegewerkschaft Druck und Papier, Hauptvorstand, no. 29. Stuttgart: IG Druck, 1978.

——. *Gewerkschaften heute: Erfahrungen – Anregungen.* Nachrichten-Reihe 27. Frankfurt am Main: Nachrichten-Verlag, 1983.

Markovits, Andrei, ed. *The Political Economy of West Germany: Modell Deutschland.* New York: Praeger, 1982.

Martin, Benjamin, and Everett M. Kassalow, eds. *Labor Relations in Advanced Industrial Societies: Issues and Problems.* Washington, DC: Carnegie Endowment for International Peace, 1980.

Mason, Timothy. *Sozialpolitik im Dritten Reich.* Opladen: Westdeutscher Verlag, 1977.

Matthöfer, Hans. *Humanisierung der Arbeit und Produktivität in der Industriegesellschaft. Demokratischer Sozialismus in Theorie und Praxis.* Colgone: Europäische Verlagsanstalt, 1977.

Mayer, Evelies. *Theorien zum Funktionswandel der Gewerkschaften.* Frankfurt am Main: Europäische Verlagsanstalt, 1973.

Mayer, Udo, *Mitbestimmungsgesetz '76: Grenzen und Möglichkeiten.* Nachrichten-Reihe 4. Frankfurt am Main: Nachrichten-Verlag, 1976.

Mayr, Hans, and Hans Janssen, eds. *Perspektiven der Arbeitszeitverkürzung: Wissenschaftler und Gewerkschafter zur 35-Stunden-Woche.* Cologne: Bund Verlag, 1984.

Meissner, Werner. *Die Lehre der fünf Weisen: Eine Auseindandersetzung mit den Jahresgutachten des Sachverständigenrats zur Begutachtung der gesamtwirtschaftlichen Entwicklung.* Cologne: Bund Verlag, 1980.

Mendius, Hans-Gerhard, Werner Sengenberger, Burkart Lutz, Norbert Altmann, Fritz Böhle, Inge Asendorf-Krings, Ingrid Drexel and Christopher Nuber. *Betrieb-Arbeitsmarkt-Qualifikation I : Beiträge zu Rezession und Personalpolitik, Bildungsexpansion und Arbeitsteilung, Humanisierung und Qualifizierung.* Frankfurt am Main: Aspekte Verlag, 1976.

Meyer, Regine. *Streik und Aussperrung in der Metallindustrie: Analyse der Streikbewegung in Nordwürttemberg-Nordbaden 1971.* Schriftenreihe für Sozialgeschichte und Arbeitertbewegung, Vol. 4. Marburg: Verlag Arbeiterbewegung und Gesellschaftswissenschaft, 1977.

Mielke, Siegfried, ed. *Internationales Gewerkschaftshandbuch.* Opladen: Leske & Budrich, 1983.

Mommsen, Hans, and Ulrich Borsdorf, eds. *Glück auf, Kameraden! Die Bergarbeiter und ihre Organisationen in Deutschland.* Cologne: Bund Verlag, 1979.

Mühlbradt, Werner, and Egon Lutz. *Der Zwang zur Sozialpartnerschaft: Hintergründe der Zusammenarbeit von Gewerkschaften und Arbeitgebern.* Neuwied/Berlin: Hermann Luchterhand Verlag, 1969.

Muhr, Gerd, ed. *Beschäftigungspolitik in den achtziger Jahren: Protokoll der DGB-Konferenz zur Beschäftigungspolitik in den achtziger Jahren am 21. und 22. Oktober 1980 in Düsseldorf.* Cologne: Bund Verlag, 1981.

Müller, Gernot, Ulrich Rödel, Charles Sabel, Frank Stille and Winfried Vogt. *Ökonomische Krisentendenzen im gegenwärtigen Kapitalismus.* Frankfurt am Main/New York: Campus Verlag, 1978.

Müller-Jentsch, Walther, and Wolfgang Streeck. "Industriegewerkschaft Bau-Steine-Erden." Unpublished manuscript, 1970.

Naschold, Frieder, ed. *Arbeit und Politik: Gesellschaftliche Regulierung der Arbeit und der sozialen Sicherung.* Frankfurt am Main/New York: Campus Verlag, 1985.

Nell-Breuning, Oswald von. *Eigentum, Wirtschaftsordnung und wirtschaftliche Mitbestimmung.* Schriftenreihe der IG Metall 64. Frankfurt am Main: Vorstand der Industriegewerkschaft Metall, 1975.

Neumann, Karl. *Konjuntur und Konjunkturpolitik.* Frankfurt am Main: Europäische Verlagsanstalt, 1972.

Noé, Claus. *Gebändigter Klassenkampf – Tarifautonomie in der Bundesrepublik Deutschland: Der Konflikt zwischen Gesamtmetall und IG Metall vom Frühjahr 1963.* Volkswirtschaftliche Schriften 141. Berlin: Duncker & Humblot, 1970.

Odhner, Clas-Erik. *Participatory Economics of Keynes Plus.* Stockholm, n.p., 1978.

OECD. *O.E.C.D. Economic Surveys, Germany.* Paris: OECD, 1974–1977.

—. *O.E.C.D. Economic Surveys, Germany.* Paris: OECD, June 1978.

—. *O.E.C.D. Economic Surveys, Germany.* Paris: OECD, 1984.

—. *Working Paper on Industrial Relations – Collective Bargaining and Government Policies – National Report: Federal Republic of Germany,* Paris: OECD, May 16, 1978.

Offe, Claus, ed. *Opfer des Arbeitsmarktes: Zur Theorie der strukturierten Arbeitslosigkeit.* Neuwied: Hermann Luchterhand Verlag, 1977.

Offe, Claus, Karl Hinrichs and Helmut Wiesenthal, eds. *Arbeitszeitpolitik.* Frankfurt am Main: Campus Verlag, 1982.

Oppenländer, Karl-Heinrich, ed. *Wirtschaftliche Auswirkungen des technischen Wandels in der Industrie.* Forschungsprojekt des RKW, Vol. 3. Frankfurt am Main: Europäische Verlagsanstalt, 1971.

Osterland, Martin, ed. *Arbeitssituation, Lebenslage und Konfliktpotential: Festschrift für Max E. Graf zu Solms-Roedelheim.* Frankfurt am Main: Europäische Verlagsanstalt, 1975.

Osterland, Martin, Wilfried Deppe, Frank Gerlach, Ulrich Mergner, Klaus Pelte and Manfred Schlösser. *Materialien zur Lebens- und Arbeitssituation der Industrie-*

*arbeiter in der BRD.* Studienreihe des Soziologischen Forschungsinstituts Göttingen. Frankfurt am Main: Europäische Verlagsanstalt, 1973.

Ostertag, Adi, ed. *Arbeitsdirektoren: Berichten aus der Praxis.* Reihe Qualifizierte Mitbestimmung in Theorie und Praxis. Cologne: Bund Verlag, 1981.

Paterson, William, and Gordon Smith, eds. *The West German Model: Perspectives on a Stable State.* London: Frank Cass & Co., 1981.

Perner, Detlef. *Mitbestimmung im Handwerk? Die politische und soziale Funktion der Handwerkskammern im Geflecht der Unternehmerorganisationen.* Cologne: Bund Verlag, 1983.

Peter, Gerd, and Bruno Zwingmann, eds. *Humanisierung der Arbeit: Probleme der Durchsetzung.* Cologne: Bund Verlag, 1982.

Peters, Jürgen, ed. *Montanmitbestimmung: Dokumente ihrer Entstehung.* Reihe Qualifizierte Mitbestimmung in Theorie und Praxis. Cologne: Bund Verlag, 1979.

Pfromm, Hans-Adam. *Das neue DGB-Grundsatzprogramm: Einführung und Kommentar.* Munich: Günter Olzog Verlag, 1982.

—. *Solidarische Lohnpolitik: Zur wirtschaftlichen und sozialen Problematik tariflicher Lohnstrukturnivellierung.* Frankfurt am Main: Europäische Verlagsanstalt, 1978.

Pickshaus, Klaus, and Witich Rossmann. *Streik und Aussperrung '78: Hafen – Druck – Metall.* Nachrichten-Reihe 13. Frankfurt am Main: Nachrichten-Verlag, 1978.

Pirker, Theo. *Die Blinde Macht: Die Gewerkschaftsbewegung in der Bundesrepublik. Teil 1 – 1945–1952, Vom "Ende des Kapitalismus" zur Zähmung der Gewerkschaften.* Berlin: Verlag Olle & Wolter, 1979.

—. *Die Blinde Macht: Die Gewerkschaftsbewegung in der Bundesrepublik. Teil 2 – 1953–1960, Weg und Rolle der Gewerkschaften im neuen Kapitalismus.* Berlin: Verlag Olle & Wolter, 1979.

—. *Die SPD Nach Hitler: Die Geschichte der Sozialdemokratischen Partei Deutschlands 1945–1964.* Munich: Rütten & Loening Verlag, 1965.

Pitz, Karl H., ed. *Das nein zur Vermögenspolitik: Gewerkschaftliche Argumente und Alternativen zur Vermögensbildung.* Reinbek-Hamburg: Rowohlt Taschenbuch Verlag, 1974.

Pless, Phillip. *Der Wille zur Tat: Gewerkschaften als gesellschaftsverändernde Kraft, Reden und Aufsätze.* Schriftenreihe Kritische Gewerkschaftspolitik, Vol. 4. Berlin: Verlag Die Arbeitswelt, 1973.

Pool, Michael. *Workers' Participation in Industry.* London: Routledge & Kegan Paul, 1975.

Pozzoli, Claudio, ed. *Grenzen gewerkschaftlicher Politik.* Jahrbuch Arbeiterbewegung, Vol. 6. Frankfurt am Main: Fischer Taschenbuch Verlag, 1979.

Projektgruppe Gewerkschaftsforschung. *Die Austauschbeziehungen zwischen Kapital und Arbeit im Kontext der sozio-ökonomischen Entwicklung: Zwischenbericht 1976 – Erster Teil, Theoretische Vorarbeiten.* Forschungsberichte des Instituts für Sozialforschung. Frankfurt am Main: Campus Verlag, 1976.

—. *Gesamtwirtschaftliche Entwicklung und Organisation der Tarifparteien.* Vol. 1 of *Rahmenbedingungen der Tarifpolitik.* Forschungsberichte des Instituts für Sozialforschung. Frankfurt am Main/New York: Campus Verlag, 1979.

—. *Strukturdaten der Metallverarbeitenden, der Chemischen und der Druckindustrie.* Vol. 2 of *Rahmenbedingungen der Tarifpolitik.* Forschungsberichte des Instituts für Sozialforschung. Frankfurt am Main/New York: Campus Verlag, 1979.

—. *Tarifpolitik 1977: Darstellung und Analyse der Tarifbewegung in der Metallverar-beitenden, der Chemischen und der Druckindustrie sowie im öffentlichen Dienst*. For-schungsberichte des Instituts für Sozialforschung. Frankfurt am Main/New York: Campus Verlag, 1978.

—. *Tarifpolitik 1978: Lohnpolitische Kooperation und Absicherungskämpfe: Darstellung und Analyse der Tarifbewegung in der Metallverarbeitenden, der Chemischen und der Druckindustrie sowie im öffenlichen Dienst*. Forschungsberichte des Instituts für Sozialforschung. Frankfurt am Main/New York: Campus Verlag, 1979.

—. *Tarifpolitik unter Krisenbedingungen: Darstellung und Analyse der Tarifbewegungen 1975 und 1976 in der chemischen Industrie und in der Druckindustrie*. Forschungsbe-richte des Instituts für Sozialforschung. Frankfurt am Main: Campus Verlag, 1977.

Prott, Jürgen. *Industriearbeit bei betrieblichen Umstrukturierungen*. Schriftenreihe Stif-tung Mitbestimmung, Hans Böckler Gesellschaft 7. Cologne: Bund Verlag, 1975.

Rajewsky, Xenia. *Arbeitskampfrecht in der Bundesrepublik*. Frankfurt am Main: Suhrkamp Verlag, 1970.

Redaktionskollektiv "express," ed. *Spontane Streiks 1973: Krise der Gewerkschaftspoli-tik*. Reihe Betrieb und Gewerkschaften. Offenbach: Verlag 2000, 1974.

Reister, Hugo. *Profite gegen Bleisatz*. Berlin: Verlag Die Arbeitswelt, 1980.

Revier-Redaktion. *Streikwinter: Der Stahlarbeiterstreik 1978–79, Eine Dokumentation*. Duisburg: Revier-Redaktion, 1979.

Richter, Wolfgang, ed. *Bauerbeit in der Bundesrepublik*. Cologne: Pahl-Rugenstein Verlag, 1981.

Riemer, Jeremiah. "Crisis and Intervention in the West German Economy: A Political Analysis of Changes in the Policy Machinery during the 1960s and 1970s." Unpublished PhD dissertation, Cornell University, 1983.

Rohde, Helmut. *Für eine soziale Zukunft*. Munich: Carl Hanser Verlag, 1975.

Roloff, Wolf-Rainer. *Interpretation und Analyse der lohn- und sozialpolitischen Zielsetzung der Industriegewerkschaft Bau-Steine-Erden*. Hilden: Selbstverlag Dr. Roloff, 1971.

*Rotbuch zu den Gewerkschaftsausschlüssen*. Hamburg: J. Reents-Verlag, 1978.

Roth, Karl Heinz. *Die "andere" Arbeiterbewegung*. Munich: C. Trikont Verlag, 1974.

Roth, Wolfgang, ed. *Investitionslenkung: Ergebnisse einer Diskussion zwischen jungen Unternehmern und Sozialdemokraten zum Problem von Markt und Lenkung*. Reinbek: Rowohlt, 1976.

Ruhr-Universität Bochum, and Industriegewerkschaft Metall. *Vereinbarung über Zusammenarbeit: Ringvorlesung 1978–79, Stahlkrise – Krise des Ruhrgebiets? Ursachen – Auswirkungen – Antworten*. Reihe: Gemeinsame Veranstaltungen Ruhr Univer-sität Bochum, IG-Metall-Bildungszentrum, Heft no. 3. Frankfurt am Main: IG Metall, n.d.

Sachverständigenrat. *Gutachten 1981–82*. Stuttgart: W. Kohlhammer, 1971.

—. *Jahresgutachten 1964*. Bundesdrucksache IV/1890. Bonn: n.p., 1964.

—. *Jahresgutachten 1965 – Stabilisierung ohne Stagnation*. Stuttgart: W. Kohlhammer, 1965.

—. *Jahresgutachten 1971*. Appendix: "Sondergutachten vom 24.5.1971." Stuttgart: W. Kohlhammer, 1971.

—. *Im Sog des Booms*. Stuttgart: W. Kohlhammer, 1969.

Sauer, Dieter, *Staat und Staatsapparat: Ein theoretischer Ansatz*. Forschungsberichte aus dem Institut für Sozialwissenschaftliche Forschung München. Frankfurt am Main: Campus Verlag, 1978.

Schäfer, Claus, ed. *Aspekte der Mitbestimmung*. WSI Arbeitsmaterielien no. 7. Düsseldorf: WSI, 1985.

Schäfer, Claus, Rainer Skiba and Hartmut Tofaute. *Personalausgaben und Einkommensfindung im öffentlichen Dienst*. Cologne: Bund Verlag, 1974.

Schäfer, Claus, Erich Standfest and Rudi Welzmüller. *Verteilung und Umverteilung unter veränderten Wachstumsbedingungen*. Cologne: Bund Verlag, 1982.

Scharpf, Fritz W. *Autonome Gewerkschaften und staatliche Wirtschaftspolitik: Probleme einer Verbändegesetzgebung*. Cologne; Europäische Verlagsanstalt, 1978.

Scharping, Rudolf, and Friedholm Wollner, eds. *Demokratischer Sozialismus und Langzeitprogramm*. Reinbek: Rowohlt, 1973.

Schmidt, Eberhard. *Ordnungsfaktor oder Gegenmacht. Die politische Rolle der Gewerkschaften*. Frankfurt am Main: Suhrkamp, 1969.

—. *Die verhinderte Neuordnung 1945–1952: Zur Auseinandersetzung um die Demokratisierung der Wirtschaft in den westlichen Besatzungszonen und in der BRD*. Frankfurt am Main: Europäische Verlagsanstalt, 1970.

Schmiede, Rudi, and Edwin Schudlich. *Die Entwicklung der Leistungsentlohnung in Deutschland: Eine historisch-theoretische Untersuchung zum Verhältnis von Lohn und Leistung unter kapitalistischen Produktionsbedingungen*. Forschungsberichte des Instituts für Sozialforschung. Frankfurt am Main/New York: Campus Verlag, 1978.

Schneider, Dieter, ed. *Zur Theorie und Praxis des Streiks*. Frankfurt am Main: Suhrkamp Verlag, 1971.

Schneider, Dieter, and Rudolf F. Kuda. *Mitbestimmung*. Munich: Deutscher Taschenbuch Verlag, 1969.

Schuchman, Abraham. *Codetermination: Labor's Middle Way in Germany*. Washington, DC: Public Affairs Press, 1957.

Schumann, Hans Gerd. *Nationalsozialismus und Gewerkschaftsbewegung: Die Vernichtung der deutschen Gewerkschaftsbewegung und der Aufbau der Deutschen Arbeitsfront*. Hanover: Goedel, 1958.

Schumann, Michael, Edgar Einemann, Christa Siebel-Rebell and Klaus Peter Wittemann. *Rationalisierung, Krise und Arbeiter: Eine empirische Untersuchung der Industrialisierung auf der Werft*. Vol. 1. Forschungsberichte der zentralen wissenschaftlichen Einrichtung "Arbeit und Betrieb." Bremen: Universität Bremen, 1981.

—. *Rationalisierung, Krise und Arbeiter: Eine empirische Untersuchung der Industrialisierung auf der Werft*. Vol. 2. Forschungsberichte der zentralen wissenschaftlichen Einrichtung "Arbeit und Betrieb." Bremen: Universität Bremen, 1981.

Schumann, Michael, Frank Gerlach, Albert Gschlössl and Petra Milhoffer. *Am Beispiel der Septemberstreiks: Anfang der Rekonstruktionsperiode der Arbeiterklasse?* Studienreihe des Soziologischen Forschungsinstituts Göttingen (SOFI). Frankfurt am Main: Europäische Verlagsanstalt, 1971.

Schuster, Dieter. *Die Deutsche Gewerkschaftsbewegung: DGB*. Düsseldorf: DGB-Bundesvorstand, 1976.

—. *The German Labour Movement, DGB*. Düsseldorf: German Federation of Trade Unions DGB, 1973.

Seidel, Heinz. *Das Verhältnis der Angestellten zur Mitbestimmung*. Frankfurt am Main: Europäische Verlagsanstalt, 1972.

Seifert, Hartmut. *Öffentliche Arbeitsmarktpolitik in der Bundesrepublik Deutschland: Zur Entwicklung der Arbeitsmarktpolitik im Verhältnis von Steuerungsaufgabe und Anpassungsfunktion*. Cologne: Bund Verlag, 1984.

Seifert, Jürgen, ed. *Grundgesetz und Restauration*. Neuwied; Luchterhand, 1977.

Seitenzahl, Rolf. *Einkommenspolitik durch Konzertierte Aktion und Orientierungsdaten*. Cologne: Bund Verlag, 1974.

Seitenzahl, Rolf, Heinz-Dieter Pütz and Ulrich Zachert. *Vorteilsregelungen für Gewerkschaftsmitglieder*. Cologne: Bund Verlag, 1976.

Sengenberger, Werner, ed. *Der gespaltene Arbeitsmarkt: Probleme der Arbeitsmarktsegmentation*. Arbeiten des Instituts für sozialwissenschaftliche Forschung München. Frankfurt am Main: Campus Verlag, 1978.

Siebert, Gerd, and Barbara Degen. *Betriebsverfassungsgesetz '72*. Frankfurt am Main: Nachrichten-Verlag, 1972.

—. *Betriebsverfassungsgesetz '72: Kommentiert für die Praxis*. Frankfurt am Main: Nachrichten-Verlag, 1979, fourth edition.

Simon, Walter. *Macht und Herrschaft der Unternehmerverbände BDI, BDA und DIHT im ökonomischen und politischen System der BRD*. Cologne: Pahl-Rugenstein Verlag, 1976.

Sozialistisches Büro Offenbach, ed. *Materialien zur Gewerkschaftsdiskussion*. Reihe Betrieb und Gewerkschaften. Offenbach: Verlag 2000, 1977.

—. *Rationalisierung, Arbeitslosigkeit, Gegenwehr: Analysen, Materialien und Erfahrungen*. Reihe Betrieb und Gewerkschaften. Offenbach: Verlag 2000, 1978.

Spiro, Herbert J. *The Politics of German Codetermination*. Cambridge, Mass.: Harvard University Press, 1958.

Statistisches Bundesamt. *Jahrbuch des Statistischen Bundesamtes*. Bonn: Statistisches Bundesamt, 1983.

Stein, Elise. *Codetermination: Its History, Development and Current Role in West Germany* Unpublished BA thesis, Hampshire College, 1984.

Steinhaus, Kurt. *Streiks in der Bundesrepublik 1966-1974*. Marxistische Taschenbücher, Reihe "Marxismus aktuell" 83. Frankfurt am Main: Verlag Marxistische Blätter, 1975.

Streeck, Wolfgang. *Gewerkschaftliche Organisationsprobleme in der sozialstaatlichen Demokratie*. Sozialwissenschaft und Praxis; Buchreihe des Wissenschaftszentrums Berlin, Vol. 7. Königstein/TS.: Athenäum Verlag, 1981.

Sturmthal, Adolf. *Left of Center: European Labor since World War II*. Urbana: University of Illinois Press, 1983.

—. *Workers' Councils*. Cambridge, Mass.: Harvard University Press, 1964.

Széplábi, Michael. *Das Gesellschaftsbild der Gewerkschaften: Eine wissenssozialogische Untersuchung der Programm-Aussagen des DGB*. Stuttgart: Ferdinand Enke Verlag, 1973.

Thum, Horst. *Mitbestimmung in der Montanindustrie: Der Mythos vom Sieg der Gewerkschaften*. Stuttgart: Deutsche Verlagsanstalt, 1982.

Thüsing, Klaus, Arno Klönne and Karl-Ludwig Hesse, eds. *Zukunft SPD: Aussichten linker Politik in der Sozialdemokratie*. Hamburg: VSA-Verlag, 1981.

Trautwein-Kalms, Gudrun, and Gerhard Gerlach. *Gewerkschaften und Humanisierung der Arbeit: Zur Bewertung des HdA-Programms*. Frankfurt am Main/New York: Campus Verlag, 1980.

Triesch, Günter. *Die Macht der Funktionäre: Macht und Verantwortung der Gewerkschaften*. Düsseldorf: K. Rauch, 1956.

Tudyka, Kurt P., ed. *Multinationale Konzerne und Gewerkschaftsstrategie*. Hamburg: Hoffman und Campe Verlag, 1974.

*Über die Verbände: Eine synoptische Selbstdarstellung der Tarifvertragsparteien*. Wiesbaden: Universum Verlagsanstalt, 1978.

Ullmann, Peter. *Tarifverträge und Tarifpolitik in Deutschland bis 1914: Entstehung und Entwicklung, interessenpolitische Bedingungen und Bedeutung des Tarifvertragswesens für die sozialistischen Gewerkschaften*. Reihe "Modern Geschichte und Politik," No. 6. Frankfurt am Main: Peter Lang, 1977.

Unterseher, Lutz. "Kollektives Arbeitsrecht und Tarifsystem." Unpublished PhD dissertation, Johann Wolfgang Goethe-Universität, 1975.

Verband der Fabrikarbeiter Deutschlands. *Festschrift zur Erinnerung an die Gründung und den 40 jährigen Kampf*. N.p., 1930.

Verein Deutscher Maschinenbau–Anstalten. *Statistiches Handbuch für den Maschinenbau*. Frankfurt am Main: VDMA, 1983.

Vetter, Heinz Oskar. *Gleichberechtigung oder Klassenkampf: Gewerkschaftspolitik für die achtziger Jahre*. Cologne: Bund Verlag, 1980.

Vetter, Heinz Oskar, ed. *Aus der Geschichte lernen – Die Zukunft gestalten: Dreissig Jahre DGB*. Cologne: Bund Verlag, 1980.

—. *Humanisierung der Arbeit als gesellschaftspolitische und gewerkschaftliche Aufgabe: Protokoll der Konferenz des deutschen Gewerkschaftsbundes vom 16. 17. Mai 1974 in München*. Frankfurt am Main: Europäische Verlagsanstalt, 1974.

—. *Mitbestimmung, Wirtschaftsordnung, Grundgesetz*. Frankfurt am Main: Europäische Verlagsanstalt, 1976.

Vilmar, Fritz, and Karl-Otto Sattler. *Wirtschaftsdemokratie und Humanisierung der Arbeit: Systematische Integration der wichtigsten Konzepte*. Cologne: Europäische Verlagsanstalt, 1978.

Vogl, Frank. *German Business after the Economic Miracle*. London: Macmillan Press, 1973.

Webber, Douglas. "German Social Democracy in the Economic Crisis." Unpublished doctoral dissertation, University of Essex, 1984.

Weber, Claudia. "Die Handlungsbedeutung von Konfliktverarbeitungsmustern unter sich veränderten sozio-ökonomischen Bedingungen." Unpublished manuscript. Institut zur Erforschung sozialer Chancen, Cologne, May 1980.

Weddigen, Walter, ed. *Zur Theorie und Praxis der Mitbestimmung*. Berlin: Duncker & Humblot, 1962.

Weiss, Gerhard. *Die ÖTV: Politik und gesellschaftspolitische Konzeptionen der Gewerkschaft ÖTV von 1966 bis 1976*. Schriftenreihe für Sozialgeschichte und Arbeiterbewegung, Vol. 7. Marburg: Verlag Arbeiterbewegung und Gesellschaftswissenschaft, 1978.

Weiss, Manfred. *Gewerkschaftliche Vertrauensleute: Tarifvertragliche Verbesserungen ihrer Arbeit im Betrieb.* Schriftenreihe der Otto Brenner Stiftung 11. Cologne: Europäische Verlagsanstalt, 1978.

Welsch, Johann. *Globalsteuerung in der Bundesrepublik Deutschland: Eine kritische Analyse der Stabilisierungspolitik seit 1967.* Cologne: Bund Verlag, 1980.

Welzmüller, Rudolf. *Preispolitik und Akkumulation.* Cologne: Bund Verlag, 1982.

Wenzel, Lothar. *Inflation und Arbeitslosigkeit.* Hanover: SOAK-Verlag, 1979.

Werner, Karl-Gustav. *Organisation und Politik der Gewerkschaften und der Arbeitgeberverbände in der deutschen Bauwirtschaft.* Berlin: Duncker & Humblot, 1968.

Wilke, Manfred, *Die Funktionäre: Apparat und Demokratie im Deutschen Gewerkschaftsbund.* Munich: R. Piper & Co. Verlag, 1979.

Willey, Richard J. *Democracy in the West German Trade Unions: A Reappraisal of the "Iron Law."* Beverley Hills: Sage Publications, 1971.

Wirtschafts- und Sozialwissenschaftliches Institut des Deutschen Gewerkschaftsbundes. *Betriebliche Beschäftigungspolitik und gewerkschaftliche Interressenvertretung.* WSI-Studie zur Wirtschafts- und Sozialforschung, No. 34. Cologne: Bund Verlag, 1977.

Witjes, Winfried. *Gewerkschaftliche Führungsgruppen: Eine empirische Untersuchung zum Sozialprofil, zur Selektion und Zirkulation sowie zur Machtstellung westdeutscher Gewerkschaftsführungen.* Soziologische Schriften, Vol. 18. Berlin: Duncker & Humblot, 1976.

Wohlgemuth, Hans. *Staatseingriff und Arbeitskampf: Zur Kritik der herrschenden Arbeitskampfdoktrin.* Cologne: Europäische Verlagsanstalt, 1977.

WSI-Projektgruppe. *Mitbestimmung im Unternehmen und Betrieb.* Cologne: Bund Verlag, 1981.

Zachert, Ulrich. *Tarifvertrag: Eine problemorientierte Einführung.* Reihe "Problemorientierte Einführungen," Vol. 10. Cologne: Bund Verlag, 1979.

Zachert, Ulrich, Maria Metzke and Wolfgang Hamer. *Die Aussperrung: Zur rechtlichen Zulässigkeit und praktischen Durchsetzungsmöglichkeit eines Aussperrungsverbots.* Cologne: Bund Verlag, 1978.

Zentralverband des deutschen Baugewerbes. *Jahrbuch des deutschen Baugewerbes 1956.* Frankfurt am Main: ZDB, 1957.

—. *Jahrbuch des deutschen Baugewerbes 1966.* Frankfurt am Main: ZDB, 1967.

Zeuner, Bodo, ed. *Genossen was nun? Bilanz und Perspektiven sozialdemokratischer Politik.* Hamburg: Konkret Literatur Verlag, 1983.

Zoll, Rainer. *Die Arbeitslosen, die könnt' ich alle erschiessen.* Cologne: Bund Verlag, 1984.

—. *Hauptsache, ich habe meine Arbeit.* Frankfurt am Main: Suhrkamp, 1984.

—. *Partizipation oder Delegation: Gewerkschaftliche Betriebspolitik in Italien und in der Bundesrepublik Deutschland.* Frankfurt am Main: Europäische Verlagsanstalt, 1981.

Zoll, Rainer, ed. *Arbeiterbewusstsein in der Wirtschaftskrise.* Cologne: Bund Verlag, 1981.

Zurhorst, Günter. *Gewerkschaftspolitik und technischer Forstschritt. Zum Problem einer basisorientierten Mitbestimmung.* Schriftenreihe Kritische Gewerkschaftspolitik, Vol. 3. Berlin: Verlag Die Arbeitswelt, 1975.

### B. Articles

Abendroth, Wolfgang. "Solidarität ist nur wirklich wenn sie konkret ist." *Gewerkschaftliche Monatshefte*. Vol. 28, no. 4 (April 1977), pp. 233–236.

—. "Das Verhältnis von Gewerkschaftsbewegung und Parteiensystem als Problem der Geschichte der Arbeiterbewegung." *Gewerkschaftliche Monatshefte*. Vol. 25, no. 4 (April 1974), pp. 205–216.

—. "Zur Funktion der Gewerkschaften in der westdeutschen Demokratie." *Gewerkschaftliche Monatshefte*. Vol. 3, no. 10 (October 1952), pp. 641–651.

Adam, Hermann. "Industrie- und Handelskammern in der Politik." *Aus Politik und Zeitgeschichte* (in *Das Parlament*), October 20, 1979, pp. 14–29.

Agartz, Viktor, "Expansive Lohnpolitik." *Mitteilungen des Wirtschaftswissenschaftlichen Institutes der Gewerkschaften*. Vol. 6, no. 12 (December 1953), pp. 245–247.

—. "Wirtschafts- und Steuerpolitik: Grundsätze und Programm des DGB." Deutscher Gewerkschaftsbund, *Protokoll – 3 ordentlicher Bundeskongress, Frankfurt am Main, 4. bis 9. Oktober, 1954*. (Düsseldorf: DGB, n.d.), pp. 423–468.

—. "Zur Situation der Gewerkschaften im liberalkapitalistischen Staat." *Gewerkschaftliche Monatshefte*. Vol. 3, no. 8 (August 1952), pp. 464–468.

"Aktion für Auslese." *metall*. Vol. 30, no. 4 (February 28, 1978), p. 4.

"Aktuelle Stunde im Bundestag zur 'Lage im Arbeitskampf' vom 25. Mai 1984." *Gewerkschaftliche Monatshefte*. Vol. 35, no. 7 (July 1984), pp. 425–435.

Altmann, Norbert, and Fritz Böhle. "Qualifikation als Ziel – Qualifizierung als Problem." *Gewerkschaftliche Monatshefte*. Vol. 28, no. 5 (May 1977), pp. 310–318.

Altvater, Elmar. "Politische Überlegungen ein Jahr nach der Wende." *Leviathan*. Vol. 11, no. 4 (December 1983), pp. 580–599.

Altvater, Elmar, and Jürgen Hoffmann. Unpublished letter to Rudolf Hickel and Axel Zerdick. Berlin, April 30, 1980.

Altvater, Elmar, Jürgen Hoffmann, and Carlos Maya. "Konzentration als Ursache von Profitratendifferenzen? Eine Auseinandersetzung mit der These vom positiven Zusammenhang zwischen Konzentration und Profitraten im 'Memorandum.'" *WSI-Mitteilungen*. Vol. 33, no. 4 (April 1980), pp. 196–206.

"An Morgenthau erinnert." *Frankfurter Rundschau*, January 21, 1985.

"Änderungsabsichten der CDU/CSU–FDP–Koalition." *Der Gewerkschafter*, Vol. 33, no. 7–8 (July–August 1985), pp. 2–3.

"Angriff aus dem Weltall." *metall*. Vol. 30, no. 3 (February 13, 1978), pp. 7–10.

Apple, R. W., Jr. "British Unions Hunting for Path back to Glory." *New York Times*, January 22, 1985.

—. "Sharp Dip in Power and Influence Hampers Labor Unions in Europe." *New York Times*, January 20, 1985.

—. "West German Unions: An Atypical Success Story." *New York Times*, January 21, 1985.

"Die Arbeitgeber sagten nur: Nein–Nirgendwo ein Entgegenkommen." *metall*. Vol. 30, no. 4 (February 28, 1978), pp. 4–7.

"Arbeitslosenzahl auf höchstem Stand seit 1948." *Frankfurter Rundschau*, February 5, 1985.

Arendt, Walter, "Rechtsgrundlage und Parxis der Aussprerrung." *Gewerkschaftliche Umschau*. Vol. 29, no. 4 (July–August 1978), pp. 2–5.

"Argumente zur Tarifbewegung '78: Gründe und Hintergründe." *metall.* Vol. 30 no. 3 (February 13, 1978), p. 6.

"Attitude Towards Strikes." *DGB Report*, No. 2 (1969), p. 22.

"Auf Dreck muss geklotzt werden." *Frankfurter Rundschau*, April 25, 1979.

Augstein, Rudolph. "Zwischen Gruppeninteressen und Gemeinwohl." *Gewerkschaftliche Monatshefte.* Vol. 26, no. 5 (May 1975), pp. 266–267.

"Aus der Redaktion." *Gewerkschaftliche Monatshefte.* Vol. 26, no. 4 (April 1975), pp. 260–263.

"Aus SPD Sicht untragbar." *Der Spiegel*, Vol. 28, no. 9 (February 25, 1974).

"Aussperrung: Seit mehr als 100 Jahren das politische Druckmittel der Unternehmer gegen die Arbeiterbewegung." *metall*, Vol. 30, no. 6 (March 30, 1978), pp. 6–14.

"Ausstieg aus der Montanmitbestimmung?" *Frankfurter Rundschau*, June 6, 1980.

Bahl, Volker. "Lohnverhandlungssystem der Weimarer Republik–Von der Schlichtungsverordnung zum Ruhreisenstreik: Verbandsautonomie oder staatliche Verbandsgarantie?" *Gewerkschaftliche Monatshefte.* Vol. 29, no. 7 (July 1978), pp. 397–411.

Bahr, Hans-Eckehard. "Gewerkschaften und die Dritte Welt." *Gewerkschaftliche Monatshefte.* Vol. 26, no. 5 (May 1975), pp. 283–286.

Balduin, Siegfried. "Gewerkschaftliche Politik zur Einflussnahme auf Arbeitsbedingungen und Beschäftigung." *Gewerkschaftliche Monatshefte.* Vol. 28, no. 6 (June 1977), pp. 345–358.

——. "Humanisierung der Arbeit als gewerkschaftliche Aufgabe." *Gewerkschaftliche Monatshefte.* Vol. 25, no. 3 (March 1974), pp. 175–182.

Balduin, Siegfried, and Hermann Unterhinninghofen. "Zur Diskussion um ein Verbändegesetz." *WSI-Mitteilungen.* Vol. 30, no. 12 (December 1977), pp. 56–67.

Bamberg, Hans-Dieter, Hans-Jürgen Kröger and Reinhard Kuhlmann. "Arbeitswelt, Gewerkschaften und Hochschulen." *Gewerkschaftliche Monatshefte.* Vol. 28, no. 2 (February 1977), pp. 82–91.

Barnouin, Barbara. "Multinationale Banken und Weltwährungssystem – Einige Anmerkungen aus gewerkschaftlicher Sicht." *Gewerkschaftliche Monatshefte.* Vol. 25, no. 5 (May 1974), pp. 290–298.

"Bauen + Umweltschutz = Arbeitsplätze." *Der Grundstein.* Vol. 36, no. 2 (February 1985), pp. 12–13.

Beck, Werner. "Chemiefaserkrise erfordert Gegenmassnahmen." *Gewerkschaftliche Umschau.* Vol. 28, no. 6 (November–December 1977), pp. 28–29.

——. "Chemie wieder im Aufwind." *Gewerkschaftliche Umschau.* Vol. 29, no. 5 (September–October 1978), pp. 13–15.

"Der Begriff glatte Parität is irreführend." *Der Spiegel.* Vol. 27, no. 46 (November 12, 1973).

"Bei Daimler flexible Arbeitszeiten." *Frankfurter Rundschau*, February 15, 1985.

Beier, Gerhard. "Leninisten führten die Feder." *ÖTV-Magazin.* No. 3 (March 1979), pp. 33–37.

"Beirat tagte in Hannover." *Gewerkschaftliche Umschau.* Vol. 29, no. 2 (March–April 1978), p. 31.

"Ein beispielhafter Streit über Schadstoffe in Lebensmitteln." *Frankfurter Rundschau*, December 28, 1984.

Benthien, Dieter. "Die Kirche muss im Dorf bleiben." *Die Quelle*. Vol. 27, no. 10 (October 1976), pp. 395–396.

——. "Durchbruch geschafft – Tor zur 35-Stunden-Woche aufgestossen." *Die Quelle*. Vol. 35, no. 7/8 (July/August 1978), pp. 390–392.

Benz, Georg. "Geschlossen gegen soziale Demontage." *metall*. Vol. 30, no. 5 (March 10, 1978), p. 3.

Bergmann, Joachim, and Walther Müller-Jentsch. "The Federal Republic of Germany: Cooperative Unionism and Dual Bargaining System Challenged." Barkin, ed., *Worker Militancy*, pp. 235–276.

"Berichte aus der Praxis." *Gewerkschaftliche Monatshefte*. Vol. 25, no. 4 (April 1974), pp. 248–255.

"Berichte aus der Praxis." *Gewerkschaftliche Monatshefte*. Vol. 28, no. 10 (October 1977), pp. 664–672.

"Berichte aus der Praxis." *Gewerkschaftliche Monatshefte*. Vol. 26, no. 2 (February 1975), pp. 107–130.

"Berichte aus der Praxis." *Gewerkschaftliche Monatshefte*. Vol. 28, no. 5 (May 1977), pp. 329–343.

"Berichte aus der Praxis." *Gewerkschaftliche Monatshefte*. Vol. 26, no. 1 (January 1975), pp. 33–62.

"Berichte aus der Praxis." *Gewerkschaftliche Monatshefte*. Vol. 28, no. 6 (June 1977), pp. 390–407.

"Berichte: Der 11, ordentliche Gewerkschaftstag der IG Chemie-Papier-Keramik (IGCPK) vom 7. bis 13. September 1980 in Mannheim." *Gewerkschaftliche Monatshefte*. Vol. 31, no. 11 (November, 1980), pp. 757–763.

"Berichte: Jugendarbeitsschutz und drei Berichte zum Thema Mitbestimmung." *Gewerkschaftliche Monatshefte*. Vol. 28, no. 12 (December 1977), pp. 761–779.

"Berichte: Zur Gewerkschaftlichen Situation nach dem Mitbestimmungsgesetz 1976." *Gewerkschaftliche Monatshefte*. Vol. 28, no. 11 (November 1977), pp. 726–733.

"Betriebsratswahl 1975." *Gewerkschaftliche Monatshefte*. Vol. 26, no. 10 (October 1975), pp. 607–636.

"Betriebsratswahl '78." *metall*. Vol. 30, no. 5 (March 10, 1978), p. 11.

"Better Working Conditions from Collective Agreements." *DGB Report*. No. 1 (1978), p. 9.

Beykirch, Heinz. "Spontaneous Downing of Tools." *DGB Report*. No. 9 (1969), pp. 77–78.

Beyme, Klaus von. "Der Konflikt zwischen Reform und Verwaltung der Wirtschafts- und Sozialordnung." (Part 1). *Gewerkschaftliche Monatshefte*. Vol. 27, no. 7 (July 1976), pp. 386–395.

——. "Der Konflikt zwischen Reform und Verwaltung der Wirtschafts- und Sozialordnung." (Part 2). *Gewerkschaftliche Monatshefte*. Vol. 27, no. 8 (August 1976), pp. 457–466.

——. "Parteien und Gewerkschaften in vergleichender Perspektive." *Gewerkschaftliche Monatshefte*. Vol. 25, no. 4 (April 1974), pp. 217–224.

—. "Politische Entwicklungstendenzen seit 1972 und die Rolle der Gewerkschaften im politischen System der Bundesrepublik." *Gewerkschaftliche Monatshefte.* Vol. 26, no. 4 (April 1975), pp. 209–218.

—. "Politische und sozioökonomische Entwicklungen seit 1974 im Lichte gewerkschaftlicher Interessen." *Gewerkschaftliche Monatshefte.* Vol. 29, no. 3 (March 1978), pp. 130–137.

Beyme, Klaus von, and Ghita Ionescu. "The Politics of Employment in Germany and Great Britain." *Government and Opposition.* Vol. 12, no. 1 (1977), pp. 88–107.

Biedenkopf, Kurt H. "Perspektiven, Möglichkeiten und Grenzen gewerkschaftlicher Politik." *Gewerkschaftliche Monatshefte.* Vol. 27, no. 4 (April 1976), pp. 217–225.

"Bild von der Gewerkschaftsjugend hängt schief links." *Frankfurter Rundschau,* June 1, 1979.

Birkwald, Reimar. "Menschengerechte Arbeitswelt." In IG Metall (ed.), *Werktage werden besser,* pp. 95–100.

*Blick durch die Wirtschaft.* March 5, 1979.

Blüm, Norbert. "Einheitsgewerkschaft und christlich-demokratische Arbeitnehmer." *Gewerkschaftliche Monatshefte.* Vol. 25, no. 4 (April 1974), pp. 238–242.

Bobke, Manfred. "Arbeitsrecht im Arbeitskampf." *WSI-Mitteilungen.* Vol. 38, no. 2 (February 1985), pp. 57–63.

Böckenförde, Ernst-Wolfgang. "Die politische Funktion wirtschaftlichsozialer Verbände und Interessenträger in der sozialstaatlichen Demokratie: Ein Beitrag zum Problem der 'Regierbarkeit.'" *Der Staat.* Vol. 15, no. 4 (Fall 1976), pp. 457–483.

Bohle, Fritz, and Dieter Sauer. "Intensivierung der Arbeit und staatliche Sozialpolitik." *Leviathan.* Vol. 3, no. 1 (March 1975), pp. 49–83.

Böker, Karlheinz. "Immer weniger Arbeitskräfte in der Zellstoff- und Papierindustrie." *Gewerkschaftliche Umschau.* Vol. 29, no. 2 (March–April 1978), pp. 18–20.

"Bonn will den Streikparagraphen vorerst nicht antasten." *Frankfurter Allgemeine Zeitung,* August 16, 1985.

"Bonner Arbeitsmarktprogramm kommt an." *Süddeutsche Zeitung,* August 8, 1979.

Bourdon, Clinton, "Craft Unions and the Organization of Work in Construction." *European Studies Newsletter.* Vol. 7, no. 2 (November–December 1977); and Vol. 7, no. 3 (February 1978).

Breidenstein, Gerhard. "Arbeitsplätze werden exportiert." *Gewerkschaftliche Umschau.* Vol. 27, no. 2 (March–April 1976), p. 5.

—. "Führt 'internationale Arbeitsteilung' zu struktureller Arbeitslosigkeit?" *Gewerkschaftliche Monatshefte.* Vol. 26, no. 12 (December 1975), pp. 760–768.

Breit, Ernst. "Fortschritt gegen, ohne oder durch die Gewerkschaften." *Gewerkschaftliche Monatshefte.* Vol. 36, no. 1 (January 1985), pp. 1–18.

—. "Gemeinsam gegen eine Politik für wenige." *Gewerkschaftliche Monatshefte.* Vol. 36, no. 8 (August 1985), pp. 449–455.

"Breit: Kohl übt Klassenkampf von oben." *Frankfurter Rundschau,* May 2, 1985.

"Bremse für Brenner." *Der Spiegel.* Vol. 16, no. 2 (January 15, 1958).

Brenner, Otto, "Die Aufgaben unserer Gewerkschaft in der gegenwärtigen Situation." IG Metall, *Protokoll über den 3. ordentlichen Gewerkschaftstag der IG Metall, Hannover, 13. - 18. September, 1984.* Frankfurt am Main: IG Metall, 1950, pp. 268–287.

—. "Sicherheit und Fortschritt durch eine starke IG Metall." IG Metall, *Protokoll des 9. ordentlichen Gewerkschaftstages der IG Metall, München, 2. bis 7. September, 1968.* Frankfurt am Main: IG Metall, n.d., pp. 210–241.

Breuer, Stefan. "Politik und Recht im Prozess der Rationalisierung." *Leviathan.* Vol. 5, no. 1 (April 1977), pp. 53–99.

Briefs, Götz. "Gewerkschaften." *Handwörterbuch der Sozialwissenschaften.* Erwin V. Beckerath, ed., Vol. 4. Stuttgart: G. Fischer, 1959, pp. 545–561.

Briefs, Ulrich. "Investitionsboom – im Ausland." *Gewerkschaftliche Umschau.* Vol. 27, no. 4 (July–August 1976), pp. 2–3.

Brinkmann, Christian. "Steigt langfristig das Niveau der Arbeitslosigkeit?" *Gewerkschaftliche Monatshefte.* Vol. 25, no. 12 (December 1974), pp. 743–755.

"Broad Popular Recognition for German Trade Unions." *DGB Report.* No. 3 (1976), p. 12.

Brügmann, Wolf-Gunter, "IG Metall – von Fesseln befreit." *Frankfurter Rundschau,* March 17, 1981.

Brunner, Margot. "Aussperrung is rechtswidrig." *metall.* Vol. 30, no. 11 (June 5, 1978), pp. 15–16.

—. "Erste Klage gegen Aussperung gewonnen: Die Unternehmer in Annahmeverzug." *metall.* Vol. 30, no. 17 (August 23, 1978), p. 15.

—. "Gericht verurteilt die Aussperrung als Verstoss gegen das Grundgesetz: '... nicht gleiche Verhandlungschance.' " *metall.* Vol. 30, no. 18 (September 6, 1978), p. 16.

—. "Das Leiden mit den 'Leitenden.' " *metall.* Vol. 30, no. 1 (January 16, 1978), p. 16.

—. "Die Scharfmacher wollen den Kampf." *metall.* Vol. 30, no. 4 (February 28, 1978), pp. 1–2.

—. "Schlichtung ohne Hoffnung?" *metall.* Vol. 30, no. 3 (February 13, 1978), pp. 1–2.

—. "Sel-Konzern verstösst gegen das Gesetz. Darum: Wirtschaftsausschuss trat zurück." *metall.* Vol. 30, no. 11 (June 5, 1978), p. 16.

Buci-Glucksmann, Christine. "Sozialdemokratie und Keynesianischer Staat." *Prokla.* Vol. 12, no. 2 (1982), pp. 9–28.

Busch, Klaus. "Führt Kapitalexport zu Arbeitsplatzexport?" *WSI-Mitteilungen.* Vol. 32, no. 9 (September 1979), pp. 493–501.

Buschmann, Karl. "Probleme der internationalen Arbeitsteilung in der Textil- und Bekleidungsindustrie." *Gewerkschaftliche Monatshefte.* Vol. 29, no. 6 (June 1978), pp. 355–367.

"Chancen für die Schwarzen? – Hoffnung auf friedlichen Wandel nicht aufgeben." *metall.* Vol. 30, no. 2 (January 30, 1978), pp. 20–21.

"The Chemical Union Demands Monthly Wages for Industrial Workers." *DGB Report.* No. 5/6 (1972), p. 19.

"Co-determination 'No Substitute for Government.' " *DGB Report.* No. 2 (1977), p. 2.

"Considerable Reduction of the Agricultural Labor Force." *DGB Report*. No. 1/2 (1973), p. 13.

Daummann, Klaus. "Lage und Bewusstsein der Angehörigen des Öffentlichern Dienstes." *Gewerkschaftliche Monatshefte*. Vol. 26, no. 6 (June 1975), pp. 355–365.

"Denkbar eng." *Der Spiegel*. Vol. 28, no. 11 (March 11, 1974).

"DGB Against Exaggerated Work Demands." *DGB Report*. No. 1 (1979), p. 9.

"DGB – Aktionsprogramm '79." *Die Quelle*. Vol. 30, no. 7/8 (July/August 1979), pp. 389–395.

"DGB Demands Quick Concept on Migration Policy." *DGB Report*. No. 3 (1977), p. 2.

"DGB Employment Programme." *DGB Report*. No. 4 (1977), pp. 3–4.

"DGB on the Reform of the Law on Abortion." *DGB Report*. No. 5 (1973), p. 4.

"DGB Resolutions." *DGB Report*. No. 3 (1975), pp. 9–12.

"DGB Stance on Construction of Nuclear Power Stations." *DGB Report*. No. 1 (1978), p. 7.

"DGB Stand on Defense against Enemies of the Constitution." *DGB Report*. No. 4 (1977), pp. 4–5.

"DGB Unions Made Clean Sweep in Works' Councils Polls." *DGB Report*. No. 4 (1975), p. 8.

Diamant, Alfred. "Democratizing the Workplace: The Myth and Reality of Mitbestimmung in the Federal Republic of Germany." Paper presented at the APSA Annual Meeting, Chicago, September 1976.

"Dicke Brieftasche immer dicker." *metall*. Vol. 30, no. 1 (January 16, 1978), p. 10.

Dieckerhoff, Lutz. – Zur Betriebsratswahl 1978. "Richtige Wahl ist Gegenmacht." *metall*. Vol. 30, no. 4 (February 28, 1978), p. 3.

Dombois, Rainer. "Massenentlassungen bei VW: Individualisierung der Krise." *Leviathan*. Vol. 4, no. 12 (December 1976), pp. 432–464.

Donges, Jürgen B. "Die Welthandelsordnung am Scheidewege: Weitere Liberalisierung oder neuer Protektionismus?" *Europa Archiv*. Series 7 (April 10, 1978), pp. 197–204.

"Die 35-Stunden-Woche ist das nächste Ziel: Stern Interview mit DGB-Chef Ernst Breit." *Stern*. Vol. 38, no. 33 (August 8, 1985), pp. 76–79.

Drexel, Ingried, and Christopher Nuber. "Die berufliche Qualifizierung von Jungarbeitern im Spannungsfeld von Betriebs- und Arbeitnehmerinteressen." *Gewerkschaftliche Monatshefte*. Vol. 26, no. 9 (September 1975), pp. 559–566.

"Drohung des DGB." *Handelsblatt*, July 17, 1980.

Droucopoulos, Vassilis. "West German Expansionism." *New Left Review*. No. 105 (September–October 1977), pp. 92–96.

"Druckgewerbe sieht schwarz." *Frankfurter Rundschau*, February 18, 1981.

"Druckindustrie spürt nichts vom Aufschwung." *Frankfurter Rundschau*, June 14, 1983.

Düll, Klaus. "Gesellschaftliche Modernisierungspolitik durch neue Produktionskonzepte?" *WSI-Mitteilungen*. Vol. 38, no. 3 (March 1985), pp. 141–145.

Düll, Klaus, and Dieter Sauer. "Rationalisierung im öffentlichen Dienst." *Gewerkschaftliche Monatshefte*. Vol. 26, no. 2 (February 1975), pp. 97–106.

Edding, Friedrich. "Über die Zunkunft des dualen Systems der beruflichen Bildung." *Gewerkschaftliche Monatshefte*. Vol. 26, no. 5 (May 1975), pp. 296–300.

"Editorial: Gewerkschaftsbewegung am Ende?" *Prokla*. Vol. 14, no. 1 (Spring 1984), pp. 3–9.

"Eight Weeks Annual Holiday by 1980." *DGB Report*. No. 1–2 (1973), p. 12.

"Einigung der Koalitionspartner." *Handelsblatt*, May 17, 1979.

Eissegg, Dietrich. "Der Streik der Metallarbeiter im Unterwesergebiet 1974." In Otto Jacobi et al., *Gewerkschaften und Klassenkampf: Kritisches Jahrbuch 1974*.

Eliassen, Kjell A. "Politische Beteiligung und parteipolitische Bindung der Gewerkschaften in Westeuropa: ein Überblick." *Soziale Welt 25* (1974), pp. 71–90.

Elvers, Gerd. "Entscheidung oder Hängepartie: Aspekte des Arbeitskampfes 1984." *Gewerkschaftliche Monatshefte*. Vol. 35, no. 11 (November 1984), pp. 683–689.

"Das Ende einer Karriere." *metall*. Vol. 30, no. 4 (February 28, 1978), pp. 9–12 and cover story.

"Energieversorgung und Beschäftigung." *metall*. Vol. 30, no. 11 (June 5, 1978), p. 8.

"Epochaler Vorgang." *Der Spiegel*. Vol. 28, no. 5 (January 28, 1974).

Eppler, Erhard. "Politischen Prioritäten – nicht 'Sachzwängen' folgen!" *Gewerkschaftliche Monatshefte*. Vol. 28, no. 10 (October 1977), pp. 643–636.

Erd, Rainer, "Der Kampf um die 6 vor dem Komma." In Rainer Duhm and Ulrich Mückenberger eds., *Arbeitskampf im Krisenalltag*, pp. 11–20.

—. "Neues Schlichtungsabkommen: Konzentration und Zentralisierung der Tarifverhandlungen in der Metallindustrie." *express*. No. 12 (December 1979), p. 6.

Erd, Rainer, and Christoph Scherrer. "Unions – Caught between Structural Competition and Temporary Solidarity: A Critique of Contemporary Marxist Analysis of Trade Unions in Germany." *British Journal of Industrial Relations*. Vol. 23, no. 1 (March 1985), pp. 115–131.

Erd, Rainer, and Rainer Kalbitz. "Gewerkschaften und Arbeitsrecht." *Gewerkschaftliche Monatshefte*. Vol. 27, no. 3 (March 1976), pp. 143–154.

"Erst Posten erobern und dann gegen Kritik abschotten." Documentation section of *Frankfurter Rundschau*, May 5 and May 7, 1979.

Esslinger, Heinz. "Bedenkliche Entwicklung." *Gewerkschaftliche Umschau*. Vol. 29, no. 3 (May–June 1978), p. 1.

—. "Gesundheitsschädlich – giftig – krebserregend." *Gewerkschaftliche Umschau*. Vol. 28, no. 4 (July–August 1977), pp. 14–15.

"Eure Bruderhand." *Der Spiegel*. Vol. 10, no. 4 (January 25, 1956), pp. 17–18.

"European Unions Put Demands for Full Employment Action." *DGB Report*. No. 1 (1978), p. 4.

Evans, J. Richard. "Labor History in the Federal Republic of Germany." *International Labor and Working Class History*. No. 10 (November 1976), pp. 20–24.

"Every Third Occupier is an Owner-Occupier." *DGB Report*. No. 3–4 (1972), pp. 8–9.

Fabian, Walter, "Zur gewerkschaftlichen Organisierung der 'Urheber Wort.'" *Gewerkschaftliche Monatshefte*. Vol. 26, no. 5 (May 1975), pp. 300–303.

"Fall Mannesmann soll kein Reinfall werden." *Frankfurter Rundschau*, July 2, 1980.

"Fast einen Tobsuchtsanfall." *Der Spiegel*. Vol. 29, no. 10 (March 3, 1975).

"FDP will die Zustimmung verweigern." *Frankfurter Rundschau*, June 24, 1980.

Feist, Ursula, Hubert Krieger and Pavel Uttiz. "Das Wahlverhalten bei der Bundestagswahl 1983." *Gewerkschaftliche Monatshefte*. Vol. 34, no. 7 (July 1983), pp. 428–436.

Feist, Ursula, and Klaus Liepelt. "Die Wahl zum Machtwechsel: Neuformierung der Wählerschaft oder Wählerkoalition aus Hoffnung – Eine Analyse der Bundestagswahl vom 6. März 1983." *Journal für Sozialforschung*. Vol. 23, no. 3 (Summer 1983), pp. 83–104.

Feldengut, Karl. "Gewerkschaftspolitik – Die europäische Gewerkschaftsbewegung und die Europäische Gemeinschaft." *Gewerkschaftliche Monatshefte*. Vol. 26, no. 8 (August 1975), pp. 496–502.

Ferlemann, Erwin. "Bilaz der Arbeitskampfes 1984 – Aus der Sicht der IG Druck und Papier." *Gewerkschaftliche Monatshefte*. Vol. 35, no. 11 (November 1984), pp. 671–683.

Fetscher, Iring. "Die Sonderstellung der Gewerkschaften im sozialen Rechtsstaat." *Gewerkschaftliche Monatshefte*. Vol. 26, no. 5 (May 1975), pp. 268–270.

Flechtheim, Ossip K. "Gewerkschaftliche Globalstrategie und futurologische Politik sind nötig." *Gewerkschaftliche Monatshefte*. Vol. 26, no. 5 (May 1975), pp. 287–291.

Fonck, Karl-Heinz. "Abgase gefährlicher als vermutet." *metall*. Vol. 30, no. 6 (March 30, 1978), p. 12.

—. "Erdgas gegen Energie-Lücken– 'Raumschiff Erde' droht Überbevölkerung." *metall*. Vol. 30, no. 4 (February 28, 1978), p. 17.

—. "Schätze im Müll." *metall*. Vol. 30, no. 5 (March 10, 1978), p. 19.

—. "Wasserversorgung: Pläne mit grossen Rohren." *metall*. Vol. 30, no. 1 (January 16, 1978), p. 19.

"Fragwürdige Methoden." *Der Spiegel*. Vol. 28, no. 14 (April 1, 1974).

Fritze, Walter. "Humanisierung der Arbeit und technischer Fortschritt." *Die Quelle*. Vol. 29, no. 4 (April 1978), pp. 208–209.

Fröbel, Folker, Jürgen Heinrichs and Otto Kreye. "The Tendency Towards a New International Division of Labor: The Utilization of a World-wide Labor Force for Manufacturing Oriented to the World Market." *Review*. Vol. 1, no. 1 (Summer 1977), pp. 73–88.

—. "Die neue internationale Arbeitsteilung: Ursachen, Erscheinungsformen, Auswirkungen." *Gewerkschaftliche Monatshefte*. Vol. 29, no. 1 (January 1978), pp. 41–54.

"Für alle etwas." *Frankfurter Allgemeine Zeitung*, March 2, 1979.

"Gar nicht vereinbart." *Der Spiegel*. Vol. 28, no. 6 (February 4, 1974).

"Das Gefährliche an Detlef." *Wirtschaftswoche 12*, March 17, 1978.

Geiss, Imanuel. "Gewerkschaften und Entwicklungsländer." *Gewerkschaftliche Monatshefte*. Vol. 26, no. 5 (May 1975), pp. 292–295.

"Gemeinsame Erklärung des DGB, der IG Metall und IG Druck." *Die Neue*, June 13, 1980.

"Genscher droht mit Koalitionsbruch." *Frankfurter Rundschau*, August 15, 1980.

Gerken, Erika. "Hessen: Die heimliche Bundestagswahl." *metall*. Vol. 30, no. 18 (September 6, 1978), pp. 11–14

Gerlach, Gerhard. "Neuere tarifpolitische Strategien der Gewerkschaften in der BRD zur Sicherung von Arbeitsplätzen und Besitzständen." *WSI-Mitteilungen*. Vol. 32, no. 4 (April 1979), pp. 221–227.

—. "Tarifbewegungen, Arbeitskämpfe und tarifvertragliche Arbeitsbedingungen im Jahre 1978." *WSI-Mitteilungen*. Vol. 32, no. 3 (March 1979), pp. 132–144.

—. "Veränderung der Arbeitsbedingungen durch 'neue Arbeitsstrukturen' in der Produktion." *Gewerkschaftliche Monatshefte*. Vol. 28, no. 6 (June 1977), pp. 381–390.

"German Entrepreneurs Are Paying Least in Social Benefits." *DGB Report*. No. 9–10 (1972), p. 12.

German Information Center, New York. *Relay from Bonn: The Week in Germany*. February 6, 1981.

"German Workers Strike Less Often." *DGB Report*. No. 7–8 (1972), p. 16.

"Germany, The Model Nation?" *Newsweek* (European edition), September 27, 1976.

"Gern behilflich." *Der Spiegel*. Vol. 32, no. 42 (October 16, 1978).

"Gesetzentwurf der Fraktion DIE GRÜNEN IM BUNDESTAG zum Verbot der Aussperrung vom 18. Juni 1984." *Gewerkschaftliche Monatshefte*. Vol. 35, no. 7 (July 1984), pp. 442–445.

"Gewerkschaften beraten über Abwehrmassnahmen." *Frankfurter Allgemeine Zeitung*, July 17, 1980.

"Gewerkschaften: Die zwei auf neuem Kurs." *Der Spiegel*. Vol. 38, no. 29 (July 16, 1984).

"Der Gewerkschaftstag hat beschlossen ..." *Gewerkschaftliche Umschau*. Vol. 27, no. 6 (November–December 1976), pp. 4–15.

"Gewisse Unruhe." *Der Spiegel*. Vol. 20, no. 19 (May 16, 1966).

Glastetter, Werner. "Die aussenwirtschaftliche Verflechtung der Bundesrepublik Deutschland – Ein Strukturproblem." *Gewerkschaftliche Monatshefte*. Vol. 25, no. 2 (February 1974), pp. 114–123.

Glotz, Peter. "Zur aktuellen Situation der SPD." *Association for the Study of German Politics (ASGP) Journal*. No. 9 (Augumn 1984), pp. 9–21.

Götz, Christian. "Die Hoffnungen, auf eine 'neue Gesellschaft' erfüllten sich nicht – 25 Jahre DGB: Anmerkungen zu einem 'Silbernen Jubiläum.'" *Gewerkschaftliche Monatshefte*. Vol. 25, no. 10 (October 1974), pp. 630–640.

Grebing, Helga. "Arbeiterbewegung und Gewalt." *Gewerkschaftliche Monatshefte*. Vol. 29, no. 2 (February 1978), pp. 65–77.

—. "Gewerkschaften als Ordnungsfaktor oder Gegenmacht?" *Gewerkschaftliche Umschau*. Vol. 24, no. 7 (July 1973), pp. 393–400.

—. "Reformstrategien in kapitalistischen Industriegesellschaften: Ein Literaturbericht (Part I)." *Gewerkschaftliche Umschau.* Vol. 26, no. 5 (May 1975), pp. 316–322.

—. "Reformstrategien in kapitalistischen Industriegesellschaften: Ein Literaturbericht (Part II)." *Gewerkschaftliche Umschau.* Vol. 26, no. 6 (June 1975), pp. 338–345.

"Grossbanken and die Kette?" *metall.* Vol. 30, no. 17 (August 23, 1978), p. 8.

Grosse, Franz. "Die Gewerkschaften in den westlichen Demokratien." *Gewerkschaftliche Monatshefte.* Vol. 3, no. 28 (August 1952), pp. 450–456.

Guha, Anton-Andreas. "Auf dem Weg in den Überwachungsstaat?" *metall.* Vol. 30, no. 16 (August 9, 1978), pp. 11–13.

—. "Aufgabe des Jahrtausends." *Gewerkschaftliche Umschau.* Vol. 28, no. 4 (July–August 1977), pp. 21–23.

Gülden, Klaus, and Horst Peter, "VW: Krisenlösung durch Entlassungen." Otto Jacobi, Walther Müller-Jentsch and Eberhard Schmidt (eds.), *Gewerkschaften und Klassenkampf: Kritisches Jahrbuch '75.* Frankfurt am Main: Fischer Verlag, 1975.

Haasis, Helmut G. "Kritik und Alternative gewerkschaftlicher Tarifpolitik am Beispiel der Industriegewerkschaft Druck und Papier." In Paul Mattick, ed., *Beiträge zur Kritik des Geldes.* Frankfurt am Main: Suhrkamp, 1976.

"Hafenarbeiter: 'Runde 7' erstreikt." *metall.* Vol. 30, no. 2 (January 30, 1978), p. 4.

Hamilton, Richard F. "Affluence and the Worker: The West German Case." *American Journal of Sociology.* September 1965, pp. 144–152.

Harten, Hans-Christian. "Entwicklungstendenzen der Berufsbildungspolitik während der Arbeitsmarktkrise." *Gewerkschaftliche Monatshefte.* Vol. 29, no. 3 (March 1978), pp. 138–149.

Hartfiel, Günter. "Die Entwicklung der Rolle und des Selbstverständnisses der Angestellten." *Gewerkschaftliche Monatshefte.* Vol. 25, no. 9 (September 1974), pp. 540–548.

Hartmann, Heinz. "Codetermination in West Germany." *Industrial Relations.* Vol. 9, no. 2 (February 1970), pp. 137–147.

—. "Codetermination Today and Tomorrow." *British Journal of Industrial Relations.* Vol. 13, no. 1 (March 1975), pp. 54–64.

—. "Managerial Employees – New Participants in Industrial Relations." *British Journal of Industrial Relations.* Vol. 12, no. 2 (July 1974), pp. 268–281.

Hartwich, Hans-Hermann. "Gewerkschaften und Parteien – Die aktuellen Probleme im Licht politikwissenschaftlicher Untersuchungen und Konzeptionen." *Gewerkschaftliche Monatshefte.* Vol. 25, no. 4 (April 1974), pp. 225–238.

—. "Die rechtspolitische Entwicklung mitgestalten." *Gewerkschaftliche Monatshefte.* Vol. 26, no. 5 (May 1975), pp. 304–308.

Hauenschild, Karl. "Energie, Wachstum und Beschäftigung: Bessere Prognosen sind notwendig." *Gewerkschaftliche Monatshefte.* Vol. 28, no. 10 (October 1977), pp. 619–622.

—. "Es geht auch um Rohstoffe." *Gewerkschaftliche Umschau.* Vol. 28, no. 6 (November–December 1977), p. 21.

—. "Wie die Gewerkschaften die Rolle der Unternehmer sehen." *Gewerkschaftliche Umschau*. Vol. 27, no. 5 (September–October 1976), pp. 8–10

Haupt, Heinz-Gerhard, and Hans-Josef Steinberg. "Tendances de l'histoire ouvrière en République fédérale allemande" *Le Mouvement Social*. No. 100 (July–September 1977), pp. 133–141.

Heinrichs, Franz. "Neues Leben auf den Halden?" *metall*. Vol. 31, no. 11 (May 30, 1979). pp. 6–7

Heiss, Martin. "Tabu Katalog fügt der Allgemeinheit Schaden zu." *Die Quelle*. Vol. 30, no. 2 (February 1979), pp. 93–94.

Helfert, Mario. "Rationalisierung, Beschäftigung, Wirtschaftspolitik." *Gewerkschaftliche Monatshefte*. Vol. 28, no. 7 (July 1977), pp. 429–438.

"Helmut Schmidt: Asserting Germany's New Leadership." *The New York Times Magazine*, September 21, 1980.

"Helmut Schmidt dankt den Gewerkschaften." *Die Quelle*. Vol. 28, no. 1 (January 1977), p. 9.

Hemmer, Hans-O., and Ulrich Borsdorf. "'Gewerkschaftsstaat' – Zur Vorgeschichte eines aktuellen Schlagworts." *Gewerkschaftliche Monatshefte*. Vol. 25, no. 19 (October 1974), pp. 640–653.

Henninges, Hasso von. "Facharbeiter im Wandel." *Gewerkschaftliche Umschau*. Vol. 28, no. 5 (September–October 1977), pp. 8–11.

Hensche, Detlef. "Works Councils and Entrepreneurial Co-determination." *DGB Report*. No. 4 (1975), pp. 2–5.

Henschel, Rudolf. "Arbeitslosigkeit: Folge einseitig quantitativ orientierter Wachstumspolitik." *WSI-Mitteilungen*. Vol. 33, no. 4 (April 1980), pp. 206–216.

—. "Arbeitslosigkeit – Folge unbewältigter Strukturänderungen." *Die Quelle*. Vol. 29, no. 2 (February 1978), pp. 75–77.

—. "Arbeitslosigkeit – Konjunkturstörung oder Strukturkrise?" *Gewerkschaftliche Monatshefte*. Vol. 28, no. 12 (December 1977), pp. 742–750.

—. "Eine Problemskizze aus gewerkschaftlicher Sicht." Unpublished manuscript, May 4, 1979.

—. "Die gewerkschaftliche Kritik am Memorandum '79." *Gerwerkschaftliche Monatshefte*. Vol. 31, no. 2 (February 1980), pp. 109–116.

—. "Memorandum '80 is eine gute Grundlage für die weitere Diskussion." *Die Quelle*. Vol. 30, no. 6 (June 1980), pp. 332–333.

Hesselbach, Walter. "Labor Market Needs Long Term Investment Programme." *DGB Report*. No. 1–2 (1977), pp. 19–20.

Hickel, Rudolf, "Kein Kraftakt." *metall*. Vol. 30, no. 16 (August 9, 1978), pp. 6–7.

"'Hier wird Geschichte gefälscht' – Kritik aus der ÖTV an Historikern aus Marburg." *Frankfurter Allgemeine Zeitung*, April 10, 1979.

Hildebrand, Eckart. "Der Tarifkampf in der metallverarbeitenden Industrie, 1978." Otto Jacobi, Walther Müller-Jentsch and Eberhard Schmidt (eds.), *Arbeiterinteressen gegen Sozialpartnerschaft – Kritisches Gewerkschaftsjahrbuch 1978/79*.

"Hilfe für Regionen mit mehr als sechs Prozent Arbeitslosen." *Frankfurter Rundschau*, June 17, 1979.

Hillgärtner, Helmut. "Schichtarbeit." *metall*. Vol. 30, no. 21 (October 18, 1978), pp. 6–7.

"Hinter 'Gesprächspartnerschaft' verschanzt." *Frankfurter Allgemeine Zeitung*, March 27, 1985.

Hirche, Kurt. "Gewerkschafter im siebten deutschen Bundestag." *Gewerkschaftliche Monatshefte*. Vol. 24, no. 2 (February 1973), pp. 83–90.

"Höchster Stand seit dem Kriegsende." *metall*. Vol. 30, no. 2 (January 20, 1978), p. 15.

Hofbauer, Hans. "Ausgewählte Daten zur Entwicklung und Struktur der Angestellten." *Gewerkschaftliche Monatshefte*. Vol. 25, no. 9 (September 1974), pp. 528–539.

Hoffmann, Jürgen. "'Amerikanisierung' der deutschen Gewerkschaftsbewegung? Probleme der gewerkschaftlichen Politik in der Bundesrepublik unter den Bedingungen des wirtschaftlichen Strukturwandels." *Gewerkschaftliche Monatshefte*. Vol. 32, no. 7 (July 1981), pp. 418–433.

—. "Einheitsgewerkschaft oder 'korporatistische Blockbildung'? Probleme einer solidarischen Interessenvertretungspolitik in der ökonomischen Krise der Bundesrepublik." *Prokla*. Vol. 11, no. 2 (Summer 1981), pp. 6–26.

—. "Ökonomische und gesellschaftliche Restrukturierungsprozesse in der Krise und gewerkschaftliche Politik." Unpublished paper, n.p., n.d.

Hoffmann, Reinhard. "Entwicklungstendenzen zur Rolle der Gewerkschaften im öffentlichen Dienst." *Gewerkschaftliche Monatshefte*. Vol. 26, no. 2 (February 1975), pp. 85–96.

"Hohe Wachstumsraten sind kein Ziel an sich." *Frankfurter Rundschau*, May 2, 1985.

Höhnen, Wilfried. "Beschäftigungssichernde Finanzpolitik: Konzepte und Probleme." *Gewerkschaftliche Monatshefte*. Vol. 29, no. 1 (January 1978), pp. 18–28.

—. "Mehr Arbeitsplätze durch öffentliche Investitionen." *Gewerkschaftliche Umschau*. Vol. 28, no. 2 (March–April 1977), pp. 10–11.

Holländer, Franz, and Dieter Schmidt. "Kooperation als Gegenstrategie." *Gewerkschaftliche Monatshefte*. Vol. 28, no. 2 (February 1977), pp. 75–82.

Hönerhoff, Dieter. "Gefahren durch Rationalisierung." *Gewerkschaftliche Umschau*. Vol. 29, no. 5 (September–October 1978), pp. 8–9.

Höpner, Thomas. "Kooperationsbeziehungen zwischen Hochschulen und der Industrie." *Gewerkschaftliche Umschau*. Vol. 28, no. 2 (February 1977), pp. 92–100.

Hoss, Dietrich. "Zum Verhältnis von gewerkschaftlichem Kampf und Sozialdemokratie: Der Metallarbeiterstreik in Baden-Württemberg 1971." In Rainer Deppe, Richard Herding and Dietrich Hoss, *Sozialdemokratie und Klassenkonflikte: Metallarbeiterstreik – Betriebskonflikt – Mieterkampf*.

"Humanising Society – A Trade Union Task." *DGB Report*. No. 3 (1977), pp. 6–8.

"IG Bau sieht keine Spaltung." *Frankfurter Rundschau*, September 3, 1984.

"IG Chemie Vorstand möchte umstrittene Praxis zementieren." *Frankfurter Rundschau*, February 20, 1979.

IG Metall. "Streik-Nachrichten." December 9, 1971.

"IG Metall-Jugend will Härte." *Frankfurter Rundschau*, January 3, 1980.

"IG Metall rügt andere Gewerkschaften im DGB." *Frankfurter Rundschau*, August 31, 1984.

"IG Metall will Montanmitbestimmung nicht ausmerzen lassen." *Frankfurter Rundschau*, June 18, 1980.

"Die IG Metall will nötigenfalls kämpfen." *Handelsblatt*, July 4/5, 1980.

"IG Metall wirft DGB-Bundesjugendschule Diffamierung vor." *Frankfurter Rundschau*, January 4, 1980.

"Im Namen des Volkes." *Das Mitbestimmungsgespräch*. Vol. 25, no. 3 (March 1979), pp. 63–86.

"Industrie-Giganten wachsen immer schneller." *metall*. Vol. 30, no. 16 (August 9, 1978), p. 8.

"Industrie kommt voran." *Gewerkschaftliche Umschau*. Vol. 27, no. 5 (September–October 1976), p. 40.

"Informieren staat spekulieren." *metall*. Vol. 30, no. 1 (January 16, 1978), pp. 6–7.

"Interview mit Hensche." *Der Spiegel*. Vol. 32, no. 25 (June 19, 1978).

Jacobi, Otto. "Über Gewerkschaften und Krise." *Leviathan*. Vol. 12, no. 2 (April 1984), pp. 238–259.

Jacobi, Otto, and Walther Müller-Jentsch. "Gewerkschaftliche Tarifpolitik in der Wirtschaftskrise." In Rainer Duhm and Ulrich Mückenberger (eds.), *Arbeitskampf im Krisenalltag: Wie man sich wehrt und warum*.

Jaeggi, Urs. "Die Gewerkschaft zwischen Theorie und Praxis." *Gewerkschaftliche Monatshefte*. Vol. 26, no. 5 (May 1975), pp. 271–274.

Jansen, Hans. "Arbeitgeberstrategie: Minderung der Realeinkommen." *Der Gewerkschafter*. Vol. 29, no. 1 (January 1981), p. 4.

——. "Die Fronten werden härter: Tarifbewegung 1981 im Rückblick." *Der Gewerkschafter*. Vol. 29, no. 7 (July 1981), pp. 4–5.

——. "Unsere Aktionen gehen weiter." *Der Gewerkschafter*. Vol. 29, no. 4 (April 1981), p. 2.

——. "Unsere Handlungsmöglichkeiten erweitert." *Der Gewerkschafter*. Vol. 27, no. 12 (December 1979), p. 1.

Janzen, Karl-Heinz. "Arbeitgeber missbrauchen den Juristentag: Zu durchsichtig und zu plump." *metall*. Vol. 30, no. 20 (October 4, 1978), p. 8.

——. "Aussperrung – Klassenkampf von oben oder legales Arbeitskampfmittel?" *Der Gewerkschafter*. Vol. 26, no. 9 (September 1978), pp. 21–28.

——. "Gerichte müssen Problem erkennen." *metall*. Vol. 26, no. 16 (August 9, 1978), p. 3.

"Jetzt kommt's zum Schwur." *Der Spiegel*. Vol. 28, no. 9 (February 25, 1974).

Johannson, Kurt. "Anpassung als Prinzip." *Gewerkschaftliche Monatshefte*. Vol. 28, no. 5 (May 1977), pp. 302–309.

Judith, Rudolf. "Montanmitbestimmung in Gefahr." Speech presented at IG Metall's special "Mannesmann Conference," Dortmund, July 3, 1980.

Jung, Volker. "Der neue Europäische Gewerkschaftsbund." *Gewerkschaftliche Monatshefte*. Vol. 24, no. 4 (April 1973), pp. 206–217.

Kalmbach, Peter. "Rationalisierung, neue Technologien, und Beschäftigung." *Gewerkschaftliche Monatshefte*. Vol. 29, no. 8 (August 1978), pp. 455–467.

"Kampf gegen Aussperrung geht bis zum Verbot weiter." *Welt der Arbeit,* June 12, 1980.

"Kampf um Arbeitsplätze-Beispiel Hamburg: Beachtliche Erfolge in der Krise." *metall.* Vol. 30, no. 3 (February 13, 1978), p. 15.

"Kampf um Teewasser organisieren; Lenin: Mit vielen kniffen an die Macht." *Einheit,* May 1, 1979.

Kassler, Erhard. "Stationen zu einem ungeliebten Gesetz." *Das Mitbestimmungsgespräch.* January 1976, p. 4.

"Keine industriefeindliche Politik mit den Gewerkschaften." *Die Quelle.* Vol. 36, no. 2 (February 1985), pp. 67–68.

Kern, Horst, and Michael Schumann. "Das Ende der Arbeitsteilung? – Eine Herausforderung für die Gewerkschaften." *Gewerkschaftliche Monatshefte.* Vol. 36, no. 1 (January 1985), pp. 27–38.

Kerr, Clark. "The Trade Union Movement and the Redistribution of Power in Postwar Germany." *Quarterly Journal of Economics.* Vol. 68, no. 4 (November 1954), pp. 535–564.

Kirchheimer, Otto. "The Transformation of the Western European Party Systems." In Joseph LaPolambra and Myron Weiner, eds., *Political Parties and Political Development.* Princeton, NJ: Princeton University Press, 1966.

Kittner, Michael. "Parität im Arbeitskampf? Überlegungen zur Forderung nach dem Verbot der Aussperrung." *Gewerkschaftliche Monatshefte.* Vol. 24, no. 2 (February 1973), pp. 91–104.

—. "Zur verfassungsrechtlichen Zukunft von Reformpolitik, Mitbestimmung und Gewerkschaftsfreiheit." *Gewerkschaftliche Monatshefte.* Vol. 30, no. 6 (June 1979), pp. 321–342.

Klauder, Wolfgang, and Peter Schnur. "Mögliche Auswirkungen der letzten Rezession auf die Arbeitsmarktentwicklung bis 1990." *Gewerkschaftliche Monatshefte.* Vol. 27, no. 12 (December 1976), pp. 738–746.

Klotten, Norbert, Karl-Heinz Ketterer and Rainer Vollmer. "The Political and Social Factors of Germany's Stabilization Performance." Paper presented for the Brookings Project on the Politics and Sociology of Global Inflation, 1980.

Kluncker, Heinz. "Energiepolitik – integrieter Bestandteil der Gesellschaftspolitik." *Gewerkschaftliche Monatshefte.* Vol. 28, no. 10 (October 1977), pp. 612–616.

Knödler-Bunte, Eberhard. "Strukturwandel des kapitalistischen Widerspruchszusammenhangs und proletarische Organisation." *Gewerkschaftliche Monatshefte.* Vol. 24, no. 8 (August 1973), pp. 295–506; and Vol. 24, no. 11 (November 1973), pp. 706–711.

"Koalitionsstreit über Mitbestimmung verschärft." *Süddeutsche Zeitung,* June 28–29, 1980.

Koch, Egmont R., and Fritz Vahrenholt. "Gift im Griff? Die unterschätzten Risiken der Chemischen Industrie." *Gewerkschaftliche Umschau.* Vol. 29, no. 5 (September–October 1978), pp. 18–23.

Kohl, Helmut. "Die Stellung der Gewerkschaften in Staat und Gesellschaft." *Gewerkschaftliche Monatshefte.* Vol. 25, no. 19 (October 1974), pp. 621–629.

Köhler, Otto. "Dr. Rebmann, übernehmen Sie!" *metall.* Vol. 30, no. 19 (September 20, 1978), pp. 6–7.

"Kommunisten an 'Knotenpunkten' in der DGB-Jugend fest verankert? Die DGB-Bundesjugendschule warnt vor DKP-Einflüssen." *Einheit*, April 1, 1979.

"Kommunistische Gewerkschaftspolitik in der Weimarer Republik." *ÖTV-Magazin*. No. 4 (April 1979), pp. 39–42.

"Krebsgefahr durch Asbest und Glasfasern." *Gewerkschaftliche Umschau*. Vol. 27, no. 3 (May–June 1976), pp. 10–12.

Krüper, Manfred. "Beschäftigung unabhängig von Lohnhöhe." *Gewerkschaftliche Umschau*. Vol. 27, no. 1 (January–February 1976), pp. 4–6.

—. "Chancen und Risiken von auslandsinvestitioner." *Gewerkschaftliche Umschau*. Vol. 29, no. 5 (September–October 1978), pp. 2–5.

—. "Chemie im Aufschwung." *Gewerkschaftliche Umschau*. Vol. 27, no. 2 (March–April 1976), pp. 2–3.

—. "Gefährdet der technische Fortschritt die Arbeitsplätze?" *Gewerkschaftliche Umschau*. Vol. 29, no. 3 (May–June 1978), pp. 2–4.

—. "Kräftiges Lohnplus-notwendig und möglich." *Gewerkschaftliche Umschau*. Vol. 28, no. 2 (March–April 1977), pp. 2–4.

—. "Lohnkostenentwicklung beeinträchtigt Wettbewerbsfähigkeit der Chemie nicht." *Gewerkschaftliche Umschau*. Vol. 28, no. 4 (July–August 1977), pp. 2–3.

—. "Muster für einen Branchenfonds." *Gewerkschaftliche Umschau*. Vol. 29, no. 6 (November–December 1978).

—. "Ohne Arbeitszeitverkürzung geht es nicht." *Gewerkschaftliche Umschau*. Vol. 28, no. 5 (September–October 1977), pp. 4–6.

—. "Streit in der Mineralölindustrie." *Gewerkschaftliche Umschau*. Vol. 29, no. 1 (January–February 1978), pp. 26–29.

Kühn, Heinz. "Zum Verhältnis zwischen der Sozialdemokratischen Partei und den Gewerkschaften." *Gewerkschaftliche Monatshefte*. Vol. 25, no. 10 (October 1974), pp. 614–620.

Kühne, Karl. "Bilanz der ersten Nachkriegsdepression in der westlichen Industriewelt." *Gewerkschaftliche Monatshefte*. Vol. 26, no. 12 (December 1975), pp. 744–759.

—. "Blutarmer Aufschwung im Schatten neuer Rezessionsdrohung." *Gewerkschaftliche Monatshefte*. Vol. 27, no. 12 (December 1976), pp. 713–728.

—. "Eurokommunismus – Ursprünge, Wirtschaftspolitik und Rolle der Gewerkschaften." *Gewerkschaftliche Monatshefte*. Vol. 28, no. 9 (September 1977), pp. 545–557.

—. "Minirezession oder Depressionsrückfall." *Gewerkschaftliche Monatshefte*. Vol. 29, no. 1 (January–February 1978), pp. 55–62.

—. "Weltwirtschaft in Sturmzeiten." *Gewerkschaftliche Monatshefte*. Vol. 25, no. 12 (December 1974), pp. 755–771.

Küller, Hans-Detlev. "Betriebliche Vermögenspolitik als Element unternehmerischer Strategie." *Gewerkschaftliche Monatshefte*. Vol. 28, no. 5 (May 1977), pp. 319–328.

Kunzmann, Alfred. "Wie sicher sind die Arbeitsplätze in der feinkeramischen Industrie?" *Gewerkschaftliche Umschau*. Vol. 28, no. 2 (March–April 1977), pp. 26–27.

Kurz-Scherf, Ingrid. "Ergebnisse und Tendenzen der Tarifrunde 1984." *WSI-Mitteilungen.* Vol. 38, no. 3 (March 1985), pp. 121–135.

—. "Tarifliche Arbeitszeit in Bewegung." *WSI-Mitteilungen.* Vol. 37, no. 9 (September 1984), pp. 513–526.

Lahner, Manfred, and Regina Grabiszewski. "Auswirkungen technischer Änderungen in der Druckerei- und Vervielfältigungsindustrie." *Mitteilungen aus der Arbeitsmarkt- und Berufsforschung.* No. 4, 1977.

Lahnstein, Manfred. "Über die Währungsunion zur Wirtschaftsunion?" *Europa Archiv.* Series 9. May 10, 1978, pp. 263–270.

Lappas, Alfons. "Zur europäischen Gewerkschaftspolitik." *Gewerkschaftliche Monatshefte.* Vol. 26, no. 8 (August 1975), pp. 457–460.

"Das lassen wir uns nicht abhandeln." *Der Spiegel.* Vol. 24, no. 6 (February 2, 1970).

"Die Leber-Party." *Der Spiegel.* Vol. 17, no. 13 (March 27, 1963).

Lecher, Wolfgang. "Gewerkschaften in Europa: Zwischen Resignation und Widerstand." *Aus Politik und Zeitgeschichte* in *Das Parliament,* December 22, 1984, pp. 29–46.

—. "Der 'Neue Arbeiter' – Differenzierung oder Vereinheitlichung der Arbeitnehmerschaft." *Gewerkschaftliche Monatshefte.* Vol. 25, no. 9 (September 1974), pp. 557–560.

—. Review of "Steurungssysteme des Arbeitsmarktes – Vergleich von Frankreich, Grossbritannien, Schweden, DDR und Sowjetunion mit der Bundesrepublik Deutschland," by Gunther Schmid. *Gewerkschaftliche Monatshefte.* Vol. 28, no. 7 (July 1977), p. 469.

—. "Überleben in einer veränderten Welt." *Die Zeit.* May 3, 1985.

Leminsky, Gerhard. "Arbeitsgestaltung als Lernprozess." *Gewerkschaftliche Monatshefte.* Vol. 24, no. 1 (January 1973), pp. 28–40.

—. "Gewerkschaftsorganisation und 'Gewerkschaftsstaat.'" *Gewerkschaftliche Monatshefte.* Vol. 25, no. 10 (October 1974), pp. 654–661.

—. "Grundfragen Überbetrieblicher Mitbestimung." *Gewerkschaftliche Monatshefte.* Vol. 28, no. 11 (November 1977), pp. 716–725.

—. "Humanisierung der Arbeit aus eigener Kraft." *Gewerkschaftliche Monatshefte.* Vol. 31, no. 4 (April 1980).

—. "Mitbestimmung am Arbeitsplatz – Erfahrungen und Perspektiven." *Gewerkschaftliche Monatshefte.* Vol. 36, no. 3 (March 1985), pp. 151–160.

—. "Der Mitbestimmungsvorschlag der Koalition." *Gewerkschaftliche Monatshefte.* Vol. 25, no. 3 (March 1974), pp. 137–142.

—. "Der Mitbestimmungsvorschlag der Koalition – Zweite Etappe." *Gewerkschaftliche Monatshefte.* Vol. 27, no. 3 (March 1976), pp. 129–134.

—. "Probleme der Betriebsverfassung." *Gewerkschaftliche Monatshefte.* Vol. 26, no. 10 (October 1975), pp. 585–589.

—. "Zum neuen Aktionsprogramm des DGB." *Gewerkschaftliche Monatshefte.* Vol. 30, no. 12 (December 1979), pp. 745–754.

"Lieber schwächer." *Der Spiegel.* Vol. 23, no. 9 (February 24, 1969).

Loderer, Eugen. "Aussperrung verbieten." *metall.* Vol. 31, no. 7 (April 19, 1979), p. 17.

—. "Einfluss durch Geschlossenheit." *metall.* Vol. 30, no. 18 (September 6, 1978), p. 3.

—. "Eugen Loderer über Aussperrung: Verbot bleibt erklärtes Ziel." *metall.* Vol. 30, no. 6 (March 30, 1978), p. 2.

—. "Eugen Loderer zur Tarifrunde 1978: Scharfmacher und Schindluder." *metall.* Vol. 30, no. 1 (January 16, 1978), p. 3.

—. "Kein Anlass zum Optimismus." *metall.* Vol. 30, no. 20 (October 4, 1978), p. 3.

—. "The Market Mechanism Will Not Be Adequate to Cope with the Problems of the Future." *DGB Report.* No. 1 (1973), p. 8.

—. "Die Montanmitbestimmung – Faustpfand der Wirtschaftsdemokratie." Speech presented at IG Metall's special "Mannesmann Conference," Dortmund, July 3, 1980.

—. "Qualitatives Wachstum, Vollbeschäftigung und Kernenergie." *Gewerkschaftliche Monatshefte.* Vol. 28, no. 10 (October 1977), pp. 616–618.

—. "Strukturelle Arbeitslosigkeit durch technischen Wandel." *Gewerkschaftliche Monatshefte.* Vol. 28, no. 7 (July 1977), pp. 409–417.

—. "Unverhohlene Kampfansage." *metall.* Vol. 30, no. 2 (January 30, 1978), p. 3.

—. "Zum Jahreswirtschaftsbericht: Katalog mit Widerspruch." *metall.* Vol. 30, no. 3 (February 13, 1978), p. 5.

Löwenthal, Richard. "Identität und Zukunft der SPD." *Gewerkschaftliche Umschau.* Vol. 33, no. 1 (January–February 1982), pp. 5–8.

Lutz, Burkart. "Die Harmonie von Stabilität , Wachstum, und Vollbeschäftigung: Das Ende einer Illusion." *Gewerkschaftliche Monatshefte.* Vol. 27, no. 8 (August 1976), pp. 479–488.

—. "Überlegungen zu einigen Zukunftsproblemen der deutschen Gewerkschaften." *Gewerkschaftliche Monatshefte.* Vol. 26, no. 5 (May 1975), pp. 274–277.

Lutz, Burkart, and Werner Sengenberger. "Die Rolle von Kollektivvereinbarungen bei der Verminderung von Ungleichheiten in den Arbeitsbedingungen." *Gewerkschaftliche Monatshefte.* Vol. 25, no. 3 (March 1974), pp. 183–192.

Mahlein, Leonhard. "Lehren aus einem Arbeitskampf." *Gewerkschaftliche Monatshefte.* Vol. 27, no. 7 (July 1976), pp. 396–406.

Markovits, Andrei. "Das Alltagsleben in deutschen Gewerkschaftszentralen: Eindrücke eines amerikanischen Sozialwissenschaftlers." *Gewerkschaftliche Monatshefte.* Vol. 30, no. 12 (December 1979), pp. 788–794.

—. "Gewerkschaften: Garanten der Kontinuität?" *Gewerkschaftliche Monatshefte.* Vol. 36, no. 8 (August 1985), pp. 465–476.

—. "The Legislative Elections of September 25, 1983: Some Thoughts and Interpretations." *German Studies Newsletter.* Vol. 1, no. 1 (Winter 1983), p. 10–13.

—. "Neuorientierung deutscher Gewerkschaftspolitik durch die Wirtschaftskrise der siebziger Jahre?" *Journal für Sozialforschung.* Vol. 21, no. 2 (Spring 1981), pp. 141–160.

—. "Problems of Social Democracy: The West German Case." Paper presented at the 1984 General Meeting of the Canadian Political Science Association held at the University of Guelph, Guelph, Ontario, June 10–12, 1984.

———. "Reflections and observations of the 1983 Bundestag Elections and their Consequences for West German Politics." *New German Critique.* No. 28 (Winter 1983), pp. 2–50.

———. "Reflections on Political and Economic Developments in the Federal Republic of Germany." Paper presented at the conference "The Federal Republic of Germany: Economics, Politics, and the Quest for Identity" held at the Centre for International Studies at the University of Toronto, December 8–10, 1983.

———. "West Germany's Political Future; The 1983 Bundestag Elections." *Socialist Review.* Vol. 13, no. 70 (Summer 1983), pp. 67–98.

Markovits, Andrei, and Christopher Allen. "The Automobile Industry and the Metal Workers Union in the Federal Republic of Germany: Changing Relationships in Crisis Conditions." Paper presented at the Second Conference of Europeanists, Washington, DC, October 1980.

———. "The Experience of Labor in a Changing Market Economy: The Ambivalence of the West German Trade Unions." Paper presented at the XIth World Congress of the International Political Science Association, Moscow, USSR, August 1979.

———. "Power and Dissent: The Trade Unions in the Federal Republic of Germany Reexamined." Paper presented at the First Conference of Europeanists, Washington, DC, March 1979, published in *West European Politics*, Vol. 3, no. 1 (January 1980), pp. 68–86.

———. "Social Democracy, Communism and the West German Trade Unions: An Old Debate Reopened." Paper presented at the annual meeting of the Northeastern Political Science Association, Newark, New Jersey, November 1979.

———. "Social Democracy, Communism and the West German Trade Unions; Changing Relations in the Crisis of the 1970s." Paper presented at the conference on socialist theory, practice and transformation in Western Europe, held at the Graduate Center, CUNY, December, 1979.

———. "Structural Change and Union Response in the Chemical Industry: The German Economy in Microcosm." Paper presented at the New York State Political Science Association, Syracuse, New York, April 1980.

———. "Trade Union Responses to the Contemporary Economic Problems in Western Europe: The Context of Current Debates and Policies in the Federal Republic of Germany." Paper presented at the annual meeting of the American Political Science Association, Washingtion, DC, September 1979; published in *Economic and Industrial Democracy*, Vol. 2, no. 1 (February 1981), pp. 49–85.

———. "The West German Unions' Role in Democratization and Participation: Social Partnership or Class Conflict?" paper presented at the XIth World Congress of the International Political Science Association, Moscow, USSR, August 1979.

Markovits, Andrei, Christopher Allen and Kenneth Gibbs. "Class Power and

Industrial Conflict in Advanced Capitalism: The Interaction of Business, Labor and the State in the Post-WWII West German Steel Industry." Paper presented at the annual meeting of the American Political Science Association, Washington, DC, August 1980.

Markovits, Andrei, and Thomas Ertman. "Das 'Modell Deutschland': Eine Herausforderung für die U.S.A." *Prokla*. Vol. 10, no. 4 (December 1980), pp. 6–31.

Martens, Helmut. "Der Streik um die 35-Stunden-Woche in der Stahlindustrie 1978/79." In Otto Jacobi, Eberhard Schmidt and Walther Müller-Jentsch, eds., *Arbeitskampf um Arbeitszeit: Kritisches Gewerkschaftsjahrbuch 1979–80* Berlin: Rotbuch Verlag, 1979.

Marth, Karlheinz. "Die Lohnkosten bieten kein Argument für höhere Preise." *Gewerkschaftliche Umschau*. Vol. 27, no. 3 (May–June 1976), pp. 2–3.

—. "Stabilität durch Begrenzung Wirtschaftlicher Macht." *Gewerkschaftliche Monatshefte*. Vol. 27, no. 10 (October 1976), pp. 587–596.

"Der Maschinenschlosser wird bald zum alten Eisen gehören." *Frankfurter Rundschau*, October 25, 1984.

"Massnahmen zur Verbesserung der Haushaltsstruktur." *Bulletin*. Bonn: Presse- und Informationsamt der Bundesregierung, September 1975.

Matthöfer, Hans. "Kernenergie – Die Bewältigung unserer Zunkunft als Chance und Risiko." *Gewerkschaftliche Monatshefte*. Vol. 28, no. 10 (October 1977), pp. 626–633.

Mayer, Paul. "Besteht wirklich eine Krebsgefahr durch Glasfasern?" *Gewerkschaftliche Umschau*. Vol. 27, no. 6 (November–December 1976), p. 25.

Mayer, Udo. "Paritätische Mitbestimmung und Völkerrecht." *Gewerkschaftliche Monatshefte*. Vol. 25, no. 12 (December 1974), pp. 771–781.

Mayr, Hans. "Der Kampf um die 35-Stunde-Woche; Erfahrungen und Schlussfolgerungen aus der Tarifbewegung 1984." *Gewerkschaftliche Monatshefte*. Vol. 35, no. 11 (November 1984), pp. 661–671.

Mechelhoff, Jürgen. "Arbeitgeber provozieren Arbeitskampf." *metall*. Vol. 30, no. 3 (February 13, 1978), p. 1.

—. "Das Täuschungsmanöver von den hohen Arbeitskosten." *metall*. Vol. 30, no. 4 (February 28, 1978), p. 6.

—. "Urabstimmung ist beantragt: In Nordwürttemberg/Nordbaden und in Nordrheinwestfalen scheiterten die Schlichtungen für die metallverarbeitende Industrie." *metall*. Vol. 30, no. 4 (February 28, 1978), p. 1.

"Mehr als linkes Gequassel." *Die Zeit*, May 4, 1979.

"Die Meisterringer." *Der Spiegel*.Vol. 12, no. 39 (September 24, 1958).

"Memorandum '79 – Eine Bewertung aus gewerkschaftlicher Sicht." *Wirtschaftspolitische Informationen*. No. 3 (June 15, 1979), pp. 1–7.

Menzel, Manfred. "Problembewältigung auf Arbeitgeberart." *Gewerkschaftliche Umschau*. Vol. 29, no. 5 (September–October 1978), p. 1.

Mertens, Dieter, and Lutz Reyher. "Zum Beschäftigungsproblem in den nächsten Jahren." *Gewerkschaftliche Monatshefte*. Vol. 28, no. 1 (January 1977), pp. 1–12.

*metall*. Vol. 31, no. 14 (July 18, 1979).

"Miese Dialektik." *Der Spiegel.* Vol. 23, no. 42 (October 13, 1969).

Minnerup, Günter. "The Bundesrepublik Today." *New Left Review,* No. 99 (September–October 1976), pp. 3–44.

Minta, Helmut. "Erfolge und Möglichkeiten einer aktiven Arbeitsmarktpolitik." *Gewerkschaftliche Monatshefte.* Vol. 29, no. 3 (March 1978), pp. 150–158.

"Mit den Experten konnten die Veteranen nichts anfangen." *Frankfurter Rundschau,* October 13, 1979.

"Mit körperlicher Kraft." *Der Spiegel.* Vol. 21, no. 34 (August 14, 1967).

"Das Mitbestimmungsgesetz ist verfassungsmässig." *Frankfurter Allgemeine Zeitung,* March 2, 1979.

Mohr, Wilma. "Weniger qualifizierte Arbeitsmöglichkeiten." *Gewerkschaftliche Umschau.* Vol. 29, no. 2 (March–April), pp. 14–17.

Moll, Rheinhard, Martin Mehrtens, Alfred Meissner and Hans-Detlef Pahl. "Arbeitszeit und Mehrarbeit?" WSI-Mitteilungen. Vol. 38, no. 2 (February 1985), pp. 80–86.

Möller, Edmund. "Der Absicherungsvertrag der IG Metall." *Gewerkschaftliche Umschau.* Vol. 29, no. 3 (May–June 1978), pp. 10–11.

Möller-Löcking, Norbert. "AFG-Regierungsentwurf wird den Aufgaben nicht gerecht." *Die Quelle.* Vol. 30, no. 2 (February 1979), pp. 112–113.

"Montanmitbestimmung mit allen Mitteln verteidigen." *Frankfurter Allgemeine Zeitung,* June 12, 1980.

"More Jobs by Forgoing Real Pay Increases?" *DGB Report.* No. 1 (1978), pp. 5–6.

"More Militancy." *DGB Report.* No. 6 (1970), p. 55.

Muhr, Gerd. "Gewerkschaften und Sozialpolitik." *Gewerkschaftliche Monatshefte.* Vol. 26, no. 3 (March 1975), pp. 137–141.

—. "Was bringt die 5. Novelle zum Arbeitsförderungsgesetz?" *Die Quelle.* Vol. 30, no. 7/8 (July/August 1979), pp. 424–425.

—. "Zur Situation der Internationalen Arbeitsorganisation." *Gewerkschaftliche Monatshefte.* Vol. 28, no. 9 (September 1977), pp. 537–545.

Müller, Gerhard. "Fragen zum Arbeitskampfrecht nach dem Beschluss des Grossen Senats des Bundesarbeitsgerichts vom 21, April 1971." *Gewerkschaftliche Monatshefte.* Vol. 23, no. 4 (April 1972), pp. 273–287.

Müller-Jentsch, Walther, and Rainer Erd. 'Innovation in the Printing Industry in the Federal Republic." Research Paper of the Anglo-German Foundation for the Study of Industrial Society, No. B0179/4E.

Münstermann, Jörg, Konrad Schacht, and Lutz Unterseher. "Handlungsfelder der Gewerkschaften." *Gewerkschaftliche Monatshefte.* Vol. 26, no. 6 (June 1975), pp. 329–337.

Murawski, Josef. "Konzentration hat ständig zugenommen." *Die Quelle.* Vol. 27, no. 10 (October 1976), pp. 393–395.

Muszynski, Bernhard. "'Social-Management'-Strategien und gewerkschaftliche Interessenvertretung." *Gewerkschaftliche Monatshefte.* Vol. 28, no. 7 (July 1977), pp. 439–448.

"Mut zur Pflicht." *Der Spiegel.* Vol. 23, no. 1–2 (January 7, 1969).

"Nach dem Karlsruher Urteil: Alle sind erleichtert." *Die Welt,* March 2, 1979.

"Nachts auf der Strasse." *Der Spiegel*. Vol. 23, no. 12 (March 17, 1969).

"Nach vier Monaten endlich ein Tarifergebnis: Löhne und Gehälter bei Eisen und Stahl gesichert." *metall*. Vol. 30, no. 4 (February 28, 1978), p. 2.

"Die Nagelprobe." *Der Spiegel*. Vol. 27, no. 46 (November 12, 1973).

Narr, Wolf-Dieter. "Was kümmert uns das Geschwätz vom Berufsverbot." *Gewerkschaftliche Monatshefte*. Vol. 27, no. 6 (June 1976), pp. 366–375.

Naschold, Frieder, "Humanisierung der Arbeit zwischen Staat und Gewerkschaften." *Gewerkschaftliche Monatshefte*. Vol. 31, no. 4 (April 1980), pp. 213–219.

—. "Zur Perspektive und Strategie einer arbeitsorientierten Gesundheitspolitik." *Gewerkschaftliche Monatshefte*. Vol. 28, no. 3 (March 1977), pp. 182–194.

Negt, Oskar. "Freizeit als Emanzipations und Orientierungszeit." *Gewerkschaftliche Monatshefte*. Vol. 36, no. 1 (January 1985), pp. 39–47.

—. "Massenmedien in der Tendenzwende." *Gewerkschaftliche Monatshefte*. Vol. 27, no. 6 (June 1976), pp. 355–366.

—. "Politische Aufgaben der gewerkschaftlichen Bildungsarbeit." *Gewerkschaftliche Monatshefte*. Vol. 26, no. 5 (May 1975), pp. 308–313.

Nell-Breuning, S. J. von Oswald. "Zum Selbstverständnis der Gewerkschaften." *Gewerkschaftliche Monatshefte*. Vol. 26, no. 5 (May 1975), pp. 277–281.

"Neue Heimat: Die dunklen Geschäfte von Vietor und Genossen." *Der Spiegel*. Vol. 36, no. 6 (February 8, 1981).

"Neue Wege der Tarifpolitik." *Der Gewerkschafter*. Vol. 27, no. 5 (May, 1979), pp. 6–7.

"Nicht Stöpseln." *Der Spiegel*. Vol. 24, no. 41 (October 10, 1970).

Nickel, Walter. "Die Wirtschaftsmacht der Gewerkschaften in der öffentlichen Meinung." *Die Quelle*. Vol. 29, no. 3 (March 1978), pp. 146–148.

"Niederlage im Nebenkrieg." *metall*. Vol. 30, no. 5 (March 10, 1978), p. 4.

Niethammer, Lutz. "Probleme der Gewerkschaften im Prozess der Integration Westeuropas." *Gewerkschaftliche Monatshefte*. Vol. 27, no. 5 (May 1976), pp. 279–287.

"The 9th Federal Congress of the DGB Sets the Points for Further Progress," *DGB Report*. No. 7–8 (1972), pp. 8–10.

"Noche einige Runden." *Der Spiegel*. Vol. 27, no. 37 (September 10, 1973).

Nolle, Doris. "IG Bau-Steine-Erden 1949–1957 – Die Entwicklung zu einer kooperativen Gewerkschaft." In Claudio Pozzoli, ed., *Grenzen gewerkschaftlicher Politik*.

Noth, Dieter, Werner Oehl and Gudrun Trautwein-Kalms. "Angestellte – Bevorzugte Objekte der neuen Rationalisierungswelle." *Gewerkschaftliche Monatshefte*. Vol. 28, no. 6 (June 1977), pp. 359–368.

"Nur für Organisierte." *Der Spiegel*. Vol. 13, no. 38 (September 16, 1959).

"Nur die Ouvertüre." *Der Spiegel*. Vol. 39, no. 31 (July 29, 1985), pp. 24–25.

Nutzinger, Hans G. "Co-determination in the Federal Republic of Germany: Present State and Perspectives". Unpublished paper, February 1977.

Oehl, Werner, "Technische Revolution in Bürobereich." *Die Quelle*. Vol. 29, no. 1 (January 1978), pp. 21–23.

Oertzen, Peter von. "Die Gewerkschaften in der Sicht der SPD." *Gewerkschaftliche Monatshefte*. Vol. 27, no. 4 (April 1976), pp. 210–216.

—. "Wie lässt sich Geschichtsschreibung im DKP-Stil messen?" *Frankfurter Rundschau*, April 11, 1979.

"Ökologischer TÜV." *Der Spiegel*. Vol. 39, no. 2 (January 7, 1985).

Osterland, Martin. "Aspekte der Lebens- und Arbeitssituation der Industriearbeiter." *Gewerkschaftliche Monatshefte*. Vol. 24, no. 8 (August 1973), pp. 457–467.

Otto, Bernd. "Tiefgreifende Strukturprobleme im Einzelhandel." *Die Quelle*. Vol. 29, no. 3 (March 1978), pp. 149–151.

"Otto der Gusseiserne." *Der Spiegel*. Vol. 12, no. 45 (November 4, 1958).

"ÖTV voll hinter Mitbestimmung." *Frankfurter Rundschau*, July 15, 1980.

Pehl, Günter. "Es blieb bei über einer Million Arbeitslosen." *Gewerkschaftliche Monatshefte*. Vol. 29, no. 3 (March 1978), pp. 168–178.

—. "Deutsche Wirtschaft 1984/85 – Weiterhin leichter Aufschwung aber kein Abbau der Arbeitslosigkeit." *Gewerkschaftliche Monatshefte*. Vol. 36, no. 1 (January 1985), pp. 48–59.

—. "Kampf dem Terrorismus: Solidarität der Demokraten muss erhalten bleiben." *Die Quelle*. Vol. 28, no. 11 (November 1977), pp. 433–435.

—. "Mitbestimmung erfüllt den Verfassungsauftrag." *Die Quelle*. Vol. 28, no. 7/8 (July/August 1977), p. 291.

—. "Eine neue internationale Arbeitsteilung setzt sich durch." *Die Quelle*. Vol. 29, no. 5 (May 1978), pp. 275–277.

—. "1978: Vielleicht etwas mehr Wirtschaftswachstum – aber kaum weniger Arbeitslose." *Gewerkschaftliche Monatshefte*. Vol. 20, no. 1 (January 1978), pp. 6–18.

—. "1975 völlig im Zeichen der Weltrezession." *Gewerkschaftliche Monatshefte*. Vol. 26, no. 12 (December 1975), pp. 769–781.

—. "1976: Wirtschaftlicher Aufschwung, aber die Arbeitslosigkeit bleibt noch." *Gewerkschaftliche Monatshefte*. Vol. 27, no. 12, (December 1976), pp. 728–737.

—. "Nur Reallohnerhöhungen garantieren das Wirtschaftswachstum." *Die Quelle*. Vol. 29, no. 3 (March 1978), pp. 131–133.

—. "Nutzung der Kernenergie bleibt ein grosses Risiko." *Die Quelle*. Vol. 28, no. 6 (June 1977), pp. 255–258.

—. "Ohne staatliche Hilfe keine Konjunkturwende." *Gewerkschaftliche Monatshefte*. Vol. 25, no. 12 (December 1974), pp. 733–743.

—. "Schafft der Verzicht auf reale Lohnerhöhungen mehr Arbeitsplätze?" *Die Quelle*. Vol. 29, no. 2 (February 1978), pp. 67–68.

—. "Steigende Gewinne und keine neue Arbeitsplätze." *Die Quelle*. Vol. 27, no. 12 (December 1976), pp. 495–497.

—. "Überholtes Konzept – politisch unbrauchbarer Rat." *Gewerkschaftliche Monatshefte*. Vol. 25, no. 2 (February 1974), pp. 73–83.

—. "Wirtschaftspolitik zwischen den DGB-Bundeskongressen 1972 und 1975: Weltwirtschaftliche Störungen waren Hauptthemen." *Gewerkschaftliche Monatshefte*. Vol. 26, no. 4 (April 1975), pp. 219–230.

Perner, Detlef. "Herr S. und der Popanz 'Gewerkschaftsstaat.'" *Vorgänge – Zeitschrift für Gesellschaftspolitik*. Vol. 17, no. 5 (May 1978), pp. 85–92.

Peters, Falk-Eckart. "Betrieblicher Datenschutz und Bundesdatenschutzgesetz." *Gewerkschaftliche Monatshefte*. Vol. 28, no. 8 (August 1977), pp. 482–489.

Pfeiffer, Alois. "Bessere Konjunktur löst nicht Arbeitsmarktprobleme." *Die Quelle*. Vol. 29, no. 1 (January 1978), pp. 12–14.

—. "Energiepolitische Perspektiven – wirtschaftspolitische Folgerungen." *Gewerkschaftliche Monatshefte*. Vol. 28, no. 10 (October 1977), pp. 607–611.

—. "Full employment is the Main Objective." *DGB Report*. No. 1–2 (1977), pp. 6–8.

—. "Der Sachverständigenrat hat seinen Gestzesauftrag verletzt." *Gewerkschaftliche Monatshefte*. Vol. 29, no. 1 (January 1978), pp. 1–6.

—. "Wirtschaftliche Entwicklung und Wirtschaftspolitik." *Gewerkschaftliche Monatshefte*. Vol. 26, no. 12 (December 1975), pp. 737–744.

"Pflock im Neuland." *Der Spiegel*. Vol. 38, no. 27 (July 2, 1984).

Pfriem, Hans, and Hartmut Seifert. "Funktion und Formwandel von Arbeitsmarktpolitik: Vom System positiver Anreize zu einer systematisierten Kontroll- und Sanktionspraxis." *WSI-Mitteilungen*. Vol. 32, no. 2 (February 1979), pp. 68–79.

Picht, Georg. "Gewerkschaftliche Aufgabe: Integrierte Infrastrukturpolitik." *Gewerkschaftliche Monatshefte*. Vol. 26, no. 5 (May 1975), pp. 281–283.

Pirker, Theo. "Die Gewerkschaft als politische Organisation." *Gewerkschaftliche Monatshefte*. Vol. 3, no. 2 (February 1952), pp. 76–79.

—. "Gewerkschaften am Scheidewege." *Gewerkschaftliche Monatshefte*. Vol. 3, no. 12 (December 1952), pp. 708–713.

—. "Staatsautorität und pluralistische Ordnung." *Gewerkschaftliche Monatshefte*. Vol. 3, no. 10 (October 1952), pp. 577–583.

Pitz, Karl. "Plus und Minus." *metall*. Vol. 30, no. 1 (January 16, 1978), p. 11.

Pöhler, Willi. "Staatliche Förderung für die Verbesserung der Arbeits-und Lebensqualität." *Gewerkschaftliche Monatshefte*. Vol. 31, no. 4 (April 1980), pp. 230–242.

"Politischer Machtkampf." *metall*. Vol. 30, no. 5, (March 10, 1978), p. 4.

Pornschlegel, Hans. "Tarifpolitische Perspektiven des technologischen Wandels." IG Metall, *Strukturelle Arbeitslosigkeit durch technologischen Wandel? Referate, gehalten auf der Technologie-Tagung der IG Metall, 24./25. Mai 1977, Frankfurt am Main*. Frankfurt am Main: IG Metall, 1977.

Prante, Otmar, "Gipfel, Gunst, Gefahr und Gewerkschaften." *Gewerkschaftliche Umschau*. Vol. 29, no. 4, (July–August 1978), p. 1.

"Prediger in der Würste." *Der Spiegel*. Vol. 38, no. 47 (November 19, 1984).

Preiss, Hans. "Für die Freiheit der Wissenschaft: Kooperationsverträge zwischen Gewerkschaften und Hochschulen." *Gewerkschaftliche Monatshefte*. Vol. 28, no. 2 (February 1977), pp. 71–75.

"Preiss; 'In der Gewerkschaft zählt nicht das Trennende, sondern die Solidarität.'" *Die Neue*, May 16, 1979.

"Privater Verbrauch – Antrieb für Wirtschaft." *metall*. Vol. 30, no. 1 (January 16, 1978), p. 10.

"Problemgebiete des Arbeitsmarktes holen auf." *Frankfurter Rundschau*, April 22, 1980.

"Problem vor Torschluss." *Der Spiegel.* Vol. 23, no. 4 (January 20, 1969).

"Productivity Advances at the Expense of Workers?" *DGB Report.* No. 4 (1977), p. 6.

"'Profitiert wie noch nie' – Meallindustrie verzeichnet Aussenhandels Rekord und gestiegene Auftragseingänge." *metall.* Vol. 30, no. 5 (March 10, 1978), p. 8.

"Die Prüfsteine des DGB und die Politik der Parteien." *Gewerkschaftliche Umschau.* Vol. 27, no. 5 (September–October 1976), pp. 2–5.

Rappe, Hermann. "Für eine klare Abgrenzung der Gewerkschaften von den Grünen." *Gewerkschaftliche Umschau.* Vol. 36, no. 1 (January–February 1985), pp. 2–8.

—. "Grenzen des Sozialstaates?" *Gewerkschaftliche Umschau.* Vol. 28, no. 6 (November–December 1977), pp. 2–3.

—. "Wir brauchen mehr qualifizierte Ausbildungsplätze." *Gewerkschaftliche Umschau.* Vol. 29, no. 3 (May–June 1978), pp. 12–15.

Rappe, Hermann, and Franz Steinkühler. "Hohe Wachstumsraten sind kein Ziel an sich." *Frankfurter Rundschau,* May 2, 1985.

"Ratsbruder ohne Wasserpredigt." *metall.* Vol. 30, no. 1 (January 16, 1978).

"Das Recht auf Arbeit." *metall.* Vol. 30, no. 11 (June 5, 1978), pp. 6–7.

Remmel, Edeltraud. "Bruderzwist im Haus Hauenschild." *Vorwärts,* April 12, 1979.

"Richters Rüstung: Für Stammesherzöge zu klein." *Der Spiegel.* Vol. 16, no. 36 (September 5, 1962).

Riester, Walter. "Der Kampf um die 35-Stunden-Woche in Nordwürttemberg/ Nordbaden–Bedingungen, Erfahrungen, Schlussfolgerungen." *WSI-Mitteilungen.* Vol. 37, no. 9 (September 1984), pp. 526–532.

Roberts, B. C. "Multinational Collective Bargaining: A European Prospect?" *British Journal of Industrial Relations.* Vol. 11, no. 1 (March 1973), pp. 1–19.

"Rohe Eier." *Der Spiegel.* Vol. 21, no. 11 (March 13, 1967).

"Rosen um Mitternacht." *Der Spiegel.* Vol. 21, no. 45 (October 30, 1967).

Roth, Jürgen. "Franz Josef Strauss und die türkischen Faschisten: Unglublicher Skandal." *metall.* Vol. 30, no. 18 (September 6, 1978), pp. 6–7.

"Ruf nach Rücktritt des IG Chemie-Chefs Hauenschild wird laut." *Frankfurter Rundschau,* March 26, 1979.

"...rührt am Nerv der Republik." *Frankfurter Rundschau,* June 18, 1980.

Sachs, Jeffrey. "Wage, Profits and Macroeconomic Adjustment in the 1970s: A Comparative Study." Paper presented at the Conference of the Brookings Panel of Economic Activity, Massachusetts Institute of Technology, Cambridge, Massachusetts, October 1979.

"Der Sachverständigenrat hat das Gesetz verletzt." *Die Quelle.* Vol. 29, no. 1 (January 1978), pp. 15–16.

Salm, Fritz. "Betriebsnahe Tarifpolitik tut not." *Der Gewerkschafter.* Vol. 6, no. 8 (August 1958), p. 8.

—. "Betriebsnahe Tarifverträge." *Der Gewerkschafter.* Vol. 6, no. 9/10 (September/October 1958), pp. 1–2.

—. "Betriebsnahe Tarifverträge, Teile 1–4." *Der Gewerkschafter.* Vol. 9, nos. 8–11 (August, September, October, November 1961).

—. "Dringliche Aufgaben unserer Tarifpolitik." *Der Gewerkschafter.* Vol. 6, no. 9/10 (September/October 1958), pp. 30–31.

Sammler, Otto, "Gewerkschaftspolitik: Die Position des DGB bei der Reform der beruflichen Bildung." *Gewerkschaftliche Monatshefte.* Vol. 26, no. 9 (September 1975), pp. 566–572.

Schacht, Konrad, and Lutz Unterseher. "Humanisierung der Arbeitswelt: Probleme für die Sozialforschung." *Gewerkschaftliche Monatshefte.* Vol. 25, no. 11 (November 1974), pp. 665–670.

—. "Spontane Arbeitsniederlegungen – Krise des Tarifverhandlungssystems?" *Gewerkschaftliche Monatshefte.* Vol. 25, no. 3 (March 1974), pp. 143–151.

Schäfer, Claus. "Gegen die Vorhaben der Bundesregierung zur Förderung betrieblicher Vermögensbildung." *Gewerkschaftliche Monatshefte.* Vol. 29, no. 1 (January 1978), pp. 28–41.

Schäfer, Egon. "Angestellte in der Industriegewerkschaft." *Gewerkschaftliche Umschau.* Vol. 29, no. 5 (September–October 1978), pp. 6–7.

Scharrer, Manfred. "Eine die Geschichte verfälschende 'Gewerkschaftsgeschichte.'" *Die Quelle.* Vol. 29, no. 11 (November 1978), pp. 606–608.

Scheel, Walter. "Schärfste Massstäbe der Selbstkontrolle." *Gewerkschaftliche Umschau.* Vol. 28, no. 6 (November–December 1977), p. 11.

Schiller, Karl. "Lebensfragen der deutschen Volkswirtschaft." IG Metall, *Niederschrift der Verhandlungen des 2. ordentlichen Gewerkschaftstages der Industriegewerkschaft Metall für die Bundesrepublik Deutschland in Stuttgart vom 15. bis 20. September 1952.* Frankfurt am Main: IG Metall, n.d., pp. 213–227.

Schleyer, Hanns Martin. "Die Rolle der Gewerkschaften aus der Sicht der Arbeitgeber." *Gewerkschaftliche Monatshefte.* Vol. 27, no. 4 (April 1976), pp. 202–210.

Schlossarek, Gerd. "Finanz- und ertragsstarke Grosschemie." *Gewerkschaftliche Umschau.* Vo. 29, no. 4 (July–August 1978), pp. 12–13.

Schmidt, Adolf. "Der Kohlebergbau im Konzept einer zukunftsorientierten Energiepolitik." *Gewerkschaftliche Monatshefte.* Vol. 28, no. 10 (October 1977), pp. 622–626.

Schmidt, Alfred. "Reformen für das Alter." *Gewerkschaftliche Monatshefte.* Vol. 28, no. 3 (March 1977), pp. 173–181.

Schmidt, Gerhard. "Öffentlicher Dienst – Für den Bürger, für die Gesellschaft." *Gewerkschaftliche Monatshefte.* Vol. 26, no. 2 (February 1975), pp. 65–69.

"Schmidt: Hände weg von Montanmitbestimmung." *Handelsblatt,* July 7, 1980.

Schmidt, Helmut. "The Role of the Trade Unions in the Federal Republic." *The Bulletin* (Archive Supplement). Bonn: Press and Information Office, April 6, 1976, pp. 1–8.

Schmidt, Rudi. "Zu den arbeitspolitischen Chancen und Grenzen neuer Produktionskonzepte." *WSI-Mitteilungen.* Vol. 38, no. 3 (March 1985), pp. 146–150.

"'Schmuddelige Kampagne gegen Kommunisten.'" *Frankfurter Allgemeine Zeitung,* April 26, 1979.

Schneider, Wolfgang. "Betriebsratswahlen 1975 – eine zusammenfassende Darstellung." *Gewerkschaftliche Monatshefte.* Vol. 26, no. 10 (October 1975), pp. 600–607.

—. "Novellierung des Betriebsverfassungsgesetzes: Angriff auf die Vertretungs-strukturen der Arbeitnehmer." *Gewerkschaftliche Monatshefte.* Vol. 36, no. 8 (August 1985), pp. 502–506.

Schneider-Zugowski, Doris. "Mehr Wettbewerb is nötig." *Gewerkschaftliche Umschau.* Vol. 28, no. 2 (March–April 1977), p. 12.

"Schon einmal dienten Feindbilder dazu, Verfolgungen einzuleiten." *Frankfurter Rundschau,* October 22, 1979.

Schumm-Garling, Ursula, "Leitung und 'Führungsstile,'" *Gewerkschaftliche Monatshefte.* Vol. 25, no. 9 (September 1974), pp. 549–557.

Schwab, Karl. "Foreign Colleagues – Neighbors on the Job." *DGB Report.* No. 1–2 (1977), pp. 12–14.

—. "Jugendarbeitslosigkeit – Was kann, was muss man tun?" *Gewerkschaftliche Monatshefte.* Vol. 26, no. 9 (September 1975), pp. 521–526.

—. "'STOP Jugendarbeitslosigkeit' – Argumente statt Parolen." *Gewerkschaftliche Monatshefte.* Vol. 28, no. 12 (December 1977), pp. 737–741.

"Schwankerei ist nicht am Platz: Spiegel Interview mit dem IG Chemie Vorsitzen-den Hermann Rappe über Friedensbewegung und SPD." *Der Spiegel.* Vol. 37, no. 26 (June 27, 1983).

Schwegler, Lorenz. "Streikrecht und Rechtsprechung." *Gewerkschaftliche Monatshefte.* Vol. 23, no. 5 (May 1972), pp. 299–309.

Schwendig, Arnd. "Die Opfer der Krise." *metall.* Vol. 30, no. 17 (August 23, 1978), pp. 11–13.

"Schwere Kiste." *Der Spiegel.* Vol. 38, no. 50 (December 10, 1984).

"Schwerpunktthema: Investitionslenkung." *WSI-Mitteilungen.* Vol. 27, no. 8 (August 1974), pp. 19–21.

Seifert, Hartmut. "Arbeitslosigkeit – Argumente und Scheinargumente." *Gewerkschaftliche Monatshefte.* Vol. 28, no. 12 (December 1977), pp. 751–760.

Seitenzahl, Rolf. "Gibt es noch eine Arbeiterbewegung? Verhältnis SPD und Gewerkschaften." Speech delivered to the SPD Unterbezirk Nürnberg, June 16, 1983.

—. "Mit der eigenen Kraft auf Sand gebaut?" *Frankfurter Rundschau,* April 20, 1983.

Seitenzahl, Rolf, ed. "Gewerkschaftsstaat oder Unternehmerstaat." *WSI-Mitteilungen.* Vol. 29, no. 8 (August 1976), pp. 36–51.

—. "Gewerkschaftsstaat oder Unternehmerstaat." *WSI-Mitteilungen.* Vol. 30, no. 12 (December 1977).

"Das Signal zum Widerstand blieb aus." *Frankfurter Rundschau,* October 13 and October 18, 1979.

"Solidarität mit den Streikenden." *Der Grundstein.* Vol. 35, no. 6 (June 1984), p. 3.

"Sozialer Frieden in Betrieben ist bedroht durch die Pläne der Koalition zur Verschlechterung des Betriebsverfassungsgesetzes." *Gewerkschaftspost.* Vol. 36, no. 2 (February 1985).

"SPD versucht den 'Brückenschlag': Arbeitsplatzsicherung und Umweltschutz nicht mehr als Gegensatz." *Frankfurter Rundschau,* March 25, 1985.

"SPD will Mannesmann durchkreuzen." *Süddeutsche Zeitung,* June 18, 1980.

Stadelmaier, Herbert. "Gegen die schrankenlose Wettbewerbswirtschaft." *Gewerkschaftliche Monatshefte*. Vol. 27, no. 10 (October 1976), pp. 608–612.

"Stahlbetriebsräte reden offen von Streik." *Frankfurter Rundschau*, July 1923, 1980.

Stammer, Otto, "Gesellschaftliche Entwicklungsperspektiven und pluralitäre Demokratie." *Gewerkschaftliche Monatshefte*. Vol. 12, no. 10 (October 1961), pp. 577–583.

Standfest, Erich. "Sozialpolitik zwischen Anpassungsproblemen und Strukturkrisen." *Gewerkschaftliche Monatshefte*. Vol. 29, no. 3 (March 1978), pp. 159–168.

"Starke Gewerkschaften – Aktive Betriebsräte." *Die Quelle*. Vol. 28, no. 12 (December 1977), p. 481.

Steffen, Jochen. "Zum Verhältnis von Sozialdemokratie und Gewerkschaften." *Gewerkschaftliche Monatshefte*. Vol. 25, no. 4 (April 1974), pp. 242–247.

Steinkühler, Franz. "An Schwierigkeiten mangelt es uns wahrlich nicht ..." *Prokla*. Vol. 14, no. 1 (March 1984), pp. 31–40.

—. "Wider die Idee, mit Arbeitslosen gegen Arbeitgeber zu kämpfen." *Frankfurter Rundschau*, March 16, 1984.

Steinmüller, Wilhelm. "Computer: Keine Gnade des Vergessens." *metall*. Vol. 30, no. 16 (August 9, 1978), pp. 13–14.

Stephan, Gunter, "DGB Trying for Greater Unionization of Salary Earners." *DGB Report*. No. 1/2 (1977), pp. 10–11.

—. "Gemeinsam Gegewart und Zukunft bewältigen." *Die Quelle*. Vol. 28, no. 11 (November 1977), pp. 443–445.

—. "Politik im Interesse der Angestellten – Die Angestelltenarbeit des DGB." *Gewerkschaftliche Monatshefte*. Vo. 25, no. 9 (September 1974), pp. 521–523.

Sternberger, Dolf, "Parlamentarismus, Parteien, Verbände." *Gewerkschaftliche Monatshefte*. Vol. 3, no. 8 (August 1952), pp. 473–477.

Sternstein, Wolfgang. "Die Grenzen der Macht – Das Lehrstück Whyl." *Gewerkschaftliche Monatshefte*. Vol. 27, no. 2 (February 1976), pp. 65–76.

Streeck, Wolfgang. "Neo-Corporatist Industrial Relations and the Economic Crisis in West Germany." In John H. Goldthorpe, ed., *Order and Conflict in Contemporary Capitalism. Studies in the Political Economy of West European Nations*. Oxford: Clarendon Press, 1984, pp. 291–314.

—. "Die organisatorische Stabilisierung der Gewerkschaften im letzten Jahrzehnt: Zur Überwindung der gewerkschaftlichen Organisationskrise der sechziger Jahre." *IIM Papers of the Science Center Berlin*, August 1978.

"Streik: 'Wir sind keine impotenten Freier.'" *Der Spiegel*. Vol. 28, no. 6 (February 4, 1974).

"Strike Days Rose to 533,697." *DGB Report*. No. 3 (1977), p. 15.

"Strike Success after 23 Days." *DGB Report*. No. 1/2 (1972), p. 11.

Sturmthal, Adolf. "Einkommenspolitik und Inflation." *Gewerkschaftliche Monatshefte*. Vol. 25, no. 2 (February 1974), pp. 83–93.

Szakats, A. "Workers' Participation in Management: The German Experience." *Journal of Industrial Relations*. No. 16 (1974), pp. 28–44.

"Der Tabu-Katalog der Unternehmer." *druck und papier*. Vol. 117, no. 3 (January 29, 1979), pp. 8–11.

"Die Tabus der Arbeitgeber: So sieht die Widerstandslinie gegen die Gewerkschaften aus." *Die Zeit*, January 26, 1979.

Tacke, Bernhard. "Terms and Conditions of Bargaining Policy 1969 – In Retrospect." *DGB Report*. No. 1 (1970), pp. 6–8.

"A Talk with Helmut Schmidt." *The New York Times Magazine*, September 16, 1984.

"Theater um Dollarverfall." *metall*. Vol. 30, no. 5 (March 10, 1978), p. 8.

Thomssen, Wilke. "Arbeiterbildung zwischen betriebsdemokratischen Bewusstsein und Aufsteigsorientierung." *Gewerkschaftliche Monatshefte*. Vol. 25, no. 11 (November 1974), pp. 671–681.

Tigges, Hans. "Aktion '77: Eine kritische Nachbetrachtung." *Gewerkschaftliche Umschau*. Vol. 29, no. 2 (March–April 1978), pp. 33–35.

"The Times Enters a New Era of Electronic Pringing." *New York Times*, July 3, 1978.

"Tips for Trade Union Work: Strengths and Weaknesses Revealed by a Demoscopic Enquiry." *DGB Report*. No. 4 (1970), p. 41.

Tofaute, Hartmut. "Ausgewählte Daten zu Struktur und Entwicklung des öffentlichen Dienstes." *Gewerkschaftliche Monatshefte*. Vol. 26, no. 2 (February 1975), pp. 69–84.

"Together for Full Employment." *DGB Report*. No. 4 (1977), pp. 5–6.

"The Trade Unions are Not a Militant Political Organization." *DGB Report*. No. 3/4 (1972), p. 6.

"Trade Union Self-Examination." *DGB Report*. 3/4 (1970), p. 27.

"Überbleibsel absoluter Unternehmerherrschaft." *Gewerkschaftliche Umschau*. Vol. 29, no. 2 (March–April 1978), p. 5

Ullmer, Richard. "Sparpolitik und Beschäftigungsprogramme." *express*. Vol. 19, no. 12 (December 15, 1981), p. 3.

"Umschau-Dokumentation." *Gewerkschaftliche Umschau*. Vol. 29, no. 4 (July–August 1978), pp. i–viii.

"Umsetzung der 38.5-Stunden-Woche; Beispielle, Modelle, Argumente." *express*. Vol. 23, no. 2 (February 11, 1985), pp. 1–6.

"Umweltschutz schafft Arbeitsplätze." *Gewerkschaftspost*. Vol. 36, no. 4 (April 1985), pp. 1–2.

"Umweltschutz schafft Arbeitsplätze." *Der Grundstein*. Vol. 36, no. 4 (April 1985), pp. 5–8

"Unsere Stärke heisst Solidarität." *Der Grundstein*. Vol. 36, no. 5 (May 1985), pp. 3–4.

"Unternehmerpräsident gibt Koalition einen Korb: Gegen Änderung des Betriebsverfassungsgesetzes." *Frankfurter Rundschau*, March 26, 1985.

"Der Unterwanderweg ist lang." *Der Spiegel*. Vol. 34, no. 3 (January 14, 1980).

Uring, Thomas von der. "Lenkungsaufgabe des Staates bei gewandelten sozialökonomischen Bedingungen." *Gewerkschaftliche Monatshefte*. Vol. 27, no. 8 (August 1976), pp. 466–478.

Velte, Peter J. "Sonderthema – Gemeinsam die Verantwortung tragen – Seit Juli 1976 gilt in der Bundesrepublik Deutschland die Mitbestimmung." *Sozial Report*. June 1976, pp. 1–19.

"Verdient die Industrie zu viel?" *metall*. Vol. 30, no. 18 (September 6, 1978), p. 8.

"Verhalten – aber stabil." *Gewerkschaftliche Umschau.* Vol. 27, no. 5 (September–October 1976), pp. 11–17.

Vetter, Ernst Günter. "Die heimliche Volksfront." *Frankfurter Allgemeine Zeitung,* July 9, 1979.

—. "Rauchzeichen der Partnershaft." *Frankfurter Allgemeine Zeitung,* March 27, 1985.

—. "Die Roten sind auf dem Marsch." *Frankfurter Allgemeine Zeitung,* April 21, 1979.

Vetter, Heinz Oskar. "Aktionsprogramm '79 ist eine Aufgabe für alle." *Die Quelle.* Vol. 30, no. 7/8 (July/August 1979), pp. 387–88.

—. "1978 brauchen wir Geschlossenheit und Festigkeit." *Die Quelle.* Vol. 29, no. 1 (January 1978), pp. 3–6.

—. "Brief an die DGB-Landesbezirke und DGB-Kreise von dem DGB-Bundesvorstand." Unpublished document. May 29, 1979.

—. "Closing Address at 8th Ordinary Federal Congress of the German Federation of Trade Unions." *DGB Report.* No. 3 (1969), pp. 9–12.

—. "DGB Independent But Not Neutral." *DGB Report.* No. 3 (1976), pp. 10–12.

—. "DGB und politische Parteien." *Gewerkschaftliche Monatshefte.* Vol. 25, no. 4 (April 1974), pp. 201–205.

—. "Energiepolitik, Umweltschutz und Beschäftigung." *Gewerkschaftliche Monatshefte.* Vol. 28, no. 10 (October 1977), pp. 601–606.

—. "Es geht um die Reformfähigkeit unserer Gesellschaft." *Die Quelle.* Vol. 28, no. 10 (October 1977), pp. 117–119.

—. "Forderungen des Deutschen Gewerkschaftsbundes zur Bundestagswahl 1976." *Gewerkschaftliche Monatshefte.* Vol. 27, no. 8 (August 1976), pp. 449–456.

—. "Für ein neues Grundsatzprogramm des DGB. *Gewerkschaftliche Monatshefte.* Vol. 27, no. 4 (April 1976), pp. 194–201.

—. "Gewerkschaften im Visier der Reaktion." *Gewerkschaftliche Monatshefte.* Vol. 25, no. 10 (October 1974), pp. 602–614.

—. "Gewerkschaftliche Solidarität in unserer Zeit." *Gewerkschaftliche Monatshefte.* Vol. 28, no. 4 (April 1977), pp. 217–225.

—. "Gewerkschaftspolitik in schwieriger Zeit." *Gewerkschaftliche Monatshefte.* Vol. 26, no. 4 (April 1975), pp. 201–208.

—. "Humanisierung der Arbeitswelt als gewerkschaftspolitische Aufgabe." *Gewerkschaftliche Monatshefte.* Vol. 24, no. 1 (January 1973), pp. 1–11.

—. "Mitbestimmung in der Krise – Krise der Mitbestimmung?" *Gewerkschaftliche Monatshefte.* Vol. 28, no. 11 (November 1977), pp. 673–678.

—. "Ownership of Large Enterprises No Longer a Privilege for Social Power." *DGB Report.* No. 4 (1976), pp. 3–7.

—. "Den technischen Fortschritt human gestalten." *Die Quelle.* Vol. 29, no. 4 (April 1978), pp. 196–197.

—. "Trade Unions Do Not Accept Unemployment as Fate." *DGB Report.* No. 1 (1978), pp. 3–4.

—. "Zum Beginn der Diskussion um ein neues Grundsatzprogramm." *Gewerkschaftliche Monatshefte.* Vol. 31, no. 1 (January 1980), pp. 1–12.

—. "Zwanzig Jahre europäische Gewerkschaftspolitik." *Gewerkschaftliche Monatshefte*. Vol. 24, no. 4 (April 1973), pp. 201–206.

"Vetter: Industrialize Developing Countries Meaningfully." *DGB Report*. No. 1/2 (1976), p. 9.

"Vetter zieht parallelen zu Weimar." *Frankfurter Allgemeine Zeitung*, June 28, 1980.

Vietheer, Heinz. "Gewerkschaften müssen Motor sein." *Gewerkschaftliche Monatshefte*. Vol. 27, no. 7 (July 1976), pp. 412–419.

"Version oder Vision? – Überlegungen zum Verhältnis der DGB-Gewerkschaft HBV zur DAG." *Gewerkschaftliche Monatshefte*. Vol. 25, no. 9 (September 1974), pp. 524–527.

Vilmar, Fritz. "Systematische Verknappung des Arbeitskraft-Angebots." *Gewerkschaftliche Monatshefte*. Vol. 28, no. 1 (January 1977), pp. 23–31.

"Der Vize-Komplex." *Der Spiegel*. Vol. 13, no. 36 (September 2, 1959).

"Vom Stolz über das Abfangen antiautoritärer Tendenzen." *Frankfurter Rundschau*, January 12, 1980.

Vornehm, Norbert. "Recht auf Arbeit, Recht auf Bildung." *Die Quelle*. Vol. 27, no. 9 (September 1977), pp. 382–384.

"Vorrang für die Vollbeschäftigung-Alternativen der Wirtschaftspolitik." *Blätter für deutsche und internationale Politik*. Vol. 24, no. 5 (May 1979), pp. 614–633.

"Vorschuss auf den Mai." *Der Spiegel*. Vol. 21, no. 49 (November 1967).

"Vorwurf der Verniedlichung kommunistischer Ziele gegen Detlef Hensche." *Frankfurter Rundschau*, September 29, 1979.

Wahsner, Roderich. "Das Arbeitskartell: Die Restauration des kapitalistischen Arbeitsrechts in Westdeutschland nach 1945." *Kritische Justiz*. Vol. 7, no. 4 (1974), pp. 369–386.

Walter, Jürgen. "Neuer Tarifvertrag setzt ein Zeichen." *Gewerkschaftliche Umschau*. Vol. 28, no. 5 (September–October 1977), pp. 2–3.

Walther, Rolf. "Jede zweite besser eingruppiert!" *druck und papier*. Vol. 23, no. 1 (January 7, 1985), p. 12.

"Warnstreiks sind Rechtens." *Frankfurter Rundschau*, September 13, 1984.

"Was Facharbeit ist, muss Facharbeit bleiben: Die IG Druck und Papier: Kampf um Tarifvertrag über neue Technik." *metall*. Vol. 30, no. 3 (February 13, 1978), p. 12.

Weber, Alfred. "Staat und gewerkschaftliche Aktion." *Gewerkschaftliche Monatshefte*. Vol. 3, no. 8 (August 1952), pp. 478–481.

Weber, Maria. "Gewerkschaftliche Hochschulpolitik." *Gewerkschaftliche Monatshefte*. Vol. 28, no. 2 (February 1977), pp. 65–71.

—. "Gewerkschaftliche Politik für Frauen im 'Internationalen Jahr der Frau 1975'." *Gewerkschaftliche Monatshefte*. Vol. 26, no. 11 (November 1975), pp. 658–665.

Wehner, Ewald, Hajo Graf Vitzthum and Rudolf Hofmann. "Beschäftigung und Arbeitsbedingungen im öffentlichen Dienst." *Gewerkschaftliche Monatshefte*. Vol. 28, no. 6 (June 1977), pp. 368–380.

"Wehner; Gruppenantrag nicht taktisch gemeint." *Frankfurter Rundschau*, July 3, 1980.

Wehner, Hans-Georg. "Die Bundesrepublik wurde zu einem 'Lohnsteuerstaat.'" *Gewerkschaftliche Umschau*. Vol. 28, no. 2 (March–April 1977), pp. 8–9.

Wehner, Herbert. "Solidarität ist Voraussetzung für Freiheit und Sicherheit." *Gewerkschaftliche Monatshefte*. Vol. 28, no. 4 (April 1977), pp. 225–233.

Wehrhart, Otto. "Erster Warnstreik gegen Werft-Stillegung." *metall*. Vol. 30, no. 20 (October 4, 1978), pp. 15–16.

Weick, Edgar. "Aus der Geschichte lernen." *express*. Vol. 17, no. 4 (April 23, 1979), pp. 8–9.

Weinberger, Marie-Luise. "Die Grünen: Vom Mythos zur Erstarrung." *Gewerkschaftliche Monatshefte*. Vol. 36, no. 8 (August 1985), pp. 489–501.

"Welche Arbeit zumutbar ist, soll im einzelfall geprüft werden." *Frankfurter Rundschau*, May 17, 1979.

Weltz, Friedrich. "Kooperative Konfliktverarbeitung." *Gewerkschaftliche Monatshefte*. Vol. 28, no. 5 (May 1977), pp. 291–309.

"Wenig dran rühren." *Der Spiegel*. Vol. 24, no. 6 (February 2, 1970).

"Wer mault, muss gehen." *Der Spiegel*. Vol. 21, no. 24, (June 5, 1967).

"Wes Brot ich ess' des Lied ich sing." *metall*. Vol. 36, no. 13 (June 22, 1984), pp. 16–17.

Wieczorek, Norbert. "Gewerkschaften und demokratische Investitionslenkung und-kontrolle." *Gewerkschaftliche Monatshefte*. Vol. 24, no. 12 (December 1973), pp. 753–757.

"Wiedererwachter Geist." *metall*. Vol. 30, no. 6 (March 30, 1978), p. 4.

Wiesner, Herbert. "Das Problem unserer Zeit: Rationalisierung und Automatisierung." *Gewerkschaftliche Umschau*. Vol. 29, no. 3 (May–June 1978), pp. 5–7.

Wiethold, Franziska. "Jugendarbeitslosigkeit – Die konjunkturellen und strukturellen Probleme aus gewerkschaftlicher Sicht. *Gewerkschaftliche Monatshefte*. Vol. 26, no. 9 (September 1975), pp. 538–550.

Wiggershaus, Renate and Rolf. "Beim 'Gewaltschutzparagraphen' geht es nicht nur um Gewalt." *Gewerkschaftliche Monatshefte*. Vol. 27, no. 10 (October 1976), pp. 597–602.

"Wille zur Kollegialität in der IG Chemie bekundet." *Frankfurter Rundschau*, April 19, 1979.

Willey, Richard J. "Trade Unions and Political Parties in the Federal Republic of Germany." *Industrial and Labor Relations Review*. Vol. 28 (October 1974), pp. 38–59.

"Willy Brandt: 'Ihr lasst mich alle allein.'" *Der Spiegel*. Vol. 38, no. 8 (February 18, 1984).

"Wir haben einen." *Der Spiegel*. Vol. 23, no. 15 (April 7, 1969).

"Wir haben Mut zum Unmut." *metall*. Vol. 30, no. 4 (February 28, 1978), p. 13.

"Wir haben Zeichen gesetzt." *Der Gewerkschafter*.Vol. 27, no. 5 (May 1979), pp. 21–26,.

"Wo alle sich verrückt benehmen." *Der Spiegel*. Vol. 16, no. 19 (May 2, 1962).

Wohlgemuth, Hermann Hans. "Zur Auseinandersetzung um die Aussperrung." *Gewerkschaftliche Monatshefte*. Vol. 30, no. 3 (March 1979), pp. 145–152.

Wolf, Ernst. "Reform des Chemie-Studiums." *Gewerkschaftliche Umschau*. Vol. 29, no. 1 (January–February 1978), pp. 22–23.

"Wollen uns fertigmachen." *Der Spiegel*. Vol. 38, no. 26 (June 25, 1984).

"Worum es in Karlsruhe ging." *Frankfurter Rundschau*, March 2, 1979.

"Die Wurzel allen Übels liegt in der unbestimmten Gesetzesformulierung." *Handelsblatt*, August 16/17, 1985.

"The Year of the Young Worker." *DGB Report*. No. 4 (1971), pp. 12–14.

Zachert, Ulrich. "Aussperrung und Gewerkschaften." *Gewerkschaftliche Monatshefte*. Vol. 29, no. 5 (May 1978), pp. 280–289.

—. "Aussperrung und Grundgesetz." *Die Quelle*. Vol. 29, no. 3 (March 1978), pp. 134–135.

—. "Gewerkschaftliche Autonomie und rechtliche Rahmenbedingungen: Die Aussperrung im Spektrum der Einschränkung von Gewerkschaftsrechten." *Gewerkschaftliche Monatshefte*. Vol. 31, no. 5 (May 1980), pp. 293–302.

—. "Mitbestimmung ohne Gewerkschaften?" *Gewerkschaftliche Monatshefte*. Vol. 30, no. 6 (June 1979), pp. 342–346.

—. "Rationalisierung-Stillegung-Arbeitsplatzverlust: Möglichkeiten und Perspektiven gewerkschaftlicher Gegenwehr." *Gewerkschaftliche Monatshefte*. Vol. 28, no. 5 (May 1977), pp. 281–291.

"Die Zeit läuft." *Der Spiegel*. Vol. 27, no. 24 (June 16, 1973).

"Zerreissproben noch und noch." *Der Spiegel*. Vol. 21, no. 11 (March 13, 1967).

Zeuner, Bodo. "Solidarität mit der SPD oder Solidarität der Klasse? Zur SPD-Bindung der DGB-Gewerkschaften." *Prokla*. Vol. 6, no. 1 (1977), pp. 1–32.

"Ziel für 1981: Einkommen sichern." *metall*. Vol. 32, no. 22 (November 5, 1980).

Zimmerman, Lothar. "Der Kampf." In IG Metall (ed.), *Werktage werden besser: Der Kampf um den Lohnrahmentarifvertrag II in Nordwürttemberg/Nordbaden*. Cologne: Europäische Verlagsanstalt, 1977, pp. 65–71.

Zinn, Karl-Georg. "Dem Krisenmanagement fehlt eine Konzeption – ein Plädoyer für mehr Interventionismus." *Gewerkschaftliche Monatshefte*. Vol. 28, no. 7 (July 1977), pp. 417–429.

—. "Politik und Sachverständigenmeinung – Sachverständigenrat und Council of Economic Advisors im Vergleich." *Gewerkschaftliche Monatshefte*. Vol. 29, no. 3 (March 1978), pp. 179–188.

Zoller, Hermann. "Darum geht's in der Druckindustrie." *Die Quelle*. Vol. 29, no. 3 (March 1978), pp. 138–139.

—. "Ein tarifpolitisches Signal." *Gewerkschaftliche Umschau*. Vol. 29, no. 3 (May–June 1978), pp. 8–10.

"Zum Memorandum '75." *WSI-Mitteilungen*. Vol. 32, no. 6 (June 1979), pp. 294–297.

"Zum Wohl." *Der Spiegel*. Vol. 25, no. 4 (January 25, 1971).

"Zusammenbrüche in ungeahnt kurzer Zeit." *Der Spiegel*. Vol. 29, no. 6 (February 3, 1975).

"Zwei Linien und ein roter Faden." *Frankfurter Rundschau*, October 6, 1979.

C. *German newspapers and magazines consulted in the course of this study*

*Das Argument*

*Aus Politik und Zeitgeschichte*

*Blätter für deutsche und internationale Politik*

*Bulletin*
*Deutscher Gewerkschaftsbund Nachrichten-Dienst*
*DGB Report* (An English periodical published by the Deutscher Gewerkschafts-
  bund, DGB)
*druck und papier*
*Die Einheit*
*express*
*Frankfurter Allgemeine Zeitung*
*Frankfurter Rundschau*
*The German Tribune* (An English weekly review of the German press, published in
  Hamburg)
*Der Gewerkschafter*
*Gewerkschaftliche Monatshefte*
*Gewerkschaftliche Umschau*
*Gewerkschaftspost*
*Der Grundstein*
*Handelsblatt*
*Journal für Sozialforschung*
*Kritische Justiz*
*Leviathan*
*links*
*metall*
*Die Mitbestimmung*
*Mitteilungen aus der Arbeitsmarkt- und Berufsforschung*
*Die Neue*
*Das ÖTV Magazin*
*Das Parlament*
*Prokla*
*Die Quelle*
*Sozial Report*
*Der Spiegel*
*Der Staat*
*Süddeutsche Zeitung*
*Die Tageszeitung*
*Die Welt*
*Welt der Arbeit*
*Westfälische Rundschau*
*Wirtschaftspolitische Informationen*
*WSI-Mitteilungen*
*Die Zeit*

D. *Individuals who participated in formal and informal interviews between
January 1, 1979 and April 15, 1985*

*Adam, Hermann.* Economist; senior editor of union-owned Bund Verlag in Cologne;
  formerly researcher at the Wirtschafts- und Sozialwissenschaftliches Institut
  of the DGB in Düsseldorf.

*Altvater, Elmar.* Political scientist; professor at the Free University of Berlin; specialist on the political economy of labor in the Federal Republic of Germany and in Europe.

*Armanski, Gerhard.* Political scientist; free-lance journalist in Frankfurt and Berlin; specialist on technology and work-related problems.

*Bahl, Volker.* Political scientist; formerly assistant editor of *Gewerkschaftliche Monatshefte*; staff member for the chairman of IG Bau-Steine-Erden; currently staff member for the chairman of the DGB's regional district of Rhineland-Palatinate.

*Bahl-Benker, Angelika.* Political scientist; staff member in IG Metall's research division on automation and technology.

*Barczinski, Jörg.* IG Metall's press secretary and chief officer of the union's media and public relations department.

*Bergmiller, Iris.* Sociologist; member of the teachers' union, Gewerkschaft Erziehung und Wissenschaft (GEW); former member of the editorial board of *express*, an independent monthly covering union-related issues.

*Beyme, Klaus von.* Political scientist; professor at the University of Heidelberg and president of the International Political Science Association (IPSA) between 1982 and 1985; expert on German and European labor movements and interest associations.

*Bieber, Hans-Joachim.* Historian; lecturer at the University of Kassel; expert on German labor, especially in the Weimar Republic.

*Birkwald, Reimar.* Bargaining specialist; former head of IG Metall's collective bargaining division at union headquarters in Frankfurt and adviser to many of IG Metall's bargaining commissions; currently IG Metall's district secretary in Hanover.

*Borsdorf, Ulrich.* Historian; researcher at the Wirtschafts- und Sozialwissenschaftliches Institut of the DGB in Düsseldorf; formerly assistant editor of *Gewerkschaftliche Monatshefte*.

*Bouillon, Rüdiger.* Economist; staff member in IG Chemie-Papier-Keramik's collective bargaining division at the union's head office in Hanover.

*Breit, Ernst.* Head of the DGB since 1982; previously head of the postal workers' union, DPG.

*Briefs, Ulrich.* Economist; researcher at the Wirtschafts- und Sozialwissenschaftliches Institut of the DGB in Düsseldorf; specialist on issues of technology and automation.

*Brügmann, Wolf-Gunter.* Journalist; specialist on trade unions for the *Frankfurter Rundschau*.

*Cremer, Dietmar.* Economist; staff member in the economics division at the DGB's headquarters in Düsseldorf.

*Deeke, Axel.* Economist; researcher at the Landesinstitut Sozialforschungsstelle Dortmund; specialist on labor market issues.

*De Hair, Achim.* Political scientist; staff member in IG Metall's media and public relations department.

*Dohse, Knuth.* Political scientist; researcher on union-related issues at the International Institute of Comparative Social Research of the Science Center Berlin.

*Dombois, Rainer.* Sociologist; researcher in industrial sociology at the University of Bremen; specialist on automation and technological innovation, particularly pertaining to the automobile industry.

*Drinkuth, Andreas.* Economist; current head of IG Metall's division on automation and technology.

*Dybowski, Gisela.* Sociologist; formerly researcher on union-related issues at the Institut für Sozialforschung in Frankfurt; currently employed by IG Metall.

*Erd, Rainer.* Lawyer and political scientist; researcher on union-related issues at the Institut für Sozialforschung in Frankfurt; former member of the editorial board of *express.*

*Esser, Josef.* Political scientist; professor at the University of Frankfurt; specialist on trade union politics and sectoral policies, particularly in the steel industry.

*Euler, Kurt.* Head of the civil service division of the DGB in Düsseldorf.

*Ferlemann, Erwin.* Head of IG Druck und Papier as of 1983; formerly member in charge of collective bargaining on this union's executive committee.

*Friedrichs, Günther.* Economist; retired head of IG Metall's division on automation and technology.

*Funke, Hajo.* Political scientist; researcher on union-related issues at the International Institute of Comparative Social Research of the Science Center Berlin.

*Gerlach, Gerhard.* Political scientist; formerly researcher at the Wirtschafts- und Sozialwissenschaftliches Institut of the DGB in Düsseldorf; currently staff member of the executive committee at HBV, the retail, banking and insurance workers' union.

*Görlich, Helmut.* Lawyer; formerly John F. Kennedy Memorial Fellow at the Center for European Studies at Harvard University; lecturer at the University of Hamburg; specialist on constitutional issues.

*Görs, Dieter.* Economist; researcher at the Wirtschafts- und Sozialwissenschaftliches Institut of the DGB in Düsseldorf; specialist on vocational education and training.

*Hauenschild, Karl.* Head of IG Chemie-Papier-Keramik between 1969 and 1982.

*Hecker, Jürgen.* Staff member of the civil service division at the DGB in Düsseldorf.

*Helfert, Mario.* Sociologist; researcher at the Wirtschafts- und Sozialwissenschaftliches Institut of the DGB in Düsseldorf; specialist on issues pertaining to the quality of work life, working conditions and other areas of industrial sociology.

*Hemmer, Hans-Otto.* Historian; currently editor-in-chief of *Gewerkschaftliche Monatshefte.*

*Hemsteg, Renate.* Sociologist; staff member of IG Metall's shop stewards division at the union's headquarters in Frankfurt.

*Hensche, Detlef.* Lawyer, journalist, political scientist; member of IG Druck und Papier's executive committee with special responsibilities for collective bargaining and the union's bi-weekly publication *druck und papier.*

*Herb, Kurt.* Former head of IG Metall's Essen district; died in 1981.

*Hildebrandt, Eckart.* Political scientist; researcher on union-related issues at the International Institute of Comparative Social Research of the Science Center Berlin.

*Hinrichs, Werner.* Lawyer in IG Metall's legal department.

*Hirsch, Joachim.* Sociologist; professor at the University of Frankfurt; specialist on unions, social democracy and social movements.

*Höhnen, Wilfried.* Economist; staff member in the economics division at DGB headquarters in Düsseldorf.

*Hoffmann, Jürgen.* Political scientist; professor at the Hochschule für Wirtschaft und Politik in Hamburg; specialist on the political economy of labor in the Federal Republic and Europe.

*Hoss, Willi.* Worker at Daimler-Benz plant in Untertürkheim in Stuttgart; co-editor and co-founder of the newspaper *Plakat*, for which IG Metall expelled him from the union; elected to the Bundestag in Bonn as a parliamentary member of the Greens in March 1983.

*Jacobi, Otto.* Economist; researcher on union-related matters at the Institut für Sozialforschung in Frankfurt; member of the editorial board of *express*.

*Janssen, Hans.* IG Metall executive committee member in charge of collective bargaining.

*Janzen, Karl-Heinz.* IG Metall executive committee member in charge of social policy, labor market issues, automation and technology.

*Jöns, Jürgen.* IG Bau-Steine-Erden executive committee member in charge of white-collar workers and the union's publications.

*Jordan, Reinhard.* Economist; researcher at the Wirtschafts- und Sozialwissenschaftliches Institut of the DGB in Düsseldorf; specialist on the steel, chemical and automobile industries.

*Judith, Rudolf.* IG Metall executive committee member in charge of the steel industry and Montanmitbestimmung.

*Jürgens, Ulrich.* Political scientist; researcher on union-related issues at the International Institute of Comparative Social Research of the Science Center Berlin.

*Kaltenborn, Wilhelm.* Political scientist; chief-of-staff in Heinz Oskar Vetter's office until May 1982, during the latter's incumbency as head of the DGB.

*Kastleiner, Erwin.* Member in charge of social policy, labor market issues and retirement plans on IG Bau-Steine-Erden's executive committee.

*Kersjes, Franz.* Chairman of IG Druck und Papier's district of North Rhine-Westphalia.

*Kittner, Michael.* Lawyer; IG Metall's senior legal counsel and head of the union's legal department; also professor of labor law at the University of Kassel.

*Kneissel, Jutta.* Economist; IG Metall executive committee senior staff member responsible for planning of long-term policy issues.

*Kohl, Heribert.* Political scientist; formerly researcher at the Wirtschafts- und Sozialwissenschaftliches Institut of the DGB in Düsseldorf; subsequently staff member of the Hans-Böckler-Stiftung (Hans Böckler Foundation) in Düsseldorf and editor of its monthly publication *Die Mitbestimmung*; currently head of the policy division of the retail, banking and insurance workers' union (HBV) in Düsseldorf.

*Krüper, Manfred.* Economist; formerly director of IG Chemie-Papier-Keramik's economics division; currently labor director at VEBA, the Federal Republic's largest state-controlled, multi-industrial conglomerate.

*Küchle, Hartmut.* Economist; researcher at the Wirtschafts- und Sozialwissenschaftliches Institut of the DGB in Düsseldorf; specialist on business cycles, international economic interdependence and investment.

*Kuda, Rudolf.* Economist; director of IG Metall's economics division; influential in the union's collective bargaining process.

*Kurz-Scherf, Ingrid.* Economist; researcher at the Wirtschafts- und Sozialwissenschaftliches Institut of the DGB in Düsseldorf; specialist on collective bargaining and director of the institute's collective bargaining and contract archive.

*Lang, Klaus.* Theologian and political scientist; formerly head of IG Metall's media and public relations department; currently head of the union's collective bargaining division.

*Lecher, Wolfgang.* Sociologist; researcher at the Wirtschafts- und Sozialwissenschaftliches Institut of the DGB in Düsseldorf; specialist on European trade unions and labor movements.

*Lehmbruch, Gerhard.* Political scientist; professor at the University of Konstanz; specialist on interest groups and their role in the politics of advanced industrial societies.

*Leibfried, Stefan.* Sociologist; professor at the University of Bremen; specialist on social policy, health policy and education.

*Leiss, Manfred.* Sociologist; staff member in IG Metall's division on works councils, the Works Constitution Law of 1972 and the Co-determination Act of 1976.

*Leminsky, Gerhard.* Economist; formerly editor-in-chief of *Gewerkschaftliche Monatshefte* and researcher at the Wirtschafts- und Sozialwissenschaftliches Institut of the DGB in Düsseldorf, specializing in the role of unions in state and society and all issues related to economic democracy and co-determination; currently director of the Hans-Böckler-Stiftung (Hans Böckler Foundation) in Düsseldorf.

*Löwenthal, Richard.* Political scientist; professor emeritus at the Free University of Berlin; expert on German social democracy and the history of the German labor movement.

*Markmann, Heinz.* Economist; director of the Wirtschafts- und Sozialwissenschaftliches Institut of the DGB in Düsseldorf.

*Martens, Helmut.* Sociologist; researcher at the Landesinstitut Sozialforschungsstelle Dortmund; specialist on union politics.

*Mehrens, Klaus.* Economist; former staff member of IG Metall's economics division, with responsibility for matters of economic conversion; currently in charge of the strategic planning division at IG Metall's head office in Frankfurt.

*Michaelis, Hans-Peter.* Political scientist; former staff member of IG Chemie-Papier-Keramik's works councils and legal issues division at the union's headquarters in Hanover; died in 1984.

*Möller-Lücking, Norbert.* Lawyer; staff member in the DGB's legal department; specialist on labor law, unemployment compensation and social policy.

*Muhr, Gerd.* Vice chairman of the DGB and member in charge of labor market policy and social policy on the DGB's executive committee.

*Mückenberger, Ulrich.* Lawyer; professor at the Hochschule für Wirtschaft und Politik in Hamburg; specialist on labor law, constitutional issues and co-determination.

*Mülhaupt, Bernd.* Economist; researcher at the Wirtschafts- und Sozialwissen-schaftliches Institut of the DGB in Düsseldorf; specialist on business cycles and banking.

*Müller, Gernot.* Economist; researcher at the Wirtschafts- und Sozialwissenschaft-liches Institut of the DGB in Düsseldorf; specialist on monetary and fiscal policy, taxation and macroeconomic growth.

*Müller, Joachim.* Director of IG Druck und Papier's collective bargaining division at union headquarters in Stuttgart.

*Müller-Jentsch, Walther.* Sociologist; former researcher on union-related issues at the Institut für Sozialforschung in Frankfurt; former member of the editorial board of *express*; currently professor of sociology at the University of Paderborn.

*Narr, Wolf-Dieter.* Political scientist; professor at the Free University of Berlin; specialist on political parties, the political process and political rights of individuals and groups.

*Naschold, Frieder.* Political scientist; formerly professor and university president at the University of Konstanz; currently director of the International Institute of Comparative Social Research of the Science Center Berlin, specializing in research concerning labor market policy, health policy and quality of work life.

*Negt, Oskar.* Political scientist; professor at the University of Hanover; specialist on political culture, political participation, interest group politics and social movements.

*Nutzinger, Hans.* Political scientist; professor at the University of Kassel; specialist on co-determination.

*Oertzen, Peter von.* Political scientist; formerly professor at several West German universities; leading SPD politician and intellectual in Lower Saxony and on the national level.

*Ötjen, Hinrich.* Educational expert. Formerly head of the DGB's youth education center in Oberursel, currently director of the DGB education center in Hattingen.

*Offe, Claus.* Sociologist; professor at the University of Bielefeld; specialist on the role of the state in advanced industrial societies, trade unions and their relations to the new social movements, and reduction of work time.

*Osterland, Martin.* Sociologist; professor at the University of Bremen; specialist on industrial relations, organization of work and labor market issues.

*Perner, Detlef.* Sociologist; researcher at the Wirtschafts- und Sozialwissenschaft-liches Institut of the DGB in Düsseldorf; specialist on union–party relations, interest group theory and employers' associations.

*Peter, Horst.* Teacher; SPD member of the Bundestag from Kassel; specialist on economy–ecology relations.

*Pfromm, Hans-Adam.* Economist; formerly chief-of-staff of the policy planning divi-sion of IG Metall's executive committee; currently labor director at the Krupp corporation.

*Piecha, Manfred.* Economist; formerly researcher at the Wirtschafts- und Sozialwiss-enschaftliches Institut of the DGB in Düsseldorf; retired.

*Piehl, Ernst.* Economist; formerly researcher at the Wirtschafts- und Sozialwissen-

currently director of the European Center for the Development of Vocational Training, in West Berlin.

*Pitz, Karl.* Economist, staff member in IG Metall's economics division; specialist on the automobile industry and asset formation.

*Rappe, Hermann.* Head of IG Chemie-Papier-Keramik since 1982 and SPD member of the Bundestag.

*Riegert, Botho.* Economist; staff member in the economics division of the DGB's headquarters in Düsseldorf.

*Rose, Gunter.* Lawyer, IG Chemie-Papier-Keramik's senior legal counsel and head of the union's legal department.

*Russig, Harald.* Lawyer; researcher on union-related issues at the International Institute of Comparative Social Research of the Science Center Berlin.

*Schäfer, Claus.* Economist; researcher at the Wirtschafts- und Sozialwissenschaftliches Institut of the DGB in Düsseldorf; specialist on asset formation, public spending and fiscal policy.

*Schauer, Helmut.* Sociologist; staff member in IG Metall's bargaining division at union headquarters in Frankfurt.

*Scheibe-Lange, Ingrid.* Economist; researcher at the Wirtschafts- und Sozialwissenschaftliches Institut of the DGB in Düsseldorf; specialist on the rights and entitlements of employees.

*Schmidt, Walter.* Economist; staff member in IG Metall's economics division; specialist on fiscal forecasting and sectoral analysis.

*Schneider, Walter.* Economist; researcher at the Wirtschafts- und Sozialwissenschaftliches Institut of the DGB in Düsseldorf; specialist on structural policy and regional industrialization.

*Seifert, Hartmut.* Economist; researcher at the Wirtschafts- und Sozialwissenschaftliches Institut of the DGB in Düsseldorf; specialist on labor market policy, flexibilization, retraining and market segmentation.

*Seitenzahl, Rolf.* Economist; formerly researcher at the Wirtschafts- und Sozialwissenschaftliches Institut of the DGB in Düsseldorf; subsequently chief policy analyst to the head of the public employees' union (ÖTV), Heinz Kluncker; currently chief-of-staff to the chairman of the railroad workers' union (GdED), Ernst Haar.

*Sengenberger, Werner.* Economist; researcher at the Institut für Sozialwissenchaftliche Forschung in Munich; specialist on labor market segmentation and the impact of technology on work.

*Standfest, Erich.* Sociologist; researcher at the Wirtschafts- und Sozialwissenschaftliches Institut of the DGB in Düsseldorf; specialist on social policy.

*Steger, Ulrich.* Economist; former SPD member of the Bundestag, currently minister of technology, science and research in the state government of Hesse.

*Steiert, Robert.* Political scientist; staff member of IG Metall's international division at union headquarters in Frankfurt.

*Steinkühler, Franz.* Former head of IG Metall's Stuttgart district; since 1983, IG Metall's vice chairman at the head office in Frankfurt.

*Streeck, Wolfgang.* Sociologist; researcher on union-related issues at the International Institute of Management of the Science Center Berlin.

*Streeck, Wolfgang.* Sociologist; researcher on union-related issues at the International Institute of Management of the Science Center Berlin.

Tiedtke, Karl-Heinz. IG Bau-Steine-Erden executive committee member in charge of vocational education, relations with works councils and co-determination.

*Tofaute, Hartmut.* Economist; researcher at the Wirtschafts- und Sozialwissenschaftliches Institut of the DGB in Düsseldorf; specialist on fiscal and tax policy, and public employees' unions.

*Trautwein-Kalms, Gudrun.* Political scientist; researcher at the Wirtschafts- und Sozialwissenschaftliches Institut of the DGB in Düsseldorf; specialist on quality of work life.

*Vitt, Werner.* Vice chairman of IG Chemie-Papier-Keramik and executive committee member in charge of co-determination, union relations with works councils and legal matters.

*Vitzthum, Hajo.* Political scientist; chief-of-staff to the chairman of the public employees' union, ÖTV, headquartered in Stuttgart.

*Vogelheim, Elisabeth.* Sociologist; former senior staff assistant for women's issues at IG Chemie-Papier-Keramik; currently head of IG Metall's women's division at union headquarters in Frankfurt.

*Volkmann, Gerd.* Economist; researcher at the Wirtschafts- und Sozialwissenschaftliches Institut of the DGB in Düsseldorf; specialist on industrial analysis.

*Wahle-Homann, Ingeborg.* Sociologist; currently assistant editor of *Gewerkschaftliche Monatshefte*.

*Welzmüller, Rudolf.* Economist; researcher at the Wirtschafts- und Sozialwissenschaftliches Institut of the DGB in Düsseldorf; specialist on technology issues, restructuration and industrial competitiveness.

*Wohlgemuth, Hans-Hermann.* Lawyer in the DGB's legal department at the federation's head office in Düsseldorf; specialist on lockouts.

*Wolter, Henner.* Lawyer; IG Druck und Papier's senior legal counsel and head of the union's legal department.

*Zachert, Ulrich.* Lawyer; formerly researcher at the Wirtschafts- und Sozialwissenschaftliches Institut of the DGB in Düsseldorf; currently professor at the Hochschule für Wirtschaft und Politik in Hamburg; specialist on lockouts, constitutional questions and co-determination.

*Zoll, Rainer.* Political scientist; holder of a professorship at the University of Bremen, the only one in the Federal Republic explicitly chartered for the study of the history and theory of the organized labor movement.

# Glossary of German terms

*Absicherungstarifvertrag (ATV)* – Protective Collective Bargaining Agreement (1978); proposal by IG Metall to enhance the job security of its membership.

*ADB* – (see *Allgemeiner Deutscher Beamtenbund*)

*ADGB* – (see *Allgemeiner Deutscher Gewerkschaftsbund*)

*AGV* – (see *Arbeitgeber Verband Eisen- und Stahlindustrie e.V.*)

*Aktiengesellschaften* – publicly held companies.

*Aktionsprogramm* – union document setting forth medium-term goals

*aktiver tarifloser Zustand* – active contractless situation; occurs after mediation efforts have failed, allowing unions the option to strike.

*Allgemeine Gewerkschaft* – single, centralized union formation supported by many leftist unionists returning to Germany after World War II; discarded in favor of the present system of seventeen industrial unions (*Industriegewerkschaften*).

*Allgemeiner Deutscher Beamtenbund (ADB)* – General German Civil Servants' Federation; pre-1933 Social Democratic union of civil servants.

*Allgemeiner Deutscher Gewerkschaftsbund (ADGB)* – General German Trade Union Federation. Largest of the pre-1933 union confederations; Social Democratic-controlled.

*Allgemeiner Freier Angestelltenbund (AFA)* – General Free Salaried Staff Association; pre-1933 Social Democratic union of white-collar employees.

*allgemeinverbindlich* – universally binding; the TVG allows the Federal Labor Court to declare a contract to be universally binding in a given industry if over 50% of that industry's employers are members of the employers' association; such a ruling can force employers to pay the same wages to unionized and non-unionized employees alike.

*Allgemeinverbindlichkeitserklärung* – declaration of general applicability; provision of the Collective Bargaining Law of 1918 which allowed the Labor Ministry to extend a regional or national contract to all firms and workers in a given industry.

*Altersgruppen* – age categories; used in the calculus to determine a worker's wage rate.

*Altersklassen* – (See *Altersgruppen*)

*Angestellte* – clerical staff.

*Angesteltenmentalität* – white-collar mentality.

*Anhänge* – appendices; the sections of a contract which set guidelines on working conditions for particular skill groups.

*Anhörungsrecht* – the right to be consulted.

*Anrechnung* – surcharge; in labor relations, refers to management's refusal to raise wages (usually during a recession) on the grounds that non-contractual remuneration (see *Leistungszulage*) has already compensated workers adequately.

*Antriebstechik* – "drive technology"; motor-production sector of the metal industry.

*Arbeiter* – blue-collar workers.

*Arbeiterklasse* – the working class.

*Arbeitgeber* – employer.

*Arbeitgeberverband Eisen- und Stahlindustrie e.V. (AGV)* – Iron and Steel Industry Employers' Association.

*Arbeitgeberverbände* – employers' associations.

*Arbeitnehmer* – employees.

*Arbeitnehmerkonferenz* – worker conference; basic organizational unit of the SPD labor organization AfA.

*Arbeitnehmervertreter* – employee representatives on the supervisory boards of some West German companies.

*Arbeitsbewertungsmethode* – methods of analyzing activities involved in a particular job; used in determining remuneration.

*Arbeitsdirektor* – labor executive; official responsible for personnel policies; elected by representatives of both labor and management in companies affected by the MMG.

*Arbeitsförderungsgesetz* – Work Promotion Law; reform package passed by the Bundestag in 1969 which provided education and retraining programs for workers facing unemployment.

*Arbeitsgemeinschaft für Arbeitnehmerfragen (AfA)* – Working Community for Workers' Issues; labor organization created within the SPD in 1972 by the party leadership and its right-wing supporters partly to counteract the growth of the leftist *Jusos*.

*Arbeitsgerichte* – three-member labor law tribunals.

*Arbeitsprogramm* – work program.

*Arbeitsring der Arbeitgeberverbände der Deutschen chemischen Industrie* (also *Arbeitsring*) – Consortium of Employers' Associations of the German Chemical Industry.

*Arbeitsvertrag* – work contract; the agreement signed by an individual worker and the employer; must meet the stipulations already agreed to by the union and works council, but may include special bonuses designed to reward certain skills.

*ATV* – (see *Absicherungstarifvertrag*)

*Aufbruchsstimmung* – "mood of opening"; describes the period of reformism and prosperity presided over by Chancellor Willy Brandt.

*Aufsichtsrat* – corporate supervisory board.

*Ausschuss zur Koordinierung der Lohn- und Tarifpolitik* – collective bargaining committee of the employers' association, BDA.

*Aussperrung* – employer-initiated lockout; *lösende Aussperrung* – dismissal lockout, in which workers are summarily fired.

*Auswahlrichtlinien* – universal selection critieria; classification of workers according to age, wage group, marital status, etc., in order to determine preferential hiring and firing practices; subject to the approval of the works councils.

*BAG* – (see *Bundesarbeitsgericht*)

*Bank der Arbeit, Angestellten und Beamten AG* – Bank for Workers, Employees and Civil Servants; financial institution founded by the ADGB unions in 1924.

*Bank für Gemeinwirtschaft (BfG)* – Bank for Social Economy; union-owned post-war descendant of the ADGB-run Bank der Arbeit, Angestellten und Beamten.

*Bauausbaugewerbe* – construction finishing industry; construction sector which includes painting, plumbing, heating and electrical installation.

*Bauhauptgewerbe* – primary construction industry.

*Bauhütten* – union-led cooperative construction movement of the Weimar Republic.

*Baunebengewerbe* – auxiliary construction industry; construction sector which includes demolition and façade-cleaning.

*Baustoffgewerbe* – construction products industry.

*BDA* – (see *Bundesvereinigung der Deutschen Arbeitgeberverbände*).

*BDI* – (see *Bundesverband der Deutschen Industrie*)

*BDZV* – (see *Bundesverband Deutscher Zeitungsverleger*)

*Beamte* – tenured civil servants for whom collective bargaining is prohibited.

*Beirat* – advisory council; among the DGB unions, the highest inter-congress union body.

*Berufsgruppe Druckformherstellung* – printing plate production professional group; IG Druck sub-group created by the union leadership in 1974 to replace the powerful typographers' section.

*Berufsgruppen* – professional groups.

*Besitzstand* – standard of living.

*betonierter Betriebssyndikalismus* – "concrete company syndicalism"; reference to the alleged strengthening of metal industry works councils as a result of monitoring loopholes in the IG Metall strike settlement of 1984.

*betriebliche Vertrauensleute* – company shop stewards; worker representatives in the chemical industry elected by the entire workforce – both unionized and non-unionized – in a given factory.

*Betriebsabsprachen* – informal plant agreements; accords reached between works councils and management which are *not* legally binding.

*Betriebsänderungen* – plant changes; any significant change in the organization, purpose or location of a particular factory, or introduction of major alterations in production techniques; the BVG stipulates that the employer must consult the works council in a given factory before implementing these changes.

*Betriebsegoismus* – "company-oriented egoism"; excessive loyalty to one's company, at the expense of worker solidarity on an industrial basis.

*Betriebsgruppen* – factory groups; set up by the SPD prior to the Bad Godesberg reforms to fight the influence of the CDU and the communists.

*betriebsnahe Tarifpolitik* – plant-level collective bargaining; policy favored by activist unions since the late 1950s to enhance union power on the shop floor at the expense of the works councils.

*Betriebsrat* – works council.

*Betriebsrätegesetz* (BRG) – Works Council Law; passed in 1920 during the Weimar Republic; called for the election of workers' councils in plants with more than twenty workers.

*Betriebsratsfürsten* – works council "princes"; reference to the power and authority of the works councils in large companies where they often use their power to undermine the representational functions of the union.

*Betriebsrenten* – plant pensions; extra pensions negotiated between works councils and management in a given factory.

*Betriebssyndikalismus* – firm-specific syndicalism.

*Betriebsvereinbarungen* – plant accords; legally binding agreements reached between management and the works council in a given factory.

*Betriebsverfassung* – works constitution; legal arrangements governing labor-capital relations on the shop floor.

*Betriebsverfassungsgesetz* (BVG) – Works Constitution Law.

*Bezirk* – region, district.

*Bezirksdelegiertenkonferenz* – district delegate conference; assembly at which local representatives of a given union meet to discuss policies and select leaders.

*Branchenfonds* – sectoral funds; "accommodationist" asset formation plan proposed by IG Chemie in the late 1970s.

*Bundesanstalt für Arbeit* – Federal Labor Office; quasi-state agency empowered by the 1969 Work Promotion Law to act as an employment clearinghouse.

*Bundesarbeitsgericht* (BAG) – Federal Labor Court; created in 1954 as a "supreme court" for labor law cases; divided into several separate courts or "senates" (*Senat*).

*Bundesarbeitstagung* – Federal Working Congress; union assembly held between official union congresses.

*Bundesausschuss* – DGB Federal Council; reviews the actions of the DGB Executive Committee (*Geschäftsführender Vorstand*) between DGB congresses; consists of the DGB Executive Committee, the heads of the DGB regional districts (*Landesbezirke*), and representatives of the member unions.

*Bundesrat* – Federal Council; West Germany's upper house of parliament, consisting of representatives from the nation's states (*Länder*).

*Bundessozialgericht* – Federal Court of Social Welfare.

*Bundestag* – Federal Congress; West Germany's lower house of parliament.

*Bundesverband der Deutschen Industrie (BDI)* – Federal Association of German Industry; the most important of West Germany's thirteen "economic associations" (*Wirtschaftsverbände*).

*Bundesverband Deutscher Zeitungsverleger (BDZV)* – Federal Association of German Newspaper Publishers; newspaper publisher employers' association.

*Bundesverband Druck (BVD)* – Federal Printing Association; employers' association of printing company owners.

*Bundesvereinigung der Deutschen Arbeitgeberverbände (BDA)* – Federal Confederation of

German Employers' Associations; lobbying organization which represents business interests on issues involving social security, unemployment and welfare programs; also the main umbrella organization for West German employers in their direct relations with labor.

*Bundeswehr* – Federal Army.

*Bürgerliches Gesetzbuch* – Civil Legal Code.

*BVD* – (see *Bundesverband Druck*)

*BVG* – (see *Betriebsverfassungsgesetz*)

*CDU/CSU* – Christian Democratic Union/Christian Social Union.

*Christlicher Gewerkschaftsbund Deutschlands (CGB)* – German Christian Trade Union Federation; post-war Christian trade-union formation and (much smaller) rival to the DGB. Formed in 1959 by Christian "extremists" who had founded the *Christliche Gewerkschaftsbewegung* (Christian Trade Union Movement), as well as members of a resuscitated DHV.

*Christlicher Metallarbeiterverband (CMV)* – Christian Metalworkers; the largest constituent member of the CGB.

*DAF* – (see *Deutsche Arbeitsfront*).

*DBB* – (see *Deutscher Beamtenbund*).

Deutsche Angestellten Gewerkschaft (DAG) – German White-Collar Workers' Union; post-war split-off from the DGB, comprising white-collar employees opposed to the *Einheitsgewerkschaft*.

*Deutsche Arbeitsfront (DAF)* – German Labor Front; National Socialist-controlled union federation formed in 1933 after the dissolution of all German trade unions by the Nazis.

*Deutsche Industrie- und Handelstage (DIHT)* – German Industrial and Commercial Assemblies; body to which all West German regional chambers of commerce belong.

*Deutsche Journalisten Union (dju)* – German Journalists' Union; journalists' sub-group within IG Druck.

*Deutsche Postgewerkschaft (DPG)* – German Postal Workers' Union

*Deutscher Bauarbeiterverband (DBV)* – German Construction Workers' Union; pre-1933, Social Democratic union; the construction sector's first industrial union.

*Deutscher Baugewerksbund* – German Construction Federation; pre-1933 forerunner to IG Bau.

*Deutscher Beamtenbund (DBB)* – German Civil Servants' Federation; post-war split-off from the DGB, comprising civil servants opposed to the *Einheitsgewerkschaft*.

*Deutscher Buchdrucker Verein (DBV)* – German Book Printers' Confederation; union representing all male, skilled workers in the printing industry; founded in 1866 (briefly renamed UVDB and VdDB at the turn of the century); revived in 1948 as part of IG Druck; dissolved in 1974.

*Deutscher Gewerkschaftsbund (DGB)* – German Trade Union Federation; name of both the present-day, non-sectarian confederation of West German unions, and the pre-1933 Christian trade union body.

*Deutscher Journalisten Verband (DJV)* – German Journalists' Association; non-DGB journalists' organization.

*Deutscher Metallarbeiter Verband (DMV)* – German metalworkers' Union; pre-war forerunner to IG Metall; founded in 1891.

*Deutsches Institut für Wirtschaftsforschung (DIW)* – German Economic Research Institute.

*Deutschnationaler Handelsgehilfenverband (DHV)* – German National Clerks' and Shop Assistants' Association; right-wing, pre-1933 union of white-collar workers, closely allied with the Nazis; member of GEDAG.

*DGB* – (see *Deutscher Gewerkschaftsbund*)

*DJV* – (see *Deutscher Journalisten Verband*)

*DMV* – (see *Deutscher Metallarbeiter Verband*)

*Drittelparitätsmitbestimmung* – one-third parity co-determination; situation in which employee representation must constitute one-third of supervisory board membership in all firms with more than 500 workers; provided for by Articles 76–87 of the 1952 Works Constitution Law.

*Ecklohn* – base wage; usually the average wage rate for a skilled, adult, male worker without special qualifications; actual wages are expressed as a percentage of this base wage.

*Effektivklauseln* – effective pay clauses; agreements favored by the unions stipulating that non-contractual remuneration (*Leistungszulage*) be considered compensation for workers possessing special skills; opposed by the employers and, to date, also by the labor courts.

*Ehrenamtliche* – active unionists who sit on their union's executive committee without monetary compensation (see also *Hauptamtliche*).

*Einheitsgewerkschaft* – unitary, non-partisan trade union.

*Einigungsstelle* – arbitration board.

*Einlassungszwang* – "the pressure to enter into arbitration"; situation in some industries whereby once arbitration is called for by one party, the other must also submit to it.

*Elektrotechnik* or *Elektro* (electro) – the electronics industry.

*Erhöhungen in festen Beträgen* – lump-sum salary raises; raises paid in fixed amounts rather than percentages; designed to reduce gap between highest- and lowest-paid workers.

*Fabrikarbeiterverband* – (see *Verband der Fabrikarbeiter Deutschland*)

*FDP* – Free Democratic Party.

*Fernsehstreik* – television strike; work stoppage in which the strikers do not actively participate (i.e. they stay at home and watch television).

*Fördertechnik* – conveyance technology; metal industry sector comprising the production of lifts, conveyor belts and elevators, etc.

*Friedenspflicht* – peace obligation; principle under which unions and employers must refrain from engaging in labor conflict while a contract is still in force.

*Funktionärstreik* – [union] functionary strike; industrial action initiated and sustained by union officials rather than the rank and file.

*Gastarbeiter* – guest workers; foreign workers "imported" to meet West Germany's labor needs during the 1960s and 1970s.

*GEDAG* – (see *Gesamtverband deutscher Angestelltenverbände*).

*Gegenmacht* – opposing (or countervailing) power; used in reference to the view held by many radical unionists that organized labor should act as a counterweight to capitalist restoration in the Federal Republic.

*Gehalt* – monthly salary.

*Geldfaktor* – "money multiplier"; the compensation per unit received by a piece-rate worker.

*gemeinnützige* – non-profit.

*Gemeinnützige Urlaubskasse des Baugewerbes (UK)* – Beneficial Vacation Fund for the Construction Sector; joint labor-management vacation pay fund started by the construction union in the British sector in 1949 to offset the hardships of sporadic unemployment in that industry.

*Gemeinwirtschaft* – business in the public interest (also refers to publicly owned property).

*gemeinwirtschaftliche Unternehmen* – publicly owned corporations.

*Gemeinwohl* – commonweal (also *Allgemeinwohl*).

*Generalkommission* – predecessor union federation to the pre-1933, Social Democratic ADGB; umbrella federation of all SPD unions.

*Gesamtbetriebsrat* – company works council.

*Gesamtbetriebsvereinbarungen* – company accords; legally binding agreements negotiated between management and company works councils (*Gesmatbetriebsrat*).

*Gesamtmetall* – (see Gesamtverband der Metallindustriellen Arbeitgeberverbände).

*Gesamtverband deutscher Angestelltenverbände (GEDAG)* – Overall Association of German Salaried Staffs' Trade Unions; confederation of white-collar workers within the pre-1933, Christian DGB.

*Gesamtverband der Metallindustriellen Arbeitgeberverbände* or *Gesamtmetall* – metal industry employers' association.

*Geschäftsführender Vorstand* – Federal Executive Committee of the DGB or any of its constituent unions; the most powerful leadership body of the DGB unions; elected by delegates at each union congress.

*Gewerbeordnung* – Basic Business Law; passed in 1869, lifted restrictions on worker organizations; carried over into the new Reich's business law (*Reichsgewerbeordnung*) after unification in 1871.

*Gewerbesteuern* – business taxes.

*Gewerkschaft der Eisenbahner Deutschlands* – German Railroad Workers' Union.

*Gewerkschaft Erziehung und Wissenschaft (GEW)* – Education and Science Union.

*Gewerkschaft Gartenbau, Land und Forstwirtschaft (GLF)* – Horticulture, Agriculture and Forestry Workers' Union.

*Gewerkschaft Handel, Banken und Versicherungen (HBV)* – Commerce, Banking and Insurance Workers' Union.

*Gewerkschaft Holz und Kunststoff* – Wood and Plastic Workers' Union.

*Gewerkschaft Kunst* – Artists and Musicians' Union.

*Gewerkschaft Leder* – Leather Workers' Union.

*Gewerkschaft Nahrung–Genuss – Gaststätten (NGG)* – Food-Processing Workers' Union.

*Gewerkschaft Öffentliche Dienste, Transport und Verkehr (ÖTV)* – Public Service and Transport Workers' Union.

*Gewerkschaft der Polizei* – Police Union.

*Gewerkschaft Textil-Bekleidung* – Textile-Clothing Workers' Union.

*Gewerkschaftsrat* – Union Council; SPD organization founded in 1968 to improve communication between the party and the unions.

*Gewerkschaftsstaat* – union state.

*Gewerkschaftstag* – union congress; one of the highest governing bodies in a DGB union.

*Gewerksverein der Bauhandwerker* – Union of Construction Craftsmen; anti-socialist, Hirsch-Duncker union of the nineteenth century; Germany's first construction union.

*Graphischer Bund* – Graphical Association; loose federation of printing unions during the inter-war period.

*Grosschemie* – "Big Chemical"; common name for the three major chemical companies in West Germany: Hoechst, BASF, Bayer.

*Grosser Senat* – large Senate; division of the Federal Labor Court (*Bundesarbeitsgericht*) which hears appeals on fundamental issues of labor law.

*Grosskapital* – big business.

*Grundgesetz* – Basic Law; the Federal Republic's constitution; ratified in 1949.

*Grundsatzprogramm* – basic program; key DGB document, periodically revised, expounds the union federation's ideological disposition and gives its views on important issues.

*Grundstoff- und Produktionsgütergewerbe* – raw materials and production goods sector of the metal industry.

*Handwerksinnungen* – craft guilds.

*Hauptamtliche* – full-time, union-paid members of a union's executive committee.

*Hauptverband der Deutschen Bauindustrie (HDB)* – Main Association of the German Construction Industry; construction industry employers' association.

*Hauptversammlung* – stockholders' assembly.

*Haushaltsstrukturgesetz* – Budget Structure Law; austerity package introduced by Schmidt and passed by the Bundestag in 1975.

*HBV* – (see *Gewerkschaft Handel, Banken und Versicherungen*).

*HDB* – (see *Hauptverband der Deutschen Bauindustrie*).

*Hirsch-Duncker Gewerkschaftsring* – conservative union organization of the pre-1933 period, named after its founders, Max Hirsch and Franz Duncker.

*IG Bau-Steine-Erden* – Construction Workers' Union.

*IG Bergbau und Energie* – Mineworkers' Union.

*IG Chemie-Papier-Keramik* – Chemical, Paper and Ceramic Workers' Union.

*IG Druck und Papier* – Printers' Union.

*IG Krawall* – "the Trouble Union"; epithet directed at the activist union IG Metall in the late 1950s because of the radicalism of its leader, Otto Brenner.

*IG Medien und Kunst, Druck und Papier* – Media, Artists' and Printers' Union; proposed "media union," resulting from a merger of IG Druck and several smaller unions representing artists and TV/radio employees; at present, the future of this proposal is unclear.

*IG Metall* – Metalworkers' Union.

*Industrie- und Handelskammern* – chambers of commerce.

*Industriegewerkschaften* – industrial unions; labor unions grouped according to industry; there are presently seventeen industrial unions in the DGB. (For specific unions, see full name; e.g. *Gewerkschaft Öfftenliche Dienst* [ÖTV], *IG Metall, Deutsche Postgewerkschaft.*)

*Instrumentarium* – "tool kit"; refers to the measures used by government to implement economic policy.

*Interessenausgleich* – interest equalization plan; such a plan must be drafted between the works council and employer in a given factory before the latter can institute major changes (see *Betriebsänderungen*).

*Internationale Metallarbeiterschaft* – International Metalworkers; union founded in 1869 by the Lasallean and Eisenach factions of the Social Democratic trade-union movement; renamed (1873) *Metallarbeiter-Gewerksgenossenschaft* (Metal Workers' Cooperative Union).

*Investitionsgüter produzierendes Gewerbe* – Investment/capital goods sector of the metal industry.

*Investitionslenkung* – investment guidance; program supported by labor in its 1963 Düsseldorf Program which demanded that the unions play a role in determining capital's investment policies via macroeconomic planning.

*Jusos* – Young Socialists (abbrev.); leftist SPD youth organization.

*Kampffähigkeit* – fighting ability.

*Kampfmassnahmen* – hostile actions, such as strikes or lockouts.

*Kampfparität* – parity of forces; the principle governing adjudication of labor disputes which holds that neither labor nor management should be able to command a monopoly of force against the other; often used as justification for upholding the rights of employers to lock out striking workers.

*Kampfregeln* – rules of combat; quasi-legal concept which proscribes the use of strikes and lockouts.

*Kanalarbeiter* – "sewer workers"; right-wing SPD members who favor an accommodationist line on labor–management relations.

*Kanzlergewerkschaften* – "chancellor's unions"; right-wing DGB unions of the late 1970s, as dubbed by their leftist counterparts in reference to the former's close relationship to Chancellor Helmut Schmidt (see also *Kanalarbeiter*).

*Kassenpolitik* – fund politics; labor strategy emphasizing wage gains through creation of industry–labor managed funds, to the exclusion of qualitative issues involving control over production and quality of work life.

*Kernkommission* – core commission; negotiating body created by the metal industry in 1971 to centralize and coordinate the collective bargaining process.

*Koalitionszwang* – the pressures of the coalition; cited by Helmut Schmidt in defense of his unpopular economic policies in order to implicate his Free Democratic coalition partners.

*Kommunistische Partei Deutschland (KPD)* – German Communist Party; declared unconstitutional in 1956; forerunner to the DKP (*Deutsche Kommunistische Partei*), which was reconstituted in 1968.

*Koordinierungsrat* – coordination council; leadership body of the *Arbeitsring*; coordinates bargaining strategy throughout the chemical industry.

*KPD* – (see *Kommunistische Partei Deutschland*)

*Kreis* – county, basic organizational unit of the unions at the local level.

*Kreisdelegiertenversammlung* – union county delegate meeting, consisting of representatives from all unions or locals in a given county (*Kreis*).

*Kreisvorstand* – union county executive committee; elected during the county delegate meeting (*Kreisdelegiertenversammlung*).

*Kündigung* – contract expiration date.

*Kurzarbeit* – short-time work.

*LAK* – (see *Lohnausgleichskasse*)

*Land* – state.

*Landesarbeitsgericht* – state labor court; state appellate court for labor law cases.

*Landesbezirke* – regional (state) districts of the DGB and most of its constituent unions; correspond roughly to the states (*Länder*) of the Federal Republic.

*Landesbezirkskonferenz* – DGB (and constituent union) regional district (state) conference; elects state executive committee (*Landesbezirksvorstand*).

*Landesbezirksvorstand* – regional district (state) executive committee; elected by delegates from all DGB unions (or constituent union locals) in a given state (*Land*); oversees union activities within each state.

*Landesverband der Metallindustriellen Arbeitgeber Nordrhein-Westfalen (LMA-NRW)* – State Federation of Metal Industry Employers of North Rhine-Westphalia; largest of the regional metal industry employers' associations.

*Landtag* – state assembly.

*Lehrling* – apprentice.

*Lehrlingsskala* – apprentice scale; limit on the number of apprentices allowed in a given industry.

*Leistungslohn* – (see *Leistungszulage*)

*Leistungszulage* – achievement bonus; the monetary differential between a union-negotiated wage rate (*Tariflohn*) and the actual remuneration paid according to a worker's performance; usually the result of special benefits arranged between employer and worker.

*leitende Angestellte* – middle management.

*lineare Prozentualforderungen* – demands for direct, percentage wage increases (see *Mischforderungen* and *Erhöhungen in festen Beträgen*).

*Lohn* – hourly wage.

*Lohnausgleichskasse (LAK)* – Wage Compensation Fund; labor–management fund set up in the construction industry in 1954 to supplement unemployment compensation.

*Lohnfortzahlungsgesetz* – Continued Wage Payment Law; measure passed by the Bundestag in the aftermath of IG Metall's 1957 strike in Schleswig-Holstein; provided wage payments during times of sickness.

*Lohngruppenschlüssel* – wage categorization.

*Lohnrahmentarifvertrag (LRTV)* – wage framework contract; contract defining wage and salary groups for a particular industry.

*Lohntarifvertrag (LTV)* – wage contract.

*Manteltarifvertrag (MTV)* – general framework contract; contract comprising guidelines on working conditions, work time, benefits and other items not involving wages or wage structures.

*Maschinenbau* – machinery sector of the metal industry.

*Metallarbeiter Gewerksgenossenschaft* – (see *Internationale Metallarbeiterschaft*)

*Metallhandwerk* – metal craft industry.

*Mischforderungen* – mixed demands; salary raises which take the form of both fixed lump-sum raises and percentage increases.

*Mitbestimmung* – co-determination; the right of workers to participate in the economic affairs of their firm.

*Mitbestimmungsgesetz* – co-determination law; passed in 1976.

*Mittelstandausschuss* – intra-CDU body representing the interests of medium-sized and small entrepreneurs.

*MMG* – (see *Montanmitbestimmungsgesetz*)

*Montanmitbestimmung* – parity co-determination as practiced in the iron, steel and coal industries; participation by labor representatives on the supervisory boards of West German firms equal to that of management.

*Montanmitbestimmungsergänzungsgesetz* – Parity Co-determination Extension Law; passed by the Bundestag in 1956 extending parity co-determination to companies in which steel, iron or coal revenues provided more than 50% of total income.

*Montanmitbestimmungsgesetz (MMG)* – Coal, Steel and Iron Co-Determination Law; passed in 1951.

*MTV* – (see *Manteltarifvertrag*)

*negative Koalitionsfreiheit* – negative coalition freedom; refers most often to the disputed "right" of a worker *not* to join a union.

*Neue Heimat (NH)* – union-owned non-profit construction conglomerate which was embroiled in scandal in the early 1980s.

*NGG* – (see *Gewerkschaft Nahrung – Genuss – Gaststätten*)

*Oberstes Schlichtungsamt* – Superior Arbitration Office; printing industry appellate arbitration board; abolished in 1973.

*Ordnungsfaktoren* – "factors of order"; often used to describe the role of unions in the Federal Republic's Rechtsstaat (constitutional state); an accommodationist's conception of the purpose of organized labor in society.

*Ortsgruppen* – location categories; criteria used in determining a worker's wage rate; originally intended to offset differences between urban and rural costs of living; today largely obsolete.

*Ortskartellen* – municipal cartels; offices set up by the DGB in towns with at least 200 DGB members to represent the DGB in local politics; responsible to the DGB county executive committee (*Kreisvorstand*).

*Ortsklassen* – (see *Ortsgruppen*)

*Ortsverein* – union local.

*Ostverträge* – "East Treaties"; treaties signed by the Federal Republic and *East European Countries* easing tensions between the two power blocks; negotiated during the social–liberal coalition led by Willy Brandt.

*ÖTV* – (see *Gewerkschaft Öffentliche Dienste, Transport und Verkehr*)

*Paritätische Mitbestimmung* – parity co-determination; worker participation in company decision-making equal to the representation enjoyed by management; introduced in the coal, iron and steel industries through the MMG of 1951 (also *Montanmitbestimmung*).

*Prämiensätze* – bonus rates; monetary incentives for piece-rate workers who exceed their production norms (see *Zeitfaktor*).

*Rationalisierungsschutzabkommen* – Rationalization Protection Agreement.

*Rechtsstaat* – constitutional state; *sozialer Rechtsstaat* – reformist constitutional state.

*Reichsarbeitsgemeinschaften* – Reich labor committees; sub-divisions of the Nazi-controlled DAF.

*Reichsarbeitsgerichte* – Reich labor courts; set up in 1919 to hear disputes between labor and management.

*Reichsbetriebsgemeinschaft Bau* – Reich Construction Union; National Socialist construction union founded in 1933 after the dissolution of the *Deutscher Baugewerksbund*.

*Reichsbetriebsgemeinschaft Druck* – Reich Printers' Union; National Socialist printers' union founded in 1933 after the dissolution of all other printing industry unions.

*Reichsbetriebsgruppen* – National Factory Groups; division of the workforce (imposed by the Nazi-controlled DAF) into 18 sectors; divisions corresponded closely to the 16 post-war industrial unions of the DGB.

*Reichstarifgemeinschaft Steine und Erden* – Reich Bargaining Community for Stone and Earth Workers; Nazi union created in 1933 for building product and quarry workers.

*Richtungsgewerkschaft* – partisan union.

*rote Filzokratie* – "red rule of entanglement"; derogatory reference to the close relationship between the SPD and the DGB; frequently cited by West German conservatives.

*Ruhreisenstreik* – Ruhr ironworkers' strike (1928); social unrest resulting from this strike action is credited with contributing to the downfall of the Weimar Republic.

*Sachverständigenrat (SVR)* – Council of Economic Advisors (also known as the "Five Wise Men").

*Schwarzfahrer* – (literally "black rider") fare-dodger, free rider; used by DGB unions in reference to non-union members who enjoy the benefits of union membership; also *Schmarotzer* ("freeloader").

*Schweigepflicht* – "obligation to be silent"; refers to the obligation imposed by the 1952 Works Constitution Law on works council members to refrain from divulging company policy information that might be damaging to the employers.

*Selbstgeschaffenes Arbeitsrecht* – self-made labor law; coined in reference to the fact that labor contracts have the force of law in the Federal Republic.

*Selbstverwaltungskörperschaften der Sozialversicherung* – independent boards which monitor state social welfare funds.

*Sockelpolitik* – fixed base wage policy; remuneration policy which favors workers in low wage categories (see also *Erhöhungen in festen Beträgen*).

*Solidaritätsbeitrag* – solidarity contribution; monetary sum paid by non-union workers in Switzerland to the unions as compensation for benefits gained as a result of unionization in their industry.

*Sozialadäquanz* – "social appropriateness"; Nipperdey's criterion for judging the legality of strike actions.

*Sozialausschüsse* – social committees; CDU labor organization.

*Sozialistischer Deutscher Studentenbund (SDS)* – socialist student organization of the 1960s and 1970s.

*Sozialplan* – social plan; before instituting major changes which will adversely affect members of the workforce, the employer in a given factory must devise a "social plan," to make restitution to those workers – usually by means of a large lump sum – and to stipulate which workers will lose their jobs.

*Sparten* – sections; in the printing industry, skilled professional craft groups.

*SPD* – Social Democratic party.

*staatsfixiert* – "fixated on the state"; description of the tradition within the German labor movement which emphasizes the importance of electoral politics, economic intervention by the state and the role of the Social Democratic Party (SPD) in securing improvements for the working class.

*staatstreu* – loyal to the state.

*Strukturpolitik* – structural policy

*Stunde Null* – "zero hour"; reference to the break with the past and the process of starting over following the end of World War II.

*SVR* – (see *Sachverständigenrat*)

*Tabu Katalog* – taboo catalogue; list of restrictions imposed by the employers' association BDA on its member organizations in dealing with labor unions; prohibited BDA members from reducing weekly work time to less than 40 hours, for example; caused major scandal when uncovered in 1979.

*Tarifausschuss* – contract committee; assists a union's collective bargaining commission (*Tarifkommission*).

*Tarifautonomie* – collective bargaining autonomy; the right of unions and employers not to submit to binding or state arbitration; more generally, the right to conduct collective bargaining freely and without fear of intimidation; cited by unionists in opposition to the employers' use of lockouts; an important tenet of contemporary labor relations in the Federal Republic.

*Tariffähigkeit* – the ability to enter contractual relationships; right enjoyed by the three parties (unions, employers' associations and individual firms) allowed by the TVG to sign collective bargaining agreements.

*Tarifgemeinschaft* – bargaining community; consortium consisting of industry (and/or labor) representatives from several regions who consult to coordinate collective bargaining strategies.

*Tarifkommission* – collective bargaining commission; major union body involved in the conduct of collective bargaining.

*Tariflohn* – contractual wage rate.

*Tarifpolitischer Ausschuss (TPA)* – Collective Bargaining Committee; Gesamtmetall's chief organ for centralized coordination of collective bargaining.

*Tarifvertragsgesetz (TVG)* – Collective Bargaining Law of 1949.

*Tarifvertragsordnung* – Collective Bargaining Law of 1918; made collective bargaining agreements legally binding.

*Tendenzschutzparagraph* – Tendency Protection Paragraph; statute prohibiting co-determination in media-related companies, ostensibly to protect the impartiality of the press.

*Tendenzwende* – turning point; describes the onset of economic crisis in West Germany during the mid-1970s.

*Treuhänder der Arbeit* – "labor ombudsmen"; Nazi functionaries who unilaterally determined wage rates for entire industries after 1933.

*TVG* – (see *Tarifvertragsgesetz*)

*Unabhängige Sozialdemokratische Partei Deutschland (USPD)* – German Independent Social Democratic Party; shortlived leftist party which broke from the SPD in 1918; dissolved in 1920 as numerous party members returned to the SPD or defected to the KPD.

*Unterbezirk* – SPD sub-district.

*Unterstützungsverein der Chemischen Industrie (UCI)* – Support Organization of the Chemical Industry; established in 1975 to provide laid-off chemical workers with funds to supplement unemployment benefits and assist elderly workers affected by technological changes in the production process.

*Unterstützungsverein der Deutschen Buchdrucker (UVDB)* – Support Organization of German Book Printers; printers' union at the turn of the century, "created" when the DBV changed its name to avoid dissolution under the anti-socialist laws (see *Deutscher Buchdrucker Verein*).

*Unvereinbarkeitsklauseln* – clauses of incompatibility; DGB decree forbidding simultaneous membership in a union and a radical left organization; passed to counter the growing power of former student radicals in the unions during the early 1970s.

*Urabstimmung* – strike vote.

*Urlaubsgeld* – vacation money; supplementary vacation bonus.

*Urlaubskasse* – vacation pay fund.

*USPD* – (see *Unabhängige Sozialdemokratische Partei Deutschland*).

*VdDB* – (see *Deutscher Buchdrucker Verein*).

*VDZ* – (see *Verband Deutscher Zeitschriftenverleger*)

*Verband der Automobilindustrie* – Association of the Automobile Industry; industrial association and member of the BDI.

*Verband der Bau-, Fabrik-, Land- und Handarbeiter* – Confederation of Construction, Factory, Agricultural and Manual Workers; union formed in 1876 as part of the Social Democratic trade-union movement.

*Verband der Fabrik-, Land- und sonstigen gewerblichen Hilfsarbeiter Deutschlands (VFD)* – Confederation of Factory, Agricultural and other Industrial Skilled Workers of Germany; skilled workers' union founded in 1890 on expiration of the anti-socialist law.

*Verband der Fabrikarbeiter Deutschlands (VFD)* – German Factory Workers' Confederation; pre-1933 union of chemical workers; major forerunner to IG Chemie-Papier-Keramik.

*Verband der Metallindustrie Baden-Württemberg (VMI)* – Federation of the Baden-Württemberg Metal Industry; second largest of the regional metal industry employers' associations.

*Verband Deutscher Zeitschriftenverleger (VDZ)* – Federation of German Periodical Publishers; magazine/journal publisher employers' association.

*Verbändegesetz* – industrial relations act; the unions have long feared passage of such an act, which would likely restrict the activities of all interest groups – particularly organized labor – in order to "safeguard" parliamentary democracy.

*Verbrauchsgüter produzierendes Gewerbe* – consumer goods sector of the metal industry.

*Verein Deutscher Maschinenbau Anstalten* – Union of German Machine Construction Works; "industrial association" and member of the BDI.

*Verein zur Förderung der Spartätigkeit und Erholung* – Association for the Encouragement of Savings and Rest; fund proposed by IG Bau and the construction industry in 1961 to provide supplementary vacation benefits of DM 80 to construction workers.

*Verfilzung* – entanglement; term used by conservatives and employers to denigrate the close relationship between the SPD and the DGB.

*Verhältnismässigkeit* – proportionality; legal term restricting the tactics used in a labor conflict to those of a "fair fight" as determined by the BAG in 1955.

*Verhandlungskommission* – negotiating committee.

*Verhandlungskreis (VK)* – bargaining circle; along with the TPA, Gesamtmetall's primary body for the coordination of centralized collective bargaining.

*Vermögensbildung* – asset formation; usually in the form of employer contributions (above wages and bonuses) to the workers' savings; also *vermögenswirksame Leistung* (individualized asset formation).

*Verrechtlichung* – "juridification"; describes the complex and routinized structure of legal regulation which sets rigid parameters on union behavior at the plant level.

*Vertragstreue* – contractual loyalty; legal concept stressing the importance of abiding by existing contracts.

*Vertrauenskörper* (also *Vertrauensleutekörper*) – literally "trusted body"; committee consisting of the shop stewards (often also the works councilors) at a given factory.

*Vertrauensleute* – union shop stewards.

*Verwaltungsstellen* – union locals.

*VFD* – (see *Verband der Fabrikarbeiter Deutschlands*)

*Volkspartei* – people's party; broad-based, catch-all party.

*Vorschriften des Richterwahlgesetzes* – guidelines governing the selection of all judges in the Federal Republic.

*Vorstand* – executive committee.

*Vorteilsausgleichskasse (VAK)* – Advantage Equalization Fund (1961); fund proposed by IG Bau to compel non-union members in the construction industry to pay a "solidarity contribution' (see *Solidaritätsbeitrag*) for enjoying the benefits of union membership.

*Vorteilsregelungen* – advantage schemes; proposals advanced by the DGB in the early 1960s to increase union membership by granting special benefits to union members; largely defeated in the courts.

*Waffengleichheit* – (see *Kampfpariät*).

*Wahlprüfsteine* – election guidelines issued regularly by the DGB stating the organization's positions and goals on key issues.

*Wende* – turning point; political realignment.

*Wirtschafts- und Sozialwissenschaftliches Institut (WSI)* – Economics and Social Science

Institute; economic research institute run by the DGB; formerly *Wirtschafts- und Wissenschaftliches Institut der Gewerkschaften* [WWI].

*Wirtschaftsausschuss* – economic committee; Article 107 of the BVG empowers company works councils (*Gesamtbetriebsrat*) to form such committees, which management must keep informed about the economic situation of the company.

*Wirtschaftsrat* – intra-CDU organization representing the interests of big business.

*Wirtschaftsverbände* – "economic associations"; business lobbying organizations.

*Wirtschaftswunder* – economic miracle; refers to West Germany's unparalleled prosperity and economic growth from the 1950s to the mid-1970s.

*WSI* – (see *Wirtschafts- und Sozialwissenschaftliches Institut*).

*ZDB* – (see *Zentralverband des Deutschen Baugewerbes*).

*Zeitfaktor* – "time multiplier"; the quantity of work a piecework employee must accomplish in a given amount of time.

*Zeitlöhner* – workers paid an hourly wage.

*Zentralarbeitsgemeinschaftsabkommen* – Central Labor Community Accord; agreement reached in 1918 between representatives of heavy industry and the Social Democratic unions, in which the former formally recognized the latter and the eight-hour day was introduced.

*Zentrales Schiedsgericht* – Central Arbitration Tribunal; arbitration body in the printing industry.

*Zentralverband der Maurer Deutschlands (ZMD)* – Central Union of German Masons; powerful, socialist construction union; founded at the turn of the century and forcibly dissolved in 1933.

*Zentralverband des Deutschen Baugewerbes (ZDB)* – Central Association of German Construction; construction industry employers' association.

*ZIP* – (see *Zukunftsinvestitionsprogramm*).

*Zukunftsinvestitionsprogramm (ZIP)* – Future Investment Program; program launched by Schmidt in 1976 to stimulate demand and decrease unemployment by increasing public investment in job-producing industries; designed in part to curry favor with DGB unions.

*Zusatzverorgungskasse (ZVK)* – Added Assistance Fund; jointly administered labor-industry fund proposed by IG Bau leader Georg Leber in 1955 to supplement the small monthly pensions for retired construction workers.

*Zweigbüros* – subsidiary offices; set up by the DGB in rural areas to improve representation of unionists in these regions; responsible to the DGB county executive committee (*Kreisvorstand*).

# Index

For Product Safety Concerns and Information please contact our EU
representative GPSR@taylorandfrancis.com Taylor & Francis Verlag GmbH,
Kaufingerstraße 24, 80331 München, Germany

Printed and bound by CPI Group (UK) Ltd, Croydon, CR0 4YY
08/05/2025
01864503-0001